Redesign of Catalogs and Indexes for Improved Online Subject Access:

Selected Papers of Pauline A. Cochrane

by Pauline Atherton Cochrane

ORYX PRESS
1985

The rare Arabian Oryx is believed to have inspired the myth of the unicorn. This desert antelope became virtually extinct in the early 1960s. At that time several groups of international conservationists arranged to have 9 animals sent to the Phoenix Zoo to be the nucleus of a captive breeding herd. Today the Oryx population is over 400 and herds have been returned to reserves in Israel, Jordan, and Oman.

Copyright © 1985 by
The Oryx Press
2214 North Central at Encanto
Phoenix, Arizona 85004-1483

Published simultaneously in Canada

Printed and Bound in the United States of America

∞™ The paper used in this publication meets the minimum requirements of American National Standard for Information Science— Permanence of Paper for Printed Library Materials, ANSI Z39.48, 1984.

Library of Congress Cataloging in Publication Data

Cochrane, Pauline Atherton, 1929–
  Redesign of catalogs and indexes for improved online subject access.

  Includes index.
  1. Subject cataloging—Data processing—Addresses, essays, lectures.   2. Catalogs, Subject—Addresses, essays, lectures.   3. Indexes—Addresses, essays, lectures.   4. Indexing—Addresses, essays, lectures. 5. Information storage and retrieval systems— Addresses, essays, lectures.   6. Information retrieval— Addresses, essays, lectures.   I. Title.
Z695.C647   1985   025.4'9'02854   85-7284
ISBN 0-89774-158-7

To my several co-authors, students, and sponsors
who provided assistance and enthusiasm when I needed it the most,
To my husband, Glynn,
who saw the thread running through my work
and encouraged me to pull it all together.

Table of Contents

Preface

"How much I know sometimes—how little at others."
—F. Scott Fitzgerald

When the history of information retrieval and library automation is written, the 1960s may be called "The Golden Age." This decade was certainly marked by rapid developments in the use of computer technology in libraries and information centers and by the almost unlimited availability of funds to research, design, and evaluate many new information systems. During that time the traditional indexing, abstracting, and retrieval methods were analyzed and criticised because designers were trying to understand what humans did to make these systems work and what it would be that computers should now be made to do. The conferences held during this period brought together engineers and scientists, linguists and psychologists, data processing personnel, and librarians. Their approaches to system design and evaluation were different, but most of them eventually understood what each had to contribute and how inadequate any one individual contribution would be. The cross-fertilization and experimentation possible then made every meeting an exciting opportunity to exchange ideas and results about system improvements.

The 1970s, on the other hand, will probably be called "The Development Decade" in the history books. With funding sources only interested in "pipeline" developments, system designers were forced to move beyond the experimental stage, and they began to make firm decisions about record formats, command language, index vocabulary, and computer system configuration for the new operational systems. Once operational, methods were designed for monitoring the use of the systems, and occasionally there would be an upgrading exercise as a new computer system was installed. By 1980, the time for experimenting, testing, and evaluating appeared to be over. Headlines were made when a new or bigger system was unveiled for another user group or when an operational system was upgraded.

Interestingly enough the 1980s may be observed by the historian of information systems and services as a return to an earlier period, for it appears to be a time of reassessment, and the online public access catalog (OPAC), although it appears to be built on an earlier design, may eventually become an entirely new system. Patterned after the information retrieval systems of the 1960s, and integrated with the library automation systems of the 1970s, the first versions of OPACs have met with mixed reviews from their users. As a public (or end user) group, these users seem to want something different from what was designed for trained information professionals. This is leading to a reassessment, and conferences are being held to discuss new system features which will have to be experimentally tested and evaluated.

The relevance of the work done in the 1960s has become evident to some because the questions asked then about user-system interface, compatibility of index vocabularies, document augmentation, computer-aided indexing, etc. all seem to have a familiar ring.

This collection brings together most of what I wrote between 1961 and 1984, a time that spans all the periods described above. Many of the papers in this collection were prepared for conferences held during this period. Rereading them brings back memories of meetings and discussions of these topics with Ralph Shaw, Pete Luhn, Mortimer Taube, Eugene Garfield, Bill Maron and Larry Kuhns, Roger Summit, Charles Bourne, Phyllis Baxendale, Naomi Sager, Phyllis Richmond, Jesse Shera, Fred Kilgour, Henriette Avram, Larry Buckland, Seymour Lubetsky, Richard Angell, Carlos Cuadra, Harold Wooster, Mike Kessler, Don Swanson, Derek Austin, Wilf Lancaster, Gerald Salton, Cyril Cleverdon, S. R. Ranganathan, Brian Vickery, Eric Coates, Bjorn Tell, Don King, Ed Bryant, and many, many others. This list of pioneers and pacesetters now reads like the Hall of Fame in our field. Luckily for our field, many of them have had their writings collected. It was an exciting 25 years, and the Golden Age was an excellent time to drop an oar into the fast moving stream of events. I always considered myself very fortunate to be around during those times.

What I have collected here has been organized around five questions which have been asked over and over again:

1. Where are we going in the redesign of catalogs and indexes?
2. What do we know about users and catalogs?
3. What can we do to improve subject access?
4. Will classification have a use online?
5. What can be learned from subject access research?

I had the time to prepare this collection while I was on leave from Syracuse University and residing in Papua New Guinea, far away from the daily preoccupation with teaching and related activities. The physical distance from the United States seemed to give me a perspective on why there might be some merit in such a collection at this time, even though I found Fitzgerald's words sobering and applicable.

The papers I wrote on library science education are not included here, but I would like to acknowledge that much of what I have gathered here represents work I did with the aid of my students and colleagues at the library schools where I have taught and done research.

During this period, I worked with the information staffs at Field Enterprises Educational Corporation, the American Institute of Physics, University of Toronto, OCLC, ERIC Clearinghouse on Information Resources at Syracuse University, Cornell University, the H. W. Wilson Company, and the Library of Congress. At all of these places I was fortunate to find information professionals who kept searching for better ways to design catalogs and indexes. They provided the impetus I needed to work on various problems and they made the search I engaged in experimental and developmental, rather than theoretical or academic. I am especially grateful to these colleagues for helping me put my work in a real setting.

I would like to thank many persons from several institutions who have financially supported my work. Unfortunately they are too numerous to name individually, so I will list them corporately:

Council on Library Resources
ERIC
Library of Congress
National Library of Medicine
National Science Foundation
OCLC Online Computer Library Center, Inc.
Rome Air Development Center
Syracuse University
U.S. Office of Education
UNESCO—General Information Programme

I appreciate the opportunity The Oryx Press has given me to publish this collection. Less than half of the selections were published in journals; many were issued as research reports and are no longer readily accessible; over one third were issued as parts of conference proceedings or as contributions to edited sets of papers by many authors; five selections were never published or distributed very widely. Thanks to The Oryx Press, readers in the 1980s can review these papers without much retrieval effort.

Port Moresby, Papua New Guinea
May 1985

Chronological List of Selections

---

c = conference paper	e = edited work	j = journal article
l = lecture notes	n = never published	r = research report

Part 1

Where Are We Going in the Redesign of Catalogs and Indexes?

Introduction

The selections chosen for this chapter span a period from 1965 to 1983. Only three of the selections were published in journals. The rest are from the "grey" literature of conference proceedings and books compiled to gather the contributions of several authors who had something to say about a current and "hot topic." It is remarkable, when you think about it, that these selections, all on the same theme, span almost 20 years. You might wonder why this topic had to be discussed over and over with no apparent resolution of the issues involved and no apparent consensus being reached. It is my contention that this has happened because the library field has not devised a comprehensive set of design concepts for their automated systems and services. As the two 1981 selections in this section describe, the basic goal of our information system design should be to provide information retrieval, and the systems we design should be for our users as well as for our library staffs. Earlier, the probable use of automated libraries by our patrons on their own seemed dreamlike, but now it is a reality hampered only by our own poor design of the systems available to them. This set of writings may help to show how far we have come.

Is Compatibility of Authority Files Practicable?

Since the title of this paper is written in the form of a question, it is possible that I could address myself to the question and answer it with one word. Although I have been tempted to take this course of action, I have not been able to decide whether the answer should be yes or no. It will thus be necessary for me to spend the next few paragraphs considering the implications. If you will bear with me, we both become a little better informed even if not satisfied.

A certain amount of confusion and ambiguity surrounds the topic of compatibility of authority files. This is partly the result of the synonym syndrome which pervades the field of information handling. Paul Howerton included a quotation from *Alice in Wonderland* on the page facing the opening of the chapter I wrote in the book he edited (Howerton, 1963). The chapter is entitled "File Organization: Principles and Practices for Processing and Maintaining the Collection." The quotation goes like this:

> When I use a word, it means just what I choose it to mean—neither more nor less.

That wasn't quite true in *Alice* and unfortunately it isn't true in our field. Paul knew it and he also knew, I believe, that it is most noticeable when we talk about "indexes, search strategies, and other file control mechanisms" and "rules for file organization." The words we hear over and over again which are relevant to the subject of compatibility of authority files also apply to the practical application of these rules. Conversations and papers on the subject often include the following words with various meanings:

> Those in favor repeat these words:
>
> standardization, centralization, cooperation, systemization, uniformity, consistency, comparability, general principles, rules, codification, convertibility, coordination and compatibility.

Reprinted with permission from *Information Systems Compatibility,* edited by Simon M. Newman, 1965, Spartan Books. Editor's Note: The examples that accompany this article are not reproduced here.

Those who worry about the consequences of efforts toward uniformity repeat these words:

> exception, alternatives, deviation, qualifications, inconsistencies, modification, local variation, individual practice, flexibility, adaptation, interpretation.

Because the problem is so vast, clarity is lacking and we are not always sure whether we are talking about compatibility of authority files or interchangeability of indexing records. Several papers in this volume concentrate on the problems of compatibility between information systems which employ different authority files for subject analysis and identification. To supplement them, I would like to spend some time discussing all the authority files and rules which might be employed by an information system.

Whatever components of the system we discuss (author-title catalog, subject index, report number index, entry for corporate source), the problem of maintaining an authority file keeps bobbing up. Whether we are bothered with a compound name for a subject or a corporate body, we will have the two problems of *choosing the elements of the name* and *selecting the particular part of the name* (if it is compound) which will serve as entry word. Whether we are bothered with the single subject term or personal author's name, we still must decide on the style of entry. Whether we are talking about a printed index in an abstract journal or a card in a library catalog, we still must record our decisions in some authority file to insure a certain degree of uniformity and consistency within the system (not to mention with other systems).

There is a long history of work on authority files in the library field. Table 1 is a sheet entitled "Examples of Rules (or Authority Files) for Uniformity in File Item Descriptions." These and other rules can help determine:

- How to find the proper descriptive elements and entry points for a given file item.
- How to choose the best items for entry of new groups of file items.
- How to integrate these new entries into the file control mechanism, yet avoid conflict, confusion and duplication.

Table 1 could have been longer, and I should have indicated that all these rules are presently undergoing change and revision. These two facts are worth remembering. They have some bearing on my final answer to the question: Is the compatibility of authority files practicable?

Table 1: Examples of Rules (or Authority Files) for Uniformity in File Items Descriptions

1. Description of File Items
   a. Rules for Descriptive Cataloging in the Library of Congress, 1949.
   b. †U.S. Atomic Energy Commission. Guide to Abstracting and Indexing for Nuclear Science Abstracts (TID-4576), Oak Ridge, Tenn., 1961.
2. Author and Title Identification
   a. Statement of Principles adopted by the I.F.L.A. International Conference on Cataloging Principles, Paris, October 1961.
   b. Cataloging Rules for Author and Title Entries. 2nd ed., Chicago, American Library Association, 1949.
   c. COS(AT)I standard.
   d. Brandhorst Jan. 1964 AD art.
   e. Chemical Abstracts—List of Periodicals, American Chemical Society, 1961 (See Example 9); Chemical Titles (list of periodicals with permanent codes for each), 1962 (see Example 8).
3. Subject Identification
   a. D.J. Haykin, Subject Headings: A Practical Guide, Washington, D. C., Government Printing Office, 1951.
   b. Subject Headings Used in the Dictionary Catalogs of the Library of Congress, 6th ed., Washington, D.C., Government Printing Office, 1957 (with supplements).
   c. Sears List of Subject Headings, 8th ed., New York, The H. W. Wilson Company, 1959 (see Example 13).
   d. †A.I.Ch.E. Chemical Engineering Thesaurus. New York, American Institute of Chemical Engineers, 1961 (see Example 12).
   e. Dewey Decimal Classification, 16th ed., Forest Press, 1958 (see Example 15); and Guide to the Use of Dewey Decimal Classification, Forest Press, 1962.
   f. Colon Classification prescribes order—not exact terms
   g. Universal Decimal Classification, Abridged English ed., British Standards Institution, 1961 (see Example 14).
4. Arrangement of Items in File Collection
   a. "LC Book Numbers" (in Cataloging Service Bulletin 14, January, 1948).
   b. †IBM 650 Automatic Information Retrieval Program, n.d.
   c. A.L.A. Rules for Filing Catalog Cards, Chicago, American Library Association, 1942.

Having stated how I intend to widen the scope of my paper, I would also like to narrow it. If I don't, you may think I am writing about something other than what I am, and I want to avoid that kind of confusion if at all

---

†rules for mechanized systems.

possible. I am not discussing the actual indexing records for file items in any information system. I am not discussing the consistency of indexers who happen to index or catalog the same file item in two different information systems. Ann Painter (1963) covered this topic quite adequately in her dissertation. I am discussing the possibility that rules or guidelines, principles of subject analysis and codes for filing may be so designed that they are capable of existing together in harmony—are compatible, and that such an effort is feasible—can be put in practice. When several information systems use these rules, they should be able to effect some degree of interchangeability and convertibility of file item descriptions.

To familiarize myself with the history which led to the publication of some of the most widely used authority files, I reread the prefaces and introductions to several of these. I would like to reproduce excerpts from these statements because this background has a bearing on the practicability of making authority lists compatible for mechanized information systems on a regional, national or international basis.

1. Background on the ALA/LC descriptive cataloging rules (Library of Congress, 1949. p. 2–4):

    Interest in cooperative and centralized cataloging in late 1800's led to the appointment of a committee of the A.L.A. to formulate standard cataloging rules which would be in accord with the system at the LC.

    During the thirty-three years which elapsed between the publication of the ALA Catalog Rules in 1908 and (1941), there was continuous advancement in the standardization of cataloging, *because* of the increased use of Library of Congress printed cards and the development of cooperative cataloging. Many questions of interpretation arose, and rules were needed to solve new types of problems . . . . [some] rules were disseminated solely through correspondences and only in reply to inquiries as to rules and practices. The unreliability of this unsystematic manner of developing and disseminating rules was realized most keenly when the cooperative cataloging program was expanded in the thirties. Other librarians, when attempting to follow the cataloging practice of the Library of Congress found that they did not know the Library of Congress rules, and that the precedents revealed by printed cards were likely to justify considerable variations.

    Rules and practice developed and recorded in this fashion tend to grow away from the principles on which they are based. . . . The Library of Congress decided, therefore, that the whole body of rules needed to be reexamined and presented in a systematic, rather than an alphabetic, order. This reexamination was carried on for several years and an attempt was made to learn the needs of other libraries for certain types of catalog data. . . . Study and criticism of the rules were invited and individuals and groups of catalogers responded. (Opinion as summarized and crystallized through A.L.A. activity . . . suggestions and recommendations were made.) Changes were also made as a result of the experience gained in using the preliminary edition and it is anticipated that further modifications will be found desirable from time to time. While it is realized that the basic principles of a cataloging system should not fluctuate from year to year it is generally admitted that change in details can be made and the rules reformulated whenever improvements are discovered.

2. Background on the code for filing (American Library Association, 1942):

The present code is based on a comparative study of filing rules which have appeared in printed codes and in manuals of library science; and also of the practices in a number of large and medium-sized public and university libraries. The comparison showed few rules with no variants; some rules where a generally accepted practice is clearly indicated; many rules where two practices are in equal use and apparently equally satisfactory; and, finally, in regard to the more perplexing problems of arrangement, a wide diversity of practice and opinion.

The code attempts to provide a set of alphabeting rules in accord with the most generally accepted usage. In addition, it offers rules for both a group and an alphabetic order of arrangement under certain types of headings. . . . In the absence of a definite knowledge as to the psychological approach of the user to the catalog, it does not seem advisable to insist dogmatically that one alternative is to be preferred to the other. . . . Consistency throughout the catalog is in general desirable but may be disregarded in special instances provided that the guide-cards at the given point show with precision the order adopted.

3. Background on the code for author and title entries (American Library Association, 1949):

Chief changes from the preliminary edition are a rearrangement of the material to emphasize the basic rules and subordinate their amplifications, and to make the sequence of rules logical so far as possible; reduction of the number of alternate rules; omission of rules of description; rewording to avoid repetition or to make the meaning clearer; and revision, where possible, of rules inconsistent with the general principles.

The A.L.A. Cataloging rules are intended to represent *the best of the most general current practice* in cataloging of the libraries of the United States. The rules are not few nor are they, in total, simple, for the materials to which they are applied are almost as multitudinous and complicated as humanity itself. The world may have become one world, but we certainly do not yet speak with one tongue nor even write our various languages in one alphabet. Our names are formed differently, our governments and institutions are variously organized, our ways of publishing are not the same.

These rules aid the cataloger in the choice of entry and form of heading so that a reasonable degree of standardization and uniformity may prevail, not only within one catalog, but especially in enterprises such as centralized and cooperative cataloging, the making of union catalogs and the compiling of biliographies. Such uniformity makes the use of a catalog (or index) easier, since the user learns what to expect.

Many know of the recent efforts to revise this code and the lengthy criticism which had been leveled at the 1949 edition and is already being leveled at the coming edition even before it is published. The same will be true of the COS(AT)I standard for descriptive cataloging for report literature (Federal Council for Science and Technology, 1963). The question of the practicability of making authority files compatible is almost answered by the editors of previous codes. It soon becomes apparent that authority files which reach the stage of use by more than one information system have the inherent characteristic of making the two systems compatible. Standardization of the width between tracks brought a very noticeable degree of uniformity between trains. An example of this in our field is the current effort to produce STAR[1] and *International Aerospace Abstracts*. With the merging of their files in mind for a mechanized information system, their authority files have *had* to be made compatible. The availability of Library of Congress cards for most of a library's collection has made it imperative for the cataloger to follow the LC rules when cataloging materials for which LC cards are not available. The result is an authority file at the Library of Congress and one at the local library that are compatible. *Consistency* within the authority file—its internal structure—will depend on a prime-mover at a central location. Jolley (1960) has some comments to make on this problem. He suggests that pure logic in the principles is not possible in our field. Although he is talking about author-title identification, his words are relevant to all types of authority files.

---

[1]Scientific and Technical Aerospace Reports.

Cataloging has been defined as the codification of existing practice, and codification means that the same treatment must be applied to
the same classes of books and that these classes must be defined by as
broad and objectively stated criteria as possible. . . . To seek for
apparent utility by sacrificing consistency is to introduce that element
of fundamental uncertainty which vitiates so much cataloging.

The principles of cataloging are short and simple, and not much
open to dispute. Many have suggested that dispute cannot be avoided
when the time comes to apply the principles. One cataloguer has
written: The plain fact is that no set of basic functions and techniques
can be set down so firmly and be so readily understood that anyone and
everyone using it as a base will come always (or even most of the time)
to the same inevitable decision about a particular problem.

If this statement is correct, then the cataloguer's task is hopeless, for
no code—however elaborate—can cover every possible exposition of a
particular bibliographic relation. In fact it is not correct—situations do arise
which cannot be dealt with unhesitatingly on the basis of agreed principles.
The soundness of the principle is not in doubt, only the manner in which it
should be applied. Such cases are not common, and no good is done by
trying too hard to bring them within a convincing logical framework. An
arbitrary and authoritative decision does less harm when its arbitrary
character is openly admitted. The perfect cataloguing code will be made up
of nine-tenths obvious development of a few basic principles and one-tenth
authoritarian cutting of the more involved "Gordian knots." The metaphor
tends to be misleading—what is needed in many cases is simply a final
choice when arguments of equal weight can be put on each side.

Only harm can be done by setting standards which are impossibly
high. No code can make certain that every book is everywhere catalogued in the same way. No catalogue can succeed always in bringing
together all the words of one author or all editions of one work. What
the cataloguer can *hope to do* is to *construct a catalogue on such lines
that it will be a source not of confusion but of instruction to its users*.
. . . For those who use the catalogue are also those who create the other
sources of bibliographic information with which the catalogue has to
be integrated and it is they who by their ignorance and indifference
create so many difficulties (Jolley, 1960. p. 138–139) (italics mine).

From this review of the development of the existing authority files
which have made several information systems and libraries compatible, it
might appear that the compatibility of authority files is inevitable. Lest you

put this paper down with undue optimism, I need only comment on one or two of the inherent problems to overcome before compatibility of *subject* authority files is a reality.

Table 2, entitled "Comparative structure of the three forms of [subject] catalogue," is from *Subject Catalogues; Heading and Structures,* by E. J. Coates (1960). Mr. Coates had this to say about the compatibility of the three forms of catalogues:

TABLE 2: Comparative Structure of the Three Forms of Catalogue

PROBLEM	MECHANISM AVAILABLE		
	Alphabetico-specific form	*Classified form*	*Alphabetico-classed form*
1 Access to correctly formulated request	Direct to subject entry	Indirect via subject index	Indirect via 'see' references for all topics not main headings
2 Synonyms	'See' reference	As above	As above
3 Hierarchical relationship. Generic-to-specific	'See also' reference	Collocation of entries	Collocation of entries
4 Hierarchical relationship. Specific-to-generic	'See also' reference (None or few in dictionary catalogue practice)	Collocation of entries	Collocation of entries
5 Collateral relationship	(a) 'See also' reference (b) Limited accidental collocation	(a) Collocation of entries to limited extent (b) Limited collocation in subject index	Limited accidental collocation of 'see' references
Illustrative example			
1 Access to correctly formulated request	RADIO ENGINEERING	Radio engineering 621.384	Radio engineering 'see' Communications— Radio
2 Synonyms	WIRELESS 'see' RADIO	Wireless engineering 621.384	Wireless engineering 'see' Communications— Radio
3 Hierarchical relationship. Generic-to-specific	COMMUNICA-TIONS ENGI-NEERING 'see also' RADIO ENGINEERING	(Collocation in classified file) 621.38—Communications 621.384—Radio	(Collocation) Communications Communications —Radio

TABLE 2: Comparative Structure of the Three Forms of Catalogue (continued)

4 Hierarchical relationship. Specific-to-Generic	RADIO ENGINEERING 'see also' COMMUNICATIONS ENGINEERING	Collocation in classified file as above	Collocation as above
5 Collateral relationship	RADIO ENGINEERING 'see also' TELEGRAPHY	(a) Collocation in classified file 621.382—Telegraphy 621.384—Radio (b) Accidental collocation in subject index Radio engineering 621.384 Radio programmes 791.4	Accidental collocation of references Radio engineering 'see' Communications —Radio Radio programmes 'see' Entertainment —Radio

Specific (or direct) alphabetical entry designed to give the enquirer immediate access to his subject is incompatible with the assembly of entries on related subjects (classed approach). The alphabetico-specific catalogue arranges headings by their affinities of spelling, the classified and the alphabetico-classed forms arrange their entries by affinities of meaning. If we arrange by affinities of meaning, it becomes necessary to provide a supplementary alphabetical list of subject headings which will direct the enquirer to the place in the catalog (or index) under which entries on the desired subject have been filed. In other words, the enquirer must make two references in every case. He must first consult the supplementary alphabetic list, and then refer to the place in the catalog to which the entry in the alphabetical list has referred him. It is on this point, the value of direct access versus display of entries on related subjects, that the great debates on the respective merits of the dictionary and classified catalogues have turned.

Great debates on indexing vocabularies are still going on—the battle still rages; I am afraid we are not yet far enough along for the following statement to apply:

In the historical development of any craft there is always a well-marked stage at which a line of intuitive and empirically minded practice is brought to an abrupt end by someone who succeeds in rationalising the best current practice into a few general principles which can thereafter be applied consciously. (Coates, 1960. p. 31).

This someone for the library profession was Charles Ammi Cutter in 1876.

This being the case, while we wait, it may be most sensible for us to consider some movement toward acceptable minimum standards of compatibility without expecting uniformity to present itself full blown. There has certainly been enough experimentation in this field. There have been some attempts to climb down from the Tower of Babel but to my knowledge, no Messiah, by the name of Cutter or Dewey, is presently available. Ranganathan (1957) is of and from another world. It appears we will have to rediscover his theories before we will apply them.

In the meantime a great many constructive efforts are getting underway: Studies sponsored by the COS(AT)I committee of the Federal Council on Science and Technology (one on a common vocabulary and another on descriptive cataloguing for report literature); cooperative effort like the National Union Catalog and the Medlars project; the mechanization of the Universal Decimal Classification schedules in all available languages and editions; the engineering terminology studies of the Engineers Joint Council. These studies should help to effect some degree of uniformity if not compatibility.

If one can learn anything from the past efforts at compatibility of authority files, these efforts were practicable because the following conditions existed:

1. There was someone devoted enough to the "cause" that he and one or two others did the necessary work of discovering the basic rules and generally accepted practice.
2. There was an outward force driving two or more information systems toward a common goal and there was a willingness to make compromise.
3. There was an inward force to centralize in an outside agency some of the effort of file organization for the information system.

and last, but not least:

4. There were basic principles underlying the processes employed intuitively to organize file collections and these were capable of description.

If these factors are at work now, and I believe they are to a certain extent for the mechanized information system, then it is appropriate to summarize some of the historical steps toward compatibility:

First stage—some one authority file is used as a "draft" for a comprehensive authority file or code of rules. Some one person or system serves as the focal point for the effort toward compatibility.

Second stage—Comments, suggestions, changes are solicited and received from interested persons.

Third stage—A preliminary edition is distributed to all interested for their comments and trial use.

Fourth stage—A first edition is approved and distributed with recommendation for its adoption and use on all new material coming into the systems who have agreed to use it.

Fifth stage—A first edition revised, or addenda, is prepared. An editorial office is maintained if frequent changes are necessary (as with classification schemes).

Sixth stage—A second edition, etc., etc.

Is the question answered? In great part, it appears that compatibility is as inevitable as harmony. But it depends on the workers in the field—just as harmony in music depends on the composer and the performers. Even though an orchestra may be following the same score, musicians can tune their instruments and play the music in such a way that they either achieve harmony or they don't.

To summarize my views, the feasibility of making authority files compatible has been demonstrated in some areas of file organization but not in others. Whether these efforts will continue or begin in the scientific and technical information field depends on the personnel involved and the environmental factors surrounding the effort.

The anniversary of the first hundred years of our country was marked by the publication of some very significant library rules or authority files: the Dewey's *Decimal Classification* and Cutter's *Rules for a Dictionary Catalog*. Perhaps the year 1976 will see the pattern repeated with significant rules or authority files being published for the field of documentation.

REFERENCES

1. American Library Association. 1942. A.L.A. rules for filing catalog cards. A.L.A., Chicago.

2. American Library Association. 1949. A.L.A. cataloging rules for author and title entries. Second ed. A.L.A., Chicago.

3. Coates, E. J. 1960. Subject catalogues: headings and structure. Library Association, London.

4. Federal Council for Science and Technology, Committee on Scientific Information. 1963. Standard for descriptive cataloging of government scientific and technical reports. Washington, D.C. Rept. PB181605.

5. Howerton, Paul W., editor. 1963. Information handling: first principles. Spartan Books, Washington, D.C.

6. Jolley, L. 1960. The principles of cataloging. Crosby Lockwood and Son, London.

7. Library of Congress. 1949. Rules for descriptive cataloging. Washington, D.C.

8. Painter, Ann F. 1963. An analysis of duplication and consistency of subject indexing involved in report handling at the Office of Technical Services, U.S. Department of Commerce. Off. of Tech. Ser., U.S. Dept. of Comm., Washington, D.C. Rept. PB 181501.

9. Ranganathan, S. R. 1957. Prolegomena to library classification. 2nd edition. The Library Association, London.

Edited comment on this paper by
Dr. Joseph H. Roe, Jr.,
National Library of Medicine

The hope expressed that someone emerge in the field of documentation to effect order out of chaos as did Charles Ammi Cutter in the field of librarianship, depends on the relative importance of the contributions of men such as Cutter and Anthony Panizzi, mid-nineteenth century Director of the Library of the British Museum.

More recently, in the United States, a dominant figure in the cataloging field has been Mr. Seymour Lubetzky, now professor of Cataloging at the University of California (Los Angeles). He has led a movement to revamp the American Library Association's *Cataloging Rules for Author and Title Entries*. This effort (Lubetzky, 1960) has attempted to provide compatibility in "main entry" cataloging on an international scale. Inherent in the revision has been an effort to simplify the "rules," eliminate the plethora of exceptions, and establish a "catalog code" based on reasonable and logical principles. This work was the subject of an international meeting at UNESCO in Paris, October 9–18, 1961. At that time there was virtually unanimous acceptance of the revised rules. However, in the United States over two years later, there is continued reluctance to adopt these new rules based primarily on the enormous *conversion costs* for certain large libraries such as the Library of Congress. Can we learn from this experience in attempting to answer the question, "Is Compatibility of Authority Files Practicable?"

REFERENCES

1. Lubetzky, Seymour. 1960. Code of cataloging rules, author and title entry, American Library Association, Chicago.

Development of Machine-generated Reference Tools

At the outset, it might be well for me to define what I do and do not mean by "machine-generated reference tools." I intend to use the term *machine* very broadly to mean any form of data-processing equipment (sorter, collater, or computer, including computerized typesetting or printing equipment). The term "machine-generated tools" includes the finished printed products, such as books, journal articles, indexes, and abstract journals, generated by use of machines; it also refers to the information available in machine-readable form. I am not going to consider as machine-generated tools those products which are merely microforms or reductions of the physical documents. The important concept underlying the term as I use it is that the "information" which the reference tool contains is potentially more readily accessible because it is in machine-readable form. This provides a flexibility for the information beyond limited use within a hardbound reference book or a catalog drawer.

The types of machine-generated reference tools I would like to discuss cover all the tools which would be included in a beginning course in reference: library catalogs, national bibliographies, union lists of serials, abstract journals, dictionaries and encyclopedias, handbooks, manuals and directories, yearbooks and almanacs, bibliographical sources, subject bibliographies and indexes, geographical sources, and government documents. Examples of any one of these types which are machine-generated (either printed or assembled) can be found. This fact of production may be unrecognized by the librarian using the tool, and the publisher may not be aware of it, either. The present physical production method for generating the physical *form* of the tools we use is important but, for the most part, out of our hands. For some time to come, most of the tools used by librarians

Reprinted by permission of the American Library Association, "Development of Machine-generated Reference Tools" in *The Present Status and Future Prospects of Reference/Information Service*, pp. 121-33; Copyright © 1967 American Library Association.

will be sold in codex form, but there are trends and developments in utilizing the machine-readable information of these tools in other ways. I do not intend to go way out and describe projected, but nonexistent, information systems which may eventually replace present tools. The stress of my argument is on the utilization of information in new ways because of its potential availability in new formats; otherwise, for example, the tapes used for printing might be considered as waste products by the printer, once the reference tool is printed. We, as buyers and makers of reference tools, will have to experiment with ways to use these by-products to best advantage.

Before discussing the potential of machine-generated reference tools, I would like to mention certain basic requirements of reference librarians which should be kept in mind when discussing all reference tools, especially those now machine generated. I do not feel enough stress has been put on these requirements as yet.

Don Swanson, in the February, 1966, issue of the *Bulletin of the Atomic Scientists,* talked about improving communication among scientists.[1] What he described as the basic requirement of the customers of our services could just as easily be described as a requirement of reference librarians—the *principle of least action.* Swanson said, "The design of any *information service* should be predicated on the assumption that its customers will *exert minimal effort in order to receive its benefits.*" Reference librarians, to provide adequate service and do their work well, also require (2) *easy access to information.* Dorothy Sinclair has asked, "Can anything be done to reduce the number of hours we spend, often fruitlessly, in checking indexes?"[2] We also need (3) *frequent updating of reference tools* which would greatly reduce the necessity of performing long retrospective searches. We should be able to place more reliance on facts and figures obtained in answer to current questions. Again, reference/information workers need (4) *less duplication in the tools they purchase and use collectively,* and this is where the greatest potential of machine-generated reference tools lies, in my opinion. We need to reduce the redundancy factor in reference tools used.

A study by Roger Greer[3] showed that, from a random sample taken from the *National Union Catalog* of books published in the United States in 1961, *Publishers' Weekly—Book Publishing Record* covered about 85

[1]Don R. Swanson, "On Improving Communication among Scientists," *Bulletin of the Atomic Scientists,* 22:9 (Feb., 1966).
[2]Dorothy Sinclair, "Meanwhile Back at the Reference Desk," *RQ,* 5:11 (Fall, 1965).
[3]Roger C. Greer, "The Current United States National Book Bibliography: An Analysis of Coverage with Recommendations for Improvement" (unpublished Ph.D. dissertation, Rutgers—The State Univ., 1964).

percent; *Cumulative Book Index,* 91 percent; *PW, BPR,* and *CBI,* together, 95 percent, with 82 percent of the items duplicated four times. In a recent National Science Foundation-sponsored study of overlap between *Physics Abstracts* and *Nuclear Science Abstracts* (Greer and Atherton, 1966, unpublished), we found that there was an overlap of more than 50 percent in coverage of identical articles between these two abstracting journals. Excess duplication in reference tools surely violates the principle of least action.

Additions to this list of basic requirements could probably be suggested, but the requirements noted may be sufficient to highlight what reference-tool producers must keep in mind, collectively, if they intend to make a contribution toward the fulfillment of the principle of least action in libraries.

The different types of reference work must also be considered before we can properly determine the usefulness of the newer reference tools available as by-products of machine processing of information for publication or compilation. The following is a list of the more or less typical kinds of reference/information work, regardless of the type of library in which it is done: answering inquiries for facts and figures—sometimes called "ready or quick reference"; preparing bibliographies; assisting readers in use of library; making interlibrary loans; maintaining special indexing and abstracting services; providing translations; collecting information on library resources; cooperating with bibliographical centers; and producing union catalogs. All of this work could be aided by combined files of reference information in machine-readable form.

Besides the so-called "reference collection" of a library, the reference librarian usually consults many "reference tools" which are available in other parts of the library, such as card catalog, process information file, and serial record file; he also obtains information outside the library, from referral centers, other libraries, direct contact with specialists, and so on. Working with this mixed variety of tools, used separately rather than collectively, is one of the problems reference librarians and library users face daily. Perhaps only sporadically, but still in actuality, the typical reference librarian is already in tune to be "on-line" to the national "system," to use Verner Clapp's phrasing—if only such a system existed. What we seem to have is H. Dubester's "un-system." Against this backdrop of requirements, activities, and display of the variety of tools available, it would seem that the time is right for librarians to organize and effect the proper use of machine records developed during the generation of existing reference tools. If we did, we might have better tools and be able to bring about greater cooperation and coordination of regional and national reference library service at no increase in cost. The combination of information in the reference tools we want to use collectively could be used in a way we have not yet imagined or adequately planned for. As Don Swanson said to me a few days ago, the problem is one of organization, not of computerization. Computerization, or automation, is simply the means to effect better organization.

Joseph Becker, back in 1947, predicted what could be expected of library (and reference-tool) mechanization:

> From the flexible arrangement of the cards, bibliographies become readily available by subject, author, and title. In special libraries, where material on one subject is concentrated, the research possibilities of gathering, sorting, filing and printing information are almost limitless. Continuous machine interfiling permits keeping current with new entry additions.[4]

It has taken almost twenty years for the library profession (and some reference-book publishers) to recognize the potentialities of computers in processing information which, when recorded only once, can be useful for multiple purposes.

It seems to me that the trend in the use of computers to generate reference tools is to follow the principle of by-product data generation, beginning with actual preparation of manuscripts for publication. The H. W. Wilson Company and the Bowker Company have done some pioneer work in the combination, cumulation, and multiple use of records for producing reference tools, but their efforts are unfortunately limited. They do not adequately provide for the combination of data from *various* sources within and without their respective companies. If we agree that such is our objective, attaining it demands greater cooperation between librarians and reference-tool publishers to consolidate their efforts at mechanization and create compatible machine records.

I would like to describe a research and development project of the American Institute of Physics (AIP) as an example of how a publisher can improve the situation. AIP publishes more than 30 percent of the world's physics research in journal form. This means that AIP has the potential capability for improving reference work in physics if all of its publications were available in machine-readable form. Imagine how easy it would be to use the information contained in these journals if it were possible to interrogate directly an information system made up of the original manuscripts and to search the indexing records provided as coded identification of each separate item in the machine text. The AIP project will provide computer programs for the production of: input for automatic typesetting (thereby helping the publisher); author and subject indexes (thereby helping

---

[4]Joseph Becker (unpublished paper, Catholic University, 1947).

readers and librarians); data for abstract journal preparation; citation index data; automatic search files for local information centers; and data for annual subject bibliographies and cumulative indexes, to mention only a few by-products. Many more reference tools can be generated with no additional keyboarding operations.

I said earlier that I would not dwell on nonexistent systems, and I meant it. Although the system I just described does not yet exist for AIP journals, the necessary technology for developing such a system is available, and we intend to do it within the next five years, beginning with manuscripts from only two journals. Accompanying this development will be the type of studies Alan Rees mentioned yesterday—psychological and environmental studies of users of physics information. We intend to study the variety of uses of this original data at places like Bell Telephone Laboratories, Massachusetts Institute of Technology, and American Society for Metals.

Many of the components of the system I have described are already in existence, behind the scenes, in many of the printshops producing the reference tools we use. For example, since January, 1966, *Psychological Abstracts* is available in print, as well as in machine-readable form, which is useful for by-product data generation. *Golden Book Encyclopedia* and the *McGraw-Hill Encyclopedia of Science and Technology* are also thus available but except for experiments in natural language searching, they have no great potential use. Several research journals are typeset and printed by computer. With slight modification, the machine record of several reference tools could be used beyond the automated printing process.

I do not have to itemize for this audience the number of library catalogs now available, in whole or in part, in machine-readable form. The numerous bibliographies with KWIC (Keyword-in-Context) indexes produced since H. P. Luhn demonstrated the method in 1958 is legion. Nor do I have to elaborate on *Index Medicus* and the backup service for mechanized retrieval searches of the medical literature, MEDLARS, at the National Library of Medicine.

Most of these machine-generated tools and services appear to have shortcomings, if the combinability and compatibility problems necessary to effect a system of these reference tools are taken into consideration. (The best summary of these shortcomings, as well as a discussion of the strong points of the KWIC indexes and other machine-generated tools, can be found in Mary Elizabeth Stevens' *Automatic Indexing: A State of the Art Report*.[5]

---

[5]Mary Elizabeth Stevens, *Automatic Indexing: A State of the Art Report* (National Bureau of Standards, 1965, Monograph 91 [Washington, D.C.: Govt. Print. Off., 1965]).

For publishers, as well as for librarians and information workers, there are many good reasons why reference tools such as dictionaries, encyclopedias, handbooks, almanacs, and bibliographies should be produced with the aid of machines which make it possible to:

1. Reduce the time lapse between a ready manuscript and time of publication
2. Increase efficiency in production techniques, i.e., reduce costs of preparation and permit complete flexibility (different type sizes and legibility insured if coded for automatic typesetting in a Photon, Linofilm, or similar photocomposing machine) of various tools in any desired format using the same data
3. Accommodate additional or by-product services or a greater variety of services than could otherwise be obtained
4. Facilitate cumulations and cooperative services
5. Attain continuous bibliographic control, as well as compilation capability, thereby making updating and revision easier
6. Provide for easy transmission of data to and from various places
7. Avoid duplication in sources normally used separately, now easily combinable.

If we compare this list with the requirements, librarians and reference-tool publishers appear to have common objectives. Chemical Abstracts Service, Engineering Index, American Petroleum Institute, and Biological Sciences Information Services have all increased their flexibility in providing additional services and have improved their present abstract journal and indexing operations by using machines for part of the work involved. In government agencies, here and abroad, there is a strong trend toward machine-generated reference tools. Atomic Energy Commission, the National Aeronautics and Space Administration, the National Library of Medicine, and even the Library of Congress beginning this fall will have part of their bibliographic reference tools on magnetic tape, and experiments in a variety of libraries throughout the country will determine the usefulness of data in this form for various purposes.

Quite obviously a great deal has happened in the last twenty years in relation to machine-generated tools for reference work, but I have had to conclude that there has been no concerted effort on the part of any group to be wholly or even partly in tune with anyone else in producing compatible tools, easily combinable for reference work. It is as though we were witnessing a rerun of an old movie covering early railroad history. This analogy will continue along the lines Miss Allen mentioned yesterday, converting our freight trains of reference service to express trains. In the early days, everyone built railroad tracks and equipment of a different gauge. Engines and trains literally could not be switched from one railroad's tracks to those of another. The east-west railroad connection was quite a feat. Today, the tapes of one library's catalog are not easily combined with those of another. The serials list of one library or a group of libraries cannot be combined with the records of any of the abstracting journals, and there has been little done to effect a combination of library catalogs and biographical directories, and so on. We still have a long way to go, and possibly only some of us are on the same gauge track.

We are now getting used to the idea of magnetic-tape libraries of legal statutes and other legal records and of computer-generated concordances (first of St. Thomas Aquinas' work in 1949, then of the Dead Sea Scrolls, Matthew Arnold's poetry, and Anglo-Saxon poetic records). Automated bibliographies of the type mentioned in the February 24, 1966, issue of the *U.S. Library of Congress Information Bulletin*[6] could be the kind of tool used in machine-readable form in several libraries. I refer here to the *Deutsche Bibliographie,* which appears weekly, contains information similar to *Publishers' Weekly,* and has an index of publishers and a combined author and keyword index automatically prepared and cumulated on a monthly, quarterly, semiannual, and five-year basis. The day may soon come when all national bibliographies are available in machine-readable form and in a computer store, where they can be used on a local, regional, or national basis, as we now use the *National Union Catalog.* Before this day is upon us, perhaps we should take stock of the possible effects and implications of these new tools and of their potential for new approaches to reference/information work.

Jesse Shera has said: "The potentialities of automation can free the reference librarian from the popular concept of a mechanical stack-boy . . . and permit the librarian to rethink the entire reference procedure. . . ." Later, he commented on the opportunity automation affords "to analyze the reference process and re-define reference service."[7] Helen Focke mentioned the need to analyze reference questions. This is a natural by-product when we use machine-generated tools, e.g., the MIT/TIP weekly monitor record. The potential may be there, but, unfortunately, the System Development Corporation research team, which completed the report on a national document-handling system for the Committee on Scientific and Technical Information last year, could not report much evidence that librarians at present were looking beyond their immediate tasks toward a larger concept of services, based on the advances in library

---

[6]"News in the Library World—Automated Bibliography," *U.S. Library of Congress Information Bulletin,* 25:111 (Feb. 24, 1966).
[7]Jesse Shera, "Automation and the Reference Librarian," *RQ,* 3:4 (July, 1964).

automation. They saw little evidence of great strides in expanded reference tools and retrieval mechanisms based on new technological developments. They felt that a "prescriptive" rather than an "adaptive" philosophy toward information-system automation was predominant at this time. This means that the computer, though used by the librarian, is regarded primarily as an aid in his work and only indirectly as an aid to the user. SDC also reported that capabilities for new applications were going untapped. (Parenthetically, I can say that many publishers of reference tools consider the computer an aid in the printing process rather than an aid to the ultimate user. Only a few farsighted publishers have looked beyond this initial operation in the long process of information transfer, which they originally initiate by the publication of information.)

In fact, the SDC team painted a very black picture:

> Unless someone with unusual foresight and influence establishes workable standardization, the history of library coordination as a mechanizable system complex may be as turbulent as the history of higher-order computer languages has been. Unfortunately, the rush of library automation efforts could be so rapid that each installation, preoccupied with attaining its own internal efficiency, might not notice the incompatibilities of its formats, codes, etc., with those of other libraries unless strong efforts—such as those that a capping agency could exert—are made to coordinate these aspects of library automation.[8]

The future development of machine-generated reference tools is bright, but there are storm clouds on the horizon. The possible effect of present-day developments may be greater duplication of effort and greater incompatibility. The requirement for positive action awaits agreement in standardizing machine-readable data and the creation of an atmosphere of cooperation among librarians, between publishers and librarians, and between librarians and users. Librarians and reference-tool publishers will have to strive toward a common technological solution of some of their problems and make an effort to avoid the duplication in services and collections of information we now have. A true "system"—an organized whole—could be effected, but a whole new field of automatic "switching centers" in the total information system will have to be established. We may get the wherewithal for this from Title III, but it will not work well if the right people do not get together.

---

[8]U.S. Federal Council for Science and Technology, Committee on Scientific and Technical Information, *Recommendations for National Document Handling Systems in Science and Technology* ([Washington, D.C.: U.S. Dept. of Commerce, National Bureau of Standards, Institute for Applied Technology; distributed by Clearinghouse for Federal Scientific and Technical Information, Springfield, Va.], 1965), Appendix A, 2: 11–6.

It would appear that I am asking for the impossible when I ask reference librarians, reference-tool publishers, and computer technologists to cooperate, but we obviously have problems in common. We should be able to work together toward acceptable solutions. At least three of the areas of responsibility of the ALA Reference Services Division, as stated in the Division's By-Laws and discussed in an article by Frances Neel Cheney, offer some guidelines for the librarian's role. They are:

> Conduct and sponsorship of activities and projects in reference services.
>
> Synthesis of reference activities . . . in the various types of libraries so as to produce a unified professional concept of the reference function.
>
> Evaluation, selection, and interpretation of reference materials.[9]

In some circles, I know there is inertia or reticence to consider new approaches to old problems because individuals feel that these approaches may be less than adequate for problems in their *own* libraries or publishing houses. It is very illuminating to present these dissenters with the evidence in the study cited earlier which documents the enormous duplication in our present national bibliographic tools; with Ann Painter's study on the inconsistency found among human indexers; and with the present lack of standards for measuring quality in existing systems. When we read daily of the new techniques for conveying information, of efforts of an M.I.T. Intrex research team to grapple with problems of developing a nationwide computer network that will make every bit of knowledge instantly available, of Radcliffe students using a computer by means of a teletypewriter in their dormitory basements while doing the laundry or drying their hair—when we read all this, we cannot continue to hide behind our own reference desks, surrounded by our own reference resources. Librarians will have to consider the impact of all these techniques on their day-to-day work, on their ready-reference questions and on their bibliographic searches.

The *Newsweek* article referred to by Miss Harris, "Good-by to Gutenberg,"[10] asked, "Who is killing Gutenberg?" It might have asked, "Who is killing Gutenberg and Marion the librarian?" The answer in the article was: rising costs, multiplying knowledge, *new techniques for conveying information,* and an exploding population. Whether you are a reference librarian in an academic institution, in a public library, or in a special library, whether you are a dictionary publisher or an index publisher, you cannot fail to admit that these are the reasons for your constant

---

[9]Frances Neel Cheney, "The Reference Services Division: A Look Before and After," *RQ*, 4:3–6, 16 (Nov., 1964).

[10]"Good by to Gutenberg," *Newsweek*, 67:85 (Jan. 24, 1966).

awareness of the pressure of time, of the limitation on manpower, and of the poverty of the tools and services you provide.

It may be that the users of our tools and libraries may solve their problems in their own way, and we may not be called upon to help. If that happens, *our* library problems may go unsolved. Don Swanson suggests that future systems must provide for more digestion, summary, and packing down of knowledge, which will permit scientists and others to progress without foundering in the backlog of published information. He states categorically:

> Present libraries and information systems wait to be used. A future information system, however, should seek out its customers. . . . We infer that future systems will provide decentralized service points and selective, direct, and continuous distribution of information to customers. Service in response to standing requests should be maximized, so that customer initiative can be minimized.[11]

He implies that, if future information services do not perform these functions, they will continue to be performed in the informal and most helpful (as well as expensive) ways in which they are performed today: the invisible college, preprint exchange groups, etc.

New information services, with libraries in focus and in tune with information and data-analysis centers, are on the horizon along with the storm clouds I mentioned earlier. The Technical Information Project within the M.I.T. library complex, the Stanford University Library plans for a computerized book catalog with remote access stations at places other than the library, and the data-analysis centers and library complex at Oak Ridge National Laboratory are examples of future relationships. But the trends are not positively in this direction; some effort on the part of catalogers and reference librarians, working closely with reference-tool publishers and information users, will be necessary.

A major shift in outlook is necessary before reference-book publishers and librarians will begin to see the need for adopting the principle of by-product data generation within their own operations. We need to try some new approaches; e.g., we need to learn from someone's efforts to combine such things as the Library of Congress catalog entries with the tape used to produce, say, the *Dictionary of American Biography;* the tape for *American Men of Science* with *Chemical Abstracts;* the special bibliographies in linguistics with the holdings of large libraries such as Harvard, Yale and Newberry; or the *Readers' Guide* with the *Union List of Serials* in a school/public library regional center. The computers we use may need to have a little more advanced storage capacity and speedier listing and

---

[11]Don R. Swanson, *op. cit.,* p. 10, 11.

list-searching processes if they are to do these things, but breakthroughs and announcements of such technological improvements have already been made. What we desperately need are more librarians who are willing to learn programming (or better still devise their own library/reference/cataloging-oriented compiler language) and librarians who will assist publishers in creating the tools they need in a way which will permit more effective and efficient reference service.

In my opinion, we should not stand by while linguists, mathematicians, and systems engineers redesign our own library-information systems. We should be involved in plans for the reference tools, which eventually will all be machine-generated for purely economic reasons.

Certain areas of research and development suggest themselves if we consider contributing to the development of machine-generated reference tools and improved reference services. These projects should be carried out by research teams which include librarians. The teams could:

1. Survey the most typical reference-work activities and the linkage of this work with various reference tools. Rothstein's comments[12] on core titles of encyclopedias, dictionaries, and almanacs in published literature reference work are worth noting here. The survey could be done by type of library, as well as by type of work, on a local and regional basis (similar to a suggestion by Verner Clapp).

2. Survey the major reference-tool publishers; determine the feasibility of increasing the data bank of machine-readable "reference" information; and estimate the changeover costs necessary to provide by-products of the type described. Such a study should include a cost-savings survey in libraries which would use these tools instead of conventional tools.

3. Plan and implement a demonstration project involving several libraries, in which machine-readable catalogs would be integrated with some machine-readable reference tools. The libraries would have a reference staff and user population capable of being trained to work with such an automated system. Perform experiments and monitor use to determine new approaches to information, new types of reference/information activity, and so forth.

4. Experiment with programmed teaching machines at appropriate points in public libraries, college campuses, and research laboratories to study ways of improving access to available information or referral services.

---

[12]Samuel Rothstein, "The Measurement and Evaluation of Reference Service," *Library Trends*, 12:463 (Jan., 1964).

No doubt many enterprising librarians in the audience have thought of many more projects which could make their work easier and the use of the library by their patrons more rewarding. Machine-generated reference tools are not a panacea; but the potential for new approaches to reference/information work, as well as greater ease in human communication, seem limitless with them and almost impossible without them.

SUMMARY

1. We need to stress a coordinated approach to information system and network development—from *origin* of information (author's manuscript to editor/publisher) to *use* of information (in library research worker's office, and the like).
2. We need to combine efforts and avoid *redo* of input operations (automatic typesetting for publisher; machine-readable cataloging for library; data compilations in information centers).
3. We should follow the *principle of least action* in information system design.
4. We should follow the *principle of by-product data generation* in machine-generated data.
5. We must make *provision for combinability and flexibility* of information records.

Bibliographic Data Bases—Their Effect on User Interface Design in Interactive Retrieval Systems

Someone, in an OECD report, conjectured that this question was posed at the very dawn of Western civilization:

> What use is the science of navigation if we do not know where to go?

Where are we going with interactive bibliographic retrieval systems? Will they only help create new bottlenecks and frustrations for the information seeker? (Is there anything worse than getting off a Boeing 747 and then driving through a traffic jam?)

This essay will follow along the lines of John L. Bennett's challenge paper for this workshop and ask more questions than it answers, prod more than it guides, and offer few solutions for the myriad of problems which lie ahead. As John said, "A key difference in interactive terminal search is that data is brought to the searcher rather than the searcher going to the data." In providing such easy access to the data we will no doubt have different classes of searchers using the file than those for whom the original bibliographic systems were designed.

Will these new users express the same needs to access data elements existent in present bibliographic data bases, or will they express some new needs?

Will it be necessary to go through several generations of system design before we discover the optimal make-up of both the bibliographic data base and the user interface?

I couldn't help thinking, as I began this paper, that we may be in the process of designing the horseless carriage but in so doing, we may have put the cart before the horse! Established data bases and bibliographic services

Reprinted with permission from *Interactive Bibliographic Search: The User/Computer Interface,* edited by Donald E. Walker, 1971, AFIPS Press, pp. 215–223.

as we know them today are often automated "as is." Such a "horseless carriage" with preconceived notions about users at the library catalog may have led us to design a limited rather than a dynamic system.

Is it possible that all our early design efforts with batch-search computer-based systems and our respect for existing indexing and cataloging styles may have put us in a conceptual straitjacket? Is a fresh look at the whole problem of "bibliographic-information retrieval" necessary?

All these questions come from someone who has spent the last five years working with existing bibliographic data bases, testing and evaluating their use within various interactive system configurations. This workshop has forced me to stop working and begin thinking about bibliographic retrieval system design. Four outstanding problem areas relating to user interface stand out as being the most worthy of our concerted attention.

THE PRINCIPLE OF LEAST ACTION

Don Swanson[1] in the February, 1966, issue of the *Bulletin of the Atomic Scientists,* described the basic requirement of the customers of our services as *the principle of least action.* He said, "The design of any information service should be predicated on the assumption that its customers will exert minimal effort in order to receive its benefits." This covers the effort the user must exert to get to the system, to understand how to use it, and to overcome any transfer problems (from one file to another, for instance) encountered before he reaches satisfaction. For the user interface feature of an interactive retrieval system, following *the principle of least action* would imply easy accessibility to computer terminals. (Even with remote access on a terminal closer to user's office or laboratory, the sign-on procedures and communications language with the bibliographic data base should be simple and straightforward, etc.)

THE PROBLEM OF COMPATIBILITY

There has been no concerted effort on the part of any group to be wholly or even partly in tune with anyone else in producing the communication language commands or field names for data in interactive bibliographic retrieval systems. Today, in 1971, one library's machine-based catalog search system cannot easily be combined with that of another library. The ANSI communications format is a step in the right direction, but few abstracting services or libraries are coordinating their efforts during system design stages. And yet, when you think of it, they have the same ultimate user in mind! More has been done in the last few years to effect a combination of machine-readable data bases for library catalogs, serials lists and abstracting data, but we still have a long way to go.

In 1966,[2] I made the following remarks, and they still seem applicable today:

1. We need to find a way to coordinate the use of bibliographic information as information networks develop. From editor/publisher to library to research worker's office, we need a truly efficient switching system for bibliographic reference retrieval. (This will facilitate the user interface problems all along the line when we think of compatible interactive systems.)
2. We need to find ways to avoid redo of input operations as bibliographic data is used over and over again: from automatic typesetting for publisher to machine-readable cataloging for library and data compilations in information centers. (If we follow the principle of by-product data generation, this will ease the transition which the user faces when he switches from one data base to another, one bibliographic style to another, etc.)
3. We should test the principle of least action in existing information systems and redesign any that are found deficient. (The impact on user interface would be great!)

THE PROBLEM OF FLEXIBILITY

Expanding on the theme of standard bibliographic data bases, I think we have to admit that the existing rules for entry and form of bibliographic references differ greatly, that they are dependent on traditions in library cataloging, styles in abstracting and indexing services and chaos in the footnote references in journal articles and monographs. None of us has yet admitted to the absolute necessity to re-think our out-dated idiosyncracies which are now called rules and "bibliographic style." Until librarians and other bibliographers free themselves from the notion of the main entry and the limitations of the established rules for added entry in catalogs and indexes, we will remain in the "horseless carriage" days of bibliographic retrieval. Nowhere more than in the handling of corporate authors do we see how the present catalogs create confusion for the user and work against the improved access of information.[3]

Caryl McAllister,[4] in the paper she presented at the recent ASIS conference in Philadelphia, covers this important point. She says the on-line catalogs and the resultant inverted file format of the access points to the cataloging records (or documents) make inappropriate the current cataloging rules for choice and form of main entry, added entries, and filing. In her opinion, and I concur, *there is no main entry,* in the usual sense of the phrase, *in an on-line catalog.* Instead, the cataloger (using MARC tapes or something similar) assigns various parts of the bibliographic information to the available access point files (author, title, subject, and call number, etc.). He can designate other information as document information, available for inspection when the document is retrieved during a search or when data elements for the document are being assembled for printing a book catalog, bibliography, or whatever. The order of the categories of information would not be as critical as they are when creating a catalog card, and the major source of cataloging difficulties and differences, namely, choice of main entry, would be eliminated.

Access to the names of persons and corporate bodies associated with a document is a problem not unlike subject access. When a user can easily access an on-line name authority file which in turn is linked to the document description file in an integrated on-line bibliographic file, are restrictive rules for describing documents necessary?

Should we launch an attack in the 1970s to free designers of bibliographic retrieval systems from these archaic practices of choice and form of main entry which are linked to the structure of the nineteenth century library catalog? If the Library of Congress calls the tune for the library world when it comes to rules and procedures for descriptive cataloging (including choice and form of main and added entries) maybe they should consider new rules to fit new forms of the catalogs, given the existence of MARC II[5] and the RECON project. Maybe they should take the lead in this area as they did in standardizing the communications format for machine readable bibliographic data.

THE PROBLEM OF AUXILIARY AIDS IN BIBLIOGRAPHIC RETRIEVAL SYSTEMS

An early concern of the designers of mechanized bibliographic retrieval systems was the ease with which the user could switch from vocabulary aids (such as a thesaurus, dictionary of terms, etc.) to the file of documents represented by indexing records. This switching was always off-line in batch processing systems, but such an arrangement is intolerable to the on-line user. Some of the earliest on-line systems provided such access (see column (d) in Table I[6]).

AUDACIOUS[7] was, to the best of our knowledge, the first on-line interactive retrieval system in which one of the widely used traditional library classification systems was the "on-line thesaurus." The user's first search words were checked against the UDC schedules. The class numbers with these keywords in their descriptions were shown and some were selected for searching a portion of the document/index file.

The user felt a certain freedom in choice of words for formulating his search. He was then provided with a "translation" of his words into the language of this particular bibliographic retrieval system.

The on-line system that is designed without such a feature will limit the effectiveness of the user. If the user interface communication language does not accommodate interaction with such vocabulary aids as well as it does for the queries with the documents-indexed data base, we will have interactive systems which are only faster-response batch systems at best. The user will continue to be just as frustrated as he is when he approaches a library catalog and finds the cross reference "Space Travel *see* Interplanetary voyages."

THE NEED FOR AN INTEGRATED BIBLIOGRAPHIC SYSTEM

The problems when several document data bases and different vocabulary control devices are assimilated into one integrated system begin to boggle the mind. Imagine trying to plan to have easy access on-line to authority files relating to just the nine systems described in Table I! Some people are now talking about the use of a "bridge language" across several indexing systems. I hope someone interested in the use of such a bridge language on-line is talking with someone who can handle the problems in the computer software and hardware areas.

TABLE 1: Some User Interface Features of Interactive Retrieval Systems (circa 1968)

(a) System Name	(b) #Docs. in Data Base	(c) Access Points	(d) Access to Authority Files On-Line	(e) Related Terms or Cross Refs Given	(f) Computer Instruction Language	(g) Computer Aided Query Formulation (Conversation)
1. AUDACIOUS (AIP)	2330	UDC description Euratom key words	UDC Schedules	Yes	Optional	Limited
2. BOLD (SDC)	6000	ASTIA Subject category index terms accession	Subject category list, index term file	Yes	Optional	Yes
3. COLEX MICRO (SDC)	2000	descriptor, author, subject /qualified by \subject country type document, subject area, date	No	No	Optional	Yes
4. GRINS (Lehigh U)	1000		Index term	Yes	No	Yes
5. MULTILIST	Varies	any chosen key term to fit application (e.g. author, subject, date, title words, subject headings)	No	No	No	No
6. MARC/MOLDS	2000	any discrete data block	Optional	Optional	No	No
7. NASA/RECON	270000	subject author corporate source report # contract # /qualified by date	No	Yes	Optional	Yes
8. TIP (MIT)	25000	author(s) location (where work done) citation identification article title (entire, keyboard) citation index bibliographic coupling	No	No	No	No
9. SUNY BIOMED COMM. NETWORK	20000	author title subject /qualified by date, lang.	No	No	No	Yes

Conceived as integrated systems, bibliographic data bases should exist on-line with related data files (circulation, union list, order files, thesaurus or classification schedule, etc.). Only then will total bibliographic retrieval system design be complete. The problem of incompatible bibliographic data bases (thesauri as well as document reference files) has to be tackled head-on if such systems are to become an operational reality. Our comparison of on-line systems in existence in 1968 (see Table I) showed great variety in certain features, e.g., access to different data elements on-line, different commands in query language use, etc. The table points up the aforementioned problems of least effort, compatibility, and flexibility.

From our table of characteristics, you could almost conclude that every system required different characteristics for its user interface. Is this really true, or were we only witnessing local variations during the early stages of a new development? I suspect that certain features of these early systems existed in order to make them "proprietary," or to handle constraints imposed by local computer facilities, etc. I know we had to ask ourselves at the time we began AUDACIOUS, MARC/MOLDS, and SUPARS: What data base redesign was needed *before* operations could begin? What could be gained from an open-ended access to the bibliographic data file rather than restricted field access? Should we consider user ease at the terminal as more important than sophisticated search operations?

Most of the papers at this workshop record new variations on this same theme of experimental development in user interface to bibliographic data bases.

The possibilities of digital-video consoles, and micro-teletransmissions screens open up ways hitherto unavailable by which documents may be transmitted. The library may provide information services to the user at work or at home, rather than requiring him to come to the library. The necessary bibliographic tools to access libraries and other data bases will become more numerous and will be available at different levels in central locations, while services will become more decentralized.

The handwriting is on the wall. If our users will access information remote from library or information centers, then it behooves us to think very positively about integrating our present-day diverse collection of data bases, each with its own user interface problems. Ritvars Bregzis[8] speaks to this point when he says that *"new patterns of research and information use will emerge as a result of machine-based bibliographic and related services. Access to documents will have to be managed and organized in a different way."*

The user who can make his own search request to the system will want and needs a *facility* not a barrier to access pertinent information. We will have to review seriously our rules and practices for creating existing bibliographic data bases and our need for compatible user interfaces. How can we promote the idea of an IBS (Integrated Bibliographic System) with and for the on-line user? Where shall we begin to formalize the input to IBS from various sources? Can we plan to combine bibliographic data and reference tools for greater user power and effectiveness? What more do we need to know about the *overlap use* of existing services before we plan an IBS?

REFERENCES

1. Swanson, Don R., "On Improving Communication Among Scientists," *Bulletin of the Atomic Scientists*, 22 Feb., 1966, 9.

2. Atherton, Pauline, "Development of Machine-generated Tools," in *The Present Status and Future Prospects of Reference/Information Service*, ed. by W. Linderman, Chicago, American Library Association, 1967, pp. 121–33.

3. S. R. Ranganathan and G. Bhattacharyya, "Conflict of Authorship; Corporate Body vs. Corporate Body," *Library Science/Documentation*, 7, 1970.

4. McAllister, Caryl, "Cataloging and Display of Bibliographic Information in an On-Line Catalog," *ASIS Conference Proceedings*, Vol. 7, p. 69–72, 1970.

5. Avram, Henriette. *The MARC Pilot Project*, Final Report, Washington, Library of Congress, 1968.

6. Atherton, Pauline and Karen B. Miller, "LC/MARC on MOLDS, an Experiment in Computer-Based Interactive Bibliographic Storage, Search, Retrieval and Processing," *Journal of Library Automation* 3, June 1970, 142–165.

See also, Welch, Noreen O., *A Survey of Five On-Line Retrieval Systems*, Mitre Corp., Washington, D.C., August 1968, MTP-322.

See also, Seiden, Herbert R., "A Comparative Analysis of Interactive Storage and Retrieval Systems. . . ." Santa Monica, California, System Development Corp., Jan. 12, 1970. TM-4421.

7. Freeman, Robert R. and Pauline Atherton. *AUDACIOUS—An Experiment with an On-Line Interactive Reference Retrieval System Using the Universal Decimal Classification as the Index Language in the Field of Nuclear Science*. American Institute of Physics, New York, April 25, 1968. (AIP/UDC-7).

8. Bregzis, R., "Library Networks of the Future" *Drexel Library Q.*, 4, 1968, 261–70.

Knowledge Space: A Conceptual Basis for the Organization of Knowledge*

by Peter P.M. Meincke and Pauline Atherton

We propose a new conceptual basis for visualizing the organization of information, or knowledge, which differentiates between the concept "vectors" for a field of knowledge represented in a multidimensional space, and the state "vectors" for a person based on his understanding of these concepts, and the representational "vectors" for information items which might be in a retrieval system which covers a subspace of knowledge. This accommodates the notion of search volume in which the user of a retrieval system can expand or reduce the subspace he searches for relevant information items which have representational vectors with components on basic concept vectors similar to his state vector. The benefits of such a new conceptual framework are explored in this article.

INTRODUCTION

Among man's major efforts have been his many attempts to classify and organize the knowledge he has accumulated, from Aristotle to Descartes, Dalgarno and Leibniz, and from Melvil Dewey to S.R. Ranganathan. "Knowledge itself," John Locke said, "is nothing but the perception of the connection and agreement or disagreement and repugnancy, of any of our ideas."

Reprinted from *Journal of the American Society for Information Science,* Volume 27, 1976. Reprinted by permission of John Wiley & Sons, Inc.
*Paper presented at the Third International Study Conference in Classification Research at Bombay, India, January 5–11, 1975.

Anatol Rapaport (1) was moved to say that:

> Life, therefore, depends essentially on an ordering process, on fighting off the general trend toward chaos, which is always present in the nonliving world. But to increase the order of anything means to make it describable with less information (less effort). And is this process not the very essence of knowledge, of science itself? . . . when scientists weave a mass of seemingly unrelated data into a monolithic theory, they are all contributing to the process of decreasing the entropy of a portion of the world, of making it more comprehensible with less effort.

Rapaport goes on (p. 260) to say that "Korzybski and others maintained that structure is the only content of knowledge . . . (and) a *measure* of structure or of the amount of organization is required" (italics ours).

Bronowski (2) contends that "One aim of the physical sciences has been to give an exact picture of the material world. One achievement of physics in the 20th Century has been to prove that the aim is unattainable . . . that there is no absolute knowledge . . . all information is imperfect. We have to treat it with humility." He describes Max Born's statement—"I am not convinced that theoretical physics is actual philosophy"—as meaning that: "The World is not a fixed, solid array of objects, for it cannot be fully separated from our perception of it. It shifts under our gaze, it interacts with us, and the knowledge that it yields has to be interpreted by us. There is no way of exchanging information that does not demand an act of judgement."

Bronowski renames the Principle of Uncertainty as the Principle of Tolerance, and hopes to fix, once and for all, the realization that all knowledge is limited. After all, he says: "All knowledge, all information between human beings, can be exchanged only within a play of tolerance."

Colin Cherry (3) thinks of science as "created in fragments like a jigsaw puzzle, in which pieces can be added, related to their neighbors but not so obviously to the whole picture." He sees all attempts at a radical recasting of the structures of science, technology and indeed all fields of knowledge, "thwarted by lack of understanding of their future *directions of growth*" (italics ours).

CLASSIFICATION AND INDEXING METHODS

The question before us, then, is: Do the various methods used by librarians, documentalists and information scientists to organize knowledge and information keep pace with the growth of knowledge and our changing constructs of it?

B.C. Vickery, some years back (4) arranged the various methods of classification and indexing in an order of increasing degrees of control. He studied these methods independently of notation, form of display or special jargon. The list of seven methods is worth repeating here, for it is the purpose of this paper to suggest an eighth method which could be the conceptual basis for a new methodology of classification and indexing. See Table 1.

TABLE 1: Existing Methods of Classification and Indexing (arranged by increasing degree of control)

1. Words chosen from title or text, with common words omitted.
2. Words chosen from text, with omission of common words and *consideration of variants*.
3. Words chosen from text, with omission of common words, consideration of variants, and *generic relationships*.
4. Words chosen from text, with consideration of *syntactical relationships between indexing terms*.
5. Any of the preceding methods, with *addition of terms not used in text*.
6. Assignment of index entries from a fixed authority list or classification scheme.
7. Assignment of index entries from authority lists or classification schemes representative of *several viewpoints* and *aspects of subject*.

INADEQUACY OF CLASSIFICATION AND INDEXING SYSTEMS

Among the major contributions of information science are the several schemes described in Items 3 to 7 of Table 1. Nevertheless, a certain amount of criticism can be laid at the feet of those who have developed and maintained these schemes because they have made few attempts to provide:

a) *Ordered structures* (mentioned by Rapoport) which would make things *describable with less information* (less effort). The tendency is simply to increase the number of descriptors in authority lists rather than to design a structure for the lists. When structures have been designed, they appear to have inherent limitations almost immediately.

b) *A mechanism for a radical recasting of the structures* of the fields of knowledge to accommodate future directions of growth which cannot be foreseen at the present time (to borrow from Cherry).

c) A way of interacting with the structures that allows for imperfect awareness of the actual descriptors and for acts of judgement (to answer Bronowski's appeal).

Classification and indexing methods rely almost entirely on the use of keywords and phrases in the representation of information items and in the description of searches for information. Obviously, words have to be used for communication during the indexing and retrieval process, but there appears to be a lack of a *conceptual framework* which could provide a suitable ordered structure and assist in the information exchange between the structure and the user, *and* between users.

There have been many attempts to discover an underlying framework by examining the words themselves. Library classifications come first to mind, but their inherent limitations make them wholly inadequate to the tasks before us.

"Library classification," S.R. Ranganathan (5) has said, "is equivalent to a representation of a multi-dimensional continuum in a single dimension. Library classification, which is subject to mechanical, dimensional and financial restrictions, has irremovable limitations imposed on it by multiplicity of helpful orders among specific subjects."

Lauren Doyle's seminal paper on semantic road maps (6) and the arrow graphs of the Euratom Nuclear Documentation System, first published in 1964 (and now in their latest edition as the INIS Terminology Charts), are examples of some recent attempts to provide structure to indexing vocabularies. These attempts do not really provide "spatial tags" which George Miller (7) considers "the obvious improvement" needed in the organization of information resources. We need to provide, according to Miller, "a spatial organization for the stored information that is more compatible with the structure of the information itself" and one which will "help exploit the user's enormous spatial imagery."

Miller criticizes the current theorizing about the man-machine interaction in information retrieval:

> There is a user who has a system of concepts, and there is an information store that also has a system of concepts. When the user discovers a gap that he needs to fill in his own system, he formulates a question about it. Since the content is missing, the question can only indicate the gap's general position in the conceptual system of the user. In order to recognize the *indicated location* (italics ours), the system being queried should have a similar conceptual organization. This interaction occurs as a dialog, and performance is determined largely by the adequacy of the concept indexing, so that the user's gaps, however characterized, can be recognized and filled quickly and precisely. It is assumed that the users will not have to learn the classification system (as they now have to for a library), because computer systems can be designed to translate a user's question, however phrased, into its own indexing system.(7)

Miller says: "I doubt whether any retrieval system that does not have a *spatial dimension* (italics ours) is going to make any kind of adequate match to concepts that characterize a user's thinking."

Mitroff and Turoff (8) and before them C.W. Churchman (9) emphasize how differences in our basic images of reality cause disagreements and differing assessments. Inquiry systems, such as those designed using any of the seven methods listed by Vickery, do not appear to accommodate differences in the philosophical bases of inquiry.

Serious lacuna exist in our field which appear to require a new method, a new structure, for organizing and representing the words and phrases we use to index and classify documents and user profiles.

MULTIDIMENSIONAL SPACE MODEL FOR KNOWLEDGE STRUCTURING

Scientists have found it useful to visualize the actual state of physical objects such as an atom in terms of a *multidimensional vector space*. The actual description of such states is given in mathematical equations or other notations (similar to words in an indexing vocabulary), but the multidimensional space construct contributes enormously to the ability to visualize these states and the relationships between them.

We are suggesting a *multidimensional space for knowledge* with the following properties:

1. CONCEPTS* CAN USEFULLY BE REPRESENTED AS OBJECTS SIMILAR TO VECTORS IN A MULTIDIMENSIONAL SPACE.

Vectors have magnitude and direction and obey precise mathematical rules. The objects we are proposing cannot be nearly as precise as vectors because of the uncertainties involved, but we do think such a construct can play a very useful role in assisting the information scientist to visualize relationships between concepts and the various processes which make up information retrieval.

Concepts could be thought of as having *direction* in the sense that they may be orthogonal to each other, if totally unrelated, and projecting in nearly the same direction in space, if closely related. Nearly related concepts would not project in exactly the same direction. The smaller the angle between them, the more closely related the concepts. Related fields in knowledge space would have certain concept vectors in common, but each field would be a different combination of concept vectors.

Marks of advances in the concept can be visualized as extensions in the length of the vector, if the origin in knowledge space represents the state of zero knowledge. Measurement of distance along concepts is not well

---

*The notion of a *concept* is something separate from terms used to label concepts.

defined in the same sense of distance along a Cartesian axis in Euclidean geometrical space. Hence, there is only a notion that one point is further out along the concept vector than another, but we are not able to say how much further. It does not appear possible to define the magnitude of concepts precisely.

The concept vectors span all of knowledge space. Since many concepts are interrelated, the number of concept vectors will be larger than the number of dimensions (orthogonal directions) in knowledge space. The task that has to be done is to determine a set of *basic concept vectors,* each of which is orthogonal to all others, in order to span all of knowledge space with the minimum number of concept vectors. As new basic concepts evolve, the dimension of knowledge space would change.

2. *THE STATE OF KNOWLEDGE OF A PERSON* CAN BE REPRESENTED IN MULTIDIMENSIONAL KNOWLEDGE SPACE BY A *STATE VECTOR,* WITH COMPONENTS ON THOSE BASIC CONCEPTS WHICH ARE "UNDERSTOOD" BY THAT PERSON

Learning a new concept can be thought of as adding to the state vector in knowledge space (or rotating it), so that the person develops a component on a concept which he has just learned. This is similar to describing the change of state of an atom as a change in the direction of its state vector in a multidimensional space. The state vector could also be thought of as repesenting a user's SDI profile.

3. BOOKS, JOURNAL ARTICLES, FILMS AND OTHER *INFORMATION ITEMS* CAN BE REPRESENTED IN THIS MULTIDIMENSIONAL KNOWLEDGE SPACE BY *REPRESENTATIONAL VECTORS* WITH COMPONENTS ON THE APPROPRIATE CONCEPT VECTORS.

Once a set of orthogonal basic concept vectors has been established, the act of classifying an information item consists entirely of determining the components of its representational vector on this set of basic concept vectors. Zadeh's fuzzy sets may play a big role here if it is desirable to have more than a crude binary designation of such components (10).

EXAMPLES OF VECTORS IN MULTIDIMENSIONAL KNOWLEDGE SPACE

The conceptual structure of knowledge space as multidimensional should help us to visualize a solution to the problems of disarray in alphabetical authority lists of words for representing concepts, the limitations of tree structures for representing the relationships between concepts and fields of knowledge, and the inherent inflexibility of the existing methods of classification and indexing.

In order to understand better the nature of a multidimensional knowledge space, we present a number of specific examples, mostly in two or three dimensions.

Concepts as Vectors in Multidimensional Space

Fig. 1 presents one dimension, which exhibits a basic concept vector, Distance (or Space or Length).

FIGURE 1. One Basic Concept Vector

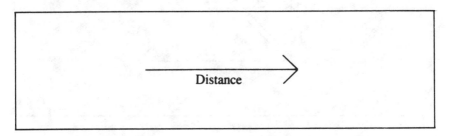

Fig. 2 presents two dimensions, which exhibit two basic concept vectors, Space and Time (orthogonal vectors).

FIGURE 2. Basic Concept Vectors (Orthogonal)

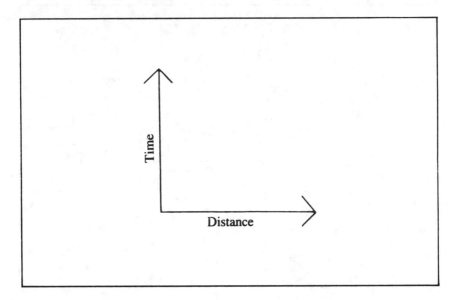

Fig. 3 presents two dimensions with a related concept vector, Motion (with components on the basic concept vectors for time and distance).

FIGURE 3. Related Concept Vector, Motion

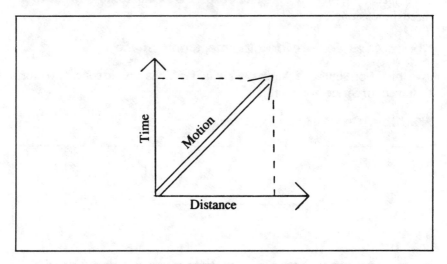

Fig. 4 presents three dimensions showing three basic concept vectors, Distance, Time, and Mass.

FIGURE 4. Three Basic Concept Vectors

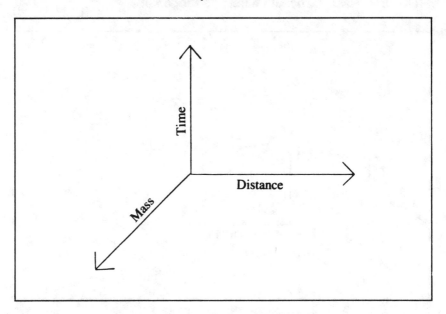

The "length" of the basic concept vectors could be represented (or "measured") and located at different regions as illustrated in Fig. 5.

FIGURE 5. Length of Concept Vectors

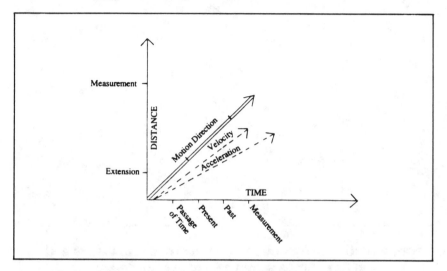

State Vectors to Represent a Person's Understanding of Concept Vectors

The knowledge space of primitive man may be thought of as having such concept vectors as space and time. Einstein and Newton's state vectors could also be thought to have components on these two concept vectors. But one can easily see how the distances out on the concept vectors, from origin, is further for Newton and Einstein than for primitive man. The state of knowledge of a person can be represented by a state vector with components on those concept vectors which he understands. It is meaningful to say that Einstein's understanding of time was deeper than Newton's, in fact it could be said that he extended or developed further the concept of time, and thereby added to the length of the concept vector. However, it is difficult to say whether his concept was twice as deep (or far), or three times as far out on the concept vector (Fig. 5). All we can do is locate Einstein's point further away from the origin of the concept vector for time than Newton's (Fig. 6).

Major insights will have to be located in knowledge space well away from the last new insight in order to accommodate the clustering of related ideas. For example, time dilation is a new concept related to Einstein's concept of time and should be located in a region near the present end of the concept vector representing time.

FIGURE 6. State Vectors and Concept Vectors

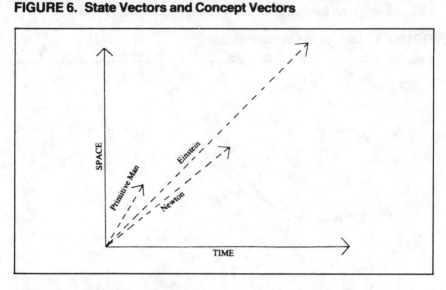

Representational Vectors for the Recorded Knowledge and Information Resources within a Field of Knowledge

This subspace of multidimensional knowledge space could be visualized as an area or volume which encompasses the known (and previously known) recorded knowledge in a field, and this would be a useful framework for more efficient retrieval of information from that subspace (Fig. 7).

FIGURE 7. Subspace of a Multidimensional Space

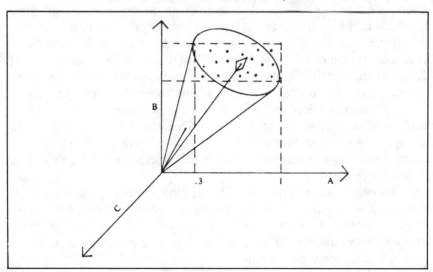

SEARCH VOLUME

A search request can be visualized as first selecting an appropriate subspace and then narrowing the search still further by confining the attention to a *search volume* within that subspace. This process would recover all the information items with representational vectors within that search volume. This is shown in Fig. 8.

FIGURE 8. Search Volume

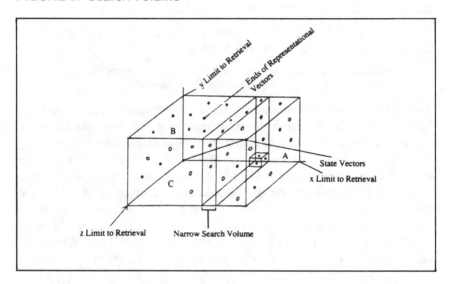

The constructs of *broader term* and *narrower term* which have been found useful in expanding or exploding searches in retrieval systems can be visualized as being related to the size of the search volume in the postulated multidimensional knowledge space. Obviously, the larger the search volume, the larger the number of items retrieved. Given attributes of the new construct, it is easy to see that a subspace of manageable dimensionality for the searcher could be easily defined, forming a search volume, specified by the coordinates on reference axes (or basic concept vectors) which mark his level of understanding. If the user would like to shrink the search volume, or shift around in a three dimensional space, the system should be able to accommodate this recasting by locating a new set of objects, locatable by replacing one or more of the concept vectors in his original search profile. Since related concept vectors would have similar directions, this would not be a difficult process.

These slight shifts and rotations would cause another "search volume" to be identified, without tampering with the original location of representational vectors for the information items in the retrieval system, since the basic concept vectors are "independently drawn" in knowledge space. Descriptors from authority lists such as thesauri would be replaced by representational vectors. The indexing records for information items would no longer be linked only to the words in use at the time of indexing. Shifts in vocabulary usage could be linked with earlier indexing records because the representational vectors would be in approximately the same subspace in knowledge space.

GENERAL DISCUSSION AND SUMMARY

We propose the following additional basis for classification and indexing to be added to the seven provided in Table 1:

> *The assignment of representational vectors as in a multidimensional knowledge space with components on basic concept vectors.*

Such a framework or structure for knowledge within a field would have such properties as flexibility for recasting as the field develops, possible rotation, and extension describable with less information (less effort).

This method would also permit the mapping of *state vectors* for the state of knowledge of a person seeking information. These state vectors would have components on the basic concept vectors, representing the "level of understanding" of those concepts by a person. This method would allow for imperfect awareness of the actual representational vectors used in the retrieval system being searched. The state and representational vectors would be in the same vicinity, since they would both have components on the concept vectors for that field, and the specified "search volume" would mark the subspace to be searched. As the interaction took place, the user could detect the optimum limits of his search.

> "Science and common-sense inquiry alike do not discover the ways in which events are grouped in the world; they invent ways of grouping. The test of an invention is the productive benefits that result from the use of invented categories. . . ." [Bruner, Goodnow, and Austin (11(]

Advantages

The benefits which emanate from a conceptual basis for representing knowledge in a multidimensional vector space include the following:

1. *Description of Relationship Between Concepts:* The structure to describe the relationships between concepts in knowledge space is more flexible and useful. It would require less information (on the part of the user) to describe and structure his search volume. As a start, three basic vectors could be used to define a subspace of manageable dimensionality.

When a field is redefined, the recasting of structures for that field of knowledge could possibly be done in multidimensional knowledge space by relating relevant representational vectors to a new set of concept vectors through a transformation.

Increased interaction between user and a retrieval system (via his state vector-profile) would take place because this conceptual basis of a multidimensional knowledge space allows for an imperfect match between a person's state vector, the representational vectors for information items within a field (as represented in some retrieval system) and the actual concept vectors which are the "objects" in the knowledge space representative of a field of knowledge.

This conceptual basis of knowledge space stretches the notion of coordinate indexing to its outer limits and hopefully moves into other dimensions, leaving behind an *area* of two or three dimensions and extending to a search *volume* with n-dimensions.

This conceptual basis stretches the notion of *broader* and *narrower* out of a hierarchical tree structure and into an umbrella-like surface where points of information can be identified, where a dense clustering of related concepts can be distinguished, and where reference axes can lead to other portions of the surface or "contents." Interfaces with other fields of knowledge can also be identified and the structure of the relationships mapped.

2. *Better Understanding of Information Transmission:* Will this bring us any closer to an understanding of the transmission of information? In most diagrams of the communication or transmission process, the change in state in the receiver is omitted. In the construct proposed here, the state of knowledge of the person could be monitored and recorded with each use of the system.

In most retrieval and inquiry systems known to the authors, there is no real differentiation made between concept vectors, state vectors, and representational vectors. This may be an inhibiting factor in improving the design of retrieval systems. The job ahead for the information specialist is to identify the best set of *basic concept vectors** to describe the paradigm for fields of knowledge. This would extend or replace the work of the past to discover basic classes and subclasses, fundamental categories, and basic isolates. It should aid in better representation of both information items and users' searches.

---

*A start in this direction would be a list of totally unrelated concepts, reduced by consensus to a basic set which would represent the paradigm in a knowledge field.

REFERENCES

1. Rapaport, A. 1953. What is Information. ETC. 1953 Summer; 10:259.
2. Bronowski, J. 1973. The Principle of Tolerance. Atlantic. 1973 December; 232(6):60–66.
3. Cherry, C. 1974. The Spreading Word of Science. Times Literary Supplement. 1974. March 22: 301–302.
4. Vickery, B.C. 1963. (Quoted and expanded in Bourne, C.P. *Methods of Information Handling*. Wiley; 1963, 13–20.)
5. Ranganathan, S.R. 1951. *Philosophy of Library Classification*, Munksgaard; 1951, 94–95.
6. Doyle, Lauren B. 1972. "Indexing and Abstracting by Association." *American Documentation*. 1972 October; 23:378–390.
7. Miller, George A. 1968. "Psychology and Information." *American Documentation*. 1968 July; 19: 286–289.
8. Mitroff, Ian I.; Turoff, Murray. 1973. "The Whys Behind the Hows.' *IEEE Spectrum*. 1973 March; 62–70.
9. Churchman, C.W. 1971. *The Design of Inquiring Systems*. Basic Books; 1971.
10. Zadeh, L.A. 1965. "Fuzzy Sets." *Information and Control*. 1965; 8: 338–353.
11. Bruner, J.S.; Goodnow, J.J.; Austin, G.A. 1962. *Study of Thinking*. Wiley; 1962.

"More" Is Not Necessarily "Better"

In President Carter's inaugural address he said:

> We have learned that "more" is not necessarily "better," that even
> our great nation has its recognized limits, and that we can neither
> answer all questions nor solve all problems.

To use those words as a theme or *text* for my remarks at this seminar, I
believe, will force many information professionals to ponder what we
would call *better* information systems and if bigger and faster information
systems necessarily lead to better information services. I'm sure you have
all seen the button or heard the phrase, "Technology is the answer. . . .
Now, what was the question?" Has our use of technology to handle more
information been the most imaginative and useful to the needers of information, or have we been guilty of using the technology because it was there?
Granted the size of the bibliographic data bases now being searched
on-line, via interactive, real-time retrieval systems, numbers well above 25
million citations. Nevertheless, the conclusion of the first part of a National
Forum on Scientific and Technical Communication, held this past fall in
Boston, was that, from a user's perspective, they (the STI users) are *not*
being served adequately. Obviously, more is not better to the user because it
means more screening of documents with conflicting information, more
sources to track down, and more cost barriers as these information systems
expect users to pay for the service. This first conference of the Forum
isolated a great many critical problems, too many, in fact, for me to
enumerate here.

BACK TO THE DRAWING BOARD

Suffice it to say that we probably must go back to the drawing board
before we can improve the situation as the user views it. Before we can say
that information technology is truly serving society, we may need to

---

Reprinted with permission from *Information Technology Serving Society,* edited by Robert
Lee Chartrand and James W. Morentz, Jr., copyright © 1979, Pergamon Press Ltd.

revamp how the present systems are designed and being managed and we may have to decide what is *better* and which questions we will answer and which problems we will solve.

There is not time this evening for a comprehensive historical perspective on the development of information systems as they exist today. Even if there were time, I would not be qualified to present such a story. My experiences have been limited to the application of computers in the modernization of bibliographic information systems. Nevertheless, my summary of developments in that area, and peripherally, developments in education, will serve to make a point and stimulate discussion. My point is this:

Until very recently, *the level of control* in information systems has been primarily inside the system (in the librarian's office or in the computer) rather than outside, i.e., in the hands of the ultimate user of the system. Early versions of the "question and answer" type of computer-based instructional programs and bibliographic searching systems required that the user answer a series of questions posed by the system. Recall "CAI (computer-assisted instruction)" in the late 60s or systems like "BOLD (Bibliographic On Line Display)," one of the first computer-based literature searching systems. These systems forced the user into a robot position, occasionally able to "command" the computer, but more often than not the human was only able to answer queries from the system, thereby proving his capability to converse with the computer! From the beginning, it should have been the other way around, but programmers and system designers were not able, or willing, to design information systems which did more to put humans in command. This prompted all the anticomputer criticism and "man as servant to the machine" propaganda. Carbonell showed the options open to a system designer quite graphically in a 1969 article (see Fig. 1).

FIGURE 1

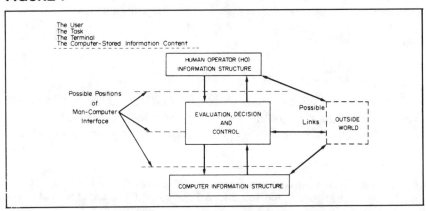

DRAMATIC CHANGES IN MAN-MACHINE INTERACTION

It is heartening to see that this trend is changing in some of our information systems. The control level for evaluation and decision is closer to the human at the computer terminal. More and more terminals are being re-designed after some human factors research has been done. The software for computer-based information systems is being rewritten to allow for more flexibility in user protocols, more error tolerance, and data base construction, and vocabulary access is becoming more responsive. Output options are increasing.

We still have a long way to go, but just as the CAI people are shifting their emphasis to "CAL (Computer-Assisted Learning)," bibliographic information systems must shift their emphasis away *from* storage *to* retrieval. In these areas the most promising advances will be in the area of relevance feedback, system memory of a user's previous searches (similar to stored SDI profiles which can be easily modified), and aids to subject searching across several data bases with varying vocabularies. Free text searching aids will need to be developed. Non-sophisticated users will need to be accommodated.

Some work out in California under William C. Mann may lead to dramatic changes in man-machine interaction. His view is that designers have implemented only one type of interaction, the command, and there are many more types of interaction between humans. If these other types are better understood, they could be used as models for more varied man-machine interactions. When problem-solving situations or information-seeking sessions between humans are analyzed, Mann found at least eight or nine other types of interactions besides the question-answer type. With a view in mind to making the man-machine interaction more versatile and suitable for problem-solving tasks, Mann's work could lead to important breakthroughs in the human becoming the master of the information systems he uses.

INFORMATION AS A REPRODUCTIVE ORGANISM

That will all be to the good, but I have another concern which may not so easily be remedied (as if the above problem were an easy problem!).

Our information systems today still live up to the complaint C. West Churchman raised ten years ago in *The Systems Approach* (p. 127):

> Information . . . has a tendency to accumulate and the more information accumulates, the more information is needed in order to keep track of the accumulation. Information in effect is a reproductive organism that has no morals and goes around generating offspring without any consideration of the *effect* of its own "population explosion." So, to design a new system that simply tries to beat the

standards of the old may be merely to design into fast-moving hardware some of the evils of information collection as well as its benefits.

Our national plans for "better" information services usually include some rationalization of the present situation regarding the *primary* sources of information (books, journals, and reports) and the *secondary* services which keep track of the accumulated primary sources (such things as library catalogs, abstracting and indexing services and their offspring such as MARC [Machine Readable Cataloging], MEDLINE, COMPENDEX, AGRICOLA, and ERIC). The managers of publishing houses, libraries, and abstracting services have been busy revamping their products and services, but rarely have these plans included a *major* thrust in the area of reducing our information base and creating *tertiary* services to repackage, consolidate, compress, or transform the information in their original packages of information. These managers designed their original information products for a select social group (scientists, engineers, biomedical researchers, and the like). They have not made many assessments to determine how their use of technology may affect their users or help them compress and consolidate information sources (see Fig. 2). Their cost-

FIGURE 2

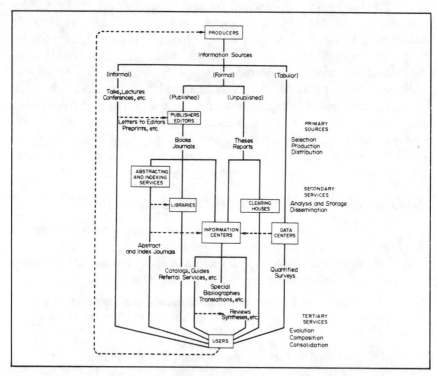

benefit studies have been efficiency or cost-savings studies rather than studies to probe into the needs for redesign of old products and design of *new* products or by-products.

MEETING USER NEEDS

We all know of some examples where new services have come into being, thanks to the use of technology. The Issue Briefs series available to the Congress from the Congressional Research Service is a fine example, but it stands almost alone as an example of a tertiary service designed to consolidate information sources.

Existing information systems and services, especially those in the STI field, are inadequate because they do not represent the best we can do to meet the needs of users.

The data bases are not integrated. The information contained within them is not coded for user groups, nor do the systems offer repackaged information products. What they put in is what you get out, even though some other possibilities might be implemented quite easily, *and* what they individually put in is what you get out, data base by data base. Merged data bases in DIALOG or ORBIT, for example, appear to be a long way off. Public interest groups, interdisciplinary research teams, and the "general public" are still among the information poor in the sense that modern information systems designers have still not found a way to serve them adequately. The needs of policy-makers and managers are also inadequately served, but they appear to have enough clout to have systems designed just for them, both in this country and on the international level.

IS THIS THE BEST WE CAN DO?

Where does this leave us? I hate to say it, but it appears we have *more* not *better* systems and services, data bases and data banks; and we have neither answered some of the questions nor solved some of the problems. Is this present state of the art a permanent condition? I hope I have not left you with that impression. There are many hopeful signs. Efforts such as "The People's Computer Company" in Palo Alto has been going since 1972. Eventually it may have a real impact as "The Whole Earth Catalog" did. Switching centers and referral services are mushrooming and information brokers are meeting the needs of those able and willing to pay for customized services. Information system designers are getting the word and some efforts are being made to be more "user oriented." Costs of computer terminals are going down rapidly and charges for computer-based searching services may come into easy reach of even the poorest graduate student by 1980. But what all these positive statements show is that there is a disorganized but optimistic scenario for the future. Is this the best we can do?

Bob Chartrand, the 1969 predecessor of this conference, quoted then Senator Walter F. Mondale, as he tried to reflect the perplexity of a national legislator:

> . . . We live *alongside* change but we have not learned to live *with* it, to accept its necessity. Most certainly, we have not yet attained the ability to harness the dynamics of change for the achievement of *social goals* of our own selection.

It appears to me that the information systems manager is perplexed in the same way, viewing now as he does the changes which technology has wrought in the services and products he can offer to a varied user market. He does not appear to have made a reassessment of his goals, nor harnessd the dynamics of change for the achievement of those goals. The National Commission on Libraries and Information Science has been making some attempts to formulate a new national information policy with goals so far reaching that every American citizen will have access to information services adequate to meet his needs. I have often wondered if the NCLIS document is being read in the libraries, publishing houses, and abstracting services of the land. If the answer is yes, I then ask, do they read it and ask, "Where do we fit in? What are we doing now that we should continue to do? What should we change? What new services should we add?" The responsiveness of some of the commercial information retrieval services may actually be in the vanguard as far as tailoring or redesigning their services for new user markets. They in turn may impact the data base suppliers and the libraries, just as the telephone company has impacted on family life styles and mobility. Will we just have to wait and see?

Most of my comments have been quite personal and unsubstantiated by facts and figures, but I didn't think an exposition was needed for such a group as this as much as a stimulant was needed. It is up to us to answer the questions I have posed:

(1) Who will be in control of the information systems we design and operate? The systems operators or the users?

(2) When will we build in more than a command and control environment into the man-machine interaction?

(3) When will we start to define our information systems in such a way that their design takes into account the varied outputs of products and services needed for a varied user clientele?

(4) When will we begin to think of the data bases as merely the raw material, not the end product, of our systems?

(5) When will we re-examine our objectives and collectively redesign our national information system components to be more compatible, more easily accessible, and more versatile for more users?

Subject Retrieval: A Marriage of Retrieval Systems and Library Automation Efforts

I appreciate the opportunity to talk on my favourite topic before such an important group. It has given me the chance to update one of my papers written in 1969, with the same title which has been lost in the oblivion of the proceedings volume for the celebration of the 100th anniversary of Purdue University.

I spoke then as a visionary, I thought, because I thought I saw something no-one else seemed to see, namely that the use of computers by libraries and by indexing and abstracting services, was bringing about a union marriage in those operations that could result in some offspring or products which would excite the whole world of information. As I said, this paper is lost—I cannot even find the proceedings volume and it has taken another ten years before I and now everyone else could really see what I saw then.

My first paper at this conference then will be more like a birth announcement than an opening address, and I hope you will forgive me for anthropomorphizing these developments in our field, but telling a brief story (or fable) may help you to remember the points I am trying to make.

Once upon a time, some eighteen years ago, Library Automation *married* Computerized Information Retrieval. Their four offspring (or children) up to 1981 are:

(Machine-Readable Cataloguing)	MARC	is 16 this year
(Integrated Library System)	ILSY	is 4
(Online Public Access Catalogue)	OPAC	is 2
(Subject Access and Retrieval of Information)	SARI	is a toddler
	and	
(Remote Delivery of Information)	REDI	is a gleam in their parent's eyes.

Reprinted with permission from *Cataloguing Australia*, Volume 7, 1981. <u>Editor's Note</u>: Illustrations 1, 4, and 5 are reprinted courtesy of OCLC from *Online Public Access Catalogs: The User Interface*, by Charles Hildreth, OCLC Library, Information, and Computer Science Series. Copyright © 1982. They are updated versions of the illustrations from this article.

As in all families, the young married couple had a very rocky start. They doted on their first-born and had a few miscarriages along the way. By their third child, OPAC, they could begin to see features of both Mom and Dad in the child. The first two, MARC and ILSY looked so much like Mom that Dad wondered if he had really played any part in their upbringing. SARI is too young for us to see her true character, and, well, REDI is only a name chosen for the gleam in their eyes.

SARI, being the fourth child, is not receiving the attention she deserves. She is almost taken for granted, but her needs are much greater than the other children, having been born handicapped. Luckily, her handicap is not caused by any brain damage. With the proper care and attention she should grow up to be one of parents' and grandparents' favourites.

Watching this family grow, with the quarrels and make-ups, the moves from one house to another, one town to another, is like a soap opera on the television where each episode seems to have a crisis and a denouement. Will they live happily ever after? Will SARI and REDI grow up loving their parents? Tune in next week and see . . . I would go on with the story, but instead let me move onto the paper.

It is difficult to believe that it was less than forty years ago that the first commercially available computer was marketed, and less than that when the first library or information centre used the computer for some library or information processing task. Electronic data processing equipment has been used in libraries for certain housekeeping functions for some time, but just recently have libraries started converting their files and catalogues for computer manipulation and even more recently have they begun to think about user access to these files. Interestingly enough, the first computer applications in the library and information services were not for the automation of acquisition or circulation control, but were in the "information retrieval" area. Subject retrieval, the theme of this conference, is another name for information retrieval or subject searching, as opposed to known-item searching by author or title. Subject retrieval has never been the specific reason for library automation efforts, but it was behind these early computer efforts. It is my thesis today that subject retrieval will now get the attention it deserves in library circles because there now is a realisation that library automation and retrieval systems should be joined because our systems designed for staff will now have to include features for our users. The organising group for this conference is to be commended for choosing the subject retrieval theme at this National Cataloguers' Conference at a time when Australia has just embarked on an automated library network which is bound eventually to include online catalogues for users as its end product. There is a lot to be learned (and unlearned) from the early developments of both library automation and retrieval systems. Where we are in the USA today is a result of those developments. The variety you can see in the searching features of online public access catalogue systems in the States (illustration 1) is graphically portrayed in the . . . recently completed OCLC research report [what] documents how several libraries or library networks have designed their newest form of their catalogues to perform subject searches. Some came to this design from their fresh experience with COM catalogues or online circulation systems and others came to this point from their use of the online computer searching of databases on such retrieval systems as DIALOG, BRS, MEDLINE, or ORBIT.

(The blanks in the columns are as interesting as the X's, as are the 1's (to be implemented in 1981).)

I hope that my presentation will help to highlight these developments and that our review of them will help you in Australia to develop plans for subject retrieval and user access which will set a new standard.

Information centres at places like NASA and ERIC, abstracting and indexing services like Chemical Abstracts led the field in the 1960's in the application of computers. They used them to produce printed subject indexes at first and later to do online searching of their files. These applications were not the typical business data processing tasks where the main purpose in using the computer would be to speed up repetitive routines. These first applications in information work were in the area now referred to as database building, bibliographic searching and for the production of printed indexes. The published reports of these early developments regarding bibliographic record formats, file maintenance, access vocabularies, batch and online searching systems did not appear in library journals and may be a part of the literature lost to librarians. I hope my paper will revive your interest in this work because it contains a great deal about subject retrieval.

Most librarians, since the fifties and even into the early seventies, viewed [all of] computer science with a great deal of fear and distrust. They have felt that too many promises and claims were being made with very little evidence of accomplishment, and they have felt the costs involved to be beyond their means. For a long time librarians insisted that their operations were different and could not be tackled by the "information and computer buffs." The suggestions to automate the cataloguing and reference functions, which have been thought to be too complicated and personalised, were not considered practicable at first. But in the USA at least a "marriage of convenience" began as far back as eighteen years ago (May 26–30, 1963, to be exact), when the Library of Congress, the National Science Foundation, and the Council on Library Resources arranged a meeting for directors of over seventy-five of the largest academic and research libraries. Information handling specialists were also invited. This invitational meeting, in the secluded setting of the Airlie Conference Centre outside Washington, DC, resulted in several contractual agreements. This Airlie Conference now serves as a benchmark for the field of library automation.(1)

ILLUSTRATION 1: OCLC, Inc. Research Project: Online Public Access Catalog Systems (Funded in part by a grant from the Council on Library Resources)

Special Search Formulation Capabilities

USER ACTION	California, University of	Claremont Colleges	Dartmouth College	Mankato State University	Mission College	Northwestern University	OCLC	Ohio State University	Pikes Peak Library District	RLG/RLIN
Controlled subject term searching*	X	X	X	X	X	X		X	X	X
Free-text term search of entire record			X							
Free-text term search in a user-selected field	X		X	X	X[6]					X
Free-text term search in user-combined fields	X		X	X						X
Free-text term search in system default field(s)		X	X[2]	X						
Word truncation for a free-text search	X		X	X						X
Explicit use of Boolean operators with search terms	X		X	X	[3]					X
Explicit use of Boolean operators on previous search set(s)	X		X	X						X
Explicit use of word adjacency/proximity operators	[1]		X							
Restrict (limit) search results by date, language, etc.	X	X	X	X		X		X		
Explicit use of relational operators	X	X	X	X		X		X		
User can view index or thesaurus terms	X		X		X[5]	X[4,5]		X[5]		
User can view search history	X		X	X					X	
User can save search statements for later execution	[1]		X	X						

X = Search capability available for user when formulating a search

* A search term may consist of a truncated word, a single word, or a multiple-word phrase.

NOTES:
1. To be implemented
2. The default includes all fields (default = user does not have to specify value or option during search).
3. Author/title and course/instructor (reserved materials) searches are implemented with Boolean "and", but user does not select and enter the Boolean operator.
4. An index display results automatically in the display of author or title multiple search results. No distinct command is available.
5. Index display results automatically in the display of subject search results. No distinct command is available.
6. Possible only in the title field when combined author/title search is utilized.

The technical experts at Airlie presented papers on such topics as the design requirements for the library of the future, library communication networks, and the automation of library systems. Some tutorial or state-of-the-art papers covered such technical points as file organisation and conversion, file storage and access, graphic storage, and output printing. These papers were distributed in advance, and the technical experts were called upon to explain some topics in simpler terms at the conference. These days of briefing and open discussion among the top decision-makers in the library field and the top system designers and technical experts in the computer and information science field made a real impact. Automation at the Library of Congress, the National Library of Medicine, and the National Agricultural Library started in full swing after this meeting. Index Medicus became MEDLARS and LC Catalogue cards became MARC some time after this meeting. Research and development efforts on a large scale in the libraries at Stanford, Chicago, Columbia, and other places began. Since that time, some regional library processing centres have been designed with a central computer utility as a keystone in their plans. One of those centres grew into OCLC, one of the world's largest online computer library centres. UTLAS began in Toronto, Canada about this same time. I may be wrong to try to establish that this Airlie conference caused and effected a relationship which has resulted in the marriage of library automation and computerised information retrieval, but nowhere else is there a better contractual agreement than that documented in the proceedings of this conference. Unfortunately *subject retrieval* was not specifically emphasised then and the various applications of computers in the library and the information industry were not properly joined for some time. Remember *MARC* was the first-born of this marriage. This marriage was rather shaky in fact. Computer technology was being applied to more and more functions and processes in libraries went unmet even though more and more sophisticated retrieval systems were being designed for use with other databases. For the most part the library systems staff seemed primarily concerned with technical processing, work simplification, and increased efficiency. The systems analysts in libraries have concentrated on (1) acquisitions, (2) circulation control, (3) serials control, *and* (4) cataloguing. Through some bibliographic utility or jobber, or on their own computers, libraries matched their systems to staff needs, and never directly considered user needs, except in the case of COM catalogues, which now appear to be very unacceptable to many library users. I tried in a paper for a conference in 1978 on the *Closing of the Catalogue* to show how users viewed the various forms of the catalogue—what they would discern as advantages and disadvantages. This is illustration 2.* As you can see, each

*Editor's Note: This illustration also appears in ''Catalog User's Access from the User's Viewpoint'' in Part 2 of this book.

ILLUSTRATION 2: Forms of Catalogs—Advantages and Disadvantages from the User Viewpoint

ADVANTAGES	DISADVANTAGES
CARD CATALOGS	
1. Alphabetical orderly parts 2. Unit entry, with all information available everywhere 3. In drawers, easy to move out 4. Printed or typed cards easy to read 5. Drawers are touchable as are cards 6. Guide cards and notes available 7. Form of catalog similar throughout life 8. Nonmediated, self-service 9. Easily updated 10. Can contain temporary information	1. Over-time, inconsistent rules of main-entry form and choice and subject-heading form and choice 2. Drawers too low or too high, where user must kneel or reach 3. No chairs to sit on 4. Must copy out all information needed by hand 5. Cryptic notes and form of entry 6. Different style of entry, different form of card in different library, for different materials 7. No "natural language" access 8. Too few cross-references 9. Drawers sometimes misfiled 10. Catalog available in only one location, even in decentralized system
COM (FICHE OR REEL) CATALOG	
1. Available at many locations 2. Several entry files (author, title, subject) 3. Can see several records at once 4. Can copy entries if printer available 5. Chair is usually provided at reader 6. Inexpensive equipment for readers, sometimes available on loan	1. Not easily updated 2. Not very readable 3. Rearrangement of output difficult 4. Cross-references often missing
ONLINE LIBRARY CATALOGS	
1. Easily updated, with changes explained 2. Can provide table lookups for authority files (author, title, subject, etc.) 3. Available at many locations 4. New access points and combinations search terms 5. Variable output formats and sorts 6. No writing by user required 7. Chair provided 8. Union lists possible	1. Need of staff assistance 2. May be expensive to user 3. Equipment failure possible 4. Queuing problems at few terminals 5. User training necessary

form has some of both. What I noticed at that time was how little was being done to provide better, improved *subject* retrieval because most libraries were more concerned with AACR2 and all the havoc it would wreak. Heavens knows, you can not fight effectively on all fronts at once, but I was disappointed to see so little attention paid to this important access service.

The processing and file-building systems in many libraries using computers have been of local origin, on local computers, maintained by local systems staff until MARC and places like OCLC, UTLAS, WLN, took off in the 1970's. When cataloguing networks were developed and vendors began providing turnkey circulation systems, all this began to change and now the use of archival tapes has forced us to think of quality control. Name authority files and subject headings, when using shared cataloguing, are now concerns of the library staff. The other papers at this conference will cover these topics with more expertise because the speakers are in the forefront of that effort.

For some of us who are concerned with access services in libraries, the searching and retrieval systems developed since the late 1960's by vendors like Lockheed and SDC have shown promise to satisfy our requirements to replace the use of conventional printed indexes with online searching. On this side of the library enterprise, the reference staff has been using the most advanced computer technology and they could see how it has helped them open up parts of their collections. The online abstracting and indexing databases they use are much like cataloguing databases, and even though they do not match their collections exactly, they have learned ways to customise output (e.g. SDI). Unfortunately, because of the expenses as-sociated with using these remote systems, the library staff is the inter-mediary, performing searches for library patrons. Rarely has the library user been instructed to do the search themselves, although this is now happening in some places. The library staff now online have become quite expert in using these systems and they can critically analyse the content of online databases, the structure of the retrieval system commands, search strategy and vocabulary problems. All these areas are grist for the mill of subject retrieval problems in library catalogues, but rarely have other library staff who are building or maintaining machine-based files and automating the other library processes listened to these staff. The true marriage of library automation and retrieval systems will come when the structure of library catalogue records are redesigned for searching. Conver-sations on these topics have to take place *before* online public access catalogues are implemented.

This dichotomy of work and interests of library automation staff and online bibliographic searchers has followed the traditional division in libraries between technical services and readers/reference services. The marriage in 1963, mentioned earlier, was really never a happy one until recently when there had been a recognition of some common interests and a decision to merge files, processes and functions into *integrated* library systems (ILS) such as that announced recently by the National Library of Medicine in their *Factsheet* dated October 1980. ILS now means one computer package for acquisition, circulation, cataloguing, public access, searching and serial control. This is the offspring I call ILSY.

In the early days, systems for circulation and cataloguing on the one hand, and systems for access and retrieval on the other, were developing in the same city (e.g. Columbus, Ohio, and Palo Alto, California), sometimes on the same university campus (Ohio State University), *with little or no interface or discussion*. The result has been incompatible command languages and features. The retrieval system vendors, meanwhile, have been concerning themselves with specialised databases, pay-as-you-serve clientele, and intermediaries, rather than end users. The library systems personnel were busy with their internal operations and staff problems. Now both groups must concern themselves with the public, with naive and inexperienced users who want subject retrieval that is easier than it was before. What can these two developments learn from each other?

At professional meetings for years, each group has been discussing their own problems. Eventually, over the years since 1963, which parallels my professional involvement in the field, some of us could see a good deal more similarity than differences in the concerns and topics being discussed. Some of the outstanding topics of the past years' meetings have direct bearing on subject retrieval [see Table 1].

Library systems staff who have been searching for good designs for COM catalogues with new formats of catalogue records have had to face the need for greater subject access. Some have succeeded partially and I was glad to see what has been done at WAIT. They have heeded some of the research findings (illustration 3). BUT . . . COM, in my opinion, is only an interim offspring and we will not see real subject access until catalogue files and online bibliographic databases are combined. The success of subject retrieval by free text searching and other features of online retrieval just can not be built into COM catalogues. All the features such as Boolean operations, truncation, and word proximity, an authority file or thesaurus, are available features for online catalogues and each feature will impact on subject retrieval. None of these can be features of COM catalogue.

All this experience with retrieval systems, then, is influencing the way online catalogue systems are being designed from the original automated technical processing systems. Local automated systems like the two at the

TABLE 1: Topics and Problems on Library Automation and Retrieval Systems (* = related to subject retrieval)

LIBRARY AUTOMATION	RETRIEVAL SYSTEMS
*search keys	*multiple database searching
cataloguing codes	*free versus controlled vocabulary searches
	vendor standards for databases
	vendor selection
	telecommunication charges
	discounts/subscriptions for user charges
*quality control	overlap of databases
shared cataloguing	
vendor versus in-house systems	
closing the catalogue	
add-on or retrospective conversion of catalogues	
integrated library systems	
circulation-catalogue linkages	
*online public access for (Novice, Inexp. Users)	*search strategy/search saves
	intermediaries
	end user training/tutorial/prompts
	friendly, forgiving user online interfaces
	human factors/equipment
known item searches	
*subject searches	
library organisation/staff retraining	reference staff retraining
database changes/updating	
costs	use charges/procedures for payment
new equipment/building remodelling	which terminal

Library of Congress (illustration 4) are showing greater variation than one could have thought possible, given the limited number of access points in the catalogue record. These online catalogues, starting from circulation systems (such as OSU), have some serious limitations where subject retrieval is concerned, but then subject retrieval in our catalogues today is rather primitive too. Some of us creating new cataloguing systems will have to show more creativity.

The evidence in a recent OCLC study, funded by CLR, clearly points to a ''Tower of Babel'' in online catalogues (illustration 5) (access points) because there are no clearly defined goals and standards for library services in the area of subject retrieval.

Just as the Airlie conference in 1963 helped to effect a union between libraries and computer technologies, conferences held in 1981 are creating the means for merging remote electronic delivery of information (REDI) and library services; the public libraries are taking the lead in this area in the USA, having formed a working group to form a membership initiative group within ALA, called The Electronic Library Association.(2)

ILLUSTRATION 3: Unheeded Research Findings About Catalogue Use (abridged, from "Closing the Catalog")(9)

1. Early studies found more known-item searches than subject searches, but more recent studies indicate that it may be premature to dismiss the subject entry as being of little value.
2. By 1970 we had findings from studies which recommended that we include the following in our catalogue records to improve the success rate of searchers: the contents notes, in-depth subject analytics, or front and back matter from book to provide greater subject access.
3. Inconsistencies in our catalogues regarding use of specific entry rule, direct and indirect entry confusion, and lack of cross references were causing many user problems.
4. By 1950 we had the recommendation that we should remove older subject cards (20 years or older) and file subject cards chronologically rather than alphabetically.
5. Most studies were recommending current terminology as entry vocabulary. A more modern, simpler, and direct entry vocabulary would increase searchers' success.
6. Reverse geographical headings for local interest material was recommended.
7. A synonym dictionary would be needed to aid computer-aided post indexing if the vocabulary from the title, notes, and contents of the book were included in the machine-readable catalogue record and provided access points for the searcher.
8. By 1905 Fletcher had suggested that we insert into our catalogue direct references to appropriate subject bibliographies and special indexes.
9. The classification scheme used in a library can provide subject access in the online catalogue, and the words in the classification schedule captions may provide the free or natural text needed for greater access to topics in the contextual areas of the schedule, thereby providing a browsing feature in online catalogues.

This will exacerbate the situation I have been describing because the new world of video technologies has the potential to effect even greater changes on library organisation and services. Some see these technologies as holding promise of faster and more cost-efficient information services, but warn that an integration into library operations will be required and systems easier to use must be devised. The warning in the June 1981 issue of the *Journal of Library Automation* reminds us that we may be back at ground zero when it comes to a second marriage of libraries with technology:

> By their natural inertia, individuals and organisations in the library community will be opposed to the acceptance of cable services, videotext, online catalogues, information retrieval, and other video technologies simply because it represents change (p. 76).

According to Thomas Harnish, from whose editorial this sentence is taken, the video technologies will help librarians and information handling specialists establish a special kind of dependence, but it will not be an easy liaison if there is resistance. REDI could be called Thursday's child, who has a long way to go.

What, you may fairly say, does all this early and recent history of library automation, information retrieval, and electronic delivery of information have to do with *subject retrieval* in the 1980's? For me, at least, it all helps to explain *why* we are where we are, in 1981. For example, we now see:

(a) Some subject access in online or COM catalogue systems look like circulation systems while others look like printed subject indexes, depending on their origins.
(b) Some librarians show great concern for subject authority control in online catalogues, while others show enthusiasm only for opening their catalogues and searching by free text anywhere in the record, abandoning main entry and controlled subject headings *per se,* adding new fields to catalogue records and allowing access to notes. Some want online indexes, dictionaries, and thesauri and cannot see how we can get there from here with LCSH.
(c) Some librarians predict that online catalogues will only be used for known-item searches and location information while others envision library catalogues becoming browsing aids with contents pages, indexes and even the full text of books available.

Command Capabilities of the Library of Congress Online Public Access Catalogs (SCORPIO and MUMS)

Functional Area I. Operational Control	MUMS	SCORPIO	Functional Area II. Search Formulation Control	MUMS	SCORPIO
COMMAND CAPABILITIES (available to, or under the control of the user)			COMMAND CAPABILITIES (available to, or under the control of the user)		
Logon (begin session protocol)	Yes	Yes	Search is default function	Yes	Yes
Select function desired	No	No	General search command is used	Yes	Yes
System has default for function	Yes	Yes	Derived search keys are required	Yes	No
Select file desired	Yes	Yes	Controlled term searching	No	Yes
System has default for file	No	No	Free-text term searching:		
Set default values for session	No	Yes	entire record	No	No
Set system message length	No	Yes	selected field(s)	Yes	Yes
Select dialogue mode	No	No	Restrict/limit search results	Yes	Yes
Edit input (erase/modify)	Yes	Yes	Boolean operators, explicit use	Yes	Yes
Interrupt online output	No	No	Relational operators, explicit use	No	Yes
Stack commands	No	No	Truncation, explicit use	No	No
Save search statements	No	No	Proximity operators, explicit use	Yes	No
Purge search statements	No	No	ACCESS POINTS		
Logoff (end session protocol)	No	Yes	Personal author	Yes	Yes
			Corporate author	Yes	Yes
			Author/title	Yes	No
			Title	Yes	Yes
			Subject	Yes	Yes
			Call number	No	Yes
			LC card number	Yes	Yes
			ISBN	Yes	No
			ISSN	Yes	No
			Government document number	No	No
			Other control number	No	No
			Additional access points	Yes	No

(d) Too few new or innovative online systems are being designed for library users. The stamp on almost every retrieval system design is that of the previous application (acquisitions or circulation) for which the system was originally designed when library staff or specially trained personnel were considered to be the only users.

Command Capabilities of the Library of Congress Online Public Access Catalogs (SCORPIO and MUMS) (continued)

Functional Area III. Output Control

COMMAND CAPABILITIES (available to, or under the control of the user)	MUMS	SCORPIO
General command to display results	Yes	Yes
Select display from predefined formats	Yes	Yes
Select specific record(s) for display	Yes	Yes
Select specific field(s) for display	No	No
Sort results for display	No	No
Merge results for display	No	Yes
Display forward (records or screens)	Yes	Yes
Display backward (records or screens)	Yes	Yes
Scroll	Yes	No
Interrupt scroll	No	No
Request offline hardcopy print	No	No
Produce online hardcopy print	Yes	Yes
Cancel offline print request	No	No

Functional Area IV. User Assistance: Information and Instruction

COMMAND CAPABILITIES (available to, or under the control of the user)	MUMS	SCORPIO
List files for review	No	Yes
List searchable fields for review	No	No
List commands for review	No	Yes
Show index or thesaurus terms	No	Yes
Show search history	No	Yes
Show time elapsed or cost	No	Yes
Show news or special messages	No	Yes
Explain system messages	No	No
Identify offline assistance	Yes	Yes
Indicate item location	No	No
Indicate item availability	No	No
Prompts or guidance comments	No	Yes
Help displays retrievable	No	Yes
Online tutorial(s)	No	No

All these differing perceptions will cause confusion and could have a harmful effect on subject retrieval in the 1980's in my opinion.

We are effecting a shift in the conception of library operations, making them more into information services; but there are some who think the library role should be limited to being a data resource, rather than a service centre. (4) This debate may cause a crisis of some dimension in library systems.

Long ago, John Kountz (5) enumerated the necessary ingredients for library automation: money, co-operation, and hardware. If we are truly to marry library automation to information retrieval, I (6) would add to that list: service conscious manpower and acceptance of the objective to aid users in their quest for information. If we are ever to redesign libraries for more efficient and effective information service, we must look beyond separate processes such as acquisition, cataloguing, circulation, and serials control and we must find personnel who can develop integrated library systems which will be evaluated on the basis of user satisfaction and not on

ILLUSTRATION 5: OCLC, Inc. Research Project: Online Public Access Catalog Systems (funded in part by a grant from the Council on Library Resources)

ACCESS POINTS*

ACCESS POINTS*	California, University of	Claremont Colleges	Dartmouth College	Mankato State University	Mission College	Northwestern University	OCLC	Ohio State University	Pikes Peak Library District	RLG/RLIN
Personal author	X	X	X	X	X	X	X	X	X	X
Corporate author	X	X	X	X	X	X	X	X	X	X
Title	X	X	X	X	X	X	X	X	X	X
Author/Title	X		X	X	X		X	X		X
Subject	X	X	X	X	X	X		X	X	X
Call number		X	X		X			X	X	X
LC card number	X		X	X	X		X		X	X
ISBN	X		X	X	X		X			X
ISSN	X		X	X			X			X
Government document number			X				X			X
Other control number	X[3]		X[1]	X[1]			X[1]	X[4]	X[5]	X[2]
Additional access points	X[8]	X[8]	X[7,8]	X[8]	X[9]	X[8]	X[6,8]	X[8]		X[7,8]
Free-text term search	X[10]	X[10]	X[11]	X[10]						X[10]

X = Access point available to user

NOTES:
1. OCLC control number
2. RLIN control number
3. 1 and 2
4. Title number
5. Barcode number
6. CODEN
7. 6 and others
8. Series title
9. Course/instructor
10. On selected fields
11. Full text and selected fields

* In some systems, access points (usually names) are combined under a single search command. In others, the specific index must be identified with the search command.

quantitative input and output measures. The readers' services function, the true information storage and retrieval process, must be made integral with other automated library processes. The emphasis on public access to our collections and services, brought on by the automation of cataloguing, the closing of the card catalogue (7), and the opening of the online catalogue(8) will require librarians who do not see themselves as warehouse keepers.

Catalogue users' searching habits must be better known to match our retrieval system features to these habits. The online system will have to provide far more assistance and instruction than we ever had for card or COM catalogues. The barriers and hurdles built into older systems, such as fixed order and single display of records, few subject searching aids, no rationale for collocation of items, and few access points must be removed if the new systems are to be an improvement over older systems.

An online catalogue user study is to get underway in the USA this fall. This study is supported by Council Library Resources and is being undertaken by RLG and OCLC research staff at more than twenty different libraries (all of those listed on illustration 1 and more). This should help to provide data about online catalogue users, their habits, perceptions, and expectations. They will also study non-users. I await the results of this study with anxiety, hoping the conclusions drawn from the data will be heeded this time.

In 1978 I compiled a table of advantages and disadvantages of different catalogue forms and unheeded research findings about catalogue use, (illustrations 2 and 3). As illustration 2 shows, no form will come without disadvantages unless we concentrate on avoiding them. Illustration 3 shows some new arrangements which would be helpful to users of our catalogues. I was startled to learn that these research findings have again been unheeded when online catalogues were designed. From the recent OCLC study of ten online catalogues in the USA (illustration 1), you can see that only half of them permit the user to view a subject index or thesaurus online. Only one allows a free text search of the whole record, only one now allows word adjacency operation. Other parts of this study show how limited the displays are. We have a lot of work to do before we can say we have made great studies in subject retrieval.

Subject retrieval in this new era will have to combine the best of our old catalogues and printed indexes with many new features made possible by the new technologies. We should avoid anything which will make catalogue use more difficult or less successful. We will need to attract users, guide them, satisfy and surprise them. It is an exciting challenge and I know that some of the other papers at this conference will help point the way.

REFERENCES

1. Markuson, B.E., ed. *Libraries and Automation,* Proceedings of the Conference . . . held at Airlie Foundation, Warrenton, Virginia, May 26–30, 1963. Washington, DC: Library of Congress, 1964. 268 p.

2. News note on REDI meeting, held in Columbus, Ohio, March 1981 in *Journal of Library Automation,* vol. 14, no. 2, June 1981, p. 121.

3. Markuson, B.E. *op. cit.*, p. 2.

4. Robinson, R.J. "Computers and Information Systems for Higher Education in the 1980's: Options and Opportunities," *Educom Bulletin,* Summer 1981, pp. 24–28.

5. Kountz, J.C. "Computers Now! Public Libraries and a Happy Union," *ALA Bulletin,* June 1968, pp. 683–687.

6. Atherton, P. "Systems Personnel: What Are Our Needs?", in *Preconference Institute on Library Automation,* Las Vegas, 1975. Chicago: American Library Association, 1975, pp. 101–126.

7. Gapen, K., ed. *Closing the Catalog.* Proceedings of the 1978 and 1979 LITA Institutes. Phoenix, AZ: Oryx Press, 1980.

8. Cochrane, P. "Improving the Quality of Information Retrieval . . .", *Online,* July 1981, pp. 30–42.

9. Gapen, *op. cit.*, p. 114, 116.

Improving the Quality of Information Retrieval-Online to a Library Catalog or Other Access Service . . . Or . . . Where Do We Go From Here?

It is probably safe to say that in 1975, anyone who was searching online was either an ORBIT user or a DIALOG user or an OCLC user or a LEXIS user. Most people [liked best] the system they learned on and kept abreast of that system and the databases on that system. Where they had a choice they would always access the system using the same telecommunications network. Sometimes this preference was forced on them because their library could not afford the various terminals needed to access the different systems. In these early years of online bibliographic searching, only trained information professionals were searching because the systems, the databases, the user-system protocols, and the offline training and instruction manuals were so confusing and inconsistent . . . especially if you *had* to use more than one system.

By 1980, the same library we described above could consolidate their training and equipment because the database formats were becoming more similar, the systems were more tolerant of differences in the terminals which could be used to access them. (Even OCLC announced access from other than their dedicated terminals.) Significant efforts were made by database suppliers and retrieval system personnel to help the inexperienced or occasional searcher by online aids, "user-cordial" interfaces and adequate training and user manuals. Nevertheless the typical library functions (searching the card catalog, circulation, interlibrary loan and acquisitions) were seen as separate online developments from those used for online bibliographic searching of abstracting and indexing databases and were being designed *de novo*.

Reprinted with permission from *Online* (July 1981), Online, Inc.

By 1985, I predict that we will have a majority of users who are occasional but serious users of several systems and multiple databases who will not always be using the assistance of an information professional. There will be a merger of in-library and remote online searching, both of online catalogs and bibliographic databases. The information industry will have settled into the ''home'' market and will be providing online aids and equipment features which will make that possible. The information professionals will see their role as one of customized service, when requested, but otherwise tutorial and educational. Remote sites such as homes, faculty offices, dormitories, corporate offices, laboratories, and staff offices will be the norm much more so than the present placement of equipment near the old card catalog or in the reference librarian's office.

If my prediction is fulfilled, what will we need to do between now and then to insure that we are doing better information searching by 1990? For one thing, we will have to understand the information seekers better than we do now or the assistance they will need will not be there. When something goes wrong online, or the user forgets to do something, or when they commit an error and can not interpret the message, or when they want to change their strategy or database . . . somehow there must be help immediately. Monitoring, advising and correcting user behavior (or the consequences of it) will have to be the rule of the day. Both databases and vocabulary aids online will have to be redesigned. No longer can the printed versions of these be the standard.

A great deal of work has brought us to our present state, and there are signs on the horizon that more will be done, but it should not continue as separate and distinct efforts. I hope there is food for thought in this article to focus our attention and direct our work toward the information scene of 1990.

Today there is little *new systems design*. Most of the developments we hear about are technical *changes,* using a micro instead of a mainframe computer system, or creating a special purpose database from discipline-oriented or comprehensive databases, or providing public access to a library's online catalog searching system, etc. The questions being asked are not how to do something better, but how to do something more cheaply; how to convert an old process or catalog into a new technical environment. Scant attention is being paid to developing new processes and services. I will venture to predict that this environment will not increase the quality of information retrieval, only change it. We will have new equipment and new users, not better service.

The dynamics of information retrieval systems today are such that most variables affecting retrieval success are not under the control of one system designer. If the designer's view is that of the stylized retrieval system of the 1960's (see Illustration 1), he may still be thinking that a change in his system's indexing procedures will have an impact on search strategy formulations, but in reality the system users' experiences may be more affected by a feature in the system which he does not control because it is a software package he has purchased or is leasing commercially.

NEEDED: AN EXPANDED VIEW

Rather than focusing on a "closed" or "in house" systems approach, the information systems analyst or designer working in the 1980's must have an expanded view which includes all the information systems available to his population of users and sources of satisfaction and retrieval success must be tracked before changes can be made in certain system components. This is a tall order, but if we really want to make improvements, we can no longer only think of replacing a card catalog with an online catalog without considering other changes as well.

There was a surprising finding in a survey of 26 participants at a working session, held at Dartmouth, July 20–26, 1980, to discuss the future development of online public access to bibliographic databases. Twelve defined the online catalog as performing the "same functions as the card catalog" and 11 said it would provide "same access points as the card catalog" (OCLC). There is no way that the online catalog will only be accessed as was the card catalog—witness the Conger chart.* Users must be studied (Atherton; Bates). No longer can we convert a printed abstracting service to an online service without considering revisions in abstracting procedures as well. The retrieval systems where these databases are searched revise the structures of the databases as part of their "loading" procedures and provide unforeseen access capabilities (See Illustration 2, Meadow and Cochrane; Atherton and others).

At the outset, I will admit that my views are biased. My grounding is in librarianship and information systems and services—with emphasis on services. As a result I usually approach every research or development project I review or participate in with the question: how will the results benefit the *users* of the information system? I tend to leave the questions about system efficiency to others.

SYSTEM SOLUTIONS OFTEN SHORT LIVED

System designers usually start from the need for improved efficiency or problems of expanded use, an overloaded document store, or the op-

---

*An online command chart—mostly of bibliographic systems—which also listed bibliographic applications for the RLIN online catalog system.

portunity to install new equipment. In and of itself, solutions to these problems may be notable but short-lived because the variety of user experiences will impose pressures on systems not foreseen by this hole-in-the-dike approach to systems design.

I know no one systems team could encompass all the aspects of today's world of information retrieval, but I think we should try to agree on a *model* of that process and then explain how our work or focus fits it. This model should be different from the 1960's, the halcyon days for individualistic information retrieval projects. I am using "model" in the sense of "description of interacting variables." A review of some impressive conceptualizations from this earlier era may help to show how much we are still influenced by the work of that period, but that a revised framework is required.[1]

Take Illustration #1.** This shows the major functions or components of an information center or service. It implies that the system designer controls all these functions and makes changes here or there (e.g. system vocabulary, or translation routine). It is implied that users use this one system with one database.

CHANGE DOESN'T ALSO EQUATE WITH IMPROVEMENT

It is my contention that no such *independent* information service exists today. I have noted that such a figure should be revised to include the free-text searching, multi-system, multi-document store environment in which this service would operate today. No one dreamed in the 60's that we would have the storage capabilities we have today and that free text searching of every word in our bibliographic records would be possible. Because of that we still do not have "free text" under systems control, nor do we have links between free and controlled vocabulary. We have *changed* our systems, but not essentially *improved* them.

Illustration #3 is more reflective of today's environment accounting, as it does, for *user and system* actions as variables in the interaction which can account for changes in results. The user-system interaction shown is an incomplete description, however, with no accounting for equipment used, varieties in databases, search complexity, etc.

---

[1]After this talk was presented, Martha Williams informed me that a Transparent System project at the University of Illinois, Coordinated Science Laboratory is working up a model which plugs in all the known pieces of research which relate to the major functions performed by the system and user in the online environment. Their work was not yet published at the time of this writing (January, 1981).

**All illustrations follow the text. Illustrations 1, 3 and 4 come from the book edited by Saracevic.

Illustration #4 is shown to remind us of the careful work done in the 1960's to observe this little understood or explained process of relevance judgements. The SDC team tried valiantly to design experiments where various variables were controlled and hypotheses tested. If their work were to be done again, because it is a core issue in determining or measuring the quality of information retrieval, their chart would need to be revised to reflect the online user of today who not only examines different documents in different databases, but who works in several retrieval systems before tracking down all documents which would be assessed for a given information requirement statement. This introduces a new set of variables which probably affect the relevance judgement—i.e., the interaction between the user and the several systems used to produce retrieval results for a single search.

USER BEHAVIOR A VITAL FACTOR

I am emphasizing the need for revision of our model of information retrieval because we have enough evidence now that it is the online user's behavior which can have such a heavy impact on the quality of information retrieval (Illustration #5 and #6). Study after study, according to Fenichel, has pointed to user behavior which must be modified by training or assistance if better retrieval results are to be obtained. The missed opportunities may be a "system error" in the global view, but most system designers would say that this is not under their control. I would disagree. They should be inventive enough to guide the user to these opportunities, or the support and training staff should emphasize this type of problem in their user training sessions. To make system changes or design experiments without taking users into account is to do research and development which may be meaningless in the long run. Illustration #6 tries to emphasize this. This chart, or model, is offered as a better view of information retrieval for the 1980's. If system changes are made, such a model would prompt the designer to discover how these changes affect the database, the searcher, and the interface. If database changes are planned, the designer should also consider effects on searchers, command languages and system features. For the online searcher in the 1980's there is a multiplicity of all these system components.

MANY VARIABLES MUST BE CONSIDERED

If the user population can search not only the single database online, but others as well, there should be some consideration for cross database indexes, the thesaurus, and other variables. In the case of the meeting cited earlier, where library catalog conversion to online public access was discussed (OCLC and RLG), the participants identified four issue areas (user and use characteristics, interface characteristics, library environment, and computing environment). The array of issue factors roughly covers the same areas as Illustration #6 but does not give the same emphasis or point up the interrelationships. In their list of issues, "Retrieval Requirements of Users" and "Retrieval Features of the Interface" and "Database Features" are not seen to be overlapping or interrelated so that the "Type of publication" (p. 25) is listed as a Retrieval Requirement and not itemized under Database Features or Record Content (p. 36–37). Interdatabase links for authority control are not mentioned. User or Searcher Proficiency online or Training for online are not mentioned, but Card Catalog Knowledge is (p. 24). These may only be minor omissions, but I am judging them to be symptomatic of an overly simplistic view of the complexity of the information retrieval scene facing the online catalog user.

BIBLIOGRAPHIC SYSTEM STUDIES MAY HELP CATALOG DESIGNERS

Some of the findings from studies of existing online bibliographic search systems (Illustration #5) may provide useful insights for the online catalog designer (Fenichel). User behavior studies have led to observations but they do not always point the way to improved search results. Should training, or system changes, or new tools be created if serious problems have been located? These studies can lead to automatic error correction, remediation, or new database features. The possible options must be considered in the context of the whole system. If a minimum of commands and logical operators are expected to be used, then an elaborate array of system commands and capabilities in training manuals for novices may not be necessary. Pocket Reminder Cards may be the best form of novice user prompting (Lancaster, p. 318–19).

If there is a noticed weakness in search strategy, for instance (second item in Illustration #6), then perhaps some new term selection aid could be designed and tested, or a different training package developed. After an analysis of ERIC user search histories, we made a suggestion for a new system tool to link free text searching to controlled vocabulary. Our focus in this ERIC/IR project was the *user* and the *database*, but we wound up focusing our suggestions on the retrieval systems where ERIC is searched (Illustration 8).

AUTOMATIC LINKS WOULD BE HELPFUL

We found that searchers were entering a free text word and were missing access to records via controlled vocabulary. Our new "tool" would allow an automatic link between title word browsing and the thesaurus (Illustration #7). We proposed that, once having checked the context in which the term *depression* is used in titles, the searcher could then see one such item, judge it to be relevant, and then automatically expand into a descriptor list which was constructed from the indexing record of all three items like it. This controlled vocabulary list of five terms could form a new search expression, increasing recall or relevant items. (This browsing process of the relevant descriptors for the selected titles cannot be done automatically now except by a routine like AID on Medline.) Such a search expression using controlled vocabulary terms would require very little effort on the part of the searcher.

On existing retrieval systems, this is a fairly laborious process. If a searcher looks for words in the title, a search expression must be developed and the search result scanned before controlled vocabulary is reviewed. Then he must enter those words. There is no efficient way to enter those vocabulary terms in a search expression from the previous output. If such an improvement were implemented on online catalogs, it would be the direct result of a user study and interpretation of a common online problem which may have been overlooked if other retrieval system features were studied.

Several changes of retrieval systems or databases could become improvements in quality of information retrieval. Transforming system commands and database access for efficiency considerations may not do it. All too often the changes come in system features and databases because of system designers' creativity and not search behavior problems. Important innovations can come from both activities, witness G. Salton's relevance feedback and T. Doczkocs' AID algorithm and the SUPARS and ERIC studies. In our ERIC online study we emphasized that there should be responsible agents for all changes and improvements and these will differ for different changes (Illustration #8 from Atherton and others; [also] Markey et al.). There is probably a need for a similar composite for library online public access efforts too. If we start with the possible foci for studies to improve quality, we may come sooner to the needed changes for online bibliographic searching in the 80's. I make a suggested start toward such an array of foci in Illustration #9. I offer it as an addendum to the OCLC-RLIN report cited earlier where a list of those who should be involved in resolving the issues is given (p. 21), but it is not linked, in that report at least, to a priority list of issues or foci.

SEARCH STRATEGY—THE REAL KEY?

Search strategy may be the real key to improvements in information retrieval quality. If it is, then we must study user behavior, both online and offline, and another set of problems can be highlighted (Bates). Illustration # 10 shows the searcher's tools at different critical decision-making stages, both before and while online. Few system manuals or tutorials (on or off line) are geared to these decision points. Tools useful at Decision Point 2 may not be the same ones needed at Stage 4, although both *now* (col. 2) are considered as a term selection function. New tools may be needed (col. 3) and will have to be incorporated into training sessions as well as online assistance procedures and index access.

Such a holistic view of information retrieval, with no system seen as independent, and no database seen in only one version, is very complex. A healthy competitive environment where solutions to specific problems are being sought is very beneficial *as long* as designers and researchers frequently review where their work fits and others see how all this can impact on several user populations. I think ten years is too long in between meetings (Walker).

REFERENCES

1. Atherton, Pauline. "Catalog Users' Access from the Researcher's Viewpoint: Past and Present Research Which Could Affect Library Catalog Design," in D. Kaye Gapen and Bonnie Juergens, eds., *Closing the Catalog*. Phoenix, Arizona: Oryx Press, 1980, pp. 106–122.

2. Atherton, Pauline and others. *Online Searching of ERIC; Impact of Free Text or Controlled Vocabulary Searching on the Design of the ERIC Data Base*. Syracuse, New York: ERIC Clearinghouse on Information Resources, 1979, ED 180 431, ED 180 432. Also Markey, Karen, Pauline Atherton and Claudia Newton. "An Analysis of Controlled Vocabulary and Free Text Search Statements in Online Searches," *Online Review*, 4(1980), pp. 225–236.

3. Bates, Marcia J. "Idea Tactics," *Journal of the American Society for Information Science*, 30(1979), pp. 280–289.

4. Conger, Lucinda D. *Online Command Chart*, Weston, Connecticut: Online, Inc., 1980.

5. Fenichel, Carol H. "The Process of Searching Online Bibliographic Databases: A Review of Research," *Library Research*, 2(1980–81), pp. 107–127.

6. Lancaster, F. W. and E. G. Fayer. *Information Retrieval Online*. New York: Wiley, 1973. (See especially SUPARS user manual in Appendix E.)

7. Meadow, Charles and Pauline (Atherton) Cochrane. *Basics of Online Searching*. New York: Wiley, 1981.

8. OCLC, Inc. and the Research Libraries Group Inc. *Online Public Access to Library Bibliographic Data Bases: Developments, Issues and Priorities*. Final Report to the Council on Library Resources. September, 1980. 62p. IR009054 (ERIC document in process).

9. Saravecic, Tefko, ed. *Introduction to Information Science*. New York: Bowker, 1970.

10. Walker, Donald E., ed. *Interactive Bibliographic Search: The User/Computer Interface*. Proceedings of a workshop held in Palo Alto, California, on 14–15 January 1971. Montvale, New Jersey: AFIPS Press, 1971.

ILLUSTRATION 1

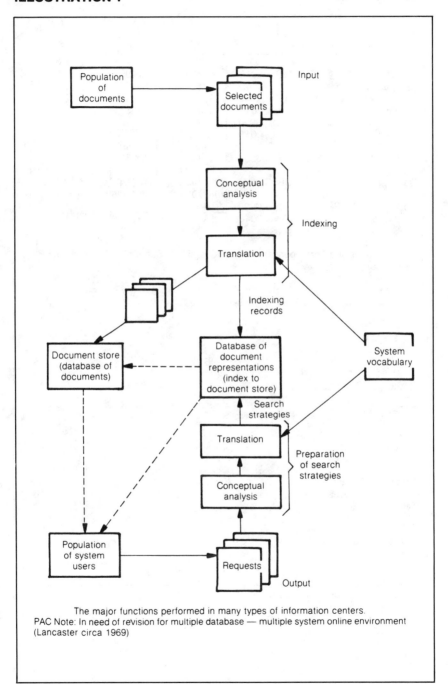

The major functions performed in many types of information centers.
PAC Note: In need of revision for multiple database — multiple system online environment
(Lancaster circa 1969)

ILLUSTRATION 2

ERIC Field Names	ERIC Codes	LRS	SDC	BRS
Accession Number	0010		/AN	.AN.
Author	AUTH 001B	AU =	/AU	.AU.
Geographic Source	GEO 004D	CP =.	/LO	.GS.
Government Level	GOV 004E	GL =	/LO	.GV.
Corporate Source	INST 001C	/CS	/OS	.IN.
Sponsoring Agency	SPON 0020	/SA	/SPO	.SN.
Title	001A	/TI	/TI	.TI.
Abstract	ABST 002C	/AB	(IN BI)	.AB.
Identifier	IDEN 0024	/ID, /ID* /IF, /IF*	(IN BI)	.ID.
Descriptor	DESC 0023	/DE, /DE* /DF, /DF*	/IT,* /IT /IW,* /IW	.MJ, MN, DE, UJ, UN.
Descriptive Note	NOTE 0026	/NT		.NT.
Language	LANG 004C	LA =	/LA	.LG.

A. ERIC Codes and Corresponding LRS, SDC, and BRS Search Qualifiers of the ERIC Unit Record.

The boxed area in the LRS, SDC, BRS columns indicates the source for the dictionary or basic index of ERIC on these systems.

	LRS	SDC	BRS
BASIC INDEX FIELDS:	CIJE: 08/79 RIE: 08/79	02/79 06/79	08/79 08/79
TOTAL	29,255	28,156	29,323
Title	9,926/TI	9,642/TI	9,958.TI.
Abstract	20,430/AB	?	?
Sponsoring Agency	7/SA	-	7.SN.
Note	2,008/NT	-	2,004.NT.
Corporate Source	792/CS	-	790.IN.
Government Level	-	-	0.GV.
Geographic Source	-	-	0.GS.

B. Field by Field Tally of Postings for Searching a Single Word, *Reading*, in the Basic Index Fields of ERIC Online (10/9/79).

ILLUSTRATION 3

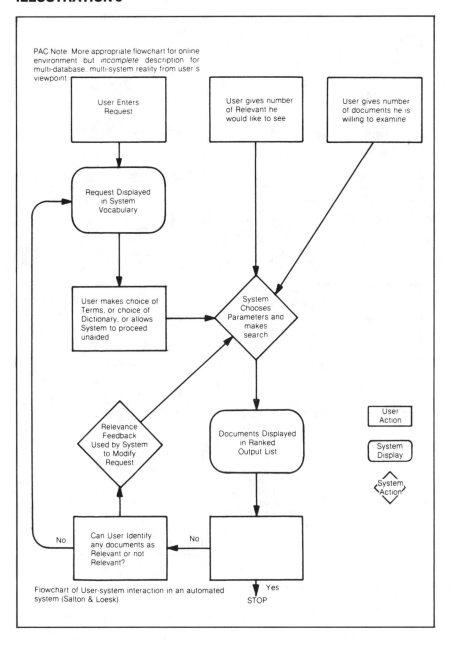

ILLUSTRATION 4

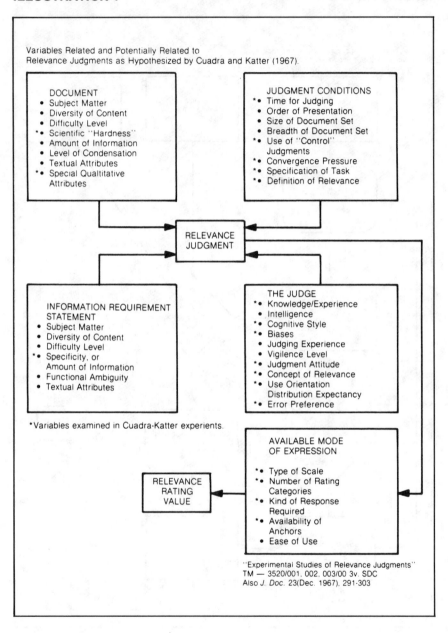

Variables Related and Potentially Related to
Relevance Judgments as Hypothesized by Cuadra and Katter (1967).

DOCUMENT
- Subject Matter
- Diversity of Content
- Difficulty Level
- * Scientific "Hardness"
- Amount of Information
- Level of Condensation
- Textual Attributes
- * Special Qualtitative Attributes

JUDGMENT CONDITIONS
- * Time for Judging
- Order of Presentation
- Size of Document Set
- Breadth of Document Set
- * Use of "Control" Judgments
- * Convergence Pressure
- * Specification of Task
- * Definition of Relevance

RELEVANCE JUDGMENT

INFORMATION REQUIREMENT STATEMENT
- Subject Matter
- Diversity of Content
- Difficulty Level
- * Specificity, or Amount of Information
- Functional Ambiguity
- Textual Attributes

THE JUDGE
- * Knowledge/Experience
- Intelligence
- * Cognitive Style
- * Biases
- Judging Experience
- Vigilence Level
- * Judgment Attitude
- * Concept of Relevance
- * Use Orientation Distribution Expectancy
- * Error Preference

*Variables examined in Cuadra-Katter experients.

AVAILABLE MODE OF EXPRESSION
- * Type of Scale
- * Number of Rating Categories
- * Kind of Response Required
- * Availability of Anchors
- Ease of Use

RELEVANCE RATING VALUE

"Experimental Studies of Relevance Judgments"
TM — 3520/001, 002, 003/00 3v. SDC
Also *J. Doc.* 23(Dec. 1967), 291-303

ILLUSTRATION 5

COLLECTION OF FINDINGS ABOUT THE ONLINE USER
(Extracted from Fenichel — 1980)

  **   Enormous individual variability in searching behavior and performance
\#**   Weakness in search strategy (not all concepts formed into search expressions, not all
       possible approaches to term selection used)
  **   Missed opportunities — did not exploit system capabilities, e.g., interactive capability
  **   Some serendipidity on and offline (explored new avenues)
  **   Little "think time" online; usually little modification at terminal
  **   User made actual errors (input, commands. spelling); did not understand error messages.
\#\#**   Used a minimum of commands and logical operators (selecting terms, combining terms,
       displaying results)
  **   Users do not adapt to differences in file structure
  **   Work speed variation influenced by search formulation, pre-search preparation, cost
       conscious attitudes, search familiarity with database and system
  **   Search effort varies: mean search times, #commands, # of descriptors, operators,
       # documents retrieved, # of concept groups
  **   Relationship found between search effort and recall
  **   Variation in search complexity may be related to institutional setting

  \#   *Major problem for experienced and inexperienced searches*
  \#\#   *Not a major problem, but can be significant barrier for very inexperienced or*
       occasional users.

ILLUSTRATION 6

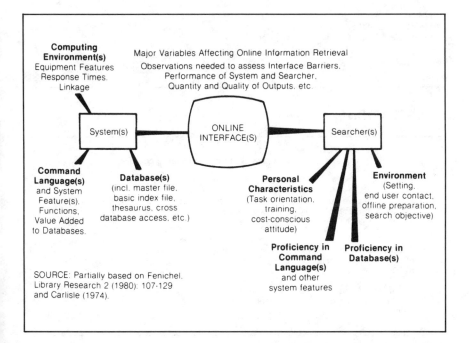

Computing Environment(s)
Equipment Features
Response Times.
Linkage

Major Variables Affecting Online Information Retrieval
Observations needed to assess Interface Barriers.
Performance of System and Searcher,
Quantity and Quality of Outputs. etc.

System(s) — ONLINE INTERFACE(S) — Searcher(s)

Command Language(s)
and System
Feature(s).
Functions,
Value Added
to Databases.

Database(s)
(incl. master file,
basic index file,
thesaurus, cross
database access, etc.)

Personal Characteristics
(Task orientation.
training,
cost-conscious
attitude)

Environment
(Setting.
end user contact,
offline preparation,
search objective)

Proficiency in Command Language(s)
and other
system features

Proficiency in Database(s)

SOURCE: Partially based on Fenichel.
Library Research 2 (1980): 107-129
and Carlisle (1974).

ILLUSTRATION 7

```
? WRAP DEPRESSION/TI
```

REF		INDEX-TERM	ITEMS	TT
w1		DEPRESSION LEARNED HELPLESSNESS	3	5
w2		DEPRESSION OPPRESSED	1	
w3		DEPRESSION RECOVERY HIGHER	1	
...		...		
w10		DEPRESSION SPEECH INITIAL	1	
w11	IRRATIONAL BELIEFS	DEPRESSION	1	
w12	LEARNED HELPLESSNESS		2	5
w13	LEARNED HELPLESSNESS	DEPRESSION CLINICAL MODEL	1	5

— MORE —

```
? T W12/8/1
EJ180832
  EFFECTS OF REAL AND RECALLED SUCCESS ON LEARNED HELPLESSNESS AND
DEPRESSION
  DESCRIPTORS: *DEPRESSION (PSYCHOLOGY)/ *PROBLEM SOLVING/ *PSYCHOLOGICAL
PATTERNS/ *PSYCHOLOGICAL STUDIES/ *PSYCHOPATHOLOGY/ *RECALL (PSYCHOLOGY)/
RESEARCH METHODOLOGY/TABLES (DATA)
  IDENTIFIERS: *LEARNED HELPLESSNESS
? EXPAND W1
```

REF	INDEX-TERM	ITEMS	RT
t1	PSYCHOPATHOLOGY	322	9
t2	PSYCHOLOGICAL STUDIES	2024	5
t3	PSYCHOLOGICAL PATTERNS	1074	21
t4	LEARNED HELPLESSNESS	44	
t5	DEPRESSION	201	

Imagined Transaction of Linkage between Free Text Title Terms
and Controlled Vocabulary.

```
FROM
ERIC/IR SPECIAL REPORT: 1979:
ONLINE SEARCHING OF ERIC (ED 180 431)
```

Is User Satisfied?

ILLUSTRATION 8

Suggestions for improvements and *responsible agents* for effecting changes.

User Groups	Retrieval systems	ERIC system
1. Establish links between user groups, ANSI, NFAIS, ASIDIC, for developing multiple data base standards	1. Provide links between basic index and the controlled vocabulary	1. Develop high quality user aids for online searching
2. Develop standards for naming of data elements, contents of ERIC basic index	2. Coordinate and announce planned reloading of ERIC files	2. Find additional ways of limiting excessive output
3. Review differences in access to data elements in ERIC online	3. Conform to ERIC standard of order of printing data elements	3. Study free text and controlled vocabulary searching

(continued)

User Groups (continued)	Retrieval systems (continued)	ERIC system (continued)
4. Study search objectives to see how they relate to requirements for system features and data elements	4. Cooperate with user groups, ANSI, NFAIS, ASIDIC, in development and implement-action of standards	4. Develop precise rules for indexing and abstracting expressions of action
5. Assess methods for improving searchers' competencies	5. Enhance online access to ERIC Thesaurus	5. Test to check savings in time and cost using various search saves
6. Suggest new system features	6. Implement new features to aid ERIC online searchers upon	6. Make available public search saves
7. Develop a review board for endorsing printed and online user aids	recommendation and review by user groups	
8. Call for coordination among retrieval systems as to reloading of ERIC master tape updates		

Source: Atherton and other (1979) or Markey (1980).

ILLUSTRATION 9

FOCI FOR STUDIES TO IMPROVE THE QUALITY OF INFORMATION RETRIEVAL

A. TYPES OF USER(S)	B. INFORMATION STORE INTRA COMPARISON	C. INTER-SYSTEM COMPARISON	D. USER- SYSTEM INTERFACE
1. Experienced or novice	1. Single vs. multi database files	1. Command languages:	1. Under system control:
2. First time or repeat user	2. Variety of access to files	2. System features	a. Instruction
3. Mediated or non-mediated use	3. Vocabulary aids on and offline	3. Database treatment — value added	b. Assistance
4. Observed search behavior and prep-aration activity (strategy & tactics) linked to other factors or user characteristics	4. Overlap in data-base coverage	4. System operational details related to files	c. Troubleshooting diagnostics
5. Question complexity	5. Database characteristics	5. Database directory assistance	d. System perfor-mance data
6. Purpose or search objective and sub-sequent library use	6. Record characteristics	6. Interface charac-teristics: terminal, equipment, etc.	2. Effected by user-system behavior:
7. Other pertinent user characteris-tics, e.g., experience and familiarity with system, files, etc.		7. Output formats	a. Level/source of control (default, override, etc.)
8. Training or assist-ance offline.			b. Search activities — commands used, file changes, data-base features used, etc.
9. Satisfaction and success measures			
10. Institutional setting — constraints, style, etc.			

Compiled by Cochrane, 1980-81

ILLUSTRATION 10

TOOLS FOR CRITICAL DECISION POINTS IN ONLINE SEARCH STRATEGY

Before Online (also online)

Decision Points	**Tools** (now in use)	**Possible Tools** (to be designed)
1. Concepts to be searched?	A. Information sheet from requester B. Pre-search interview data C. Thesauri for relevant databases. D. Dictionaries and glossaries	A. Merged thesauri lists across databases B. Free-text/thesauri linkages
2. Terms — in what form?	A. Inverted file wordlists B. Thesauri C. Words in title and abstracts of some relevant items D. Classification schedules or category lists E. Database user manuals	A. Concept-search/saves B. Access to sample searches with similar concept groups
3. Features of retrieval system use?	A. Retrieval system user manual specific to database to be searched B. Sample searches C. Sessions from update briefings	A. Analytic charts with system features arranged by search objectives

While Online

4. Unfavorable results — how to react?	A. Information sheet from requester B. Online thesauri C. Database dictionary list online D. Brief search analysis	A. Relevance feedback B. System compensation for common errors C. Diagnostics and corrections D. System aids for search tactics E. Ranking or weighting algorithms F. Explicit error messages and "conversational" suggestions to correct error
5. Revise search logic?	A. Pre-search strategy notes B. System user manuals	A. System aids for idea tactics B. Online search review assistance

Source (in part): C. Meadow and P. Cochrane, *Basics of Online Searching.* Wiley, 1981

A Forward Look—Online Library Catalogs in 1990 and Beyond

If the right interaction takes place, it is a safe assumption that library catalogs of the 21st century will contain references to all information items in library collections; not just books, but also journal articles, maps, filmstrips, videodiscs, etc. It is also safe to say that these catalogs will be made up of acquired records, gleaning from large bibliographic utilities those records which reflect individual library holdings.

At the present time, OCLC represents the largest bibliographic utility with customers online to acquire records which they then use to make up local online catalogs (or card catalogs). OCLC is able to customize each library's archival tape after the library's staff has examined the master OCLC file and made choices and selections from it.

Another large bibliographic file is in the making. As in a jigsaw puzzle, it represents the missing piece which could make each library's catalog more truly reflect the information content of the library.

For over eighty years, libraries (especially school and public, but also academic and special) have acquired periodical collections which match the periodicals indexed in the H. W. Wilson Company indexes (Reader's Guide, Applied Science & Technology Index, Art Index, Social Science Index, etc.). Every high school student in the country is taught to use the Reader's Guide and to find articles in their library's collection which they can use as background for term papers, speeches, etc. There are over 100,000 subscribers to the family of H. W. Wilson indexes in print. Most of these are libraries with limited holdings (their journal collections would not go back more than ten years for many titles).

Slowly but surely HWW is going online, creating a database for each index which they can use to continue to print the indexes as well as to offer an online bibliographic searching service. The internal computerized services at HWW will support the creation of the databases and the centralized

Never published; written in 1982.

searching service (called WILSONLINE—modeled after ELHILL at the National Library of Medicine).

Such a centralized searching service may only be an interim measure. Most libraries, if the trend continues, will want to serve their clientele locally, on their own computers, with their own database—going off site only when those services have not fulfilled a need and when the patron can and will pay for that additional service. How then can portions of the HWW database which match their holdings be added to their Local Online Catalog? Possibly by a process even simpler than the present operations on OCLC . . . the library's periodical holdings (journal title and volume data) can be matched automatically against the HWW Master File and a customized tape generated for changing and updating the library's online catalog file. Instead of putting the latest issue of the printed Reader's Guide on the shelf, the library would load a customized tape from HWW (via OCLC?) which would reflect their new journal holdings. VIA OCLC???? Yes, because the expertise for such a service is there, and because the volume of business would not easily be supported by the computer system at HWW. Just as OCLC is the wholesaler and retailer for MARC, so could it be for HWW.

I think it is worth exploring such a possibility, don't you? What is the alternative? A slow, chaotic development of local online catalogs, with a segmented market of and for bibliographic databases.

A Paradigm Shift in Library Science

In other places I have gone on record concerning the unheeded research findings from catalog use studies. I suggested that these studies should be reviewed again, and the most constant recommendations should be incorporated into the design of the new form of library catalogs. What I failed to observe at that time was that some of the findings had been heeded by the library profession but that other findings were not heeded because they were not strong enough to cause a paradigm shift, in Kuhn's terms. In *The Structure of Scientific Revolutions,* Thomas Kuhn describes how research findings, which are substantiated and verified, can challenge scientific "truths" and can cause a scientific community to shift away from common wisdom to a new consensus about what is truth for them.

The paradigm shift in librarianship that did not occur, even though some research showed a certain tendency, has to do with the primary activity or activities at the library catalog. Common wisdom since Cutter's time has been that most users of the library want a catalog where they can find a particular item, a known item. Because we believed that to be true, we have invested a great deal of professional effort in providing catalogs that can help users perform that task par excellence. Generations of catalog specialists have produced descriptive catalog codes, standard unit records in card and MARC form, and have invested greatly in name authority projects. The strength of our belief in this truth is shown in our national bibliographical tool, the NUC, which only provides access to known items, as does the first national online bibliographic utility, OCLC. In recent times we have held international conferences, created international standards, and organized a Universal Bibliographical Control project—all devoted to bibliographic description of known items. Belief in the paradigm that the catalog was for known-item searching is very strong indeed.

Most catalog use studies, until recently, seemed to confirm that this belief was a correct one. But now we have findings from several *online* catalog use studies that dispute this "truth." The CLR/OPAC survey, recently completed (reported in this journal and elsewhere), online catalog transaction log analyses, focused group interviews, and data and statistical reports from several libraries (including the Library of Congress and the University of California Library System) attest to the "fact" that the great majority of library users are performing *topical subject* searches, not author/title or known-item searches. That is the overwhelming finding from these studies. It was also the finding from some earlier catalog use studies, but this time the weight of the evidence cannot be ignored or unheeded.

The important question is: What impact will these findings have on the professional work of librarians, the catalog codes, the efforts to standardize and internationalize our bibliographic records? If the findings are accepted as the "new truth" about catalog use, we may see a perceptible shift in professional work, with greater attention being paid to subject analysis and subject access in library catalogs. I don't expect a pendulum swing away from descriptive cataloging, but there may be just enough of a shift for balance so that the profession, the international scene, and the national libraries and bibliographic utilities will devote more resources to the improvement of this aspect of library catalog design. If this does not occur, we may find the *technology* of online library catalogs dictating the *science* of online library catalogs. That would be unfortunate for subject analysis and subject access are greatly aided by computers and other technologies, but the underpinnings of OPAC developments should be a firm understanding and professional agreement about what subject analysis and subject access *is* or *should be*.

We really don't know if augmented MARC records and keyword access are good enough to replace LCSH. Such an extremist view (which I personally do not advocate) needs to be justified and verified. We really don't know if LCSH online or a new library thesaurus will be the answer to improved subject access. We need to arrive at some professional consensus about it. As library scientists, we need to concentrate on these issues before we confirm which OPAC feature and what online authority and bibliographic records will be universally adopted. We cannot assume, as before, that subject authority formats will match name authority formats. The functions of known-item access and subject access are different and will require different codes, formats, and links to bibliographic records.

The challenge for the library profession now is *not* how to convert card catalogs to online catalogs, but how to convert unifunctional catalogs into multifunctional catalogs where known-item and topical-subject searches can both be successfully completed. Cutter will not roll over in his grave, but he may sit up and take notice! As will Ranganathan, Haykin, M. Taube, Metcalf, J. C. M. Hanson, Bliss, and C. Martel!

Part 2

What Do We Know About Users and Catalogs?

Introduction

All of these selections are primarily literature reviews. There have been many studies of catalog use and catalog design, but only a few have formed a part of the "common wisdom" of our profession. All too often the results of these studies have been ignored by catalog designers. From the 1973 selection (which introduced Indian librarians to some of the catalog research carried on at that time in the USA) to the 1983 selection (which is an expansion of a paper presented at an ALA Preconference) I have made the same plea: let's listen to the researchers who have found out how our library catalogs are being used, and when they tell us about user problems let's listen to them and redesign accordingly at the first opportunity. With online catalogs now seen to be a necessity in the modern library the requirement to monitor the system's use can be met very easily and the results can be quite rewarding, both for the library user, the library staff, and the library researcher.

Putting Knowledge to Work: Five Lectures by Pauline Atherton

INTRODUCTION

Attracted by Dr Ranganathan's Work

It is indeed an honour for me to be here with Dr Ranganathan and his students in his home-land. I have introduced myself to many groups in the United States as an apostle of Ranganathan. Now I have the opportunity to tell a group in his own land why I have given myself such a title.

FIRST IMPRESSION

More years ago than I care to remember, even at my age, I heard of Ranganathan. It was in a course on the History and Theory of Cataloguing at the University of Chicago; I had already received my Master's Degree in Library Science and was working as a librarian. It was in this advanced course that I first learned of the "Father of library science in India." Let me recall for you what my first impressions were when I pursued the request that Mrs Ruth French Strout made of me in a seminar to find out something about Ranganathan's catalogue code and report back to the class. I remember them quite well because my immediate impression upon reading the five statements called "The Five Laws of Library Science" in the first book by Dr Ranganathan that I found was one of amusement. Yes, I smiled, and thought to myself, "how simple he makes it all sound, when really it is much more complicated!"

Depth of the Five Laws

After that, I thought about these five short statements and decided that no more really needed to be said to force me to think seriously about the most important areas of library service, evaluation, and management. Ever since that day fifteen years ago, I have been guided by those words when I pursued advanced technological developments and applied them to library and information work, or when I would begin a class on the organisation of information, cataloguing, or library in society. I have written these five statements on every blackboard in every classroom where I have taught and I will continue to do so, because they offer me (and my students) the guidance and the rationale we need when we critically review how we follow the cataloguing practices which prevail, how we evaluate the libraries we use, visit, or work in, and how we work to improve the practices we follow and the library services we manage. Because these five statements have served as my guiding star throughout my professional library career, I would like to use them as the framework for my Sarada Ranganathan Lectures, being delivered at the Documentation Research and Training Centre which Dr Ranganathan helped to found.

An Opportunity to Review

I appreciate the invitation to deliver these lectures in Bangalore. This has served as my needed opportunity to pull together my thoughts on the topics which mean a great deal to me; namely, library education, library use, system evaluation, and improvements in the principles and practices of cataloguing and classification based on assistance from computers and empirical research. Because I am so deeply touched by this opportunity, I may tend to be overly personal in my remarks rather than purely scientific and scholarly. Hopefully, this will not detract from my presentation too much. I hope that my review of several studies on these topics recently completed by my colleagues in the United States (some of them former students) will add the substance needed to make these lectures as beneficial to the listener (or reader) as they are to the writer. . . .

LECTURE #1

LAW 1: BOOKS ARE FOR USE: HOW TO SEE TO IT!

Improvising the Usability of Documents

During the 1960's in the United States, a great many developments have taken place in trying to improve the usability of documents (all printed forms of messages and data, that is, recorded knowledge). More often than not, the headlines are made when a bigger or better computing system is used, but we should not confuse ourselves: the improvements came because a competent staff investigated the problems presently faced by users trying to get documents to use, investigated the user himself, and his channels of communication, and the media he selects to find information. Only when they were sure that he values the use of documents above other media have they tried to improve his access by the use of computers or other mechanical devices. Many studies and efforts could be cited and their findings quoted, but let one study of physicists serve as an example.

Media for Information and Communication

Twelve different media were cited by the physicists surveyed as best performing seven information functions:

*1. Articles in periodicals read in *own, or library copy*;
2. Reprints they collect;
*3. Manuscripts (including drafts) they receive from author;
4. Technical reports distributed within own institution;
5. Technical reports distributed by other than own institution;
6. Telephone conversations;
*7. Face-to-face discussions with persons working in their institution;
8. Face-to-face discussions with persons not currently working in their institution (e g, at scientific meeting, etc);
9. Oral presentations made at scientific meetings or conferences;
10. Copies of oral presentations (including lecture notes and conference proceedings);
11. Private correspondence; and
12. Other.

Needs of Readers, or Information Dissemination Function

The following were considered to be the main objectives of use of the different media mentioned. . . .

1. General awareness of current state of physics;
2. Find out who is working in what area or on what problems;
3. Source of specific ideas for work *in progress*;
4. Source of specific ideas for *new* work;
5. Inform others of my research activities;
6. Getting up-to-date in a new area; and
7. Browsing stimulation.

The study showed the high value of articles in periodicals and manuscripts in respect of all the seven of the information functions. With this

---

*Found to be most important.

knowledge, the American Institute of Physics proceeded with their plans for a computer-based information system to publish and disseminate information in the field of physics in printed form. Because face-to-face discussions with persons were the second most important media with respect to meeting the information needs (3) and (4) above, the American Institute of Physics expanded its responsibility for organising meetings for the members of its member societies. They have sought new and better ways of performing these important information dissemination functions because they recognise that "books are for use."

Conference on Interconnection of Computer-based Information Networks

LIBRARY NETWORK

A recent conference in USA at Airlie, near Warrenton, Virginia, brought one hundred leaders in the American library and communications world together to discuss and make recommendations for national policy regarding library and information networks. Without the dedication that *books are for use,* it would have been difficult for some to agree to certain recommendations because they conflict with their institutional objectives. For the greater good, then, the group established certain goals for *library network services.* I cite them here to indicate how far Dr. Ranganathan's first law can be pursued.

At the CICIN meeting sponsored by ALA, we agreed that *it is a legitimate need of every library or information centre to call upon information networks to identify, locate and make available all forms of materials and services and to provide efficient and dependable information delivery services to the ultimate seeker of information.* This implies a freer interinstitutional communication structure.

MAKING READERS AWARE OF INFORMATION

We agreed at the Airlie Conference that the major goal in the provision of information services through a library network should be to facilitate *learning* in its broadest sense. Libraries and other information centres at the present time are able to provide the storage, retrieval, and display systems for information that can be utilised by a *limited* number of patrons with a fairly well defined need and clearly articulated demand for services. Use of these services is conditioned by the perceived expectation of satisfaction on the part of the user. Success reinforces usage and disappointment leads the patron to seek elsewhere or to let his needs go unfulfilled. To have continued use of our libraries and information centres, initiative must be taken by the service agency to make their services known to potential users. They must develop the means and take a more active role in identifying and defining a patron's need for information. Let us call these *awareness* services—one of our first tasks.

BIBLIOGRAPHICAL SERVICE: MEDIATION

To use information for learning, the perceived need for information must be translated into the provision of information to meet that need. This *mediation function* depends on the interpretation of the need, and on the availability and use of *directory systems* and *consulting services* that lead to the eventual delivery of the information and information services needed. Thus, the second function to be performed by a service network of libraries and information centres is the provision of information *about* information and information systems. We call this *bibliographic* or *intellectual* access.

PHYSICAL ACCESS TO DOCUMENTS

In addition to this intellectual access, provision for physical access by *delivery* systems will make information available in the place, time, and form that is best suited to the user. It is recognised that the problems of resource management and control in a network will be exceedingly complex, but that these problems must be solved with a primary view towards the more expeditious delivery of informational media to meet service demands.

EVALUATION OF SERVICE

Even with a network with objectives to provide awareness, mediatory access, and delivery service, we still agreed at the CICIN conference that the network must provide an *evaluation* service both to aid the user in guiding his behaviour, and sensing his opinion. We need the necessary feedback mechanisms at all levels which will make such a network adaptive to changing patterns of need and use. In this sense, the network is itself a learning mechanism which is aware of both its parts and the environment in which it operates and is able to modify its behaviour accordingly.

Change of Pattern of Service

These five services—awareness, mediation, access, delivery, and evaluation—describe the user-system interface in terms of the benefits to be provided by an information network. This delineation of services at Airlie seems to be a natural extension of the First Law if we put it into a larger context of library and information networks. There should be no mistake that, what is being contemplated under the term library and information, something quite new and different from conventional library systems is envisioned. It is a new medium for the dissemination of knowledge. Are we librarians prepared for such a change in our professional lives?

Such developments as information networks and system evaluation studies in the US have brought about a general awareness that either books are for use or libraries should not be supported and stay in business. Many people have strongly criticised "traditional library service" in the United States and have questioned whether the established methods are the ones to perpetuate.

Impact on Library Education

Such reports as *Libraries at Large, Library Response to Social Change,* and the new ALA Policy on Education and Manpower force us in library education in the United States to engage in some self-evaluation and reassessment of our curriculum. We have to ask ourselves: how do we teach the new version of the First Law of Library Science? I am not sure library education in India is undergoing such upheaval, but reflections on developments in one country may quite possibly have some relevance for our colleagues elsewhere. The following remarks are offered in that spirit.

Students in American library schools are asking for a new curriculum and for class activities which are relevant to today's and tomorrow's libraries. Should we admit that library education goals need to be re-vamped? Can we stem the tide of increasing irrelevancy of many of our libraries today? One possibility I suggested in a talk I delivered in Texas in the Spring of 1970 was to "put knowledge to work" in today's library schools. Knowledge about librarianship, I contended, exists in the form of library research and development efforts which are available but not always integrated quickly into a library school curriculum. D W MacKinnon (8) said this about the word *knowledge:*

> "Knowledge is the result of playing with what we know, that is, with our facts. *Ledge,* the second element in the word *knowledge,* means apart. A knowledgeable person in science is not, as we are often wont to think, merely one who has an accumulation of facts, but rather one who has the capacity to have sport with what he knows, giving creative rein to his fancy in changing his world of phenomenal appearances into a world of scientific constructs."

A knowledgeable person in librarianship, then, would be someone who has the facts as well as the experience of using these facts, taking them apart as a young boy might examine a clock. If the object of library science education would be to develop creative and knowledgeable librarians, then the stage must be set for this. Passive learners do not make creative librarians. Passing an examination or series of examinations is not the best criterion for judging professional promise, or certifying that someone is a knowledgeable person.

Instead of the usual array of admission tests, lectures, class work, term papers, reading lists, and oral reports, I ask you to imagine a library school which would operate as follows.

ADMISSION TO LIBRARY COURSE

The object of the *admission procedure* would be to determine if the student has the potential to develop in professional competence and take his full responsibility as a librarian. To ascertain this potential, he would be interviewed by ''library school representatives'' (professional librarians in the field near the student's home who know the library school's objectives). This new student would also be interviewed by faculty and students currently enrolled in the school. These interviews would be designed to determine the candidate's capacity for independent thinking, intelligence, and potential competence as a professional librarian.

INITIAL ORIENTATION

As for curriculum content and method of presentation, the transmission of basic facts, skills and techniques would be by means of an independent study programme. Faculty would be on call for special classes or meetings on certain topics but would not have regular classes as such covering these basic skills. Some faculty might run laboratories where exercises in basic skills could be performed or they might operate experimental libraries as part of their teaching/research load. This activity might require anywhere from one to three months of the student's time, depending on his rate of development and on a consensus of what we consider to be *the* basic skills or knowledge.

RESEARCH ON SPECIFIC LIBRARY PROBLEMS

After this initial orientation and basic learning period, the student would be placed in direct contact with various research problems associated with library developments. Either formal courses or directed field work would be arranged for this portion of his education. The faculty would approach this phase of library education as colleagues rather than as teachers of the students. The students would help choose the subject matter and possible projects which would have relevance for their own purposes and development. Real problems in libraries could form the basis for projects; sometimes the work would be brought to the school's laboratory and at other times, the *students* and *faculty* would study and work at the library in the field. Any problem deemed manageable could be pursued with the guidance of the faculty and the librarians in charge. In this way, the necessary theories and principles, methods and advanced knowledge could be introduced and assimilated. The students could play with the basic knowledge they acquired during the first phase of their library education. This type of educational experience would approximate the clinical and laboratory experience in many other graduate programmes such as the biosciences, social work, forestry, dentistry, etc. The faculty's research interests and the student's objectives in learning would be blended during this phase.

ASSESSMENT OF STUDENT WORK AND EVALUATION OF PROGRAMME

The evaluation of students and of such an innovative library science programme would take some careful rethinking of our present evaluation procedures. They say creativity of thought is facilitated when self-criticism and self-evaluation are basic. If the student has had a chance to select learning experiences considered relevant to him, then he will willingly choose direction, participate responsibly in the learning process and live with the consequences of his choices. The faculty must be prepared for him to evaluate his own exercises because this will be much more important than the evaluation of others. When the time eventually comes for the quality of his completed students and research and the other products of his learning to be certified, this evaluation could be done by the faculty and by representatives of librarianship as a whole.

IN DRTC

It is interesting that in the Documentation Research and Training Centre, the programme for education in documentation has already been implementing some of the ideas I have just mentioned. For instance, even though the Centre admits to the documentation course only either professionally qualified librarians or persons with a Master's Degree in a subject and at least two years' library experience, an initial two months orientation programme is gone through. This, I understand, helps the students who have come with varied educational background and library experiences to accustom themselves to the habit of systematic thinking, deriving the theory and practice of library service from the Laws of Library Science, express ideas clearly using the appropriate technical terminology of the subject.

Close contact between student and teacher is emphasised in maintaining a student-teacher ratio conforming to the prescriptions of a sound theory of education, and by making the course a residential one.

The student's interest and abilities are stimulated by minimising the number of lectures and using more of class discussions, tutorials, colloquia, seminars, and project work. The lectures are mainly for raising the curtain, as it were, to point to some areas of research in the field. That some of the students are able to turn out pieces of research in library science even while they are undergoing the course is an indication of the effectiveness of the methods used.

It is also noteworthy that evaluation of student work and of the effectiveness of the programme is based on project work—individual and cooperative—in each of the subjects rather than on answering a two-hour or three-hour question paper.

The Challenge

CHANGE OF PROGRAMME NEEDED

Will faculty in library schools be willing to admit that a series of courses, no matter what their content, is not sufficient preparation for the responsibilities the student should assume upon graduating? It is difficult to see a working alternative if we are to implement in the United States the proposed ALA statement of the objective of the master's programmes in librarianship. The ALA statement says, "the objective . . . should be to prepare librarians capable of participating and engineering the change and improvement required to move the profession constantly forward." Concentrating on the tasks and routines in today's libraries will not do this nor will a purely academic library education. We need to relate the library school student to the library profession's present problems and future needs.

TWO PHASES OF LIBRARY EDUCATION

If knowledge in librarianship is to be seriously pursued, we must find the capacity to have sport with what we know. No longer can we assume that knowledge in librarianship is merely the accumulation of brick-upon-brick of content and information—that is something to be taught in a basic set of courses or learned on the job. Instead, we should look at library education as a two phase operation; first we will have to master certain skills and facts, and secondly we will have to approach some of the problems of librarianship as researchers and scholars. Library schools should be where this happens, where fledgling librarians sprout their wings under the guidance of experienced professionals.

CHANGE OF ATTITUDE CALLED FOR

If this approach sounds interesting to you, there is a crucial question for students, library educators and librarians alike: can we abandon some of the assumptions we now have about library education? Students quite often assume that courses and experiences in library school will be like their other classes; faculty expect to teach course by course and assume it is difficult to innovate; librarians would find it difficult to fit both library school faculty and students into their work-a-day world. Everyone will need to be re-oriented if we are to develop a programme whose graduates will be tomorrow's decision-makers in libraries. We will all have to work to find ways for the students to demonstrate that they are able to make original, significant contributions to professional practice.

RELATE LIBRARY EDUCATION TO LIBRARY PROBLEMS

Such a school, as I envision, would include direct experimental confrontation with research problems and other practical, ethical and philo-sophical problems. The students would relate their educational experiences to the real problems being faced today and those likely to come up in the near future. Before such a school could open its doors, several librarians would have to agree to have their libraries designated as "library education experimental stations"; library educators would have to accept their role as researchers and field workers; and students would have to assume their role as colleagues working on more than studying library problems.

Library Education Experimental Project

A PERSONAL NOTE

This past year, we tried to put part of this plan to work for such a library school at the Syracuse University. We established something called the LEEP Laboratory. Before I can begin to describe it, I would like to tell you some personal history to put it all into some context.

More than ten years stretch between my library school days as a student and my being a member of the faculty at Syracuse University School of Library Science. During much of that time, I was engaged in documentation research (later called information storage and retrieval systems) in the field of scientific information. Libraries and librarians were not the stars of the drama I witnessed during those years, although I thought we had a lot to contribute as well as a lot to learn from the whole endeavour. When I returned to library education and tried to relate some of the excitement I felt about the developments in information systems, I met the same looks and attitudes that you do when you show your slides of Europe to a group that has never been there. Gradually, I realised that what I had witnessed could only come alive if the audience was given first-hand experiences; if, in other words, they were able to play with their knowledge and have sport with what they knew. The problem was: How to bring information storage and retrieval concepts into a traditional library school with no strong resources or faculty in special librarianship or computers.

PROVIDING REAL EXPERIENCE OF AUTOMATION

The United States Office of Education and the Library of Congress came to my rescue with financial and technical resources to help us transform some of the class discussion of library automation and information storage and retrieval systems. We created LEEP, the Library Education Experimental Project. It is a laboratory environment where the students and faculty have experience with a computer-based catalogue, developed from the MARC Pilot Project data from the Library of Congress. We have learned to use the MARC records in the computer as a library user now uses the cards in a card catalogue. Students and faculty began to evaluate the bibliographic control system within a library by contrasting it with this new tool. Some students are taking the initiative and are engaged in independent projects where they work with a librarian in the field to study and suggest improvements in existing systems. The impact of MARC in libraries has been brought home to every student regardless of his orientation to school, public, academic, or special libraries because every student in the school experiences some use of MARC when he takes courses in cataloguing, reference service or bibliography. All of these courses have assignments of one kind or another which bring the student to the LEEP Laboratory.

A COOPERATIVE EFFORT

LEEP had as consultants the two librarians in the Syracuse area most directly involved with advanced library automation projects—Ron Miller of the Five Associated University Libraries and Irwin Pizer of the Biomedical Communications Network. They advised us as we developed the LEEP Laboratory. Some of our students in turn contributed something to their research efforts. More than three hundred students at Syracuse during 1969–70 had at least a brush with the computer-based MARC catalogue. The students say they went away feeling less fearful about the "machine." Some of the faculty were glad that LEEP existed because they were able to demonstrate certain concepts and new developments instead of merely talking about them.

LEEP-BY-MAIL SERVICE

At an institute in the Adirondack Mountains in October 1969, faculty from twenty library schools came to see what we had done. At that time, we implemented a LEEP-by-Mail service. Now students in other library schools, where computing facilities and the MARC data base are not as accessible, can perform MARC searches in our LEEP laboratory and they too can put this knowledge to work, testing the potential of MARC, etc! As of this date, some fifty or more students in two library schools in New York and Philadelphia are using LEEP.

Faith in Collective Effort

I have great faith in the combined efforts of librarians, students and faculty in library schools today. Together we will find a way to insure that books are used and that this will be our first goal. The absolute essential for success will depend, of course, on our willingness to have sport with what we know. Librarianship is a practical world but it is on the edge of a new existence. If we look at ourselves in a playful way and use the knowledge we gain, we could make our education more relevant and our graduate librarians more professional. If we make an effort to establish a *quid pro quo* relationship between the field of library work and library education, we can insure the implementation of the First Law of Library Science.

Philip H Rhinelander said, "Education ought to be ultimately not a matter of systems, nor of organisations, or of structures, or of theories, but of individuals who *encounter* one another, who respect one another, who can speak to one another, despite disagreements, and who can *listen*" (18). Such an opportunity as this is my education, my encounter, and my chance to listen as well as speak.

LECTURE #2

LAW 2: EVERY READER HIS BOOK: HOW TO KNOW THE READER IN SEARCH OF HIS BOOK

> There are some things which cannot be learned quickly, and time, which is all we have, must be paid heavily for their acquiring.
> —Ernest Hemingway

Need for "Use Studies"

Most libraries appear committed to the doctrine of service to patrons, to facilitating the reader's search for his book. Oftentimes, however, doubts have arisen in our minds as to whether or not we are providing those facilities which, in fact, best meet the needs of patrons. Out of these doubts have come numerous "use studies" in the United States and elsewhere which contribute to our knowledge of the reader (or user) and sometimes provide us with the information needed to redesign our libraries to give better performance.

Catalogue Use Studies

The 1960's have seen a great many surveys of use studies, accompanied with justifiable criticism of the research methodologies used and the unreliability of the findings. Two studies in the United States have recently been reported, which rise above these criticisms and serve as fine examples of how to investigate the following questions:

1. Who uses the library?
2. For what purpose is the card catalogue consulted?
3. With what success is the catalogue consulted?
4. How was the catalogue card utilised? Which items on the card were used? Do different classes of users make different use of the items on the catalogue card?
5. Would a hypothetical reduced catalogue meet the needs of most users of the card catalogue (that is, would a catalogue, consisting of author, title, subject headings, call number, and date of publication, suffice)?

Because this area of library research is so important, I would like to concentrate on these two studies of the user at the card catalogue, explaining the methodology used in some detail, the most interesting findings, and the implications of their work for improvement of library services in general. Consider this information exchange with me serving as the catalyst, since neither Richard Palmer (10) nor Ben-Ami Lipetz (6) can be here to discuss their work first hand. I will leave behind, in India, however, their reports, with the compliments of the authors. They gave me permission to discuss their work in detail with you. For this, I am grateful.

POPULATION STUDIED

The Palmer study consisted of the users of the University of Michigan General Library card catalogue. The sample, obtained by means of a two-stage probability sampling model, consisted of 5,067 users of the card catalogue who completed questionnaires during an eight-week survey during the Fall Term of 1967.

The Lipetz study was conducted in the Sterling Memorial Library of Yale University. The pattern of traffic flow in the catalogue area was determined by means of frequent traffic counts that were continued for more than a year. The observed traffic flow was used as the basis for designing the interview schedule that would encompass a thoroughly representative sample of catalogue users.

The Lipetz study at Yale went beyond catalogue use and traced the users' starting clues at the catalogue through to use of books and the front matter from these books and their representation on catalogue cards.

Palmer reviewed over eighteen card catalogue use studies and found all but five lacking in their definition of population studied. This is a basic concern in research design and the connection between knowledge of our population and our stated goals of service is very straightforward. One cannot create an ideal tool of any sort on a rational basis (whether that tool be a conventional catalogue, a computerised catalogue, or any other device for any other application) without knowing a good deal about the purpose or purposes for which the tool is to be used, and about the manner in which the users interact with the tool (11).

The careful way in which Palmer and Lipetz established the population for their user surveys deserves repeating.

Methodology

POPULATION STUDIED: UNIVERSITY OF MICHIGAN LIBRARY

Palmer chose the actual users of the University of Michigan General Library card catalogue as the survey population. In the process of establishing the population for the user survey at Michigan, he rejected as the survey population such possible populations as all individuals officially connected with the University of Michigan or all users of the University of Michigan General Library because it was not possible to establish from available data that the characteristic of these potential populations matched the population of the users of the card catalogue.

In order, however, to provide some background on the general environment in which the survey was conducted, it is noted that the study was conducted at the University of Michigan General Library card catalogue room during the Fall Term, 1967, at which time the student enrollment at the University of Michigan totalled 37,283. Of those enrolled, 21,087 were undergraduates, 9,729 were graduates, and 3,698 were graduate-professionals. Included in the 37,283 students were 2,769 who were enrolled in credit extension (mostly graduate). The faculty numbered more than 3,800; other academic staff, about 2,500; and non-academic staff, including part-time employees, totalled about 13,700. As indicated above, these categories of potential patrons were not selected as the survey population because the configuration of their use of the card catalogue could not be predicted from available data and because users other than those officially connected with the University of Michigan would be likely to use the card catalogue during the eight-week survey period.

During the survey period (September 11 to November 5, 1967), 186,768 persons passed through the turnstiles at the entrances to the University of Michigan General Library. Thus, an average of 23,346 persons per week patronised the General Library during the eight weeks of the survey. These patrons were not, however, selected as the survey population because the configuration of their use of the card catalogue could not be predicted from available data.

It was therefore the decision of this study that actual users of the University of Michigan General Library card catalogue during the survey period would comprise the survey population. It was further decided that no attempt would be made to ascertain the exact number of such users. Rather, a team of students conducted a physical head count of patrons using the card catalogue during one week, February 20–26, 1967, during the 101 hours that the library was open. The count came to a total of 5,778 persons. On the basis of this count, it was estimated that approximately 48,000 persons would use the card catalogue during the survey period. This estimated number of persons constituted the survey population. The survey was then designed to sample not less than ten per cent of this estimated population, or not less than 4,800 patrons. It was determined that a ten per cent sample, clustered and systematically randomized, should provide findings of statistical reliability at the .05 level of significance, for which a reasonable confidence interval could be computed, and from which useful predictions regarding the total user population could be made.

POPULATION STUDIED: YALE UNIVERSITY

Lipetz chose a similar survey population (7), namely, the actual users of the card catalogue at the Yale University Library, but his technique for sampling this population involved a careful observation over a total of 62 weeks of the traffic flow at the card catalogue.

Traffic Flow Management

Lipetz thought that the determination of the pattern of people entering the catalogue area was a key factor in the later design of an interviewing schedule which would yield a clearly representative sample of catalogue users. The pattern of entry to the catalogue was determined by having observers assigned to count the number of people entering the catalogue area through different entryways during different times of day and days of the week. Observers were stationed where they could observe simultaneously either the front three aisles into the catalogue or the rear two aisles into the catalogue. For a period of five minutes' duration, they would count the number of persons entering each of the aisles being observed. Timing periods were rigidly predetermined to cover different hours of the day, different days of the week, and even different tenths of each hour. Observation assignments were rigidly scheduled; the schedule repeated every seven weeks. Observations were continued over a total of 62 weeks so as to provide a ten-week overlap period for determination of any annual variation in traffic which might occur. (During this 62-week period, there was a 5-week interruption in observations, during the late summer, while shifting of catalogue drawers was going on; the abnormal shifting activity tended to interfere with traffic flow).

The total amount of time during which traffic was counted was somewhat over 4 per cent of the time that the library was open during the total time span involved. For practical reasons, the coverage was more intense during weekday working hours (6 per cent) and lower during evening hours and weekends (about 2.5 per cent). However, observed traffic was also lower (by about one-fourth) during evening hours and weekends. Tallies of traffic counts by hour, day and entryway for the first ten weeks of observation were used as the basis for designing the interviewing schedule. Traffic counts were continued during the interviewing period to check on the continuing validity of the pattern observed during those first ten weeks and to provide a rational basis for weighting of interview results if the interview schedule should prove to be biased with respect to observed traffic.

Several other traffic measurements were made in addition to the counts of persons entering the catalogue area: At precise preassigned times, observers would follow anyone entering the catalogue to observe where he went (which catalogue drawer), how long he stayed at the catalogue, and how many call-number notations he wrote down. Intervals for conducting these observations were scheduled in exactly the same pattern as intervals for gross traffic counts so as to cover all times of catalogue availability.

Observers of catalogue traffic were instructed to avoid counting those library staff members who regularly work in the catalogue area (filers, verifiers, reference librarians). The intent of the measurements was to count, as far as possible, only the "consumers" of the catalogue service, rather than the suppliers and interpreters.

Methods for the collection of data differed in the two studies, but both appear to have been rigorous applications of the statistically reliable methods they chose to employ. They are explained here to illustrate how two different methods can be employed for achieving the same objective. The survey periods were at first approximately the same—eight weeks at Michigan and ten weeks at Yale, but Yale continued their interviewing over a full year. The questions asked and techniques used varied as the following excerpts from the two reports show.

SAMPLING: MICHIGAN UNIVERSITY LIBRARY

At Michigan, the population was defined as the users of the card catalogue during the survey period, September 11 to November 5, 1967 (12). The sample size was established as ten per cent of the population. A one-page questionnaire, including an illustrative catalogue card, with items on the card identified by means of red exponential numbers and a list of items on the catalogue card numbered in red placed immediately below the illustrative card, was selected as the survey instrument. Questionnaires were distributed to selected patrons as they entered the catalogue room and were collected as they left.

A two stage probability sample using systematic selection was chosen for the survey. (See ["Population Studied: University of Michigan Library"]). The estimated figure of 48,000 patrons was based, as mentioned earlier, on a physical head count of users conducted during the week ending 26 February 1967. In this two-stage probability sample, the frame of the sample was taken to be all users of the General Library card catalogue during the eight-week period, September 11 to November 5, 1967. The hours of the week in which the library was open were the first-stage sample units, and the users in each of the selected hours were the second-stage sample units. The outline of the sample design is as follows:

1. Measures of size were assigned to hours (clusters) according to the probable number of users in each of them. As it was expected that there would be some random fluctuation in the number of users, the measures of size were corrected to the nearest unit of twenty to simplify the operation.
2. Under-sized clusters (hours when few users were expected) were linked or combined to insure that each selected cluster would yield a reasonable number of users.
3. The method of selection used was probability proportional to size in the first-stage and probability inversely proportional to size in the second stage in order to give an overall equal probability of selection to each user.
4. Systematic selection was employed in both the first-stage and second-stage selections.

Questionnaire

A survey team composed of eleven students enrolled in the Department of Library Science conducted the survey. During systematically selected hours, questionnaires were handed to a random sample of about twenty patrons as they entered the catalogue room, were completed by the patrons while in the catalogue room, and were collected by the survey team as the patrons left. The survey team was available throughout the 240 survey hours to answer any questions that the patrons surveyed might have about the questionnaire.

The survey team found that such outside factors as weather, football games, or major campus events, occasionally caused the actual number of patrons who utilised the catalogue room during a survey hour to drop below the estimated number of patrons who would use the card catalogue as listed in the sampling procedure. To obtain the desired twenty completed questionnaires per hour on these few occasions, the survey team reduced the interval between sampling units, or patrons, by one. Questionnaires were given to each (a-1)th patron, so that, for example, in an hour when every fifth patron was to have been given a questionnaire, one was given to every fourth patron. Since this procedure modified the basic sampling pattern, it increased the chance for selection of the patrons using the catalogue during these hours. As these changes were made rarely, they are unlikely to have any noticeable effect on the findings of the survey.

Of the 5,073 patrons who were given questionnaires, 4,456 completed them, giving a completion rate of 88 per cent. The rejection level was, therefore, 12 per cent. The total of usable survey units was 5,067.

The questionnaire used at Michigan sought information on a variety of aspects of catalogue use. (See ["Items of Information Collected"]). A question was also asked as to whether or not a hypothetical computer catalogue consisting of five items per entry, namely, name of author, title, subject headings, call number (including location), and date of publication, would meet their needs, and if not, what additional catalogue card items of information would be required.

Patrons were instructed to answer questions in accordance with their specific use of the catalogue on this particular occasion. Answers were not to reflect previous recollected use of the catalogue.

Since the clustering of hours and thus of samples taken in this survey introduced a higher level of probability that the sample population may not represent the total population as nearly as a simple random sample would, the design effect and related statistical measures were computed.

INTERVIEW SCHEDULE

The schedule for conducting interviews with the Yale catalogue users was based on observed traffic flow into the catalogue during an initial *10-week observation period*. Projection of observed traffic for this period suggested that the annual traffic into the catalogue would be of the order of

300,000. (Full-year traffic observations later showed this estimate to be low.) When one adjusted this count to omit individuals who were found to be entering the catalogue area merely to use it as a shortcut between the front entrance and the main reading room, the indicated annual total of real catalogue users was closer to 250,000. It was decided that about 2,500 interviews or more (that is, at least something approaching one per cent) should be attempted.

The interview schedule adopted at Yale (8) called for an interviewer to be at a particular entryway to the catalogue area at a specified time on a specified day of the week. The first individual other than library staff to enter the catalogue through that entryway during the next six minutes and to begin to use the catalogue would be the person to be interviewed. (If no one entered during that interval, no one was interviewed until the next assigned time and place.) Interview assignments were set up on a revolving schedule much like the schedule for traffic measurements. As with traffic measurements, the schedule for interviewing during the evening and weekend periods was made lighter than during the regular weekday periods; this was done with the knowledge that compensations could be made later by weighting the results of actual evening and weekend interviews somewhat more heavily than the results of weekday interviews in compiling final statistics.

Interview content and technique were designed to elicit quite specific information from catalogue users, with a minimum amount of bias due to prompting or leading by the interviewer. The method adopted made use of an interview guide in the form of a multiple-part questionnaire which interviewers were required to follow uniformly. Interviews would begin with very vague, nondirective questions (''Please tell me precisely what you were about to do at the catalogue the moment I interrupted you.''), in order to give the user full opportunity to state whatever he happened to regard as important or significant.

The underlying pattern of the interview identifying rather quickly the basic type of search which the user was about to make in the catalogue (for example, a search for the purpose of borrowing a specific known document; a search for finding documents on a specific subject; a search for the identity of documents from a specific source, as by a particular author or by a particular organisation; a search for descriptive bibliographic information regarding a known document without any intent of borrowing the actual document). Identification of this basic type of search would then determine which of several possible lines of questioning to follow in the remainder of the interview.

When it appeared that no more useful information could be gathered regarding the immediate search being conducted by the user, the interview would be terminated with a series of questions on the user and his personal background (but not his name). Background questions related to the user's status at Yale, his field of specialisation, the length of his residence in the Yale community, and the general level of his use of the Sterling Memorial Library and other libraries at Yale.

ITEMS OF INFORMATION COLLECTED

Questions asked during the main portion of the interview were intended to bring out everything of possible document-finding value that the user knew about the material he desired at the time of starting his search. This would include, as appropriate, the type of document (whether an ordinary book, or periodical, report, etc), descriptive data (author, title, date, publisher, etc), physical characteristics of a document (size, colour), contents (index, illustrations, bibliography), terms in the name of subject, translation specification, edition specification, and so forth. The questions also established whether or not the user was already familiar with the material he wanted, how he had first learned of the existence of the material, the connection in which he wanted to make use of the material, and the particular clue which he intended to use to begin his search of the catalogue. Particular pains were taken to record descriptive data elements exactly as they were known to the user, taking nothing for granted: If the data came only from his memory, he was asked to spell out the name of the author and the longer title words; if the data came from class notes or duplicated lists which he had brought to the library, these were photocopied by the interviewer.

Both the Michigan and the Yale studies uncovered a great deal of information about the user of a card catalogue in search of his book. From the selected catalogue users, the following information was obtained:

1. The user's status: undergraduate, graduate, special student, library science student, faculty, teaching fellow, university staff (except Library), university library staff, or other.
2. The user's school, department, or field of interest.
3. Whether the language of the work or information which the user was seeking was in English or a foreign language.
4. The subject on which the user desired a work or information.
5. The purpose for which the user came to the catalogue: class assignment, personal use, teaching, research, or other purpose.
6. The approximate date of publication of the desired work or information.
7. The object of this specific catalogue use: a specific work, information on a subject, bibliographic information, or other.
8. Which items on the catalogue card were used.

FOLLOW-UP

At Yale, at the conclusion of the interview, the user was left alone to complete his catalogue search. However, he was observed discreetly from a distance. The amount of time spent at the catalogue and the number of catalogue drawers searched were noted on the interview record. As the user was leaving the catalogue area, he was stopped again and asked whether his search had been successful. If the answer was affirmative, he was asked to let the interviewer copy any call numbers that he had found in the catalogue that satisfied his search needs. Users who were not certain whether their searches had been successful, but who were going elsewhere in the library to find out (usually these were people who had identified a potentially useful stack area by finding some representative class numbers in the catalogue and who intended to browse the stack for known and/or unknown documents) were given a self-mailing follow-up form on which they could conveniently note any call numbers that were subsequently found to satisfy their needs.

Objectivity in Study

Several months were spent at Yale in developing and testing the interview outline and technique before starting the full year's run of data collection for the project. Only very minor changes were made as the year progressed. Five individuals performed practically all of the interviews. A comparison of the results of interviews conducted by different interviewers was made about four months after the start of the interviewing year; no serious biasing of results could be associated with the interviewers compared. Therefore the interviewing technique was judged to be quite objective, as had been hoped.

The interviewing schedule that was adopted at Yale provided for a maximum of some 2,700 interviews during the full year studied. Because of various random factors (for example, no user at the catalogue at the scheduled time and place, unexpected library closings, or illness of the interviewer), the number of interviews actually completed in the year was 2,134.

Findings

The numerous tables and charts in the two studies document the findings from their work. I have a series of slides which highlight these findings which it would be appropriate to show at this time.

TRAFFIC PATTERN

The traffic studies in the Lipetz study are unique and deserve special attention. Both the figures for catalogue use *and* borrowing are remarkably similar. They both show only two significant seasons: the regular academic year and the summer vacation period. The activity pattern of the regular academic year is punctuated by irregular declines that are associated with holidays and recesses, but the mean and median for the academic year appear to be very close. Even so, Dr Lipetz felt that the complexity of the traffic pattern strongly justified the original decision to conduct interviews throughout an entire year, with representative coverage of different days of the week, hours of the day, periods within the hour, and portals of entry to the catalogue area.

A clear pattern of the catalogue traffic variation with day of the week was observed, however. It can be seen that the rate of use of the catalogue is heaviest during the early part of the week, especially on Tuesdays, and that it is lowest on Saturdays and Sundays, as one would expect.

USER STATUS

Both studies found that more use is made of the library card catalogue by graduate students than by other classes of users.

Faculty rank below undergraduates and graduate students in terms of absolute use of the catalogue.

OBJECTIVES OF USE OF CATALOGUE

Most of the users seek a known item at the card catalogue. The Yale study differentiated between four basic types of objectives in using the catalogue:

1. In a *document search* (often called a "known item" search), the catalogue user is aware of the existence of some particular book or other publication that he wants to locate;
2. In a *subject search*, the catalogue user is interested in both identifying and locating one or more documents pertaining to some known topic;
3. In an *author search*, the catalogue user is aware of the name of some author, publisher's series, or other source of literature and is interested in identifying and possibly selecting specific documents from that source; and
4. In a *bibliographic search*, the catalogue user is interested in using the catalogue itself to supply or verify bibliographic information regarding a known document; he is not interested in locating and using the document.

The distribution of searches among these four basic types is given in Table 1. The distribution was determined in two different ways, yielding two different results. The first column is based on the *immediate* objective of the catalogue user at the moment of his approach to the catalogue. Most of the questions asked during an interview pertained to this immediate objective. The distribution of *underlying* objectives is given in the second column of Table 1.

TABLE 1. Distribution of Search Ojbectives

Search Type	Immediate, %	Underlying, %
Document	73	56
Subject	16	33
Author	6	6
Bibliographic	5	5
	100	100

About a third of the catalogue users are basically interested in subject or topical information, but half of these users attempt to use a document search to make do for a subject search. In terms of underlying interest, document searches account for only 56 per cent (not 73 per cent) of catalogue use.

It is interesting to note that no significant variations in the distribution of search objectives with respect to season of the year, academic status of user, departmental affiliation, or newness to the Yale library were detected in this study.

OTHER FINDINGS AT MICHIGAN

The group at Michigan analysed their data a little differently and came up with the following findings: The card catalogue is used primarily for academic purposes.

1. The catalogue is used most heavily for preparing class assignments.
2. Few patrons use the catalogue as a source of bibliographical data.
3. Few users seek foreign language materials; the proportion of users seeking them increases as the educational level increases.

FAILURE OF SEARCH

Both studies found that most users are successful in using the card catalogue. Only approximately 15 per cent of the searches turned up nothing at all or could be counted as unsuccessful. Yale analysed the 256 unsuccessful searches to learn more about the reasons for failure. Some 31 per cent apparently failed because of faulty search techniques or because of failure to persevere. The desired document was catalogued under entries known to the user at the time of the interview, but unfortunately he missed the clue! A table from the report shows this analysis of follow-up document searches.

USE OF THE ITEMS OF INFORMATION IN AN ENTRY

The use of different items of information on the catalogue card was carefully analysed in both studies. The Michigan study by Palmer meticulously analysed the use of over twenty items and found that many items appearing on the catalogue card are seldom used. A hypothetical reduced computer catalogue would appear to meet the needs of most users of the card catalogue. Few users, they found at Michigan, would require more than a five-item catalogue, and the number of additional catalogue items desired increases slightly as the educational level of the patron increases.

MAIN ENTRY: LEADING SECTION

The Yale study found something very interesting for anyone who has considered challenging the right of main entry to be all important in library cataloguing. Their results would seem to show that neither the name of author nor the title of document has an overwhelming advantage as candidate for the leading section of the main entry and for preferred search approach. There seems to be an advantage to the title approach, but only a slight one. One can question why there is such a strong tendency for library users to approach the catalogue by name of author if the title approach is just about as good if not better.

Computer-Based Catalogue

The analysis of failures in searching the catalogue could not be compensated or in computerised catalogue, unless a near-human facility compensating for inadequacies in search clues were built in. The computer will fail to select unless it is given some definite programme that will cause it to ignore particular kinds of mismatches. Until such methods are available, Dr Lipetz concluded that it seems highly unlikely that computer methods of document finding will seriously rival document finding capacity of human beings. He recommended further intensive research work on the user of our catalogues and the relative-offs in usefulness and cost of including additional data elements in a computerized record. If, as Dr Palmer at Michigan found, a five-item catalogue record suffices, then we need to study the interface between the user and such a new catalogue before we proceed much further toward library automation.

Improving Catalogue Use

Having learned so much about the reader in search of his book, one of the most important conclusions seems to be that user-education or self-education methods need to be improved before our libraries can give efficient service. Increasing the complexity and accessibility of the catalogue offers comparatively little potential for improvement of the success rate of searches currently attempted. Improving the convenience of the catalogue use might attract heavier use of the catalogue and the library collection. Providing access through a greater variety of title-liek entries is a promising approach to helping document search. Filing by date within subject headings is a promising approach to helping search by name of subject. Data elements other than name of author, title, and subject are of most value in resolving many searches in which the entry clues are ambiguous or inaccurate.

With this much new information about the user, it is well to turn our attention to the next law of library science, and consider our techniques for every book finding its reader.

LECTURE #3

LAW 3: EVERY BOOK ITS READER—HOW EVERY BOOK CAN BE FOUND BY ITS READER

Catalogue and Readers' Requirements

STRUCTURE OF CATALOGUE

Cataloguers have a view of library service which in many ways is most distorted and at the same time most central. Without their efforts at bibliographic control where would library service be? Without some form of listing the items in a library, how could anyone ever find anything? Nevertheless, some people are now asking—even with the help of the cataloguer's effort, why do we not seem to find what is available? Has the time come for us to carefully analyse what happens when a cataloguer performs the present ritual of describing books for readers? Many of us have embarked upon such a study only recently because the availability of MARC (Machine Readable Cataloguing) has given us access to current catalogue information in a form easy to manipulate for study. The accessibility of all the information on a catalogue card as access points instead of only three or four elements (main entry, title, subject, call number) makes it possible to match the individual user's words used in a subject search with any portion of the catalogue record allows us to study our present cataloguing rules for main and added entry and test their potency compared to other elements.

Some of us (including students in library schools, such as Syracuse) are asking:

1. Is the main entry form we establish for corporate bodies really useful to the reader in search of a particular book?
2. Is our rule for main and added entries for works by more than three authors valid if we are trying to describe a book accurately?
3. Are there other items of information on the catalogue card that are more descriptive of the book's content than the main and added entries we have established for it? If yes, shouldn't these be more accessible for the user in search of material on a given subject?
4. Is our strict control over the names of subjects we use in cataloguing essential if we maintain an integrated bibliographic retrieval system, with catalogues, name and subject authority files, and biographical reference sources available at one and the same time in the computer?

VIEW AS A WHOLE

I am not sure that we can completely uproot all of our present practices and rules for descriptive and subject cataloguing. Nor am I sure that we can indict today's cataloguers as persons with a myopic view, that is, do they see service to users for the mountain of books still needing cataloguing. It is safe to say that their work does necessitate their view of each and every book as an entity to be handled separately. Only rarely do they get a chance to view the whole scene of which their individual effort is but a small part. Many of them view their work as assembly, or piece work. Most libraries are not equipped with aids or devices which would facilitate the work of cataloguers so that they could see the true impact on the library catalogue as they catalogue individual works. How many cataloguers know how close their description of a book comes to matching the user's clue words when he is in search of that book? The two studies I discussed in the previous lecture provide some useful information about book descriptions in card catalogues and their use by university scholars. This brings us a little closer to an awareness of this important relationship—the book and the reader—but we still have a long way to go.

Investigation

In this lecture I am quite proud to report on some work a few students at Syracuse have done to enlarge our understanding of this subject. With the

availability of MARC tapes from the Library of Congress and some computerized retrieval programs from IBM, we were able to study cataloguing
records very carefully, and compare the retrieval of books from a catalogue
having traditional access points with retrieval from a catalogue with unlimited access points.

MARC FORMAT

Before I begin to discuss our findings, perhaps an explanation of the
MARC format is necessary. It is not important for this discussion to be very
detailed in this explanation, nor for that matter, entirely up-to-date. For
example, we began our work using MARC I records. This was during the
MARC Pilot Project at the Library of Congress. Since March 1969, the
Library of Congress has been distributing MARC II records. The MARC II
format is much more elaborate in identifying and tagging fields and elements of information. Our work with MARC I records could also be done
with MARC II records, if we chose. For the purposes of our study,
however, which format we used was not as important as the information
content. It was the content of a Library of Congress catalogue card, created
by cataloguers following the rules for main entry, descriptive cataloguing,
subject cataloguing and classification that we were scrutinizing. What they
created was now accessible in ways they never imagined, and we were
curious to find out how useful their descriptions of books were for machine
searching.

The figure of a MARC I record explained and set beside the printed
catalogue card for Mao Tse-tung's book entitled *Basic tactics*, shows how

---

MARC Pilot Project
Bibliographic Listing   0) LC Card No. 66–018912

Filed Field Information :   *Supplement   Conference   Juvenile*
  1) *Type of Entry* 2) *Form of Work* 3) *Biblio* 4) *Illus* 5) *Maps* 6) Number 7) Conference 8) Work
    Personal Author Monograph Yes None None None No No
  9) *Language Data:* 10) *Publication Data:*
    Class *Lang 1* *Lang 2* *Key Date 1 Date 2* *Place Name Height*
    Translation Eng Unk Single 1966 NYNY PGR 21CM

Name of Variable Field	*Tag*		
Main Entry	10	Mao, Tse-Tung, 1893-1	Mao, Tse-tung, 1893—
Title Statement	20	Basic Tactics. Translated and with an Introd. By Stuart R Schram. Foreword by Samuel B Griffith II	Basic tactics. Translated and with an introd by Stuart R Schram. Foreword by Samuel B Griffith, II. New York, Praeger [1966]-
Imprint Statement	30	New York, PRAEGER 1966	viii, 149p. 21 cm.
Collation Statement	40	VIII, 149 P. 21 CM	Bibliographical footnotes.
Notes	60	Bibliographical Footnotes.	
Subject Tracing	70	Guerrilla Warfare.	1 Guerrilla warfare I. Schram, Stuart
Pers Author Tracing	71	Schram, Stuart R, Ed and Tr	R. and tr. II. Title
Title Tracing	74	T	U240.M28 355.425 66-18912
L C Call Number	90	U240.M28 1966	Library of Congress
Dewey Class Number	91	355.425	

every field of information on the catalogue card is not only analysed but explicitly tagged.

In the actual machine readable record on magnetic tape or punched cards, the field tag 10 would appear directly before the main entry line, field tag 20 would appear before the title statement, tag 70 would appear before the subject entry, tag 90 before the Library of Congress call number, and tag 92 before the Dewey class number. Additional information about the work in hand is described in coded fashion, in what are called fixed-length fields. For example, in character position 21 on the MARC I record, a code would appear which indicated the type of main entry. For example, Mao Tse-tung is a personal main entry. Therefore, the code P would appear in character position 21. If the book's main entry were a government body, a code letter G would appear in character position 21, S for Society, R for Religious body, T for Title main entry, and so on. If the notes section of the catalogue card made reference to a bibliography, there would be an X in character position 23. On this figure all of these fixed field codes have been translated for ease of use of the reader. For example, the listing reads "yes" under *Biblio* in the Fixed Field portion. This is a translation of the coded information on the MARC record, indicating that there is an "X" in character position 23.

Reformatted MARC Record

When we reformatted the MARC records for use with the IBM Document Processing System, we knew that *every* group of characters on the MARC record bounded on either side by spaces would be considered a keyword, accessible for searching. That meant that the Dewey Class Number was a Keyword, by definition. So was every word in the title statement including *and, with, by* (unless we instructed the computer to ignore them as common words). This also meant that every word in a subject heading was now a keyword, not only the first word as is true in our catalogues. As if through a glass darkly, I saw the first glimmerings of something like a classified catalogue approach available to American Library users! Is this too big a concept to grasp over so many miles? The workings of the computer program for accessing the information on the MARC records is fairly complicated, but the use of the MARCS/DPS system as it was called was not—luckily. All that the user needed to do was to structure his searches in English-like sentences, combining keywords with logical operators (such as *and, or*), availing himself of some useful modifiers or delimiters. He could for example specify that two keywords had to be side-by-side in a MARC record or he should not want to see the record. He could specify which field (or sentence) to search for his particular keyword. This was very useful when searching the file by using Dewey class numbers as keywords. A three-digit Dewey number looks like any other three-digit number to the computer, and we knew that the collation contained the number of pages in a book, and numbers appeared elsewhere. By phrasing his search in the following way, he could exclude any three-digit numbers other than those in the Dewey Class number field:

> L1   355 ($);
> L2   L1 AND T92(SEN);

We knew that the field tag numbers would be confounded with other two-digit numbers when the MARC record was processed by the Document Processing System, so we instructed the computer programmer to insert the letter T before every field tag number. This gave us a group of unique keywords representing the MARC field tags.

Library Education Experimental Project

FACILITY

With such a laboratory facility at our disposal, we proceeded to study catalogue records and test the finding of books by new search strategies. We called this laboratory LEEP (Library Education Experimental Project). During its first year-and-a-half, it was supported by the US Office of Education. Now it is maintained by Syracuse University as an integral part of the educational facilities available to students and faculty in the School of Library Science.

SAMPLE CATALOGUE

For the studies reported here in detail we used a sample catalogue of approximately 10,000 books in the social sciences, representing titles published primarily in 1967–68. It was a stratified sample of the larger MARC Pilot Project file of approximately 48,000 titles. We were able to create such a sample by computer manipulation of the file because we had analysed the content of the entire file during the earlier stages of LEEP.

MAJOR OBJECTIVE

Most of the projects the library school students developed centered around the third question I asked at the outset of this lecture: Are there other fields of information on the catalogue card that are more descriptive of the book's content than the main and added entries we have established for it?

If the answer was found to be yes, we intended to tell the world of librarianship so they could begin to consider making such data more accessible. This new information, we felt, would help justify library automation and MARC records not on the basis of efficiency of library operations but on the basis of the third law of library science, namely *every book its reader*.

SEARCHES

Many students, more than two hundred in fact, performed searches using MARCS/DPS. They performed these searches while they were students in reference and bibliography classes, cataloguing and technical services classes, or in advanced courses in information systems. Several students went beyond one or two searches, and two of them organised their work into a small research study and wrote down their findings in a fashion suitable for publication. One report is in the process of being published by *Library resources and technical services* and the second is almost ready for submission to the *Journal of the American Society for Information Science*. My report of their work will be the first public report. I have their permission to report their work to you and I am indeed proud to do so.

Study 1

OBJECTIVE

One student, Mrs Judith Hudson, was interested in finding all the relevant information in the MARCS/DPS file for *area studies* bibliographies. This is not a simple matter in a traditional card catalogue and she was not sure which would be the most efficient way to find documents in a machine-based catalogue, such a MARCS/DPS. She set out to:

1. Discover the optimum search strategy to find at least 95% of the relevant documents in our computer-based catalogue on an area of the world;
2. Discover what other methods to use if one search strategy is not optimum; and
3. Determine why non-relevant document references would be found.

If possible, she hoped that her study would allow her to recommend search strategies which would minimize "false drops" and maximize "hits."

DEFINITION

The first step in constructing the searches was to begin defining terms and geographic areas. Area studies or area research are considered to be "the interdisciplinary study of a given geographic region, country or group of countries (considered as a unit), which takes account of the socially significant data about the area, including the history of the people, their economic and political development and their use of natural resources" (24). "Area studies . . . may treat the topography, ethnography, natural resources, religion, sociology, economy, law, government, history, culture (or any combination of these) for an area, large or small" (23).

The area to be studied was the Middle East. Later on in the study, it was decided to examine another area as a check on the results of the Middle East Study. Latin America was chosen.

It was decided that "the Arab countries, inclusive of North Africa, together with Israel, Turkey, Iran and Afghanistan—often called collectively the Near East or Middle East . . . constitute a regional unit" (4). Latin America was defined as "that part of the Western hemisphere that lies south of the border of the United States and of the Florida Strait. It includes Middle America (Mexico, Central America and the West Indies) and South America" (3).

SEARCH STRATEGY

In order to find all the relevant MARC records from the file, four different types of searches were written:

1. Searches for keywords—English language words and phrases—for example, Middle East, Palestine, etc.
2. Searches for *Library of Congress* (LC) *Classification* numbers on the area—for example, DS36, F1869, etc.
3. Searches for *Dewey Classification* numbers on the area—for example, 956, 972, etc.
4. *"If-scan" searches*—The "If-scan" function enables the user to scan a specified field of the record portion of the MARC/DPS record for a given character or character string. In this case, we specified that the computer scan the field called DDCNO, which is the Dewey Classification number, for an area code. Such a search for the area code 56 (Middle East) would yield such Dewey numbers as 560.956, 321.00956, etc.

PREPARATION FOR SEARCH

Search by Keyword

The first step in preparing the keyword searches was to compile a list of words and phrases which would yield records relevant to an area study. We examined the Dewey and LC Classification Schedules for the two areas and listed all of the relevant words and phrases we could find. To this list were added such words as geographical names, names of religions, and famous people representative of the area, etc. Each word and phrase was checked in our index list of keywords in MARCS/DPS to see if the word appeared in the file of 8,000 MARC records. If a word was not listed in this index, it was discarded.

The words which remained formed the *keyword searches*. They were combined according to DPS vocabulary and syntax rules in such a way as to find every MARC record which contained any one or more of the specified words or phrases regardless of where it might appear in the text portion.

Search by Class Number

The LC and Dewey Classification searches were prepared by examining the LC and Dewey schedules to determine the appropriate class number on the area. These class numbers were checked in the 'index list.' If they appeared in this index, the DPS search was written to find every MARC record which contained the specified LC or Dewey Classification numbers.

"If-scan" Search

The "If-scan" search was prepared for the applicable area notations from the Dewey Classification Area Table (2). All MARC records having a Dewey class number built with these area notations were to be retrieved.

EXAMPLES

Searches were run on MARCS/DPS. The Middle East searches were as follows:

Keyword Searches

Search Number 206

```
L1    DEAD & SEA(+1);
L2    MOUNT & CARMEL(+1);
L3    TEL & AVIV(+1);
L4    IBN & SAUD(+1);
L5    BENI & KURT(+1);
L6    PALESTINE, ISRAEL, JORDAN, ARAB($);
L7    ANTIOCH, PALMYRA, SMYRNA, SUMERIANS, TYRE, UR;
L8    JEW($), JERUSALEM, BETHLEHEM, EMMAUS, MEGIDDO,
      NAZARETH;
L9    NEGEV, NEGEB, CAPPADOCIA, HEROD, HUSSEIN, JUDEA,
      AFGHANISTAN;
L10   L6 & T10 (NOT SEN);
```

L11   PERGAMON & T30 (NOT SEN);
L12   MEDINA, DARIUS, BAHRAMPOUR, ISMAIL, MAHMUD;
L13   L1, L2, L3, L4, L5, L6, L7, L8, L9, L10, L11, L12;
LIST OFFLINE, TEXT, SUBJECTS

Search Number 207
L1   MIDDLE & EAST (+1);
L2   NEAR & EAST (+1);
L3   UNITED & ARAB(+1) & REPUBLIC (+1);
L4   TURKEY, TURKS, CYPRUS, SYRIA, LEBANON;
L5   IRAQ, IRAN, PERSIAN, MESOPOTAMIA, EGYPT($);
L6   ASIA & MINOR (+1);
L7   MOROCCO, ALGERIA ($), TUNIS ($), LIBYA, SUDAN;
L8   ARMENIA, ISLAM ($), BEDOUIN;
L9   EUPHRATES, ANATOLLA, ANKARA, ARARAT, ADEN, MOS-
       QUE, MUSLIM ($);
L10   BABYLON ($), KURDISH, KISH, BEIRUT, LEVANT;
L11   L1, L2, L3, L4, L5, L6, L7, L8, L9, L10;
LIST OFFLINE, TEXT, SUBJECTS;

LC Searches

    Search Number 208
L1   DS1($), DS2($), DS313($), DS326($), DS38($), DS43.S5,DS44($),
       DS48.F53, DS49($);
       DS53($); DS62($), DS70.6($), DS71.07($), DS80.9($), DS84($),
       DS89.T($);
L3   DS99($);
L4   L1, L2, L3;
LIST OFFLINE, TEXT, LCCALL:

Dewey Searches

    Search Number 209
L1   915.6($), 955($), 956($);
L2   L1 & T92 (SEN);
46 LIST OFFLINE, TEXT, DDCNO;

RECORD OF SEARCH RESULT

The method used for recording the information gathered in the searches was straightforward: Once run, each of the searches resulted in a print-out, with statistics and document references which met the search criteria. Each MARC record in the MARC/DPS file has a unique number and that document number was used for identification of individual MARC records.

Each MARC record selected was examined and the following information was recorded:

1. Document number;
2. Is it relevant (R), questionable (Q), or not relevant (NR)?;

3. Search number;
4. Kind of search; and
5. Keyword(s) which caused the record to be selected.

For keyword searches other than LC or Dewey class numbers, the location (by MARC tag number) where the keyword appeared was recorded. For example, here's one document record:

Doc No 4469		RXQ NR
Search No	Kind	KW
208	LC	DS 80.9
209	DC	956.92
210	IFSc	956.92
207	KW	Lebanon

Side 1

FINDINGS

The findings of Mrs Hudson's study are a little startling for any of us who hoped to prove that searching the file by class number would be more useful than any other keyword approach. The following table points up how few relevant documents were found using either the LC or DC numbers, when compared to keywords found anywhere in the MARC record.

Doc No 4469					
KW	T10	T20	T60	T70	Other
Lebanon		X		X	

Side 2

AREA: MIDDLE EAST

Search Strategy	Relevant Hits	Precision ratio R ret / T ret	Recall Ratio R ret / Total R
KW	101	40.6%	97.1%
LC	36	14.4	34.6
DC	26	10.4	25.0
IF Sc	21	8.8	20.1
KW & LC	103	41.3	99
KW & DC	103	41.3	99
KW & IF SC	102	40.9	98
KW & LC & DC	104	41.7	100

AREA: LATIN AMERICA

Search Strategy	Relevant Hits	Precision ratio R found / T found	Recall ratio R found / Total R
KW	143	33.4%	98.6%
LC	60	14.1	41.3
DC	47	11.0	32.4
IF Sc	36	8.4	24.8
KW & LC	145	33.9	100
KW & DC	144	33.7	99.4
KW & IF SC	143	33.4	98.6
KW & LC & DC	145	33.9	100

Annotation

Total R is 104 (Middle East), 145 (Latin America)

T found for any single search strategy is the sum of documents found using it alone or in any combination with other strategies.

ANALYSIS OF FINDINGS

The analysis of the placement of the keywords in the MARC record is at the heart of the problem. Where do the keyword hits and false drops come from? The table [on the next page] tells an interesting story which looks consistent or area studies searches for two parts of the world. The fields for author and imprint often yielded non-relevant reference, or false drops. These same fields were never the only reason for the retrieval of a relevant MARC record. It appeared that keyword searches restricted to fields for the title, series notes, notes, and subject headings eliminated many false drops without sacrificing the finding of any relevant records. The table also shows that the fields for title *and* subject heading (T20 and T70 in the MARC I records respectively) are the most effective for finding relevant documents. Keywords in the title field can be both useful and a nuisance, according to these findings.

TABLE 4: Keyword Hits by MARC Data Field

KEYWORDS IN DATA FIELD	MIDDLE EAST			LATIN AMERICA		
	RELE-VANT	QUES-TION-ABLE	NON-RE-LEVANT	RELE-VANT	QUES-TION-ABLE	NON-RE-LEVANT
Single field hits:						
T10 (author)	0	0	9	0	0	11
T20 (title)	8	1	12	9	5	15
T30 (imprint)	0	3	11	0	1	10
T60 (notes)	2	2	3	3	2	16
T70 (subject heading)	19	1	7	16	5	5
Hits in more than one field:						
T20/T70 (title and subject heading)	70	0	7	49	4	15
T20/T60/T70 (title, noter and subject heading)	9	0	0	7	0	1

To find documents on an area of the world, then, we concluded that the keyword search seems optimum, with the use of LC numbers and then Dewey class numbers following for exhaustivity. The homonym problem caused a great many false drops during such searches and seems unavoidable with an "uncontrolled" vocabulary of keyword searching such as that done in MARC/DPS. For example, Israel (the country) and Israel (the surname) cannot be distinguished.

Conclusion

Mrs Hudson [came to these conclusions]: The fact that keyword searches were better than searches using a classification system was not surprising. Material on a given geographic area is not easily found on the shelf in any library. It is scattered because other aspects of the material are highlighted and used for primary subject access. The subdivisions of subject headings, more than the geographical codes in DC, appear to provide access to some of this material. To access the subdivisions, however, a catalogue record must be in machine readable form and the programming system used for searching the records must allow access to any word in the subject field, not just the first word. MARC/DPS is such a system. Our results show that two MARC I fields (title and subject) provide access to the relevant documents for an area study search. Neither is sufficient alone.

We are not certain that our findings hold true for other kinds of subject searches (for example, biographical, political, historical, literary, etc). Much more work along the lines described here will have to be done before the class numbers (either LC or DC) on MARC records should be discarded as subject access points in a mechanized document finding system. Before we can say that the title and subject headings fields should be considered the primary routes of subject access to library materials, someone will have to test the entire system more rigorously than we have here.

Study 2

OBJECTIVES

Michael Ubaldini, a recent graduate of the School of Library Science at Syracuse University, delved a little more deeply into MARC searching than Mrs Hudson. He refined some of the objectives of her work and pinpointed for very close scrutiny the placement of keywords in various MARC fields. He had eight objectives when he undertook his research:

1. To analyse *keyword searches* (phase 1) to determine if there were any well-defined *relationships* between finding relevant documents and specifying which tagged MARC fields should be searched.
2. If such relationships existed, to determine if an increase in the *precision ratio* could be effected by such field specification.
3. If so, to determine the subsequent effect on the *total estimated recall*.
4. If the effect on the total estimated recall was favourable, to determine the sequence in which the tagged fields should be searched to insure high precision and equally high recall.
5. To determine the effect of restricting searches to *single fields*; to compare these results with *multiple-field* searching; and to conclude which method, if either, is better for obtaining high precision and recall.
6. To determine what part, if any, the following *search characteristics* played in the question of tagged field specification: subject area searched, search author, length and degree of specificity of the search.
7. To construct keyword, LC, and DC searches (phase 2) on one topic to *test* the results of phase 1 (steps 1–6 above).

8. To compare the results concerning tagged field specification of Judy Hudson's report on *area studies* with the results of his work and to determine if her recommendations could be extended to all *keyword* searches.

The concept of single-field versus *multiple-field* searches is an important one. Some document finding systems allow selection only by

TABLE 8: Unique documents found by single-field keyword occurrences (Analogous to KWIC indexing)

FIELD	Total Docs found	Rele-vant	Non-rel.	Quest.	Preci-sion Ratio %	T Esti-mated Recall %
T10 (main entry)	4	3	0	1	75	3
T20 (title)	36	30	5	1	83	27
T30 (imprint)	4	0	4	0	0	0
T40 (collation)	0	-	-	-	-	-
T51 (series)	3	0	3	0	0	0
T60 (notes)	9	6	3	0	67	5
T70 (subject headings)	32	23	6	3	72	21
T7 + (corporate author)	6	1	5	0	16	1
T80 (copy information)	0	-	-	-	-	-
TOTAL RESULTS	79	51R	23N	5Q	65	48

TABLE 9: Documents found by multiple-field keyword occurrences (Phase 1 results)

FIELD	Total Docs found	Rele-vant	Non-rel.	Quest.	Preci-sion Ratio %	T Esti-mated Recall %
T10 (main entry)	27	13	10	4	48	12
T20 (title)	122	78	30	14	64	70
T30 (imprint)	20	9	8	3	45	8
T40 (collation)	2	2	0	0	100	2
T51 (series)	25	5	18	2	20	5
T60 (notes)	59	30	20	9	51	27
T70 (subject headings)	107	76	19	12	71	69
T7 + (corporate author)	28	10	17	1	36	9
T80 (copy information)	1	1	0	0	100	1
TOTAL RESULTS*	162	95	44	23	59	86

*These total results do not represent the arithmetic sums of their respective columns because one keyword may have appeared in many fields of a document retrieved by the keyword strategy.

single-field keyword occurrences. The KWIC indexing of article *title words* (analogous to field T20 in the MARC I records) is an example. It allows access to the contents of these articles solely by the indexing of keywords in the titles of the articles indexed. This may, in fact, be desirable. Allowing specified keywords to be indexed and accessed from multiple parts of an article (for example, abstract, affiliation) may cause the finding of many irrelevant drops, but may insure a substantially higher number of additional relevant documents to be selected.

TABLE 10: Documents found by multiple-field keyword occurrence (Phase 2 results)

	Total	Documents Retrieved			Preci-sion Ratio %	Total Est. Recall %
		Rele-vant	Non-rel.	Quest.		
Documents retrieved by *all* strategies	43	14	20	9	33	100
Documents retrieved by *keywords*	19	12	1	6	63	86
Documents retrieved by *LC* class nos	16	6	8	2	38	43
Documents retrieved by *DC* class nos	23	10	12	1	44	72
Field(s) specified or keyword search						
T 10 (main entry)	0	-	-	-	-	-
T 20 (title)	6	5	0	1	83	36
T30 (imprint)	0	-	-	-	-	-
T40 (collation)	0	-	-	-	-	-
T51 (series)	0	-	-	-	-	-
T60 (notes)	3	1	1	1	33	7
T70 (subject headings)	15	11	0	4	73	79
T80 (copy information)						
T 20 or T70	0	-	-	-	-	-
T 20 or T60 or T70						
T 10 or T 20 or T60 or T70	16	11	0	5	69	79
	19	12	1	6	63	86
T 20 or T30 or T60 or T70	19	12	1	6	63	86

FINDINGS

Ubaldini's findings show interesting differences if single-field searches are compared with multiple-field searches.

CONCLUSION

He summarised his results as follows:

1. Analysis of the table of single-field keyword occurrences indicates that the most useful fields for finding *relevant* MARC records may be ranked as follows:

   T20 (title)
   T70 (subject headings)
   T60 (notes)
   T10 (main entry)

   The ranking would be different if the precision ratio were used as the sole criterion because the number of non-relevant retrievals in these fields varies.

2. Analysis of the table of multiple-field keyword occurrences supports the validity of this sequence. The table which records the results of the test keyword search (phase 2), shows that all 12 relevant documents were retrieved by specifying only fields T20, T60 and T70 to be searched.

3. Single-field keyword searching was not as effective as multiple-field searching. 79 of a possible 162 documents were retrieved by the single-field keyword strategy. Of these 79 documents, 51 were assessed as relevant (a precision ratio of 65 per cent). By allowing keyword occurrence in all fields, 95 relevant documents were retrieved (a precision ratio of 59 per cent). Multiple-field retrievals gave a slightly lower precision ratio, but the increase in the total estimated recall was critical, an increase from 48 per cent to 86 per cent. This would mean, for example, that a KWIC indexing of all the fields of the MARC record would furnish less than half of the relevant documents in the data base while multiple-field searching would furnish over 6/7 of the relevant documents. From another viewpoint, allowing multiple-field searching nearly doubled the total number of relevant documents retrieved, with little cost to the overall precision.

4. Using MARCS/DPS, relevant documents were selected by the occurrence of one or more of a number of specified keywords in the *titles* of these documents (field T20). Manually searching an alphabetically arranged card catalogue by the title of a document would have selected only those documents which had a specified keyword as the *first word* of its title. Analysis of the first indexable word of a sample of 20 relevant documents selected by searches analysed in this report indicates that only 40 per cent of these

documents would be retrieved by a manual search of a card catalogue which contained entries for these documents. That is, for the searches studied here, approximately only 28 per cent of the total number of relevant documents in the card catalogue would be selected by a manual search compared to the retrieval of 70 per cent by use of computer access.

5. Using MARCS/DPS allowed the keyword searching of the *notes* portion of a catalogue entry (field T60). Some of the documents selected in this study could not have been found by a manual search of a card catalogue under title or subject heading. One example is the case of a compilation of articles in which the article titles are given in the notes. A few of the documents retrieved by the search on Shakespearean drama, for example, were retrieved solely by keyword occurrence in the notes. In the light of the results of this report, the ability to search this part of a catalogue entry for specified keywords may be a very valuable facility.

6. In summary, when one considers the title, notes, and subject entries, the occurrence of specified keywords in these fields taken together rather than in any *one* of these fields alone, the total number of relevant documents found is increased by 26 per cent while the precision ratio is decreased by only 3 per cent.

Comparison of Findings

The following statement of Mrs Hudson is corroborated by the results of Mr Ubaldini's report: "The fields for *title* and *subject heading* (T20 and T70 respectively) are the most effective for retrieving relevant MARC records." However, her statement that the "author, imprint, and title fields (T10, T30, and T20 respectively account for most of the non-relevant keywords hits," may not be extended to all keyword searches as is evidenced by the analyses in Ubaldini's report.

In her report, Mrs Hudson recommends that the following fields be searched to obtain high precision and recall in an area study: "filing or conventional title (T15), title statement (T20), series, traced (T50), series not traced (T51), notes (T60), and subject headings (T70)." The results of Ubaldini's report do not confirm the wholesale extension of her recommendations for area studies to all keyword searches. They do confirm the searching of fields title, notes, and subject. However, since *no* keyword occurrences in his study were noted in fields for conventional title or series (traced), it is not expedient to recommend that they be searched in all keyword searches. In his report, field T51 (series, not traced) was responsible for retrieving 3 documents (all non-relevant) by single-field keyword occurrence and 25 documents (18 non-relevant) by multiple-field keyword occurrence. In multiple-field searches, T51 was responsible for selecting 5 relevant documents, all of which would have been selected anyway if field T51 had been excluded from being searched. Therefore, the recommendation that field T51 be searched in an area study does not appear to be easily extended to all keyword searches.

Remarks

Ubaldini's conclusions have great impact on the future of cataloguing as we know it today. If we are to continue to obey the third law, it is possible that we will have to revise our practices quite dramatically. We cannot ignore much longer such statements as the following: The most productive fields for subject searching, as determined by the results of this report, are title, notes and subject headings. Specifying additional MARC fields for searching will either result in (a) a greater decrease in precision with little increase in recall, or (b) the selection of *no* additional MARC records.

Requiring that all the keywords (specified in a search) be found in a single field *critically reduces* the number of relevant MARC records selected by the search. The resulting recall ratio is likely to be lower than is desired by the users of the system.

The use of LC subject headings as a means of access to catalogue entries of monographs may not be as useful as is generally accepted. It appears, from the results of this report, that a KWIC index of the monograph titles for specified keywords would have selected a greater number of relevant MARC records than searching the subject headings for these keywords, without appreciably lowering the precision ratio of the search. The necessity for LC subject headings in the MARC record is put in serious doubt. Nevertheless, the results of this report also point to the conclusion that searching the subject heading field *in addition to* the title and notes fields did select many more relevant records than searching the titles and subject headings alone.

LECTURE #4

LAW 4: SAVE THE TIME OF THE READER. A PLEA FOR UNITED ACTION!

A Measure of Efficiency

In the one hundred years since Melvil Dewey and Charles Ammi Cutter were young librarians, we have erected a great many devices for bibliographic control. The studies I reviewed in earlier lectures are a few of the recent attempts to find whether these devices assist or prevent the reader's access to the documents he seeks. These studies have just scratched the surface of what we need to know about the match between a user's information needs and the systematic description of our information resources—the documents.

In communications research, they speak of the *gatekeeper function*. Library catalogues are a form of gate in the communication process between reader and book, and cataloguers and reference librarians are gatekeepers of a sort. By what criterion do we measure the performance of our task? I submit that the fourth Law of Library Science should be used. In constructing the catalogue and other library tools, do we save the time of the reader or do we add to the time he must spend before he can put to use the information resources we have collected for his use? Many studies in libraries centre around increased efficiency of the library staff in performing certain functions, but very few are cost/effectiveness studies of the information seeker.

Making Students' Experience It

As a feeble attempt to make library science students aware of the need to evaluate our functions in this light, I usually require beginning students in cataloguing to chart their own path of information seeking from known information need to information satisfaction. They measure the steps and the minutes it takes to go from their study desk to an index or the library catalogue, to the book shelf or circulation desk, and finally to the book itself. It is usually a revelation to them when they add up the steps and can count their efforts in hundreds of feet, when they add up the minutes and can see that one such search took almost a half-hour! After this, they seem to take much more interest in "saving the time of the reader" and they also seem to have this law uppermost in their minds whenever we discuss anything which may set up hurdles for the user. For example, the establishment of main entry for corporate bodies or conference proceedings always bothers a new class in cataloguing because a comparison of the title page and the catalogue card shows very few common elements, oftentimes. They ask, "How can we continue to do this and still say we are saving the time of the reader who has a known item in mind?" Needless to say, I am at a loss for words on such occasions and quickly switch the subject to automated library catalogues where, I hope, we will have freer access to all the information we store.

Focus on the Reader

DESIGNING FOR BETTER USE

It is not an easy problem to solve. How can we measure our present efforts to save the time of the reader (and the staff) when the library is such a complex organisation and no one function can be changed without having a rippling effect throughout the organisation? We can begin at one obvious place, in my opinion. We can begin to concentrate on knowing more about the reader. This awareness will force us to design or redesign our information centres and libraries to facilitate their use. This new point of view (new for many) can effectively transform many libraries with no real modernisation effort such as automation being necessary. I have visited many public libraries in the United States, in large cities and small towns, and I always enter the building with the fourth law on my mind. I murmur to myself, ''How does this library save the time of the reader?'' By observing where the information signs are, where the librarian sits, where the card catalogue stands, where the book return is located, how a reader signs out a book, and how the catalogue user is aided in his search, I can tell very easily if the library is enforcing the fourth law. Equipment is not the only essential to save the time of the reader. The spirit of willingness to serve or to help the reader help himself is more essential.

SUBJECTIVE TIME

More than the 'objective time,' the 'subjective time' of the reader is important. While waiting in a queue to use a particular catalogue drawer, or to get a book charged or discharged, although the objective time may be only a couple of minutes, it might appear as waiting for hours for the busy reader. Even an additional minute he takes to find the appropriate catalogue entry for his document can increase his impatience and frustration. This is true also of locating a document on the shelves using the call number, etc. This subjective time varies from reader to reader and even with one and the same reader from one context to another.

Principle of Least Action

When I became interested in the use of computers for information storage and retrieval, I noticed how easily this fourth law could be ignored even though increased efficiency was supposedly the objective of the system. Don Swanson said in the February 1966 issue of the *Bulletin of the atomic scientists* that ''the design of any information service should be predicated on the assumption that its customers will exert minimal effort in order to receive its benefits.'' Users of such services, he said, operate under *the principle of least action.* If this be so, then we must take the user into account every day of our existence and be sure that every attempt is made to save his time as well as our own. The problem is one of organisation, not of computerisation. The conference on library and information networks in my country, which I spoke of in the first lecture ([Conference on Interconnection of Computer-based Information Networks]) placed more importance on agreements to effect compatibility, combinability, and multiple use of records than on any other problem. We may consider it inefficient to type catalogue cards for the same book that was catalogued before in another library, but imagine the poor reader who must use several different bibliographical sources only to come up with a list of known items which he must now trace through several different libraries. Without union lists and greater cooperation between librarians and publishers of indexes, bibliographies, etc, we add enormous workloads to the users of our services.

Standarisation and Simplification

I must apologise because I do not know too much about the efforts in India to save the time of the reader and the staff in your information centres, but when I surveyed efforts in the United States a few years ago, I had to conclude that there has been no concerted effort on the part of any group to be wholly or even partly in tune with anyone else in producing compatible tools, easily combinable for bibliographical reference work. Title abbreviations for serials, for example, differ in different reference works; libraries create union lists of serials with no aids to ease this problem. It is as if we were building railroads, each on a different gauge track so that no equipment or trains could pass from one company's tracks to another.

A research team from System Development Corporation painted even a blacker picture in their report to the US Federal Council for Science and Technology, Committee on Scientific and Technical Information:

> "Unless someone with unusual foresight and influence establishes workable standardisation, the history of library coordination as a mechanisable system complex may be as turbulent as the history of higher-order computer languages has been. Unfortunately, the rush of library automation efforts could be so rapid that each installation, preoccupied with attaining its own internal efficiency, might not notice the incompatibilities of its formats, codes, etc, with those of other libraries unless strong efforts—such as those that a capping agency could exert—are made to coordinate these aspects of library automation" (22).

It is possible that the users of our tools and libraries may solve their problems in their own way, and we may not be called upon to help. But should we sit passively and wait to be called to help? I think not, if we adhere to the fourth law. Don Swanson suggests that information systems should provide for more digestion, summary, and packing down of knowledge, which will permit the library user to progress without floundering in the backlog of published information. He states categorically:

> "Most present libraries and information systems wait to be used. A modern information system, however, should seek out its customers . . . we infer that these systems will provide de-centralised service points and selective, direct, and continuous distribution of information to customers. Service in response to standing requests should be maximised, so that customer initiative can be minimised" (21).

Points for Consideration

With such words to guide us, we must ask ourselves: Are we following the fourth law? More specifically we might ask: What are we doing to effect a positive plan to meet the following needs:

1. We need to stress a coordinated approach to information system and network development—from *origin* of information (author's manuscript to editor/publisher) to *use* of information (in library, research worker's office and the like).
2. We need to combine efforts and avoid *redo* of input operations (automatic typesetting for publisher; machine-readable cataloguing for library; data compilations in information centres).
3. We should follow the *principle of least action* in information systems for every library user.
4. We should follow the *principle of by-product data* generation in machine-generated data.
5. We must make *provision for combinability and flexibility* of information records.

Cooperation

WORK TOGETHER

For all these projects, we need to work together across state and national borders and across *library* borders. We need a unifying force— provided by some governmental authority or by our own professional zeal to accomplish our stated goals. Dr Ranganathan in his life-time of work, shows us the way, but now we collectively must do what one man tried to do single-handed forty years ago. Our task is more difficult because we do not have a unifying body-force he has. Can we strive for it? Let us share the ideas about how to begin.

HOLISTIC APPROACH

There is another sense in which united action or integrated effort is essential. The requirements and psychology of readers are complex; they are dynamic and changing. No single tool of the library—classification, cataloguing, reference service—can all by itself satisfy the varied demands of each of the readers. Only through an integrated use of the several tools can greater efficiency be achieved to the satisfaction of the Laws of Library Science. This is the right approach, the holistic approach.

LECTURE #5

LAW 5: A LIBRARY IS A GROWING ORGANISM

> "Finding out what we want should become a major object of our attention . . . there is a vast difference between letting changes occur and choosing the changes we want to bring about by our technological means."
>
> —Bertrand de Jouvenal
>
> "Utopia for Practical Purposes" —*Daedalus* (Summer, 1965)

The Human Side

In my own interpretation of Ranganathan's Five Laws of Library Science, I come full circle when I review the impact of the fifth law on my efforts and interests in librarianship. If we are to develop library service, we must effectively control the system which facilitates the interactions between reader and book. To insure proper growth we need librarians who are educated in such a way that they believe in facilitating this interaction in everything they do.

Professional Education

Library education for me has become the focal point where the library profession's growth can be nurtured and guided. Libraries *are* people (both readers and literature and *not* collection of books). Library education puts me in touch with librarians who are struggling with the notion of professionalism for the first time, who are eager to learn what we know; and because they are a captive audience, I can also tell them what we do not know. Our struggles to understand ourselves and our work can be laid out before a class and they can have sport with what we know. Many of them have stimulated me to rethink the role of the librarian in society, and the place of technology in the library. These exchanges have been very exciting and I welcome every new class with open arms because I am convinced that personal growth comes through our interaction with others.

In the United States, we are engaged in a reexamination of the library profession, our work and our education, our relationship with other professionals in the information business. This creates an aura of crisis for some, but for others it has helped to clarify how we can accommodate growth, change, and new perspectives.

Professionalism

Several years ago, a sociologist by the name of William J Goode discussed the professional nature of librarianship. He felt that librarianship fell somewhere in the middle of a professional-nonprofessional continuum. To him, librarianship was engaged in a struggle for full professional recognition.

In this struggle, he felt librarianship had certain advantages. One, librarianship is a full-time occupation specialising in a certain area and is not subordinate to any other group, in the same status as nursing is to doctoring in medicine. Related to this is that librarians have a sense that their occupation is unique. Two, librarians are closely attached to learning which is a prime source of occupational prestige in the society. In addition, an increasing number of librarians are trained in professional schools, some of which are associated with universities and offer a doctorate. Three, librarians belong to professional associations, at local, state, and national levels. Four, librarians have formulated a code of ethics.

But Goode did feel that librarianship lacked two key attributes that keep it from becoming fully accepted as a profession. One, a prolonged specialised training in an abstract body of knowledge. Two, a collectivity or service orientation, in terms of professionally defined ''needs'' of its clients, rather than what its clients simply ''want.'' I shall explain.

In terms of the knowledge base, Goode maintained that librarianship had failed to develop a general body of scientific knowledge dealing with information storage and retrieval, but depended upon rather rule-of-thumb, local regulations and rules, plus a major cataloguing system for most of its day-to-day work. Even now, some librarians express doubt about the importance of formal education for librarianship. Goode maintained that the public did not believe that the librarian has a knowledge base specific to his occupation. He felt that the public views librarians as gatekeepers and custodians to a ''stock room'' of books and periodicals. This aspect, if true, seems to be intensified by the fact that the public largely meets only the unskilled and semi-skilled help in libraries and judges the trained librarians, who work mostly away from the eyes of the public, by the performance of the help. Even today some librarians seem to be particularly sensitive to being referred to as "gatekeepers" or some similar term. This is not to deny that others particularly seem to be proud of being called "book-keepers."

Library Management

According to Goode, another factor related to the knowledge base is that the librarian begins to assume administrative tasks earlier than in most other occupations. Much of this administration is not specific to librarianship, for it consists instead of integrating human beings in a corporate enterprise and not in pushing back the frontiers of knowledge in the field. Some librarians even argue that such an administrative emphasis is properly a central task of librarians. In fact, status or prestige today seems to be achieved in the field mostly by administration, that is, in taking on more administrative responsibility rather than being distinguished as a specialist.

When the administrative ladder no longer is the only way to increased status, we may be closer to calling librarianship a true profession. As the problems of handling information increase, many will have to do research similar to those I described if we are ever to cope with the fifth law. There are problems of values and changes in values of what is significant information and what is insignificant. Coping with growth may mean that we need ways of dispersing the avalanche of information so that the reader will not be overwhelmed. Efforts called SDI (Selective Dissemination of Information) come to mind very quickly. The natural extension of such efforts can be made an integral part of a library if librarians will handle *information*, not as we do today in libraries (storage and retrieval functions), but in a way that will both create and destroy it! By selecting and evaluating information, we give priorities to the contents of our storehouses. We make value commitments and we say that our choices are unbiased. Is this truly the case? Let us say that a librarian has five hundred rupees to spend. The physics department wants a reference book that costs almost the full amount. The history department wants some early works which cost about five hundred rupees. Who gets that priority? How does the librarian decide? Is history more important than physics or vice versa? If a librarian decides on some sort of compromise, what values does he use to decide who gets what? Is a compromise a "good" thing? Why? As librarians, you know that you make similar decisions nearly every day. You decide, within certain limits, who gets what. You are faced with limits of time, finance, etc. Within the contexts of these limits, you make choices about what knowledge is to be available. You are determining the growth of the library by your decisions!

Growth of Knowledge

Alvin M Weinberg, who was chairman of the President's Science Advisory Committee, said that "those who control information will become a dominant priesthood in the science of the future." He is right. If our choices emphasise certain areas of science, those areas will benefit to the possible detriment of other areas. If our choices emphasise science areas, humanities areas may unduly suffer as a result. In part, our choices determine the areas of knowledge of the present and of the future. We are part of the process of knowledge creation and destruction. We should recognise this responsibility in all of our libraries and make our decisions based on more knowledge wherever possible. That is why I tried to describe some research studies in these lectures, the finding of which will affect library practice. It is a fact of life that the library is a growing organism *if* the library's staff is engaged in pursuing the other four laws. How we put our knowledge to work—the knowledge we have of ourselves and of our users—will determine our growth rate and the evaluation that society makes of the importance of our contribution.

Bibliographical References

1. Atherton (P), Dr S R Ranganathan. (Library resources and technical services. 14; 1970; 582–4).
2. Dewey (M). Dewey decimal classification and relative index. Ed 17. 1967. V2 (revised). NY, Lake Placid, Forest Press.
3. ENCYCLOPEDIA AMERICANA. International ed. 1968. New York, American Corporation.
4. Ferguson (CA). Language study and the Middle East. (Annals of the American Academy of Political and Social Science. 356; 1964; 77).
5. Graves (FH). The five laws of library science. (Special libraries. 49; 1958; 271).
6. Lipetz (B-A). User requirements in identifying desired works in a large library. New Haven, Yale University Library. 1970 June.
7. ———. P 14–6.
8. ———. P 16–20.
9. Mackinnon (DW). Nature of creativity. (*In* creativity and college teaching. Proceedings of a conference held at the University of Kentucky. 1963. Kentucky. College of Education, University of Kentucky, Lexington. (Bulletin of the Bureau of School Service. 35, Number 4; 1963; P 33).
10. Palmer (R). User requirements of a university library card catalog. 1970. (Thesis, PhD. University of Michigan). [Unpublished].
11. ———. P 66–8.
12. ———. P 66–6, 73–4, 82–3.
13. Ranganathan (SR). Five laws of library science. 1931. Madras. Madras Library Association.
14. ———. Scientific method, library science and march of digvijaya. (*In* Author's Five laws of library science. Ed 2. 1957. Chapter 8).
15. ———. Social bibliography or physical bibliography for librarians. 1952. Delhi, Delhi University.
16. ———. P 14–6.

17.———. *Ed*. Documentation and its facts. 1963. Sec B 17. Bombay, Asia Publishing House.

18. Rhinelander (PH). Education and society, (Key reporter. 1968 Autumn).

19. Shera (JH). Sociological foundations of librarianship. 1970. Sec E75. Bombay, Asia Publishing House.

20. Sayers (WCB). Preface. (*In* Ranganathan (SR). Prolegomena to library classification. Ed. 2. 1957. P 19).

21. Swanson (D). On improving communication among scientists. (Bulletin of atomic scientists. 1966. Feb; 10–11).

22. System Development Corporation. Recommendations for national document handling systems in science and technology. 1965. Appendix A, 2: 11–6).

23. Winchell (CT). Guide to reference books. Ed 8. 1967. Chicago. American Library Association.

24. Zadrozny (JT). Dictionary of social science. 1959. Washington, Public Affairs Press.

Catalog Users' Access from the Researcher's Viewpoint: Past and Present Research Which Could Affect Library Catalog Design

The prospectus for my part of this Institute reads as follows:

> This presentation will explore what the results of research studies have already demonstrated about the manner in which users access library collections, and how that access might be affected positively or negatively by the use of alternative catalogs, *AACR II,* and possible changes in subject structure.

I have found myself unable to write a paper with the answers this prospectus would lead one to expect. The reason for my failure, I believe, is not that there has been no research on user access to library collections but that there has been no research which links present practices and user experiences with the prospective publication of new cataloging rules, with hypothesized alternatives to the card catalog, or with nonexistent plans for changes in subject access. Library service is not known for its careful systems planning, analysis, design, evaluation, and redesign of any of the subsystems. There are no pilot plant models of various library subsystems where we could test the impact of alternatives in redesign of services, the revision of catalog forms, or the reorganization of collections. People in England have been trying for some years to get funds for an ideal test collection, but this is still not a reality. Project Intrex was a bust in this area although the group tried very hard. The monitoring reports of systems we have already changed, for example, reports of shifts from the book catalog to the Computer Output Microform (COM) catalog, do not stand up as

Reprinted by permission from *Closing the Catalog: Proceedings of the 1978 and 1979 Library and Information Technology Association Institute,* edited by D. Kaye Gapen and Bonnie Juergens, pp. 105–22. Copyright © 1980 by The Oryx Press, 2214 N. Central at Encanto, Phoenix, AZ 85004-1483. <u>Editor's Note</u>: The Appendix to this article is not reproduced here.

system evaluation reports. I must report, then, at the outset, that I have found no research with the linkages I would like to see from present to planned changes in library catalogs so that we could check positive and negative effects.

The dilemma of seeking and not finding reminded me of the famous joke about the drunk who, on a very dark night, is searching for something under a lamppost. A policeman comes upon the man who is on his knees. The drunk tells him that he is looking for his keys which he says he lost "over there," pointing out into the darkness. Not unexpectedly, the policeman asks him, "Why, if you lost the keys *over there*, are you looking for them under the streetlight?" The drunk answers, "Because the light is so much better here."

If we continue to rely on past research studies that tell us about users of card catalogs, I fear we will be like the drunk looking where the light is so much better. Granted, this small circle of light around the card catalog does cast a little light on the darkness before us. For that reason it is a good place to start, but I think we do need to explore the darker areas too before we can hope to find the answers we seek.

As I reviewed the catalog use studies done over the last 50 years (yes, 50, according to James Krikelas' review in volume 3 of *Advances in Librarianship*), I found that the studies could be separated into two parts: work concentrating on the form and access points in the catalogs of the library and work concentrating on the users of the library and its catalogs. Very few researchers established experimental conditions where the effect of changing one could be seen to affect the other. Daniel O'Connor's doctoral dissertation at Syracuse in 1978, Marcia Bates' work at Berkeley in 1972, and the Chicago study in the mid-1960s on the Requirements Study for Future Catalogs are somewhat different from the others. Unfortunately, these studies were done outside the operational environments where technological changes were being considered and where decision makers were planning the format changes of catalogs and the rules for description of the library's collections. When Wilf Lancaster undertook to summarize all the known evaluation work in this area, he decided to concentrate on only a few studies: the American Library Association (ALA) study of the 1950s, the University of Chicago study mentioned above, three Michigan studies done in the late 1960s, the Ben Lipetz study at Yale also done in the late 1960s, and a United Kingdom study of the 1960s reported in several parts. I have taken the liberty of quoting excerpts from the Appendix to his chapter on catalog use studies to summarize for this audience the important findings from these studies. This is our present small circle of light. The Appendix in Lancaster's book was prepared during 1973–74 by a graduate student at the University of Illinois, Alan Meyer. I have excerpted and have also made here certain additions to this list of findings in order to emphasize what would be useful to us as we venture into the darkness of alternative forms of catalogs, new cataloging rules, and possibly new forms of subject access. The Appendix to my paper follows the outline of the Appendix in Lancaster's chapter. Findings are organized as follows:

I. Findings about the behavior of catalog users.
   1. Most people remember titles better than authors.
   2. Most people do not persevere in catalog searches. More than 50 percent will look up only one entry and then stop, regardless of whether or not they have found what they are looking for. Most subject searches are attempted under a single subject heading. Only a small proportion of the searches (26 percent) where a search length is less than ten cards are in a conventional catalog.
II. Findings about known-item searches.
   1. Searching under author requires an average of five times as many card examinations as searching under title. With inaccurate bibliographic information, which is very common, that ratio increases considerably.
   2. Permuted title indexes greatly raise the success rate of searching for incomplete and half-remembered titles.
III. Findings about subject searches.
   1. About 50 percent of all users think up a subject heading or entry word that gets them an entry or *see* reference in the catalog on the first try.
   2. Subject headings are not specific enough to meet the needs of most users.
   3. Subject searches very often fail because the user cannot tell from the cards s/he finds whether or not the books they represent are relevant to his/her needs.
IV. Findings about the physical structure of the catalog.
   1. An abbreviated catalog with five elements in citation (author, title, call number, subject heading, and date of publication) would satisfy 84 percent of user requirements. This satisfaction rate could be raised to 90 percent if a sixth item, contents note, were added.
   2. Future catalogs should incorporate principles of redundancy and multiple-access routes to a much greater extent than they do presently. Unquestionably, title entries are of special importance, with each word accessible as a separate alphabetic entry with suitable provision for entry by means of singular/plural and other types of word-form variations, as well as synonyms.[1]

Although there is some merit in reviewing these findings, I must stress the need to look beyond these studies and investigate the impact of other variables on our future plans. Movements toward resource sharing, library cataloging networks, and online bibliographic retrieval may have a greater impact on our plans than any knowledge we may have gained from studies about the users of card catalogs in university and public libraries.

The half century of catalog use and user studies has still not uncovered the master design for our catalogs, even though some valiant efforts were made to bring forth some generalizations about possible improvements. We seem not to have heeded, nor even correctly interpreted, some of these findings.

It is a fact that some studies have seemed to contradict others. I don't know if that is our rationale for ignoring all research. The debate still rages as to whether we can design catalogs for all our users. In 1946 Marie Prevost said, "Once the diverse nature of the users of the catalog is recognized, it becomes a patent absurdity to speak of cataloging according to the 'public' mind, as if that mind were a single entity." She then added that,

> logically, there are two alternatives in attempting to construct a subject catalog for the use of the public. One is to try to incorporate in it all the entries which any of [the] different classes of users may conceivably look for. The other is to construct it according to a system which can be understood by librarians—the group which uses it most and which alone is in a position to help those who don't understand it. The first alternative is obviously impossible. . . . Even if it were possible . . . the resulting tool would be so huge, so unwieldy, and so confused, with the same subject appearing under various terms, that it would defeat its own purpose. . . . Our present practice . . . represents a hopeless attempt to combine the two intrinsically incompatible alternatives.[2]

By 1958 the ALA Catalog Use Study was telling us that those same librarians do not have a good understanding of the catalog themselves, as evidenced by their low success in searching. Perhaps this shook us up. By 1972 Marcia Bates was telling us that subject experts left the catalog unsatisfied more often than naive users because of the illogic and inconsistencies in our use of the rules for direct and specific entry of subject headings. But still no one heeded the researchers' findings.

If we put all these findings together, we come away from catalog use studies quite discouraged about the present state of use of our catalogs, with no sure guidance about improvements and the impact of changes. Some studies concentrated on success rates of catalog searches and concluded that more than 66 percent of the known-item searches were successful. They usually did not explain the one-third failures as system errors. No one has replicated these studies or redesigned the survey to gather comparative data for various forms of the catalog, or with new cataloging rules for entry and description, or new modes of subject access. So we are still not very far ahead after 50 years and more than 200 catalog use studies. We still do not know which changes will be improvements or disasters from the users' point of view.

Rather than being totally discouraged by this review, I would like to help bring a little more intensity to that small center of light under which we are working. Toward that end, I have prepared a table entitled, "Unheeded Research Findings and Recommendations about Catalog Use" (*see Table 1*). These statements by researchers appear to have fallen on deaf ears or were presented before their usefulness could be ascertained. I think they deserve a review at this time.

TABLE 1: Unheeded Research Findings about Catalog Use

1. Early studies found more known-item searches than subject searches, but more recent studies indicate that it may be premature to dismiss the subject entry as being of little value.
2. By 1970 we had findings from studies which recommended that we include the following in our catalog records to improve the success rate of searchers: the contents notes, in-depth subject analytics, or front and back matter from book to provide greater subject access.
3. Inconsistencies in our catalogs regarding use of specific entry rule, direct and indirect entry confusion, and lack of cross-references were causing many user problems.
4. By 1950 we had the recommendation that we should remove older subject cards (20 years or older) and file subject cards chronologically rather than alphabetically.
5. Most studies were recommending current terminology as entry vocabulary. A more modern, simple, and direct entry vocabulary would increase searchers' success.
6. Reverse geographic headings for local interest material were recommended.
7. A synonym dictionary would be needed to aid computer-aided post-indexing if the vocabulary from the title, notes, and contents of the book were included in the machine-readable catalog record and provided access points for the searcher.
8. By 1946 we were advised that conceptual limitations in our existing schemes of access would plague any new catalog form.
9. User access in a large academic library would average about 1000 catalog searches per week. There is some correlation of this use and actual circulation statistics within the same library. Catalogers searching a catalog would take, on the average, 24 minutes per title and would access (or search) the catalog at 1.4 points per title.
10. More effective user training would improve the success rate of catalog users.

TABLE 1: Unheeded Research Findings about Catalog Use (continued)

11. The classification scheme used in a library can provide subject access in the online catalog, and the words in the classification schedule captions may provide the free or natural text needed for greater access to topics in the contextual areas of the schedule, thereby providing a browsing feature in online catalogs.

12. New forms of catalogs should include opportunities for searchers to ask for help from a staff member, look in a bibliography related to their subject, request an interlibrary loan, check the uncataloged file, or find a suitable substitute.

These unheeded findings point to improvements in the catalog which would facilitate user access to the library's collections. By concentrating on these features, I hope to bring to your attention some alternatives in design which we can incorporate now as we plan for change. As a collective enterprise, via OCLC, Inc., or some other shared cataloging project, we might make some changes, suggested by these past studies, in library catalogs. None of the findings in Table 1 would involve revolutionary or costly changes in our catalog conversion projects. From the users' point of view, each would be seen as an incremental change which was not difficult to comprehend.

Rearranging subject cards by date is something very straightforward for a computer-based Computer Output Microform (COM) catalog. This feature is already in online bibliographic retrieval systems as a sort option for offline prints.

Our inconsistent use of direct and indirect entry for subject headings could be repaired by a permuted subject entry list like the ERIC Thesaurus "Rotated Descriptor Display." Both COM catalogs and online catalogs could provide this easily.

A profusion of cross-references in an online name or subject authority file is not a big project to implement and such a service could be an adjunct to another online system in a library, even if the full catalog file were only available as a COM product.

Inserting notes about subject bibliographies in our COM or online catalogs could be done quite easily.

Signaling a need for a reference librarian after a person searches the catalog unsuccessfully would not be too difficult to design into a computer terminal used by the public for online catalog searching.

Examining such a list of unheeded research findings could serve as a checklist for those redesigning our catalogs at the present time. It could open up a renewed interest in approaching system redesign from the user's point of view. Considering the objectives of our new catalogs, we must reach beyond the objectives of an OCLC system or even the University of Toronto Library Automation System (UTLAS) and Bibliographic Automation of Large Library Operations Using a Time Sharing System (BAL-LOTS) because these were originally designed not for library users but for library staffs.

Twenty-five years ago, in 1953, Dake Gull found "no trend towards any physical substitute which will replace the card catalog in the near future as the basic record of each library." By 1963, when David Weber cited Gull's words in a paper, he concluded that "the character of the American library catalog has not changed in other than minor respects since the beginning of libraries in this country, [but] some major changes seem certain in the years ahead."[3]

Now, 15 years later, we admit that change is at hand, but we seem to think of the need for change resulting from system changes rather than from the research findings which have found our systems inadequate for our users. This startling fact has caused me a great deal of concern. We should not take the position I did early in this paper that previous studies in catalog use are not of much value for our present redesign efforts. I do want to emphasize the need to review previous findings and recommendations. Improved user access and a higher success rate for the information searcher must still be our goals, and the best way to check our achievements is to observe the user.

Unfortunately, the work done in the past may have been based on a faulty construct and we may need to rethink user studies entirely if they are to be useful for system redesign. Daniel O'Connor said at a Library and Information Technology Association (LITA) conference in September 1978:

> Many librarians erroneously assumed that information needs really existed somewhere inside a user's head. An information need predisposed individuals to exhibit some information-related behavior. It was—and still is—felt that by describing use, information needs can be inferred and future use predicted, which then allows for the design of appropriate services and systems.

He concluded that this construct, with the assumption that users' behavior is a constant, is "ill-conceived and clouds our thinking."[4]

I believe, as Dr. O'Connor does, that we have made our mistake by concentrating solely on the uses of the card catalog. We should be studying the total information-seeking behavior of the individuals who appear at the catalog and elsewhere in the library. We will be studying different forms of the catalog, but we will be forced to examine the observable responses and behavior of individuals. In this manner, we can systematically account for similarities and differences in information seeking. According to O'Connor, for each person studied, we should record data on a variety of variables. In the long run, we will begin accounting for individual variability in a systematic fashion. Observable responses and behaviors of individuals in conjunction with conventional use surveys will tell us what we need to know about information seeking and users, and this in turn will help us redesign our systems.

Another area of past research needs to be improved. Lancaster, in his review of catalog use studies, tried to bring together findings about the user and findings about the catalog, but he did no more than list them. The interrelationships between these user and catalog characteristics still need to be described. From the following lists of user and catalog characteristics, one cannot draw positive or negative correlations.

TABLE 2: User Characteristics and Catalog Characteristics

1. Accuracy of information brought to catalog	1. Average number of entry points/items
2. Type of approach made to known item	2. Extent of title entries
3. User training and expertise	3. Number of cross-references provided
4. Perseverance, diligence, and intelligence	4. Size and complexity of catalog
	5. Quality of labeling and guidance given in catalog

As Table 2 indicates, if we knew more about the individuals at the catalog, we might be able to see how certain catalog characteristics affected their information-seeking behavior. If we knew whether certain studies were or were not studying typical persons, we could make certain conclusions about the value of these studies to us. Differences in the user characteristics should be contrasted with catalog characteristics. The reported changes or conditioning of an individual's behavior by the existing capabilities of the catalog being used should be assessed. In many of the studies reviewed by Krikelas, Lancaster, Montague, and others, information was collected about the users (age, sex, educational background, skill at catalog use, resourcefulness and persistence as a catalog user, familiarity with catalog rules, confidence-expectations-attitudes toward catalog's associational structure, satisfaction with retrieved information, knowledge of topic being searched, ability to discriminate what is/what is not relevant, motivation for search, recall ability), but rarely did the researcher correlate this information with the features of the catalog being searched. Such research is long overdue in our field. The work of young researchers like

Bates and O'Connor may take us a long way, but we also need a national effort to bring in the required findings in time for our 1980 changes.

Again, our circle of light is very small and our trek into the outer darkness is at hand. This plea for needed research stems from the urgency I feel because of the forces we have marshaled to make big changes in library catalogs over the entire world. Such an undertaking should not be set in motion without some reliable research in user behavior and some investigation of the interaction of users with the forms of catalogs we plan.

The form of the catalog and related files has been much discussed at this Institute, but I wonder how many of those discussions focused on the features of alternative forms from the user's point of view. Would we reach the same conclusions about the designing of our catalogs if we scanned a list of advantages and disadvantages of each catalog form as viewed by the user? I started such a list as an exercise before beginning this paper. I present it here in hopes that more of you will look at the list and expand it, observing how changes we plan in the form of the catalog may or may not be advantageous. Maybe some new, as yet unplanned, features need to be added. Maybe the unheeded research findings mentioned earlier can help us think of some improvements which the technological changes make feasible and practical. We should be trying to wipe out the disadvantages of the previous catalog form, but a glance at this list in Table 3 shows that this may not totally be possible.

In summary, some results from previous research suggest changes in card catalogs which could be reviewed for their applicability to alternate forms of the catalog. But we would be in error if we stopped there and went on about our business, redesigning catalogs just because of changes in rules for entry. These system changes should not be our only concern as we drastically alter the forms of our catalogs. The information-seeking behavior of our users needs also to be explored. Participant-observation techniques used by anthropologists may be more appropriate than survey studies with predetermined question-and-answer sets.

The unheeded research findings of previous studies need to be reviewed again by system designers. Such farsighted work as Don Swanson's 1963 design of a computer terminal for a dialogue with the catalog is an example. Such a seminal paper has missed its audience all these years and needs to be revived and reviewed. Even with the rapid changes in computer technology, it may be that his design is still appropriate. The AUDACIOUS Project which Robert Freeman and I worked on in the mid-1960s may also merit reviewing. The idea that a classification schedule like the *Universal Decimal Classification* (UDC) could be used by an information seeker for search terms in context with the logical organization of the library's collection is an idea that has never been tested with real users. O'Connor's file preference study was a good beginning in an experimental study but should be expanded into a real system evaluation effort.

As we begin to look beyond the circle of light we now have, I do hope we will give more attention to the users for whom the catalogs are being designed. Please allow our researchers in the field to explore the darkness ahead of us!

Afterword

There is no way to come to understand the real options involved in the future unless you start to become involved in creating them. . . . The time when you could be objective and noninvolved and still learn has passed.—*Robert Theobald*

TABLE 3: Forms of Catalogs—Advantages and Disadvantages from the User Viewpoint

ADVANTAGES	DISADVANTAGES
CARD CATALOGS	
1. Alphabetical orderly parts 2. Unit entry, with all information available everywhere 3. In drawers, easy to move out 4. Printed or typed cards easy to read 5. Drawers are touchable as are cards 6. Guide cards and notes available 7. Form of catalog similar throughout life 8. Nonmediated, self-service 9. Easily updated 10. Can contain temporary information	1. Over-time, inconsistent rules of main-entry form and choice and subject-heading form and choice 2. Drawers too low or too high, where user must kneel or reach 3. No chairs to sit on 4. Must copy out all information needed by hand 5. Cryptic notes and form of entry 6. Different style of entry, different form of card in different library, for different materials 7. No "natural language" access 8. Too few cross-references 9. Drawers sometimes misfiled 10. Catalog available in only one location, even in decentralized system
COM (FICHE OR REEL) CATALOG	
1. Available at many locations 2. Several entry files (author, title, subject) 3. Can see several records at once 4. Can copy entries if printer available 5. Chair is usually provided at reader 6. Inexpensive equipment for readers, sometimes available on loan	1. Not easily updated 2. Not very readable 3. Rearrangement of output difficult 4. Cross-references often missing

TABLE 3: Forms of Catalogs—Advantages and Disadvantages from the User Viewpoint (continued)

ONLINE LIBRARY CATALOGS	
1. Easily updated, with changes explained 2. Can provide table lookups for authority files (author, title, subject, etc.) 3. Available at many locations 4. New access points and combinations search terms 5. Variable output formats and sorts 6. No writing by user required 7. Chair provided 8. Union lists possible	1. Need of staff assistance 2. May be expensive to user 3. Equipment failure possible 4. Queuing problems at few terminals 5. User training necessary

REFERENCES

1. F. Wilf Lancaster, *The Measurement and Evaluation of Library Services* (Arlington, VA: Information Resources Press, 1977). Appendix, prepared by Alan Meyer, pp. 69–72.

2. Marie Prevost, "An Approach to Theory and Methodology in General Subject Headings," *Library Quarterly* 16 (April 1946): 140–41.

3. David C. Weber, "The Changing Character of the Catalog in America," in *Library Catalogs: Changing Dimensions,* edited by Ruth French Strout (Chicago: University of Chicago Press, 1964), p. 33.

4. Daniel O'Connor, "Determining User Needs: Information Seeking Behavior," 1978. (Manuscript to be published.)

BIBLIOGRAPHY

Altman, Ellen. "On My Mind: Reactions to a COM Catalog." *Journal of Academic Librarianship,* vol. 3, no. 5 (November 1977): 267–68. (ERIC Document EJ 172 265)

Aroeste, Jean, et al. *UCLA Working Group on Public Catalogs. Final Report.* January 1976.

Atherton, Pauline. "Books Are for Use: Evaluation of MARC Records in Online Subject Retrieval Systems." *The Information Age in Perspective.* Proceedings of the ASIS Annual Meeting. November 1978, pp. 17–20.

Books Are for Use. Final Report of the Subject Access Project. Syracuse, NY: Syracuse University, 1978. (ERIC Document ED 156 131)

Putting Knowledge to Work. Delhi, India: Vikas, 1973. (See pp. 86–118 for review of Yale, Michigan, and Syracuse studies of catalog and readers' requirements.)

Bates, Marcia. "Factors Affecting Subject Catalog Search Success." *Journal of the American Society for Information Science* 28 (May 1977): 161–69. (Also available as Ph.D. dissertation from Xerox Microfilms 74-15639.)

"System Meets User: Problems in Matching Subject Search Terms." *Information Processing and Management* 13 (1977): 267–375.

Bath University, Comparative Catalog Study:
Paper 1—P. Bryant, "The Background to BUCCS."
Paper 2—A. Needham, S. Morris and P. Bryant, "Methodology."

Paper 3—A. Needham, "Performance of Four Physical Forms of Catalogue."

Paper 4—A. Needham and J. Spencer, "Catalogues on Rollfilm."

Paper 5—A. Needham, "Performance of Four Orders of Catalogue."

Paper 6—A. Needham, "Classified KWOC Catalogues."

Paper 7—P. Bryant and A. Needham, "Costing Different Forms of Library Catalogues."

Paper 8—A. Needham, "User Reactions to Various Forms and Orders of Catalogue."

Paper 9—J. H. Lamble, P. Bryant, and A. Needham, "Incidental Discoveries of the BUCCS Project."

Paper 10—J. H. Lamble, P. Bryant, and A. Needham, "The BUCCS Project: Conclusions and Recommendations."

Bath, England: Bath University, 1975 (British Library, Lending Division, Fiche Nos. BLRDR 5240 through 5249).

Blackburn, Robert. "Two Years with a Closed Catalog." *Journal of Academic Librarianship* 4 (January 1979): 424–29.

Brittain, J. M. *Information and Its Users: A Review with Special Reference to the Social Sciences*. New York: Wiley, 1971.

Childers, Thomas, et al. *Book Catalog and Card Catalog: A Cost and Service Study*. Towson, MD: Baltimore County Public Library, March 1967 (ERIC Document ED 019 099).

Cox, Carolyn M., and Juergens, Bonnie. *Microform Catalogs: A Viable Alternative for Texas Libraries*. Dallas, TX: AMIGOS Bibliographic Council, November 1977 (ERIC Document ED 149 739).

Dubester, Henry. "Studies Related to Catalog Problems." *Library Catalogs: Changing Dimensions*. Edited by Ruth French Strout, pp. 97–105. Chicago: University of Chicago Press, 1964.

Elrod, J. McRee. "Year's Work in Cataloguing and Classification." *Library Resources and Technical Services*. vol. 17, no. 2 (Spring 1973): 175–200 (ERIC Document EJ 083 174).

Freeman, Robert, and Atherton, Pauline. *AUDACIOUS: An Experiment with an Online, Interactive Reference Retrieval System Using the Universal Decimal Classification as the Index Language in the Field of Nuclear Science*, Report AIP/UDC-7 under National Science Foundation Grant GN-433. New York: American Institute of Physics, April 1968.

Hazen, Dan C. "The Assumption of Automation (Or: The Card Catalog is Dead! Long Live the Card Catalog!)," *Cornell University Libraries Bulletin* 1 (Summer 1978).

Head, J. W. "The Effect of Bibliographic Format and Content on Subject Retrieval: A Comparative Study of Four Cataloguing Styles." Ph.D. Dissertation, University of Wisconsin, Madison, 1972.

Hill, Jean, and Brown, Nancy. "COM Catalogues at the University of Guelph Library." *Microform Review* 7 (July 1978): 213–16.

Hudson, Judith. "Searching MARC/DPS Records for Area Studies: Comparative Results Using Keywords, LC, and DC Class Numbers." *Library Resources and Technical Services*, vol. 14, no. 4 (Fall 1970): 530–45.

INTREX: Report of a Planning Conference on Information Transfer Experiments. September 3, 1965. Edited by Carl F. J. Overhage and R. Joyce Harman. Cambridge, MA: MIT Press, 1965. (See also subsequent progress reports reviewed in the *ASIS Annual Review of Science and Technology*.)

Irwin, R. R. "The Use of the Card Catalog in the Public Library." Master's Thesis, University of Chicago Graduate Library School, 1949.

Jacobs, Peter J. "Automated Catalogs for the Library." Williamsport, PA: Brodart, June 1978.

Keen, E. M. "Prospects for Classification Suggested by Evaluation Tests Carried Out 1957–70." In *Classification in the 1970's: A Discussion of Development and Prospects for the Major Schemes*. Edited by Arthur Maltby, pp. 209–10. London: Bingley, 1972.

Krikelas, J. "Catalog Use Studies and Their Implications." *Advances in Librarianship,* vol. 3. Edited by M. J. Voigt, pp. 195–220. New York: Seminar Press, 1972.

——. *The Effect of Arrangement on the Use of Library Catalogs: An Experimental Study of a Divided and a Dictionary Catalog. Final Report.* Urbana, IL: Illinois University, Library Research Center, October 1967 (ERIC Document ED 020 767).

Lancaster, F. Wilf. *The Measurement and Evaluation of Library Services.* Arlington, VA: Information Resources Press, 1977.

Martyn, John. "Information Needs and Uses." *Annual Review of Information Science and Technology,* vol. 9. Edited by C. A. Cuadra. Washington, DC: American Society for Information Science, 1974.

McCarn, Davis. "Online Systems: Techniques and Services." *Annual Review of Information Science and Technology,* vol. 13. Edited by M. Williams, pp. 90–94. New York: Knowledge Industry Publications, 1978.

Meincke, P. P. M., and Atherton, P. "Knowledge Space: A Conceptual Basis for the Organization of Knowledge." *Journal of the American Society for Information Science* 27 (1968): 18–24.

Montague, E. "Card Catalog Use Studies, 1949–65." Master's Thesis, University of Chicago Graduate Library School, 1967.

North, John. "Card Catalog to COM." *Library Journal,* vol. 102, no. 18 (October 15, 1977): 2132–34 (ERIC Document EJ 170 243).

O'Connor, Daniel. "Determining User Needs: Information Seeking Behavior." Manuscript to be published, 1978.

——. "The Interactive Influences of Person and Situation Characteristics on Expectations . . . on Relevance Judgments and File Preference Choices by Undergraduates Searching Alphabetical and Classed Subject Catalogs." Ph.D. Dissertation, Syracuse University, School of Information Studies, 1978.

Paisley, W. J. *Information Source Preference as a Function of Physical and Psychological Distance from the Information Object. Report.* Syracuse, NY: Syracuse University, 1966 (ERIC Document ED 026 101).

Palmer, R. P. "User Requirements of a University Library Card Catalog." Ph.D. Dissertation, University of Michigan, 1970.

Prevost, Marie Louise. "An Approach to Theory and Methodology in General Subject Headings." *Library Quarterly* 16 (April 1946): 140–51.

"Programme of Catalogue Research," *Newsletter* (J. H. Lamble, Project Head, The Library, University of Bath, Claverton Down, Bath, BA27A4, England).

Quigley, H. "Investigation of the Possible Relationship of Interbranch Loan to Cataloging." *Library Quarterly* 14 (1944): 333–38.

Raffel, Jeffrey A., and Sheski, Robert. *Systematic Analysis of University Libraries: An Application of Cost-Benefit Analysis to the MIT Library.* Cambridge: Massachusetts Institute of Technology, 1969.

Richmond, Phyllis. "Research Possibilities in the Machine-Readable Catalog: Use of the Catalogue to Study Itself." *Journal of Academic Librarianship,* vol. 2, no. 5 (1976): 224–29.

Sacco, Concetta N. "Book Catalog Use Study." *RQ,* vol. 12, no. 3 (Spring 1973): 259–66 (ERIC Document EJ 080 063).

Slight, Owen E. "The Segmented Subject Catalogue: A Free-Vocabulary Subject Approach to Library Materials." *Library Automated Systems Information Exchange Bulletin* (1976).

Strout, Ruth French, ed. *Library Catalogs: Changing Dimensions.* Chicago: University of Chicago Press, 1964.

Swanson, Don R. "Dialogues with a Catalog." In *Library Catalogs: Changing Dimensions.* Edited by Ruth French Strout, pp. 113–25. Chicago: University of Chicago Press, 1964.

Tagliacozzo, R., and Kochen, M. "Information-Seeking Behavior of Catalog Users." *Information Storage and Retrieval* 6 (1970): 363–81.

Tagliacozzo, R.; Rosenberg, L.; and Kochen, M. "Access and Recognition: From Users' Data to Catalogue Entries." *Journal of Documentation* 26 (1970): 230–49.

Task Force on The Future of the Cornell University Library Card Catalog. Report Number 1 with Appendices 1-8. Ithaca, NY: Cornell University Library, December 1977.

Virginia Beach Dept. of Data Processing. *Cost-Benefit Analysis of a Catalog System for the Virginia Beach Department of Public Libraries.* Virginia Beach, VA: Virginia Beach Dept. of Public Libraries, January 1978 (ERIC Document ED 153 657).

Weber, David C. "The Changing Character of the Catalog in America." *Library Catalogs: Changing Dimensions.* Edited by Ruth French Strout, pp. 20–33. Chicago: University of Chicago Press, 1964.

Catalog Use Studies—Since the Introduction of Online Interactive Catalogs: Impact on Design for Subject Access*

by Pauline A. Cochrane and Karen Markey

1981-1982: THE TRANSITION FROM CARD TO ONLINE CATALOGS

1981–1982 may well be the year that marks the changeover in library catalogs from card to online, just as the turn of the century marked the transition to a standard card catalog at the Library of Congress and other libraries in the United States. As we all know, neither date represents a clear-cut transition, but this year and this conference may well mark a change in trend and direction. The remarkable difference between these two historic developments in the library profession is that the turn of the century marked a trend toward standardization, but 1981–1982 marks a trend toward experimentation in library catalog design. The experimentation is so great that we are now beginning to hear a sound of alarm that online public access catalog (OPAC) designers may be using librarians and patrons as guinea pigs to try out for a time some unique features of their online catalogs or a number of different commands for accessing catalog information.

During such a time, it is fortunate that the Council on Library Resources (CLR) has had the foresight to monitor the effects of this experimentation on OPAC users (Ferguson et al., 1982). Their support of

Reprinted with permission from *Library and Information Science Research*, Volume 5, Number 4, 1983.

*Article is based on Pauline A. Cochrane's presentation at the RTSD/RASD/LITA Preconference on "Prospects for the Online Catalog," on July 8, 1982 in Philadelphia, PA. Correspondence and requests for reprints should be sent to Karen Markey, Office of Research, OCLC, 6565 Frantz Road, Dublin, Ohio 43017.

discussion among the many organizations planning OPACs (Ferguson & Kaske, 1980; Russell, 1982; McCarn, 1983) is having a moderating effect. Historians of library system design and the user-system interface will someday reflect on this period and will be able to trace the beginnings of online catalogs. Research, funded by the Bibliographic Systems Development Project (BSDP) of the Council on Library Resources, and coordinated by CLR Program Officer C. Lee Jones, has been dubbed Online Public Access Catalog Evaluation Projects, or CLR-OPAC. These are landmark data-gathering and analysis projects facilitating statistical comparisons, trend analyses, feature analyses, and qualitative analyses of user reactions to OPACs. To our knowledge we have never had such carefully orchestrated and focused research projects in librarianship. The *Public Library Inquiry* in the early 1950s may have had more scope, but it was limited to public libraries. The ALA *Catalog Use Study* of 1958 (Jackson, 1958), monumental as it was, did not have the correlative studies that mark the present CLR-OPAC efforts. The important card catalog use studies, performed at Yale (Lipetz, 1972) and at the University of Michigan (Palmer, 1972; Kochen, 1970), were statistically sound, but they were hardly generalizable according to the many reviewers of catalog use studies (Atherton, 1980; Hafter, 1979; Markey, 1980), because each of these studies was limited to a single institution, with all of its idiosyncracies.

However, 1981–1982 not only marks a new era for library catalogs, it also heralds a new era of catalog use studies. Catalog use studies have traditionally been associated with descriptive surveys and questionnaires. Thanks to technology, catalog use studies can now go beyond such methods. Today, studies of online catalogs employ transaction log analysis, protocol analysis, and focused-group interviews, as well as the more familiar descriptive surveys and questionnaires. We will address the methods employed by online catalog use studies, the limitations of each, and the types of research questions that each method can answer.

As we observe online catalogs and online catalog use today, the very *act of observing* is changing the course of the development of the online catalog. Nowhere was this more dramatically demonstrated than at a meeting at the University of Denver in January, 1982, when the preliminary findings of the CLR-OPAC Evaluation Projects were presented. These findings caused several participants to say that "common wisdom is in error, sacred cows are dying, we must change the way in which we have designed our catalogs. If the public wants sophisticated subject searching and they are using the catalog to search by subject more than by author or title, then online catalog systems will have to be redesigned" (Besant, 1982).

Based on those preliminary observations, libraries have begun to revamp their original OPAC design or to revise specifications for their new online catalogs. Some have attempted to improve subject access by changing the indexes of their libraries' online databases, providing access to words and phrases *within* subject heading strings and/or titles, rather than merely matching card catalog access points. Some are providing online displays of alphabetical lists of subject headings and their related terms.

Preliminary findings of the CLR-OPAC Evaluation Projects were an incentive for improving subject access to OPACs. The impediments to change are not technological, but technical. What is hindering system designers from making improvements is the unavailability of the Library of Congress Subject Headings (LCSH) in a form easily manipulated and updated. Subject access in the card catalog was wholly different from that in the online catalog. As is well known, the reason for the limited amount of subject searching in the card catalog was attributed to "the inadequacy of the present system" (Lipetz, 1972). A majority of online catalog users are doing subject searching and have been vocal in suggesting improvements and reporting problems.

With a new form of the catalog in the making, we now have the opportunity to make changes for our users that we never before thought possible. This new phenomenon is causing us to change the online public access catalog even as we observe it, because the opportunity now exists to start over. The next three to five years may well be the formative period for online catalog development. After that, no doubt we will have too much invested, and changes will again be considered too costly. To take full advantage of this opportunity to conduct studies and compare systems, we should use research and operational data to make decisions. Hopefully, the findings and conclusions will benefit our library staff and patrons, because our choice of one format design over another, one terminal over another, and one subject access feature over another, will be soundly based.

METHODS FOR STUDYING ONLINE CATALOGS

In card catalog use studies, we have used surveys, questionnaires, and microsystem evaluations. The few online catalog use studies that predate the CLR-OPAC Evaluation Projects also employed questionnaires which asked patrons about their most recent catalog search, e.g., type of search, purpose, satisfaction, etc. (Dowlin, 1980; Pease and Gouke, 1982; Pritchard, 1981; Pawley, 1982; Moore, 1981). Granted some other systems analysis techniques are taught in library schools and practiced by library systems analysts when time and money permit, but suppliers of turnkey systems and the programmers of library automation efforts for single libraries neither awaited the results of online catalog use studies nor performed a formal cycle of benchmark tests, user feedback, revisions, more tests, feedback, and revisions. Unfortunately, they probably had their hands full meeting the deadlines specified in proposals, contracts, or agreements. Enhancement of existing OPACs and development of future ones should then be based on analyses of library patron and staff experiences, problems, and needs. Without these analyses, designers would be "flying blind," for there would be no common wisdom yet about optimum OPAC design.

The CLR studies grew out of the Dartmouth Meeting in August 1980, which gathered 25 library administrators involved in the planning, development, and/or implementation of online public access catalogs (Ferguson & Kaske, 1980). Participants identified four priority areas for systematic study and cooperative effort.

1. Analyzing user requirements and behavior
2. Monitoring existing OPACs
3. Developing cost management methods
4. Developing distributed computing and system linkages

Following the Dartmouth meeting, CLR sponsored J. Matthews & Associates (JMA), Research Libraries Group (RLG), and OCLC Online Computer Library Center, Inc. to construct a survey instrument to collect information to analyze library user requirements of OPACs and user behavior, i.e., the first priority area of the Dartmouth Conference. Eventually, the survey instruments were pretested, revised, and administered at 29 libraries by several organizations: JMA, the Library of Congress, OCLC, RLG, and the Division of Library Automation of the University of California (UC/DLA). Besides these organizations, the National Library of Medicine (NLM) administered the user survey instruments of the CLR-OPAC Evaluation Projects at NLM to obtain user reactions to two candidate systems from which to choose a permanent online catalog (Online Catalog Study, 1982). The CLR-sponsored studies and the NLM study are of considerable interest. Besides the administration of questionnaires to users and nonusers of online catalogs (Anderson et al., 1982; Matthews, 1982a; Ferguson, 1982; Markey, 1983a; University of California, 1982, 1983b), there were:

- Focused-group interviews with library patrons and staff (Markey, 1983a)
- Individual and group interviews with library staff at research libraries (Ferguson, 1982)
- A feature analysis project (Hildreth, 1982b)
- System monitoring with transaction log analysis (Tolle, 1983; Larson, 1983)

These studies are important, because they employed several methods to study library patrons' reactions to OPACs, user experiences and behavior, system features, patron use of and reactions to system features, and system performance.

Early in 1981, we had the opportunity to critique the original proposals for the group of studies now referred to as the CLR-OPAC Evaluation Projects. We asked some "So what?" questions, because much money and time were about to be spent in executing these study plans. The proposals received by CLR included system monitoring, patron interviews, self-administered surveys of users and nonusers of online catalogs, system simulation, online controlled retrieval tests, and data collection of staff and expert observations. We remarked then that the data collected would only help answer questions that matched the stated research objectives. Put another way, we warned that not all questions would be answered by a single methodology:

- If we wanted answers to questions about *user behavior online*, we should rely more on system monitoring and expert observation than on statistical analysis of self-administered questionnaires completed by OPAC users and nonusers.
- If we wanted to *compare* OPACs with regard to *usefulness or effectiveness*, we would do well to rely on online controlled retrieval tests, feature analyses, and system performance reports, rather than on survey data or interviews with library patrons and staff.
- If we wanted *feedback from the user*, e.g., reactions to system features from different groups of clientele, knowledge about why some groups are not using or will not use online catalogs, etc., then we must rely on survey instruments, interviews with library staff, and focused-group interviews with library staff and patrons.
- If we want to *design the user-system interface* to be more user-friendly or reconstruct the database, then we may have to rely on expert opinion and laboratory tests more than on user reactions to existing systems.

There are certainly more questions that can be asked of online catalog use studies, particularly ones of interest to libraries planning for OPACs, for example:

- Do you want to know what is the *best* online catalog according to experts or to OPAC users?
- Do you want to know how to index the library's online database?
- Do you want to learn how to retrain your staff to deal with the online catalog user?

- Do you want to install LCSH as an online thesaurus?
- Are you trying to choose the best visual display terminal?
- Do you want the best displays and user prompts for subject searching?

Since there can be so many different reasons for being interested in online catalog use studies, using Figure 1 may help us determine the focus of different studies (Cochrane, 1981).

FIGURE 1: Major Variables Affecting Online Information Retrieval

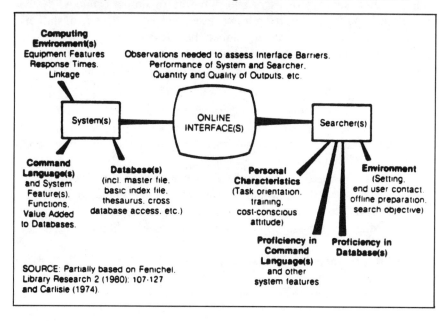

We will learn about the *system* from Charles Hildreth's (1982b) book *Online Public Access Catalogs: The User Interface,* which was the result of a CLR grant to OCLC. It is an excellent state-of-the-art review and *system* comparison. But keep in mind, this study's focus was not on the cost of these systems nor on searchers per se. No one study could focus on all the variables shown in Figure 1.

Hildreth's study of ten operational OPACs is an unusual catalog *use* study, because it did not involve a survey of users, but a survey of systems and the computer-based features that can affect use and performance. Hildreth collected available documentation of ten operational features with available documentation and with features of the other OPACs, under study. He then outlined system command capabilities by four functional areas—operational control, search formulation control, output control, and user assistance (Figure 2)—and took ten operational OPACs, including two at the Library of Congress, and displayed their features against this template. The chapters on dialogue modes and the user-system interface are state-of-the-art reviews, in which Hildreth has collected the best expert opinion that the literature of the man-machine interface has to offer and made a significant contribution by reviewing and interpreting the literature in the light of online catalogs. The monograph concludes with a glossary of terminology from such diverse fields as computer science, human factors engineering, ergonomics, and information and library science to cover the terminology of OPACs. Hildreth's *Online Public Access Catalogs* will be a ready reference tool for all interested in OPACs for some time to come. But do not expect this publication to tell you that System A is the best or even better than any others. This work is a *functional analysis* of the computer-based systems, *not a comparative evaluation*. As Lee Jones says in the introduction to the monograph: "It is hard not to make some comparisons between systems. Remember though, that they are not comparable systems. They use different equipment and software, and all were developed under different conditions." Look to Hildreth's work when you are writing

FIGURE 2. Functional Areas in OPAC User-system Interface*

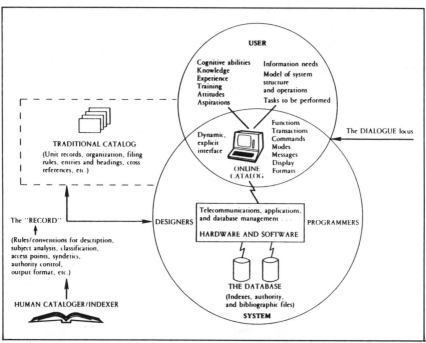

*(Source: Table 2 in Hildreth (1982b, p. 14).

specifications or trying to decide if a vendor is supplying something beyond the state-of-the-art or something less than that. Look to Hildreth's work for a background summary of the variations across systems. Look there to see what may cause different user problems. Look there to see the common attributes of the systems. We will not describe the monograph's findings in this report, but it is worth noting what Hildreth and the research staff at OCLC did accomplish:

1. Reviewed and evaluated the offline and online documentation and other evidence bearing on each OPAC's functional features and command languages.
2. Documented *in a uniform format* the functions and commands of each OPAC.
3. Provided a *common, systematic framework and format for comparing each OPAC system's* functional capabilities and command languages.
4. Provided a *uniform terminology* and working definitions for command-based capabilities and related system features, capable of denoting the many varieties found in existing systems, which have often been described with conflicting or vague terminology.
5. Identified and illustrated all interface characteristics and components that could impact on the effective use of the system's functional capabilities.
6. Reviewed and described how three OPAC systems supported and implemented these user-perceived functional features at the file access and retrieval level, given their particular hardware/software configurations.
7. Reviewed the recent literature on interface design and experimentation.
8. Identified crucial interface design alternatives (viewed from the user's point of view).

OCLC and CLR have given us a very important study. However, those looking for data on system cost, reliability, efficiency, and search performance will have to look elsewhere. Meanwhile, Hildreth (1983) has continued to reflect on OPAC developments and the designer's search for the ideal catalog.

When developing specifications for your library's online catalog, review Markey's (1983b) study of required features for an online catalog, which were based on an analysis of the process of searching the traditional subject catalog using protocol analysis, i.e., the analysis of subject searchers' spoken thoughts, which were collected as they performed their subject search at the traditional library catalog. The Markey study was undertaken by OCLC's Office of Research and addresses *system features* in Figure 1. Protocols were collected at high school, public, university, and college libraries. A coding scheme, based on the scheme used by Penniman (1975) to describe states in online bibliographic searches of the BASIS retrieval system, was applied to analyze the protocols used in subject searching of traditional library catalogs. The result of the protocol analysis was a composite model of the process of subject searching in the traditional library catalog. A subset of the composite model is shown in Figure 3. This subset of the composite model illustrates a typical approach to subject

FIGURE 3. Ad Hoc Process Model of a Bookshelf Browsing Subject Search*

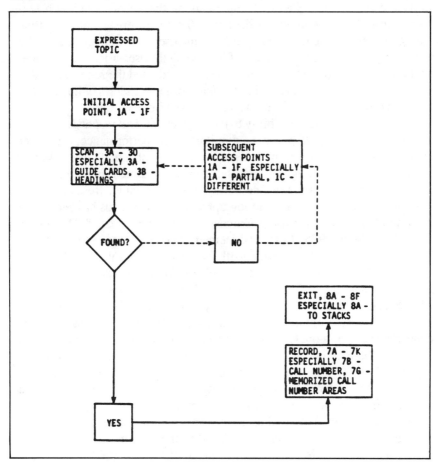

*(Source: Figure 19 in Markey, 1983b, p. 85)

(Note: Dotted line indicates process which frequently occurs, but did not occur in the search modeled.)

searching, namely, the bookshelf browsing search, in which the searcher consults an access point in the catalog, scans the first half-dozen cards, memorizes the most frequent class number, and exits to consult the books shelved in that class number area.

The model of bookshelf browsing and others that Markey presented suggests features for an online public access catalog that are required to support the present search tactics employed by searchers of the traditional library catalog. Markey's study tells us a great deal about the process of searching the library's traditional subject catalog and a set of minimum features that an online catalog must support to assist the user and must perform at least as well as our traditional subject catalogs. The Markey study did not cover the cost of implementing the set of "minimum features" in OPACs. Although it described the characteristics of the online public access catalog that is *unique* (i.e., the user-system interface), it did not cover the necessary ingredients for building the user-oriented interface, as the Hildreth book did. Look to Markey's study and the required OPAC features it covers when evaluating the features in a vendor's online catalog or when developing specifications for your own library's OPAC.

The computer has the ability to record every system response and user action input into the OPAC (e.g., monitor system performance, track user errors, record every command entered by users, number of items displayed, etc.) Thanks to technology, we now have a very accurate way of finding out exactly what people input to the library's online catalog. Research using system monitoring of online bibliographic retrieval systems has been done by a number of investigators (Fenichel, 1980–81; Mittman & Dominick, 1973; Penniman, 1975, 1981) and seemed "a natural" for extension to the study of online catalogs. Prior to the CLR-OPAC Evaluation Projects, several OPACs collected statistical information about user transactions, e.g., the University of California's MELVYL, Mankato State University's MSUS/PALS, and Syracuse University's SULIRS. These three OPACs and others were programmed to collect data about every transaction that occurred at one or more OPAC terminals. Such data were called transaction logs, and the method used to study such logs is known as transaction log analysis. Figure 4 shows an example of part of a user's online transaction at an OPAC terminal at Syracuse University. The Syracuse OPAC records the date and time of the transaction, the nature of the transaction as a read or write statement, the length of user input or system response, and the actual information input by the user or displayed by the system.

The analysis of transaction logs can tell us:

- Total number of online transactions and/or online search sessions over a given time period
- Frequency of commands entered by users

- Mean length of a user's online search session
- Number of retrievals or ''prints available'' after an input access point
- Most frequently used access points, e.g., author, title, subject, subject keyword, etc.
- Number of errors by type of error and number of errors per online search session

FIGURE 4. Transaction Log Record Format and Example from Syracuse University's SULIRS

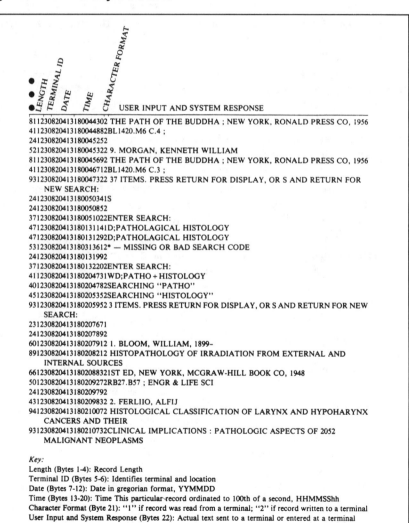

USER INPUT AND SYSTEM RESPONSE

```
811230820413180044302 THE PATH OF THE BUDDHA ; NEW YORK, RONALD PRESS CO, 1956
411230820413180044882BL1420.M6 C.4 ;
241230820413180045252
521230820413180045322 9. MORGAN, KENNETH WILLIAM
811230820413180045692 THE PATH OF THE BUDDHA ; NEW YORK, RONALD PRESS CO, 1956
411230820413180046712BL1420.M6 C.3 ;
931230820413180047322 37 ITEMS. PRESS RETURN FOR DISPLAY, OR S AND RETURN FOR
    NEW SEARCH:
241230820413180050341S
241230820413180050852
371230820413180051022ENTER SEARCH:
471230820413180131141D;PATHOLAGICAL HISTOLOGY
471230820413180131292D;PATHOLAGICAL HISTOLOGY
531230820413180313612* — MISSING OR BAD SEARCH CODE
241230820413180131992
371230820413180132202ENTER SEARCH:
411230820413180204731WD;PATHO + HISTOLOGY
401230820413180204782SEARCHING "PATHO"
451230820413180205352SEARCHING "HISTOLOGY"
931230820413180205952 3 ITEMS. PRESS RETURN FOR DISPLAY, OR S AND RETURN FOR NEW
    SEARCH:
231230820413180207671
241230820413180207892
601230820413180207912 1. BLOOM, WILLIAM, 1899–
891230820413180208212 HISTOPATHOLOGY OF IRRADIATION FROM EXTERNAL AND
    INTERNAL SOURCES
661230820413180208832 1ST ED, NEW YORK, MCGRAW-HILL BOOK CO, 1948
501230820413180209272RB27.B57 ; ENGR & LIFE SCI
241230820413180209792
431230820413180209832 2. FERLIIO, ALFIJ
941230820413180210072 HISTOLOGICAL CLASSIFICATION OF LARYNX AND HYPOHARYNX
    CANCERS AND THEIR
931230820413180210732CLINICAL IMPLICATIONS : PATHOLOGIC ASPECTS OF 2052
    MALIGNANT NEOPLASMS
```

Key:
Length (Bytes 1-4): Record Length
Terminal ID (Bytes 5-6): Identifies terminal and location
Date (Bytes 7-12): Date in gregorian format, YYMMDD
Time (Bytes 13-20): Time This particular-record ordinated to 100th of a second, HHMMSShh
Character Format (Byte 21): ''1'' if record was read from a terminal; ''2'' if record written to a terminal
User Input and System Response (Bytes 22): Actual text sent to a terminal or entered at a terminal

- Patterns of OPAC searches, e.g., probability of entering a certain command given the entry of the same or a different command
- Pattern of OPAC searches which have the greatest probability of resulting in an error or series of errors
- Average 5 minutes of catalog activity during a week (number of active terminals, number of logons and logoffs, average response time, average idle time, etc.)

These data provide more information than we have ever known about card catalog use. However, there are still some shortcomings to this methodology for a catalog use research objective. Some systems do not have logon and logoff commands. This has made it difficult to differentiate a *search* or *session* of one user from that of the next. A *search* may not be defined the same in two different OPACs. Few systems require a logon identification before OPAC use begins, so OPAC users are usually anonymous. The transaction log analysis performed by Tolle (1983) on data from the Library of Congress, Syracuse University, Ohio State University, and Dallas Public Library involved an elaborate programming effort to parse the data by session, because only one of the four systems had logon and logoff procedures. Borgman's (1983) transaction log data from Ohio State University was supplemented by human observers' recording the arrival times of library patrons at OPAC terminals. Time stamps on Ohio State transaction logs were then matched with arrival times recorded by human observers to determine online search sessions of individual OPAC users. In transaction log analysis, patterns of online searching (i.e., the probability of a user's proceeding to one state or command given his most recent state or command) are discovered. Parsing individual search sessions from transaction logs yields data from which conclusions are drawn to describe transitions from one state to another, not from one search to another search. Larson's (1983) analysis of transaction logs from the Library of Congress, the University of California, Mission and West Valley Colleges, and Northwestern University did not involve parsing individual search sessions. From those transaction logs that record information input by users and the computer's responses, we obtain a gold mine of data about searching vocabulary vs. system (i.e., LCSH) vocabulary. These data have not yet been analyzed formally, but some diagnostic investigation has begun at Northwestern University, the University of California, and Syracuse University (private communication).

Few OPACs have a logon or logoff procedure. This is useful for privacy reasons, but makes transaction log analysis difficult if one wants to draw conclusions about an individual search session. A system like Paper-Chase, in a hospital environment, can request a logon and carefully track a user's success or failure (Cochrane, 1982b). PaperChase asks each user to comment and can, on an hourly basis, review these comments and provide some assistance when necessary. Few OPACs in other environments have such a capability, but it is interesting to note it here.

Even though these system-monitoring reports usually do not include any identification of the user, they will be very valuable for assessing online users' behavior, input, and system performance. When transaction logs are matched with questionnaire data, they can provide very interesting data to compare what library patrons' say they have entered into the OPAC (i.e., through the questionnaire approach) with what they actually have entered into the OPAC (i.e., through transaction log analysis), and to match patterns of online searches (i.e., through transaction log analysis) with types of library patrons (i.e., through analysis of demographic data on questionnaires). In this way, users' online questionnaire responses could be matched with their OPAC transactions. The University of California's study of MELVYL (Larson, 1983) involved cross-checking users' questionnaire responses about type of search with what users actually input into the OPAC. Capturing verbal protocols at the OPAC, i.e., searchers' spoken thoughts, and matching protocols with transaction logs would provide us with the most reliable data about the type of search(es) performed by OPAC users, e.g., title, subject, author/title, etc., and the perseverance of OPAC users. From studies of transaction logs can come system improvements, better user assistance, possibly better staff and user interfaces (Johnson, 1982), and a better understanding of online catalog use.

In a review of a single day's *transaction log* at Syracuse University's (SULIRS) online public access catalog (Wyman, 1982) and from a review of statistics from MELVYL (Larson, 1982), we came up with a fairly long list of findings that could become suggestions for system improvements if these problems were found to occur quite frequently. Here is a sampling of the findings from SULIRS and MELVYL data and our subsequent observations:

1. *Many users retrieve nothing.* (On MELVYL at the University of California, 30% of the searches retrieved zero hits week after week.) If this finding holds up, a system might be designed to print the following message whenever this condition occurs:
   - "Sorry you found nothing here. Try the card catalog as the computer catalog does not list all the holdings in this library."

     or
   - "Sorry you found nothing here. Listed below are some related terms which may have been used to index items of possible interest." (List of terms would come from LCSH tracings matched against the OPAC's index.)

or
- "Sorry you found nothing here. You may also check appropriate indexes found near the computer catalog or ask the librarian for some assistance."

or
- "Sorry you found nothing here. Perhaps your search was mislabled or misspelled. Ask the librarian on duty for assistance."

A detailed examination of zero-hit searches might turn up the need for vocabulary aids online, for example, cross-references or classification tables as prompts for search strategies (Cochrane, 1982a; Hildreth, 1982a; Markey, 1983a).

2. *Many users retrieve too much and view only some of the search results.* If this finding holds up (and it has on MELVYL for several months—15 percent of the searches retrieved more than 100 hits), a system improvement might be to interpose a message or an option such as the following:
   - "Your search retrieved more than 100 items. Would you like to see the results displayed by call number, with the most frequent listed first?"

   or
   - "Your search retrieved more than 100 items. Would you like to see a list of the subject headings used on these items, with the most frequent first?"

3. *Many users make a common error of not typing in their search as required.* For instance, they may use a colon where a semicolon is required. They may specify AU (i.e., the field label for an author search), when a free text search should be done. They may frequently type their search as a phrase, failing to include a command verb or data element tag. Why can't the system, if this is a common error, replace the colon with a semicolon and rerun a search? Where a data element has been specified and the search retrieved nothing, why not automatically perform a free text search?

4. *Many users use heavily posted common words in a free text search and this adversely affected system response time.* Rather than penalize the searcher who has to wait longer, why not, if this is a common occurrence, check every word entered against a table of most frequently used words and interpose a system message which says something like the following:
   - "You have entered a word that occurs in this catalog more than 500 times. Would you like to scan the following call number ranges where your term appears most frequently? We will then

display some items for you to get more specific terms or call numbers for your search.''

or

- ''You have entered a term that occurs in this catalog more than 300 times. Listed below are more specific terms which may help you retrieve fewer items.'' (List of terms would be composed of ''see also'' references from LCSH.)

As you can see from the above, transaction logs can give us data that we could not have found any other way, and the data allow us to take corrective actions, which we can predict will help a sufficient number of users.

During this formative stage of development of OPACs, analysis of transaction logs can help system designers decide which user problems warrant careful and immediate attention and identify for improvement those system features that are never used. From system monitoring statistics and/or transaction logs kept on a periodic basis at Mankato State University, the University of California, Syracuse University, and other libraries, we can learn a great deal about the use and abuse of the new feature of free text searching, the need for better vocabulary aids online, and the potential of various data elements in the catalog record for improving searches online. Without the computer's assistance, none of these data would be so readily available.

The method of more traditional catalog use studies (namely self-administered questionnaires) was the primary data collection method employed in the CLR-OPAC Evaluation Projects by the five CLR-supported organizations. Questionnaires were completed by OPAC users and non-users in all types of libraries—public, academic, academic research, community college, and federal and state libraries, and in system-wide library environments as well as single-library settings. We now have, from standard and pretested data collection instruments, results that were obtained by using standard and documented data collection procedures and analyzed by using standard and documented techniques. Thus, others can carry out similar studies, such as that at the National Library of Medicine, which utilized the CLR user questionnaire to study two prototype OPACs shortly after the five CLR-supported organizations administered the user questionnaire in 29 libraries throughout the U.S.

The five organizations have completed the following documents, which are available through ERIC: data collection manuals (Research Libraries Group, 1982, Markey, 1982), pretest instruments (Markey, 1982), actual study instruments (Ferguson et al., 1982), and a sampling plan (Baratz, 1982). ERIC is also the source of the final reports of each organization: JMA (Matthews, 1982a), Library of Congress (Anderson et al., 1982), OCLC (Tolle, 1983; Markey, 1983a; Kaske & Sanders, 1983);

RLG (Ferguson, 1982); and University of California (1982, 1983b; Larson, 1983).

The results of the aggregate of 29 libraries were covered in one of the final reports of the University of California (1982). All five organizations submitted reports to CLR about the findings of the group of libraries at which they administered the user and nonuser questionnaires. Rather than duplicating each other's reports, some of the reporting organizations adopted a viewpoint that reflected the goals and interests of the reporting organization.

For example, Ferguson's report (RLG) covered research libraries and OPAC use, and Anderson's report (Library of Congress) enumerated findings that Anderson intended to pursue at LC to improve the library's systems. In general, the reports from the five organizations about findings on the individual system (or library) level supported aggregate findings with regard to—

1. Demographic characteristics of OPAC users and nonusers:
   - Academic library patrons visit the library on a more frequent basis than do public library or federal and state library patrons. The largest percentage of first-time library users are at federal and state libraries.
   - OPAC users visit the library more frequently than do OPAC nonusers.
   - Per library visit, OPAC users at academic libraries consult the OPAC less frequently than do OPAC users at public libraries. The largest percentage of first-time OPAC users are at federal and state libraries.
   - A greater percentage of men than women are OPAC users.
   - Older adults are likely to be OPAC nonusers.
2. Online searches of the OPAC:
   - OPAC users search by subject more than any other search type.
   - OPAC users' searches at academic libraries are course-related and at public libraries are for personal interest.
   - At least 40% of OPAC users find all that they were looking for or more than they were looking for. Finding the object(s) of the online search is related to frequency of OPAC use, i.e., frequent users of the online catalog find more items of interest than infrequent users.
   - Most OPAC users first heard about the OPAC by seeing a terminal in the library.
3. Problems with OPAC features. The following features were problems at nearly every library where user questionnaires were completed:

- Increasing the result when too little is retrieved.
- Remembering what is included in the OPAC.
- Finding the correct subject term.
- Reducing the result when too much is retrieved.

4. General attitudes toward the OPAC:
   - Over 75% of OPAC users expressed favorable attitudes toward the OPAC. Nonusers also expressed favorable attitudes, but were less exuberant than were OPAC users.
   - OPAC users who found what they were searching for and/or found other things of interest in the OPAC were the most satisfied users.
   - The most frequent reasons for OPAC nonuse was that nonusers had not yet taken training sessions on use or did not have enough time to learn.

5. Improvements to the OPAC and OPAC services:
   - OPAC users want subject searching improvements, notably online related word lists and the ability to search books' tables of contents, summaries, or indexes.
   - OPAC users want more terminals, particularly in buildings other than the library.
   - OPAC users want access to titles of journal articles in OPACs.

In general, the results enumerated above held true at all 29 libraries. With regard to Figure 1, survey results shed light on the *searchers* of online public access catalogs. When there were individual differences in patrons' responses between libraries, results obtained from the focused-group interview method were especially helpful (Markey, 1983a).

OCLC's study of online public access catalogs involved focused-group interviews with library patrons and staff. A focused-group interview requires that a group moderator lead a group of about six to twelve individuals through an open, in-depth discussion. The moderator follows an interview schedule containing open-ended questions and focuses the discussion on relevant subject areas in a nondirective fashion, but is free to pursue relevant ideas that emerge in conversation. Group members challenge, interact, and stimulate one another, and their remarks provide researchers with insights, spontaneous thoughts, and language not likely to occur in individual interviews.

The results obtained through focused-group interviews also address the *searcher* in Figure 1, and, more specifically, the searcher's reactions to, perceptions of, and needs for the system and for the online interface. The OCLC interview team conducted a total of 70 focused-group interviews with library patrons, who were users or nonusers of OPACs, and with library technical and public services staff. Not only did focused-group interview results provide insight into and assistance in interpreting quantitative survey results, but they also provided a means of collecting information about groups whose needs, perceptions, and attitudes toward the OPAC were virtually lost in aggregate statistics or who were not included in the questionnaire administration, e.g., university faculty, youngsters, older adults, etc.

Figure 5 is a composite outline of the themes that emerged in focused-group interviews at the six libraries where they were conducted. Many of the remarks made in interviews were specific to system or interface characteristics of each library's particular OPAC(s). For example, patron users of one library's OPAC wanted to be able to find out whether books were checked out of the library when viewing retrieved bibliographic records; surprisingly, the library's OPAC already had such a capability. What library patrons needed was a suggestive prompt in brief record displays to direct them to full-record displays where circulation information resides. Thus, focused-group interviews can provide both information about specific patrons needs to assist local system designers in the improvement of the library's OPAC and generalized information about patron needs to assist system designers in general. The following are examples of subject areas where the focused-group interview technique was useful in interpreting questionnaire findings or in providing fresh insights into areas that questionnaire findings did not cover or scarcely covered.

FIGURE 5. Outline of Themes Emerging from Focused-Group Interviews

```
        I. EXISTING SYSTEM(S)
           A. Problems
                1. Screen (and paper) displays
                2. Order or form of output
                3. Terminal availability
                4. Downtime/response time
                5. Commands
                6. Equipment
                7. Physical layout
                8. Many postings
                9. Common words
               10. Relearnability
           B. Advantages
                1. Sophisticated search capabilities, i.e., commands/functions/
                features
                2. Time saver
                3. Printout
                4. Databases (includes union catalog capability)
                5. Circulation information
                6. Services
                7. Patron satisfaction
```

FIGURE 5. Outline of Themes Emerging from Focused Interviews (continued)

    C. Improvements
       1. Equipment
       2. New Services
       3. Enhancements to commands/functions/features
       4. New commands/functions/features
       5. Access at home or locations other than library
       6. Order of output
       7. Screen and paper displays
  II. CARD TO COMPUTER TRANSITION
    A. Patrons' Expectations of the OPAC
       1. Database contents
       2. Circulation
       3. Slowness of the OPAC
       4. About learning to search
    B. What was Good in the Card Catalog Should be in the OPAC
       1. For subject searches
       2. In general
    C. Fear of, Frustration with, or Insecurity Using the OPAC
    D. Change in Search Habits
    E. Privacy at the OPAC
 III. DATABASE
    A. Problems
       1. Finding the right subject heading
       2. Ambiguous codes and abbreviations
       3. Currentness and coverage
       4. Indexing and database accuracy
       5. Updating
    B. Improvements
       1. Subject headings and subject heading displays
       2. Shelflist-related displays
       3. Name and subject cross references
       4. Periodicals, indexes, and reference books
       5. Enhancement to the MARC record
       6. Holdings information
       7. "Community" information
       8. Other bibliographic information in the library
       9. Full bibliographic information
      10. Other databases
 IV. USER ASSISTANCE
    A. Printed Instructions
    B. Librarian's Assistance
       1. On-the-spot assistance
       2. Classes, workshops, etc.
       3. Publicizing the OPAC
       4. Librarians' needs
    C. Librarians—Expectations of Library Users
    D. Computer Assistance
       1. Computer-assisted instruction
       2. Naive and experienced modes
       3. Prompts, error messages, computer responses, help screens
    E. Predefined Search Tactics for the OPAC Interface

- Resistance of older adults to the OPAC
- Ease of acceptance of the OPAC by youngsters
- Reasons why the attitudes of OPAC users are favorable toward the OPAC
- Reasons why OPAC nonusers have unfavorable attitudes toward the OPAC and/or will never use it
- Change in library users' search habits since they began using the library's online catalog
- The nature of OPAC users' problems with specific OPAC features
- Reasons why library catalog searchers have difficulty finding the right subject heading
- Improvements and enhancements to and enrichment of the OPAC's bibliographic database and addition of information other than bibliographic information to the OPAC
- Improvements and enhancements to existing OPAC features and services and future OPAC services
- Improvements to offline and online assistance for OPAC users

One CLR-sponsored study of online public access catalogs included personal and group interviews of library staff at the three academic research libraries studied (Ferguson, 1982). The purpose of the interviews was to provide insights into quantitative questionnaire results. Library staff observations included remarks about:

- Patron acceptance, apprehension, or nonuse of online catalogs
- Patrons' difficulties with OPAC features
- Improvements and enhancements to and enrichment of the OPAC's bibliographic database
- Improvements to existing OPAC services
- Impact of the OPAC on the library, library staff, and patrons

Libraries with online public access catalogs that were studied agreed to this exposure in the hope of increasing staff and user awareness, understanding, and knowledge of their library patrons' reactions toward OPACs, e.g., their acceptance, use, attitudes, needs, etc.

In contrast, Siegel et al. (1983) conducted a comparative evaluation of two prototype OPACs at the National Library of Medicine (NLM), where the findings of the evaluation would be used to *select* an interim OPAC for NLM. Siegel employed three methods in the evaluation: (a) a self-administered questionnaire completed by OPAC users (which was the same instrument constructed for and used in the CLR-sponsored OPAC Evaluation Projects); (b) a comparison online search experiment performed by library patrons; and (c) a sample online search experiment performed by library staff. The selection of an OPAC for the NLM was very much dependent upon NLM *searchers'* reactions to the candidate systems and to the systems in online retrieval experiments and upon the results that searchers obtained in online retrieval experiments (see Figure 1).

Three methods were used simultaneously over a three-month period for the following reasons:

- Produce a comprehensive data set pertaining to online catalog use at the NLM,
- Distribute equitably and realistically the response burden among participating patrons and staff,
- Weave across the three study methods a common thread of similarly worded questions relating to a set of dependent and independent variables.

Assigning these variables in an overlapping fashion across three methods, it is hoped, yields a high degree of confidence in the strength and reliability of study findings (Siegel et al., 1983, 506).

Siegel's focus on the "strength and reliability of study findings" was important in the context of his study because of its far-reaching end result, i.e., the selection of an OPAC for the NLM. Future studies of OPACs, whose results are used to select systems or have a different, but comparable, effect on library staff and patrons, should involve at least two methods and yield data about variables that overlap across methods to ensure the "strength and reliability of findings."

All of the techniques described—self-administered questionnaires, OPAC transaction logs, focused-group interviews, feature analysis, and online search and retrieval experiments—have provided a mountain of data and definitive answers to some research questions. As OPACs are redesigned, instruments used in these recent studies could be used again for additional user feedback. By this iterative pattern of studies, we can obtain information about users that will affect decisions about online catalog design over and over again, as librarians focus on different, but interrelated, decisions about their online catalogs.

NEW DIRECTIONS FOR OPAC RESEARCH

Unfortunately, upon review of the above studies, we still do not have the answers to some of the questions relating to human factors or ergonomic aspects of online catalogs and costs of online catalogs. There is much literature available in the ergonomics and human factors areas that provides guidelines and recommendations for environments where computer terminals are used. Galitz's (1980) focus is on office automation; however, he gives simple explanations of and guidelines for the many factors present in office environments, where computer terminals are used, that require the

attention of office system designers, e.g., lighting, acoustics, workstations, user/computer system interfaces, etc., that may be generalized to
library automation environments. McCormick and Sanders (1982) published a comprehensive textbook of human factors whose chapters on
workspace and workspace arrangement, environment, and application of
human factors data cover topics of interest to the library setting, but the
discussion of these topics is generalized to the many working settings in
which computers are present. Ergonomic requirements for visual display
terminals workplaces, e.g., desk height, viewing distance, lighting requirements, etc., and health and safety aspects of working with visual display
terminals are detailed by Cakir, Hart, and Stewart (1980), and Miller
(1983). There are no basic textbooks or manuals that treat human factors or
ergonomics specifically from the library viewpoint. Tijerina (1983) has
made recommendations to help operators at VDT workstations control
glare and reduce postural problems based on a review of the human factors
and ergonomics literatures. Operators of VDT workstations who spend
many continuous hours working at VDTs will benefit from reading and
following Tijerina's recommendations.

There were a few questions in the user survey instrument that asked
OPAC users about the suitability of or problems with lighting, noise, glare,
computer equipment, and writing space, but only the focused-group interviews with library staff, who spend long hours working at VDTs,
revealed their concern about the health aspects of their job.

The recent OPAC Evaluation Projects centered primarily on users'
acceptance of OPAC features and their acceptance of the OPAC as a new
medium for the library catalog. We still need to run timed tests and
controlled experiments to get answers to how much noise, glare, lighting,
and other factors will present problems for the online catalog user, especially staff members who may spend from four to seven of their workday
hours at the VDT (Matula, 1981). The focus in such a study would be on
OPAC *workstations* and *equipment* like the video display terminal and
attached printer. Staff may complain long before public users, because
much more of their working day may be at the VDT. Our effort should be to
see that neither has cause to complain.

Information about the costs of online catalogs has been difficult to
collect. The fact that OPACs are such recent additions to libraries' automation efforts has undoubtedly contributed to this difficulty. Matthews
(1982b; Matthews & Williams, 1983) has been very outspoken about
preparing libraries for implementation of OPACs and includes cost figures
in his recent monograph on OPACs (Matthews, 1983). The Wye Conference (McCarn, 1983), sponsored by CLR in December 1982, included a
study of the costs of online catalogs, which will be published in summer

1983 (University of California, 1983a). Ghikas (1983) sent questionnaires requesting cost information from libraries that had implemented online catalogs and reported preliminary findings at the 1983 LITA/RTSD pre-conference on online catalogs. The published report will detail cost figures that Ghikas indicated at the preconference were difficult to collect.

Data from online catalog use and user studies are still only indicative and not predictive. Without a conceptual model of user behavior, we will have to continue to take the variable-by-variable approach. George D'Elia (1980) has said that "a priori model building and testing is essential to move beyond description to explanation or, ultimately, prediction of user behavior." D'Elia's research interest was in predicting public library use. Someone should begin this kind of research in the online area. The work of Penniman (1981), Borgman (1983), and Tolle (1983) in system monitoring and transaction log analysis of OPAC search sessions could be expanded to include simultaneous protocol analysis, i.e., searchers' spoken thoughts, to provide us with a truer picture of the process of and patterns in OPAC searching. Data analyses of transaction logs and protocols could be used to develop a conceptual model of online catalog use. This research area poses some great challenges.

Findings from online catalog use studies are toppling, if not negating, a number of findings of traditional catalog studies (Mandel & Herschman, 1983). This leads to the conclusion that either the present users of library catalogs have different requirements or that the capabilities of library catalogs using the new technology may be able to better match what catalog searchers have wanted to do all along, but could not do with the older forms of catalogs. This new form, the online library catalog, and its use for information searching affects the core activities of libraries. There will always be a continuum of catalog users—some novices at subject searching and other novices in the manipulation of the tool. At the online catalog, subject experts may be novice computer searchers, while others will be novice searchers, but expert computer users. For all, we need to provide optimum systems. By monitoring and polling this diverse user activity, we can make changes for the better to accommodate and meet the needs of all library patrons and staff.

More than anything else, these past two years of research have made one thing fairly clear—we have probably misnamed the new form of library catalog. Yes, it is online, but the truly operative word to describe what we as a profession must design is an *interactive* library catalog for public and staff. *How the user and the system interact* is the important thing, not that the interaction occurs "online." If our choice of adjectives will affect our focus and our efforts, then we cannot change the nomenclature too soon.

REFERENCES

Anderson, R., Reich, V. A., Wagner, P. R., and Zich, R. (1982). "Library of Congress Online Public Catalog Users Survey: A Report to the Council on Library Resources." Library of Congress, Office of Planning and Development, Washington, DC.

Atherton, P. (1980). Catalog users' access from the researcher's viewpoint: Past and present research which could affect library catalog design. *In* "Closing the Catalog: Proceedings of the 1978 and 1979 Library and Information Technology Association Institutes" (D. K. Gapen and B. Juergens, eds.), pp. 105–122. Oryx Press, Phoenix, AZ.

Baratz, D. (1982). "Sampling Plan." Research Libraries Group, Inc., Stanford, CA.

Besant, L. (1982). Early survey findings: Users of public online catalogs want sophisticated subject access. *American Libraries 13*, 160.

Borgman, C. L. (1983). "End User Behavior on The Ohio State University Libraries' Online Catalog: A Computer Monitoring Study." OCLC, Dublin, OH. (OCLC Research Report OCLC/OPR/RR-83/7.)

Cakir, A., Hart, D. J., and Stewart, T. F. M. (1980). "Visual Display Terminals." Wiley, New York.

Cochrane, P. A. (1981). Improving the quality of information retrieval . . . Where do we go from here? *Online 5*, 30–42.

Cochrane, P. A. (1982a). Classification as a user's tool in online public access catalogs. *In* "Universal Classification," pp. 260–267. (Proceedings of the 4th International Study Conference on Classification Research, Augsburg, Federal Republic of Germany, June 28–July 2, 1982.) Indeks Verlag, Frankfurt.

Cochrane, P. A. (1982b). Friendly catalog forgives user errors. *American Libraries 13*, 303–306.

D'Elia, G. P. M. (1980). The development and testing of a conceptual model of public library user behavior. *Library Quarterly 50*, 410–430.

Dowlin, K. E. (1980). On-line catalog user acceptance survey. *RQ 20*, 44–47.

Fenichel, C. H. (1980–81). The process of searching online bibliographic databases: A review of research. *Library Research 2*, 107–127.

Ferguson, D. (1982). "Public Online Catalogs and Research Libraries: Final Report to the Council on Library Resources." Research Libraries Group, Inc., Stanford, CA.

Ferguson, D., and Kaske, N. K. (1980). "On-line Public Access to Library Bibliographic Data Bases: Developments, Issues, and Priorities." OCLC, Inc., and The Research Libraries Group, Inc., Columbus, OH, and Stanford, CA (ED 195 275.)

Ferguson, D., Kaske, N.K., Lawrence, G. S., Matthews, J. R., and Zich, R. (1982). The CLR public online catalog study: An overview. *Information Technology and Libraries 1*, 84–97.

Galitz, W. O. (1980). "Human Factors in Office Automation." Life Office Management Association, Inc., Atlanta, GA.

Ghikas, M. W. (1983). Costs and funding for public access: Hard dollars and difficult decisions. *In* "Online Catalogs; Online Reference, Proceedings of the 1983 LITA/RTSD Preconference" (B. Aveney, ed.).

Hafter, R. (1979). The performance of card catalogs: A review of the research. *Library Research 1*, 199–220.

Hildreth, C. R. (1982a). Online browsing support capabilities. *In* "Information Interaction" (A. E. Petrarca, C. I. Taylor, and R. S. Kohn, eds.), pp. 127–132. (Proceedings of the 45th ASIS Annual Meeting, Columbus, OH, October 17–21, 1982.) Knowledge Industry Publications, White Plains, NY.

Hildreth, C. R. (1982b). "Online Public Access Catalogs: The User Interface." OCLC, Dublin, OH.

Hildreth, C. R. (1983). "Pursuing the Ideal: First and Second Generation Online Public Access Catalogs." *In* "Online Catalogs; Online Reference, Proceedings of the 1983 LITA/RTSD Preconference" (B. Aveney, ed.).

Jackson, S. L. (1958). "Catalog Use Study." American Library Association, Resources and Technical Services Division, Chicago, IL.

Johnson, M. F. (1982). "An Analysis of the Log of an Online Public Access Catalog." Washington University, School of Medicine Library, St. Louis, MO. (Unpublished manuscript.)

Kaske, N. K., and Sanders, N. P. (1983). "A Comprehensive Study of Online Public Access Catalogs: An Overview and Application of Findings: Final Report to the Council on Library Resources, Volume III." OCLC, Dublin, OH. (OCLC Research Report OCLC/OPR/RR-83/4.)

Kochen, M. (1970). "Integrative Mechanisms in Literature Growth: Final Report." University of Michigan, Mental Health Research Institute, Ann Arbor, MI.

Larson, R. R. (1982). "MELVYL Transaction Logs." University of California, Berkeley, CA. (Private communication.)

Larson, R. R. (1983). "Users Look at Online Catalogs; Part 2: Interacting with Online Catalogs; Final Report to the Council on Library Resources." University of California, Berkeley, CA.

Lipetz, B. (1972). Catalog use in a large research library. *Library Quarterly 42*, 129–139.

Mandel, C. A., and Herschman, J. (1983). Online subject access—enhancing the library catalog. *Journal of Academic Librarianship 9:* 148–155.

Markey, K. (1980). "Analytical Review of Catalog Use Studies." OCLC, Inc., Columbus, OH. (OCLC Research Report OCLC/OPR/RR-80/2). (ED 186 041).

Markey, K. (1982). "Pilot Test of the Online Public Access Catalog Project's User and Nonuser Questionnaires: Final Report to the Council on Library Resources." OCLC, Dublin, OH. (ED 221 165).

Markey, K. (1983a). "Online Catalog Use: Results of Surveys and Focus Group Interviews in Several Libraries: Final Report to the Council on Library Resources, Volume II." OCLC, Dublin, OH (OCLC Research Report OCLC/OPR/RR-83/3.)

Markey, K. (1983b). "The Process of Subject Searching in the Library Catalog: Final Report of the Subject Access Research Project." OCLC, Dublin, OH. (OCLC Research Report OCLC/OPR/RR-83/1.)

Matthews, J. R. (1982a). "A Study of Six Online Public Access Catalogs: A Final Report Submitted to the Council on Library Resources, Inc." J. Matthews & Associates, Inc., Grass Valley, CA.

Matthews, J. R. (1982b). 20 Qs & As on automated integrated library systems. *American Libraries 13*, 367–371.

Matthews, J. R. (1983). "Public Access to Online Catalogs: A Planning Guide for Managers." Online, Inc., Weston, CT.

Matthews, J. R., and Williams, J. F. (1983). Oh, if I'd only known. *American Libraries 14*, 408–412.

Matula, R. A. (1981). Effects of visual display units on the eyes. A bibliography. *Human Factors 23*, 581–586.

McCarn, D. B., ed. (1983). "Online Catalogs: Requirements, Characteristics and Costs; Report of a Conference Sponsored by The Council on Library Resources at the Aspen Institute, Wye Plantation, Queenstown, Maryland, December 14–16, 1982." Council on Library Resources, Inc., Washington, DC.

McCormick, E. J., and Sanders, M. S. (1982). "Human Factors in Engineering and Design." McGraw-Hill, New York.

Miller, R. B. (1983). Radiation, ergonomics, ion depletion, and VDTs: Healthful use of visual display terminals. *Information Technology and Libraries 2*, 151–158.

Mittman, B., and Dominick, W. D. (1973). Developing monitoring techniques for an on-line information retrieval system. *Information Storage and Retrieval 9*, 297–307.

Moore, C. W. (1981). User reactions to online catalogs: An exploratory study. *College and Research Libraries 42*, 295–302.

Online catalog study at NLM. (1982). *National Library of Medicine News 37*, 1–2.

Palmer, R. P. (1972). "Computerizing the Card Catalog in the University Library: A Survey of User Requirements." Libraries Unlimited, Inc., Littleton, CO.

Pawley, C. (1982). Online access: User reaction. *College and Research Libraries Research Notes 43*, 473–477.

Pease, S., and Gouke, M. N. (1982). Patterns of use in an online catalog and a card catalog. *College and Research Libraries 43,* 279–291.

Penniman, W. D. (1975). "Rhythms of Dialogue in Human-computer Conversation." Unpublished dissertation, The Ohio State University.

Penniman, W. D. (1981). "Modeling and Evaluation of On-line User Behavior: Final Report to the National Library of Medicine." OCLC, Dublin, OH.

Pritchard, S. M. (1981). "SCORPIO: A Study of Public Users of the Library of Congress Information System." Library of Congress, Washington, DC. (ED 198 801).

Research Libraries Group. (1982). "Public Online Catalogs and Research Libraries: Final Report to the Council on Library Resources." Stanford, CA.

Russell, K. W., ed. (1982). "Subject Access; Report of a Meeting Sponsored by The Council on Library Resources, Dublin, Ohio, June 7–9, 1982." Council on Library Resources, Inc., Washington, DC.

Siegel, E. R., Kameen, K. Sinn, S. K., and Weise, F. O. (1983). Research strategy and methods used to conduct a comparative evaluation of two prototype online catalog systems. *In* "Proceedings of the National Online Meeting—1983, New York, NY, April 12–14" (M. E. Williams and T. H. Hogan, comps.). Learned Information, Medford, NJ.

Tijerina, L. (1983). "Optimizing the VDT Workstation: Controlling Glare and Postural Problems." OCLC, Dublin, OH.

Tolle, J. E. (1983). "Current Utilization of Online Catalogs: Transaction Log Analysis: Final Report to the Council on Library Resources, Volume I." OCLC, Dublin, OH. (OCLC Research Report OCLC/OPR/RR-82/2.)

University of California, Division of Library Automation and Library Research and Analysis Group. (1982). "Users Look at Online Catalogs: Results of a National Survey of Users and Non-users of Online Public Access Catalogs: Final Report to the Council on Library Resources." University of California, Berkeley, CA.

University of California, Division of Library Automation and Library Research and Analysis Group (with the assistance of J. R. Matthews). (1983a). "Costs and Features of Online Catalogs: The State of the Art; Prepared for the Council on Library Resources." Unpublished draft.

University of California, Division of Library Automation and Library Studies and Research Division. (1983b). "University of California Users Look at MELVYL: Results of a Survey of Users of the University of California Prototype Online Union Catalog; Final Report to the Council on Library Resources." University of California, Berkeley, CA.

Wyman, J. (1982). "SULIRS Transaction Logs." Syracuse University, Syracuse, NY. (Private communication.)

Part 3

What Can We Do to Improve Subject Access?

Introduction

The selections in this chapter span a long period, 1963–1984. Since this is the most central theme in all of my writings, that is not surprising. This chapter more than any of the others shows how I kept weaving in and out of the two worlds of library service and information science. When I was writing for one audience, I would have to describe as almost new concepts what were known to be basics by the other group—for example, the first 1963 selection reads like an early library science textbook on automation. The third 1981 selection, on the other hand, reads like an introduction to indexing and abstracting for an Information Retrieval course. As I mentioned in several selections in Part 1, there has not yet been enough cross-fertilization in our field. I tried to do this for my students at Syracuse when I introduced Subject Analysis to them (see the 1981 selection).

The other theme throughout these selections is the admonition "not to throw the baby out with the bath water." There are many good points about traditional catalogs and indexes which will be lost if we redesign for the online environment without remembering those good points. The idea is to preserve the best of the old and work to remove the constraints of the new medium.

Besides the 1981 class notes, two papers in this section were never published (the 1979 and 1983 selections), but they received some circulation. The second 1984 selection is in press as this is being written, but I have included it here for the reader who may never see the conference proceedings volume.

File Organization: Principles and Practices for Processing and Maintaining the Collection

INTRODUCTION

From the days of the Alexandrian Museum (350 B.C.) to the present we have been faced with the problem of file organization. Ever since Callimachus, chief librarian of the ancient Alexandrian library, compiled his first catalog we have heard cries for new solutions to this problem. It is not the purpose of this chapter to provide a new solution. Instead we shall attempt to describe the paths that everyone takes in order to show how many of the seemingly new ways are basically very similar to the old. The old approaches may now be implemented in part by machines, but the sequence of operations and procedures of the machines are very often determined by the same rules that have been used for many years. The common principles of file organization will be emphasized.

The reader, it is assumed, is either a novice to the field of information handling or is more concerned with managing (rather than performing) the processes involved in file control. For this reason, the processes and the underlying theory of the *work* of information handling will not be discussed in great detail. Also for this reason, some definitions are here given to provide proper orientation for the subject.

- *File Item*—any written, printed, or otherwise recorded item of information or communication which has found its way into a file or collection. (Sometimes called *document*.)
- *File Organization*—an orderly collection of file items under control by some mechanism which permits ready access to file items upon request. (Sometimes called *document store*.)
- *File Control Mechanism*—any system employed for managing, describing, listing, and locating file items. Usually this mechanism

Reprinted with permission from *Information Handling: First Principles,* edited by Paul W. Howerton, 1963, Spartan Books.

is separated from the file collection; e.g., library catalog, journal index, bibliography. (Procedures include: cataloging, classifying, or indexing and filing.)

- *Authority Lists or Codes of Rules*—lists of accepted forms for headings and entries in file control mechanisms; rules for style and order or arrangement of descriptions of file items; guidelines to prevent inconsistency, scattering of related material, etc. (Sometimes called rules for bibliographic and subject description, the cataloging conventions, or the "grammar" of the descriptor language.)

This chapter stresses the principles and processes of effective file management which apply to any type of information handling system.

- The overall objectives of file organization.
- The basic elements of description of file items, i.e., how a document is identified in a catalog or index.
- The various stages and processes involved in information handling.
- The authority for the choice of entry and style of the file control mechanisms.
- The necessity for continuous maintenance and control of the file.

Numerous examples of file control mechanisms and their methods of employment are used in this chapter for illustration. Several of the following charts and table show the process involved, although not in great detail. It is assumed that the interested reader will fill in the details from the literature of documentation and library science, data processing and computer technology, starting with the suggested readings given at the end of this chapter.

The major theme of the chapter can be expressed as follows: the usefulness of what comes out of a file depends entirely on *what* has been put in and *how* it has been put in.

GENERAL CONSIDERATIONS

Reasons for Filing. Any collection of file items is usually organized and maintained for a particular reason. The reason will (or should) affect the procedures and devices used for organizing the file items and the rules and devices used for developing file control mechanisms. The following statements, taken from three separate sources, are all succinct and similar. They can serve as reminders of the basic objectives of *any* proposed or operating system of file organization and control.

The Five Laws of Library Science.[1] Here are five useful reminders of the function and purpose of a library:

---

[1] From S. R. Ranganathan, *The Five Laws of Library Science,* London, G. Blunt and Sons, 1957.

1. Books are for use.
2. Every reader his book.
3. Every book its reader.
4. Save the time of the reader (and the staff).
5. The library is a growing organism.

OPERATING CONSIDERATIONS[2]

1. The items selected should be pertinent to the interest of the users.
2. The interest of the person(s) indexing the items should reflect the interest of the users.
3. The keywords should be such that the user's inquiry can be easily transformed into appropriate keywords.
4. There should be no short cuts in selecting keywords at the expense of not characterizing the concepts of an item.
5. All requests should be answered with a minimum of delay.
6. Because the contents of information systems are in a constant state of change, the indexing system selected should provide for a simple method of entering new items and deleting obsoleted ones.

OBJECTIVES[3]

1. To enable a person to find a book of which either the author, the title, or subject is known.
2. To show what the library has by a given author, on a given subject, in a given kind of literature.
3. To assist in the choice of a book as to its edition (bibliographically), and as to its character (literary or topical).

Type of Control Mechanisms. The type of material in the collection may, to some extent, affect the type of file control mechanism used, as well as the rules, procedures, and devices employed to manage and maintain the file. If we disregard differences based on format of file items and take an overall view, we see a good deal of similarity among many different control mechanisms both ancient and modern. Callimachus, as head of the Alexandrian library, had to read, handle, and classify papyrus rolls and clay tablets. In a nineteenth-century library, Charles Cutter had to cope with books, manuscripts, pamphlets, and periodicals. The manager of today's scientific information center has to maintain file controls for abstracts,

---

[2]From *General Information Manual; An Introduction to Information Retrieval,* Brochure E20-8044, International Business Machines Corporation, Data Processing Division, White Plains, N.Y., 1960, p. 11.
[3]From Charles A. Cutter, *Rules for a Dictionary Catalogue,* U.S. Government Printing Office, 1876–1904.

news reports, proprietary reports, classified reports, foreign literature, translations, books, preprints, patents, and monographs. Callimachus chose to describe his material by title, author's name, *incipit* (i.e., the first few words of the text), and subject of the file item. We believe he recorded these descriptions in classified order. Cutter, as librarian of the Boston Atheneum (1868–1893), also chose author, title, and subject descriptions to identify his material, but added cross references, form (i.e., poetry, essay, etc.) and language entries to his catalogs. He displayed his descriptions in an alphabetically arranged dictionary as well as subject-classified arrangements, first in books and later on cards. Indexers and information handlers today identify documents and other material by listing many of the same basic elements of descriptions on cards or in printed lists—using conventional presses or computers. Some of these basic elements are listed below. If one examines a book or journal article carefully, many of these descriptive elements can be identified.

SOME POSSIBLE CHOICES FOR BASIC ELEMENTS OF DESCRIPTION OF FILE ITEMS

(Any or all of these elements of descriptions may be used as heading for file item descriptions—see Examples 1–4.)

1. File Item—Identification (as a bibliographic unit)
   a. Report number and title
   b. Journal title, article title, volume, issue number, page number
   c. Book or monograph title
   d. Accession number
   e. Publisher or distributor
   f. Date
2. Author or Producer—Identification
   a. Author(s), editor, translator
   b. Name of producer (sponsoring organization)
   c. Affiliation of author
3. Subject—Identification
   a. In natural language
   b. In abbreviated notation
   c. In machine language

Mechanism of File Control. Characteristics of the mechanism employed for file control and the use to which it will be put will often determine how it is prepared and the amount of description it will contain. Answers to the following questions will help determine how various mechanisms should be prepared:

- Is the library or information center staff the only user of this file control mechanism?
- Must this mechanism facilitate self-service use of the file items?
- What parts of the entire operation of file organization and maintenance does this mechanism control?
- Will this mechanism need to be followed by an intermediate step (a second mechanism) before the file items themselves are accessible?
- Will it be necessary to up-date or replace this mechanism periodically—in part or entirely?

Some of the descriptive elements may appear in one mechanism but not in another. Examples of the variety of file-control mechanism and their

FIGURE 2.1. Flow chart for maintenance of the file and indexing information—system control.

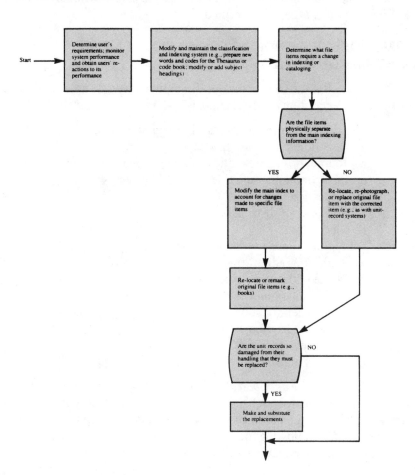

uses are given below and in Figs. 2.1 through 2.7,[4] and Examples 1–6. Careful study of this material will provide a systematic approach to most of the processes and types of control mechanisms employed in information handling. The actual step-by-step procedures for preparing file item descriptions will not be outlined here. Explanations of such procedures can be found in textbooks for library cataloging and in the opening chapters contained in the authority lists given [below].

FIGURE 2.2. Flow chart for acquisitions.

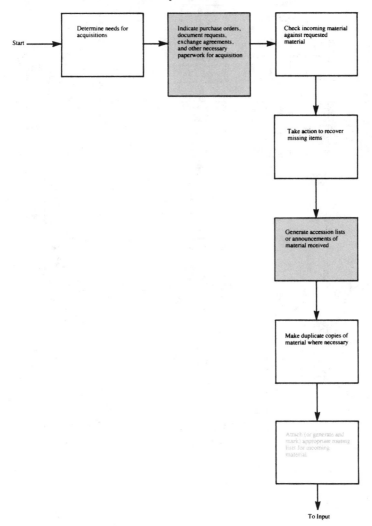

[4]Reprinted, with permission, from C. P. Bourne et al., "Requirements, Criteria, and Measures of Performance of Information Storage and Retrieval Systems" (AD 270 942), Stanford Research Institute, December, 1961, pp. 46–52.

FIGURE 2.3. Flow chart for input.

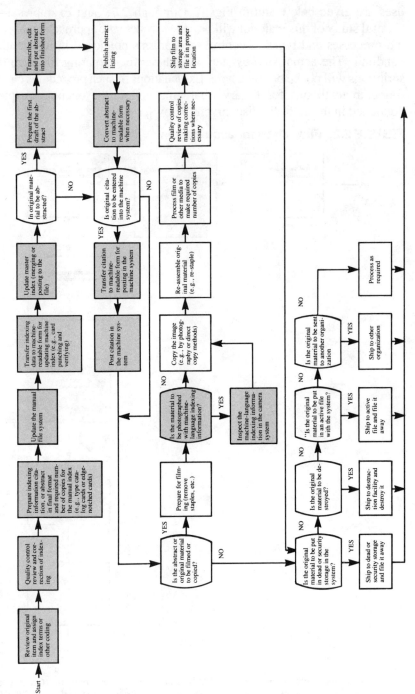

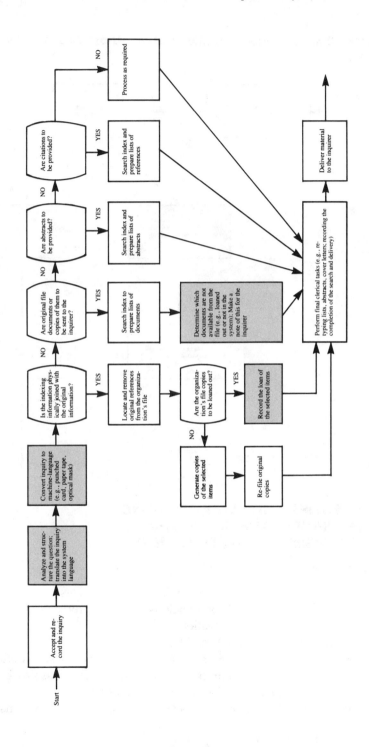

FIGURE 2.4. Flow chart for search.

FIGURE 2.5. Flow chart for refile or return of borrowed material.

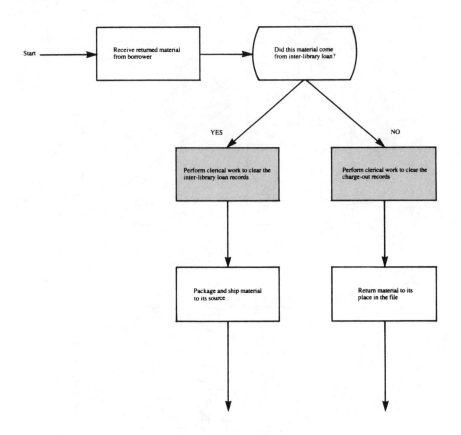

STAGES OF INFORMATION HANDLING WITH EXAMPLES OF FILE CONTROL MECHANISMS AND SYSTEM CONTROL

System Control

- Rules for choice and form of descriptive elements
- Rules for filing and abbreviations, notes, and references
- Rules for coding or notation
- Lists of preferred or forbidden terms
- Records of cross references for variant spellings, variations of author, title, or subject descriptions, and relationships between various headings in file control mechanisms
- Record of different treatment of file items in outside systems

FIGURE 2.6.   Flow chart for document requests and interlibrary loan.

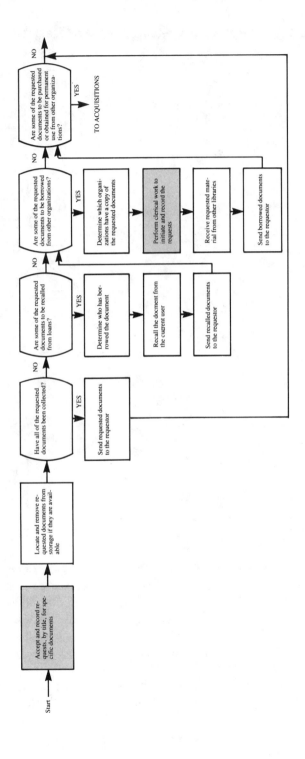

FIGURE 2.7. Flow chart for system conversion or establishment.

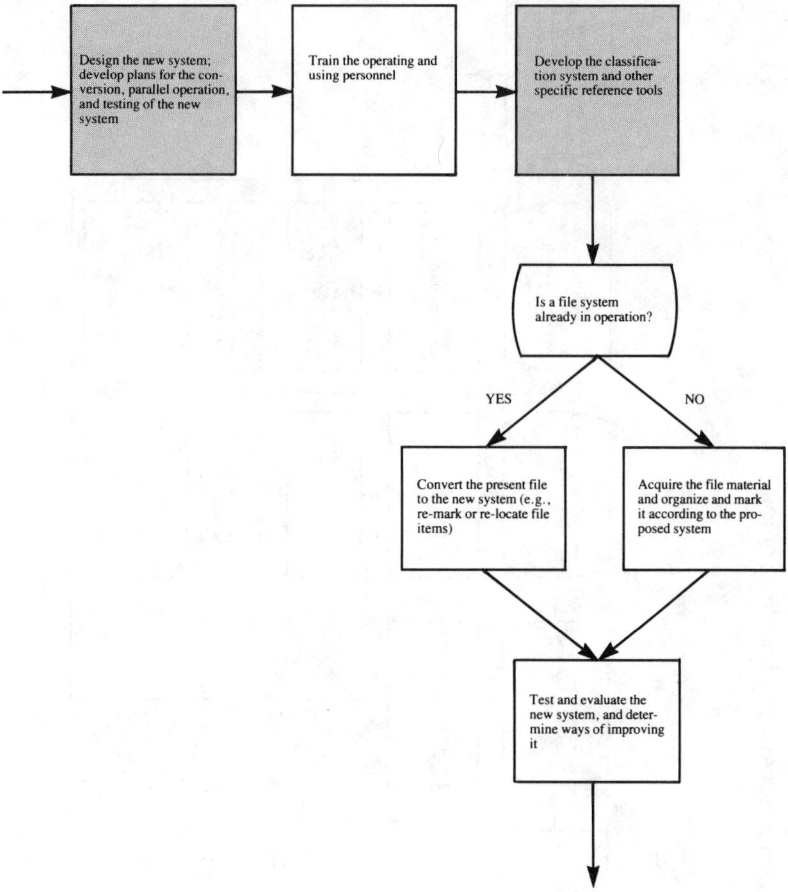

File Control Mechanisms (see also Figs. 2.1–2.7 and Examples 1–4):

1. *Acquisition stage*—request forms; order blanks; accession lists
2. *Input stage*—library catalog with author, title, subject, and cross references (card or book form); abstracts in journal format with indexes for author, subject, report number, etc.; machine-manipulated subject term and/or document cards with machine printed lists for author, date, report number, etc.
3. *Search, response, loan and return stages*—search request forms; file item loan slip; search products such as bibliographies, etc.

Figures 2.1–2.7 facilitate a systematic review of various file control mechanisms in the context of the work done in information handling. When the acquisition records, the catalog cards, and the search-request forms are viewed in terms of their function at a particular stage, one can see why they contain different descriptive elements and take various forms. The shaded areas in Figs. 2.1–2.7 represent the operations involved in the preparation and maintenance of the file control mechanisms.

Example 1, a typical library accession list, lists four descriptive elements: code for subject of file item and its shelf location, author, title, date.

Examples 2 and 3, an abstract card and a library catalog card, record these same elements of description but include many more—e.g., affiliation of author, source, number of references, subject of file item in words and two different cataloging subject codes, etc.

Example 4, a search request form used in a machine-supported document indexing system, lists subject and scope of search, code for machine search, requester, etc.

Example 5, a report number index, records report number, abstract number, and source and cost of file item. The abstract (file item) contains the other descriptive elements.

Example 6 displays a complete set of cards prepared for a file item. If the complete set for Examples 2 and 3 were shown, there would be at least four cards, one for each of the numbered headings.

EXAMPLE 1. From Engineering Library (University of Rochester, N.Y.), "Books Received, Feb. 1–Aug. 1961."

Z 06...			60
QC0020	COURANT RICHARD	METHODS OF MATHEMATICAL PHYSICS	MC
QC0271	COXON W F	TEMPERATURE MEASUREMENT & CONTROL	60
QA0261	CRAIG HOMER VINCENT	VECTOR & TENSOR ANALYSIS	43
TL0671.6	CRANDALL STEPHEN H	RANDOM VIBRATION ED2	59
QC0481	CULLITY BERNARD D	ELEMENTS OF X-RAY DIFFRACTION	56
QD0457	DANIELS FARRINGTON	EXPERIMENTAL PHYSICAL CHEM ED. 5	56
TK0140	DAVENPORT WALTER R	BIOGRAPHY OF THOMAS DAVENPORT	29
T 0175	DAVIES OWEN L	DESIGN & ANALYSIS OF INDUS EXPER ED.2 REV.	56
TN0672	DAWIHL W	HANDBOOK OF HARD METALS	55
QD0549	DEAN ROBERT B	MODERN COLLOIDS	48
TA0455	DE DANI A	GLASS FIBRE REINFORCED PLASTICS	60
TJ0009	DEL VECCHIO ALFRED	DICT OF MECHANICAL ENGINEERING	60
Q 0123	DE VRIES LOUIS	FRENCH-ENGLISH SCIENCE DICTIONARY ED. 2	51
T 0010	DE VRIES LOUIS	GERMAN-ENGLISH TECH & ENGR DICTIONARY	50
UG0630		DICT OF GUIDED MISSILES & SPACE FLIGHT	59
UG0030	DOW RICHARD B	FUNDAMENTALS OF ADVANCED MISSILES	58
VK0571.5	DRAPER CHARLES S	INERTIAL GUIDANCE	60
QD0518	DREISBACH ROBERT R	PRESS VOL TEMP RELNSHIPS ORG COMPOUNDS ED. 3	52
TA0455	DUFFIN DANIEL JOHN	LAMINATED PLASTICS	58
ZTP845	DUNCAN GEORGE S	BIBLIOGRAPHY OF GLASS	60
QA0076	ECKERT WALLACE J	FASTER, FASTER	56
QC0039	ECKMAN DONALD P	INDUSTRIAL INSTRUMENTATION	50

EXAMPLE 2.   Abstract card—U.S.A. AEC Office of Isotopes Development.

OID 1352   USSR

Ryskin, G. ÍA.
    DIFFUSION COEFFICIENT MEASUREMENT
    BY RADIOACTIVATION ANALYSIS OR THE
    ISOTOPIC DILUTION METHOD. (Izmerenie
    koeffifŝientov diffuzii metodami
    radioaktivafŝionnogo analiza i izotopnogo
    razbavleniiâ; Text in Russian.) Fizika Tverdogo
    Tela, 1, no. 6: 952-954, June 1959. 6 refs.
    DLC, Unbound periodical

In case of very small diffusion coefficients
$(D \cong 3 \times 10^{-17}$ sq cm/sec), the customary methods
of diffusion analysis contain many errors. In these
cases, activation or isotope dilution analyses give
more exact results. The first method consists in the
preparation of the diffusing metal and the diffusion
medium, the annealing of both, the separation of the
metal and medium, the bombardment of the medium
                                              (over)

1. Metals--Diffusion
    --Measurement
I. Ryskin, G. ÍA.
II. Akademiiâ Nauk SSSR.
    Leningradskiĭ Fiziko-
    Tekhnicheskiĭ Inst. [Acad.
    Sci. USSR. Leningrad Inst.
    Physics and Technology]

U.S. Atomic Energy
Commission
Office of Isotopes Development

EXAMPLE 3.   Library of Congress Catalog Card.

Canada. *Bureau of Statistics.*
        Revised index of industrial production, 1935–1957 (1949=
    100) Ottawa, Queen's Printer, 1959.

        122 p.   diagrs., tables.   26 cm.

        At head of title: Dominion Bureau of Statistics.   Research and
    Development Division.   Business Statistics Section.
        "Reference paper (formerly no. 34, revised)"
        Bibliography: p. [49]

        1. Canada—Indus.   I. Title: Index of industrial production, 1935–
    1957.

    HC111.A4   1957   338.0971   59—46136

    Library of Congress   [8]   Printed in U. S. A.

EXAMPLE 4. Machine Search Request form. (Reprinted with permission from "Machine Literature Processing; Demonstration Manual," Technical Information Group, Paulsboro Laboratory, Research Department, Socony Mobil Oil Co., Inc., Rev. April 1, 1960, p. 24.)

MACHINE SEARCH REQUEST   RD-1565M Rev. (7/25/58) (Front)

NAME Harold Myers   SMX — 56-16C

PHONE 204   DATE April 16, 1956

SUBJECT:
Hydrocarbon isomerization - primarily gasoline range - C_5 to C_{12}

BACKGROUND:
Bodkin has searched Patents for this subject back to 1908 (via C.A.) and previous T.I.G. search on butane isomerization and subject file search through T.I.G. file

SCOPE:
Journal References from 1952 to ICTA 11 No. 14

Patent References from 1952 to PG 11 No. 8

PRINCIPAL CODE: 11 F   12 5/8   13 R   14 .6/8

STATISTICS: DATE

Number of References Retrieved	182	
Time for Machine Data Processing	6 hrs.	4-20-56
Time for Reference Duplication	3 hrs.	4-25-56
Total Time	9 hrs.	

CODE DEFINITIONS:

F. 5/8 - hydrocarbon isomerization
G. 9 - catalytic process
R. z/6/8. 1 - gasoline or naphtha hydrocarbon fraction
R. z/6/8. 7 - normally gaseous hydrocarbon fraction
R. (no z) 6/8. 2 or 3 or 4 or 5 - aliphatic·hydrocarbons
                              1-20 carbon atoms

These records are part of a continuous operation of file control. All the processing steps involved in preparing these separate file control mechanisms should be integrated to increase consistency and efficiency and to reduce duplicate effort.

EXAMPLE 5. Report Number Index in Nuclear Science Abstracts.

Report No.	Abstract No.	Availability		Report No.	Abstract No.	Availability
75	16-11052	$1.25 OTS as PB-161576		65	16-10102	Dep.(mc), $8.60(fs), $3.05(mf) OTS
NEVIS–	(Misc.)			103	16-10265	Dep.(mc); $1.60(fs), $0.80(mf) OTS
99*	16-10958			106	16-11236	Dep.(mc); $8.60(fs), $2.96(mf) OTS
NMI–	(Misc.)			127	16-11343	Dep.(mc); $4.60(fs), $1.55(mf) OTS
2100	16-10435	Dep.(mc); $1.60(fs), $0.80(mf) OTS		128	16-10133	Dep.(mc); $2.60(fs), $0.83(mf) OTS
2102	16-10534	Dep.(mc); $1.60(fs), $0.80(mf) OTS		149	16-10103	Dep.(mc); $7.60(fs), $2.60(mf) OTS
7210	16-11150	Dep.(mc); $4.60(fs), $1.46(mf) OTS		ORO–		
7242	16-11233	Dep.(mc); $1.60(fs), $0.80(mf) OTS		482	16-10189	Dep., $0.50(OTS)
NP–	(AEC File No. for Non-AEC Reports)			501	16-11153	Dep., $2.00(OTS)
10640(Suppl.I)	16-10535	OTS		524	16-10541	Dep.(mc); $1.10(fs), $0.80(mf) OTS
11300	16-10816	Dep.(mc)		PATENTS	(British)	3s. 6d. each, U.K. Patent Office
11301	16-10817	Dep.(mc)		889,234	16-11106	
11303	16-10308			889,294	16-10655	
11305	16-9743			889,307	16-10095	
11312	16-10454			889,351	16-10448	
11314	16-10188			889,388	16-11173	
11344	16-11335			889,424	16-11310	
11347	16-10482			889,427	16-10449	
11355	16-10959			889,465	16-11107	
11356	16-10536			889,477	16-10138	
11357	16-9731			889,536	16-11174	
11370	16-10620			889,554	16-10115	
11385	16-11336			889,636	16-11175	
11387	16-10537			889,674	16-10116	
11388	16-9977			889,702	16-11176	
11390	16-10818	Dep.(mc)		889,758	16-11177	
11400	16-10538			889,775	16-10042	
11402	16-10539			889,890	16-11108	
11404	16-11337			889,902	16-11178	
11405	16-10132			889,923	16-10139	
NP-tr–	(AEC File No. for Non-AEC Translations)			890,061	16-10140	
821	16-10489	OTS		890,145	16-10092	
846	16-10370	Dep.(mc); $1.60(fs), $0.80(mf) JCL		890,330	16-11179	
848	16-9854	Dep.(mc); $3.60(fs) $1.28(mf) JCL		890,410	16-10117	
NR–					16-10141	

INDEX 94

REPORT NUMBER INDEX

Ready-made file control mechanisms (available from Library of Congress, H. W. Wilson Company, Nuclear Science Abstracts, etc.) are often used. For the reader interested in flow charts giving more details of these operations, the book, by L. Schultheiss and D. Culbertson is recommended.[5]

AUTHORITY FOR THE CHOICE OF HEADING AND ENTRY OF DESCRIPTIVE ELEMENTS

Since the time of Callimachus we have been striving for standardization of the rules for library catalog entries. Such standardization, by creating uniformity, would facilitate use of several file collections for a given problem. Homemade and ready-made file control systems would be more compatible. Left to our own devices without any record of previous practice, we have often found it necessary to formulate a new set of rules, but the work of earlier "information handlers," when examined carefully,

---

[5]Louis A. Schultheiss, Don S. Culbertson, and Edward M. Heileger, *Advanced Data Processing in the University Library,* Scarecrow Press, 1962.

EXAMPLE 6. Complete Set of Cards for a File Item—prepared for machine literature searching. (Reprinted with permission of Technical Information Group, Paulsboro Laboratory, Research Department, Socony Mobil Oil Co.)

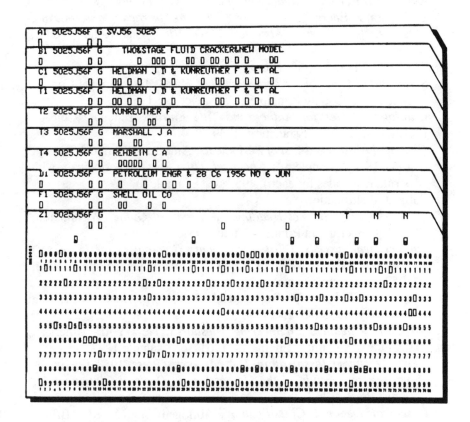

can be found to be useful for directions in preparing a library catalog card or input for a computer-operated index. Some early projects for standardization have not been successful or of lasting value. The reasons for this are many. On the other hand, the efforts of others have stood the test of time; the work was soundly based on fundamental principles and objectives. Less lasting efforts quite often were merely compendia of existing variations. All these attempts and efforts at standardization stand out as major accomplishments in a field where variety and rule-of-thumb practices have too often been the rule, not the exception. A few of the best-known sets of rules or authority files for standardized entry and description are listed below.

EXAMPLES OF RULES (OR AUTHORITY FILES) FOR UNIFORMITY IN FILE ITEM DESCRIPTIONS

1. Description of File Items
   Rules for Descriptive Cataloging in the Library of Congress, 1949.
   U.S. Atomic Energy Commission. *Guide to Abstracting and Indexing for Nuclear Science Abstracts* (TID-4576), Oak Ridge, Tenn., 1961.
2. Author and Title Identification
   Statement of Principles Adopted by the I.F.L.A. International Conference on Cataloging Principles, Paris, October 1961.
   Cataloging Rules for Author and Title Entries. 2nd ed., Chicago Amerian Library Association, 1949.
   Chemical Abstracts—List of Periodicals. American Chemical Society, 1961 (See Example 9); *Chemical Titles* (list of periodicals with permanent codes for each), 1962 (see Example 8).
3. Subject Identification
   D. J. Haykin, *Subject Headings: A Practical Guide,* Washington, D.C., Government Printing Office, 1951.
   Subject Headings Used in the Dictionary Catalogs of the Library of Congress, 6th ed., Washington, D.C., Government Printing Office, 1957 (with supplements).
   Sears List of Subject Headings, 8th ed., New York, The H. W. Wilson Company, 1959 (see Example 13).
   A.I.Ch.E. Chemical Engineering Thesaurus, New York, American Institute of Chemical Engineers, 1961 (see Example 12).
   Dewey Decimal Classification, 16th ed., Forest Press, 1958 (see Example 15); and *Guide to the Use of Dewey Decimal Classification,* Forest Press, 1962.
   Universal Decimal Classification, Abridged English ed., British Standards Institution, 1961 (see Example 14).
4. Arrangement of Items in File Collection
   "LC Book Numbers" (in *Cataloging Service Bulletin* 14, January, 1948).
   IBM 650 Automatic Information Retrieval Program, n.d.
   A.L.A. Rules for Filing Catalog Cards, Chicago, American Library Association, 1942.

These and other rules can help determine:

   (1) How to find the proper descriptive elements and entry points for a given file item.
   (2) How to choose the best terms for entry of new groups of file items.
   (3) How to integrate these new entries into the file control mechanism, yet avoid conflict, confusion, and duplication.

Whether the entries for the file control mechanism are obtained ready-made or are "homemade," it is absolutely necessary to record the decisions being followed for entry and style of descriptive information used in this particular mechanism. Most systems have come to an untimely end because this rule was ignored. Following the rule may be extremely dull, wearing, and time-consuming, but such records are the *sine qua non* of

EXAMPLE 7. Abbreviations used in catalogs of the Engineering Library, University of Rochester, N.Y.

```
                          ENGINEERING LIBRARY
                  BOOKS RECEIVED FEB. 1 - AUG. 1, 1961

                            ABBREVIATIONS

   ABS         ABSOLUTE                    ABSB     ABSORBTION, ABSORB
   ADV         ADVANCE, -S, -D, -MENT      AGIT     AGITATION
   ALUM        ALUMINUM                    AMER     AMERICAN, AMERICA
   ANAL        ANALYSIS, ANALYTIC          ANN      ANNALS, ANNALES, ANNUAL
   ANTILOGS    ANTILOGARITHMS              APP      APPLIED
   APPL        APPLICATION                 ASSN     ASSOCIATION
   BIOL        BIOLOGY, BIOLOGICAL         BR       BRITISH
   BROADCSTRS  BROADCASTERS                CAL      CALCULUS
   CHEM        CHEMICAL, CHEMISTRY         CIRC     CIRCUIT
   CO          COMPANY                     COEFF    COEFFICIENT
   COLLOQ      COLLOQUIUM                  COMP     COMPOUNDS
   COMPR       COMPRESSIBLE                COMB     COMBUSTION
   COND        CONDUCTOR                   CONF     CONFERENCE
   CONG        CONGRESS                    CORR     CORRELATION
   DICT        DICTIONARY                  DIOX     DIOXIDE
   CYL         CYLINDER, CYLINDRICAL       DIFF     DIFFERENTIAL
   DISSOL      DISSOLUTION, DISSOLVE       DRAFT    DRAFTING
   DSGNRS      DESIGNERS                   DETERM   DETERMINATION
   ECON        ECONOMIC                    EDUC     EDUCATION
   ELEC        ELECTR, -ICAL, -ONICS, -ICITY  ELEM  ELEMENTS, ELEMENTARY
   ENG         ENGINE                      ENGR     ENGINEERING
   ENGRS       ENGINEERS                   ENGY     ENERGY
   EQUILIB     EQUILIBRIUM                 EQUIV    EQUIVALENT
   EST         ESTIMAT, -E, -ING, -ION     EXCHR    EXCHANGER
   EXPLOSN     EXPLOSION                   EXPER    EXPERIMENTS
   FLU         FLUID                       FOUND    FOUNDREYMEN
   FNDN        FOUNDATION                  FUND     FUNDAMENTAL
   GAS         GASEOUS                     GEN      GENERAL, GENERALIZED
   GEOG        GEOGRAPHY                   GRAD     GRADUATE
   HI          HIGH                        HS       HISTORICAL WORK
   HT          HEAT                        INDUS    INDUSTRIAL, INDUSTRY
   INFO        INFORMATION                 INST     INSTITUTE, INSTITUTION
   INT         INTERNATIONAL               INTL     INTERNAL
   INTRO       INTRODUCTION                IONIZ    IONIZING, IONIZATION
   J           JOURNAL                     KIN      KINETIC, KINETICS
   LIQ         LIQUID, LIQUIDS             LAB      LABORATORY
   LT          LIGHT                       LIT      LITERATURE
   LOGS        LOGARITHMS                  MAN      MANUAL
   MANAG       MANAGEMENT                  MANUF    MANUFACTURER, MANUFACTURING
   MAT         MATERIALS                   MATH     MATHEMATICS, MATHEMATICAL
   MC          MONOGRAPHIC CONTINUATION    MEAS     MEASURE, MEASUREMENT
   MECH        MECHANICS                   METALL   METALLURGY, METALLURGICAL
   METH        METHOD, METHODS             MIXT     MIXTURE
   MOLEC       MOLECULAR                   NAT      NATURAL
   NATL        NATIONAL                    NO       NUMBER
   NUM         NUMERICAL, NUMERISCHE       NOS      NUMBERS
   NS          NEW SERIES
   ORG         ORGANIC                     OPERA    OPERATIONAL
   PART        PARTIAL                     PHYS     PHYSICS, PHYSICAL
   POLYM       POLYMERS                    PRAC     PRACTICAL
   PHILA       PHILADELPHIA                PRESERV  PRESERVATION
   PRESS       PRESSURE                    PRIN     PRINCIPLES
   PROC        PROCESS, PROCESSING         PROB     PROBLEM, PROBLEMS
```

EXAMPLE 8. Code for periodicals in *Chemical Titles,* with list of words not used in permuted title index. (Reproduced with permission of American Chemical Society, from April 5, 1962 issue.)

successful file organization. So long as few rules exist on paper, and so long as decisions are made on the basis of individual understanding of the problem and individual conception of underlying principles, inconsistency in practice is inevitable.

Editor's Note: Example 8 was not available for more legible reproduction.

EXAMPLE 9. Full title of periodical, with abbreviation (in boldface type), library location, history of title changes, place of publication. (Reproduced with permission of American Chemical Society, owners of copyright, from *Chemical Abstracts List of Periodicals*, 1961, page 327.)

EXAMPLE 10. From "Thesaurus of ASTIA Descriptors," 1st ed., May 1960, p. 113.

EXAMPLE 9   EXAMPLE 10

EXAMPLE 11. From "ASTIA Thesaurus Code Manual," June 1961, p. 8.

EXAMPLE 12. Page C19 of *Chemical Engineering Thesaurus, a Word-book for Use with the Concept Coordination System of Information Storage and Retrieval:* Part Two, Chemical Terms, 1961. (Reproduced with permission of the American Institute of Chemical Engineers.)

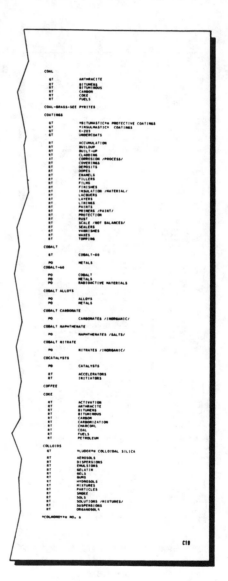

EXAMPLE 11   EXAMPLE 12

EXAMPLE 13. Excerpts from pp. 127 and 157 of *Sears List of Subject Headings*, 8th ed., New York, H. W. Wilson Company, 1959.

Chemistry, Organic—Synthesis 547.
    See also **Plastics; Synthetic products**
    x Chemistry, Synthetic; Synthetic chemistry
    xx **Plastics**

Chemistry, Pathological. *See* **Chemistry, Medical and pharmaceutical; Physiological chemistry**

Chemistry, Pharmaceutical. *See* **Chemistry, Medical and pharmaceutical**

Chemistry, Photographic. *See* **Photographic chemistry**

Chemistry, Physical and theoretical 541
    See also

Atomic theory	**Molecules**
Atoms	**Nuclear physics**
Catalysis	**Periodic law**
Colloids	**Quantum theory**
Crystallography	**Radiochemistry**
Electrochemistry	**Thermodynamics**
Ions	

    x Physical chemistry; Theoretical chemistry
    xx **Nuclear physics; Physics; Quantum theory**

Chemistry, Physiological. *See* **Physiological chemistry**

See Dewey Decimal Classification & Relative Index for interpretation of numbers

---

        —univer.
    xx **Examinations**
Colleges and universities—Finance. *See* **Education—Finance**
Colleges and universities—U.S. 378.73
    x American colleges; U.S.—Colleges and universities
Collisions, Railroad. *See* **Railroads—Accidents**
Colloids 541.3; 547; 660.29
    xx **Chemistry, Physical and theoretical**
Colonial architecture. *See* **Architecture, Colonial**
Colonial furniture. *See* **Furniture, American**
Colonial history (U.S.) *See* **U.S.—History —Colonial period**
Colonial life and customs (U.S.) *See* **U.S. —History—Colonial period; U.S.— Social life and customs—Colonial period**
Colonies 325.3
    Use for works on general colonial policy. Works on the policy of settling immigrants or nationals in unoccupied areas are entered under **Colonization.** Works on migration from one country to another are entered under **Immigration and emigration.** Works on the movement

See Dewey Decimal Classification & Relative Index for interpretation of numbers

EXAMPLE 14. *Universal Decimal Classification.* **1961 Abridged English Edition. British Standards Institution B.S. 1000A., p. 67.**

54.084	Measuring apparatus. Instrumentation
.09	Uses. Applications
541	**GENERAL, THEORETICAL AND PHYSICAL CHEMISTRY**
541.1	**Physical chemistry**
.11	Thermochemistry. Chemical thermodynamics
.12	Chemical mechanics. *Cf.* 536.77
.121	Chemical statics. Equilibrium. Phase (systems)
.122	Homogeneous equilibrium
.123	Heterogeneous equilibrium
.124	Chemical kinetics. Mechanism of reaction
.125	Reaction limits. *Cf.* 541.42
.126	Spontaneous reactions. Explosions
.127	Velocity of reaction: mass action law
.128	Catalysis. *Cf.* 542.97
.13	Electrochemistry. Electrolysis
.131	Electrochemical equivalent. Faraday's laws
.132	Electrolytic dissociation. *Cf.* 537.56
.3	Hydrogen ion concentration (pH)
.133	Conductivity and resistance of electrolytes
.134	Electromotive force and (potential) series
.135	Electrolytes and electrolysis. Polarization
.14	Photochemistry. *Cf.* 535.217
.15	Radiation chemistry. *Cf.* 541.28
.17	Topochemistry (regional reactions)
.18	Colloid chemistry. Capillary chemistry
.182	Disperse systems. Colloids, suspensions, etc.
.2/.3	Gas dispersion medium. Aerosols
.2	Mists. .3 Smokes, dusts
.4/.6	Liquid dispersion medium. Sols, etc.
.41	Emulsions. .45 Foams
.6	Sols, gels and suspensoids
.8	Solid dispersion medium. Solid sols
.183	Contact systems. Adsorption
541.2	**Atomic theory.** *Cf.* 530.14; 539.18
.22	Stoichiometry: proportions, equivalents
.23	Atomic weight. Determination (*by* .08)
.24	Molecular weight. Determination (*by* .08)
.25	Atomic and molecular volumes
.26	Parachor
.27	Chemical properties revealing atomic structure
.28	Radiochemistry: dependence of chemical properties of radioactive atoms on nuclear changes. *Cf.* 541.15; 546.79
541.4	**Chemical compounds.** *Cf.* 54–3
.41	Generalities. Compounds and mixtures
.42	Reactivity and decomposition (limits)
.43	Free elements
.44	Hydrogen compounds. Hydrides
.45	Oxides. Acids. Bases
.451	Oxides. 542 Acids. .454 Bases
.456	Neutral oxides. .457 Amphoteric oxides
.459	Peroxides
.48	Salts
.481	Basic. .483 Neutral. .484 Acid
.486	Double salts
.49	Complex compounds
541.5	**Valency. Affinity. Bonds**
* .56	Electrovalency: [1957] *see* 541.573
.57	Bonds, linkages
.571	Primary, homo- and semi-polar bonds. Covalency
.572	Secondary, chelate, dipole, resonance bonds
.573	Ionogenic bonds. Electrovalency
541.6	**Chemical structure in relation to properties**
.61	Structural formulae

541.62	Chemical isomerism. Tautomerism. Mesomerism
.63	Stereochemistry. *Cis*-transisomerism
.64	Macromolecular chemistry. *Cf.* 678
.65	Optical properties. Mutarotation, etc.
.651	Chromogenic groups, batho-, hypso-, vario-, halo-chromism. Chromo-isomerism
.66	Thermochemical properties. *By* :536.42, etc.
.67	Electrical, magnetic properties
.68	Mechanical properties and chemical structure
.69	Physiological properties: taste and smell; odori-, aromato-phoric groups. *Cf.* 543.92
541.7	**Allotropy. Physical isomerism**
.72	Enantiotropy
.73	Monotropy
541.8	**Solutions and solubility in general.** *Cf.* 532.73
541.9	**Classification systems** for elements and compounds, *e.g.* Mendeleev's periodic table
542	**EXPERIMENTAL AND PREPARATIVE CHEMISTRY. Laboratory equipment and technique.** 542.4/.9 *broadly as* 66.04/.09
.1	Laboratory fittings, layout, etc. *Cf.* 727.5
.2	Laboratory apparatus and technique in general
.23	Vessels. Beakers. Dishes. Funnels. Tubes
.24	Stands. Tripods. Tongs and holders
.26	Tubing. Jointing, sealing materials. Lutes
.3	Volume, density, weight determination. Graduated, calibrated vessels. *By* :531.73/.75
.4	Heating and cooling. *Broadly as* 66.04
.47/.48	Drying. Distillation
.5	Flame. Blowpipe
.6	Treatment and operations with liquids: solution, filtration, washing, etc. *Broadly as* 66.06
.7	Operations with gases. *Broadly as* 66.07
.8	Electrical and electrochemical operations
.9	Chemical operations. *As* 66.09, *e.g.*
.92	Destruction. Decomposition
.97	Catalysis. *Cf.* 541.128
543	**ANALYTICAL CHEMISTRY.** *Cf.* 614.3
	Denote material analysed by colon here, and determined constituent(s) by further :546, *etc. Optionally, omit the 543 and colon together the UDC nos. for material and constituent* (*adding* .06), *e.g.* 543:669.14:546.28 *or* 669.14:546.28.06
	Analysis of steel: determination of silicon
−1	State of material under analysis. *As* 54–1
−4	Reagents, standard solutions, indicators, etc.
543.05	Sampling and preparation (Equipment by :542.)
543.06	Procedure, types of analysis and determination
.061	Qualitative analysis, detection, identification
.062	Quantitative analysis, estimation
.063	Micro-analysis, semi-microanalysis
.064	Trace analysis, impurities
543.08	Measurement and instrumentation. Physical, instrumental methods of analysis. *As* 53.08
543.2	**Special chemical methods of analysis and assay**
.21	Wet separation, assay. Gravimetric analysis
.219	Spot tests
.22	Dry separation, assay: cupellation, bead, blowpipe
.24	Volumetric analysis, titration: alkali- and acidi-metry, oxidation and reduction, precipitation
.25	Electroanalysis, electrolytic and other methods
.253	Polarographic analysis

EXAMPLE 15. *Dewey Decimal Classification,* 16th ed. 1958, p. 439. (Reproduced with permission of Forest Press, Inc.)

Physics

532	**Mechanics of fluids**

Former heading: Liquids, hydrostatics, hydraulics

Comprehensive works on mechanics of gases and liquids

For mechanics of gases, see 533; hydraulic engineering, 627; hydraulic power engineering, 621.2

[.076]   Problems and questions

           Class in 532.9

[.083]   Tables

           Class in 532.9

.1   **Mechanics of liquids (Hydromechanics)**

           Including properties of liquids [*formerly also* †541.32]

           Class pressure [*formerly* †532.1] in 532.2

           For hydrostatics, see 532.2; hydrodynamics, 532.5

.2   Hydrostatics

           Equilibrium and transmission of pressure [*formerly* †532.1] in liquids

           Class buoyancy [*formerly* *532.2] in 532.3

.3   Buoyancy [*formerly* *532.2]

           Including Archimedes' and Pascal's principles, stability of floating bodies

.4   Density measurements of liquids

           Including specific gravity measurements, e.g., hydrometry

.5   Hydrodynamics

           Liquids in motion

.51   Theories of liquid flow

           Including kinetic theory of liquids

532.52–532.6 Liquid flow variations

.52   Flow thru orifices and nozzles

           Including rate of discharge, pressure-velocity relationships

.53   Flow over weirs and spillways

           Including gravitational problems, gravity model tests

.54   Flow thru pipes and tubes

.55   Flow thru bends and irregular enclosures

EXAMPLE 16. Code and coding sheet for machine-literature processing.... File item being analyzed is same as that described in Example 6.

The following examples of authority files illustrate how decisions can be recorded and how instructions for the use of this or that term or symbol can be explained.

Examples 7–9 record abbreviations and codes for words and journal titles. These records control manual and machine operations. Examples 1 and 7 are obviously related. Examples 8 and 9 control two different but related publications, *Chemical Titles* and *Chemical Abstracts*. Example 8 includes a record of words which the machine will bypass in performing permuted title indexing. Example 9 includes a library location record for each journal as well as information and cross references regarding changes in the titles of journals.

Examples 10–14 are taken from several subject authority lists. They demonstrate the variety of ways a subject may be controlled. Example 10 provides information about style of heading, scope of heading, cross references to related headings or descriptor. Example 11 gives the machine code for Example 10. The code is primarily a serial code, not a subject code.

Example 12 is based on the same basic rules for choice of entry but the relationship to other terms is shown by symbols: GT (generic to), RT (related to), or PO (post on).

Example 13, in two parts, is similar to Example 10. It also records the terms to use, cross references and scope notes. The Dewey Decimal Classification (DDC) numbers are more than a machine code as they represent the subject in a classification scheme.

Example 14, which is one page from the Universal Decimal Classification (UDC), shows how this classification would arrange colloids in an arrangement similar to that suggested in Example 13. Careful examination of this classified arrangement of Theoretical and Physical Chemistry and the terms under *Colloids* in Examples 10–13 will show that they all treat the subject in a similar way. The UDC, when originally devised, used the DDC as a guide.

Example 15, taken from the 16th edition of the DDC, is an excellent record of decisions and revisions, scope notes, and cross references. Such a record is invaluable if a mechanism is to grow and change with the file collection.

All of these examples are published. When used within a given organization they serve as the basis for the record of decisions in that

---

Editor's Note: Example 16 was not available for legible reproduction.

organization. If the printed version is not followed exactly, it should be modified. See for instance, Example 13, where the classification number and cross references have been marked or changed.

Example 16 is a combination code sheet and record of decisions. It records the subject analysis which produced Example 6. Example 16 is taken from a book which is a combination of a code of rules and a manual of procedures, forms, and techniques. As such it is an excellent example of a valuable working tool, instructional manual, and guide for the user of the file collection and file-control mechanisms. To be most useful, such records of decisions must be complete and must record all the decisions and rules governing processes in flow-chart order. Several of these manuals do exist, but more are needed. Sometimes they exist only in single-copy editions—a file of 3 × 5 cards in the top-drawer of the chief cataloger's desk. [Editor's Note: Example 16 was not available for legible reproduction.]

SUBJECT CONTROL OF FILE ITEMS

Rules governing the bibliographical elements which serve to identify file items in a collection are not completely standardized, but they are more or less consistent from one file-control mechanism to another or, from one information-handling system to another. The arrangement will vary more than the form of the elements. Mechanisms for subject control of file items are another matter. Part of the problem is the burden of tradition, plus the fact that designers and architects of subject control mechanisms do not always consider user requirements. Often the systems they develop do not reflect a fundamentally sound approach to subject analysis. Dr. Frank Landee states the repercussions of such an approach:

> We are so impressed with the equipment we have, and what it will do, and with the wonderful promises that manufacturers make to us with regard to the next generation of equipment, that we think that we have a wonderful thing going for us. So we feel we've got a whole lot of ready-made answers and we spend our time looking for questions that these answers will fit. . . . Why do we computer-oriented people make such a backwards approach? Really we don't have much choice. We come to meetings like this or we read the literature and publication that is going to engulf us all. And there we sit with all those nice answers and we think, "Oh Boy! When those people with such problems hear about us they'll be beating our doors down." And so we sit, and sit, and sit, and sit—nothing much happens. . . . I used to think they were holding out on us. I dont think so any longer. On the whole, I don't think they understand their own problems very well. . . . Secondly, I am sure they don't really understand what it is that we can do for them. . . . This works both ways, of course. *We don't really understand them or their problems too well, either.* You need some way of attracting their attention, and some way to start them thinking

and some method of feedback so you will *know what they are thinking*.[6] (Italics added.)

Both user requirements and a disciplined technique for subject analysis are necessary if a useful and reliable subject control mechanism is to be devised. The development of such a mechanism can be carried out in a systematic way within the framework of the processes shown in the flow charts (Figs. 2.1–2.7). A suggested method for such a systematic development is given below. The work of members of the Classification Research Group and S. R. Ranganathan provided the basis for this method.

STEPS IN THE CONSTRUCTION AND APPLICATION OF A SYSTEMATIC METHOD FOR HANDLING THE SUBJECT CONTROL OF FILE ITEMS

1. Come to an understanding of the commonly accepted *categories for* dividing the 3 characteristics of a given field of knowledge to be handled.
2. Isolate every distinctive category; recognize every *relation* between and among the categories.
3. Organize the categories (of terms and characteristics) into suitable facets (the sum total of the divisions of each aspect of these grouped categories); assign an order in which the facets are to be used (the most helpful sequential arrangement).
4. Fit the schedule of facets with a notation that will permit the fully flexible combination of terms that is needed.
5. Provide an index for the terms or characteristics as they appear. The alphabetical key to the subjects will lead into the materials in the systematic arrangement at the exact level of approach and will list all the distributed facets.
6. Analyze the content of a file item according to the prescribed facet formula; fuse the terms listed under each facet, so that the subject content of the file item is described adequately. Apply the prescribed notation to the fused or faceted analysis. Add to the alphabetic index any new terms generated by the analysis.[7]

When the construction and application of such a method is considered in such general terms, it becomes clear that it is not realistic to speak of indexing *or* classification, natural language *or* symbolic notation. The

---

[6]*American Documentation,* 13, January 1962, pp. 39–40.
[7]For more detail and examples, the following are recommended: B. C. Vickery, *Faceted Classification* (London, 1960), S. R. Ranganathan, *Elements of Library Classification* (London, 1959), and *Classification and Indexing in Science* (New York, 1959).

intellectual effort and the basic procedures are similar, even if the physical manifestations of the effort (and the quality of the mechanism) are different. In S. R. Ranganathan's article on natural, classificatory, and machine languages,[8] he explains the interrelationships of these languages and the control processes associated with them; the example shown earlier also points to the same conclusion:

> Natural language is frequently inadequate for scientific communication and description. In semantics and mathematics, artificial languages have been developed for mechanizing the process of thinking. The development of any artificial language requires the initial use of natural language as a meta-language, but the artificial language thus created (e.g., classificatory language) can then be used as a meta-language to develop another artificial language of greater efficiency for a particular purpose (e.g., machine language). Classification involves the naming of subjects in an artificial language of ordinal numbers or symbols. Machine language is not made of symbols but of mechanical "bits" such as positioned punches and magnetic spots. The parallelism between the emergency and development of classificatory language and machine languages, and the increasing recognition of the need for classification in constructing expressive rather than purely extensional code symbols in machine coding, suggest the value and economy of using classificatory language as a bridge language between natural and machine language. This is the case whether the machine language is used for literature searching or in searching for entities having a combination of specified properties or values.

The "language" chosen for subject control of file items determines what comes out when searching for file items and how quickly it comes out. No amount of speed will lessen the degree of disappointment if the quantity of irrelevant material or missed file items is inordinately high. If adequate control is not built into the subject control mechanism before searching begins, the search product will be disappointing. The theme of this chapter bears repeating: the usefulness of what comes out of a file depends entirely on what has been put in and how it has been put in.

Vickery lists several levels of control of descriptor language. He makes no distinction between natural language or notation schemes, giving both as examples of the same level of control. The following data are based on Vickery's list,[9] with new examples added:

---

[8]*Annals of Library Science,* 6, September 1959, pp. 65–8.
[9]B. C. Vickery, *On Retrieval System Theory,* London, Butterworth & Co., Ltd., 1961, pp. 50–51.

SOME SCHEMES FOR THE CONSTRUCTION OF SUBJECT CONTROL MECHANISMS

1. Terms selected from documents—no rules for barred terms (except connecting words, etc.).
   Examples: Early Uniterm files
   Early KWIC (Keywords in Context) indexes
2. Terms selected from documents—rules to bar synonyms.
   Example: Amateur alphabetical indexes and subject heading lists
3. Terms in document fitted to fixed vocabulary of generic descriptors.
   Examples: Early classification schemes
   Systems based on thesauri
4. Specific and generic descriptors linked hierarchically.
   Examples: Dewey Decimal Classification (DDC)
   A.I.Ch.E. Chemical Engineering Thesaurus
   Library of Congress (LC) Subject Heading List
5. Display of relationships by analysis of categories of terms used to describe subject content.
   Examples: Faceted classifications
   Semantic factoring—(Western Reserve University System) WRU
6. Correlation of descriptors.
   Example: Correlative indexes
7. Weighting of descriptors, interfixing rules, regulated sequence of descriptors, role indicators.
   Examples: Faceted classifications with relational indexing
   Some alphabetical indexes based on thesauri, with links and roles designated
   Probabilistic indexing

The notation of a classification scheme or the numerical code for machine manipulation (see Examples 11, 14, 15) are devices for mechanizing the arrangement which has been decided upon by the originator of the system. Sorting and replacement are facilitated by this notation. It is important to remember when applying the notation that sorting for specific as well as generic searches must be facilitated. If the notation is merely an accession-order arrangement, this fact may facilitate some sorting procedures during the acquisition stage but it will not permit efficient sorting for subject searching. Step 4 [above] is sometimes overlooked by those who erroneously believe that the speed of the machines which are now available can overcome this inherent weakness in accession arrangement of entries in the file-control mechanism.

In summary, the basic operations in subject control are the analysis of the subject of each individual file item into its elements and the synthesis of these elements into a preferred systematic arrangement. It is not necessary to enumerate specific subjects in an authority file of terms or classification scheme, but only to state the matrix from which the specific subjects can be deduced. Additions will always have to be made to meet the objectives stated very early in this chapter. Continuous revision and evaluation are musts for any method. The method described [above] is called *facet analysis* by Ranganathan. As one reviewer of his work said, "undoubtedly [it is] of value since it seems to be constantly in the process of being rediscovered, renamed, and applied, with some degree of variation, on a fairly extensive scale by documentalists."

J. Farradane[10] summarizes the American search for subject control mechanisms, and in so doing makes an accurate comparison of several existing methods:

> . . . In the United States the well-known difficulties of traditional "family-tree" classifications led most of those concerned with detailed information retrieval to the abandonment of classification as a principle, and to the adoption of various methods of keyword coordination instead. This had not given the desired results, and various attempts have been made to rediscover means of obviating synonyms, express relations between concepts, and indicate cognate and generically related terms, but the rediscovery of classification is apparently yet to come. One of the latest gimmicks to be thus tried is the "thesaurus principle."
>
> . . . For information-retrieval the word thesaurus has, however, been loosely used for a system of standardizing terms and avoiding synonyms, which would be better done by a cross-reference index, and for indicating higher- and lower-class terms (very arbitrarily), which would be much better done by a classified system. Furthermore, different thesaurus lists are being prepared by workers in different special subjects, so that coordination of effort will soon be impossible. . . . The rather vague methods of possible combination of concepts are far from adequate, and the synthesizing methods of "facet" classifications offer the possibility of more accurrate denotation of complex subjects.

Farradane may be too critical of the American scene, but careful scrutiny of seemingly new methods of subject control does show an underlying similarity to the ordered array and grouping found in older methods.

10J. Farradane, "The Challenge of Information Retrieval," *Journal of Documentation,* 17, December 1961, p. 237.

MAINTENANCE OF COLLECTIONS AND CONTROL MECHANISMS

Figures 2.1 and 2.7 describe in general terms the operations involved in conversion from one system to another or in the maintenance (revision, up-dating, etc.) of an operating system. Standard textbooks on technical processes in libraries cover the details of inventory, weeding, rebinding, and withdrawal processes involved in maintenance of the file collection. It is not necessary to repeat these lessons here.

The operations involved in maintenance of the file control mechanisms are not adequately covered in standard texts. Systematic review of subject headings, cross references, codes and terms in the thesaurus, additions and revisions of the notation and index of a classification scheme are arduous tasks left in the hands of a few. Often only the originator of the system devotes time and effort to these tasks.

The people applying the rules do not often have time to think about the logic underlying them. Time is rarely allotted for a systematic review of the application of the rules at regular intervals. These conditions, it goes without saying, require correction if the system is to work with optimum efficiency.

The file control mechanism—all the entries and descriptions of file items—and the rules governing these operations need constant review. When a new file-item description is being prepared it is usually checked against the authority file. A system-wide check is also necessary. An experienced librarian who has just made the switch from conventional library cataloging to the type of cataloging shown in Example 1 offers this advice on the maintenance of file control mechanisms: "Don't forget lots of emphasis on cross-references and tracings, tracings, tracings [other subjects in the catalog under which this item may be found]. In other words, if you don't keep track of what you did or where things are, you'll regret it. We learned that the hard way." The librarian gave the following example:

> Coxon, Wilfred F
> Coxon, W F

A large number of "corporate bodies" had to be redone because of variations in the way they had been abbreviated:

> Royal Society
> Royal Soc London

A systematic review of all the file-control mechanisms and the application of the rules will improve efficiency and service. Staff discussions of the rules and procedures will point up varying viewpoints and practices.

Such discussions often lead to improvements in the rules and instructions as well as greater consistency in the application of the rules. A comparison of several systems of file organization is most illuminating. The examples of subject-control mechanisms in this chapter, for example, could serve as the basis for such a comparison. Comparison of the various forms of the other basic elements of description (names of authors, abbreviations, etc.) or cross references could also serve as a constructive way of reviewing one's own system.

If all the stages of information handling are in flow-chart order, all the file-control mechanisms under continuous review, and all the rules and procedures susceptible to change and improvements, the information handler need not fear the words of Ecclesiastes: "Of making many books there is no end."

The newcomer to the field of information handling might well heed the advice of A. R. Meetham, reviewer of B. C. Vickery's book, *On Retrieval System Theory* (see footnote [above]) "a newcomer . . . would have been saved six months, spend mainly on the retrieval of information about retrieval, if the book had been ready earlier. No one else now needs to enter the field through quite such a prickly hedge."[11]

For the reader interested in the devices and techniques (coding, punched-card systems and the like), a new book by Charles P. Bourne is recommended: *Devices and Techniques for Information Processing, Storage and Retrieval,* New York, John Wiley & Sons, Inc. (in press).

Other than these books and those cited in the chapter, a regular reading or scanning of the following periodicals will turn up either articles of interest or reviews and references to pertinent literature: *Journal of Documentation, American Documentation, Revue de la Documentation, Library Resources and Technical Services, Special Libraries,* and *Journal of Chemical Documentation.*

A few cumulative indexes, bibliographies and annual reviews for this field are available. Besides those which appear in the above periodicals, there are: (1) Charles P. Bourne, "Bibliography on the Mechanization of Information Retrieval" (Stanford Research Institute, 1958 to date); (2) *Bibliographie de la Documentation et de la Bibliothèconomie,* (International Federation for Documentation, 1951 to date); (3) Paul C. Janaskc, ed., *Information Handling and Science Information; a Selected Bibliography, 1957-1961* (Washington, D.C., American Institute of Biological Sciences, 1962); (4) M. Spangler, *General Bibliography on Information Storage and Retrieval* (General Electric Company, Computer Department, Technical Information Series R62CD2, 1962).

---

[11]*Journal of Documentation,* 17, December 1961, p. 251.

An Action Plan for Indexing

To supplement the considerations in the two preceding letters, I should like to point out that the AIP Documentation Research Project benefits greatly from the advice of its advisory committee, composed mostly of working physicists who have some interest in documentation problems. Its members are Paul Camp, chairman, R. T. Beyer, F. G. Brickwedde, M. M. Kessler, Gilbert King, J. B. H. Kuper, Jerry B. Marion, K. G. McKay and S. Pasternack. A nuclear physicist has been a regular consultant for several years and a consulting chemical physicist was added to the staff last year.

The Documentation Research Project, supported by the National Science Foundation, has embarked on a plan for indexing physics research papers that should result in the improvement of the many reference retrieval tools for physicists: subject indexes to the journals that they read, abstract journals that they search, new current awareness tools, mechanized information centers, and even the new SDI systems (Selective Dissemination of Information). The plan has been evolving for some time. The 1962 survey of physicists to acquire data needed to develop a reference retrieval system (PHYSICS TODAY, April 1962, p 52) provided the basic information for its development. Experiments with aid-to-indexing forms (PHYSICS TODAY, February 1965, p 76) were another part of the overall plan. A US-UK *Science Abstracts* working party coordinates the efforts in the United States and Great Britain. . . . Thanks to the cooperative effort of physicists, journal editors, indexers, computer specialists, and documentalists, we are well along toward meeting the objectives stated below.

OBJECTIVES OF THE AIP-DRP INDEX PROJECT

1. *Multicoordinate index vocabulary* for various fields of physics designed for mechanized retrieval and mechanized production of indexes.
2. *Improved indexing* of papers *at time of publication* to provide quicker access to content of papers by way of various abstract-

Reprinted with permission from *Physics Today*, Vol. 1, No. 1, pp. 58–59 (1966). © American Institute of Physics. Written while Associate Director of AIP/DRP.

journal indexes, information and data centers, and mechanized retrieval systems.

3. *Combined and compatible vocabulary* of categories and index headings for analytic subject indexes in AIP journals and for *Physics Abstracts* and its indexes.
4. *Author assistance* in analysis of papers for indexing in journal and abstract journal indexes.
5. *Centralized index production* at AIP for volume and cumulative journal indexes, for both author and subject indexes, for all AIP journals (including translation journals).
6. *Common style* of entry for each article, letter, and abstract in author and subject indexes.

It appears essential to undertake this work in units that correspond to the various major fields of physics. Dividing physics into the most appropriate categories is a problem in itself and we need to consult with physicists about it. This is one of the objectives of our current study of *Physics Abstracts* and *Current Papers in Physics*. Without waiting for a best answer, indexing studies are in progress in the following fields:

1. *Nuclear physics.* Continued effort at Lawrence Radiation Laboratory (Livermore) and USAEC/DTIE, Oak Ridge, and UKAEA (Harwell) to develop multicoordinate indexes, review and revise existing indexing vocabulary used in AIP, AEC, EURATOM, and *Physics Abstracts* systems. Plans are to expand the effort with assistance from the NASNRC Nuclear Science Subcommittee on Techniques for the Distribution of Scientific Information.
2. *Chemical physics.* Continued effort at AIP-DRP and Columbia University under the direction of Dr. Rita G. Lerner to improve subject indexes in the *Journal of Chemical Physics* and build a multicoordinate index for chemical physics. Review and revision of the *Physics Abstracts* index in this area is also planned.
3. *Acoustics.* Continued effort of the JASA Editorial Committee to improve the journal index and develop new index vocabulary for this area.
4. *Solid-state physics.* Expanded effort to review and revise existing indexes under the direction of AIP journal editors, with the cooperation of physicists in the APS Solid-State Division.
5. *Geophysics, plasma physics, etc.* Review and revision by individual cooperating physicists of index headings used in *Physics Abstracts*.
6. *Optics, mathematical physics, instrumentation, etc.* Assistance from editors and authors of recent journal papers by way of the aid-to-indexing forms to improve index vocabulary.

7. *Overall index vocabulary control*. A subcommittee of the AIP Publication Board has been appointed to effect greater uniformity in AIP journal indexes and to study index headings used in *Physics Abstracts*.

8. *Interface problems* with the information systems designed for other disciplines. By cooperating with the Atomic Energy Commission, Engineers Joint Council, American Chemical Society, American Society for Metals, Bell Telephone Laboratories, Institution of Electrical Engineers and others in their thesaurus revision and other efforts, AIP hopes to achieve greater compatibility among physics, chemistry and engineering information systems. The plans for this cooperative effort are only in the beginning stage at this time.

As these projects advance, we intend to keep the physics community informed so that everyone who has a contribution to make will be encouraged to make it.

Universal Subject Access (USA); Can Anyone Do It?

First, let's *define* what UNIVERSAL SUBJECT ACCESS is.

It's *universal*—not just *U.S.*, not just *libraries,* not just *books,* not just *library catalogs.* It has no limits, no geographical limits, no limit on type of information service, and no limit on type of information item. The term does not necessarily refer to a centralized subject authority file.

At a Subject Access Workshop[1] sponsored by the Council on Library Resources (CLR) in October, 1978, the assembled invited participants had 20 definitions of *subject access.* The Planning Committee members for that workshop were composed of representatives of a large research library, a book publisher, NFAIS and LC, Chemical Abstracts and a university-computer-based searching service. Their own definition of subject access reflected a focus much wider than some individual participants who were only thinking of the subject tracing on a library catalog card. Their definition reads as follows:

> By subject access is meant:
>
> *the use* of words, phrases or symbols to represent the intellectual content of recorded knowledge for purposes of *organization* and *retrieval.*

This definition does *not* state *who* does the organizing or the retrieving and that is very *important.* Nor does it state *what* the recorded knowledge items are nor *where* they are. Subject access is seen both as a process performed by information professionals and librarians *and* the process performed by persons trying to retrieve the information.

At that workshop my definition was somewhat different and yet related to the CLR workshop definition.

> By subject access I meant:
>
> The *approaches* to subject matter in a collection. The approach may be *systematic* (as in the classified arrangement of books on

---

Never published; written in 1979. Based in part on presentation at Dallas American Library Association Meeting.

a library shelf) or the approach may be *topical* (as in the subject headings in the card catalog) or the approach may be "*natural or free*" (as in the title words or words in an abstract or subject description if they are for matching with query words online).

These definitions emphasize that both processes: *subject cataloging* and *retrieval* by the searcher are part of *subject access*.

Please Note: USA (Universal Subject Access) would *not mean* a Single Standard Authority File for Subject Cataloging. It should mean the appropriate access systems of a library and other information collections which make possible the accessing of information by users anywhere.

Is *USA desirable*? Maybe not from some points of view because certain power bases in librarianship and the information would fear central control and the changes it would bring.

But it is *necessary* from a user's point of view who has or will have even more information at his/her fingertips but will become frustrated and confused by the lack of vocabulary control or aids for searching across data bases/indexes/catalogs.

So. . . Desirable? Yes. Possible? Yes. If we benefit from past errors and false starts.

We need to start with some understanding about how pieces will fit together.* For example:

1. Within a *USA* effort, individual libraries or information services need not, would not, and should not be expected to adopt a common subject indexing language which they would apply to all items.

2. In the *USA* system, a *responsible agency* would work to *maintain* subject authority files for specific library networks or designated data services where controlled vocabulary was used for the production of special tools, e.g., subject catalog to a specific library collection, a published index or abstracting journal, etc. (See Figure 1)

3. The transmission of information to users would call for the use of a communication or switching mechanism to mediate between local subject heading "languages" if these files are linked in networks.

4. There would need to be a *responsible agency* for developing this switching mechanism between sublanguages and coordinating sys-

---

*At the time of presentation of this paper I had not yet seen the final report of the Subject Access Workshop (ref. 1). Nevertheless my remarks here and their recommendations excerpted in appendix are very similar. The striking difference between us is their pessimism about any centralized effort. Instead of creating a responsible agency outside present groups, they would have present groups step forward to carry out their action recommendations.

tems for user access. This agency would have no special audience of users of its own. It would be responsive to those closest to user audiences. (See Figure 1)

5. For cross data base searching, the responsible agency would develop *searching thesauri* for *online* users.

FIGURE 1: Universal Subject Access—Configuration with Responsible Agency

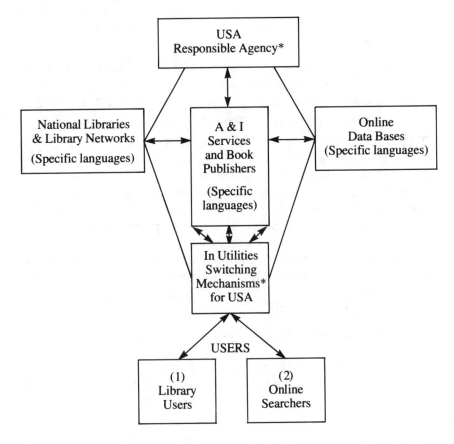

*Functions:
1. System for switching from one language to another
2. Searching thesauri for online catalog and data base searching.
3. Coordinate revision efforts for universal subject access tool.

There are *both political* and *technical* problems in developing a *USA* effort. We would need to tackle it as the *Bibliographic Service Development Program* at the Council on Library Resources has been described in *Library Journal* this spring (April 1, 1979, p. 771–72).

In my opinion, the 5-year plan for a *Bibliographic Service Development Program* at CLR (with C. Lee Jones, Program Officer) may provide impetus for *coordination* of efforts of existing bibliographic networks which could lead to a *USA* effort. To do this, BSDP would have to attempt coordination of libraries, book publishers, bibliographic utilities and A & I services. Without such an effort, the concept of *USA* is not possible.

For *political* reasons we need a *responsible agency* to:

a. coordinate/develop parts of the *USA* effort and to manage the switching mechanisms between *parts,*
b. research common problems and launch review and revision projects which have *system-wide effects* like LCSH.

Why should LCSH be revised only by staff at LC when it is a national subject authority file used in small, medium and large libraries, in library networks and at other information sites (PAIS, etc.)?

For *technical* reasons we need a *responsible agency* which can review the impact and utility of new technology in the USA effort. We need to assess how the NLM efforts across several online files, which has resulted in an online thesaurus revision and control program, can be of use in a *USA* effort.

Unfortunately, within the information world, our record of national subject access efforts is dismal. It is a record of no starts or small starts which got us *nowhere*.

To mention two such efforts:

1. *1969 ALA Atlantic City:* Institute on the Subject Analysis of Library Materials.
   Papers by 1) J. Harris, 2) J. Daily and 3) W. Kurmey, among others, pointed to weaknesses in LCSH and other efforts at vocabulary control.

Ten years ago in 1969, after that conference, an ALA committee was founded: ALA-RTSD-CCS-CPRX Subcom. MICRO. Its recommendations were for ALA/LC Liaison Group to develop a theoretical framework for LCSH. NOTHING CAME OF IT. An autopsy at this point might point to its demise because of the hierarchical problems of any subcommittee of a committee of a section of a division of ALA.

2. The mid 1960's saw attempts at compatibility of index vocabularies among the abstracting services. It began with the Datatrol concordance project for ASTIA-AEC-NASA thesauri. Not much

came of it because the computers at the time could not process all the word-form variants and maintain records of relationships. Also this effort at coordination was not carried out by any responsible agency. Not COSATI or any other group became such an agency.

Let's learn from past efforts. Where should we put a *USA* effort? May I suggest that we *not* put such an effort in ALA. Also, do not put such an effort in LC. It would be better to put a *USA* effort in a place like IFLA, NCLIS or CLR where all libraries and information services can be heard from.

If we were to start with an LCSH revision project at such an agency, the printed debate between J. Fitzgerald and C. Ishimoto of Harvard College Library (in *American Libraries,* May 1979, p. 233) and Michael Gorman could be aired and resolved. As they pointed out there is a need for collaboration of bibliographic utilities, LC, and other interested and responsible agencies in revising LCSH. They consider Michael Gorman's idea of a *bibliographic democracy (American Libraries,* March 1979, pp. 147–49) as unworkable. I would tend to agree, but even William Welsh sees that LC should not go it alone (*American Libraries,* June 1979, p. 293) and he speaks of a "distributed system."

My suggestion of a *responsible agency* is not as narrowly focused as either the Harvard, Gorman, or LC positions. No one has expressed plans for what is to happen to LCSH in the 1980's. How would LC's present revision effort fit into a *USA* effort?

We all agree that the LCSH system is in need of revision,[2] but *consensus* on the most useful structure for a national subject headings system is *nonexistent,* and LCSH's terminology is now considered less than useful in many types of libraries, especially in those designing and implementing online public access catalogs (OPAC). The history of LCSH changes is spotty as the three figures (3–5) at the end of this paper attest. Something needs to be done.[3] A responsible agency for the *USA* effort might be a first step.

A *responsible agency* for *USA* could tackle such a problem as revision of LCSH in the context of new technology for vocabulary control and for online catalog use, new means of subject access across various library networks and data bases serving different types of users could be devised. The Library of Congress should not have to support such an effort alone, for LCSH is now an international subject authority file which many libraries and information services use. The coordinated effort at LCSH revision and other subject access projects could be undertaken by such a *USA* agency. It could coordinate its effort with international efforts such as UNISIST/ BSO, ICSU/AB, etc. I am not suggesting another ALA committee, but a funded and responsible agency for research and development.

The modernization of LCSH, along the lines suggested by modern thesaurus construction (see Figure 2) and related standards[4] and research reports[5] could be the first effort of such a responsible agency for *USA* with decentralized, but coordinated work. It could follow somewhat the lines of the ERIC/Vocabulary Improvement Project[6] about which I am familiar. It would not be an easy effort. Is it politically and technically acceptable and possible? I don't know. I think a centralized effort—only at LC—is impossible because it imposes too great a burden on them.

A revision of LCSH under the aegis of a USA agency might be the basis for the first edition of *USSH, The United States List of Subject Headings,* if this USA were to begin primarily as an American effort. Such a list would represent LC practice as preferred but would represent means for subject switching as well. If feasible this would follow along the lines of multilingual and macro/micro thesaurus developments.

FIGURE 2: Displays and Features in a Modern Thesaurus

Lead-In Term ⟍   **ALPHABETICAL DISPLAY**

➤ Achievement Prediction

USE ACHIEVEMENT TESTS

➤**ACHIEVEMENT RATING**   *Jul. 1966*
CIJE 184   RIE 267
Descriptor ⟋   SN The process of comparing
                         achieved performance and
                         the ranking assigned to
                         compared performances
                     UF Achievement Comparison
                     NT Grades (Scholastic)
                     BT Evaluation
                     RT Academic Achievement
                         Academic Records
                         Achievement
                         Achievement Tests
                         Awards
                         Grading
                         Merit Rating Programs
                         Pass Fail Grading
                         Progressive Retardation
                         Rating Scales
                         Report Cards
                         Student Evaluation

ACHIEVEMENT TESTS *Jul. 1966*
CIJE 460   RIE 127
UF Achievement Prediction
NT College Entrance Examinations

FIGURE 2: Displays and Features in a Modern Thesaurus (continued)

TWO-WAY HIERARCHICAL TERM DISPLAY

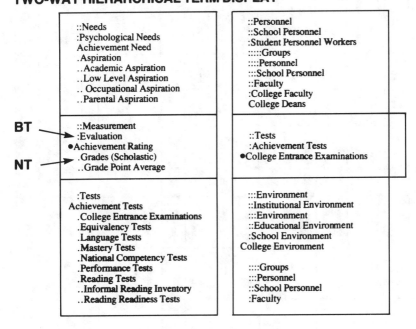

BT

NT

ROTATED DESCRIPTOR DISPLAY

FIGURE 3:   Record of Changes for 14 Related Subject Headings in LCSH (Editions 1-8)

Subject Headings	Date of First Appearance as Lead-In	Date of First Appearance as Subject Heading	Date of Last Appearance	Date of Greatest Change	Features of LCSH: Direct/Indirect	Class code and/or range	Number of X References	Number of s.a. References	Number of XX References
Feminism	1928	1974		1974	Indirect	range	2(1974-5-)	5(1974)▲ 10(1977)	1(1974-5-)
Sex (Biology)		1910-14		1975		-1974: range 1974-: 3 class codes	1(1910-14)▲ 7(1973) 5(1975-)	0(1910-14)▲ 2(1975-)	1(1975-)
Sex (Psychology)		1910-14		1957		range▲1948 1948▲class code	2(1957-1975)	1(1943-48)	1 4th and 5th editions only
Sexual Ethics		1910-14		1943		class code	3(1943)▲ 4(1975-)	4(1910-14)▲ 12(1977)	7(1943) ▼5(1977)
Wife Beating		1910-14	Discontinued in 1974	1943	Indirect (1977)	class code			1(1943) 2(1974-5-)
Woman		1910-14	Discontinued in 1974	1973		3 ranges and 3 class codes	2(1943) -2(1973)	ca 10(1910-14)▲ ca 21(1973)	5(1943-73)
Women		1910-14		1974	Indirect (1974-)	3 ranges and 3 class codes	3(1974-)	15(1974)▲ 21(1977)	3(1974) ▲(1977)
Women-Rights of Women		1910-14	Discontinued in 1974	1974		ranges	3(1943)▲ 5(1974-)	2(1910-14 -1974)	2(1943-1974)
Women's Rights		1974			Indirect	ranges	5(1974-)	3(1974-)	2(1974-)
Women-Social and moral questions		1910-14	cancelled in 1974 as term for post 1940 literature	1974			1(1943-1973)	5(1910-14)▲ 8(1973)	2(1943) ▼1(1973)
Women, Negro		1919				class code	2(1943-)		1(1957-)
Women as authors		1910-14	1973	1973	Indirect (1943)▲	range	1(1943-1973)	3(1910-14)▲ 4(1973)	3(1943) ▲4(1973)
Women Authors		1973 (8th Edition)		1973	Direct	range	2(1973-)	4(1973-)	2(1973-)
Women in Charitable work		1910-14		1943		class code		3(1910-14-)	4(1943) ▲5(1977)

FIGURE 4: Record of Changes of one Heading in LCSH (Editions 1–8)—From Inclusion to Cancellation

Subject Heading: WOMAN—SOCIAL AND MORAL QUESTIONS	Features in LCSH: Qualifier	Direct/ Indirect	LC Classi- fication	Scope notes	s.a.	X	XX	Subdivisions
1st edition					Divorce Prostitution Woman–Charities Woman–Crime Woman–Societies Woman and clubs			
2nd edition					Same, plus: Woman in public life			
3rd edition					Same			
4th edition					Same	Feminism	Ethics Social problems	
5th edition					Same	Same	Same	
6th edition					Same, plus: Delinquent women purged: Woman—Crime	Same	Same	
7th edition					Same, plus: Women in public life	Same	Same	
8th edition					Same, plus: Vietnamese Conflict, 1961- —Women World War, 1939–45—Women	Same	Same	
1974–75 suppl. WOMEN-Social and Moral questions	cancelled			Here are entered works written, for the most part, before 1940 and cataloged before 1974 which moralize on the position of women in society. This heading is no longer used by Library of Congress.			Ethics	

FIGURE 5: Record of Changes in Cross Reference Structure in LCSH (Edition 1 to 8)

Subject Heading: SEXUAL ETHICS	Features in LCSH: Qualifier	Direct/ Indirect	LC Classi- fication	Scope Notes	s.a.	X	XX	Subdivision
1st edition			HQ 31		Chastity, Free love, Prostitution, Sex and Religion			
2nd edition			Same		Same as above			
3rd edition			Same		Same, plus: Birth Control, Hygiene, Sexual			
4th edition			Same		Same, plus: Sex crimes	Ethics Sexual purity Social purity	Birth Control, Conception— Prevention, Ethics, Hygiene, Sexual Marriage, Prosti- tution, Social ethics	
5th edition			Same		Same as above		Same, *but* purged: Birth control	
6th edition			Same		Same, plus: Promiscuity		Same	
7th edition			Same		Same, plus: Dating		Same	
8th edition			Same		Same, *but* Dating qualified— Dating (Social custom)	Same, plus: Sexual Behavior	Same	—Juvenile literature
1974–75 suppl.			Same		Same as above	Same	Same	Same
1974–76 suppl.			Same		Same as above	Same	Same	Same
1977 suppl.			Same		Same, plus: Contraception, Premarital sex Sterilization (Birth Control) Moral and religious aspects	Same	Same, *but* purged: Conception—Prevention	Same

Such an effort would require several planning steps, which might parallel ERIC/VIP, but there would of necessity have to be different arrangements for collecting background data and responses from users.

The following might be considered a blueprint for the USSH Project over a 3–5 year period.

1. Under the aegis of BSDP at CLR, *appoint a USSH Project Coordinator*—someone who is acceptable to the LC Processing Department Head and Subject Catalog Division Chief. Not necessarily an LC employee, but he/she must be an experienced LCSH cataloger with administrative or research experience.

2. *Appoint a USSH Project Executive Committee* (3–6 members) who can represent the various types of libraries who use LCSH and would use USSH as their system/network subject indexing language.

3. *Form a USSH Project Group* (no more than 40 members) to serve as a "manageable" sounding board with semi-annual meetings as the project proceeds. The makeup of this USSH Project Advisory Group would represent large subject areas and types of user groups. All those serving on such a committee or in such a group would *themselves* be involved in the USSH effort, at least on a part-time basis.

4. The USSH Project Coordinator and Executive Committee would draw up plans and a timetable for systematic data collection, LCSH review and revision, and USSH development. They should also draw up tentative rules and procedures for revision (see Step 7 below).

5. *The data collection phase* would involve steps to obtain information on each main heading in LCSH (print and nonprint and subdivision practice). Once collected it could be assembled in a way similar to Figures 3–5 of this paper, but in addition, *usage data* at LC and elsewhere would have to be collected. (Name subject headings might be excluded from such a study as they fall under National Name Authority File Project.) A representative group of library catalogs (in card form and online) could be searched for usage data over a time series (e.g., before 1940, 1941–1970, 1971–date) as well as a search of MARC and REMARC. Searching the file in one or another of the library networks and large OPACs could uncover usage data by type of library as well as information about other main headings used and not "controlled" by the present LCSH editor, entry vocabulary, etc.

6. This assembled data, plus the display of each main heading in LCSH would form the *Background Information Sheets* which

would be *assembled* by broad subject areas and *reviewed* by cooperating library staffs and representatives of user groups. This *Review Phase* would help to collect revision suggestions. (This step could parallel that phase in ERIC/VIP almost exactly.) The USSH Executive Committee would make the distribution of the assignments of terms to cooperating groups. (The existing AAT Project is an example of this stage.)

7. Priorities, principles and procedures for the *decentralized revision effort* would have to be established. The first order of business would have to be decisions about the USSH would look like—more like LCSH or more like the ERIC, MESH or Psychological Abstracts thesauri (see Figure 2). Would date of adoption, scope note, indexing history, RT, BT-NT relationships be delineated? Would each heading be linked to one or more LC class number or range? What form of heading (inverted, natural order, etc.) would be preferred?

8. A *communication mechanism* to facilitate a decentralized but coordinated revision effort would have to be implemented—perhaps something more advanced than the *ERIC Play Thesaurus*. This tool (see Figure 6) incorporated suggestions, comments, and approved changes into the existing thesaurus file so that all 20 ERIC/VIP reviewers, spread out across the country, could see the suggested changes and their impact on other terms as the work progressed. Ten different editions of this ''Play Thesaurus'' came out over the course of one year. (The MESH online file with software to provide for search and read and write capabilities is a possible candidate if an online connection between all revisors could be effected.)

9. A *research effort* running parallel with the above steps could uncover in certain critical subject areas new vocabulary which should be added to USSH and which features of OPACs for subject access could be improved. There could be checks of special collections, vocabularies of online data bases, online usage reports and other sources. This data would be made available to USSH workers. . . .[5]

10. For a brief period, a nearly final, but still preliminary machine-readable edition of USSH could be used for cataloging and accessing books at LC and several cooperating libraries. The features and vocabulary of this ''new LCSH'' should be field-tested by catalogers and online public access catalog users before an Editorial Committee would prepare the first edition of USSH for publication and adoption. The printed and machine-readable

FIGURE 6: Play Thesaurus of ERIC Descriptors Third Edition May, 1979 (Excerpts)

```
CLASSROOM FURNITURE                 JUL66
 UF  FURNITURE (CLASSROOM)
 BT  FURNITURE
 RT  CLASSROOMS
     EQUIPMENT STORAGE
     FURNITURE ARRANGEMENT
     FURNITURE DESIGN

CLASSROOM FURNITURE (D AA) **       APR79
 RT  EQUIPMENT STORAGE

CLASSROOM GAMES                     JUL66
 BT  GAMES
 RT  CLASS ACTIVITIES
     CLASSROOMS
     EDUCATIONAL GAMES

CLASSROOM GAMES (D JC) **           APR79
 RT  CLASSROOMS

CLASSROOM GUIDANCE PROGRAMS         JUL66
 BT  GUIDANCE PROGRAMS
 RT  CLASSROOM ENVIRONMENT
     CLASSROOMS
     GROUP GUIDANCE
     GUIDANCE SERVICES

CLASSROOM GUIDANCE PROGRAMS
(1968 1979) (A CG)
 USE COUNSELOR TEACHER CONSULTATION (A
     CG)

CLASSROOM GUIDANCE PROGRAMS (D      APR79
CG)
 BT  GUIDANCE PROGRAMS (D CG)
 RT  CLASSROOM ENVIRONMENT (D CG)
     CLASSROOMS (D CG)
     GROUP GUIDANCE (D CG)
     GUIDANCE SERVICES (D CG)
 COM TRANSFER POSTINGS TO NEW TERM
     "COUNSELOR TEACHER CONSULTATION"
     (CG); CANNOT EVALUATE CHANGES THAT
     ARE SUBMITTED WITHOUT ANY
     JUSTIFICATION -- HOW WAS IT
     DETERMINED THAT DOCUMENTS POSTED
     WITH THIS TERM ARE CONCERNED
     SPECIFICALLY WITH COUNSELOR-
     TEACHER INTERACTIONS? -- SHOULDN'T
     THE TERM ALSO BE MERGED WITH "GROUP
     GUIDANCE"? (AA)

CLASSROOM GUIDANCE PROGRAMS (D      APR79
JC) **
 RT  CLASSROOMS

CLERGY (A SO) **                              APR79
 UF  CLERGYMEN (1968 1979) (A SO) **
     MINISTERS (A SO) **
     PARSONS (A SO) **
     PREACHERS (A SO) **
 NT  PRIESTS (A SO) **
 BT  PERSONNEL (A SO) **
 RT  CHURCHES (A SO) **
     CHURCH WORKERS (A SO) **
     NUNS (A AA) **
     RELIGION (A SO) **
     RELIGIOUS CULTURAL GROUPS (A SO) **
     RELIGIOUS EDUCATION (A SO) **
     RELIGIOUS ORGANIZATIONS (A SO) *
     THEOLOGICAL EDUCATION (A AA) **

CLERGYMEN                                     JUL66
 UF  MINISTERS
     PARSONS
     PREACHERS
 NT  PRIESTS
 BT  PERSONNEL
 RT  CHURCHES
     CHURCH WORKERS
     RELIGION
     RELIGIOUS CULTURAL GROUPS
     RELIGIOUS EDUCATION
     RELIGIOUS ORGANIZATIONS

CLERGYMEN (1968 1979) (A SO) **
 USE CLERGY (A SO) **

CLERGYMEN (D SO) **                           APR79
 UF  MINISTERS (D SO) **
     PARSONS (D SO) **
     PREACHERS (D SO) **
 NT  PRIESTS (D SO) **
 BT  PERSONNEL (D SO) **
 RT  CHURCHES (D SO) **
     CHURCH WORKERS (D SO) **
     RELIGION (D SO) **
     RELIGIOUS CULTURAL GROUPS (D SO) **
     RELIGIOUS EDUCATION (D SO) **
     RELIGIOUS ORGANIZATIONS (D SO) **
 COM MERGE POSTINGS TO NEW DESCRIPTOR
     "CLERGY" (SO)

CLINICS                                       JUL66
 UF  CLINICAL SERVICES
     TREATMENT CENTERS
 NT  DENTAL CLINICS
     HEARING CLINICS
     ITINERANT CLINICS
     MENTAL HEALTH CLINICS
     PRESCHOOL CLINICS
     PSYCHOEDUCATIONAL CLINICS
     READING CLINICS
     RURAL CLINICS
     SPEECH CLINICS
 RT  CASE STUDIES
     CLINICAL DIAGNOSIS
     CLINICAL EXPERIENCE
     CLINIC PERSONNEL (SCHOOL)
     FACILITIES
     HEALTH
     HOSPITALS
     MEDICAL TREATMENT
     MEETINGS
     PROBLEM SOLVING
     SERVICES

CLINICS (A EC) **                             APR79
 NT  SPEECH AND HEARING CLINICS (A EC)
     **

CLINICS (A SP) **                             APR79
 RT  HEALTH FACILITIES

CLINICS (D CG)                                APR79
 NT  MENTAL HEALTH CLINICS (D CG)

CLINICS (D EC) **                             APR79
 NT  HEARING CLINICS (D EC) **
     SPEECH CLINICS (D EC) **
```

Legend: (DCG), (AJC) are codes to *add* or *delete* on recommendation of a revisor (CG, JC indicate subject area expert; AA is ERIC lexicographer). COM=comment; * not approved; ** approved by lexicographer. 1979 entries are suggestions of VIP effort; all other dates with terms signify existing descriptors in use.

version of USSH would display linkages between vocabularies as well as preferred terms.

11. The Editorial Committee would meet annually with a permanently employed lexicographic staff to review comments, prepare for new editions, etc. The project coordinator would report annually on the USA effort.

BIBLIOGRAPHY

1. *The Subject Access Problem—Opportunities for Solutions*; a workshop (18–20 October 1978) sponsored by The Committee for the Coordination of National Bibliographic Control. Report issued by the Council on Library Resources in July 1979. 46p. (With papers by F.W. Lancaster and M. Fischer in appendices—10 and 13 pages respectively).

2. Monika Kirtland and Pauline Cochrane. *Critical Views of LCSH*. ERIC/ IR 1981.

3. Carol Mandel. *Online Subject Access*. Report to BSDP of CLR. August 1981.
   Pauline Cochrane. "Online Subject Access" *Research Libraries in OCLC* (January 1982), 1–7.
   See also preliminary findings of CLR-sponsored research on Online Catalog Use, reported in January, 1982 before ALA Midwinter. Especially remarks of Robert Zich from LC and OCLC report by Charles Hildreth on Features of OPACS.
   William H. Mischo. *A Subject Retrieval Function for the Online Union Catalog*. OCLC Report No OCLC/DD/TR-81/4. 20 Nov. 1980.

4. British Standards Institution. "Guidelines for the Establishment and Development of Monolingual Thesauri," BS5723: 1979. (Available from BSI, 2 Park Street, London). See also UN15157 documents on thesaurus construction.

5. To mention only a few research reports:
   Gertrude London. A Classed Thesaurus as an Aid to Indexing, Classifying and Search. New Brunswick, N.J., Rutgers University, Graduate School of Library Service. 1966. PB173954.
   Tamas E. Doszkocs. "AID, an Associative Interactive Dictionary for Online Searching," *Online Review* 2 (June 1978), 163–173.
   Eugene Wall, "Vocabulary Building and Control Techniques," *American Documentation* (April 1969), 161–64.
   Robert Niehoff, "Switching Vocabularies," JASIS.
   Pauline Atherton. *Books Are for Use;* Final Report of the Subject Access Project. Syracuse University, School of Information Studies, 1978.

Pauline Atherton. "Findings About Subject Searches," Appendices A-2 & 3 in "Catalog Users Access from the Researcher's Viewpoint: Past and Present Research which could affect Library Catalog Design," *Closing the Catalog* (Oryx Press, 1979).

Richard S. Marcus. "Networking of Retrieval Systems," seminar presentation at the National Library of Medicine, March 8, 1977.

6. Barbara Booth. "A 'New' ERIC Thesaurus, Fine-Tuned for Searching," *Online* (July 1979), 20–29.

APPENDIX

Excerpts from the Report: The Subject Access Problem—Opportunities for Solution

A Workshop Sponsored by the Committee for the Coordination of National Bibliographic Control, 18–20 October, 1978. (Report issued July, 1979)

I. Major Themes:
   1. *Diversity,* even though *useful, commonality* was the intention of the workshop.
   2. *Serious communication and understanding gaps* between the practitioners in the various communities of interest.

II. Provocative Assumptions:
   p.38—"Work to improve subject access must take into account the fact that there is no one way that can be applied to all areas. However, there are useful linkages among approaches and activities that appear desirable but which do not yet exist."

   p.39—". . . universal standardization should not be an end in itself. Carefully selected standardization can be a useful, even necessary, tool in the reduction of redundant effort; and local standardization (by subject area or use environment) is a tool in effective system design. *Interlinkage* among the various communities of interest is more practical and acceptable than any attempt at absolute uniformity."

III. Action Recommendations:
   The following action recommendations each require an agent for an organizing initiative, a funding source (possibly separate), and a set of people and organizations to do the work. The planning committee does not assume the authority to designate such participants by listing them in this report. Real progress can be accomplished only if those who have the capability to perform the work, those who can benefit, and those who can facilitate progress through providing study and development funds will step forward and take initiative and responsibility. By

stating desired and specific actions in the paragraphs that follow, the planning committee hopes to provide a catalyst for that to happen.

1. Interlinkage of library and A & I produced subject-access tools.
   <u>Actions</u>: Several demonstration projects, etc.
2. Toward a system view of future subject-access mechanisms.
   <u>Actions</u>: Research project
3. Gaps in subject-access tools for the general public.
   <u>Actions</u>: Analytic study.
4. Subject access for the humanities.
   <u>Actions</u>: Research and follow-up task groups for humanists.
5. Subject access to monographs.
   <u>Actions</u>: No suggestions have widespread applicability for the unsolved problem, but maybe a research project in the use of computer-controlled composition tapes.
6. Subject-access authority files.
   <u>Actions</u>:
   1) Include in BSDP work means to link subject-access vocabularies.
   2) Workgroup to define codes to guide construction and use of vocabularies.

Introduction to Subject Analysis

I. Definitions of Important Terms Used Over and Over Again:

1. Subjects—words and concepts—topics in a knowledge field— (can be in concept and form, simple or basic, compound, complex, composite, biased)

2. Subject Access Scheme—a particular system of *indexing rules, indexing language,* and *procedures* used and developed by an information service to create tools which facilitate use of their service

3. Subject Analysis—conceptual grasp of *meaning of terms* in a *controlled vocabulary and the relations* (syndetic structure) between them (see VIII below)

4. Subject Entry—the *heading* created by an indexer to give access for a particular item in a collection—all the subject entries created for an item form its *indexing record*—all the entries for all the items create a *catalog* (i.e., a *file*, a *data base*, a *catalog*, or an issue of an abstracting/indexing service). *Entries* are also called *subject terms*

II. Objectives of Subject Access Scheme:

1. To show, via certain tools, what is available on a particular *subject* in a particular information service

2. To show what exists, which is related to *subject of inquiry*

3. To construct a *catalog* and to *arrange* the items in the collection of the service

4. Must permit users to eliminate what is *not* wanted

5. Must reduce probability of error in indexing and in searching, as far as possible

III. (a) Catalog for Subject Entries can be:

1. Alphabetico-classed/indirect
2. Alphabetico-specific/direct

Class notes; written in 1981.

    3. Classified
    4. Precoordinated or postcoordinated
    5. Syndetic
(b) Classified Arrangements of items in catalog or on "shelf" can be:
    1. Hierarchical (genus-species, part-whole)
    2. Faceted (precoordinated)
    3. Analytico-synthetic
    4. Enumerative
    5. Systematic
IV. Index Language (Controlled Vocabulary or Intermediate Language) is used for indexing and for translating and matching inquiries. It can be:
    1. List of subject headings
    2. Thesaurus
    3. Classification scheme (outline and index)
V. Index Languages should have the following characteristics:
    1. Comprehensiveness for subject or knowledge fields covered by information service
    2. Flexibility
    3. Minimal complexity
    4. Browsability—provision for collection of related subjects to minimize scattering
    5. Currency of terminology
    6. Revisable—hospitable to new concepts and sub-fields
    7. Appropriate treatment of "distributed relatives"
    8. Control of synonyms
    9. Sufficient access vocabulary for entry to used *headings* or *subject entries*
    10. Allow for specificity and exhaustivity of indexing
    11. Comprehensible "notation" in subject entry
VI. *Index Language* and Subject Access *Scheme* will usually provide *Rules* for *Headings (Subject Entries)*. Entries are made of multiple words. The rules and language will display how to create:
    1. A citation order of parts of the entry
    2. The arrangement of *isolates* within *facet* in index language display (category or classes)
    3. Additional access entries needed in catalog for improved matching of indexing record and inquiry
    4. A complete display of all relationships between entries in index language

VII. *Subject Access Scheme* for *Organizing and "Indexing"* should include *rules to indexer and notes to user* (external and internal guidance) as well as display of the *Index Language*.

VIII. *Indexing Process* requires both *subject analysis* and translation of analyzed concepts into the *index language* and creation of *indexing record* (tracing) for the item and a *file* of all indexing records.

IX. In general, the steps in the *indexing process* would include:

ANALYSIS
(IDEA PLANE)

1. Scanning the item, noting key topics
2. Converting this into a succinct summary—concept analysis

DESCRIPTION
(VERBAL
PLANE)

3. Placing the terms in the subject area summary into order of priority
4. Adding the general/basic class into which summary belongs
5. Adding other concepts (for time or place, etc.) as steps of division allowed in subject access scheme

CREATION OF
INDEXING
RECORD
(NOTATION
PLANE)

6. Searching the *index language* under broad class/concepts to find specific *index terms/notation* for key concepts; building the *indexing record* (the class number, *subject entry*) being as specific as index language and rules permit
7. Providing for alternative approaches via access terms (see, see also)
8. Checking to see that all major key topics in item have been indexed

X. Examples of *Indexing Languages* which should be examined:
   1. LCSH—Library of Congress Subject Headings (8th ed.)
   2. *Thesaurus of ERIC Descriptors* (7th ed.)
   3. *Sears List of Subject Headings* (10th ed.)
   4. Any others of your choice

Options for Automated Subject Access: A Personal Assessment

1) What could automated subject access be but should *not* be:
   a) Automated online library *card* catalogue with only *direct match* access by subject headings.
   b) Automated online *printed* index with only direct match access by *single entry*.

2) What *should* automated subject access be but will not be for some time:
   a) Direct question answering in *natural languages* going beyond reference citation. This is *automatic* subject access and out of scope.
   b) Self-service probing of a library's contents.

3) What can automated subject access be and may be:
   a) Improved access to information in books, journals, films, and other media in the library's collection.
   b) Direct access to either a local, a regional, a state or national bibliographic service with links into Circulation and ILL procedures.
   c) Integrated *multi*-database searching systems from a single service station (for cross-system, cross-database) using free and controlled term searching, Boolean search strategy, and search saves.
   d) Direct access to library from remote locations for both topical and reference searching.
   e) Computer-aided indexing and vocabulary maintenance system.
   f) Computer-aided system for both online vocabulary *construction* as well as searching.

Reprinted with permission from *Cataloguing Australia*, Volume 7, 1981.

ILLUSTRATION 1.

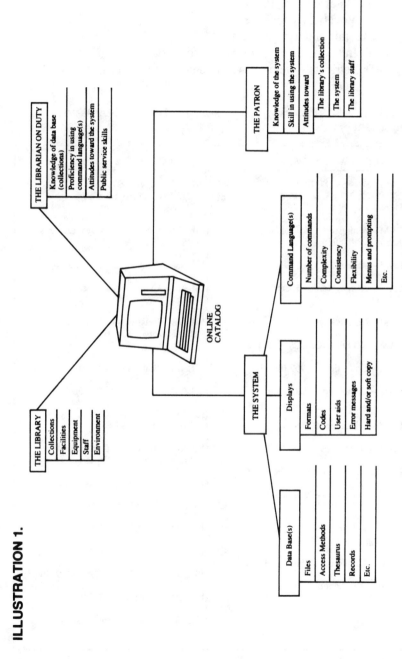

THE LIBRARY
- Collections
- Facilities
- Equipment
- Staff
- Environment

THE LIBRARIAN ON DUTY
- Knowledge of data base (collections)
- Proficiency in using command language(s)
- Attitudes toward the system
- Public service skills

THE PATRON
- Knowledge of the system
- Skill in using the system
- Attitudes toward
  - The library's collection
  - The system
  - The library staff

ONLINE CATALOG

THE SYSTEM

Data Base(s)
- Files
- Access Methods
- Thesaurus
- Records
- Etc.

Displays
- Formats
- Codes
- User aids
- Error messages
- Hard and/or soft copy

Command Language(s)
- Number of commands
- Complexity
- Consistency
- Flexibility
- Menus and prompting
- Etc.

NOTE: This chart is based in part on Fenichel, *Library Research* 2:107–127 (1980–81), and notes of Pauline (Atherton) Cochrane.

4) *But* if it does become any of the (3) above, this is bound to have *impact* on:
   a) Cataloguing rules and procedures
   b) Database generation
   c) Vocabulary for indexing
   d) Staff and user training
   e) Indexing efforts (micro/macro thesauri)
   f) Retrieval system software/features—commands, etc. (See Illustration 1)

ILLUSTRATION 2. Browsing LCSH—Logical or Word-by-Word Arrangement

LCSH Word-by-Word		LCSH Online—in parts
ISLAM. 297(9); J297; J915.3; 297.1972; 297.63; See also: Dervishes	M	(ISLAM. 297(9); J297; J915.3 (297.1972; 297.63; See also: (Dervishes
ISLAM—Addresses, Essays, Lectures R297; 297.08; 956		(ISLAM—Addresses, Essays, Lectures. (R297; 297.08; 956 (
ISLAM—Africa. 276; 297.096	F	(ISLAM—Collections. Q909.09767 (
ISLAM—Africa, North—History. 209.61		(ISLAM—Controversial Literature. (291
ISLAM AND ART. 709.67		((ISLAM—Relations—Christianity— (*Bibliography*. Ref 016.29724
ISLAM AND ECONOMICS. 330.122		
ISLAM—Collections. Q909.09767		(ISLAM—Education. 370.956 (
ISLAM—Controversial Literature. 291		(ISLAM—History. 297(2); 956(2) (
ISLAM—Education. 370.956	T	(ISLAM—Relations—Christianity. (276; 291; 297.1972 (
ISLAM—History. 297(2); 956(2)		(ISLAM—Relations—Christianity— (*Bibliography*. Ref 016.29724 (
ISLAM IN EAST AFRICA. 896.92109		(ISLAM—Relations—Judaism. 291 (
ISLAM—Relations—Christianity. 276; 291; 297.1972	CH	(ISLAM—20th Century. 297
ISLAM—Relations—Christianity— Bibliography. Ref 016.29724		(ISLAM AND ART. 709.67 (
ISLAM—Relations—Judaism. 291	C	(ISLAM AND ECONOMICS. 330.122 (
ISLAM—20th Century. 297		(ISLAM IN EAST AFRICA. 896.92109
	G	(ISLAM—Africa. 276; 297.096 (
		(ISLAM—Africa, North—History. (209.61

Because automated subject access will affect both the file of cataloguing records and the subject authority file, I think it best to review subject access possibilities first separately, without the subject authority file being evident to the users. By this I mean they search our machine-readable file by a system which allows access to index points but does not show anything which is much beyond what is available on the cataloguing records. The question is, what are the things we can do online or produce as printed products *from our MARC records* that would provide user tools for better subject access? This could be done, on demand, for each user or as library products (sometimes called bibliographies). I will try to list them:

1) Online (or as a print-out—COM or hard copy) *an index list* of all subject tracings in alphabetical order (with or without catalogue entries). With it would be our COM subject catalogue.
2) Online (or as a print-out) such a list with cross-references (see and see also) created by comparing our list with LCSH tapes.
3) Online (or as a print-out) a KWIC alphabetical list of every tracing (with or without *see* cross-references)—much like the ERIC rotated descriptor display.
4) Online (not as a print-out) access to *every* word in title or subject field, not only *first* word in title, (although such a capability is useful for known element searching). (See Illustrations 3–5.)
5) Classified arrangement (online or as print-out) (possibly abridged class number for better groups), with or without captions for class numbers, created by comparing class numbers in cataloguing records with machine-readable file of classification schedules. . . .

If the option is to produce such lists, either in response to individual user searches or as general library tools, there are problems or decisions associated with each. They are problems of filing, display, and highlighting, and content.

Choices must be made if any portion of catalogue record will be displayed in each list. Just as with COM catalogues, because the machine-readable catalogue record is very flexible, all or only some of it can be rearranged and shown online, in full or partially, and in different order in different places.

For example, if you decide to create a printed list of alphabetical subject headings as a guide to your collection because your COM catalogue does not have cross-references, do you include (as in Illustration 2), the call numbers associated with each subject heading; if yes, in what order (numerical, or as here, in column 1, ranked by number of items).

If you decide to do this online, will the limited amount of information on one screen force you to rearrange headings so that filing sequence does not split subjects and all subdivisions of one type are together, as in column 2 of Illustration 2. (This is a serious COM catalogue display problem too.)

At WAIT in their COM subject catalogue, the subject ISLAM covers eight screens. The subject is subdivided, of course, but the filing breaks up subject in strange way, with compound headings (---) interspersed with subdivisions on second screen. Not being able to display all of ISLAM at once can cause some user difficulty.

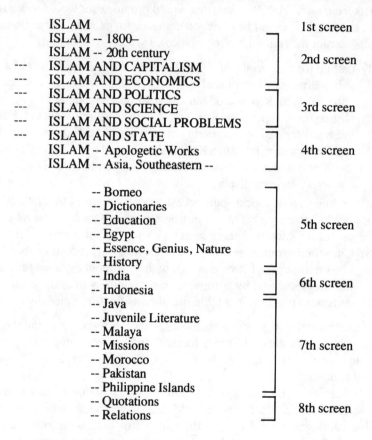

ISLAM	1st screen
ISLAM -- 1800–	
ISLAM -- 20th century	
--- ISLAM AND CAPITALISM	2nd screen
--- ISLAM AND ECONOMICS	
--- ISLAM AND POLITICS	
--- ISLAM AND SCIENCE	3rd screen
--- ISLAM AND SOCIAL PROBLEMS	
--- ISLAM AND STATE	
ISLAM -- Apologetic Works	4th screen
ISLAM -- Asia, Southeastern --	
-- Borneo	
-- Dictionaries	
-- Education	
-- Egypt	5th screen
-- Essence, Genius, Nature	
-- History	
-- India	6th screen
-- Indonesia	
-- Java	
-- Juvenile Literature	
-- Malaya	
-- Missions	7th screen
-- Morocco	
-- Pakistan	
-- Philippine Islands	
-- Quotations	8th screen
-- Relations	

For the new form of our catalogues, and for index listings, we may have to rethink our filing rules, use of subdivisions, and arrangement of data elements in our catalogue record displays.

These are not easy decisions to make and user preferences should be taken into account.

The options are almost endless, even when you are working with the catalogue records alone.

Important options have to do with which data elements are accessible for searching in a combined basic index or as a "known element" search (see Illustrations 3–5). The example of ERIC on three different systems (Illustration 6) is now duplicated by MARC records on all the online catalogues. What is being searched when SULIRS, MELVYL or MUMS or LUIS say you can do a title search, or the ubiquitous keyword search? Are you searching all title fields—as traced or as written, both uniform and as on the piece? What are the stop words in the system? Compare MLA's choice to PAIS in Illustrations 3 and 5.

If you begin to *think of automating subject authority lists* (see Lancaster)(3) and develop authority control files (as at LC, NLM, MLA) to aid indexers, subject catalogues, and also users, what are the options for displaying information from those files? Luckily, this is something that can be solved for us at some central agency like a national library. They can create the file and the software to display it, as on MEDLINE, where MESH is online as a file for searching and updating. But these agencies need to be responsible to all the possible uses they and others will make of the thesaurus file.

Some options here are like those suggested earlier, but even more varied:

1) The automated subject authority file (either something like LCSH or LCC, DDC, etc.) could be listed in print or displayed online, with headings alone, with main headings and subdivisions, with indexing notes, syndetic structure, etc. (as in MESH, annotated and unannotated). ERIC thesaurus, during a revision process, was printed with *comments* (messages to and from different clearing-houses and the lexicographer).

    (a) This file could help when revisions are made and either new or dead headings are created. . . .

2) The subject authority file could be listed in classified order or KWIC-ed. (Illustration 6—ERIC rotated descriptor display.) This list could also contain *see* references.

3) The file could be shown with postings (for different libraries—if catalogue file contains holdings). See Illustration 8.

4) Online, this file could be merged with keyword-title word lists displayed as in Illustration 8 line R2–R21, so that user could make selection.

5) If a class schedule is in machine-readable form, there could be *links* between *words* in class captions and subject headings used on catalogue records. (This is an important area for further research.)

ILLUSTRATION 3.   MLA Bibliography. Dialog File 71.

Sample Record

DIALOG Accession Number

AN = $\dfrac{7635876 \qquad 76\text{-}2\text{-}000150a}{}$

Discordant Voices: The Non-Russian Soviet Literatures, 1953–1973 ←——— /TI
AU = ►Luckyj, George S.N.
PU = Oakville, Ontario: Mosaic, 1975. 149 pp.
PY = Doc Type: festschrift
DT = Note: "Editorial Note," vii; "Some Statistics," 145; "Selected   } /NT
Bibliog. Secondary Sources in Eng.," 145–49
Descriptors: literature—collections, analyzed—East European ←——— /DE

DC = Descriptor Codes: 0201000007

Search Options
Basic Index

Page	Suffix	Field Name	Examples
71-3	None	Basic Index (includes Descriptor, Note, Title)	E Literature S Non(W) Russian
71-3	/DE	Descriptor[1]	S East European(F) Collections /DE
71-6	/NT	Note	S Editorial(W) Note/NT
71-7	/TI	Title	S Discordant(W) Voices/TI

[1] Also /DF.

ILLUSTRATION 4.   Philosopher's Index. Dialog File 57.

Sample Record

DIALOG Accession Number
052017
AU = How to Apply the Categorical Imperative ←——————— /TI
Potter, J. R., Nelson
JN = ►Philosophia, (Israel), 5,395-416, 0 75
LA = ►Languages: English
DT = ►Doc Type: Journal Article
JA = ►Journal Announcement: 105

A Procedure for successfully (i.e., without the use of subsidiary moral premises) applying the "Universal Law" formulation of Kant's categorical imperative is outlined, using as a model application Kant's argument that it is wrong to make a lying promise. Also included is an account of "maxims" and of the "contradition" resulting when we attempt to universalize an immoral maxim, and a discussion of how the action is to be described for the purposes of moral evaluation (a causal criterion of action-description is proposed).   ◄/AB

Descriptors: Ethics; Categorical Imperative; End; Description; Maxim ←——— /DE
Named People: Kant ←————————————————————————— NA =

ILLUSTRATION 4. Philosopher's Index. Dialog File 57. (continued)

Search Options   Basic Index

Page	Suffix	Field Name	Examples
57-3	None	Basic Index (includes Abstract, Descriptor, and Title)	E Moral S Immoral
57-3	/AB	Abstract	S Universal(W) Law/AB
57-5	/DE	Descriptor[1]	S Ethics/DE
57-6	/TI	Title	S Categorical(W) Imperative/TI

[1] Also /DF

ILLUSTRATION 5. PAIS International. Dialog File 49.

Sample Record

DIALOG
Accession   AN =
Number

      0 200219   761002395
      Who rules the giant corporation?
      "the legal image is virtually a myth: in nearly every large
YR = American   ◄—/TI
      business corporation, there exists a management autocracy."
AU = ► Nader, Ralph and others
JN = ► Bus and Society R, p 40-8 Summer '76,
LA = ► Languages: Engl
      Excerpted from their forthcoming book entitled, "Taming the
      giant ◄————————————————————————————————— /AB
      corporation."
      Descriptors: *Corporations—Size: *Management ◄——————— /DE

Retrieval Methods

Subject or Text Searching

Page	Suffix	Field Name	Examples
49-3	None	Basic Index (includes Abstract, Descriptor, and Title fields)	E Economics S Political
49-6	/AB	Abstract	S Taming(W) Giant/AB
49-4	/DE	Descriptor	S Management/DE
49-3	/TI	Title	S Giant(W) Corporation/TI

ILLUSTRATION 6.

ERIC Field Names	ERIC Codes	LRS	SDC	BRS
Accession Number	0010		/AN	.AN.
Author	Auth 001B	AU=	/AU	.AU.
Geographic Source	Geo 004D	CP=	/LO	.GS.
Government Level	Gov 004E	GL=	/LO	.GV.
Corporate Source	Inst 001c	/CS	/OS	.IN.
Sponsoring Agency	Spon 0020	/SA	/SPO	.SN.
Title	001A	/TI	/TI	.TI.
Abstract	Abst 002c	/AB	(IN BI)	.AB.
Identifier	Iden 0024	/ID,/ID* /IF,/IF*	(IN BI)	.ID.
Descriptor	Desc 0023	/DE,DE* /DF,/DF*	/IT,*/IT /IW,*/1W	.MJ,MN,DE, UJ,UN.
Descriptive Note	Note 0026	/NT		.NT.
Language	Lang 004c	LA=	/LA	.LG.

*ERIC Codes and Corresponding LRS, SDC and BRS Search Qualifiers of the ERIC Unit Record.

ILLUSTRATION 7. ERIC Rotated Display for Integration Descriptors.

	INSURANCE
	INTEGERS
	INTEGRATED ACTIVITIES
	INTEGRATED CURRICULUM
	INTEGRATED PUBLIC FACILITIES
CLASSROOM	INTEGRATION
COLLEGE	INTEGRATION
	INTEGRATION EFFECTS
FACULTY	INTEGRATION
GRADE A YEAR	INTEGRATION
	INTEGRATION LITIGATION
	INTEGRATION METHODS
NEIGHBORHOOD	INTEGRATION
PERSONNEL	INTEGRATION
	INTEGRATION PLANS

ILLUSTRATION 7. ERIC Rotated Display for Integration Descriptors (continued)

RACIAL	INTEGRATION
	INTEGRATION READINESS
SCHOOL	INTEGRATION
SOCIAL	INTEGRATION
	INTEGRATION STUDIES
TEACHER	INTEGRATION
TOKEN	INTEGRATION
VOLUNTARY	INTEGRATION
	INTEGRITY
	INTELLECTUAL EXPERIENCE
	INTEGRATION
	INTEGRATION
ANTI	INTELLECTUALISM

ILLUSTRATION 8.

? EXPAND (RACIAL INTEGRATION)

REF INDEX-TERM	TYPE	ITEMS	RT
R1 RACIAL INTEGRATION		111	30
R2 DESEGREGATION..	U	107	1
...			
R5 SOCIAL INTEGRATION	B	47	27
R6 AFFIRMATIVE ACTION	R	38	22
R7 ANTI SEGREGATION PROGRAMS	R	2	5
...			
R11 CLASSROOM INTEGRATION	R	217	32
R12 COLLEGE INTEGRATION	R	12	5
R13 FACULTY INTEGRATION	R	9	6
R14 GRADE A YEAR INTEGRATION	R	☐	3
R15 INTEGRATED PUBLIC FACILITIES.. . ..	R	☐	3
R16 INTEGRATION EFFECTS	R	52	3
R17 INTEGRATION LITIGATION METHODS	R	31	3
R18 INTEGRATION METHODS ·.	R	56	6
R19 INTEGRATION PLANS	R	31	1
R20 INTEGRATION READINESS	R	5	2
R21 INTEGRATION STUDIES	R	20	2

ILLUSTRATION 8. (continued)

	TYPE	ITEMS	RT
...			
R 26 RACE RELATIONS	R	105	16
R 27 RACIAL SEGREGATION	R	45	16

I am excited about the potential of automated subject access in our COM and online catalogues. Even without *automatic* subject access, I am excited. The potential of *automatic* searching, where the computer "does the walking" and suggests subject headings after you enter a word (as in Paper Chase), and then suggests related headings for your particular complex search, is all beyond this paper, but it is not unrelated. Maybe now the unheeded research findings I spoke of in an earlier paper (in "Closing the Catalogue")(1) and our new findings about library users, and especially about catalogue users (5) will bring us to the point where we will see our catalogues and subject authority files as dynamic tools, able to respond as required, providing different display and output options. We can begin to see this happening in online retrieval system operating on other bibliographic databases (4). Why not in our library catalogues?

Maybe now we can also update and change our subject vocabularies more easily, analysing free text fields for new concepts and headings (2). We should not settle for less and the result is going to be *worth* the effort. The end result will either be a strengthened LCSH, or a new vocabulary for our catalogues. It will either be improved access via classified arrangement or it will sound the death knell of classification in libraries. The 1980's will probably bring about an international effort at Universal Subject Control or it will force us to recognize the impossibility of such a dream. That is the challenge and I, for one, am excited about it, aren't you?

REFERENCES

1. Gapen, K. "Closing the Catalogue."
2. Christ, J. "Concepts and Subject Headings."
3. Lancaster, F. W. "Vocabulary Control."
4. Meadow, C. and Cochrane, P.A. "Basics of Online Searching."
5. Markey, K. "Catalogue Use Studies." *OCLC Report* (in ERIC, EDH).

Subject Access in the Online Catalog

Several articles[1,2] for different audiences have broadcast the changes which are taking place in research libraries because of technology and the growing acceptance of shared resources, bibliographic networks, and computerized holdings lists. For the library user these changes will eventually mean improved subject access and better document delivery. For the library staff and the keepers of our cataloging traditions, it is becoming a time to assess traditional ways and means of access, maintenance of cataloging files, and authority files.[3]

Nowhere is this assessment and redesign of library files and look-up procedures more evident than in the design of online public access catalogs (OPAC). A soon-to-be-published OCLC research report, "The User Interface in Online Public Access Catalogs,"[4] funded in part by the Council on Library Resources (CLR), documents the existing diversity in access, ease-of-use, indexing, and specialized search capabilities of twelve operating online catalogs. Rather than summarize that report (which will be highlighted in a future issue of this journal), I will use it as a backdrop for comments I would like to make about subject access—that all important and little understood process.

The title I have chosen for this article is identical to that of a recent CLR report[5] by Carol A. Mandel, prepared for the BSDP (Bibliographic Service Development Program). My reason for this choice is again to use its recommendations as a backdrop for comments I would like to make. The recommendations of the CLR/BSDP report are to:

- Understand the relationship between library bibliographic records and researchers' subject searches;
- Enrich the search terms available in library bibliographic records;
- Enrich the entry vocabulary for subject search;
- Get the most from the controlled vocabulary; and
- Develop and promote standards for their user interface in the online library catalog.

Reprinted with permission from *Research Libraries in OCLC: A Quarterly*, January 1982, pp. 1–7.

Many may see these two reports as covering different territory, but I see the CLR/BSDP recommendations as most important for the design of online catalogs even though this design at present seems to rest in the hands of many different library system designers or vendors. The recommendations in the CLR report are aimed at the Library of Congress from where, for the most part, our bibliographic records and controlled vocabulary improvements come. But the report also calls for studies of subject searches and for standards for the user interface in online catalogs.

VOCABULARY

My major focus, as in the CLR report, is on Library of Congress Subject Headings (LCSH) as it is now our principal vocabulary for online subject searching, just as it has been our principal vocabulary in card and COM catalogs. If we are to judge from a recent bibliography of critical views of LCSH[6] and catalog use studies,[7] the CLR/BSDP recommendations could not have come at a better time, for the library world is busy building machine-readable databases and ''new'' subject indexes to them for online access. This is the best time to re-think how we will allow patrons to search these files (e.g., LCSH match or keyword free text searches), how we will help them search, and what we will display for their perusal.

What the Library of Congress will do with LCSH and other authority files online[8] will have a profound effect on every library's online catalog. The CONDOC (Consortium to Develop an Online Catalog) requirements, reported by Joseph R. Matthews,[9] ranked an online authority control file for names and subject headings with cross references fourth out of forty features. Surprisingly, consortium members ranked call number access third, and keywords in titles access twelfth. These features and some of the ''unheeded research findings about catalog use''[10] may all affect subject access routes to library collections someday, but not all the implications of these are being weighed carefully by some system designers as I will show later. Some features can already be seen to have unfortunate consequences for subject searching in an online catalog.

In this brief paper, I would like to review subject access via card, COM, and online catalogs and itemize some of the improvements and unfortunate consequences already evident in the newest online forms of a library's catalog. I will end with some personal recommendations about online catalog design for improved subject access.

At the outset I want to acknowledge the assistance and enlightenment I received from OCLC staff, especially the Office of Research under Neal K. Kaske, who kept me informed of all the research, in progress or recently reported,[11-14] which had an effect on my own perspective of the developments which could affect online catalogs in general, and subject access in particular.

FORMS OF THE CATALOG

Through the years since Charles Ammi Cutter and the beginning of LC's card distribution service, we have created several physical forms of the catalog in our libraries, but the card, COM, and online forms appear most prevalent at this time. Although card and COM catalogs allow the same subject access points, those of online catalogs are different from card and COM catalogs. Each form of catalog presents different styles of entry and arrangement. Each form (see Table 1) displays records in different ways, arranging these records using a different sorting rule, and often displays differing amounts of information about each item. Each seems to have advantages the other forms do not.

Noticeably different in each online catalog examined by Hildreth[4] is the amount of useful information provided about subject access. The diversity of subject access approaches in online catalogs can be represented by a continuum from the post-coordination of Boolean search operations, permuted subject headings and titles to the precoordination of subject headings and their subdivisions. The added subject access routes in various online catalogs would appear to improve access, but, in fact, vary from OPAC to OPAC and may already be confusing users. (see Figures 1–6)

TABLE 1. Different Routes to Subject Access in Library Catalogs

Form of Catalog	Subject Access Points & Style of Heading	Display of Records (Content & Filing Order)	User Aids to Other Access Points, for Improved Search Results
Card Catalog	LCSH or Sears S.H. complete word by word match; words in controlled order, with subdivisions for form, geographic, chronological, topical aspects; some headings contain inversions and phrases for compound concept headings	Standard, predefined "unit" records alphabetically sorted by main entry; display of main term "hits" affected by filing order of form, geographic, chronological and topical subdivisions.	Printed on separate cards and filed within catalog: 1) Cross references (see) from lead-in term to used heading 2) Cross reference (see also) to more specific or related headings. 3) General reference to common subdivisions or unnamed specific headings
COM Catalog	Same as above.	Predefined abridged "unit" records may have data elements rearranged for easier scanning. Filing order as above, or by most recent date of publication.	Above not usually included; reliance on use of printed copy of LCSH or separate "Subject Guide" prepared from tracings and LCSH cross reference structure.
Online Catalog	Wide diversity of approaches. In some, same as above. In others, "uncontrolled" keyword access to title words and subject heading words from record or selected field with or without Boolean operators, proximity operators, truncation. In others, same as above plus "uncontrolled" keyword access to title words and subject heading words from record or selected field with or without Boolean operators, proximity operators, truncation; Call number searching (truncated to class number or in full); Rare option: display of LCSH for choice of all search-related headings; Derived search keys may be required for designated fields; Free text term search may be in combined fields; Search sets may be combined.	*Index* lists online, sometimes with postings information for LCSH terms or keywords, call number, etc. Brief or full catalog records with data elements rearranged; sorting rule yields non-conventional display of records (e.g. by accession number, or latest date in, or first words in record, etc.); sorting not usually controlled by user.	May be browsable index lists for headings and terms in searchable fields; use of machine-readable LCSH and name authority files as separate file for browsing and term selection; in-context field searching; restrict or limit results by some parameter (e.g., language, date, format or material); rare option: save search for later execution; error messages, user prompts and help messages.

USER INTERFACE

Searching in five different online catalogs is shown in Figures 1–6. These are all large research or public libraries whose users might occasionally use any of the other catalogs. When they do, they may be confused not only by the different user interfaces (different command entry techniques, different capabilities, different reports and messages), but they will probably also be confused by the displays of catalog records, the arrangement and content of these records and the various record fields where their search words were searched in the file. This may be why the CLR/BSDP report recommends standards for the user interface and improved entry vocabulary.

Table 1 summarizes the different subject access points, displays and user aids in card, COM and online catalogs. Progressively, it would appear that subject access is improving. But is it? When we review the advantages of earlier forms of the catalog, we can see that not all those features are kept

TABLE 2. Forms of Catalogs—Advantages and Disadvantages from the User and Staff Viewpoint (Revision of Table in Ref. 10) (*=Characteristic Related to Subject Access)

–Advantages–	CARD CATALOGS	–Disadvantages–
User: 1. Alphabetical, orderly parts 2. Unit entry, with all information available everywhere *3. Guide cards and notes available with reference to related entries 4. Form of catalog similar throughout 5. Nonmediated, self-service 6. Easily updated 7. Can contain temporary information		1. Over time, inconsistent rules of main-entry form and choice of form of subject heading 2. Must copy out all information needed by hand 3. Cryptic notes and confusing form of entry 4. Different style of entry, different form of card in different library for different materials *5. No "natural language" access *6. Too few cross references 7. Catalog available in only one location, even in decentralized system
Staff: *1. Name and subject authority control 2. Collocation or works, authors		1. Error-ridden filing; misplaced cards *2. Expensive, labor-intensive to maintain, new, old entries x-ref structure *3. Limited access — one arrangement 4. Reproducibility difficult 5. Inflexible 6. Limited information — no holding information, only crude location information

–Advantages–	COM (FICHE OR REEL) CATALOG	–Disadvantages–
User: 1. Available at many locations 2. Several entry files (author, title, subject) *3. Can see several records at once *4. Can copy entries if printer available 5. Inexpensive equipment for readers, sometimes available on loan		1. Not easily updated 2. Not very readable *3. Rearrangement of output impossible *4. Cross-references not listed *5. Reliance on "offline" authority list like LCSH which is not specific to catalog entries 6. Guidance within catalog not available *7. No "natural language" access.
Staff: 1. Reduces delay in listing new items 2. Saves money spent in filing cards *3. Subject headings may be checked against machine-readable LCSH for quality control		1. Some updates costly *2. May not be user-oriented 3. Incomplete record of library's holdings if no retrospective conversion

–Advantages–	ONLINE LIBRARY CATALOGS	–Disadvantages–
User: 1. Easily updated, with changes explained *2. Can provide table lookups or browsing in authority files (author, title, subject) 3. Available at many locations *4. New access points and combinations; search terms may be natural language *5. Can provide online user assistance 6. Can see several records at once 7. Union lists possible		1. Need of staff assistance on occasion 2. Equipment failure possible 3. Queuing problems 4. User training necessary *5. Cross references and general notes not present *6. Terms too common — may abort search 7. Variable output formats and sorts may be confusing 8. Printer not always available
Staff: 1. Less expensive to maintain than card catalog 2. Can provide more location information 3. Resource sharing and listing at many locations *4. Better access to subject words and names may be possible 5. Subsets of catalog possible *6. Various sorts possible		1. Some forms costly to be updated *2. May not have user-oriented retrieval system (which is friendly, forgiving, acceptable) 3. Incomplete record of library's holdings if no retrospective conversion *4. Authority files and x-ref structure used may not represent specific catalog's headings

or improved in the newer form. One might say we are "throwing the baby out with the bath water." I recently revised a table developed for an earlier paper[10] which shows that not all is coming up roses in online catalogs (Table 2). I have marked those advantages and disadvantages of each form of catalog which affect subject access.

Figures 1–6 indicate the variety now seen in online catalog design.

TABLE 3. Unfortunate Consequences of Present-Day Online Subject Access Procedures

1. In those OPACs in which content of the catalog record (i.e., unit record) is more accessible, this access is less controlled. All words in the title field(s) are now accessible except for those words on a "stop list." The fields used to build "title" keyword searches may not be uniform across online catalogs.

2. In those OPACs which require letter-for-letter matches with LCSH and titles, punctuation (especially hyphens), word order, and abbreviations may cause problems in searching unless treatment before indexes is explained to user.

3. The controlled vocabularies (e.g., LCSH, LCC, DDC) exist in the online index (created from the catalog records) only as a subset of used headings or class numbers. These indexes include "uncontrolled" or unrecorded use of subdivisions and Cutter numbers. There are no lead-in terms (see references) and no see also references online in these lists usually. The call numbers appear as unexplained codes.

4. Common words in titles or subject headings (e.g., history, basic, education, literature, America, etc.) which cannot be placed on a stop word list, slow transaction throughout and may be prohibited or placed in background processing for Boolean searches or proximity checks.

5. Allowing keyword searches in a combination of fields (e.g., title and subject heading, or both subject headings in a record) may cause false drops. The retrieval techniques needed to prevent this, such as proximity operators, may not be present.

6. The filing order of the subject heading entries in the index lists (e.g., main LCSH and all subdivisions) may cause confusion by not following the LCSH printed order or the order of headings in the card catalog. Main heading and subdivisions may be interspersed with inverted or compound headings. (See figures 1-6)

7. The number and kind of heading indexes in which the user may browse vary from OPAC to OPAC.

8. Entry of Boolean operators exist as explicit or implicit procedures from OPAC to OPAC, or within a single OPAC.

SUBJECT INDEXES

These catalogs and several others examined this past year (see OCLC report cited earlier[4]) may be incorporating features with unfortunate consequences for online subject access. I have identified six such consequences already (see Table 3) which lead me to conclude that we are not necessarily making improvements when we make changes for increased subject access.

FIGURE 1. Browsing in Online Index—Library A

```
User: SIS/ISLAM
     11      1 ISLA, JOSE FRANCISCO DE,   1703-1781
     12     63 ISLAM
     13*     1 ISLAM (THE ARABIC WORD)
     14*     2 ISLAM AND ART
     15      1 ISLAM AND CAPITALISM
     16      5 ISLAM AND ECONOMICS
     17      1 ISLAM AND POLITICS
     18      1 ISLAM AND POLITICS—ADDRESSES, ESSAYS, LECTURES
     19      1 ISLAM AND POLITICS—INDONESIA
     20      1 ISLAM AND POLITICS—IRAN
         PAGE 2 of 3    FOR OTHER PAGES ENTER PS AND PAGE NUMBER
                        FOR TITLES ON A SPECIFIC SUBJECT ENTER SBL/
                        AND LINE NUMBER

User: PS3
     21      1 ISLAM AND POLITICS—IRAN—MISCELLANEA
     22      1 ISLAM AND POLITICS—MALAYSIA—KELANTAN
     23      1 ISLAM AND POLITICS—MISCELLANEA
      •
      •
      •

User: SIS/ISLAM—ADDRESSES, ESSAYS, LECTURES
     11      3 ISLAM IN LITERATURE
     12     23 ISLAM—ADDRESSES, ESSAYS, LECTURES
     13      6 ISLAM—AFRICA
     14*     1 ISLAM—AFRICA—ADDRESSES, ESSAYS, LECTURES
     15      1 ISLAM—AFRICA—BIBLIOGRAPHY
     16      1 ISLAM—AFRICA—CONGRESSES
     17*     1 ISLAM—AFRICA, NORTH—HISTORY
     18      1 ISLAM—AFRICA, SUB-SAHARAN—BIBLIOGRAPHY
     19      3 ISLAM—AFRICA, WEST
     20*     1 ISLAM—AFRICA, WEST—ADDRESSES, ESSAYS, LECTURES
         PAGE 2 OF 3    FOR OTHER PAGES ENTER PS AND PAGE NUMBER
                        FOR TITLES ON A SPECIFIC SUBJECT ENTER SBL/
                        AND LINE NUMBER

User: PS3
     21      1 ISLAM—AFRICA, WEST—HISTORY—ADDRESSES, ESSAYS, LECTURES
     22      5 ISLAM—APOLOGETIC WORKS
     23      1 ISLAM—ASIA
     24      1 ISLAM—ASIA, SOUTHEASTERN
     25*     1 ISLAM—ASIA, SOUTHEASTERN—CONGRESS
     26      5 ISLAM—BIBLIOGRAPHY
     27      2 ISLAM—BIOGRAPHY
     28*     1 ISLAM—CHAD
     29*     1 ISLAM—COLLECTED WORKS
     30*     1 ISLAM—COLLECTIONS
```

Indicates number of items retrieved under each subject heading *beginning* with *Islam*.
(Note: filing arrangement of main heading, main heading with subdivisions an dcompound main heading, total number of subject heading entries in list beginning with *Islam* not reported.)

For example, allowing access to "free or uncontrolled text" such as keywords in titles and subject headings is a mixed blessing. False drops or long lists may frustrate users of online catalogs (see Table 3, #4). To be able to search call numbers, but not to be shown what the call number means, may be confusing to a user.

Some of the findings of the studies summarized by Markey[7] show users' impatience at the catalog. Usually users will consult a single subject heading and no more. If they continue to behave this way online, we may need to prompt or assist them by automatically displaying additional search terms. Few of the existing online catalogs do this for users, and our authority files are not now set up to help that process. A more important

FIGURE 2. Browsing in Online Index List—Library B

```
User: BROWSE SU ISLAM
      Browse request: BROWSE SU ISLAM
      Browse result: 254 subject headings found in the subject index

        1. Authority (Islam)
        2. Bibliography — Bibliography — Islam
        3. Birth control — Religious aspects — Islam
        4. Birth control — Religious aspects — Islam — Congresses
        5. Blasphemy (Islam)
        6. Christianity and other religions — Islam
        7. Christianity and other religions — Islam
        8. Christianity and other religions — Islam — Addresses, essays, lectures
        9. Christianity and other religions — Islam — Bibliography
       10. Christianity and other religions — Islam — History
       11. Christianty and other religions — Islam
       12. Civilization, Islam
       13. Classification — Books — Islam
       14. Communism and Islam
       15. Communism and Islam — Sudan
       16. Creation (Islam)
       17. Dar'ul Islam Rebellion, 1948-1962
       18. Darul Islam Movement
        •
        •
        •
       37. Islam
       38. Islam (The Arabic word)
       39. Islam — Addresses, essays, lectures
       40. Islam — Africa
       41. Islam — Africa — Addresses, essays, lectures
       42. Islam — Africa — Bibliography
       43. Islam — Africa — Congresses
       44. Islam — Africa, East
       45. Islam — Africa — History
       46. Islam — Africa, North — History
       47. Islam — Africa, Northwest — History
       48. Islam — Africa, Sub-Saharan — Bibliography
       49. Islam — Africa, West
       50. Islam — Africa, West — History — Addresses, essays, lectures
       51. Islam — Algeria
       52. Islam — Algeria — Addresses, essays, lectures
       53. Islam and art
       54. Islam and capitalism
```

Reports every subject heading with word *Islam*. Number of items retrieved per subject heading is *not* indicated.
Note: filing arrangement of main heading, subdivisions and compound main heading.

FIGURE 3-A. Browsing in Online Index with Single Term—Library C (Display 1)

```
User: BRWS ISLAM
      BRWS   TERM FILE:LIBRARYC; ENTRY TERM:ISLAM
      B01   ISLA, JOSE FRANCISCO DE//(AUTH = 2)
      B02   ILSA, JUAN DE//AUTH = 1)
      B03   ISLAHI, AMIN ASHAN//(AUTH = 4)
      B04   ISLAHI, MUHAMMAD YUSUF//(AUTH = 2)
      B05   ISLAKUTSHELWA SIBONA NGOMOPHO//(TITL = 1)
      B06 + ISLAM//(TITL = 39; INDX = 831)
      B07   ISLAM (THE ARABIC WORD)//(INDX = 1)
      B08   ISLAM & FAMILY PLANNING//(TITL = 1)
      B09   ISLAM & I.E. DAN KEBUDAYAAN KEBANGSAAN//(TITL = 1)
      B10   ISLAM & NATIONALISM IN THE SUDAN/ / (TITL = 1)
      READY FOR NEW COMMAND (FOR NEXT PAGE, XMIT ONLY)
```

Indicates cumulative number of hits in index (title keywords) *and* all subject headings beginning with *Islam* (index). Title keywords and subject headings alphabetically *preceeding* and *following* Islam are displayed.

FIGURE 3-B. Browsing in Index with LCSH Subdivision—Library C (Display 2)

```
User: BRWS   ISLAM—CONTROVERSIAL LITERATURE
      BRWS   TERM FILE:LIBRARYC: ENTRY TERM:ISLAM—CONTROVERSIAL LITERATURE—
      B01   ISLAM—CHINA—HISTORY//(INDX = 1)
      B02   ISLAM—COLLECTED WORKS//(INDX = 9)
      B03   ISLAM—COLLECTIONS//(INDX = 1)
      B04   ISLAM—CONGRESSES//(INDX = 12)
      B05   ISLAM—CONGRESSES—HISTORY//(INDX = 1)
      B06 + ISLAM—CONTROVERSIAL LITERATURE//(INDX = 9)
      B07   ISLAM—CONTROVERSIAL LITERATURE—ADDRESSE//(INDX = 1)
      B08   ISLAM—DICTIONARIES//(INDX = 6)
      B09   ISLAM—DICTIONARIES—ARABIC//(INDX = 2)
      B10   ISLAM—DICTIONARIES—MALAY/ / (INDX = 2)
      READY FOR NEW COMMAND (FOR NEXT PAGE, XMIT ONLY):

User: R B6
      SET 3           9: RETR INDX/ISLAM —CONTROVERSIAL LITERATURE
      READY FOR NEW COMMAND
      DISPLAY 3
      FILE:LIBRARYC; TITLE/LINE—SET 3                         ITEMS 1-3 OF 9
      1. 70-97135:MARTIN, MALACHI.  THE ENCOUNTER.  NEW YORK, FARRAR, STRAUS AND
         GIROUX, 1970, C1969.  XVI, 488 P, 22CM.
         LC CALL NUMBER: BM585 .M365
      2. 73-157725:JONES, LEWIS BEVAN.  THE PEOPLE OF THE MOSQUE. CALCUTTA,
         ASSOCIATION PRESS, Y.M.C.A, 1932.  XIII, 355 P, 19 CM.
         LC CALL NUMBER: CP161 .J6 1932B
      3. 75-546281:NOSOWSKI, JERZY.  POLSKA LITERATURA POLEMICZNO-ANTYISLAMISTYCZNA
         XVI, XVII I XVIII W.  WARSZAWA, AKADEMIA TEOLOGII KATOLICKIEJ, 1974-.  V.
         , 25 CM.
         LC CALL NUMBER: DR479.P7 N67
      READY FOR NEW COMMAND OR NEW ITEM NBR (FOR NEXT PAGE, XMIT ONLY):
```

Browsing list shows nearby LCSH subdivisions.

feature in online catalogs than Boolean operations or proximity searching may be subject search prompts and aids.

Because our present practices of constructing subject term indexes do not usually enhance the existing controlled vocabulary, a user's search terms may not match a controlled vocabulary term or a title keyword. Studies have shown that a searcher is likely either to give up or choose a term broader than an accepted term. Perhaps with system guidance an online searcher could be led to other search terms by means of hierarchical displays of related terms or by viewing an outline of the subject area closest to the search terms. (Our library classification schedules, with some modifications, might help here.)

DESIGN OF FUTURE SYSTEMS

At the present time, users apparently have low expectations of what assistance they will get at the library catalog.[11,12] Online catalog users could be pleasantly surprised by a system response that automatically presents broader, narrower and related terms. Users could then select terms by line number, and search online catalogs provide such assistance now.

The present picture is not quite as dark as I have painted it. Several of the recommendations made by earlier researchers of catalog use are now being incorporated into online catalogs:

- *Geographic Term Access* is facilitated online, through access to every word in the subject heading phrase (including subdivided and inverted adjectival terms for geographic terms).
- Some *current terminology access* can be found when title word searches are permitted. They, in turn, can serve as hooks to find tracings and call numbers which can be searched systematically.
- Some systems allow *search output to be limited* by publication date, by language, or by form.
- A *browsing feature*, if call number search is possible, permits a scan of the shelves at the online catalog. (Shades of the classified catalog!)

These are all improvements, to be sure, but each improvement needs to be assessed to see if it brings along some disadvantages or if it might not require some additional file maintenance or redesign. Several online catalog system designers are concerned about costs and system efficiency. User efficiency will also have to be considered.

A few subject access features now being incorporated into online catalogs appear to imitate features that have been available for some time on such systems as DIALOG, NEXIS/LEXIS, MEDLINE, ORBIT and BRS. Database suppliers have had to reassess the design of their databases as free

FIGURE 4-A. Online Single Term Subject Search—Library D (Display 1)

```
User: FIND S 'ISLAM'
      NUMBER OF HITS = 1429    [FIND]    SEQUENTIAL RECORDS    1 TO 6
         1 ISLAM DICTIONARIES.
           HUGHES, THOMAS PATRICK, 1838-1911.
             A DICTIONARY OF ISLAM; 1896.
             BP40 .H8 1896
         2 ISLAM ALGERIA.
           RINN, LOUIS MARIE, B. 1838.
             MARABOUTS ET KHOUAN. 1884.
             BP65.A5 R5
         3 ISLAM PERIODICALS.
           ORIENTE MODERNO. ROMA,
             D461 .07
         4 ISLAM PERIODICALS.
           REVUE DES ETUDES ISLAMIQUES. PARIS,
             BP1 .R53
         5 ISLAM.
           MEYERHOF, MAX, 1874-1945.
             LE MONDE ISLAMIQUE. [1926]
             BP161 .M5
         6 JERUSALEM IN ISLAM.
           IBN AL-FIRKAH, IBRAHIM IBN :ABD AL-RAHMAN, 1262-1329.
             BA:ITH AL-NUFUS ILA ZIYARAT AL-QUDS AL-MAHRUS 1935.
             BP187.5.J47 A18
```

Note report of hits, automatic display of six records, order of entries and abbreviated record.

FIGURE 4-B. Online LCSH Subject Search—Library D (Display 2)

```
User: FIND S 'ISLAM—CONTROVERSIAL LITERATURE'
      :PAGE S 'ISLAM—CONTROVERSIAL LITERATURE'
      NUMBER OF HITS = 9    [FIND]    SEQUENTIAL RECORDS    1 TO 6
         1 ISLAM CONTROVERSIAL LITERATURE.
           MARTIN, MALACHI.
             THE ENCOUNTER. [1970, C1969]
             BM585 .M365
         2 ISLAM CONTROVERSIAL LITERATURE.
           JONES, LEWIS BEVAN.
             THE PEOPLE OF THE MOSQUE; 1932.
             BP161 .J6 1932B
         3 ISLAM CONTROVERSIAL LITERATURE ADDRESSES, ESSAYS, LECTURES.
           NOSOWSKI, JERZY.
             POLSKA LITERATURA POLEMICZNO-ANTYISLAMISTYCZNA XVI,
             XVII I XVIII
             W. : 1974-
             DR479.P7 N67
         4 ISLAM CONTROVERSIAL LITERATURE.
           DE WILDE, JAMES COPRAY, 1896-
             THE RISING TIDE OF ISLAM / C1976.
             BP173.5 .D48
         5 ISLAM CONTROVERSIAL LITERATURE.
           MAKATOV, IRSHAD AGARZAEVICH.
             ATEISTY V NASTUPLENII : 1978.
             BP169 .M24
         6 ISLAM CONTROVERSIAL LITERATURE.
           MARKS, STANLEY J.
             THREE DAYS OF JUDGEMENT: / 1981.
             BL2730.M37 T57
```

Note report of hits, display of records, etc.

text searching (in title and abstract) became available. Proximity operators and other devices to refine search output, such as searching by document type, geographic aspect, or date of publication, have been added as separate access points to be combined with subject terms. OPACs may have to do the same, which may require reloading of subject tracings and revising LCSH subdivision practice.[13] The CLR/BSDP recommendations do not specifically refer to this problem, but data represented in Figures 1–6 point directly to the need to pay particular attention to LCSH subdivisions.

FIGURE 5. Online Subject Search and Retrieval in Library A

```
User: SIS/ISLAM—ADDRESSES, ESSAYS, LECTURES
      11    3 ISLAM IN LITERATURE
      12   23 ISLAM—ADDRESSES, ESSAYS, LECTURES
      13    6 ISLAM—AFRICA
      14*   1 ISLAM—AFRICA—ADDRESSES, ESSAYS, LECTURES
      15    1 ISLAM—AFRICA—BIBLIOGRAPHY
      16    1 ISLAM—AFRICA—CONGRESSES
      17*   1 ISLAM—AFRICA, NORTH—HISTORY
      18    1 ISLAM—AFRICA, SUB-SAHARAN—BIBLIOGRAPHY
      19    3 ISLAM—AFRICA, WEST
      20*   1 ISLAM—AFRICA, WEST—ADDRESSES, ESSAYS, LECTURES
      PAGE 2 OF      FOR OTHER PAGES ENTER PS AND PAGE NUMBER
                     FOR TITLES ON A SPECIFIC SUBJECT ENTER SBL/
                     AND LINE NUMBER

User: SBL/12
      PAGE 1 OF 3            23 MATCHES.        FIRST         0 SKIPPED.
      01 BP20167 /    / Islam, past influence and present challenge //1979
      02 BP20G551 /   / We believe in one god ://1979
      03 BP20M29I7 /  / Islamic perspectives ://1979
      04 BP165G561975 / Giorgio Le / Individualism and conformity in classical I/1977
      05 DS35.4A2E84 /   / Essays on Islamic civilization ://1976
      06 BM42D67 /    / Drei Wege zu dem einen Gott ://1976
      07 BP88M313R512 / Ma:hm:ud,   / Du dout a la foi //1975
      08 BP165N312 / Nasr, Seyy / Islam ://1975
      09 BP20M42 /    / M:elanges d'islamologie :1974
      10 BP20I7 /     / Islamwissentschaftliche Abhandlungen ://1974
      ISLAM—ADDRESSES, ESSAYS, LECTURES          FOR MORE ENTER PG2

User: PG2
      PAGE 2 OF 3            23 MATCHES.        FIRST         0 SKIPPED.
      11 BP20S921973 / Symposium / Studies on Islam ://1974
      12 BP170N3 / Nadvi, Abu / Speaking plainly to the west //1973
      13 BP161M191971 / Macdonald, / Aspects of Islam./1971
      14*S.297SCH86D / Schuon, Fr / Dimensions of Islam;/1970
      15*S.297M451968 /   / The Macdonald presentation volume;/1968
      16*S.297N186I / Nasr, Seyy / Ideals and realities of Islam./1967
      17 BP165C5 / Charnay, J / Normes et valeurs dans l'Islam contemporain,/1966
      18 DS33N6 / Nohara, Sh / Ajia no rekishi to shis:o //1966
      19*S.910.091ST49 / Stewart-Ro / The traditional Near East,/1966
      20 BP165C55 / Chirri, Mo / Inquiries about Islam./1965
      ISLAM—ADDRESSES, ESSAYS, LECTURES          FOR MORE ENTER PG3

User: PG3
      PAGE 3 OF 3            23 MATCHES.        FIRST         0 SKIPPED.
      21*S.297C447I / Chirri, Mo / Inquiries about Islam./1965
      22*S.297J223L / Jamali, Mo / Letters on Islam./1965
      23 BP25G34 / Gam:o, Rei / Isur:amu ://1958
      ISLAM—ADDRESSES, ESSAYS, LECTURES          ALL RETRIEVED
```

Order of list of 23 items retrieved is by date of publication.

As online subject access systems are designed or redesigned, let us hope we will see some of these features:

- Automatic interaction between searcher and computer system so that the best list of search terms can be found.
  This feature may require word-list browsing prompts, displays of command options or a search-term ''menu.'' At each step, the searcher would be shown the number of hits for the term as entered *and* the result using related terms. (''Related'' could be determined by conventional indexing rules and authority files as well as by automatic rules such as stemming routines, frequency of occurrence in a retrieved set, etc.) This feature would ease the burden on the searcher to think of, or key in, additional terms.

FIGURE 6. Online Subject Search for Islam—Library E

```
  User: SUBJECT ISLAM

                                  MASTER BIBLIOGRAPHIC DATA BASE
  SUBJECT SEARCH ISLAM
        SUBJECT                   TITLE                        CALL NUMBER
  01  ISLAM                       ALLAH THE GOD OF ISLAM MOSLEM 297 F545A
  02  ISLAM                       AVICENNA ON THEOLOGY—1ST ED  297.2 A957A
  03  ISLAM                       HOUSE OF ISLAM               297 C885H2
  04  ISLAM                       IDEALS AND REALITIES OF ISLAM 297 N264I
  05  ISLAM                       INTERPRETATION OF ISLAM      297 V396I
  06  ISLAM                       INTRODUCING ISLAM            297 W749I
  07  ISLAM                       ISLAM                        297 E24I
  08  ISLAM                       ISLAM                        297 G957I
  09  ISLAM                       ISLAM                        297 R147I
  10  ISLAM                       ISLAM                        297 W724I
  11  ISLAM                       ISLAM BELIEFS AND PRACTICES  297 T839I
  12  ISLAM                       ISLAM BELIEFS AND INSTITUTION 297 L232I
  13  ISLAM                       ISLAM FILMSTRIP              297 I82
  14  ISLAM                       ISLAM IN MODERN HISTORY      297 S663I
  15  ISLAM                       ISLAM THE PROPHET AND THE PEO 297 I82
  LINE #:__ __        **PRESS 'ENTER' TO CONTINUE**
  SUBJECT_ _ _ _ _   _ _ _ _  _ _ _  _ _ _      AUTHOR_ _ _ _ _ _ _ _ _ _  _ _  _ _
  TITLE_ _ _ _ _ _ _ _ _  _ _  _ _  _            CALL NUMBER_ _ _ _ _ _ _ _ _  _ _ _ _ _  _ _ _ _
    •                                     •                              •
    •                                     •                              •
    •                                     •                              •
  16  ISLAM                       ISLAM THE STRAIGHT PATH      297 M848I
  17  ISLAM                       ISLAMIC REVELATION IN THE MOD 297.1972W346I
    •                                     •                              •
    •                                     •                              •
    •                                     •                              •
  26  ISLAM                       WHAT IS ISLAM                297 W346W
  27  ISLAM—AEL                   WE BELIEVE IN ONE GOD THE EXP 297 W361
  28  ISLAM-ADDRESSES ESSAYS LECTURE INQUIRIES ABOUT ISLAM     297 C541I
  29  ISLAM-ADDRESSES ESSAYS LECTURE LEGACIES ABOUT ISLAM      909 S291L
  30  ISLAM-AFRICA                CHRISTIAN AND MUSLIM IN AFRIC 276 K53C
    •                                     •                              •
    •                                     •                              •
    •                                     •                              •
```

Note: no report of hits is given; form of catalog record listed includes only subject heading, title and call number; sorting order of records is alphabetically arranged by five-character subject key, then title (mixing together Islam and Islamic subject headings); and use of abbreviations is inconsistent for subject subdivisions. This list continued until 124 items (or nine screens) were displayed. There is no way to review previous screens.

- Automatic display of some retrieval items for relevance feedback and iteration of the above feature using different selection rules.
- Automatic display of logical outlines (or classified lists) to select search terms in context: some broader, some coordinate, some narrower. This may help increase output or sharpen precision of search.
- Automatic display of limit options (language, date of publication, etc.) This could help reduce output of search.

Moreover, certain steps will have to be taken to correct the present construction of index lists for browsing online. The CLR/BSDP report refers specifically to this, and no National Subject Authority File Service[8] should proceed until these points are considered.

The Dartmouth Conference Report[14] and the Hildreth study[4] point to the complexity of the problems surrounding online public access catalog design. The Hildreth report contains a figure which illustrates this complexity very well (represented here as Figure 7).

As we move from the traditional world of the card catalog and the catalog record generated by human catalogers into the dynamic explicit environment of the online catalog, we face a myriad of possibilities in hardware, software modes, messages and displays. We can see that the tasks to be performed by the user and the explicit functions which the

FIGURE 7. The User Interface in Online Information Retrieval (figure 2c in Ref. 4)

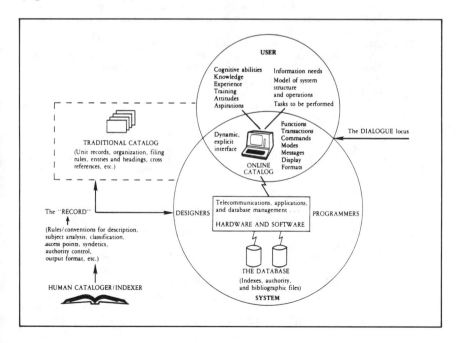

system can perform by way of assistance, training and transactions make subject access different from what it was in the card or even the COM catalog.

The variety now evident in the features of existing OPACs is evidence of the opportunities available to the system designer. What is not quite so evident is which new features will become uniform across all systems and which will have unfortunate consequences and have to be removed or reworked.

My observations in this article are based on experience. I have only been able to highlight some glaring problems. Others will be reported, I am sure, by other observers. Critical observations are an important part of system design, especially if we are at a crossroads in the organization of information resources and access to our library collections.

REFERENCES

1. Black, George. "Prospects for Research Libraries" *Science* 213 (August 1981), p. 14.

2. Smith, John Brewster and Schleifer, Harold B. "Research Libraries in Transition" *AAUP Bulletin* (May 1978), p. 78–81.

3. Cochrane, Pauline. "Improving the Quality of Information Retrieval—Online to a Library Catalog or Other Access Service . . . or . . . Where Do We Go from Here?" *Online* (July 1981): p. 30–42.

4. Hildreth, Charles. "The User Interface in Online Public Access Catalogs: An Analysis of Functions, Dialogue Techniques, and Command Languages." "Final Report to the Council on Library Resources," (in press).

5. Mandel, Carol A. "Subject Access in the Online Catalog: a Report Prepared for the Council on Library Resources, Bibliographic Service Development Program" (August 1981), p. 30.

6. Cochrane, Pauline A. and Kirtland, Monika. "I. Critical Views of LCSH . . . II. An Analysis of Vocabulary Council in LCSH." ERIC Clearinghouse on Information Resources, Syracuse University, 1981. (An ERIC Information Analysis Product).

7. Markey, Karen. "Analytical Review of Catalog Use Studies." OCLC Research Report, (1980) ED 186041.

8. Bausser, Jaye. "Authority Files and the Online Catalog" *RTSD Newsletter* 6 (Nov-Dec 1981), p. 65–66.

9. Matthews, Joseph R. "Requirements for an Online Catalog" *Technicalities* 1 (October 1981), p. 11–13.

10. Atherton, Pauline. "Catalog Users' Access . . . Past and Present Research Which Could Affect Library Catalog Design" in *Closing the Catalog*. Oryx Press (1980), p. 105–122.

11. Kaske, Neal K. and Sanders, Nancy P. "Evaluating the Effectiveness of Subject Access: The Views of the Library Patron" in Proceedings of the 43rd ASIS Annual Meeting (1980), Vol. 17. White Plains, NY: Knowledge Publications, Inc., p. 323–325.

12. Kaske, Neal K. and Sanders, Nancy P. "On-line Subject Access: The Human Side of the Problem" *RQ* (Fall 1980), p. 52–58.

13. O'Neill, Edward T. and Aluri, Rao. "Subject Heading Patterns in OCLC Monographic Records." OCLC Research Report, (1979) ED 183167, also in abbreviated form in *Library Resources and Technical Services* 25 (Jan–Mar 1981), p. 63–80.

14. Kaske, Neal K. and Ferguson, Douglas. "Outline Public Access to Library Bibliographic Data Bases: Development, Issues and Priorities. Final Report to the Council on Library Resources." OCLC, Inc. and RLG, Inc., (September 1980), 79p.; ED 195275.

Trends in the Improvement of Online Retrieval Services which Preserve the Desirable Features of Printed Indexes and Catalogs

With the growing use of online retrieval systems and catalogs by naive and inexperienced users, system designers are groping for new features which will ensure successful searching, return business, and lower frustration levels. Many systems now incorporate online tutorials, better user manuals, prompts for subsequent user choices on every screen, vocabulary searching aids such as online thesauri, browsing through the index, automatic ranking of documents on the basis of vocabulary matches, etc. Even with all these improvements over the original design back in the late 60's, most system designers have not systematically looked at the good features of printed indexes and card catalogs to be sure that there isn't some feature that was very good but somehow has been lost in the online environment. This paper will review some of those desirable features and comment on how they could be incorporated into online systems.

1. FORMAT considerations for easy scanning on printed page include "white space"—blank lines and indentations, typefont changes, 2-column spreads, and running heads or captions for each column or page.

These format features allow the user to scan and map out what is above and below the exact match initially made on the page. Immediately related headings can be seen; cross references to other pages and headings that are relevant, but located elsewhere, can be found easily. The number of hits and the arrangement of the list of items retrieved can be easily discerned. There is a division of a long list (rarely does a list of references or citations appear in print which is longer than 50 lines—somehow some way of subdividing it has been made).

2. INDEXING practices have evolved over the years to help array article citations on the printed page in those long lists in a helpful

---

Never published, written in 1983.

way. Subdivisions for aspects of the subject (form of work, place and specific aspects) are very necessary. Related topics file immediately behind a major heading.

3. General reference notes to the user keep down the long list of references (e.g., See also all entries beginning with. . . .)

4. The placement of *see also* references at the head of a list has served as a prompt to help revise a search or to add on other searching places if enough material is not found.

5. *See* references in the same alphabet as headings used for indexing have served as spelling prompts, variants based on a popular or scientific terminology, level of specificity at which a topic has been indexed etc. All the following references are examples of these printed aids.

   Family. See Families.
   Family law. See Domestic relations.
   Family planning. See Birth control.
   Family camping. See Camping.
   Family budget. See Budget, Household.

6. Citations begin with TITLE first because this has been proven to be the most useful data element for browsing purposes. Author and bibliographic citation are only useful after an item has been deemed relevant by its title. The indexer's enhancement of the title is evidence of its importance.

Online user studies have shown over and over again that these features of printed indexes would be helpful online. Users are asking for "browsing" capability, aid in finding related terms, ways of increasing or descreasing results, help in spelling, desire to go backwards and forwards in lists.

The move to link thesauri and bibliographic databases online will help the user only if they are designed to display lists of related terms in a helpful way at the right time in the search. If the user must leave a screen of citations, switch to a thesaurus file, note related terms, and then continue a search, a lot will be lost in ease of use over printed indexes. If the only prompts to the user are written as error messages with not any help for revising search then and there on that very screen, a lot will be lost over the easy scan and new choice of terms on a printed page. If the related terms must be rekeyed instead of chosen by a stroke or two, then online will take more effort than the use of the printed index. If the output from a search is not organized for easy scanning and choice for printing, then again, the printed index will have it all over the online retrieval system.

Some consideration for a split screen, user prompts, menu-driven options and better browsing of related terms must be made before online searching will be as good as searching in a printed index or catalog.

Modern Subject Access in the Online Age

by Pauline A. Cochrane with
Brian Aveney and Charles Hildreth

Subject access is the process of finding information in a *collection of items* by *matching search words* with the *vocabulary* found in the *index* or *catalog records* for the collection, with *words found in the items* themselves, or with other *related words* or *clues* provided in the *file* being searched.

WHAT SUBJECT ACCESS IS ALL ABOUT: THE USER

I recently read the following rhetorical question in a review of the 12th ASIS mid-year meeting:[1] "'. . . what difference does it make that a given search could have been better[?]''

This comment responded in part to a question from the audience about the wisdom of promoting end-user searching. The words jumped off the page at me. I almost shouted out loud: "It had better make a difference if we care about user satisfaction at all!''

The audience at this meeting was primarily information specialists trained to serve as intermediaries on DIALOG, BRS, MEDLINE, and similar online retrieval services. Many of them seriously question the development of end-user-oriented systems such as online public access catalogs, DIALOG's Knowledge Index, and BRS/After Dark, because users of these information services will need more and different training.

Most libraries will have no alternative but to train "end users" because they won't have enough library staff to "mediate" for every online catalog user. Those already involved in training online catalog users or designing online user tutorials are now talking about frequent and infrequent users, or competent and incompetent users, rather than "information

Reprinted by permission of the American Library Association, "Modern Subject Access: In the Online Age" with Brian Aveney and Charles Hildreth, from *American Libraries* 15:7, pp. 527–29 (July/August 1984).

specialists'' or ''end users.'' These new user-group terms will be more helpful in understanding such systems. This last lesson in our course will concentrate on the user of our subject access systems.

In Lesson Two (*AL*, March, p. 145–148+), we illustrated how catalog and index records are being transformed by computer searching systems. For example, searches by single words can be displayed online and browsed before the searcher selects bibliographic references; and related terms (more specific, more general) can automatically be shown after a search yields no results. We have easily traced these changes, but until now we could not do the same for users' search strategies. The tracking of their search paths in catalogs and indexes has been possible only in projects that used participant-observation techniques, in information-seeking case studies, or in controlled tests at the catalog or printed index.[2]

Now information from online catalog transaction logs (printouts showing each step in all searches done in a system) helps us to see how users search and to identify the obstacles they encounter during online searches. We don't identify individual users on these logs, but we can make some interesting observations nonetheless.

Nearly all online catalogs today can track how the system is being used. An example is this transaction I was able to review from a log at the Library of Congress:

Steps	User:	Computer response
1	Find publi re	0 items
2	Find s public relations	904
3	Find public relations quarterly	2
4	Find public relations, business	17

Obviously this person caught the misspelling of *public* but still sent it as a search to the online computer system. The computer responded that there was nothing in the file: 0 items. Then the user made a correct subject (s) search and retrieved 904 items! (The search was done against a file of more than one million LC MARC records.) The user immediately tried to narrow the search, first by using a known journal title and then by adding the word *business* to *public relations*.

From the transaction log, I cannot tell whether this search could have been better from the user's point of view. The 17 items finally retrieved may have included the information being sought. However, I know the search could have been improved from a system point of view. The system response in step 1 could have been:

> ''Do you mean *public relations*? If yes, there are 904 items with this subject heading. If too many items were retrieved, enter another word to combine with your first term; this will reduce the results.''

Such a system response would have saved the time of the user and the system, thereby obeying Ranganathan's fourth law of library science: Save the time of the reader and the staff. The revised transaction log would look like this:

Steps	User:	Computer response
1	Find public re	[stem match; 904 items reduce results by AND (new term)]
2	business	17 items

Whether you call this a "fifth generation" system, because the computer made some inferences about what the user was trying to do, or a "user-friendly" system, I think you will agree that such improvements could be a step in the right direction for online catalogs and other information services.

Online catalog transaction logs are rich mines of raw data that must be analyzed in detail before we can understand how to improve search effectiveness and design online user training. Pioneer efforts in user training have concentrated on teaching system commands, computer terminal basics, and certain search protocols. These lessons are essential because they allow the user initial access to the online services. But as the box below (content borrowed from Charles Hildreth[3]) shows, there are several more obstacles along the path to the user's retrieval goal. Recent online catalog user studies[4] document this path. Viewing the situation from the user's point-of-view, maybe we should be asking:

How do we contribute to or help overcome the obstacles a searcher encounters at the online information service?

Are the access points for our records and files—the entry vocabulary and references provided in our thesauri—more critical than the records themselves?

Should we adopt user satisfaction as a system goal?

How can we achieve a balanced use of scarce resources to satisfy users *and* transform the library's technical processes into an "integrated library system"?

The path to online catalog access

START: DOCUMENT OR INFORMATION NEED ● Input/display terminal devices ● search and retrieval functions ● command entry techniques ● database access points ● entry vocabulary ● index construction ● system-to-user dialogue ● results display manipulation and interpretation ● FINISH: RETRIEVAL GOAL.

We know from library automation literature that we can achieve many efficiencies by using one machine-readable record in a central file for different functions, such as circulation and acquisition, rather than maintaining separate files and systems for each function. We now face another challenge: to improve these systems for both staff and public use. It appears that most public users need more information about the content of a file, better access to the system vocabularies used for subject access, and an explanation of search results.[5]

I do not see one path to improved subject access. I wish that our profession could repeat the process that occurred in the late 1960s when we reached a consensus that MARC should be the standard format for the interchange of bibliographic data. I don't see a similar consensus on what we should do to improve subject access. However, opinions from two more "experts" on the role of the Library of Congress *Subject Headings* in improving subject access present challenges as provocative as Marcia Bates's in 1977.

Unified access an obsolete concept

Why do librarians persist in the task of creating unified access to all subject areas? The idea of a common thesaurus for all fields is bankrupt. In fact, librarians ceased trying to control all literatures (e.g., journal articles) many decades ago.

Monographic literature is of primary interest to past-looking fields such as literature and history. For these fields continuity is important and LCSH should not be dramatically changed. Additional headings per title and improved syndetics do make sense since these do not impact continuity.

The model of separate orientalia catalogs and specialized tools like *Chemical Abstracts* will prevail increasingly. Libraries must look to provide access to a panoply of specialized services targeted at specific user groups. Both thesauri and searching techniques will vary from field to field.

Diversity is the model for the future. We should not waste resources dramatically overhauling a tool aimed at a diminishing portion of our constituency.

BRIAN AVENEY
Director of Research and Development
Blackwell North America
Oswego, Ore.

LCSH Needs Hierarchical Restructuring

Experts have long pointed out the inadequacies of subject vocabularies and subject catalogs used to access library collections. But an imperative for improving subject access was not felt or heeded, perhaps because of constraints imposed by manual forms of the catalog or the belief that most searching was for "known items." Now the users of online catalogs are agreeing with the experts. Subject access is *the* problem of information access today.

The key findings on online catalog use and user preferences are easy to summarize: subject searching is the predominant searching mode; subject searching is more problematic and less likely to be successful than other searching modes; online catalog users place the highest priority for improved systems on a cluster of subject searching enhancements; and users prefer the one-stop, self-service approach when they search for information.

Subject access in the online environment is a multidimensional, multi-institutional problem (not just an LC problem). The fundamental ingredients in this problem mix are *vocabulary* and *technology*. New computer-based technologies offer a gold mine of solutions. But, as Marcia Bates feared, many designers of online catalogs have simply transferred "the austerity-based LC subject heading approach to expensive computer systems."

The online catalog design process is becoming more rational, open, and user-oriented. Designers are agreeing on desirable retrieval functions and how to present them in a more uniform, easy-to-use interface. Online catalog use is being monitored and user feedback is leading to seemingly overnight improvements. With all its shortcomings, the LC list of subject headings is the nearest thing we have to a common subject vocabulary authority system in this country. It would be unrealistic to abandon LCSH in the online catalog environment.

This is not the place to refute the claim that free-text, Boolean searching capabilities, properly used, will solve the subject access problem. This approach has and will continue to provide only partial solutions. What is needed is an enrichment and expansion of the subject content in our MARC records. Adding to MARC records subject terms based on in-depth, part-by-part indexing of new works should be a decentralized activity throughout the library community. Subject terms should derive from a restructured, consistently rule-governed LC subject authority list.

A comprehensive, standard subject authority record format must be redefined by consensus of those who must accommodate it in their online systems. The authority format in the LCSH tapes is woefully inadequate, lacking much of the information and guidance found in the printed edition of LCSH. However, before a new authority format can be defined, the call for restructuring LCSH into a hierarchical thesaurus—with broader and narrower terms—must be answered.

Many opportunities for improving our subject vocabulary system would arise during the hierarchical restructuring of LCSH. Conceptual gaps would be identified and new subject terms added. New lead-in terms (*see* references) could be added. Consistency could be achieved in the forms of subject terms and subheading patterns. The resulting syndetic structure would provide the related terms and subject vocabulary guidance users of today's online library catalogs are demanding.

CHARLES HILDRETH
Research Scientist
OCLC, Inc.
Dublin, Ohio

SUMMING UP: QUESTIONS FOR THE PROFESSION

How would you and your colleagues respond to these comments? Can we implement a model of diversity? Can we redesign the MARC format for subject authorities?

Will we improve our focus on the obstacles to subject access if we do as Aveney suggests and no longer work to change LCSH? Should we use several controlled vocabularies together in our online catalogs? Should we change our systems from exact-match routines to freer matches with interactive searching and relevance feedback mechanisms that explain to users what is happening in a search? (This was implied in the revised transaction log mentioned earlier in this lesson.) Should we work toward linking our systems to personalized information services on microcomputers?

The questions come in a torrent when you take a broad view of subject access. If these were exam questions I could not expect you to give complete answers after such a short course; but I hope this series and especially the responses from the experts will stimulate you to ask the library and information profession to try to come up with the answers!

NOTES

1. Newman, Linda, "Online Age: Assessment & Directions." *ASIS Bulletin* (August 1983), 28–29.
2. Cochrane, Pauline A., and Karen Markey, "Catalog Use Studies—Since the Introduction of Online Interactive Catalogs: Impact on Design for Subject Access." *Library and Information Science Research* 5 (Winter 1983), 337–363.
3. Hildreth, Charles, *Online Public Access Catalogs: The User Interface.* Dublin, Ohio: OCLC, 1982, p. 114.
4. See such books as the following:
(a) Matthews, Joseph. *Public Access to Online Catalogs: A Planning Guide for Managers.* Weston, Conn.: Online, Inc., 1982. (b) *Online Catalog, The Inside Story, A Planning & Implementation Guide.* Edited by William E. Post and Peter G. Watson, RRI, 1983.
5. Matthews, Joseph R., and Gary S. Lawrence, *Using Online Catalogs; A Nationwide Survey.* New York: Neal-Schuman, 1983. Esp. Chapter 6.
Markey, Karen, "Thus Spake the OPAC User." *Information Technology and Libraries* 2 (December 1983), 381–387.
Markey, Karen, *Subject Searching in Library Catalogs.* Dublin, Ohio: OCLC, 1984.

Subject Access—Free or Controlled? The Case of Papua New Guinea

In 1876, Charles Ammi Cutter said, "The *ideal catalogue* would give under every subject its *complete* bibliography, not only mentioning *all the monographs* on that subject, but *all works* which in any way illustrate it, including all parts of books, magazine articles, and the best encyclopedias that treat of it. . . ." After surveying library catalogues throughout the United States during this centennial year, he had to conclude, "This can rarely be done, because it is beyond the ability of librarians and the means of libraries."[1]

Now, more than 100 years later, we seemed poised and ready to assess our ability to create the ideal catalogue, given that we now have different resources and new technologies to assist us.[2] It may be well to take time to review what Cutter meant by *ideal* and determine if we are headed in that direction with our online public access to library files. In summarizing his survey findings, he noted the existence of four types of catalogue:

1) The dictionary catalogue
2) The alphabetico-classed catalogue
3) The classed catalogue
4) The combined catalogue

He commented on how these four types bring works together, how they may separate related subjects or parts of classes, and what information they might conceal. He also summarized with what ease or difficulty each type of catalogue might be used for specific or general questions. His analytic framework is still valid today and will provide the foundation for

Reprinted with permission from *Online Public Access to Library Files; a National Conference at Bath University,* 1984. (To be published by Elsevier.)

[1]"Library Catalogues" in *Public Libraries in the United States,* Part I, 1876 Report [Champaign, Illinois, University of Illinois, Graduate School of Library Science, Monograph Series, Number 4 (reprint)], p. 549. Italics mine.
[2]Carol Mandel. Private communication, June 1984.

my remarks about subject access in online catalogues as they are presently being designed. I will try to illustrate my remarks by specific examples using a search for information on Papua New Guinea. I have chosen this case because I am writing this in that country and it has received international prominence recently by the visit of the Pope and Prince Charles and the Commonwealth leaders. Given this burst of publicity I feel sure many people are rushing to their library catalogues to find out more about PNG!

Some of the catalogues they may be using are card catalogues; others may be online catalogues. The questions we could raise about their success in finding information are similar to Cutter's:

1) Have the catalogues brought works on PNG together;
2) Have they separated related subjects or parts of classes;
3) What information have they concealed;
4) How easy or difficult was it to ask specific or general questions about Papua New Guinea.

For me this will be a useful way to get into the subject of how online subject access is to be provided and whether free text access and/or controlled vocabulary access are essential. Just as Cutter expressed a preference for the type of catalogue he called a *combined* catalogue which came closest to have ideal characteristics, I have in many places expressed my preference for online systems that combine both the free text and controlled access routes. The evidence has been in for some time but the designers of our systems have not yet seen fit to incorporate the features which will assure this flexible access.[3] For that reason I will enumerate features and link them to Cutter's ideal catalogue concept and use the case of Papua New Guinea for illustration.

Online catalogues (and before them card or book catalogues) should have the following capabilities:

a) Access to subjects and their relationships
b) Access to records for works on these subjects
c) Browsing of subject or term lists
d) Browsing of retrieved records
e) Assistance in focusing search words to match subjects in file
f) Displaying of subject records
g) Displaying/printing of catalogue records for works

The first word in these seven capabilities is worth remembering (access, browsing, assistance, and displaying) because it helps maintain our focus

---

[3]Karen Markey. *Subject Searching in Library Catalogs; Before and after the Introduction of Online Catalogs*. OCLC, 1984. ISBN 0-933418-54-X.

on *function* as we describe more precisely what catalogues must do to demonstrate these capabilities. If we don't maintain this focus on function it is very easy to stray and focus on catalogue records *per se,* or subject authority files *per se,* or alphabetical indexes/inverted files for the catalogue records, etc.

If we don't concentrate on function we can also stray into the area of retrieval system design *per se,* which could lead to questions of how to program the computer rather than how to aid the user.[4] For that reason I will enumerate capabilities as they might be seen by the user at the catalogue.

CATALOGUE CAPABILITIES—MOVING TOWARD THE IDEAL CATALOGUE

1. A capability to *access* catalogue records[5] if the author, title, or subject are known, provided the *word* in a search statement *matches* the word in the respective data fields of a record.

   For example, you would find records with the subject "Papua New Guinea" if you asked to search the subject field and if you entered the word "Papua New Guinea." (*Word* here is meant to imply identical length in characters of search statement and data element. Given this capability, any subject heading with the *subdivision* "Papua New Guinea" would not be matched because the *main* heading with that subject heading would not have been part of the "word" in the search statement.)

2. A capability to *browse a list of access words* which have come from either the catalogue records and/or auxiliary files. The first word in the phrase usually determines the sort. Several identical lines (or entries) from many records would be displayed as one line, followed by posting of the number of occurences. Any difference in the string of characters would cause a separate listing. These "word" lists can be call numbers, subject headings, titles, etc.

   For example, you could browse such a list beginning at the entry "Papua New Guinea" and find Papua Niugini, Papua-New Guinea, Papua-New Guinea (Ter.), Papua-New Guinea (Terr.), and Papua, New Guinea. Each would be listed separately because they are not identical matches . . . to the computer. (see Figure 1)

4Pauline A. Cochrane, "Modern Subject Access in the Online Age," *American Libraries* (February 1984), 80–83.

5It goes without saying that the ideal online catalogue will eventually record and access all types of information items, as envisioned by Cutter in 1876. See figure 3 in article cited in footnote 4.

3. A capability to *display catalogue records* which meet the search criterion. These may be full or brief records in a sorting order usually determined by the system—maybe by record number, in chronological order, or in order by date entered into the system. This capability online represents a sharp deviation from previous practice where "main entry" ruled the sort.

FIGURE 1. Browsing List Online Covering Four Screens—Entries beginning with word PAPUA...

```
BRWS TERM FILE:LCCC; ENTRY TERM:PAPUA
B01 PAPSTWAHL DES JAHRES 1903, UNTER BESONDERER/ (TITL=1)
B02 PAPSYS, ANTANAS//(AUTH=2)
B03 PAPTISTELLA, RUDCLE//(AUTH=2)
B04 PAPU, EDGAR//(AUTH=3)
B05 PAPU, LETITIA//(AUTH=1)
B06+PAPUA//(INDX=35)
B07 PAPUA & NEW GUINEA, A GUIDE TO GROWTH//(TITL=1)
B08 PAPUA AND NEW GUINEA CONFERENCE//(CONF=1)
B09 PAPUA AND NEW GUINEA IN COLOUR//(TITL=1)
B10 PAPUA AND NEW GUINEA SOCIETY OF VICTORIA//(CORP=6)
B11 PAPUA AND NEW GUINEA, LAND OF TOMORROW//(TITL=1)
B12 PAPUA DISTRICT COMMITTEE//(CORP=1)
B13 PAPUA GUINEA//(INDX=1)
B14 PAPUA NEW GUINEA--//(CORP=52; TITL=16; INDX=531)
B15 PAPUA NEW GUINEA AS AN EMERGENT STATE//(TITL=1)
B16 PAPUA NEW GUINEA BATTLEFIELDS//(TITL=1)
B17 PAPUA NEW GUINEA BRANCH//(CORP=5)
B18 PAPUA NEW GUINEA COOKBOOK//(TITL=1)
B19 PAPUA NEW GUINEA COOKERY//(TITL=1)
B20 PAPUA NEW GUINEA CREATIVE WRITING INDEX, 19//(TITL=1)
READY FOR NEW COMMAND (FOR NEXT PAGE, XMIT ONLY):


BRWS TERM FILE:LCCC; BEGIN WITH:PAPUA NEW GUINEA
B01+PAPUA NEW GUINEA DEVELOPMENT PROBLEMS//(TITL=1)
B02 PAPUA NEW GUINEA DRAMA (ENGLISH //(INDX=1)
B03 PAPUA NEW GUINEA EDUCATION//(TITL=1)
B04 PAPUA NEW GUINEA FICTION (ENGLISH)//(INDX=1)
B05 PAPUA NEW GUINEA IN LITERATURE//(INDX=1)
B06 PAPUA NEW GUINEA INSTITUTE OF APPLIED SOCIA)
B07 PAPUA NEW GUINEA LEGAL MATERIALS//(TITL=1)
B08 PAPUA NEW GUINEA LITERATURE//(INDX=1)
B09 PAPUA NEW GUINEA LITERATURE (ENGLISH)--//(INDX=4)
B10 PAPUA NEW GUINEA MUSEUM--(CORP=3; INDX=2)
B11 PAPUA NEW GUINEA POETRY (ENGLISH)//(INDX=2)
B12 PAPUA NEW GUINEA POLITICS, THE ECONOMY, TRA//(TITL=1)
B13 PAPUA NEW GUINEA PORTRAITS//(TITL=1)
B14 PAPUA NEW GUINEA RESORCE ATLAS//(TITL=1)
B15 PAPUA NEW GUINEA STAMPS, 1971-1976//(TITL=1)
B16 PAPUA NEW GUINEA TRADE//(TITL=1)
B17 PAPUA NEW GUINEA UNIVERSITY OF TECHNOLOGY//(CORP=2)
B18 PAPUA NEW GUINEA; PROSPERO'S OTHER ISLAND//(TITL=1)
B19 PAPUA NEW GUINEA, A TRAVEL SURVIVAL KIT//(TITL=2)
120 PAPUA NEW GUINEA, ITS ECONOMIC SITUATION AN/ (TITL=1)
READY FOR NEW COMMAND (FOR NEXT PAGE, XMIT ONLY):
```

FIGURE 1. Browsing List Online Covering Four Screens—Entries beginning with word PAPUA. . . (continued)

```
BRWS   TERM FILE:LCCC; BEGIN WITH:PAPUA NEW GUINEA: AN  INTER-
INDUST
B01+PAPUA NEW GUINEA: AN INTER-INDUSTRY STUDY//(TITL=1)
B02 PAPUA NEW GUINEA: GEOGRAPHY AND CHANGE//(TITL=1)
B03 PAPUA NEW GUINEAN HISTORY & POLITICS//(TITL=1)
B04 PAPUA NIUGINI//(TITL=1)
B05 PAPUA NOVA GVINEIA//(TITL=1)
B06 PAPUA NUGINIRI TATAMA//(TITL=1)
B07 PAPUA UJ-GUINEA//(TITL=1)
B08 PAPUA-NEUGUINEA//(TITL=1)
B09 PAPUA-NEUGUINEA, ALTE KULTUR, JUNGE KIRCHE,//(TITL=1)
B10 PAPUA-NEW GUINEA//(CORP=1; INDX=16)
B11 PAPUA-NEW GUINEA (TER.)--//(CORP=4; INDX=58)
B12 PAPUA-NEW GUINEA (TERR.)//(INDX=2)
B13 PAPUA-NEW GUINEA: BLACK UNITY OR BLACK CHAO//(TITL=1)
B14 PAPUA, NEW GUINEA//(TITL=2; INDX=4)
B15 PAPUA, NEW GUINEA (TER.)//(INDX=1)
B16 PAPUAN IMPRINTS--//(INDX=1)
B17 PAPUAN LANGUAGES--//(INDX=19)
B18 PAPUAN LANGUAGES OF OCEANIA//(TITL=1)
B19 PAPUAN POETRY--//(INDX=3)
B20 PAPUAN WONDERLAND//(TITL=1)
READY FOR NEW COMMAND (FOR NEXT PAGE, XMIT ONLY):

BRWS TERM FILE:LCCC; BEGIN WITH:PAPUANS
B01+PAPUANS//(INDX=12)
B02 PAPUANS & NEW GUINEANS IN ECONOMIC DEVELOPM//(TITL=1)
B03 PAPUC, GHEORGHE//(AUTH=1)
B04 PAPUC, ION//(AUTH=1)
B05 PAPUDRE//(TITL=1)
B06 PAPULI, NONDA//(AUTH=1)
B07 PAPULOV, GEORGII NIKOLAEVICH//(AUTH=6)
B08 PAPUNEN, HEIKKI//(AUTH=3)
B09 PAPUNEN, PENTTI//(AUTH=1)
B10 PAPUNYA TULA ARTISTS' COMPANY//(INDX=1)
B11 PAPURU SOSHO//(TITL=3)
B12 PAPUS, LE "BALZAC DE L'OCCULTISME"//(TITL=1)
B13 PAPUSS, VLADILENS//(AUTH=1)
B14 PAPUZZI, ALBERTO//(AUTH=2)
B15 PAPWORTH, D. S//(AUTH=2)
B16 PAPWORTH, KNG--//(INDX=1)
B17 PAPWORTH, JOHN//(AUTH=2)
B18 PAPWORTH, JOHN BUONAROTTI//(AUTH=1)
B19 PAPWORTH, JOHN WOOLY//(AUTH=1)
B20 PAPWORTH, WYATT ANGELICUS VAN SANDAU//(AUTH=2)
READY FOR NEW COMMAND (FOR NEXT PAGE, XMIT ONLY):
```

4. A capability related to browsing, which *rotates subfield words* in a data field to provide greater access and matching. This may help to overcome some of the inherent weakness in capability #1.

   If ''Papua New Guinea'' is the subdivision in a subject heading field, it would appear in such a list as would the main heading

"New Guinea," and the user could approach the file more flexibly and find more words that match with "some" of the search statement.

5. A capability to *find records in which several words have/have not been used,* no matter what the position or length of the data fields specifically accessed. This is called the "free text" approach by many and is associated with Boolean operators (and, or, not). If a phrase forms the search statement, the system processing may consider this a Boolean statement with each word combined with the others by means of an implicit "and." This again can overcome weaknesses mentioned above. Other systems process the phrase using "or" operator or by weighting the retrieval on the basis of the number of words in the phrase matched.

   In the case of a search statement like "Papua New Guinea," any record would be retrieved if all three words were in the record, or in a given field, depending on how the match was structured. Unless the matching were relaxed, a record with "New Guinea" alone would not be retrieved.

6. A capability to *find records* when only *word stems* are specified in a search.

   For example, if the search term was Papua, records with a subject heading "Papuan people" would be retrieved along with Papua New Guinea, etc. Given the length of the browsing lists mentioned in both 2 and 4 above, this capability could increase retrieval substantially, if it were done automatically, because users might not scroll far enough in a list to catch all the variants of a stem. (see Figure 1)

7. A capability to display name and subject records which in turn display the cross references between and among these records as well as other pertinent information which may assist the user. A related and more powerful capability would be to allow for an automatic retrieval of records entered under all or some of these related headings.

   For example, the independent country now called Papua New Guinea has been known by several other names when it was a territory of Great Britain, later Australia, etc. Dates for each previous name would be recorded on such a record and the user, by choice, could determine which records should be retrieved.

8. A capability to *assist the user by redirecting* him/her from words in the search statement to synonymous or related indexing words. This is usually called the "entry vocabulary" capability and is

FIGURE 2: Browsing List of Class Numbers (truncated call numbers) in vicinity of DU740.

```
BRWS TERM FILE:LCCC; ENTRY TERM:CALL DU740
B01 CALL DU710//(LCNO=4)
B02 CALL DU715//(LCNO=2)
B03 CALL DU720//(LCNO=12)
B04 CALL DU739//(LCNO=3)
B05 CALL DU740//(LCNO=237)
B06 CALL DU740.2//(LCNO=17)
B07 CALL DU740.4//(LCNO=1)
B08 CALL DU740.42//(LCNO=59)
B09 CALL DU740.5//(LCNO=5)
B10 CALL DU740.62//(LCNO=2)
B11 CALL DU740.7//(LCNO=1)
B12 CALL DU740.72//(LCNO=2)
B13 CALL DU740.75//(LCNO=7)
B14 CALL DU740.76//(LCNO=1)
B15 CALL DU740.9//(LCNO=10)
B16 CALL DU742//(LCNO=9)
B17 CALL DU744//(LCNO=54)
B18 CALL DU744.35//(LCNO=12)
B19 CALL DU744.5//(LCNO=26)
B20 CALL DU746//(LCNO=10)
READY FOR NEW COMMAND (FOR NEXT PAGE, XMIT ONLY):
```

associated with a "see" or "use" reference in controlled vocabulary lists. There are refinements of this capability which exist in online systems that automatically match "related" words in documents and display the records in some ranked output.

In the case of Papua New Guinea, a system with this capability could "translate" call numbers for this country, and, for example, display records with LC class "DU740" even though the subject heading was "Daribi" or Arapesh tribe," because the system would have "equated" DU740 with Papua New Guinea.

9. A capability to *help the user broaden or narrow the search* by displaying a list of related (more specific) headings and a list of other headings (broader, or loosely related). Accompanying this could also be some notes about scope, historical usage of the headings, etc. This capability is missing in systems which operate exclusively in a "free text" environment and is most often associated with a "controlled vocabulary" searching system, but may not always appear within the online system. It may only be available in a printed thesaurus, if the thesaurus records have not been loaded for manipulation in the online catalogue.

10. A capability to *find all monographs classed at the same place*. At the present time, this is usually a two-step process after the user

has determined the relevant records in the field and their class numbers appear to match most of the time.

In the case of Papua New Guinea, the number the user would find most frequently occurring would be DU740, if the library were classed by the L.C. Classification scheme. (see Figure 2)

11. A capability for *messages to the user* which would help correct errors of syntax in system commands and redirect search strategies.

In the case of Papua New Guinea, depending on which of the above capabilities were available, one user message might be directed at variant spellings and forms of the search words.

12. The capability to *present a systematic outline of a subject* so that different aspects of the subject can be displayed and references to other parts of the outline (more general, more specific, or related) can be highlighted. (see Figure 3)

In the case of Papua New Guinea, such a display would describe where material on the politics, economics, anthropological, ethnological features of Papua New Guinea could be found and also where the birds, alligators, river, etc. of Papua New Guinea are to be found. Then the separation of these subjects could be overcome.

13. The capability of *presenting the user with a choice* of either an alphabetical or a systematic access route into the file. This could overcome the anarchy of the alphabet in scattering related subjects (e.g., Papua New Guinea and New Guinea) and present more relevant information on a given screen of 24 lines. (see Figure 4)

14. The capability to *present a systematic display of works* on a subject. Just as shelf browsing allows someone to come upon general works which may contain parts on a more specific subject, so would such a systematic display provide such access. (see Figure 5) This might also be a way to incorporate notes about related files, like journal indexes and pamphlet files, which normally do not appear in online catalogues.

If there were an online catalogue with all these capabilities, I think you would agree with me that we would have combined free text and controlled subject access, but would we have an *ideal* catalogue? I might venture to guess that we might not unless we would incorporate some additional features which would preserve the simplicity of the system from the user's point of view. Our automatic retrieval results and frequent displays of this or that might cause confusion and distraction. Features conceived as necessary in online catalogues were never contemplated by Cutter: for example, "user friendliness." A sensitivity to the complexities we can build into computer-based catalogues may put a brake on some of these capabilities being developed unless we attend to these human factors in our design.

As I investigated the case of Papua New Guinea in both the Library of Congress online catalogue and in the catalogue of the University of Papua New Guinea I began to see how much danger there might be in designing the ideal, but unusable, online catalogue.

FIGURE 3: Systematic Outlines of a Subject in an Online Catalogue

---

User: Christianity in Papua New Guinea

System Response: CHRISTIANITY IN PAPUA NEW GUINEA

  BR Christianity

140-1500 Church History
500-1500 By Country
1490-1499 Oceania. Pacific Islands
***1495.N5 NEW GUINEA *** LCSH: Christianity (Indirect)

****

User: Economic conditions in Papua New Guinea

System Response: ECONOMIC CONDITIONS IN PAPUA NEW
                GUINEA

HC Economic History and Conditions
94-1085 By region or country
681-695 Pacific Ocean Islands
***683.5 PAPUA NEW GUINEA *** LCSH: Papua New Guinea—
                         Economic Conditions
****
User: Papua New Guinea

System Response: PAPUA NEW GUINEA

More than 1000 items on this subject. They can be grouped as follows:

1. Christianity in Papua New Guinea
2. Economic History and Conditions in Papua New Guinea
3. Melanesian Poetry
4. Papuan language
   etc.

CHOOSE ONE OF THESE GROUPS to browse through items on a more specific topic, or rephrase your search.

FIGURE 4: Choice of Alphabetical or Systematic Subject Display in Online Catalogue

User: Papua New Guinea
System Response: PAPUA NEW GUINEA
   The library contains more than 1000 items on this subject. You may view these items, or have your set of items printed, in any order you specify:

   A—Alphabetical by title or subject heading
   S—Systematically by class number

   TYPE THE LETTER A or S.

FIGURE 5: A Systematic Display of Records on a Subject in an Online Catalogue

NOTE: User in Figure 4 typed the letter S. The following is a portion of that output. The order would be quite different if the output were either in title or subject heading order.

```
                        68-128176
Joyce, Roger.
   New Guinea. Melbourne, New York,
Oxford University Press [1960] 32 p.
illus., maps, ports. 19 cm. Australian
explorers
      Bibliography: p. 32.
      New Guinea--Discovery and
   exploration.
DU740.J69

                        72-186110
Lea, David Alexander Maclure.
   New Guinea, the territory and its
people [by] D. A. M. Lea and P. G.
Irwin. Melbourne, New York, Oxford
University Press [1971] 116 p. illus. 25
cm.
      Bibliography: p. 105-107.
      Papua New Guinea.
   ADDED ENTRY: Irwin, Peter George.
      joint author.
DU740.L427 1971
```

```
                        72-471416
Anderson, James L., 1941-
   New Guinea, produced and photographed
by James L. Anderson. Text by Donald M.
Hogg. Sydney, Reed [1969] 216 p. illus.
(part col.), map. 30 cm.
      Title on two pages.
      Papua New Guinea--Description and
   travel.
   ADDED ENTRY: Hogg, Donald M., joint
      author.
DU740.A56 1969

                        76-184666
Mann, Milton B., 1937-
   New Guinea, by Milton and Joan Mann.
Tokyo, Palo Alto, Calif., Kodansha
International [1972] 93 p. illus. 19 cm.
This beautiful world, v. 34
      Bibliography: p. 130.
      Papua New Guinea--Description and
   travel.
   ADDED ENTRY: Mann, Joan, joint
      author.
DU740.M373
```

   The Library of Congress does not have the comprehensive collection of works on Papua New Guinea—the University of Papua New Guinea has that collection. Nevertheless, the size of the monographic collections at L.C. on this subject must be approaching more than 1000 titles. To retrieve *all* of these works when you ask for something on Papua New Guinea would be a disservice to the user, unless some additional assistance is provided to cull through such a retrieval result. (Imagine what would happen if you asked to view books on U.S. History at the Library of Congress, or to view books on Darwin at the British Museum, etc.) We have created devices in the past for alleviating this problem (e.g., subdivisions, class number refinements, etc.) but new devices must be designed for the online environment. Opening up Pandora's box with free text searching is not the whole answer by any means. Neither is the exact replica of Cutter's combined catalogue the answer. We will have to go back to the drawing board and develop new access routes, new browsing displays, new systematic and alphabetical displays, new record displays, and new user messages if we are to move toward the ideal online catalogue.

This was all brought home so vividly by the case of Papua New Guinea, but I feel sure that every reader of this paper could relate even better to the problem by choosing a subject of great personal interest. As I noted how the online catalogue exhibited results and displays to the user in search of information on PNG, each capability seemed to be a mixed blessing at best.

The weaknesses of capability 1 have already been noted. The faults of capability 3 are excessive length and redundancy; the faults of 5 and 6 are overwhelming and common words like "new" could bring down the system. Capability 7 would confound the retrieval result if it were executed automatically before the users could make the decision about how far back in history they wanted to go. Capabilities 8 and 9 would require a real overhaul of subject heading lists like the *L.C. List of Subject Headings* (LCSH) before they could display meaningful relationships which could be easily followed by the user while online. Capability 10 in the raw would only confuse the searcher. If the class numbers in the retrieval result were ranked, but not identified, it would not be easy to use this capability to narrow or redirect a search. The neighborhood of the class number would also have to be explained to provide useful assistance. (see again Figures 2 and 3)

Forty-four different L.C. classification ranges represent materials on Papua New Guinea. Without some explanations of what is where and how these ranges are subdivided, no searcher could make heads or tails out of their retrieval results, short of listing all the records and organizing them to suit themselves. If we think we have some systematic arrangements of the library's collections, then it behooves us to use the online environment to present those systematic displays in some useful fashion. We have spent much time and money in designing signs and billboards around our libraries to direct shelf browsers. Now I believe we must invest some time and effort in better systematic displays online. The unfortunate case, however, is that these signs and displays will have to be customized and presented to the user when needed or they will not be useful. This is quite a challenge for our profession.

As I analyzed the possibilities possible in providing capabilities 10-14, I realized the potential symbiotic relationship between classification and subject headings, even in the LC system. I need not tell this audience about the strength of thinking of subject headings and class numbers together, but the American library audience needs to hear this again and again because they abandoned trying to create a combined catalogue about the time Cutter did his survey in 1876! As a result, the tools used by cataloguers to do classifying and subject analysis have fallen on hard times and do not now provide us with ready-made tools to provide both alphabetical and systematic displays of subjects for the online user. During the discussion of this paper, perhaps you can record if the British tools are in better shape for the task ahead. What I think will be needed is some way of using either subject headings and their relationships when the user needs assistance in reducing or increasing search results or rephrasing a query or the classification system if it can do the job better and quicker. My analysis of the class number ranges and the subject headings with subdivisions for the case of Papua New Guinea (Figure 3) may help you see what I am driving at. If someone is interested in the role of Christianity in PNG, they could be directed to Christianity subdivided by place. But if they are not satisfied by the result, they could be directed to the LC Class number range, BR 500-1500 which divided the Pacific Islands, A-Z, where by browsing, additional titles might be found. The same would be true for almost every subject.

The subject heading or place name in an alphabetical list will rarely give you a comprehensive picture of the available resources, and the syndetic structure of the subject heading cross references may lead too far from the subject. The notes and references in both the subject heading list and the classification schedules could also tie in with the search strategies associated with free text searching, but not until the system designer and lexicographer see their way clear to combining these capabilities.

As I mentioned earlier there are no existing tools being used in libraries to create catalogue record information which are immediately usable by library searchers to retrieve those records. It may appear a mammoth effort to begin to produce ''searching thesauri'' but the necessity for such a tool will become more and more apparent as time goes on, especially if we monitor online catalogue use as some libraries are doing by reading transaction logs.[6]

Subject access online can not be equated with subject analysis alone or the preparation of thesauri and class schedules. It must include the design of messages for user assistance during the search process online. Again, I

---

[6]Pauline A. Cochrane and Karen Markey, ''Catalog Use Studies—Since the Introduction of Online Interactive Catalogs: Impact on Design for Subject Access,'' *Library and Information Science Research*, 5 (1983), 348.

noticed in the case of Papua New Guinea, that it would not be enough to merely display some index or browsing screen or display the actual records retrieved. What was needed was a message to the user about the error of his way of searching or helpful hints about other places to look if the result was unsatisfactory. Several libraries, notably the Library of Congress, Stanford University, Northwestern, and the University of California are taking the lead and designing some of these messages and online tutorials. But the first versions of these messages are almost always too wordy, poorly designed from a graphics point of view, and desperately in need of user testing before they become finished products with predictable results.

The work with controlled vocabulary tools needed to be done before these messages can generate useful guidance represents a revolution in the design of these tools. The ERIC Thesaurus, in print, now exhibits some different features because the editor began to think of it as a searcher's tool, e.g., a rotated descriptor display with Use references, a two-way hierarchical display, footnotes to explain relationship codes, etc. No one to my knowledge has looked at the LCSH with the same goal in mind. Maybe someone at this conference knows of work in Britain to create user tools for online catalogue searching which would revise the displays of the Dewey classification schedules or some other authority files.

I only know of the recent OCLC Research Project to use the Dewey schedules in an online catalogue. This is taking the status quo as far as you could go, but Karen Markey and her associates will not address the bigger issues of change, redesign, etc.

SUMMARY

I began this paper focusing on Cutter's ideal catalogue and his survey of the existing catalogues being of four types, only one of which, the combined catalogue, appeared to approach the ideal, if its capabilities to assist the user in finding information on a subject were uppermost. I proceeded to enumerate what the capabilities of an online catalogue would be if it were to approach the ideal, but I quickly cautioned the reader that the increased power to perform certain operations might not really result in user satisfaction if these capabilities were designed crudely and if the background tools normally used by cataloguers, but now useful to users as well, were not redesigned.

The question is not free text vs. controlled searching, nor is it Boolean vs. non-Boolean searches. The question is "How can we create a catalog that brings works together, does not separate related subjects or conceal information, and allows the user to search with ease and little difficulty no matter whether the query is specific or general." If that is our focus we may come closer than Cutter did to the ideal catalogue.

Part 4

Will Classification Have a Use Online?

Introduction

The 1961 and 1965 selections predate any use of classification in the online environment, but they are included to show where I am coming from. All my research reports and commentaries assume the utility of classification beyond mere shelf arrangement, but during the early years of library automation I felt the need to convince the American library community that classification could play a role in computer-based systems. These writings represent the arguments I tried to present and the 1967–68 research demonstrated that it could be a useful tool online.

The 1965 selection, more than any other selection in this book, is included for very personal reasons. The debt I owe S. R. Ranganathan is so enormous that I would find it difficult to compile any selection and not include it.

The second 1968 selection represents, for the record, the fun Phyllis Richmond and I had in the early days of the Classification Research Study Group in the United States. We were trying to emulate the Classification Research Group in England and we did this by preparing papers on classification for any and every professional meeting we attended. By and large the audiences did not heed our sage advice about looking at classification in a new light, but by 1982 there was a more perceptible interest in the subject— witness the two selections for that year, one for a national invitational meeting in the U.S. and the other for an international conference.

A Suggested Classification for the Literature of Documentation

by Pauline Atherton and Virginia Clark

"One would expect to find, in the field of documentation, an altogether exemplary organization of the literature on the subject. An informed survey of the pertinent abstracting services, however, discloses that unfortunately this ideal situation does not exist."

—Helen L. Brownson, "Abstracts of Documentation Literature,"
American Documentation VI (1955), 63–7

INTRODUCTION

The lament quoted above from a 1955 issue of *American Documentation* needs only a change of date to make it an appropriate comment on the condition of documentation bibliography at this decennial review of documentation. So busy have the documentalists been in mapping paths through the bibliographic undergrowth of other subject fields that the literature of documentation itself has been left to flourish largely uncontrolled. The lack of a widely accepted definition of the term "Documentation"—and particularly the difference between American and European usage of the term—have added to the problems of searching out "documentation" from among the many labels under which pertinent information masquerades.

Students enrolled at the University of Chicago, Graduate Library School during the spring quarter, 1960, in GLS 304: The History and Theory of Classification, undertook as a class project the formulation of a classification scheme for the organization of documentation literature. Existing definitions were discussed and compared—and challenged. It was decided to proceed empirically: to examine the literature which called itself documentation to see whether any significant patterns or groupings could

Reprinted from *American Documentation*, Volume 12, January 1961, pages 38–40. Reprinted by permission of John Wiley & Sons, Inc. <u>Editor's Note:</u> Appendix I is not reproduced here.

be discerned. A substantial sample of such documentation literature was provided by the instructor, Herman Henkle, director of the John Crerar Library, Chicago, from that library's special (and largely un-cataloged and un-classified) collection on documentation. This collection consists of books, pamphlets, reprints and photographic copies of periodical articles, and also bound volumes of such periodicals as *American Documentation* and the *Journal of Documentation*. The class divided into several small groups, each of which worked out at least a partial classification. The classification scheme presented here had its beginnings in that class project, although it has been slightly modified as the result of comparison with other schemes.

PRINCIPLES OF CONSTRUCTING A CLASSIFICATION SCHEME—GENERAL

This classification is, first, by the very means of its construction around a given pile of literature, a classification of literature rather than an attempted ideal schematic of a subject field. It has, second, been evaluated during its formulation and is now submitted for further evaluation by the six basic building rules for special classification stated by the late David J. Haykin (*AD: VIII:* (1) 51 – 2) and I quote:

"To meet the retrieval needs of a library with highly specialized collections, a classification system should meet the following criteria:

"1) It should be detailed enough to provide for individual concepts, facts, processes or groups of them represented by the literature of the special field.

"2) It should provide for various aspects pertinent to such facts, such as history (origin and development), psychology (personal and group reactions or attitudes), legislation, management, instrumentation, process and utility.

"3) If possible, it should be structurally and notationwise capable of being integrated, or at least related to a general system of classification. (Example: the Army Medical Library Classification which can be used with the LC system)

"4) It should employ a pure or, in any case, a simple notation in which the order of the symbols is universally understood and accepted.

"5) It should serve primarily as a means of retrieval rather than shelf location, but conceivably, lend itself to both.

"6) It should lend itself to machine operation since special classifications are to prove more effective if used as a coding system for machine retrieval."

The principal features of this classification will now be described with reference to Mr. Haykin's prescriptions. At this point you may wish to refer to the appendix to the classified guide—it contains the outline of the classification scheme as it has thus far developed.

1) *Regarding Detail.* The classification presented provides, besides a general section, six main avenues of approach to the topic of documentation: acquisition of documents, document description, document analysis, diffusion of information in documents, application of instrumentation techniques to several subject areas, and subject name index of persons, firms, and trade names. Each literary unit to be classified is placed in as many sections as are applicable. The sections cover:

   a. The several aspects of the overall procedure which a document undergoes as it becomes part of a collection, with emphasis on the intellectual aspects of the process. There are three main sections: document acquisition, document description, i.e., discussions of cataloging, coding and entry problems generally; and document analysis, i.e., discussions of indexing, classification, and subject heading work.

   b. The several aspects of the procedure by which the information in the documents collection is distributed or diffused, i.e., circulation, individual use, editing, publication, and reproduction.

   c. The subject field in which documentation is being done.

   d. The specific names of tools, theories or persons under discussion. These six sections, together with the general section (where material on general theories, personnel education and training, administration, and equipment would be classified) are conceived of as adjacent files. As the bulk of material or the conveniences of management dictate, these sections serve as the means of subdividing one another, in chain index style. The scheme is thus hospitable to almost infinite refinement, depending on the demands of the use situation. For an example of this, see the last page of the appendix, under Suggested Procedure, step 2. The scheme as presented here is at its simplest, but the scope notes and footnotes in the Classified Guide to *American Documentation* and the appendix include suggestions for handling subdivision and multiple classification procedures.

2) *Mr. Haykin's second point—provision for point of view.* Mr. Haykin felt that specialized classifications should provide for various aspects of the subject such as history management, instrumentation, etc. The general section .00—.09 provides form numbers which may be applied at any point in the classification. It should be noted here that the material on equipment and mechanization of the documentary processes is grouped under 085.

3) *Mr. Haykin's third criterion had to do with the relation of the special scheme to existing scheme.* The classification presented here was first conceived of as development of the Dewey Decimal Classification Number 008 (unused in the 16th ed.) or 010 (bibliography). Form and geography numbers could be borrowed from Dewey. The alphabetical personal and trade name section could use Cutter numbers if necessary. There is no special significance to the numbers assigned to class section for this paper. There is scarcely evidence of hierarchy in the notation—and then only in .2 and .3. Relationships are the important concepts to be displayed in the notation. The sections could be notated using other symbols to fit other schemes. It is the concept of multiple analysis and notation for relationship which are important, and they can be attained under any system of notation.

4) *Mr. Haykin's remark on notation* is universally understood and accepted. The Arabic numerals used probably come as close as any other symbols to being universally understood. The advantages of decimal reading of these symbols, for purposes of expansion at any point in a sequence, are also widely appreciated. The order of the Roman alphabet, used in .09 and .6, is also widely familiar.

5) *Regarding means of retrieval rather than of shelf location.* The nature of this scheme, with its concomitant of complex class numbers, is designed for information retrieval. Possibly, the first number assigned to any document or literary unit could become, arbitrarily, a shelf number. The nature of publication in the field of documentation, however, suggests a serial number unrelated to classification as the simplest shelf arrangement. The large number of contributions to documentation literature appearing as periodical articles would be automatically removed from the possibility of individual shelf classification by their format. The amount and importance of the monographic literature in the field does not seem to warrant its strait-jacket control over the notation to be used.

6) *Suitability for machine operation.* The literature of the field supplies evidence of the fact that similar schemes have generally proved eminently suitable for machine use.

The rest of this paper appears as two appendices. One is an application of this scheme to the literature of documentation represented in the last ten years of one publication, *American Documentation.* We hope that this paper will achieve its triple goal. As a classified guide to the major articles in *American Documentation,* 1950–1960, we hope it supplies a needed subject approach to the contents of that periodical, while at the same time contributing to the decennial review theme of this meeting. At a glance, one can easily see which aspects of the field have received the most attention. One can also see which aspects received attention in the early part of the decade and which are just beginning to receive attention. The articles are listed within each section, in chronological order (unless alphabetical arrangement is specified by CAPS in Title). The third and most important goal we hoped to achieve in presenting this paper to you, was to offer a possible model—or at least a stimulus to rival creations—for the organization of future bibliographies of documentation. We sincerely hope that the person reviewing the literature of documentation at the 1970 meeting of the American Documentation Institute will not have to repeat Miss Brownson's lament quoted at the beginning of this paper. The acute problems of coordinating the information about our own field are surely as important as those in metallurgy and chemistry. Our present indexing services either duplicate or omit valuable material of interest to us. The organization of the information in such bibliographic tools does not provide sufficient control. Librarians and information officers are trying to find a way to break the traditional patterns of the vast output of information. They need the help available in the published literature if they could only find what existed on their particular problems. Experience is less expensive if we get it second-hand. Perhaps the ADI could provide the support for such an undertaking.

The second appendix is the proposed scheme.

APPENDIX II. Suggested Classification for the Literature of Documentation

.00   DOCUMENTATION—general
Should be distinguished from literature on book collecting, bibliomania, subject, national, and general bibliographies, catalogs, etc., by the following delimiting *definition:*
"the group of techniques necessary for the ordered presentation, organization, and communication of recorded specialized knowledge, in order to give maximum accessibility and utility to the information contained."
—Mach & Taylor, *Documentation in Action* (1956)
In this most general section, classify material treating the field as a whole or material relating to the field's background problems in bibliographic organization, the nature of scholarship, etc.

.01–.09 *Analytical or form subdivisions*
Besides using this notation for a general treatment of the subject, any of these subdivisions may apply to a more specific aspect of the subject. When this is the case, and when the size of the collection or the nature of the use made of it warrants such close classification, this notation may be "attached" to the basic notation without affecting the arrangement, e.g.,

.1(09) for material covering the history of the acquisition of documents. Such "attachments" may be made whenever necessary to show relationships, point of view, or more minute analysis.

.01 DOCUMENTATION THEORY—General
This section would include material on the research and development of the field as a whole.

.014 DOCUMENTATION TERMINOLOGY
General discussions of symbolism, notation, etc.

.02 DOCUMENTATION BIBLIOGRAPHIES

.03 DOCUMENTATION DICTIONARIES

.04 ADDRESSES, LECTURES, ETC. (see also .00)

.05 DOCUMENTATION PERIODICALS

.06 PROFESSIONAL DOCUMENTATION ORGANIZATIONS
Include here materials on the activities, history, organization of such organization. Commercial firms should be represented by type of work in .1–.4 or by name in .6 and not in this section.

.07 PERSONNEL AND STAFF—EDUCATION, TRAINING, RECRUITMENT, ETC.

.08 ADMINISTRATION OF DOCUMENTATION SERVICES— General
Included in this section would be reports of individual documentation agencies, their organization and administration. Also material on the general aspects of administration—planning, budgeting, coordinating, etc.

.081 THEORETICAL ASPECTS OF DOCUMENTATION SERVICES—OBJECTIVES, ETC.
To distinguish from .01, this section would deal with the organization of such services rather than the field as a whole.

.082 COOPERATIVE PROJECTS IN THE ORGANIZATION OF DOCUMENTATION SERVICES

.083 ECONOMIC, FINANCIAL, AND COMMERCIAL ASPECTS OF DOCUMENTATION SERVICES

.084 LAWS, PATENTS, STANDARDS AFFECTING DOCUMENTATION

.085 EQUIPMENT— General
Included here would be general material on the equipment used to perform various processes. See specific process section (.1–.4) for mate-

rial on equipment used in only that process. See also .6 for material on equipment which is featured in the literature.

.09   HISTORICAL AND GEOGRAPHICAL DISTRIBUTION OF DOCUMENTATION SERVICES
This section could be arranged alphabetically or expanded in notation to include DC numbers for the geographical region.

.1   ACQUISITION, PROCUREMENT, AND MAINTENANCE OF A DOCUMENTS COLLECTION
This section could be subdivided if the size of the collection would warrant it. Suggested subdivisions would be: selection, acquisition, physical storage, filing, discarding, etc.

.2   DOCUMENT DESCRIPTION— General

.21   DOCUMENT DESCRIPTION—CATALOGING PROCESS (Entry, etc.)

.22   DOCUMENT DESCRIPTION—CODING Process (Posting, etc.)

.3   DOCUMENT ANALYSIS— General

.31   DOCUMENT ANALYSIS—CLASSIFICATION

.32   DOCUMENT ANALYSIS—INDEXING

.33   DOCUMENT ANALYSIS—SUBJECT HEADINGS

.34   DOCUMENT ANALYSIS—TRANSLATION FROM ONE LANGUAGE TO ANOTHER

.4   DIFFUSION OF INFORMATION IN DOCUMENTS COLLECTION— General
Besides the following subdivisions, the section might be further subdivided for the following topics: circulation, literature searching processes, bibliography, abstracting, etc.

.41   DIFFUSION OF INFORMATION—EDITORIAL AND PUBLISHING CONSIDERATIONS

.42   DIFFUSION OF INFORMATION—REPRODUCTION PROCESSES

.5   APPLICATION OF DOCUMENTATION TECHNIQUES
Arranged by subject area where techniques were applied. This arrangement could be alphabetical or the notation extended to include the DC number for that subject, e.g., .502, for the application of documentation techniques to the field of librarianship. Please note that the history of such an application could be classified as .502(9)

.6   NAME INDEX FOR PERSONS, FIRMS, AND TRADE NAMES
Only a subject index, not an author file. (See also the above classes, especially .06, .085, .22, and .42)

Suggested Procedure:
1. Classify material in as many sections as are appropriate.
2. Use simple notation as given above or "attach" any other number to it to show relationship, form of literature, or point of view. Such attachments should be enclosed in separate parentheses, e.g., .22(32)(01) would be the notation for material on the theory of coding and indexing. This material could also be classified .32(22)(01) if the emphasis and point of view warrants such multiple classification.

Ranganathan's Classification Ideas: An Analytico-Synthetic Discussion*

The following quotation is from the opening sentences of Ranganathan's *Prolegomena to Library Classification:*

> When one is engaged on a problem, the most useful ideas occur suddenly. They seem at once to cast a flood of light over murky tracts of half-formed thought, and promise reward to further exploitation. . . . These surprise ideas present themselves as ready-made wholes, coming at the oddest moments.

I agree with him wholeheartedly. This spring, while waiting for a bus in the rain, I looked at a puddle of water. An idea suddenly occurred to me. I thought that puddle of water could very well be a universe of knowledge, dark and muddy, maybe shallow, maybe deep (I couldn't tell from looking at it—I would have had to step in or measure it to find out). The drops of rain falling into the puddle lose their individual identity just as the information in books and articles in a library does. As I gazed at the drops of rain falling into the puddle, I watched them make circles ever widening; the circles from one raindrop intersected circles made by another raindrop. This, I thought, is an apt description of the effect made by the information in books and articles on the universe of knowledge. . . . A book may treat a topic in minute detail, but its content can reverberate throughout all fields of knowledge. Sometimes the thought-content of one article intersects the thought-content in several books and articles. When we classify a book or article for future use, we try to provide a means for doing something similar to "retrieving" a raindrop from a puddle, if such a thing could be done! Now the person retrieving a raindrop would have to know, among other things, the molecular structure of the raindrop—what foreign material it

*First written as a talk before Classification Research Study Group at McGill University, Montreal, in June, 1960; revised for publication in January, 1965.

contained (such as dust and microscopic life) and he would need to record what happened when the raindrop broke the surface tension of the puddle. In comparison, the classifier would need to analyze the content of the book (or article) into isolated ideas or "facets" of the subject mentioned. He would need to know if it contained any material foreign to the major subject discussed or if it presented an unusual combination of ideas which would affect the potential use of the book or article. He would need to record the relationship of this book or article to the rest of the material on that subject which has already been recorded. Standing in the rain that day, I thought of *what* the classifier, with his puddle of knowledge and raindrops of books and articles, would need to know about Ranganathan's ideas on classification. I thought of this because this classifier is intuitively applying some rules of classification which Ranganathan has now formalized. To know all the rules may make each classifier's work more consistent with every other and could make the work of each easier.

So here I am, about to embark on an explanation which I hope will help you understand his ideas, his theories, and procedures so that you can retrieve information from your own muddy puddle, if you have one.

This is not a sales talk for the Colon Classification, the library classification system devised by Ranganathan. This paper is intended to be a personal analysis and synthesis of his writings on the subject of classification—nothing more. If it should motivate you to read further on your own, so much the better. Appended to this paper is a list of suggested readings.

As one reads Ranganathan, it is apparent from the very outset that his approach to the subject of classification is different from the usual approach. He starts with an explicitly-stated set of *postulates* or guidelines and a set of principles, in the form of stated canons. He then proceeds as a *classificationist*. He develops a classification system (the Colon Classification) and determines its consistent application of the canons. The everyday work of the *classifier* is governed by these same postulates. That is why his work goes far beyond his own system.

Ranganathan's close association with mathematics throughout his life has caused him to approach classification in this way. (Classification has sometimes been called the mathematics of librarianship.) The result has been a number of publications with many significant ideas and a new approach to old problems. What has been said about mathematics may now be said about library classification. An enormous change in attitude took place in mathematics around 1800 which is responsible for many contributions to modern mathematics. This change in attitude came about when mathematicians realized that Euclid's postulates need not be regarded as "self-evident truths" at all, but rather as mere man-made assumptions. The result in mathematics has been a new-found freedom where various mathematical systems could be created and where mathematics could be applied to many practical problems. Perhaps Ranganathan's work will help change *librarians'* attitudes and will provide them with a new-found freedom from the enumerative classification such as DC and LC. It would seem to me that we are more than ready for such a change in attitude—if not in large, old libraries, at least in new, small ones and the new information centers. The proper classification system for the retrieval of documents from muddy puddles in our libraries, information centers, and computerized retrieval systems is not one which fixes a single number or term to the raindrop *before* it falls in but one that can identify facets of information in each document when it is required to do so. (It has been noted that if an ordinary shipping tag were affixed to each molecule of a pint of water and the result mixed with all the waters of all the oceans, the only things one would see when observing an ocean would be shipping tags.)

There are indications that new classification systems being devised today to solve our practical problems have applied some of Ranganathan's ideas. Jessica Melton, in a paper on the compatibility of the Colon Classification and the Western Reserve University System (used in their mechanized information retrieval system), points up a similarity in method which can be explained only in terms of the application of ideas Ranaganathan has expounded.[1] Vickery, in his book, *Classification and Indexing in Science,* acknowledges his debt to Ranganathan. The work of the Classification Research Group in England is a direct result of their study of Ranganathan's work and an application of it. We get the most satisfactory explanation of his ideas in the reports of this group. Many of these reports are in the CRSG Loan Collection at the SLA Classification Center located in Cleveland at Western Reserve University.

Even though Ranganathan's approach to the subject of classification and the approach of his followers is similar, the outward appearance of their work is not. The notations used are not universally accepted. Each worker has devised his own notation. His followers apply his methods within a restricted universe, usually a special library, while he has tried to develop a satisfactory classification system for all knowledge. His explanation of the need for a universal classification system cannot be denied: "experience has shown that the entire field of knowledge is at the bottom so inter-related that progress in any portion of it affects every other portion sooner or later. Special classifications are thus outmoded . . . a universal classification is therefore, more suited." Nevertheless, his early idea that one man can devise such a system is untenable. Such a universal classification would have to be worked out by several subject specialists applying the same method of classification to their respective fields. To elaborate on this, I will need to define classification, *what* and *why* we classify, and *how* to go about it.

DEFINITION OF CLASSIFICATION

Ranganathan defines library classification as "an uncovering of the thought content of a written or expressed unit of thought." In all its minutest details he thinks classification is what it should be only when the thought-content as a whole is uncovered—all the *phases* (meaning relationships or influences with other subjects) are apprehended; all the *facets* (meaning thought-units or isolated ideas corresponding to a class or fundamental category of concepts) are expressed; and all *the foci* (meaning the specific *characteristics* of the material being analyzed) are uncovered. To say it in one sentence, he thinks that classification is the method by which a written or expressed unit of thought is exhaustively analyzed in terms of entirety rather than in terms of parts.[2] He defines classification in still another way which is not contradictory but is related more to the use of the term as a "scheme" rather than as an "act." In his "Library Classification Glossary" he calls classification a scheme or statement showing the filiatory sequence (meaning hierarchy) of the classes fitted with terminology and notation. Such a scheme may be an *analytico-synthetic faceted* classification involving analysis of a subject into its facets according to a set of postulates, the translation of the facets into ordinal numbers on the basis of a notation system for facets and their relationships, then a synthesis of these numbers into a class number. Such a scheme does not provide ready-made class numbers for every subject. Or a classification scheme may be *enumerative* where there is a schedule of ready-made numbers and an enumeration of most of the classes. At the Dorking Conference Ranganathan described the enumerative classification as one suited to a relatively finite and lethargic universe of knowledge, but found the analytico-synthetic classification was needed to face the challenge of the infinite, ever-growing, and turbulent universe of knowledge.

THE WHAT AND WHY OF CLASSIFICATION

The what of classification for most of us today is that turbulent universe of knowledge, that muddy puddle I described earlier. In his paper for the GLS Conference on Bibliographic Organization in 1950, Ranganathan tried to describe the behavior (or tactics) of knowledge by means of a diagram which incorporates some mathematical concepts based on Boolean algebra.

In this diagram (Figure 1) he includes the counter-tactics of classification which represent an attempt to organize that knowledge. He gives specific examples of these conditions or tactics in *Elements of Classification,* but it is not difficult to think of many more. A few examples serve as illustration: (1) *Denudation*—current electricity would be the smaller circle

within the larger circle of electricity; (2) *Dissection*—Judaism and Bud-
dhism would be co-ordinate classes or segments in the large circle of
Religion; (3) *Lamination*—Biochemistry would be the shaded area and the
large circles would be biology and chemistry; (4) *Loose-assemblage*—(the
formation of a new subject by bringing one subject into relation with
another but with no forming or sharpening the first subject). The one
example which comes to mind is Documentation which is a loose assem-
blage of librarianship and communication theory. Table II explains some of
the tactics of classification which Ranganathan identifies in Figure 1.

FIGURE 1*

TACTICS OF FIELD OF KNOWLEDGE				COUNTER-TACTICS OF CLASSIFICATION		
Diagram		*Name*	*Result*	*Focus* [a]	*Notation* [b]	*Result*
1		Denuda-tion	*Subordi-nated* classes or *chain* of classes	Sharper *focus*	Decimal-fraction nota-tion	Infinite hospi-tality in *chain*
2		Dissec-tion	*Co-ordi-nate* classes or *array* of classes	Addi-tional *focus*	Octave nota-tion	Infinite hospi-tality in *array*
3		Lamina-tion	*Composite-*class	Com-pound *focus*	Faceted nota-tion	Infinite hospi-tality in *facets* [a]
4		Loose-as-semblage	*Com-bination-*class	Complex *focus*	Phased nota-tion	Infinite hospi-tality in *phases* [a]

*Source: S. R. Ranganathan. ''Colon Classificaton and Its Approach to Documentation. In
Jesse H. Shera, ed. *Bibliographic Organization*. Chicago, University of Chicago Press,
1951, p. 97.
[a] See definition given earlier in this paper.
[b] See Table II for examples.

Ranganathan has described satisfactorily *what* we are trying to classify and he has also expressed the *why* of classification:

> Few workers are able to name their specific subjects exactly. It is a broader or a narrower subject that is usually thought of. Workers can get full satisfaction. . . . only if the arrangement throws the entries in the order of filiation of their specific subjects. But the ruthless indiscriminate scattering of specific subjects which is caused by alphabetical arrangement is notorious. . . . (In a classified arrangement), the reader or library user finds all that he was vaguely conscious of having wanted; and indeed it is only then that he is enabled to know the exact thing he wanted. The helpful filiatory way, in which entry follows entry, brings to his notice everything bearing on his field of work, exactly, exhaustively, and expeditiously.[3]

By now it should be obvious that a classification scheme which does not provide counter-tactics for the tactics and complications of knowledge, will not prove satisfactory for very long. A satisfactory scheme must have certain qualities if it is to be a useful component of a retrieval system. These qualities have been outlined by Ranganathan:

Helpful Qualities in a Classification Scheme Which Provide for Revision and Perpetuation

1. Individualization of every subject in the classes.
2. Infinite hospitality in *array* (co-ordinate within a class or co-ordinate classes).
3. Infinite hospitality in a *chain* (subordinate within a class).
4. Infinite hospitality in facets when there is a compound focus caused by lamination of two basic classes.
5. Provide for phase analysis (compound or complex class).
6. Permanence of meaning and absence of homonyms within the scheme.
7. Provide for elimination of synonymous class assignments.
8. A mixed notational base: digits of more than one conventional group.
9. Mnemonically useful digits.

Tests for these qualities in any scheme can be made by assessing its provision or arrangement for an application of the following canons:

The Canons of Classification

(See list of suggested readings at end of paper for titles of books which explain these canons in detail.)

For Characteristics (Foci)

1. Canon of Differentiation	4. Canon of Ascertainability
2. Canon of Concomitance	5. Canon of Permanence
3. Canon of Relevance	6. Canon of Relevant Sequence
	7. Canon of Consistency

The Canons of Classification (continued)

For Array
8. Canon of Exhaustiveness
9. Canon of Exclusiveness

10. Canon of Helpful Sequence
11. Canon of Consistent Sequence

For Chain
12. Canon of Decreasing Extension

13. Canon of Modulation

For Filiatory Sequence
14. Canon of Subordinate Classes

15. Canon of Co-ordinate Classes

For Terminology
16. Canon of Currency
17. Canon of Reticence

18. Canon of Enumeration
19. Canon of Context

For Notation
20. Canon of Relativity
21. Canon of Expressiveness

22. Canon of Mixed Notation

THE HOW OF MAKING A CLASSIFICATION SCHEME

Having analyzed the difficulties, it would have been unfortunate if Ranganathan had not provided a method of solution. His classification scheme is a direct result of his analysis of the problem. Like Euclid in mathematics and Rameau in music, his work must be recognized as the basis for an understanding of the theories, techniques, and procedures in library classification. In his many writings on the subject, he has presented the theory which must underlie a classification scheme if it is to provide all the detail, variety, flexibility, and simplicity required for modern information indexing.[4] He has also provided the method for the application of such an analytico-synthetic classification scheme once it is devised—it is called *facet analysis*. Any classification scheme which meets the standards or canons of classification will be an acceptable device. For that reason, the rest of this paper will be an explanation of the steps in the construction of an analytico-synthetic faceted classification scheme and an application of it by means of facet analysis. It would be folly to devise an analytico-synthetic faceted classification on the basis of my exposition of the method (which is really a dangerous condensation of a rather complicated process), but if all this sounds like a reasonable idea, then, by all means, follow up with the reading of Ranganathan's *Prolegomena* and Vickery's book, *Faceted Classification,* or test the classification scheme you use against the canons of classification. Might we not all be better off today if Melvil Dewey could have checked his scheme against these canons?

If you know the subject you wish to classify, it should not be too difficult for you to follow the steps outlined in Table I. First you determine and establish the primary or *fundamental categories* which would divide the field according to helpful characteristics. Ranganathan, working with the whole universe of knowledge, uses the fundamental categories—Space, Time, Matter, Energy, Personality—because these can be applied equally well to any field after they are translated into the language of the field. Vickery, working within a restricted universe, e.g., soil science, divided the field into property, part, measure, parent material, process, and operation. J. Binns analyzed the subject field of electronic, mechanical, and electrical engineering into the fundamental categories of industries and professions, plants and machines, components, materials, physical phenomena, operations, agent (meaning instruments and equipment), language and form of publication, and geographical divisions.

Once you have established these primary or fundamental categories, terms can be groups in these categories. The sequence in which these categories should be combined needs to be decided upon and the facets under which individual terms (*foci* or *isolates* of the scheme) will be grouped need to be determined. In a limited field, it is helpful to maintain a glossary of terms with an indication of the proper facet for each term. The analysis of the terms into facets should not depend on the interpretation of each classifier. The classification-maker should provide this guidance.

Next the schedule of facets is fitted with a notation that permits a flexible combination of terms. Only in this way can you provide for all the tactics of knowledge: denudation, dissection, lamination, and loose-assemblage.

TABLE I: Steps in the Construction and Application of a Faceted Analytico-Synthetic Classification

---

Inherent Concepts: Characteristics; facets; array of classes; chain of classes; filiatory arrangement; terminology of the scheme; notation

Steps:

1. In a given field of knowledge, establish a basis for dividing the field by helpful *characteristics*. Isolated ideas can be grouped into *categories* by applying these characteristics of division. An *array of co-ordinate classes* will be derived from the consistent use of one and the same characteristic.
2. Organize the *categories* into suitable *facets* (basic class, isolate idea, or thought unit—not a subject in itself) and assign a helpful sequence in which they are to be used.

TABLE I: Steps in the Construction and Application of a Faceted Analytico-Synthetic Classification (continued)

3. Fit the schedule of facets with a notation that will permit the fully flexible combination of word groups that is needed.
4. Provide an index for the terms or word groups (*foci* or *isolates* of a given facet).
5. Classify material by using the standardized procedure for facet analysis (postulational approach to classification):
   a. Idea Plane: Analyze the subject into its facets and name the isolates in each facet.
   b. Idea Plane: Rearrange the names of the isolates so as to conform to the syntax of the classificatory language adopted.
   c. Verbal Plane: Change the name of each isolate into the standard terminology found in the scheme of classification.
   d. Verbal and Notational Planes: Translate the name of the isolate in each facet into isolate number with the aid of the schedule for the facet and the devices applicable to it.
   e. Notational Plane: Synthesize the basic class number and the different isolate numbers into the class number with the aid of connecting symbols.

THE HOW OF CLASSIFYING BY FACET ANALYSIS

The method of facet analysis using a classification scheme devised as described above is rather simple. It has been compared to the work of an apothecary compounding a mixture according to any given prescription. The thought-content of the document gives the prescription. The short schedules for the facets give the ingredients. The connecting symbols and the digits (includes letter, punctuation marks, and other symbols for relationships) correspond to the adhesives and other materials used to bind all the ingredients into a state of consistency and stability.

The application of facet analysis is shown in Table II. Three different classification systems are used: Ranganathan's Colon Classification, Vickery's classification scheme for Soil Science, and Phyllis Richmond's for the History of Science. Facet analysis can best be applied when you use a faceted classification scheme, but it is not essential. If you don't, just be prepared to go as far as you can until the fixed notation (such as DC) will not allow you to open the door of hospitality to a new (or sharper) focus of a given subject.

TABLE II: Application of Facet Analysis Using Three Different Classification Systems

1. Start with the title of the work.
   Ranganathan: Leaf-virus of wheat and spraying of chemicals in Michigan in 1958
   Vickery: Salinity in relation to irrigation
   Richmond: The Black Death and men of learning
2. Derive from the "raw" title the full descriptive title, remembering to include the *Basic Class* into which this work falls.
   R: Disease of leaf of wheat caused by virus and curing by spraying of chemicals in Agriculture (BC) in Michigan 1958
   V: Salinity (a property) in relation to irrigation (an operation) in Soil Science (BC)
   Ri: Influence of Bubonic plague (Black Death) on men of learning (medieval education) in History of Science (BC) Western Society, 14th C. Europe
3. Analyze the title in terms of isolates or units of thought. These *isolates* must be attached to the basic class and cannot be a subject in themselves.
   R: Disease Leaf Wheat Virus Curing Spraying Chemicals Agriculture (BC) Michigan 1958
   V: Soil Salinity relation to Irrigation Soil Science (BC)
   Ri: Bubonic plague influence medieval education History of Science (BC) Western Society 14th C. Europe
4. Transform the isolates into fundamental categories:
   R*: Disease (E) Leaf (P) Wheat (P) Virus (P) Curing (E2) Spraying (E3) Chemicals (P) Agriculture (BC) Michigan (S) 1958 (T)
   V: Salinity (Property) related to Irrigation (Operation on Soil) Soil Science (BC)
   Ri: Bubonic Plague (Medicine-Disease) influence Medieval Education (non-scientific subject) Western Society (Cultural milieu) History of Science (BC) 14th Century (Time) Europe (Space)
5. Arrange isolates in standard facet order. Sharpen the *focus* of the facet. This arrangement is important when more than one isolate falls into the same fundamental category.
   R. Agriculture (BC) Wheat (P) Leaf (P2) Disease (E) Virus (P2) Therapy—Curing (E2) Chemical (P3) Spraying (E3) Michigan (S) 1950's (T)
   V: Soil Science (BC) Salinity (Property) Irrigation (Operation on Soil)
   Ri: History of Science (BC) Bubonic Plague (Medicine-Disease) Medieval Education (Non-scientific subject) Western Society (Cultural milieu) in 14th Century (T) Europe (Space)
6. Transform *facet numbers* into standard notational terms.
   R: J (BC) 382 (P) 5 (P2) 4 (E) 23 (P2) 6 (E2) 3 (P3) 5 (E3) 7381 (S) N5 (T)
   V: Soil Science (BC) 6s (specific physico-chemical property) 4f (irrigation—operation on soil)

*(E)—Energy; (P)—Personality; (S)—Space; (T)—Time.

TABLE II: Application of Facet Analysis Using Three Different Classification Systems (continued)

Ri: WC (Scientific subject—Medicine) J3E (non-scientific subject) V (cultural milieu) 31 (space/time)

7. Synthesize *facet numbers* and class numbers, using facet and relationship indicators.

R: J382, 5:423:63:5.7381.N5

V: 6s/4f

Ri: #WC(7)$J3E¢V@31   Note: (7) is indicator for *phase* relationship

CONCLUSION

This brief explanation may help to explain why some people are so enthusiastic about Ranganathan's work. B. I. Palmer,[5] in his review of the 5th edition of the Colon Classification, had this to say:

> Ranganathan has elevated the study of classification from the description of vague feelings and the drawing of remote analogies to an objective science. The notation reveals the hierarchy of the scheme, has mnemonic features, and produces an infinitely flexible tool which reflects unerringly in a formalized way each phase and facet, each twist and turn of a specific subject. The notation matches microthought at deeper and deeper levels by a notation of greater length and complexity. . . . He has shown us the full potentialities and limitations of notation and provided us a method of analysis which lies at the back of all constructive work that is being done in the field of classification today.

Ranganathan's own system is well worth study by those who contemplate constructive developments in bibliographic classification, but even without the study of Colon, a great deal can be learned from his thoughts on classification theory in general. Anyone attempting to make a new classification or devise a thesaurus of terms would benefit from a serious exploration of analytico-synthetic faceted schemes.

The range of Ranganathan's ideas goes beyond the library field. Information science (better called *informatology,* the study of information handling and processing techniques) has also felt the effect. It would probably be impossible to estimate the extent to which consciously or otherwise, the WRU system and other mechanized systems have been influenced, even guided, in their development by Ranganathan.

The following statement by Ennis[6] struck me with double force when I was trying to summarize my thoughts on classification theory and

Ranganathan's contributions to our work in the muddy puddle called the universe of knowledge:

> . . . there is a continuum of effects as a given technological change echoes more and more distantly through society, somewhat similar to the way the disturbance rings of a pebble thrown into a lake spread out in widening and weakening circles. The problem is to know when to stop looking for effects—either because they are too distant in time or too distant in social space from the point of origin.

ACKNOWLEDGEMENT

The author is indebted to Phyllis Richmond, Robert J. Howerton, and John S. Rippon for their helpful criticism when this paper was first written.

REFERENCES

1. Melton, Jessica. "A Note on the Compatibility of Two Information Systems." *Technical Note* No. 13 AFOSR TN 60-261. March 8, 1960.

2. Ranganathan, S. R. *Classification and Communication.* Delhi, University of Delhi, 1951. p. 185.

3. ———. "Classification and International Documentation." *Revue de la Documentation,* 14:154-77. 1947.

4. For a short essay outlining Ranganathan's contributions to classification theory, see Palmer, Bernard I. *Itself an Education.* London, The Library Association, 1962. p. 46–57.

5. Palmer, B. I. Review of *Colon Classification,* 5th ed. *Journal of Documentation,* 14:17. 1958.

6. Ennis, Philip H. "Technological Change and the Professions." *Library Quarterly,* 32:195. July, 1962.

LIST OF SUGGESTED READINGS

Ranganathan, S. R.
  Colon Classification; Basic Classificaton. 6th ed. completely rev. London, Asia Publishing House, 1960.
  "Colon Classification and Its Approach to Documentation." *in* Shera, Jesse, ed. *Bibliographic Organization.* Chicago, University of Chicago Press, 1951. pp. 94–105.
  Elements of Library Classification. 2d ed. London, The Association of Assistant Librarians, 1959.
  "Library Classification Glossary." *Annals of Library Science,* V. September, 1958.
  Philosophy of Library Classification. Copenhagen, E. Munksgaard, 1951.
  Prolegomena to Library Classification. 2d ed. London, Library Association, 1957.
Vickery, B. C.
  Classification and Indexing in Science. 2d ed., enl. New York, Academic Press, 1959.
  Faceted Classification. London, Aslib, 1960.
  On Retrieval System Theory. London, Butterworths, 1961.

American Institute of Physics/ UDC Project AUDACIOUS

File Organization and Search Strategy Using the Universal Decimal Classification in Mechanized Reference Retrieval Systems*

by Robert R. Freeman and Pauline Atherton

Abstract

Starting from a model of contemporary mechanized retrieval systems and the characteristics of indexing languages used therein, the authors develop a rational basis for use of the Universal Decimal Classification (UDC) in this context. Practical design considerations for the use of UDC in a mechanized retrieval system are discussed. Examples are reported of the use of UDC as the indexing language with the Combined File Search System, an existing retrieval system for the IBM 1401, used by several large information centers in the United States. Finally, the authors discuss how UDC might be used as a query language in a typical retrieval system of the near future in which the user interacts directly with the computer-stored document reference file.

The authors conclude that it is technically feasible to use UDC in mechanized retrieval systems and that, under certain conditions, it may be desirable. Some of these conditions are the existence of large files already indexed by UDC, staff already trained for its use, and extensive international use or exchange of materials of the system.

UDC 025.3 + 025.4UDC:651.53 + 651.838.8:681.322.04/.06

*Excerpts from a paper presented at the F.I.D./I.F.I.P. Conference on Mechanized Information Storage, Retrieval, and Dissemination, Rome, June 15, 1967. American Institute of Physics/UDC Project, Report No. AIP/UDC-5 National Science Foundation Grant GN-433, September 15, 1967. Editor's Note: Figure 1 is not reproduced here.

Explanation of UDC numbers:

025.3	*—Cataloging and indexing-Information retrieval systems*
025.4UDC	*—Decimal classifications-U.D.C.*
651.53	*—Methods of file organization*
651.838.8	*—Electronic methods of selection from files*
681.322.04/.06	*—Digital computers-data representation (.04), data conversion (.05), and programming aspects (.06)*

CHARACTERISTICS OF UDC AS AN INDEXING LANGUAGE IN THE CONTEXT OF MECHANIZED RETRIEVAL SYSTEMS

Authority File

The UDC is an example of an indexing language of the type illustrated in the model mechanized retrieval system (Figure I). It consists of (a) a controlled and structured set of descriptors organized and displayed in a file with a variety of devices to facilitate comprehension of the structure and meanings and (b) a set of rules of formation used to specify relationships among descriptors used to represent a given document.

The major principle upon which UDC is being continuously developed is that of general characteristics, or facets. Its name indicates that it is a decimal classification, i.e., one in which each node of a tree of related descriptors may have up to ten nodes connected to it. However, this is *not* the case at the most basic level. The basic division of the stock of descriptors in UDC is into *six facets*, two *form* facets and four *content* facets, as illustrated in Figure II.

Unfortunately, the development of the UDC was begun before the advent of the facet principle. It has been recognized (9) that the general subject facet has not one unifying characteristic, but several. An internationally controlled instrument like the UDC can only respond slowly to greatly varying philosophies and practical needs. A concession to the need for further facets was the development of what might be termed "subordinate descriptors." These "subordinate descriptors" make explicit recognition of unifying characteristics in various parts of the general subject facet. However, the subordinate descriptors have meaning only through use with a normal descriptor.

The ten primary divisions of the general subject facet have been referred to as the "main classes," while all other facets were known as "auxiliaries." In rules of formation, emphasis has been placed on a definite order for stating the descriptors to be used to represent a document and on a definite order for stating the descriptors to be used to represent a document and on a definite order for filing such records. This has meant that descriptors from facets other than the general subject facet could not serve as direct points of entry in a document index produced using UDC. The only apparent reason for this practice has been the necessity to severely limit the number of entries in a manual card file for reasons of cost and sheer physical size. An example of the full use of the UDC indexing for one document is given in Figure III.

No theoretical reason makes any of the entries shown in Figure III auxiliary to any other and incapable of serving as a valid point of entry to a file. The example, besides illustrating this point, reveals the other two characteristics of UDC to be considered, the rules of formation and the notation.

FIGURE 2. Form and Content Facets in UDC with Standard Notation

Facets		Standard Notation
Form facets:		
1.	language	$= \ldots$
2.	form of work	$(0 \ldots)$
Content facets:		
3.	place	$(n \ldots) \quad n = 1$ to 9
4.	race	$(= \ldots)$
5.	time	" $\ldots$ "
6.	general subject	absence of notational signal

Rules of Formation

The rules of formation of the UDC have been exhaustively and critically discussed by Perreault (10), who has advanced proposals for additional and revised rules. For the purposes of this paper, we will only corroborate his principle points of criticism:

(1) the rules lack specificity, i.e. too many possible relationships must be represented by too few devices;

(2) the rules are weak in that they do not permit nonlinear relationships to be coded in a linear expression, thus resulting in ambiguous expressions;

(3) the rules are ambiguous in application, i.e. two indexers may encode the same relationship differently.

The conclusion which must inevitably result is that the rules of formation, as they presently exist, are of no practical value in a mechanized retrieval system, other than to separate descriptors.

FIGURE 3. Example of UDC Indexing of a Document

Document Title: Distribution and Seasonal Movements of Saginaw Bay Fishes.

UDC in statement form:

    597:591.9:591.52(285:71:73)"1964/1966"(047+084.3)

UDC in index entry form with English equivalents:

(047)	Technical Reports
(084.3)	Maps
(285)	Lakes
(71)	Canada
(73)	United States
"1964/1966"	Events of 1964 - 1966
591.52	Animal Habitats and Migrations
591.9	Geographical Distribution of Animals
597	Ichthyology. Fish.

Notation

UDC and other indexing languages which make use of a non-natural language notation are frequently criticized on the ground that such notations introduce unnecessary complications for the user. However, as we have seen in the system model presented above, many mechanized systems convert natural language descriptors to a non-natural language descriptor surrogate or code at the input stage (see Figure 1). The latter is then used for all internal processing and retrieval purposes. For mechanized retrieval systems, the advantage would appear to rest with the indexing language with a notation which not only uniquely identifies the descriptors, but reveals relationships among them. This notation, to be most useful, should reveal relationships between descriptors in the indexing language as well as between the descriptors used to index a particular document.

The idea of mechanical assignment of individual UDC numbers (e.g., the nine numbers in Figure III), via lookup in a machine-readable table of natural language descriptor equivalents has not yet been tried, but there does not seem to be any reason why it cannot be done. Such a step would relieve human indexers and searchers from any concern with the UDC notation, while retaining the advantage of the notation. The relational indicators might be more difficult to do in a purely mechanical way, unless a rather strictly controlled form of natural language input were used. UDC has been used to mechanically structure a merged vocabulary of alphabetic descriptors from sixteen different agencies in the field of atmospheric sciences in the United States (11). This work, if carried still further, could show the way toward structuring purely alphabetic descriptor lists.

Regardless of how the notation is derived and assigned, it is necessary for the system designer and programmer to understand the significance of the notation and how it should be handled in a mechanized retrieval system. UDC notation consists of strings of digits, interspersed for visual covenience with decimal points, at intervals of three digits, and other symbolic indicators. There are also various symbols assigned to signal the facet to which the descriptor belongs and to signal subordinate descriptors. There are, in addition, symbols which are the notational manifestation of the rules of formation, i.e. connectives which specify certain relationships between two UDC numbers when used to describe the complex content of a document.

UDC has developed a set of filing rules for the numbers which is based on philosophical reasoning about the degree of concreteness of the facets and other considerations. Such matters generally lose their importance when one is concerned with a mechanized retrieval system.

It would be more efficient to store a notation in the computer which preserves the concepts and relationships of the UDC, but uses a somewhat differing set of symbols from those shown in Figure II. There are several reasons for holding this opinion:

(1) Some of the notational devices of UDC serve the function of visual convenience; this function is meaningless in a computer.

(2) Some of the notational devices use the same punctuation symbols. The order of sorting these characters, arbitrarily defined for each type of computer, causes some problems when they are interspersed among digits in UDC numbers, especially if the user desires to adhere to UDC filing rules (12).

(3) Some of the notational devices require recognition of two characters in order to differentiate between devices. For example, the

FIGURE 4. UDC Index Numbers Encoded for Storage and Retrieval by Computer

Type	Name	Normal Form	Encoded Form	Example	Encoded Form
Content Facet	General Subject	n	Cn	551.524.63	C55152463
Form Facet	Language	=n	En	=30	E30
Form Facet	Form of Work	(0n)	Fn	(084.3)	F843
Content Facet	Place	(mn)	Pmn	(265)	P265
Content Facet	Race	(=n)	Rn	(=30)	R30
Content Facet	Time	"n"	Tn	"475"	T475
Subordinate Content Facet	Point of View	.00n	Vn	55.002.2	C55V22
Subordinate Content Facet	Special Auxiliary	-n	Wn	62-451	C62W451
Subordinate Content Facet	Special Auxiliary	.0n	Xn	62.018.7	C62X187
Connective	Synthetic Connective	n'n	nYn	546.32'13	C54632Y13
Connective	Inclusive Connective	n/n		543/546	C543
Connective	Relative Connective	n:n		543:546	C546
Connective	General Connective	n+n		543+546	(Connectives
Connective	Subordinate Connective	n(n)		543(546)	not encoded)

Note: n = a set of digits, any of which may be any of the digits, 0 ... 9.
    m = a digit from 1 to 9.

equals sign has one meaning by itself and another if it is preceded
by a parenthesis.

(4) Two of the devices (.0 and .00) incorporate a meaningful use of
what is otherwise a convenience symbol, the decimal point.

The authors have found it convenient to transform conventional UDC
numbers to a more efficient notation in the computer during an editing stage
which takes place as the data are converted to their representation on
magnetic tape, a step common to most information retrieval systems. The
symbols selected for this special form are purely arbitrary; any set which
meets external criteria could be used.* The rules of transformation should
be so clear from the example below as to not require formal statement.

The particular system selected for use, which will be described next,
makes use of an inverted file, in which the connectives are not meaningful
and therefore not used. However, the reader should carefully differentiate
between this practical consideration and the theoretical criticism offered
above.

TOWARD USE OF UDC IN AN INTERACTIVE RETRIEVAL SYSTEM

During the course of the project, the authors observed with interest the
development of several experimental interactive retrieval systems. Such
systems are characterized by the user's ability by means of instruments of
direct communication between himself and the computer, to become a part
of an iterative process which leads to a direct answer to his query. We
became convinced that the concept of such a retrieval system (1) provides a
closer analogue to the man-system interaction that takes place in a
conventional manual library or information center than does a computer
batch processing system and (2) at the same time this interaction helps to
overcome some of the physical access problems of manual systems, such as
the need to manipulate large books and card files. In short, the interactive
retrieval system appears to be a reasonable prototype for future systems, at
least in concept.

We investigated several of the experimental systems to determine
possibilities for demonstrating the use of UDC in this context. Use of UDC
in such a mode appears to be feasible. Because the design of interactive
systems is such a new area, from the standpoints of both file processing and
hardware for man-machine interaction, it seems worthwhile to document
our general conception of how a user would interact with our UDC-indexed

---

*The set suggested here is thought to improve upon that suggested by Freeman in 1964 (12),
although the latter accomplishes the purpose.

files. Results of an experiment with an existing interactive system will be reported in a subsequent report of this project.

The instruments of man-machine communication vary, generally consisting of one or more on-line keyboard instruments, cathode ray tube display scopes, and light pens. The keyboard instruments, which provide communciation from as well as to the computer, combine several aspects:

(a) keys which identify specific characters, such as the letters of the alphabet, the digits, and some punctuation characters;
(b) keys which identify symbols of broader scope, such as types of bibliographic data;
(c) keys which facilitate, file processing, such as scanning rapidly through a file to a certain point, then stepping along item-by-item;
(d) keys which regulate communication with the computer, such as "transmit message" or "erase display."

Let us assume, for this hypothetical example, that we have a single on-line typewriter equipped with all these keys and a display scope.*

Step One: Negotiation of Query

The user, a meteorologist, after identifying himself to the system and establishing his right of access to the system, is ready to begin negotiation of his query. He is interested in atmospheric radioactivity in the Arctic regions. The computer has stored a file of nuclear science literature and, as the authority file for the index language, the UDC *Special Subject Edition for Nuclear Science and Technology.*

The user types "radioactivity?" on his keyboard. The authority file has several descriptors in which this term is used, so the system displays the alternatives for a more specific choice:

```
RADIOACTIVITY                          539.16
RADIOACTIVITY IN ATMOSPHERE            551.510.7
RADIOACTIVITY IN EARTH                 550.378
RADIOACTIVITY IN OCEANS AND SEAS       551.46:539.16
RADIOACTIVITY IN RIVERS                551.48:539.16
RADIOACTIVITY STANDARDS                539.16.081
```

*This description is a simplified composite of our observations of the Bibliographic On-Line Display System (BOLD) (19), NASA/RECON (20), and MULTILIST (21).

"Radioactivity in the atmosphere" clearly describes one part of his query, but to be sure, he asks for a display of related descriptors by typing "551.510.7?". The system responds with the display:

```
 551.51         STRUCTURE, MECHANICS, AND THERMODYNAMICS
                OF THE ATMOSPHERE
 551.510.3      PHYSICAL PROPERTIES OF THE ATMOSPHERE
 551.510.4      COMPOSITION OF THE ATMOSPHERE
 551.510.5      GENERAL STRUCTURE OF THE ATMOSPHERE
►551.510.7      RADIOACTIVITY OF THE ATMOSPHERE
 551.510.71     NATURAL RADIOACTIVITY
 551.510.72     ARTIFICIAL RADIOACTIVITY
 551.510.721    RADIOACTIVE FALL-OUT  Cf. 614.73, 628.511
 551.511        MECHANICS AND THERMODYNAMICS OF THE
                ATMOSPHERE
```

Two cross references appear to require further checking, so he types "614.73?" and gets the display:

```
 614        PUBLIC HEALTH AND SAFETY
 614.3      FOOD AND DRUGS.  SANITARY INSPECTION AND CONTROL
 614.4      PREVENTION OF INFECTION, EPIDEMICS, ETC.
 614.6      DISPOSAL OF THE DEAD
 614.7      HYGIENE OF AIR, SOIL AND WATER.  POLLUTION
►614.73     FALL-OUT IN GENERAL, Cf. 551.510.721
                FOR SAMPLING METHODS, USE 614.73:543.053
 614.8      ACCIDENTS.  SAFETY ORGANIZATIONS AND PROCEDURES
```

On typing "628.511?" he sees the display:

```
 628        PUBLIC HEALTH ENGINEERING
 628.1      WATER SUPPLY.  DRINKING WATER IN GENERAL
 628.3      SEWAGE.  DISPOSAL OF SEWAGE
►628.511    ATMOSPHERIC POLLUTION
 628.515    WATER POLLUTION
 628.543    INDUSTRIAL WASTE DISPOSAL
 628.8      INDOOR CLIMATE ENGINEERING
 628.9      ILLUMINATING ENGINEERING
```

Both 614.73 and 628.511 are sufficiently related, he thinks, that they should be used as search terms. Since he also wishes to limit his search to material on Arctic regions, he types "Arctic?" and sees the display:

```
        ARCTIC REGIONS    (98)
```

Let us now agree that he is satisfied that he has found the descriptors he wishes to use for a search.

Step Two: Search Formulation and Reference Retrieval

The user decides to accept as output any reference which is indexed by the descriptor for Arctic Regions (98) and by any of the terms he believes may be linked to atmospheric radioactivity. He now types the query:

$$``[551.510.7{+}614.73{+}628.511]{*}(98)"$$

The + sign is to be interpreted as the Boolean "or" and the * sign as "and." The system very soon responds with this display:

```
[551.510.7+614.73+628.511]*(98)

1 DOCUMENT FOUND:

DOCUMENT NO.  19-20157

TITLE:   ARTIFICIAL RADIOACTIVITY OF GROUND LEVEL AIR AT
         HAYES ISLAND (FRANZ JOSEF LAND) IN 1960 AND 1961.

SOURCE:  GOSUDARSTVENNYI KOMITET PO ISPOLZOVANIYU ATOMNOI
         ENERGII, SSSR

AUTHORS: DAVYDOV, E.N. AND MALAKHOV, S.G.

UDC:  614.73(98)"1960/1961"
      614.73:546.655.02.144
      614.73:546.36.02.137
      614.73:546.42.02.90
      614.73:539.165
```

The document was retrieved by the coordination of the query with the first indexing record displayed above, 614.73(98)"1960/1961." Note the other descriptors: 614.73 (fall-out) related to 546.655.02.144 (cerium-144), 546.36.02.137 (cesium-137), 546.42.02.90 (strontium-90), and 539.165 (beta radioactivity and decay).

Step Three: Search Output

The user decides to keep a record of this document for reference. He touches a key which commands the transfer of the display to the typewriter.

A myriad of factors would be considered in the design of a system of the type described. This simple example is intended only to illustrate how one might make use of the UDC for a structured authority file and document representation file in an interactive system.

CONCLUSIONS ON THE USE OF THE UDC IN MECHANIZED REFERENCE RETRIEVAL SYSTEMS

Our studies of the UDC in mechanized reference retrieval systems, while not yet complete, serve as a basis for some conclusions. The purpose of the work described in this paper has been to bring the light of practical experience to bear on an area in which there had previously been only speculation, thus providing guidance for the information system planner who is faced with deciding what role, if any, the UDC should play in a particular system.

First and most obvious, there is no longer any doubt that the UDC can be used as the indexing language in a mechanized system. Judgment must be based on the subtler question of whether it *should* be used. There are two major considerations:

(a) The adequacy of the indexing language, with regard to both specificity of the descriptors and the mechanism for keeping up to date, for the particular application. This aspect is outside the scope of this general study, except as experimental data may serve to illustrate such problems.

(b) The comparative adequacy of UDC with respect to problems associated with the design of mechanized systems.

Contemporary information retrieval system design emphasizes a partnership between man and machine. In this scheme, man performs the intellectual task of analysis, while the machine takes over the clerical task of replacing the indexer's natural language expressions by codes through which the machine can most efficiently represent terms and their interrelationships.

The meaning of efficiency must have something to do with the optimal use of resources to attain a goal, but what is optimal frequently involves policies of a given organization. At least at this point in time, the characteristics of available hardware heavily influence the design of a particular system. The UDC may be able to match the efficiency of machine processing of other, well-known existing indexing languages, but this is yet unproven. Marron and Snyderman have given an analysis of the economics of one system which uses a hierarchical code indexing language (22). More work along this line is needed before comparative efficiencies can be determined.

The preceding remarks have been made with the present notational manifestation of the UDC descriptors in mind. As we have already seen, the present notation, based largely on the need for visual convenience and manual processing, can be translated to forms more suitable for machine processing. Our investment in modifying a system designed to operate with alphabetic descriptors (CFSS) so that UDC could be used instead was not great in either time or money.

If some of the notational problems inherent in the present UDC, described earlier in this paper, are resolved, a new notation which is even better could make the UDC more useful for machine processing of information. This raises the question of the degree to which the present structure of UDC has been constrained by the need to adhere to a decimal notation. The capability of the mechanized system to assign a code for internal use from the indexer's natural language input means that such a code need not even be readily recognizable to human eyes, but there is something traditionally useful in a code of the latter type.

Our *second conclusion, then, is that the UDC, as it presently exists, probably cannot function as efficiently in a mechanized system as an indexing language designed specifically for machine processing, but no barriers exist to the successful use of the UDC in either a batch processing or interactive mode.* In general, system planners will want to consider the UDC if there are compelling reasons.

Several such reasons might be mentioned here. (1) An organization, through many years of use, may have built up large files and a skilled staff based on the use of UDC. (2) The ability to use UDC could save the not-insignificant cost of developing an indexing language. (3) The idea of an internationally used indexing language may have appeal for organizations for whom international exchange of materials is important. No barrier exists to the successful use of UDC in a mechanized retrieval system in cases where conditions such as these prevail.

REFERENCES

1. R. H. Richens, "An Abstracting and Information Service for Plant Breeding and Genetics," Chapter 17 *in* R. S. Casey, J. W. Perry, M. M. Berry, and A. Kent, *Punched Cards: Their Applications to Science and Industry, 2nd Edition*, New York, Reinhold Publishing Co., 1958.

2a. M. Rigby, *Mechanization of the UDC*, Final Report on NSF Grant GN-131, Washington, American Meteorological Society, June 3, 1964. PB166412.

2b. M. Rigby, "Experiments in Mechanized Control of Meteorological and Geoastrophysical Literature and the UDC Schedules in These Fields," *Rev. Int. Doc., 31*(3), 103–106 (1964).

3. American Documentation Institute, *Annual Review of Information Science and Technology, Volume 1* (Carlos A. Cuadra, Editor), New York, Interscience, 1966.

4. P. Atherton, "File Organization: Principles and Practices for Processing and Maintaining the Collection," Chapter 2 *in* Information for Industry, Inc., *Information Handling: First Principles* (P. W. Howerton, General Editor), Washington, Spartan Books, 1963.

5. C. W. Cleverdon and J. Mills, "The Testing of Index Language Devices," *ASLIB Proceedings, 15*(4) 106–130 (1963).

6. J. Perreault, *Towards Explication of the Rules of Formation in UDC* (to be published).

7. J. C. Gardin, *SYNTOL*, pp. 20–47, Volume II of the Rutgers Series on Systems for the Intellectual Organization of Information (Susan Artandi, Editor), New Brunswick, New Jersey, Graduate School of Library Service of Rutgers, the State University, 1965.

8. J. Mills, "Classification as an Indexing Device," pp. 428–441 *in* FID/CR Committee on Classification Research, *CLassification Research, Proceedings of the Second International Study Conference* (Pauline Atherton, Editor), Copenhagen, Munksgaard, 1965.

9a. E. deGrolier, *A Study of General Categories Applicable to Classification and Coding in Documentation*, pp. 17–42, Paris, UNESCO, 1962.

9b. H. Wellisch, "A Generally Applicable Material Facet for the UDC," *FID News Bulletin*, 16(9), 93–94 (1966).

10. J. Perreault, *op. cit.* and "Categories and Relators: a New Schema," *Revue Internationale de Documentation*, 32(4), 136–144 (1965).

11. Interdepartmental Committee for Atmospheric Sciences, *ICAS Vocabulary (Preliminary Edition)*, Washington, January, 1966.

12. R. R. Freeman, "Computers and Classification Systems," *Journal of Documentation*, 20(3), 137–145 (1964).

13. R. R. Freeman, *Research Project for the Evaluation of the UDC as the Indexing Language in a Mechanized Reference Retrieval System: an Introduction*, Report AIP/DRP UDC-1, New York, American Institute of Physics, October 1, 1965. NSF Grant GN-433.

14. D. D. Prentice, *The Combined File Search System*, Preprint of a paper presented at the 1965 Congress of the F.I.D., Washington, 15 pp., dated March 11, 1965 (revised). See also reference 16.

15. D. D. Prentice, G. deGraw, A. Smith, and I. A. Warheit, *1401 Information Storage and Retrieval System (The Combined File Search System), IBM 1401 General Program Library Number 1401-10.3.047 (Version 2)*, San Jose, California, IBM Corporation, April 21, 1965.

16a. I. A. Warheit, *The Combined File Search System: A Case Study of System Design for Information Retrieval*, Preprint of a paper presented at the 1965 Congress of the F.I.D., Washington, 9 pages. Updated.

16b. I. A. Warheit, "The Direct Access Search System," *AFIPS Conference Proceedings, Vol. 24; 1963 Fall Joint Computer Conference*, pp. 167–172, Baltimore, Spartan Books, 1963.

17. W. D. Climenson, "File Organization and Search Techniques," p. 113, Chapter 5 *in* American Documentation Institute, *Annual Review of Information Science and Technology*, (Carlos A. Cuadra, Editor), New York, Interscience, 1966.

18. British Standards Institution, *Universal Decimal Classification, Abridged English Edition, 3rd Edition*, BS1000A: 1961 (F.I.D. No. 289), London, 1961, pp. 5–10.

19. H. Borko and H. P. Burnaugh, *Interactive Displays for Document Retrieval*, Report No. SP-2557, Santa Monica, California, System Development Corporation, 4 August 1966.

20. National Aeronautics and Space Administration, *NASA/RECON User's Manual*, Washington, October, 1966. Contract NASW-1369.

21. N. S. Prywes, "Browsing in an Automated Library through Remote Consoles," *in Computer Augmentation of Human Reasoning*, (M. A. Sass and W. D. Wilkinson, Editors), Washington, Spartan Books, 1965.

22. H. Marron and M. Snyderman, Jr., "Cost Distribution and Analysis in Information Storage and Retrieval," *American Documentation*, 17(2), 89–95 (1966).

American Institute of Physics/UDC Project AUDACIOUS

Audacious—An Experiment with an On-Line Interactive Reference Retrieval System Using the Universal Decimal Classification as the Index Language in the Field of Nuclear Science*

by Robert R. Freeman and Pauline Atherton

The report describes an experimental system for remote direct access to files of computer-stored information which has been indexed by the Universal Decimal Classification (UDC). The data base for the experiment consisted of references from a single issue of Nuclear Science Abstracts. The Special Subject Edition of UDC for Nuclear Science and Technology was also stored in the computer so that users could discover how to translate their questions from natural language to logical statement containing UDC numbers.

The authors conclude that the technical feasibility of use of existing classification and indexing tools, such as UDC, has been demonstrated. However, detailed attention to all facets of man-machine communication is a necessity if systems are to be designed which will be voluntarily used. AUDACIOUS is reviewed and criticized from this point of view.

Finally, the authors conclude that the use of UDC in an on-line, interactive system may have important ramifications for the development of international information networks. Conversion tables (schedules) already exist which would allow speakers of many languages to search files indexed by UDC without regard to national or linguistic boundaries.

UDC 025.3+025.45UDC:651.53+651.83.0121: [621.385.832]:654.1.026.012.1:02:621.039

*Reprinted from American Institute of Physics, UDC Project, Report No. AIP/UDC-7, National Science Foundation Grant GN-433, April 25, 1968. Editor's Note: Figure 4 is not reproduced here.

Explanation of UDC numbers

025.3	*-Cataloging and indexing-information retrieval systems*
025.45UDC	*-Decimal classifications-UDC*
651.53	*-Methods of file organization*
651.83	*-Indexing and retrieval methods*
.012.1	*-Experimental testing and evaluation*
621.385.832	*-Cathode ray tubes*
654.1	*-Telegraphic telecommunications systems*
.026	*-Special purpose systems*
.012.1	*-Experimental testing and evaluation*
02	*-Libraries*
621.039	*-Nuclear science and technology*

INTRODUCTION

Over the course of the past twenty-odd years, mechanized systems have been developed to assist in the organization, search, and retrieval of increasingly large amounts of information. Until fairly recently, the translation and structuring of questions for such systems was a process of such a degree of complexity that an intermediary specialist's help was required. Furthermore, economic considerations have demanded that the timing of the processing of questions be a function of system—rather than user—convenience.

However, it has now become increasingly common to speak of interactive systems, i.e. those in which users enter directly into the search process, obtaining a result through a series of successive exchanges with the system. Interactive systems consequently offer a return to the flexibility of the traditional library.

In the United States, the same period of ferment in the field of documentation has gradually evolved a fairly widespread consensus on a set of principles for developing a thesaurus for the indexing and searching of scientific and technical literature. This particular type of thesaurus is exemplified by the DOD-LEX, EJC, ASM, NASA, and ERIC thesauri.

Their use has tended to be among abstracting and indexing services and information centers, all of which are concerned with in-depth coverage of detailed technical materials. Pioneering experiments with interactive systems have concentrated all of their attention upon the use of either thesauri of the type described or the natural language of document titles, abstracts, and other text.

In special libraries and other centers in which direct, often public, access to a physical collection of documents is particularly important, arrangement of the collection by the Dewey Decimal Classification or the Library of Congress Classification is most common. In recent years, some trend toward greater use of the LC Classification is evident. The Library of Congress's own MARC project creates a new level of importance for the development of techniques for handling such classification by machine.

Throughout the remainder of the world, however, the Universal Decimal Classification (UDC) is the most extensively used tool. The Soviet *Referativnyi Zhurnal* alone provides UDC numbers with each of the approximately 600,000 abstracts it publishes yearly. Moreover, it is used for both of the purposes mentioned above, indexing a file of documents in detail or arranging the file. With the increasing use of mechanized data processing systems in the handling of scientific information, the question arose as to whether the UDC was suited to use in this context. The current American Institute of Physics UDC Project has now given an affirmative answer.[1]

Furthermore, the UDC provides an internationally accepted, controlled (N.B.-not closed) vocabulary and a (largely) digital code which may be readily used by anyone who has a table (schedule) which translates his natural language to the code. This provides one answer to the dilemma pointed out recently by Baxendale: ". . . indexing design and practice seem to be moving in a direction counter to that of the information system planner. Where the planner is projecting 'integrated' centralized systems or networks of information systems, the continuing growth of very specialized information nuclei, responsive to a specific clientele with its unique professional dialect, seems to be working against centralization."[2]

The prospect of international information networks with on-line users in the relatively near future and the knowledge that large files of UDC-indexed documents are continuing to be created led us to investigate the

[1]R. R. Freeman and P. Atherton, *File Organization and Search Strategy Using the Universal Decimal Classification in Mechanized Reference Retrieval Systems.* Report AIP/UDC-5 under NSF Grant GN-433. American Institute of Physics, New York, September 15, 1967.
[2]P. Baxendale, "Content Analysis, Specification, and Control," Chapter 4 in American Documentation Institute, *Annual Review of Information Science and Technology* (C.A. Cuadra, Ed.), Interscience, New York, 1966. p. 72.

feasibility of an interactive information retrieval system using the UDC. We have named the experimental system which is described in this paper AUDACIOUS, an acronym for *A*utomatic *D*irect *A*ccess to *I*nformation with the *O*n-Line *U*DC *S*ystem.

BACKGROUND

The UDC has sometimes been pictured, quite wrongly, as a rigid hierarchical structure of mutually exclusive classes, which the innocent user may only approach by proceeding from the most general levels downward. It is in fact a semantic structure which may be entered by natural language and which displays semantic closeness by its hierarchy and other relationships of a less close nature by thorough cross referencing.

To illustrate that UDC can, in fact, be used quite similarly to other information languages, we determined to make use of an existing interactive retrieval system. Relatively few such systems were in existence at the beginning of 1967, at least to any degree of public availability. None, to our knowledge, were yet in full "production" operation, i.e. available to the clientele of an information system without the required intercession of a specialist in the use of the system.

SOME EXISTING INTERACTIVE SYSTEMS

Our search for a suitable experimental system led us to Dr. Noah S. Prywes at the University of Pennsylvania. Prywes and his associates had designed the MULTI-LIST real-time information storage and retrieval system,[3] implemented several versions of it, and described its application in principle to a library of a million documents.[4]

A somewhat modified version of the MULTI-LIST system was then being developed by the Information Systems Division of Xerox Corporation. In July, 1967, Xerox, through its University Microfilms Division announced a service, called DATRIX,[5] based upon storage and retrieval of information relating to doctoral dissertations. Discussions with Xerox staff members led us to the conclusion that there should be no difficulty in demonstrating the ability to search a file of UDC-indexed document references using DATRIX. The present report presents details of our experience with this system.

---

[3]N. S. Prywes and H. J. Gray, "The Multi-List System for Real-Time Storage and Retrieval," *IFIP Conference Proceedings 1962*, pp. 112–116.

[4]N. S. Prywes, "Browsing in an Automated Library Through Remote Access," *in* M. A. Sass and W. D. Wilkinson, Eds., *Computer Augmentation of Human Reasoning*, Spartan Books, Washington, 1965. pp. 105–130.

[5]*DATRIX*, Xerox Education Division, University Microfilms Library Services, Ann Arbor, Michigan, (no date).

Several conceptually similar systems have been or are being developed. We shall mention several here to help establish the context of this study, without attempting a complete cataloging of the available material. Another early development, still being used and improved, was M. M. Kessler's TIP system.[6] Users could query a file of physics literature for document references which contain occurrences of specified title words, author names, journal references, or bibliographic citations. No attempt was made to provide either for control of the vocabulary used or for a dialogue with the system in the first version of the system. TIP operates in a time-sharing mode, with a teletypewriter input-output device.

The BOLD system,[7] developed at System Development Corporation, provides two additional capabilities which are of interest here. First, starting from a display of the most general categories of a classification, a user can ask for successive displays of the subclasses subsumed by a given class, i.e. he may "go down the hierarchy" until he finds classes which describe his current question. Second, he may ask to see a display of all indexing terms (classes) in which a given word or root is present. Both techniques enable the user to convert his free language to the controlled language of the system. BOLD, as implemented in early 1967, operated in a time-shared mode, with CRT display, light pen, and teletypewriter for input-output functions.

Two similar systems were reported during 1967, both designed to allow a number of dispersed users to simultaneously retrieve document references from a NASA collection of around 300,000 references. Both DIALOG[8] (Lockheed Corp.) and RECON[9] (Bunker-Ramo Corp.) provide the user with the second of the two capabilities described for BOLD, the conversion of free language to a controlled language. Both systems use keyboard input and CRT display output, with DIALOG also providing a printer at the terminal.

OBJECTIVES OF AUDACIOUS

Earlier studies, including those cited in the previous section, had demonstrated the feasibility of on-line, user-directed searching of files of

---

[6]M. M. Kessler, "The MIT Technical Information Project," *Physics Today, 18,* 28–36 (March, 1965).

[7]System Development Corporation, *The BOLD User's Manual for Retrieval,* Report TM-2306/004/00, Santa Monica, California, September 6, 1966.

[8]R. K. Summit, "DIALOG: An operational on-line reference retrieval system," *Proceedings of the Association for Computing Machinery National Meeting-1967,* 51–56.

[9]D. Meister and D. J. Sullivan, *Evaluation of User Reactions to a Prototype On-Line Information Retrieval System,* Report NASA CR-918. Contract NASw-1369, prepared by Bunker-Ramo Corporation, Canogn Park, California. Contains appendix: NASA/Recon User's Manual, pp. 31–58.

bibliographic references, with varying capabilities for interaction between user and system. Our objectives in conducting the present study were:

(1) to demonstrate that it was possible to use UDC as a search tool in an interactive retrieval system, thereby extending the range of experience with such systems.

(2) to observe and report on any special characteristics or peculiarities of the use of UDC in this context. In particular, we were concerned with the ease with which a user could familiarize himself with and use the system. Recent research in the information-seeking behavior of individuals indicates the selection of a channel for acquiring information is governed even more by the user's perception of ease of use and familiarity with the system than by his judgement of the reliability of the system or expectation of amount of information to be obtained.[10,11,12]

(3) to add a new technique, or perhaps a fusion of existing techniques to the repertoire of interaction strategies available to the user. We have seen that, where a controlled vocabulary is available, interactive systems have offered the user two choices of discovery procedures for converting his own language to that of the system. The two were (a) entry to an alphabetic array of terms, including the one which the user specified, and (b) descent through successive levels of hierarchy from broadest to most specific concept.

DIRECT ON-LINE ENTRY INTO A HIERARCHICALLY-ARRAYED LIST OF TERMS

The new technique to be introduced in AUDACIOUS would provide for direct entry into a hierarchically-arrayed list of terms according to terms specified by the user. If the terms are present in remotely connected branches of the hierarchy, the system would display this fact to the user, then allow him to select one or more places to enter the hierarchy. *Note* that the user is exploring an array of terms, commonly called a UDC schedule or

---

[10]T. J. Allen and P. G. Gerstberger, *Criteria for Selection of an Information Source,* Working Paper No. 284-67, Sloan School of Industrial Management, Massachusetts Institute of Technology, Cambridge, September, 1967.

[11]Victor Rosenberg, "The Application of Psychometric Techniques to Determine the Attitude of Individuals Toward Information Seeking and the Effect of the Individual's Organizational Status on These Attitudes," pp. 443–454 *in* American Documentation Institute, *Progress in Information Science and Technology, Proceedings of the 1966 Annual Meeting,* Santa Monica, Calif.

[12]W. J. Paisley, *Information Source Preference as a Function of Physical and Psychological Distance from the Object,* Institute for Communication Research, Stanford University, Stanford, California, July, 1966.

systematic tables, not a file of document references at the point in which we are interested at the moment. Some other interactive retrieval systems require the user to check a machine-stored thesaurus, some a printed book-form thesaurus kept near the console, and still others, none at all.

The hierarchical array is a semantic structure which serves to suggest to the user related terms in the system, either directing him along a path to a more satisfactory expression of his question or helping to assure him that he has found such an expression.

If the semantic structure is generally agreeable to most users and is up to date,[a] then one of the central purposes of an interactive system, that of facilitating the accuracy of searches, is fulfilled. To the extent that semantically-related concepts may be represented by terms which cluster alphabetically, an alphabetical list may accomplish the purpose also. However, careful attention to the cross-reference structure is mandatory with the latter.

SYSTEM DESCRIPTION

In this section, we shall concentrate on those aspects of the system of which the user is most aware. That is to say, in discussing hardware, we shall be most interested in the console with which the user communicates with the system and vice-versa; in discussing software, we shall be more interested in the interaction procedures and query language than in the method of organization and processing of the files. We do not discount the importance of other aspects, but since our methods called for making use of an existing system, we shall leave the matter of advocacy or criticism of some aspects to others whose objectives differ from ours.

Files Processed

The user of AUDACIOUS has access to two files, namely an authority file (the list of terms referred to in ["Direct On-line Entry into a Hierarchically-arranged List of Terms"]) and a document reference file. His goal is to retrieve references from the latter which satisfy his question. The former exists for the dual purpose of (a) aiding him to refine his formulation of a question by leading him through a newtwork of semantically-related concepts and (b) providing for him the symbolic codes which the system uses to represent those concepts.

---

[a]It is well known that the UDC, at present, contains many examples of outdated structures. However, this is a practical problem which is of trivial importance to the argument presented here.

THE DOCUMENT REFERENCE FILE

Any real mechanized information system would operate on a large file, probably of the order of 50,000 items upward to millions. However, for reasons of economy and convenience, we decided that our limited goals could be satisfied by use of a small subset of such a large file. A further requirement was that the subject matter of the file be in an area in which the UDC is relatively up-to-date in terminology.

Accordingly, we acquired, in machine-readable form, the bibliographic data from one issue of *Nuclear Science Abstracts* (Volume 19, No. 11, June 15, 1965). The issue contained 2,330 items out of an annual total of about 50,000 items. The issue was indexed by UDC for us by an ad-hoc group of information specialists at several installations of the United Kingdom Atomic Energy Authority.[b]

The items of data in the document reference file included (1) personal author(s), (2) title, (3) either corporate author and report number or journal reference, (4) translation data where applicable, (5) UDC indexing records, and (6) Euratom keyword indexing records.[13] Only the latter two were available to the user as access points to records in the file; the remainder of the record was used only for display purposes. This point reflects only that our interest lay in searching by subject, not a technical limitation of the system.

THE AUTHORITY FILE

A special edition of the UDC, bringing together in a compact volume all of the parts of the UDC pertinent to nuclear science and technology, was published several years ago.[14] The edition was largely an outgrowth of a code of practice developed through active use of UDC by the United Kingdom Atomic Energy Authority.

The systematic tables of the UDC presented therein (see example, Figure 1) were converted to machine-readable form. Each record consisted of (1) a UDC number, (2) an English language description of the concept represented by the number (referred to hereafter as a "heading"), and (3) frequently, added scope notes and cross-references which serve to clarify and delimit the meaning and to suggest related concepts in other parts of the

---

[b]Details of the use of UDC in indexing this file are presented in report AIP/UDC-8, in preparation.

[13]*Euratom Thesaurus of Indexing Terms, 2nd Edition,* Report EUR-500e, European Atomic Energy Community, Directorate for Dissemination of Information, Center for Information and Documentation, Brussels, December, 1966.

[14]*Universal Decimal Classification, Special Subject Edition for Nuclear Science and Technology,* FID No. 351, International Federation for Documentation, The Hague, 1964.

FIGURE 1. Examples of Systematic Tables of the UDC*

621.039.574.3	Production reactors. Reactors used primarily for the production of fissile materials. Cf. 621.039.577
.5	Reactors used primarily for isotope production
.576	Reactors used primarily for the production of heat. (District heating. Process heat) Reactors in which the heat flux (with or without the radiation flux) is used for chemical processing
.577	Production of electrical power, e.g. 621.039.577-182.3 Portable power reactors, package reactors. For nuclear power stations, use 621.311.2:621.039
.578	Propulsion reactors Subdivide by :... 621.039.578:623.827 Submarine reactors 621.039.578:625.282 Reactors for locomotives 621.039.578:629.12 Reactors for ship propulsion in general 621.039.578:629.135 Reactors for aircraft propulsion 621.039.578:629.19 Reactors for rockets and interplanetary craft
621.039.58	Safety considerations: Siting. Containment. Fault analysis. Reactor hazards. Subdivide by.02 auxiliaries
.583	Siting in regard to population distribution, effluent disposal, rural amenities, etc.
.584	Overall (outer) structural containment to prevent the release of radioactive material through incident or fault, e.g. underground containment. Cf. 621.039.536, 621.039.538
-733	Filters and scrubbers to prevent release of radioactive particles
.586	Fault analysis generally
.587	Safety devices and circuits
.588	Reactor excursions, accidental and deliberate. Cf.621.039.514
621.039.59	Treatment of reactor products. Chemical processing of spent fuels and fuel elements. Separation of fissile and fertile materials
621.039.6	CONTROLLED THERMONUCLEAR DEVICES. FUSION REACTORS For specific types, use 621.039.62...subdivisions
.61	Theory and experiments. Cf. 533.9 Subdivide further by .02 auxiliaries subdivided as 621.039.62 For plasma reactions, statistical behaviour and dynamics, use 621.039.61:533.9 For plasma dynamics: waves, oscillations, resonances; turbulence, stability, pinch effect. use 621.039.61:533.95
.616	Operational behaviour. Loss mechanisms. Plasma production and formation
.617	Temperature distribution
.619	Experiments
.62	Thermonuclear devices classified by type
...12	Confinement by z field
...13	Confinement by v field
.623	Devices using externally applied closed magnetic lines (Stellarartor, Astron, etc.)
.624	Devices using externally applied open magnetic lines (Mirror machines, DCX, OGRA, Cusp Geometry, Ion Magnetron)
.626	Devices using internally generated closed magnetic lines, e.g. Toroidal pinch, Zeta, hard-core, etc.
.627	Devices using internally generated open magnetic lines, e.g. Linear pinch, sheet pinch, linear unpinch
621.039.629	Other devices, e.g. Rotating plasma, radio frequency confinement, etc.

621.039.63	Components
.633	Fuels, e.g. H, H², H³, He, Li
.634	Containment vessels; including liner materials, using :669... where appropriate
.637	Associated elctrical equipment. Power supply units. Energy storage and switching devices Subdivide by :621.3... where appropriate
.64	Heating mechanisms
.643	Electrical and magnetic, e.g. Joule, induction, h.-f., magnetic pumping
.646	Thermodynamic, e.g. adiabatic compression, shock waves
.647	Injection (electron, ion, neutral, plasma)
.66	Operational measurements. Diagnostics Subdivide broadly as 53.082 and further by the auxiliary 02 (as 621.039.62)
.665	Optical phenomena (including spectroscopic methods)
.667	Electrical, electrodynamic and nuclear phenomena
.4	Electromagnetic and electrodynamic methods
.6	Perturbation methods (probes)
.9	Nuclear methods (e.g. neutron production)
.67	Controlled thermonuclear devices and fusion reactors classified by purpose. Subdivide as 621.039.57
.68	Safety and siting Subdivide broadly as 621.039.58
.7	RADIOACTIVE WASTE MANAGEMENT The following numbers may be attached to any subdivision
.1	Physical form in which wastes occur
.13	Gaseous
.14	Liquid
.16	Solid
.73	Treatment of wastes
.733	Evaporation
.734	Precipitation
.735	Ion exchange processes
.736	Fixation in solids
.738	Separation and purification of fission products prior to use as radiation sources Subdivide by :546...02
.74	Storage and transportation of wastes. Details by :621.6 and :656
.743	Storage
.746	Transportation
.75	Waste disposal Subdivide by :628...for other disposal methods than those under 621.039.73
.76	Waste monitoring
.762	Land
.763	Fresh waters
.764	Marine waters
.766	Air
.77	Utilization of wastes, fission products
.8	APPLICATIONS OF ISOTOPES GENERALLY (include here applications of both radioactive and stable isotopes) For precautions against accidents in handling isotopes, use 621.039.8:614.8 For remote handling, use 542.1:541.28 For transport, use 656.073.436:539.16
(085) 621.039.8.002	Isotope catalogues and price lists Production and preparation of isotopes for use Subdivide by :..., e.g. 621.039.8.002:621.039.554 Production in reactors 621.039.8.002:621.384.6 Production in particle accelerators

*Source: *Universal Decimal Classification, Special Subject Edition for Nuclear Science and Technology*, FID No. 351, International Federation for Documentation, The Hague, 1964. Page 30 reproduced here.

semantic network. The third part of the record was not distinguished from the second during processing by the computer.

The method of access to the authority file should be carefully noted. Transmission from the user of a request for one or more words or word roots according to procedures described below is sufficient to evoke a display of all places in the authority file containing those forms. All words in a heading are treated as a set. If the request contains the members of the set or of any subset, the record is displayed. (see ["TERM"] and Appendix 4). No consideration of syntax is permitted. It should be absolutely clear that the user is not required to know in advance the exact wording of any heading or any other fixed vocabulary, such as that found in the A/Z index of most printed UDC schedules. The A/Z index of the *UDC Special Subject Edition for Nuclear Science and Technology* was not used in the present study. Instead, the user had available what is analogous to a KWIC index to the UDC systematic tables.

CODING OF UDC NUMBERS

All UDC numbers in both files were coded according to the scheme suggested in an earlier report (reference 1 . . .) , with the slight exception that the letter U was used accidentally as a facet prefix for main class numbers instead of C. In addition to the reasons given in the cited report, UDC numbers were required to be encoded because nonprefixed integers were assigned a special function, explained below in the description of the user's personal working file.

Internal File Structures

The records of both files are stored internally as a single file with a tree structured, threaded list organization. We shall here describe this structure only briefly, as it is well documented elsewhere[15] and it does not concern the user, according to whose viewpoint this report is chiefly written. The reader should also be aware of the existence of the view that list-organized files are less efficient than a combination of serial and inverted files for large document reference files,[16] one side of a controversy into which we have no basis for entering.

The file in the present case has several keys (means of access), namely, words which appear in UDC headings, UDC numbers, and Euratom keywords. A portion of the computer's disc storage contains a

[15]N. S. Prywes (1962), *op. cit.*
[16]E. G. Fossum and G. Kaskey, *Optimization and Standardization of Information Retrieval Language and Systems,* Final Report under contract AF49(638)1194, Univac Division of Sperry-Rand Corporation, Blue Bell, Pennsylvania, 28 January, 1966. AD 630 797.

record of each UDC number and each Euratom keyword which has been used to index at least one item in the document reference file. Following each UDC number or Euratom keyword is the disc address of the first document reference in the file in which it has been used. Similarly, for each word used in a UDC heading, the disc address of the first UDC number in which the word appears is given.

These items may be thought of as the contents of "level 2" of the tree structure and the UDC authority file and the document reference file as "level 3." Associated with each UDC number and Euratom keyword in the document reference set is the address of the next document reference in which that number of keyword is used. Likewise, associated with each heading word in the authority file is the address of the next record in which that word is used. This chain of terms and addresses is referred to as a list and the fact that any one record may be a member of more than one list is referred to as the threaded list technique. "Level 1," which resides in the computer's core memory, contains a coarse division of level 2, such that the area of the disc in which the level 2 entry which satisfies a query will be found if it exists may be quickly determined. Note that only the general area and not the exact disc address is determined in level one.

To further clarify the method of file organization for the reader who is accustomed to manual information systems, let us consider a file of periodicals. It is desired to provide an article index in the most compact form possible, while maintaining the file itself in chronological order of publication of each issue. According to the threaded list technique, an index would be prepared which gives only the first article in which each index term is used. For each index term, we would then mark each successive article with the volume and page numbers of the next article to which that term was applicable. The list structure allows us to avoid looking at every article in the file, while at the same time being more physically compact than an inverted (or coordinate) file. For a technical discussion of the relative merits of the various techniques of file organization in a computer-based information retrieval system, the reader is referred to the articles cited above.

Hardware

The system operated on an IBM 7044 computer with 32K core memory and extensive associated disc storage and tape units. The files are loaded from tape to disc at the beginning of use of the system and another tape unit is used to maintain a record of the use of the system. The contents of this tape may be printed, using the high speed printer, if the users or the system operator wish to retain a record. Communication between the system and the user takes place through a console which contains a key-

FIGURE 2. Hardware Configuration for AUDACIOUS

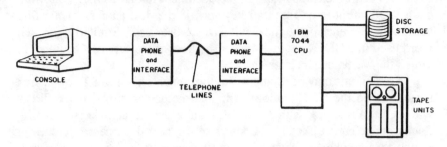

board and a CRT display. The console, connected via telephone lines to the computer, as shown in Figure 2, may be operated at a remote location. Our work was carried out with the console at Syracuse University, some 80 miles from the Xerox computer center in Rochester, New York.

The version of the system under which AUDACIOUS operated was not associated with a time-sharing executive system. Consequently, the user of the single console had full control of the computer at all times (provided, of course, that no errors occurred to require computer operator intervention). While this condition could not exist for economic reasons in a real system for public use, it proved advantageous for the experiment. Responsive times following user commands to the computer were fully satisfactory, which may not always be the case when messages must enter a queue in a time-shared environment. (Xerox Corporation is reportedly reprogramming the DATRIX system to operate in a time-shared mode on third generation equipment.)

CONSOLE CHARACTERISTICS

A Raytheon DIDS-400 Terminal Unit was made available for AU-DACIOUS as part of the DATRIX configuration. While it is possible to operate several such consoles by means of a switching unit, only one was involved in the present work. The unit, which is connected to the computer via an interface unit, data phone, and telephone line, contains a cathode ray tube which can display up to 520 characters on 13 lines of 40 characters each and a keyboard. The keyboard (see Figure 3, Keyboard Layout and Controls) contains 43 character keys, with a total of 59 characters (including space), and 12 control keys for 11 functions (two shift keys). Figure 4 is an illustration of the console used.

The console has three functions, namely (1) to allow transmission of user messages to the computer, (2) to receive and display messages from the computer, and (3) to permit editing and formatting of text before it is transmitted. The basic control device is the "cursor," a blinking character

FIGURE 3. Console Keyboard and Controls

Keyboard Controls

Name	Function	Keyboard Notation
Transmit	Initiates transmission of displayed data to computer	XMIT
Erase Line	Clears data on cursor marked line to the right of and including the cursor position	ER LN
Erase Message	Clears data on entire screen to the right of and below the cursor and including cursor position	ER MSG
Frame Reset*	Returns cursor to origin (first position, first line)	FR RST
Cursor Line Return*	Advances cursor to the first position on the following line	LN RST
Cursor Advance*	Advances cursor one position	
Cycle Right*	Automatically steps cursor ahead until button is realeased	
Cursor Backspace*	Backspaces cursor one position	
Shift*	Accesses characters shown on top part of character keys -- operates similar to typewriter shift key	SHIFT
Carriage Return	Inserts CR symbol, clears remainder of line, and advances cursor to start of following line (standard on Model 402 Display Units only)	CR
End of Message	Inserts end of message character	EOM

*These controls do not alter message but move the cursor (marker character) about the screen to enable the operator to enter data, or edit messages as desired.

which appears on the screen to indicate the current position at which action will be initiated by striking a key on the keyboard. The uses of some of the remaining function keys will be seen in the following section.

QUERY LANGUAGE

In this section we shall consider the features of the language in which the user must communicate with the system in order (1) to gain access to the program and the files, (2) to express his questions, and (3) to transmit his commands to the system. Use of the query language and other features of user-system interaction will be discussed in the following section.

System Access

The user initiates use of the system by turning on the console power and using the dataphone to dial the number of the computer data transmission interface. Completion of this connection causes the computer's executive system to load and give control to the program. The latter causes the files to be loaded from tape to disc storage, after which the message, "console ready, send your password" is transmitted and appears on the console screen.

The user must then establish his right of access to the data in the files. He does this by transmitting the code "UDC" to the system.

Message Transmission

All messages are defined by positioning the cursor over (i.e. at the same position on the screen) the first character to be sent and the end-of-message character immediately after (to the right of) the last character of the message. A message is transmitted by pressing the XMT control key.

Command Verbs

The AUDACIOUS system provides a limited repertory of words through which the user expresses the action which he wishes the system to take. This set of command verbs may be conveniently grouped according to the files or portions of the program which are called into use.

SWITCHES

Having gained access to the system, the user must tell it at which points he wishes to conduct searches, to receive instruction, and to terminate his use of it. Four commands are available.

BROWS. This command tells the sytem that the user is ready to conduct a search. The peculiar spelling results from certain details of the development of the system which are of no consequence here.

HELP. This command calls for a series of displays which provide instruction in the use of the commands and in the required query syntax. . . . These instructions are reproduced in Appendix 3.

PUNT. The inexperienced user may find that, at some point in the course of a dialogue with the system, he forgets how to operate certain features of the console. The PUNT[c] command signals the system to provide instructions in the use of the console. The console-operating instructions are reproduced in Appendix 2.

QUIT. Use of the command "QUIT" terminates the user's connection with the computer. The system transmits an acknowledgement of receipt.

COMMANDS INVOLVING EXAMINATION OF THE AUTHORITY FILE

The two commands described here provide the capabilities for beginning interaction between user and system.

TERM. Unless a user is familiar with the UDC number of numbers which represent the topics in which he is interested, he must determine this information before he can specify the conditions for a search. The use of the command "TERM X" where X is any word causes the system to display all items in the UDC schedule (authority file) in which the word X is present. If the X is suffixed by an asterisk, the resulting display includes all items in which X or a word which begins with X is present. Finally, the command Term $X_1 X_2....X_n$ causes display of all items which contain all n members of the requested set of words. The words may stand in any order or relationship to each other. The user tutorial explains the use of TERM as follows:

> You may begin a search by entering words describing your interests. The system will respond with a set of codes and their English equivalents which contain all of the words you entered. Suppose you are interested in 'FUSION REACTORS'. You may enter
>
>   TERM FUSION
>
> followed by the end-of-message symbol. The system will respond with the following:
>
> | U5391753 | CHAIN REACTING FUSION |
> |---|---|
> | U660465 | FUSION, MELTING, SMELTING |
> | U536652 | HEAT OF FUSION |
> | U6210396 | CONTROLLED THERMONUCLEAR DEVICES. FUSION REACTORS |
>
> Note that the word 'FUSION' is present in all of the English equivalents. If you had entered TERM FUSION REACTORS, the only line

---

[c]For the benefit of readers who are not familiar with this familiar borrowing from American football terminology, PUNT refers to the action of willingly transferring control of the flow of action to the opposition when it becomes probable that not doing so will result in a forced transfer under less favorable circumstances.

displayed would have been U6210396 CONTROLLED THERMO-NUCLEAR DEVICES. FUSION REACTORS., because both 'FUSION' and 'REACTORS' were present.

Incidentally, in any of the commands where English words are used (such as the 'TERM' command just explained, you may specify roots or stems of words, by placing an asterisk (*) after the desired root or stem). For example, TERM FUSION REACT* will call for any English equivalent containing the word 'FUSION' in addition to any other word beginning with the letters R-E-A-C-T. The response to the command TERM FUSION REACT* would be the same as before, that is U6210396 CONTROLLED THERMONUCLEAR DEVICES. FUSION REACTORS.

SCAN. Having been presented with a display through the use of the TERM command, the user may wish to examine the UDC concepts which are most closely related to a given displayed item; i.e. he may wish to see a portion of the UDC schedule. For this purpose, the SCAN command is used. Along with SAVE, description of which follows, SCAN is the only command which generally presumes that a display is already present on the screen.

In order to execute the command the user types SCAN and then, manipulating the cursor with appropriate control keys, places a plus sign immediately to the left of the UDC numbers which he wishes to see in hierarchical array. When the command is transmitted, the system responds with a display of a portion of the UDC schedule (authority file) in the immediate area of each of the indicated UDC numbers, in the order in which they appeared in the original display. Although the use of SCAN is normally based on an existing display, the user is permitted to enter the command "SCAN +X", in which X is any UDC number, regardless of whether it is keyed in or part of a display.

Temporary personal file commands. Another file, not previously explained, may be addressed by the user and the system. It takes the form of a temporary personal file, or "scratchpad" which is designed to help the user to remember UDC numbers which represent concepts of immediate interest. Twenty separate items may be kept in this file. As an added convenience, once the user had entered a UDC number in this file, he may thenceforth refer to the UDC number by its file line number, for example when formulating a search.

SAVE. The SAVE command, executed in the same manner as the SCAN command, causes the UDC numbers marked with a plus sign by the user to be entered on the next available "lines" of the personal file. The file is often called the "SAVE file." Note carefully that UDC numbers are saved, not document references as in some other similar systems.

DISPLAY. This command causes the contents of the personal file (or "SAVE file") to be displayed. While primarily intended as a means of reference when a search is being formulated, the DISPLAY command may also be used to check that a prior SAVE command was correctly executed.

CLEAR. This command clears the contents of the personal file. The file is cleared automatically only when the program is first loaded. Consequently, each successive user must issue a CLEAR command when commencing his use of the system. If he is concerned with the privacy of his interests, he must also remember to CLEAR the file before he leaves the console.

The user tutorial explains the use of the SAVE, DISPLAY and CLEAR commands as follows:

> If you wish to have the system remember any of the codes, e.g. U6210396, on the present screen, you may do so by using the 'SAVE' command. Place the word 'SAVE' on the top line, clearing the remainder of the line. Then place a plus sign (+) directly to the left of each code you wish to save, for example save +U6210396. Put the end-of-message symbol on the bottom line and transmit the entire screen. The codes you have marked with a plus will be entered in a personal file called a 'SAVE FILE'. If the system has more codes to show you, it will then display them. If there is no response, this means there are no more codes to see and the system awaits your next command. You may put a plus sign in front of any number of codes on any screen. All marked codes will be saved.
>
> At any point you may examine what you have saved by entering the command DISPLAY (followed by end-of-message). If you had previously saved U6210396 and nothing else, the response to 'DISPLAY' would be 1.U6210396. U6210396 has thus become the number 1 entry in your personal SAVE FILE. The SAVE FILE is cumulative. Every time you save codes, they are 'ADDED' to the SAVE FILE. If you wish to delete all of the entries in your SAVE FILE, use the command 'CLEAR' (followed by end-of-message).

COMMANDS TO EXECUTE A DOCUMENT REFERENCE SEARCH

Two commands cause the system to search the document reference file. While the command verbs are easily understood, the formulation of the entire command may become complex, owing to the rules of syntax. The latter are explained in a separate section below.

COUNT. Under many normal circumstances, a user wishes to have only a small number of references displayed to him. To avoid consuming time to find an unwanted number of references, the user may tell the system to "COUNT X', where X is a UDC number, a Euratom keyword, or a correctly formed logical expression of several. Suffixing an asterisk causes a number or keyword to be treated as a root form, as in the TERM command. The system responds to the command by displaying "N RE-FERENCES FOUND."

FIND. The FIND command is executed in the same manner as the COUNT command. The system then displays either "0 REFERENCES FOUND" or the first reference which satisfies the query.

The user tutorial explains the use of the FIND and COUNT commands as follows:

> When you have identified the codes which represent the terms of your question, you may ask the computer to search for document references. There are two commands that you may use, 'FIND' and 'COUNT'. The 'COUNT' command allows you to check quickly on the number of references which satisfy your request. If there are more than you wish to examine, you may have to modify your request.
>
> You have found the codes which represent the topic 'FUSION REACTION' by using the 'TERM', 'SAVE', 'DISPLAY' and 'SCAN' commands. You found that the code for 'FUSION REACTORS', is U6210396. To search for documents about 'FU-SION REACTORS', you have two choices of commands, COUNT and FIND. The 'COUNT' command will tell the computer to display the number of references about 'FUSION REACTORS'. For exam-ple, if you type
>
> COUNT U6210396
>
> at the top of the screen, the computer will display
>
> ITEM COUNT = N
>
> where N is the number of references about fusion reactors.
>
> If N is large you may want to reduce the number by using codes which make your request more specific. If you feel that the number of references is too large, you may return to the 'TERM', 'SAVE', 'DISPLAY', 'SCAN', command sequence. If the number is satis-factory, you may ask for a display of the references about 'FUSION REACTORS', by typing
>
> FIND U6210396
>
> to which the computer will respond
>
> RESULTS OF RETRIEVAL
>
> and then below will appear the first reference which answers your question. If there are too many references to fit on the screen at one time, the question
>
> DO YOU WANT MORE OUTPUT
>
> will appear on the next-to-the-last line on the screen. You may answer 'YES' or 'NO.'
>
> If the computer does not find anything to answer yur question, it will display
>
> RESULTS OF RETRIEVAL NO ITEMS FOUND END OF
>   OUTPUT.
>
> PLACE NEW DESIRED COMMAND AT TOP OF SCREEN.
>
> Frequently you can locate additional references on specific as-pects of your question. For example, you might wish to find refer-ences about 'PARTS OF FUSION REACTORS'. This can be done by

placing an asterisk (*) directly to the right of the code. Thus, the above command would be

FIND U6210396*

For your convenience, when you use either 'FIND' or 'COUNT' commands you may refer to codes you have saved by the number of the line in your personal file. For example, if the code for 'FUSION REACTORS' is on the line numbered 1 of your personal file, and the code for 'REACTOR SAFETY PROCEDURES' on line 2, you could find references about 'FUSION REACTOR SAFETY PROCE-DURES' by typing

FIND (1 'AND' 2)

Note that when more than one code is used, you must enclose the codes within parentheses.

If you want references about 'FUSION REACTORS' except those on 'RESEARCH SAFETY PROCEDURES', you would send

FIND (1 'AND' 'NOT' 2)

If you want references about either 'FUSION REACTORS' or 'REACTOR SAFETY PROCEDURES', you would send

FIND (1 'OR' 2)

Note that the words 'AND', 'OR', 'NOT', must be enclosed by apostrophes.

Now let's assume you have four codes in your personal file and you want references on any of these topics. You would then type

FIND (1 'OR' (2 'OR' (3 'OR' 4)))

Note that each time you use the word 'OR' you must enclose the codes in a new set of parentheses. It may be helpful to look at it in this way

(1 'OR' X)

X = (2 'OR' Y)

Y = (3 'OR' 4)

This rule applies only to the use of 'OR'.

Suppose again that 4 codes were saved in your personal file and that you wanted references about either concept 1 or 2 but that the document also must be about either concept 3 or 4. Type

FIND (1 'OR' 2) 'AND' (3 'OR' 4)

DISPLAY-CONTROLLING PSEUDO-COMMANDS

More frequently than not, the response to a given command exceeds the capacity of the display screen. The system provides means for advancing to the next display in succession, returning to the previous display, returning to the first display of a series, and terminating the display series before completion.

YES/NO. When the system's response exceeds display capacity, the next-to-the-last line of the screen will read "DO YOU WANT MORE OUTPUT?" The pseudo-command "YES" causes more data to be displayed. The pseudo-command "NO" terminates the display series and causes the system to display "PLACE YOUR NEXT COMMAND AT THE TOP OF THE SCREEN."

Plus-Box and Double-Plus-Box. One reserved character, which appears above the letter L on the keyboard (see Figure 2) is referred to as the "plus-box," from its shape $(+)$. Transmitting a command consisting of a single plus-box causes the previous one of a series of displays to be returned to the screen. A command consisting of two plus-boxes causes reversion to the first display of a series. Owing to the especially artificial manner of execution of these two commands, we did not provide instruction in their use for the experimental users of AUDACIOUS.

Command statements and phrases for document reference search.

A query consists of one of the command verbs, FIND or COUNT, and a phrase in the form of one or more controlled subject descriptors in a specific syntactic arrangement. The descriptors may be of three types, namely

(1) UDC numbers, with or without asterisk suffix (see ["TERM"]),
(2) Euratom keywords, or
(3) the numbers of "lines" in the user's temporary personal file (see ["Temporary Personal File Commands"]), which act as surrogates for the UDC numbers or keywords stored on those "lines." We have described the manner in which the user is able to discover how a topic in which he is interested is coded in the UDC (see ["Comments Involving Examination of the Authority File"]). In the case of Euratom keywords, it is necessary for the user to have prior knowledge of the correct keywords, since the Euratom thesaurus was not available for access in AUDACIOUS.

QUERY SYNTAX

A query is completed by use of the logical connectives 'OR', 'AND', and 'NOT' (including the single quotes) and arrangement of descriptors in groups of two by the use of parentheses, as shown below.

The form of expression used is referred to as "conjunctive normal form." If we let the symbol C represent a class which is defined as either a specific descriptor or the absence of a specific descriptor ('NOT' descriptor), then a primary expression (PE) can be:

$PE = C_1$
or $PE = (C_1 \text{ 'OR' } C_2)$
or $PE = (PE_1 \text{ 'OR' } PE_2)$
and a secondary expression (SE) can be:
$SE = (PE_1 \text{ 'AND' } PE_2)$

or SE=(SE$_1$ 'AND' PE) or SE=(SE$_1$ 'AND' SE$_2$)

For example, if we are interested in any of the descriptors J, K, L, M, or N occurring in the same document with both Y and Z

Then PE$_1$=J

    PE$_2$=(K 'OR' L)

    PE$_3$=(M 'OR' N)

    PE$_4$=(PE$_1$ 'OR' PE$_2$)=(J 'OR' (K 'OR' L))

    PE$_5$=(PE$_4$ 'OR' PE$_3$)=((J 'OR' (K 'OR' L)) 'OR' (M 'OR' N))

    PE$_6$=Y

    PE$_7$=Z

    SE$_1$=(Y 'AND' Z)

    SE$_2$=(PE$_5$ 'AND' SE$_1$)=(((J 'OR' (K 'OR' L)) 'OR' (M 'OR' N))

    'AND'

    (Y 'AND' Z))

The difficulty of correctly executing such a complex expression, easily imagined, is discussed below. Fortunately, since UDC numbers themselves often represent a pre-coordination of several subjects, searches of this level of complexity are not common with the UDC as the tool for controlling vocabulary.

Failure to execute correctly the syntax of a query results in display of the message "BAD EXPRESSION", but no diagnostics are given.

INSTRUCTION IN THE USE OF AUDACIOUS

We have seen that the use of AUDACIOUS requires the user to know or to learn how to

(1) gain access to the system;

(2) translate natural language to a controlled indexing language, the UDC;

(3) use a restricted set of command verbs to direct the action of the system; and

(4) formulate queries in a definite, sometimes complex syntactic pattern. Although a person who is highly motivated by interest in the system quickly becomes adept at its operation, the same is not true of the casual user who wishes to locate references, but has no interest in knowing about the UDC or any of the hardware or software aspects of the system.

Consequently, it is of the utmost importance to provide instruction in the use of the system in the most easily comprehended fashion. Various techniques of instruction might be suggested, e.g.

(1) oral instruction through group lectures or personal tutoring techniques;

(2) printed instructions placed in the vicinity of the console;

(3) audio-visual techniques (e.g. film loop or microfilm reader near console);

(4) use of the computer to display a set of instructions;

(5) computer-assisted instruction (CAI) with interaction between the user and the system used to measure the user's learning pattern.

Limitations of time and money eliminated consideration of audio-visual and CAI techniques. We felt that oral instruction was unrealistic for a real environment except where the clientele of the system are members of a restricted group known to the system manager.[d] Printed instructions suffer the disadvantages that they are susceptible to removal from the location of the console and do not permit reinforcement if the reader is confused. The computer-displayed instructions, on the other hand, are more tedious to read owing to the physical characteristics of the CRT display and the need for repeatedly transmitting a command to cause the display to advance to the next "page" of instructions.

We chose a combination of printed and displayed instructions. The complete instructions were made available through the display system, while the limited set of instructions which dealt with access to the system and manipulation of the console were also distributed in printed form to users who wished to have them.

In addition to seeing the instructions upon commencing use of the system, the user also could recall the console-operating instructions and the system-operating instructions by means of the commands PUNT and HELP, respectively, as already explained. The sets of instructions are reproduced as Appendices 1 and 2.

The reader may observe that the system operating instructions commence with a "table of contents" which direct the user to the "page" or "screen" on which the instructions for use of a given command verb begin. When a user commands HELP, he may only wish to refresh his knowledge of a specific command. Unfortunately, the limitations of time precluded programming of the instructions to be able to branch directly to the instructions for a given command. Hence, the table of contents was provided to aid the user in skipping rapidly through the series of displays to a certain point by merely counting "pages" or "forms."

The limitations of the project also precluded any systematic treatment of the learning patterns, problems, and degree of success of the experimental users. However, a discussion of related problems appear below.

---

[d]Meister and Sullivan (ref. 9) chose this approach when testing a system for scientists at NASA installations.

DISCUSSION AND EVALUATION

Although interactive information retrieval systems are often thought of as having an important future role as a tool for extending the utility of today's libraries, a methodology for evaluating such systems seems to be almost totally lacking. In fact, knowledge of how to evaluate information retrieval systems of any type, while evolving from the use of strictly quantitative methods toward recognition of important behavioral factors, is not well established. Clues to the problem of evaluation of interactive man-machine systems may well be found in the literature of human factors engineering, the psychology of learning and decision-making, and computer-assisted instruction. Considering such an investigation of methodology beyond the scope of this report, we shall attempt only a subjective evaluation, based on the more limited published knowledge which relates directly to information retrieval systems.

Our primary objective, as already stated, was to demonstrate the feasibility of the use of UDC in an interactive reference retrieval system. The outcome of the work reported here leaves no doubt of an affirmative answer to this problem. The examples shown in Appendix 4 are adapted from searches which were actually run with the experimental AUDACIOUS system. In addition to the use of UDC for searches, it was also possible to make on-line searches using Euratom keywords and manual searches using the *Nuclear Science Abstracts* subject index.

If a system such as AUDACIOUS were being tested for possible use in a real information system, it would be necessary to state a certain behavioral goal. That is, for a defined user population, we would have to show that a study of user attitudes leads to the conclusion that the system probably would be accepted and consistently selected as an information source. We had neither a well defined user population nor a test of acceptance or attitude change.

However, a subjective summary[e] of the reactions of perhaps fifty people who participated in the demonstrations as users or observers leaves little doubt that AUDACIOUS, as it existed, would not have been accepted in a real information system without some extensive modification. The participants were physicists, engineers, graduate library school students and faculty, computer-assisted instruction specialists, and information system designers and managers. This conclusion reflects no discredit on the designers of AUDACIOUS, but rather indicates the pioneer stage of development of interactive systems and the time and financial constraints which we ourselves imposed.

---

[e]The summarization was aided by the existence of tape recorded reactions and comments made by users in both the tutorial and search (BROWS) modes.

Some of the factors involved in user reaction to AUDACIOUS may be gleaned from reports cited above. In addition, we have found an extensive review of the behavioral effects of various characteristics of technical reports by Ronco *et al.* to be useful.[17] After listing the factors which appear important to us, we shall comment on each one in turn in terms of its possible relationship to AUDACIOUS.

Possible Factors Affecting User Attitudes Toward Interactive Retrieval Systems

In this section we shall discuss the following factors: (1) perceived ease of use, (2) credibility, (3) satisfaction with response time, (4) satisfaction with methods of communication with the system, and (5) satisfaction with characteristics of reports from the system. There are several other factors which merit brief attention for the sake of greater completeness.

One, of course, is the monetary cost involved. We have no data, since the demonstrations were run in an admittedly uneconomic fashion. Another factor is the perceived utility or benefit resulting from use of the system. A final additional factor might be the user's satisfaction (or lack of it) in using a system in which there are interpersonal relationships involved and none of the familiar mnemonic cues available, such as the color and actual spatial position of a document, points discussed recently by Miller.[18]

Perceived ease of use

A user's attitude toward use of an information system is likely to be a product of training, retention of learning, past experience, habit, familiarity, and motivation. In the case of interactive retrieval systems, the first two have a particularly important role. We have described the choice of methods for instructing the user. . . .

Although the sets of instructions (reproduced in the appendices) were improved during the course of the experiment, our judgement is that most users perceived that AUDACIOUS was difficult to use. The major reasons appear to be lack of practice exercises, the lack of opportunity for questions to be answered[f], the lack of diagnostic feedback when an error was made, and the inability of the user to call for instruction in the use of a particular command without going through the full set of instructions.

---

[f]Questions were answered informally, of course, but not as a formal part of the training.
[17]P. G. Ronco, J. A. Hanson, M. W. Raben, and I. A. Samuels, *Characteristics of Technical Reports that Affect Reader Behavior: A Review of the Literature,* Institute for Psychological Research, Tufts University, Medford, Mass., (1965?). NSF Grant G25112.
[18]G. A. Miller, "Psychology and Information," a lecture presented to the Annual Convention of the American Documentation Institute, New York, 1967.

Credibility

Information system evaluation studies have generally emphasized objective performance measures which may be used as a managerial quality control tool. The user, on the other hand, almost undoubtedly formulates a subjective judgement of performance, albeit in not such precise terms as "recall" and "precision" ratios. This judgement, which we shall call "credibility" may also be influenced by the total amount of information presented to the user.

During the AUDACIOUS experiment, in contrast to an operational system situation, users were able to make parallel on-line searches using UDC and Euratom keywords and manual searches using the subject index to the issue of *Nuclear Science Abstracts* used as the data base. The fact that widely differing sets of document references were frequently retrieved by parallel searches tended to reduce the level of credibility considerably. However, one should recall that in none of the three cases was the indexing done with this particular type of system in mind.

Satisfaction with Response Time

In the case of an interactive retrieval system, response time refers to the time elapsed between the transmission of a command from the console user and the completion of a display which responds to the command. Operating on an IBM 7044 which was completely dedicated to this one task, AUDACIOUS gave highly satisfactory response times, generally on the order of 10 seconds or less.

Those cases in which greater response times were observed tended to confirm reports by others that user tolerance of response times greater than, say, 20–30 seconds is quite low. This situation was particularly evident because there was no response from the computer to acknowledge that the command had been received and was being processed.

Satisfaction with Methods of Communication to the System

Communication to the system may be viewed as having the distinct facets, namely those of the query language, the UDC, and the hardware.

Since our comments will emphasize deficiencies, we shall begin by reiterating our satisfaction that AUDACIOUS was a successful first trial. Given improved training and motivating techniques and devices we have little doubt that the use of AUDACIOUS could have been successfully taught within one hour. Even so, improvements in the system itself may provide for faster learning, better retention, and more effective and satisfying use.

QUERY LANGUAGE

The query language, described in previous sections, contained a small number of easily learned words as command verbs. The principle deficiency of the query language was the complex format in which the user was required to state the logical relationships among search terms, including precise requirements for use of parentheses and of single quotes around the connectives, or, and, and not. A possible improvement in the latter case would have been the use of reserved keys to represent the connectives, resulting in a saving of keystrokes and a reduction in errors.

Communication to the system was further hindered by a lack of adequate diagnostic messages to enable the user to correct his errors. For example, a single mistake in balancing parentheses following a FIND or COUNT command led only to the message "BAD EXPRESSION."

The command "BROWS" (sic) did not serve any discernible purpose for the user. Yet is was necessary to remember to issue the command whenever going from the tutorial to the search mode. Consequently, it was a source of error and dissatisfaction.

Similarly, it was necessary to answer "yes" or "no" to questions displayed by the system at frequent intervals (For example, "Do you want more output?") before one could proceed with other commands. Our brief experience indicated that the user's desire often involves abrupt changes in search tactics, the progress of which is needlessly hindered by a requirement to answer "no" before going on.

The ability to use the asterisk as a signal that a requested term is a root form was extremely valuable. It may even be desirable to assume that every requested term is a root form unless signalled to the contrary, thus reversing the use for the asterisk.

THE UDC IN AN INTERACTIVE SYSTEM

With the exception of the authors, most users of AUDACIOUS were familiar with UDC only in a very general way or not at all. Similarly, American library users in general are not accustomed to classed catalogs, the most nearly related of traditional library tools.

Not unexpectedly, therefore, some of the experimental users found that the alternative of using Euratom Keywords to request a search was easier to grasp, since there was no need to learn to comprehend a non-natural language code. However, at least one physicist expressed the opinion that physical scientists are so accustomed to numerical codes that the UDC numbers pose no special communication problem.

It was also suggested that the UDC numbers be used as internal codes, without their ever being displayed to the user, if he so desired. All communication to and from the system would be in (controlled) natural language terms. The idea is sufficiently appealing to warrant investigation. However, for the user who frequently makes searches for the same topic(s) and who is willing to learn a few numbers there is an advantage in the compact numerical code of the UDC. By analogy, it is simpler to dial a familiar telephone number than it would be to dial the name and address of the person one is calling.

One deficiency of AUDACIOUS proved to be inflexibility with respect to variations in spelling (e.g. anti-neutron vs. antineutron) and inconsistency in use of singular and plural forms. Most communication problems of this type could be readily corrected if the UDC schedule had been devised with the present use in mind.

HARDWARE

Although the console served the purpose, there was little doubt that user communication with the system was seriously hindered by it, especially for the inexperienced user. A basic improvement would be the use of reserved function keys to alleviate the need for typing out the command verbs, the logical connectives, and the display-controlling pseudo-commands (see ["Display Controlling Pseudo-Commands"]). In addition, the excessive amount of manipulation of the cursor for the purpose of defining the beginning and end of a message to be transmitted could be eliminated by adoption of a reserved "start of message" character to complement the existing "end of message" character. In both cases, the use of a light pen in place of function keys is a possible alternative.

Satisfaction with Characteristics of Reports from the System

User satisfaction with communication from the system to him is likewise a complex matter. If not others also, it is at the least a function of these factors: record content, organization, format, language, display legibility, and display format.

RECORD CONTENT

Record content refers to the unresolved question of how much information and what types of information need to be shown to a user to enable him to make a decision with regard to further information seeking. The content of records displayed to users of AUDACIOUS consisted of bibliographic data, i.e. journal references, title, personal author(s), authors' affiliations, corporate author(s) or issuing organizations, and report numbers, where applicable. In a high percentage of cases in the brief experimental period, the document title alone was sufficient to establish probable relevance to a given question. In some cases, the ability to consult an abstract was desirable. However, too few of the users were regular professional users of the nuclear science literature to permit any conclusions to be drawn.

ORGANIZATION

The order in which the items of the bibliographic record were displayed was determined by their appearance in the original magnetic tape record copies from a tape prepared in 1965 by the U.S. Atomic Energy Commission. No data on the effect of record organization on user satisfaction can be reported, owing to the limited nature of the experiment. However, a user option to select the content and organization which is to be displayed appears intuitively conducive to increased user satisfaction.

FORMAT AND DISPLAY FORMAT

The format, i.e. the manner in which the parts of the record are layed out with respect to each other, was generally adequate, except for the journal reference or technical report identification. The flaws in this format, resulting from our use of an unmodified tape record format not intended for this purpose, lay mainly in incomprehensible spacing.

The display format is constrained by a limited number of lines and character positions per line on the display screen. Two unsatisfactory points were noted by most users. First, in all displays, including the tutorials, the UDC schedule, and document references, there was no attempt to make a logical or otherwise psychologically satisfactory break when it was necessary to divide a system response among several successive screens. Second, the system did not automatically clear the entire screen when a new response which covered only a portion of the screen was displayed. Both the resulting residual displays and the illogical breaks mentioned above were a source of confusion and error.

LANGUAGE

The only significant problem of language was the extensive use of abbreviations, many of them highly condensed. This result was a consequence of using data in a way not intended.

LEGIBILITY

The brightness, shape, and spacing between characters and between lines was entirely adequate in a small, well lit room. There were no objections to the all-upper-case characters.

CONCLUSION AND RECOMMENDATIONS

AUDACIOUS was, to the best of our knowledge, the first on-line interactive retrieval system in which one of the widely used traditional classification and indexing tools was used. While the UDC was the tool in this case, the success of the experiment may be generalizable to other tools, such as the Dewey and Library of Congress Classifications. The ability to use Thesauri and Keyword lists has already been demonstrated elsewhere. One suggestion we would make for future investigation is to explore the use of UDC in conjunction (rather than in parallel, as we did) with a suitably detailed thesaurus. UDC might be used to rapidly narrow the portion of the file to be searched to a small size, the thesaurus then being used for detailed interaction with that subset of the file.

The problem of user preferences for interacting with the system via natural language versus a numeric or other code also needs to be investigated. We have pointed out arguments for both cases in ["Discussion and Evaluation"].

For system designers, clearly, the most important implication of the results of AUDACIOUS is the need for careful consideration of the user viewpoint in all facets of the design of an interactive retrieval system. A system which is a technical success can fail to impress an information system user in many areas, some of which we have discussed.

AUDACIOUS also has implications for information system designers in a broader sense. Improvements during the past few years in communications and computer technologies strongly indicate that networks of libraries and information centers, whose resources are linked electronically, will be feasible in the not-too-distant future. Users will be able to conduct searches by means of a dialogue with the system, with access to distant as well as geographically nearby files of information. Such networks need not be confined within national borders; Dubon,[19] for example, has outlined a possible European Information Network, in which various national centers, each specializing in a given subject area, would exchange information cooperatively.

---

[19]R. J. Dubon, "Implementation of International Information Retrieval Center," pp. 339–46 in *Progress in Information Science and Technology: Proceedings of the American Documentation Institute, Vol. 3,* Santa Monica, California, Adrianne Press, 1966.

The very concept of an international network raises the question: what manner of indexing would serve adequately for users who do not share a common natural language. One solution is to use the language in which the largest volume of literature is written, i.e. English. This solution undoubtedly serves well in a situation in which the user must submit his question through an intermediary analyst who is skilled in both the subject matter and in English. However, it is open to question whether the average non-native speaker, even though he may be able to converse with another person in English, would be able to carry on a successful dialogue with a computer-based information file.

Another solution might be to make use of a form of indexing that is not dependent on natural language—which suggests the UDC. Without commenting on the present adequacy of the UDC, it should be emphasized again that schedules, or guides, for conversion between UDC, and natural languages already exist for some sixteen languages. Kepple[20] has pointed out the advantage of the UDC as a tool for an international library because it is not language-dependent. Use of a classified card catalog by a scientist without the aid of a librarian is somewhat analogous to the 'on-line' retrieval situation.

A third solution, requiring greater effort to implement it, would be to permit indexing and searching to be done using a controlled natural-language vocabulary of local choice. A part of the system would then be a table of equivalences between the UDC and the natural language vocabulary. The result would be to take advantage of the hierarchical notation of the UDC without even requiring that the user be familiar with the UDC. In addition, since the UDC would be the internal form of indexing, users in any center could direct queries to the file, without regard to the original language in which the indexing was done.

ACKNOWLEDGEMENTS

The cooperation and interest shown by the administration, the School of Library Science, and the Department of Physics of Syracuse University in making facilities available for the demonstration of AUDACIOUS are gratefully acknowledged. We also wish to acknowledge the helpful assistance of Messrs. Kenneth Fishell, Robert Bundy, and Ronald Miller, all of the Center for Instructional Communication, Syracuse University, and Miss Sue Ford of the School of Library Science. The development of AUDACIOUS also owes much to Xerox Corporation staff members Carey Dobbs, Ronald Furman, and Harry Kaplowitz.

---

[20]R. R. Kepple, ''Serving Readers in a Special International Library,'' *College and Research Libraries, 28* (3), 203–207, 216 (1967).

APPENDIX 1: PRINTED OPERATING INSTRUCTIONS FOR AUDACIOUS

1. Turn on the console
2. Put Dataphone in "Talk" mode
3. Dial [----] (Telephone number of data set at computer)
4. Wait for high pitched tone
5. Press "Data" button on Dataphone
6. Hang up Dataphone
7. Adjust intensity of screen, clear screen (push Frame Reset (FR RST) and Erase Message (ER MSG) keys).
8. When system is loaded a message will appear on the screen:
   CONSOLE READY
   SEND YOUR PASSWORD

The cursor (blinking symbol) will be at the spot where you should begin typing the password, UDC, followed by end-of-message symbol (EOM). Backspace the cursor (using left arrow key) until it is over the first character of the password. Press the transmit key (XMT).

9. If the password is acceptable, go to step 10. If unacceptable, the system will reply with an error message, allowing another try. Repeat the procedure in 8.
10. System will respond:
    "If you want help, type 'YES,' if not, type 'NO' and send."
11. If you respond 'YES', the Console operating procedure tutorial will follow. (See text). You must then follow through the entire tutorial (4 screens), after which you will be given the choice of whether you want help on the UDC system or not (go to 12).
12. If you respond 'NO' to the question in 10, system will respond: "If you want help type 'HELP'. If not, place command at top of screen."
13. If you respond 'HELP' the UDC tutorial will follow. Every screen will have the question 'DO YOU WANT MORE OUTPUT?' If you type YES, a new screen will appear. If you answer NO, the screen will be cleared and the message 'END OF OUTPUT. PLACE NEW DESIRED COMMAND AT TOP OF SCREEN.'
14. After leaving the UDC tutorial, either by following it to its end or by answering 'NO' in the middle, the legitimate commands are HELP, FIND, COUNT, TERM, SAVE, DISPLAY, SCAN, CLEAR, UDC, PUNT. These are described in the UDC tutorial. To use these, enter browse mode by sending command 'BROWS.'

APPENDIX 2: CONSOLE OPERATING TUTORIAL

Screen 1

When you type, nothing is sent to the computer until you depress the 'XMT' key (upper right of keyboard). To send a message, you must place an 'EOM' character after the last character to be sent to the computer. Then place the 'CURSOR' (blinking symbols) over the first character to be sent and hit 'XMT'.

Type 'MORE'. Then hit 'EOM' key, then hit left-arrow key five times. Then 'XMT'.

Screen 2

OK. You have just used one of the 'editing' features—moving the cursor to the left. The right-arrow moves it to the right, one position at a time. The dotted-right arrow moves it to the right until you release the key. The 'FR RST' key moves the cursor to the top left of the screen. 'LN RST' moves it down a line at a time. With these and the above, you can move the cursor anywhere on the screen. Now send 'MORE' as you did before.

Screen 3

You're doing fine. Now, to actually edit, you may move the cursor over any letter and either erase it using the SPACE bar or type a new letter right over the old one. You may erase everything on the same line as the cursor and to the right of it. Use 'ER LNE' (erase line) key. You may erase everything to the right of and below the cursor. Use 'ER MSG' (erase message) key. Now send 'MORE'.

Screen 4

Note that to erase the screen, use 'FR RST' followed by 'ER MSG'. Other than these editing features and the way you send a message, the keyboard looks and acts like a typewriter. Use the 'SHF' key for 'upper case'—i.e., -,=, etc. Type 'MORE' to continue. Typing 'QUIT' at any time terminates your connection to the computer.

APPENDIX 3: TUTORIAL FOR THE AUDACIOUS SYSTEM
Table of Contents

Introduction to the System

This is the UDC Interactive Retrieval System. With this system you will be able to search for references from *Nuclear Science Abstracts* June 15, 1965. To make the computer work for you, there are commands which you should type on the top line of the screen. You may begin a search by entering words describing your interests. The system will respond with a set of codes and their English equivalents which contain all of the words you entered. Suppose you are interested in 'FUSION REACTORS'. You may enter

TERM FUSION

followed by the end-of-message symbol. The system will respond with the following:

U53191753	CHAIN REACTING FUSION
U660465	FUSION, MELTING, SMELTING
U536652	HEAT OF FUSION
U6210396	CONTROLLED THERMONUCLEAR DEVICES. FUSION REACTORS

Note that the word 'FUSION' is present in all of the English equivalents. If you had entered TERM FUSION REACTORS, the only line displayed would have been U6210396 CONTROLLED THERMONUCLEAR DEVICES. FUSION REACTORS, because both 'FUSION' and 'REACTORS' were present.

Incidentally, in any of the commands where English words are used (such as the 'TERM' command just explained) you may specify roots or stems of words, by placing an asterisk (*) after the desired root or stem. For example, TERM FUSION REACT* will call for any English equivalent containing the word 'FUSION' in addition to any other word beginning with the letters R-E-A-C-T. The response to the command TERM FUSION REACT* would be the same as before, that is U6210396 CONTROLLED THERMONUCLEAR DEVICES. FUSION REACTORS.

If you wish to have the system remember any of the codes, e.g. U6210396, on the present screen, you may do so by using the 'SAVE' command. Place the word 'SAVE' on the top line, clearing the remainder of the line. Then place a plus sign (+) directly to the left of each code you wish to save, for example save+U6210396. Put the end-of-message symbol on the bottom line and transmit the entire screen. The codes you have marked with a plus will be entered in a personal file called a 'SAVE FILE'. If the system has more codes to show you, it will then display them. If there is no response, this means there are no more codes to see and the system awaits your next command. You may put a plus sign in front of any number of codes on any screen. All marked codes will be saved.

At any point you may examine what you have saved by entering the command DISPLAY (followed by end-of-message). If you had previously saved U623096 and nothing else, the response to 'DISPLAY' would be 1.U6210396. U6210396 has thus become the number 1 entry in your personal SAVE FILE. The SAVE FILE is cumulative. Every time you save codes, they are 'ADDED' to the SAVE FILE. If you wish to delete all of the entries in your SAVE FILE, use the command 'CLEAR' (followed by end-of-message).

If you would like to find out whether there are codes which represent related but broader or narrower concepts, you may do so by using the 'SCAN' command. To do this type 'SCAN' immediately followed by the code and the end-of-message symbol. You may save any of the new codes displayed.

When you have identified the codes which represent the terms of your question, you may ask the computer to search for document references. There are two commands that you may use, 'FIND' and 'COUNT'. The 'COUNT' command allows you to check quickly on the number of references which satisfy your request. If there are more than you wish to examine, you may have to modify your request.

You have found the codes which represent the topic 'FUSION REAC-TION' by using the 'TERM', 'SAVE', 'DISPLAY', and 'SCAN' commands. You found that the code for 'FUSION REACTORS' is U6210396. To search for documents about 'FUSION REACTORS', you have two choices of commands, COUNT and FIND. The 'COUNT' command will tell the computer to display the number of references about 'FUSION REACTORS'. For example, if you type

COUNT U6210396

at the top of the screen, the computer will display

ITEM COUNT = N

where N is the number of references about fusion reactors. If N is large you may want to reduce the number by using codes which make your request more specific. If you feel that the number of references is too large, you may return to the 'TERM', 'SAVE, 'DISPLAY', 'SCAN', command sequence. If the number is satisfactory, you may ask for a display of the references about 'FUSION REACTORS', by typing

FIND U6210396

to which the computer will respond

RESULTS OF RETRIEVAL

and then below will appear the first reference which answers your question. If there are too many references to fit on the screen at one time, the question

DO YOU WANT MORE OUTPUT

will appear on the next-to-the-last line on the screen. You may answer 'YES' or 'NO'.

If the computer does not find anything to answer your question, it will display

RESULTS OF RETRIEVAL NO ITEMS FOUND END OF OUTPUT.

PLACE NEW DESIRED COMMAND AT TOP OF SCREEN.

Frequently, you can locate additional references on specific aspects of your question. For example, you might wish to find references about 'PARTS OF FUSION REACTORS'. This can be done by placing an asterisk (*) directly to the right of the code. Thus the above command would be

FIND U6210396*

For your convenience, when you use either 'FIND' or 'COUNT' commands you may refer to codes you have saved by the number of the line in your personal file. For example, if the code for 'FUSION REACTORS' is on the line numbered 1 of your personal file, and the code for 'REACTOR SAFETY PROCEDURES' on line 2, you could find references about 'FUSION REACTOR SAFETY PROCEDURES' by typing

FIND (1 'AND' 2)

Note that when more than one code is used, you must enclose the codes within parentheses.

If you want references about 'FUSION REACTORS' except those on 'REACTOR SAFETY PROCEDURES', you would send

FIND (1 'AND' 'NOT' 2)

If you want references about either 'FUSION REACTORS' or 'REACTOR SAFETY PROCEDURES', you would send

FIND (1 'OR' 2)

Note that the words 'AND', 'OR', 'NOT', must be enclosed by apostrophes.

Now let's assume you have four codes in your personal file and you want references on any of these topics. You would then type

FIND (1 'OR' (2 'OR' (3 'OR' 4)))

Note that each time you use the word 'OR' you must enclose the codes in a new set of parentheses. It may be helpful to look at it in this way.

(1 'OR' X)

X=(2 'OR' Y)

Y=(3 'OR' 4)

This rule applies only to the use of 'OR'.

Suppose again that 4 codes were saved in your personal file and that you wanted references about either concept 1 or 2 but that the document also must be about either concept 3 or 4. Type

FIND (1 'OR' 2) 'AND' (3 'OR' 4)

These are all the commands you need to make searches. Remember them:

TERM	SCAN
SAVE	COUNT
DISPLAY	FIND
CLEAR	

If you ever need help in using the system, send 'HELP' from the bottom line of the screen.

If you need the console operating instructions at any time, send 'PUNT' from the bottom line.

Now you are ready to begin your search. First send the word

BROWS

from the top line of the screen. After the response, place your command (TERM, SAVE, DISPLAY, CLEAR, SCAN, COUNT, FIND) on the top line of the screen.

APPENDIX 4: EXAMPLES OF SEARCHES USING AUDACIOUS

Five searches, which were run using AUDACIOUS during November, 1967, are recorded on the following pages. Readers who may wish to review the full abstracts of the references retrieved will find them in *Nuclear Science Abstracts,* Volume 19, Number 11, June 15, 1965. The location of the abstract number in the display is indicated under question one. It is impossible to reproduce the exact contents and format of the material on the display screen at any one time; the reader should be aware that the following pages represent only an approximation which is intended to convey the significant features of the user-system interaction.

QUESTION 1: Literature on Nuclear Reactions

S t e p	Initiator: User (U) or System (S)	Message (▪ shows position of end-of-message symbol)
1	U	BROWS ▪
2	S	BROWS MODE ENTERED
3	U	TERM NUCLEAR REACTIONS ▪

4	S	U5391754 539.175.4 CYCLIC NUCLEAR REACTIONS
		U5391728 539.172.8 PRODUCTS. NUCLEAR REACTIONS ACCORDING TO PRODUCT
		    PARTICLES (IRRESPECTIVE OF INDUCING PARTICLES)
		U539172 539.172 INDIVIDUAL NUCLEAR REACTIONS. EXCEPT FISSION FURTHER
		    SUBDIVISION OF ANY OF THE NUMBERS 539.172
		U53917013 539.17.013 RESONANCE EFFECTS IN NUCLEAR REACTIONS
		U53917 539.17 NUCLEAR REACTIONS. NUCLEAR DATA IN GENERAL
		COMMAND OKAY.
		PUT NEXT COMMAND AT TOP OF SCREEN.

5	U	COUNT U53917* ▪
6	S	ITEM COUNT = 9 COMMAND OKAY. PUT NEXT COMMAND AT TOP OF SCREEN.
7	U	FIND U53917* ▪

8	S	RESULTS OF RETRIEVAL
		ITEM 1
		1921393 PHYS. REV. V138 APR266583898398 1112UCES
		DENSITY PROPAGATOR FOR A SELF-BOUND FERMION SYSTEM. II. LINEAR RESPONSE AND
		    INELASTIC ELECTRON SCATTERING.
		WEIZMANN INST. OF SCIENCE. REHOVOTH, ISRAEL. REINER, A. S.
		ITEM 2
		1921266 UCRL-11828 108 109 1112UWLG
		NUCLEAR SPECTROSCOPY WITH TWO-NUCLEON TRANSFER REACTIONS.
		LAWRENCE RADIATION LAB., UNIV. OF CALIFORNIA, BERKELEY.
		GLENDENNING, NORMAN K.
		ITEM 3
		1921225 AECL-2168 FEB 6517 1112UWLG (SM-60/50)*
		FISSION DATA AND NUCLEAR TECHNOLOGY.
		ATOMIC ENERGY OF CANADA LTD., CHALK RIVER (ONTARIO). HANNA, C. C.
		ITEM 4
		1921196 AWRE-0-81/64 DEC 6447 1111UCES
		DICE MK.IV -- THE PREPARATION OF NUCLEAR DATA INTO A FORM SUITABLE FOR MONTE
		    CARLO CALCULATIONS USING THE IBM703 COMPUTER.
		ATOMIC WEAPONS RESEARCH ESTABLISHMENT, ALDERMASTON (ENGLAND).
		KERR, W. M. M. PARKER, J. B. ED.
		ITEM 5
		1921117 MACMILLAN COMPANY T 65234 1108UMJT
		TABLES OF COULEMB WAVE FUNCTIONS (WHITTAKER FUNCTIONS). TRANSLATION OF TABLITSY
		    VOLNOVYKH KULONOVSKIKH FUNKTSII.
		LUKYANOV, A. V. TEPLOV, I. V. AKIMOVA, M. K.
		ITEM 6
		1921076 INDIANA UNIV. 6453 1107UWLG
		KINEMATIC ANALYSIS OF PRODUCTION REACTIONS.
		HIGGINS, JOHN REID
		ITEM 7
		1920938 UCRL-11828 9 10 1107UWLG
		DIGITAL COMPUTER CALCULATION OF MATRIX ELEMENTS OF NUCLEAR INTERACTIONS.
		LAWRENCE RADIATION LAB., UNIV. OF CALIFORNIA, BERKELEY.
		REDLICH, MARTIN C. BAER, ROBERT M.
		ITEM 8
		1920762 MEM. ROY. ASTRON. SOC. V 69 65 21 81 1102UDCW
		THE EQUILIBRIUM DISTRIBUTION OF NUCLIDES IN MATTER AT HIGH TEMPERATURES.
		DEPARTMENT OF APPLIED MATHEMATICS AND THEORETICAL PHYSICS, CAMBRIDGE, ENGLAND.
		CLIFFORD, F.E. TAYLER, R. J.
		ITEM 9
		1919735 UCRL-11828 JAN 65289 0200UWLG
		NUCLEAR CHEMISTRY DIVISION ANNUAL REPORT, 1964.
		LAWRENCE RADIATION LAB., UNIV. OF CALIFORNIA, BERKELEY.
		HOLLANDER, J. M. ED. REYNOLDS, F. ED.
		    CUNNINGHAM, B.B. ED.
		END OF RETRIEVAL
		COMMAND OKAY.
		PUT NEXT COMMAND AT TOP OF SCREEN.
		
		TIME FOR RETRIEVAL WAS 0015.4 SEC.

Annotation pointing to the COUNT step: NUCLEAR SCIENCE ABSTRACTS ABSTRACT NUMBER

QUESTION 2: All Papers Dealing with Tritanum

Step	Initiator: User (U) or System (S)	Message (∎ shows position of end-of-message symbol)
1	U	BROWS ∎
2	S	BROWS MODE ENTERED
3	U	CLEAR ∎
4	S	COMMAND OKAY. PUT NEXT COMMAND AT TOP OF SCREEN
5	U	TERM TITANIUM ∎
6	S	U669295 669.295 TITANIUM
		U661882 661.882 TITANIUM COMPOUNDS: OXIDES (WHITE), ETC.
		U553494 553.494 TITANIUM, ZIRCONIUM AND HAFNIUM ORES
		U54682 546.82 TITANIUM GROUP
		U 546821 546.821 TITANIUM
7	U	SAVE
		+U669295 669.295 TITANIUM
		+U661882 661.882 TITANIUM COMPOUNDS: OXIDES (WHITE), ETC.
		+U553494 553.494 TITANIUM, ZIRCONIUM AND HAFNIUM ORES
		+U54682 546.82 TITANIUM GROUP
		+U546821 546.821 TITANIUM ∎
8	S	VALUES SAVED.
9	U	SCAN +U66188 ∎
10	S	U6618 661.8 METALLIC COMPOUNDS MINERAL PIGMENTS. CF. 669
		U66188 661.88 GROUPS IV AND V METALS. AS 546.8.
		U661.881 661.881 TIN COMPOUNDS: STANNATES, ETC.
		U661882 661.882 TITANIUM COMPOUNDS: OXIDES (WHITE), ETC.
		U661886Y887 661.886/.887 ANTIMONY AND BISMUTH COMPOUNDS
11	U	DISPLAY ∎
12	S	1. U669295
		2. U661882
		3. U553494
		4. U54682
		5. U546821
13	U	COUNT (1 'OR' (2 'OR' (3 'OR' (4 'OR' 5))))∎
14	S	ITEM COUNT = 5
		COMMAND OKAY.
		PUT NEXT COMMAND AT TOP OF SCREEN
15	U	FIND (1 'OR' (2 'OR' (3 'OR' (4 'OR' 5))))∎
16	S	RESULTS OF RETRIEVAL
		ITEM 1
		1920524 TID-20625 V 4R 1 B 64265 0903UJMJ
		WELDING PROCEDURES. VOLUME FOUR. PROCEDURE SPECIFICATIONS, WELDING PROCEDURES,
		AND PROCEDURE QUALIFICATION TEST RECORDS (HSW-7600 THROUGH HW S-8091 SERIES).
		GENERAL ELECTRIC CO., RICHLAND, WASH. HANFORD ATOMIC PRODUCTS OPERATION.
		ITEM 2
		1920505 JAERI-1071 OCT 6443 J0903UJMJ
		DEVELOPMENT OF BONDING METHODS FOR GRAPHITE MATERIALS.
		JAPAN ATOMIC ENERGY RESEARCH INST., TOKYO.
		ANCO, YOSHIO TOBITA, SHOZO FUJIMURA, TADATO
		ITEM 3
		1919831 OCT 649 0201UJGB (CONF-721-11)*
		DETERMINATION OF HYDORGEN IN ZIRCONIUM ALLOYS BY ISOTOPIC EQUILIBRATION.
		FROM 8TH CONFERENCE ON ANALYTICAL CHEMISTRY IN NUCLEAR TECHNOLOGY, GATLINBURG,
		TENN., OCT. 1964.
		ASHLEY, R.W. DENOVAN, A. S.
		ITEM 4
		1921801 NUCL. INSTR. METHODS V34 APR 65 100 102 1112UCES
		COMPARISON OF THE NEUTRON YIELD FROM DEUTERIDED ERBIUM AND TITANIUM TARGETS.
		SERVICES ELECTRONICS RESEARCH LAB., BALDOCK, HERTS, ENG.
		LARGE, L. N. HILL, H.
		ITEM 5
		1920775 SOVIET ASTRON. AJ (ENGLISH TRANSL.) V 8 T MAR 65 725 730 1102UDCW
		DETERMINATION OF THE EXCITATION TEMPERATURE IN THE SOLAR ATMOSPHERE. TRANSLATED
		FROM ASTRON. ZH., V 41 907-13 (SEPT.-OCT. 1964).
		INST. OF TERRESTRIAL MAGNETISM, IONOSPHERE AND THE PROPAGATION OF RADIO WAVES,
		ACADEMY OF SCIENCES, SIBERIAN SSR
		TEPLITSKAYA, R. B.
		END OF RETRIEVAL
		COMMAND OKAY.
		PUT NEXT COMMAND AT TOP OF SCREEN.

QUESTION 3: Methods for Presenting or Inhibiting the Corrosion of Zirconium

S t e p	Initiator: User (U)or System (S)	Message (▐ shows position of end-of-message symbol)
1	U	BROWS ▐
2	S	BROWSE MODE ENTERED.
		COMMAND OKAY.
		PUT NEXT COMMAND AT TOP OF SCREEN.
3	U	TERM CORROSION ▐
4	S	U6690188 669.018.8 CORROSION RESISTANT ALLOYS SUBDIVIDE AS 620.193
		U62103955336 621.039.553.36 CORROSION AND COMPATIBILITY. CORROSION LOOPS
		U62103954455 621.039.544.55 TO IMPROVE CORROSION RESISTANCE
		U620197 620.197 PROTECTION AGAINST CORROSION. CF. 669.2/.8...69
		U6201942 620.194.2 STRESS CORROSION
		U620194 620.194 MECHANICAL INFLUENCES ON CORROSION
		U6201938 620.193.8 BIOLOGICAL ACTION CAUSING CORROSION
		U6201936 620.193.6 ACTION OF LIGHT. PHOTOCHEMICAL CORROSION
		U6201935 620.193.5 CORROSION BY HIGH TEMPERATURE GASES
		U62019347 620.193.47 CORROSION BY ORGANIC SUBSTANCES SUBDIVIDE AS 547
		U62019346 620.193.46 CORROSION BY OTHER INORGANIC SUBSTANCES SUBDIVIDE AS
		546... . E.G. 620.193.46.11 CORROSION BY H
		U62019343 620.193.43 CORROSION BY MOLTEN SALTS
		U62019342 620.193.42 CORROSION BY ALKALINE SUBSTANCES IN GENERAL
		U62019341 620.193.41 CORROSION BY ACIDS IN GENERAL
		U62019327 620.193.27 CORROSION BY SEA WATER
		U62019324 620.193.24 CORROSION BY CARBON DIOXIDE (ALL TEMPERATURES)
		U62019323 620.193.23 CORROSION BY WATER OR STEAM (ALL TEMPERATURES) INCLUDING
		HERE AIR-WATER MIXTURES
		U62019322 620.193.22 CORROSION BY AIR OR OXYGEN (ALL TEMPERATURES)
		U62019321 620.193.21 ATMOSPHERIC CORROSION. ACTION OF CLIMATE IN GENERAL
		U6201932 620.193.2 CHEMICAL CORROSION
		U620193013 620.193.013 ELECTROCHEMICAL THEORY OF CORROSION
		U62019301 620.193.01 THEORY OF CORROSION
		U620193 620.193 CORROSION IN GENERAL. COMPATABILITY. RESISTANCE TO ATTACK.
		PHYSICAL AND CHEMICAL EFFECTS
		COMMAND OKAY.
		PUT NEXT COMMAND AT TOP OF SCREEN.
5	U	DISPLAY ▐
6	S	SAVE FILE IS EMPTY.
7	U	SAVE +U62019323 ▐
8	S	VALUES SAVED.
9	U	DISPLAY ▐
10	S	1. U62019323
11	U	TERM ZIRCONIUM ▐
12	S	U669296 669.296 ZIRCONIUM
		U553494 553.494 TITANIUM. ZIRCONIUM AND HAFNIUM ORES
		U546831 546.831 ZIRCONIUM
		COMMAND OKAY.
		PUT NEXT COMMAND AT TOP OF SCREEN.
13	U	SAVE
		+U669296 669.296 ZIRCONIUM
		U553494 553.494 TITANIUM, ZIRCONIUM AND HAFNIUM ORES.
		U546831 546.831 ZIRCONIUM ▐
14	S	VALUES SAVED.
15	U	DISPLAY. ▐
16	S	1. U62019323
		2. U669296
17	U	FIND (1 'AND' 2) ▐
18	S	RESULTS OF RETRIEVAL
		ITEM 1
		1920492 J. NUCL. MATER. V 15 65 263 277 0901UJMJ (AERE-R-4702)*
		FURTHER STUDIES ON THE INHIBITION OF BORIC ACID OF THE OXIDATION OF ZIRCONIUM IN
		HIGH PRESSURE STEAM.
		ATOMIC ENERGY RESEARCH ESTABLISHMENT, HARWELL, BERKS, ENG.
		BRITTON, C. F. ARTHURS, J. V. WANKLYN, J. N.
		END OF RETRIEVAL
		COMMAND OKAY.
		PUT NEXT COMMAND AT TOP OF SCREEN.

QUESTION 4: References to any of the "Inert" Gases

S t e p	Initiator: User (U)or System (S)	Message (▉ shows position of end-of-message symbol)
1	U	BROWS ▉
2	S	BROWSE MODE ENTERED
3	U	CLEAR ▉ (I.E. CLEAR THE USER'S PERSONAL FILE)
4	S	COMMAND OKAY
		PUT NEXT COMMAND AT TOP OF SCREEN
5	U	TERM INERT GAS*▉
6	S	U661939 661.939 INERT, RARE (ZEROVALENT) GASES. AS 546.29
		U660961 66.096.1 TREATMENT WITH INERT GASES
		U62103953436 621.039.534.36 HELIUM AND INERT GASES
		U54629 546.29 ZEROVALENT ELEMENTS. INERT GASES
		COMMAND OKAY
		PUT NEXT COMMAND AT TOP OF SCREEN
7	U	COUNT (U661939 'OR' (U660961 'OR' (U62103953436 'OR' U54629)))▉
8	S	ITEM COUNT = 7
		COMMAND OKAY
		PUT NEXT COMMAND AT TOP OF SCREEN
9	U	FIND (U661939 'OR' (U660961 'OR' (U62103953436 'OR' U54629))) ▉
10	S	RESULTS OF RETRIEVAL

```
ITEM 1
1921616    J. NUCL. ENERGY             P AV 19  FEB 65  91 100 1201UDCW
THE DETERMINATION OF LONG-LIVED KRYPTON AND XENON ISOTOPES IN MAGNOX REACTOR
    COOLANTS, AS A MEANS OF DETECTING CERTAIN FUEL ELEMENT FAILURES.
UNITED KINGDOM ATOMIC ENERGY AUTHORITY, SEASCALE, CUMBERLAND, ENG.
FRENCH, R. L. D.            OCKENDEN, D. W.
ITEM 2
1920862    PROC. PHYS. SOC. (LONDON)   V 85   FEB 65  363 373  1103UMJT
EXCITATION IN RARE GAS ION-ATOM COLLISIONS IN THE ENERGY RANGE 100-400   KEV.
UNIVERSITY COLL., LONDON.
THOMAS, E. W.             GILBODY, H. B.
ITEM 3
1920850    PHYSICA             V 31  JAN 65    94 112 1103UDCW
IONIZATION CROSS SECTIONS FOR ELECTRONS (0.6-20KEV) IN NOBLE AND DIATOMIC GASES.
STICHTING VOOR FUNDAMENTEEL ONDERZOEK DER MATERIE, AMSTERDAM.
SCHRAM, B. L.    DE HEER, F. J.    VAN DER WIEL, M. J.    KISTEMAKER, J.
ITEM 4
1920847    PHYS. REV. LETTERS        V 14   MAR2965 489 490 1103ULBS
MULTIPHOTON IONIZATION AND THE BREAKDOWN OF NOBLE GASES.
OHIO STATE UNIV., COLUMBUS.
TOMLINSON, RICHARD G.
ITEM 5
1920833  J. QUANT. SPECTRY. RADIATIVE TRANSF*V  5  JAN 65 87 89 1103UDCW  ER
THE CALCULATION OF BOUND-FREE TRANSITION PROBABILITIES AND THEIR APPLICATIONS TO
    THE CONTINUUM SPECTRA OF THE RARE GASES.
UNIVERSITAT, KIEL.
SCHLOFTER, DIETER
ITEM 6
1919992    J. CHEM. PHYS.     V 42    APR 16523212327 0207UEJH  (UCRL-11631)*
DETERMINATION OF THE EXCITATION FUNCTIONS FOR FORMATION OF METASTABLE STATES OF
    SOME RARE GASES AND DIATOMIC MOLECULES BY ELECTRON IMPACT.
UNIV. OF CALIFORNIA, BERKELEY.
OLMSTED, JOHN III      NEWTON, AMOS S.      STREET, K. JR.
ITEM 7
1919931    ZH. TEKHN. FIZ.    V 35    JAN 65 117 122RO203UDCW
RESONANCE CHARGE EXCHANGE IN INERT GASES.
SMIRNOV, B. M.           CHIBISOV, M. I.
END OF RETRIEVAL
COMMAND OKAY.
PUT NEXT COMMAND AT TOP OF SCREEN.

TIME FOR RETRIEVAL WAS  0005.2 SEC.
```

QUESTION 5: Use of Radiation for Polymerization of Cellulose

S t e p	Initiator: User (U) or System (S)	Message (⁋ shows position of end-of-message symbol)
1	U	BROWS ⁋
2	S	BROWSE MODE ENTERED
3	U	CLEAR ⁋
4	S	COMMAND OKAY. PUT NEXT COMMAND AT TOP OF SCREEN.
5	U	TERM CELLULOSE* ⁋
6	S	U661728 661.728 CELLULOSE DERIVATIVES. CF. 678.54
		U67746 677.46 CELLULOSE FIBRES
		U6785 678.5 PLASTICS, ESPECIALLY SEMI-SYNTHETIC PLASTICS (BASED ON CELLULOSE, PROTEINS, ETC.)
		U67854 678.54 PLASTICS BASED ON CELLULOSE OR DERIVATIVES. CF. 661.728:677.46
		U678542 678.542 BASED ON CELLULOSE: VISCOSE, CUPROMMONIUM
		U678546 678.546 BASED ON (SINGLE) CELLULOSE ETHERS
7	U	SAVE
		+U661728 661.728 CELLULOSE DERIVATIVES. CF. 678.54
		+U67746 677.46 CELLULOSE FIBRES
		+U6785 678.5 PLASTICS, ESPECIALLY SEMI-SYNTHETIC PLASTICS (BASED ON CELLULOSE, PROTEINS, ETC.)
		+U67854 678.54 PLASTICS BASED ON CELLULOSE OR DERIVATIVES. CF. 661.728:677.46
		+U678542 678.542 BASED ON CELLULOSE: VISCOSE, CUPROMMONIUM
		+U678546 678.546 BASED ON (SINGLE) CELLULOSE ETHERS ⁋
8	S	VALUES SAVED.
9	U	TERM POLYMER* ⁋
10	S	U54W126 54-126 POLYMERIZED STATE OF SUBSTANCE
		U54164 541.64 POLYMERISM. MACROMOLECULAR CHEMISTRY. CF. 66.095.26, 678.
		U66V952 66.095.2 ISOMERIZATION. POLYMERIZATION. CF. 678
		U66V9526 66.095.26 POLYMERIZATION
		U66V95268 66.095.268 POLYMERIZATION WITH BETA- AND GAMMA RAYS
		U6787 678.7 SYNTHETIC POLYMERIZATES: RUBBERS, RESINS, ETC.
11	U	SAVE
		+U54W126 54-126 POLYMERIZED STATE OF SUBSTANCE
		+U54164 541.64 POLYMERISM. MACROMOLECULAR CHEMISTRY. CF. 66.095.26, 678.
		+U66V952 66.095.2 ISOMERIZATION. POLYMERIZATION. CF. 678
		+U66V9526 66.095.26 POLYMERIZATION
		+U66V95268 66.095.268 POLYMERIZATION WITH BETA- AND GAMMA RAYS
		+U6787 678.7 SYNTHETIC POLYMERIZATES: RUBBERS, RESINS, ETC. ⁋
12	S	VALUES SAVED ⁋
13	U	SCAN +U678 ⁋
14	S	U67/68 67/68 VARIOUS INDUSTRIES AND CRAFTS BASED ON PROCESSABLE MATERIALS
		U678 678 MACROMOLECULAR MATERIALS. RUBBER AND PLASTICS.
		U6784 678.4 RUBBERS AND NATURAL MACROMOLECULARS
		U6785 678.5 PLASTICS, ESPECIALLY SEMI-SYNTHETIC PLASTICS (BASED ON CELLULOSE, PROTEINS, ETC.)
		U6786 678.6 SYNTHETIC POLYCONDENSATES: RESINS, FIBRES, ETC.
		U6787 678.7 SYNTHETIC POLYMERIZATES: RUBBERS, RESINS, ETC.
		U6788 678.8 OTHER MACROMOLECULAR MATERIALS
15	U	DISPLAY ⁋
16	S	1. U661728
		2. U67746
		3. U6785
		4. U67854
		5. U678542
		6. U678546
		7. U54W126
		8. U54164
		9. U66V952
		10. U66V9526
		11. U66V95268
		12. U6787
		[HERE ARE SEVERAL WAYS THE USER MIGHT FORMULATE HIS SEARCH, GIVEN THE UDC NUMBERS HE HAS SAVED IN HIS "PERSONAL FILE".]

QUESTION 5: Use of Radiation for Polymerization of Cellulose (continued)

S	Initiator: User (U)or System (S)	Message (▧ shows position of end-of-message symbol)
17	U	COUNT (1 'OR' (2 'OR' (3 'OR' (4 'OR' (5 'OR' 6))))) 'AND' 7 'OR' (8 'OR' (9 'OR' (10 'OR' (11 'OR' 12))))) ▧
18	S	ITEM COUNT = 20 COMMAND OKAY PUT NEXT COMMAND AT TOP OF SCREEN
19	U	COUNT (1 'OR' (2 'OR' U6785*) 'AND' 7 'OR' (8 'OR' U66V952*)) ▧
20	S	ITEM COUNT = 5 COMMAND OKAY PUT NEXT COMMAND AT TOP OF SCREEN
21	U	COUNT (1 'OR' (2 'OR' U6785*) 'AND' 11) ▧
22	S	ITEM COUNT = 1 COMMAND OKAY PUT NEXT COMMAND AT TOP OF SCREEN
23	U	FIND (1 'OR' (2 'OR' U6785*) 'AND' 11) ▧
24	S	RESULTS OF RETRIEVAL ITEM 1 1919960 VDDIT-93 RADIATION-INDUCED GRAFT POLYMERIZATION ON CELLULOSE, A LITERATURE SURVEY. AKTIEBULAGET ATOMENERGI, STOCKHOLM (SWEDEN) HOLM, HANS I. END OF RETRIEVAL COMMAND OKAY PUT NEXT COMMAND AT TOP OF SCREEN

Bibliography of AIP/UDC Project Reports, with Abstracts*

1. Freeman, Robert R., *Research Project for the Evaluation of the UDC as the Indexing Language for a Mechanized Reference Retrieval System: An Introduction,* New York, American Institute of Physics, Report AIP/DRP UDC-1, October 1, 1965. NSF Grant GN-433.
   The report describes the five areas of activity which lead toward the aim expressed in the title: (1) to develop a complete English-language version of UDC in both hierarchical and alphabetical arrangement in machine-readable form; (2) to develop techniques for automatic file maintenance and photo-composition of UDC editions; (3) to develop a computer-based reference retrieval system which uses UDC as its indexing language; (4) to collect a set of UDC-indexed document files in machine-readable form in various subject areas; and (5) to conduct tests with the aid of experimental user groups which will lead to an evaluation of the UDC in the desired context. Data are also given on the organization of the project.

---

*Originally prepared for appendix in final AIP/UDC project reports.

2. Freeman, Robert R., *Research Project for the Evaluation of the UDC as the Indexing Language for a Mechanized Reference Retrieval System: Progress Report for the Period July 1, 1965-January 21, 1966,* New York, American Institute of Physics, Report AIP/DRP UDC-2, February 1, 1966. NSF Grant GN-433.
The report reviews activities involving collection of English, French, and German schedules of the Universal Decimal Classification (UDC), translation of some schedules, further development of a mechanized (IBM 1401) UDC file maintenance system, experiments with automatic alphabetic indexing of UDC schedules, automatic typesetting and composition of UDC schedules, selection of equipment and rules for keyboarding the UDC into machine-readable form, and initial steps toward collections of UDC-indexed documents and a retrieval system for test and evaluation purposes. Detailed appendices deal with considerations of creating machine-readable UDC records on punched-paper tape for subsequent computer processing.

3. Freeman, Robert R., *Modern Approaches to the Management of a Classification,* Report AIP/UDC-3 under National Science Foundation Grant GN-433, New York, American Institute of Physics, October 1, 1966. Presented at the Seminar on UDC and Mechanization at the 32nd Conference of the International Federation for Documentation, the Hague, September 20, 1966. Also published as ''The Management of a Classification: Modern Approaches Exemplified by the UDC Project of the American Institute of Physics,'' *Journal of Documentation, 23* (4), 304–320 (December, 1967).
The report views the problem of managing a classification, such as the Universal Decimal Classification (UDC), as an example of the broader class of problems known in the system analysis and data processing field as "file management." The characteristics of file management are listed and related specifically to the UDC. The uses of data processing equipment for the creation, maintenance, manipulation and display of files are discussed. The development of a prototype file management system for the UDC is reviewed. Appendices illustrate the progress of the project and summarize the present status of the UDC in the English language.

4. Russell, Martin, and Freeman, Robert R., *Computer-Aided Indexing of a Scientific Abstracts Journal by the UDC with UNIDEK: a Case Study,* Report AIP/UDC-4 under National Science Foundation Grant GN-433, New York, American Institute of Physics, April 1, 1967.
This paper is a case study of the adoption by *Geoscience Abstracts* of UNIDEK, a novel computer-compiled systematic subject index based on the Universal Decimal Classification (UDC) of the International Federation for Documentation (FID). Events leading to a decision to adopt the system, some theory of indexes, problems involved in conversion, and some of the results achieved are reivewed.

5. Freeman, Robert R., and Pauline Atherton, *File Organization and Search Strategy Using the Universal Decimal Classification in Mechanized Reference Retrieval Systems,* Report AIP/UDC-5 under National Science Foundation Grant GN-433, New York. American Institute of Physics, September 15, 1967. Presented at the FID/IFIP Conference on Mechanized Information Storage, Retrieval, and Dissemination, Rome, June 15, 1967. Published in *Proceedings of the Conference,* North Holland Publishing Co., (forthcoming).

   Starting from a model of contemporary mechanized retrieval systems and the characteristics of indexing languages used therein, the authors develop a rational basis for use of the Universal Decimal Classification (UDC) in this context. Practical design considerations for the use of UDC in a mechanized retrieval system are discussed. Examples are reported of the use of UDC as the indexing language with the Combined File Search System, an existing retrieval system for the IBM 1401, used by several large information centers in the United States. Finally, the authors discuss how UDC might be used as a query language in a typical retrieval system of the near future in which the user interacts directly with the computer-stored document reference file.

   The authors conclude that it is technically feasible to use UDC in mechanized retrieval systems and that, under certain conditions, it may be desirable. Some of these conditions are the existence of large files already indexed by UDC, staff already trained for its use, and extensive international use or exchange of materials of the system.

6. Freeman, Robert R., *Evaluation of the Retrieval of Metallurgical Document References Using the Universal Decimal Classification in a Computer-Based System,* Report AIP/UDC-6 under National Science Foundation Grant GN-433, New York, American Institute of Physics, April 1, 1968.

   A set of twenty-five questions were processed against a computer-stored file of 9,159 document references in the field of ferrous metallurgy, representing the 1965 coverage of the Iron and Steel Institute (London) information service. A basis for evaluation of system performance characteristics and analysis of system failures was provided by using questions which had previously been processed by the American Society for Metals against a data base which contained many of the same documents. The Cuadra-Katter model for describing the system evaluation environment was used. The results, which were highly satisfactory, led to observations and recommendations which contrast the requirements for class definition, indexing policy, and search strategy between manual and computer-based systems which use UDC.

7. Freeman, Robert R. and Pauline Atherton, *AUDACIOUS-an Experiment with an On-Line, Interactive Reference Retrieval System Using the Universal Decimal Classification as the Index Language in the Field of Nuclear Science,* Report AIP/UDC-7 under National Science Foundation Grant GN-433. New York, American Institute of Physics, April 25, 1968.

The report describes an experimental system for remote direct access to files of computer-stored information which has been indexed by the Universal Decimal Classification (UDC). The data base for the experiment consisted of references from a single issue of *Nuclear Science Abstracts*. The *Special Subject Edition of UDC for Nuclear Science and Technology* was also stored in the computer so that users could discover how to translate their questions from natural language to logical statement containing UDC numbers.

The authors conclude that the technical feasibility of use of existing classification and indexing tools, such as UDC, has been demonstrated. However, detailed attention to all facets of man-machine communication is a necessity if systems are to be designed which will be voluntarily used. AUDACIOUS is reviewed and criticized from this point of view.

Finally, the authors conclude that the use of UDC in an on-line, interactive system may have important ramifications for the development of international information networks. Conversion tables (schedules) already exist which would allow speakers of many languages to search files indexed by UDC without regard to national or linguistic boundaries.

8. Atherton, Pauline, Donald W. King, and Robert R. Freeman, *Evaluation of the Retrieval of Nuclear Science Document References Using the Universal Decimal Classification in a Computer-Based System*, Report AIP/UDC-8 under National Science Foundation Grant GN-433, New York, American Institute of Physics, May 1, 1968.
A single issue of *Nuclear Science Abstracts*, containing about 2,300 abstracts, was indexed by UDC, using the *Special Subject Edition of UDC for Nuclear Science and Technology*. The descriptive cataloging and UDC-indexing records formed a computer-stored data base. A systematic random sample of 500 additional abstracts, taken from a collection of about 196,000, was also indexed by UDC. An experimental design was developed such that the potential results of retrieval tests with the full collection could be inferred from actual results obtained from the two smaller data bases.

Sixty questions were collected from nuclear science research organizations in North America and Europe. Two search analysts, neither of whom was familiar with the policies and practices of the indexers, formulated logical search statements with UDC numbers. The resulting queries were processed against the UDC-indexed data bases. They were also processed by two other information services. Twelve questions, a subset of the original sixty, were chosen for more detailed analysis. The results are presented in the report.

9. Freeman, Robert R., and Pauline Atherton, *Final Report of the Research Project for the Evaluation of the UDC as the Indexing Language for a Mechanized Reference Retrieval System*, Report AIP/UDC-9 under NSF Grant GN-433. New York, American Institute of Physics, May 1, 1968.
The background, objectives, and accomplishments of the project are reviewed briefly. Specific areas discussed are English language UDC schedules, a computer-based UDC file management system, data bases for retrieval experiments, batch-process and on-line, interactive information retrieval systems,

and retrieval system evaluation. The conclusions deal with the usefulness of the UDC for mechanized retrieval systems, needed research, needed organizational effort, and a proposed international seminar. Several appendices summarize the current state of the UDC in English and the availability of magnetic tape and microfilm files developed by the project.

Subject Analysis of Library Science Literature by Means of Classification Systems: Outline of Criteria Needed for Evaluation

by Phyllis Richmond and Pauline Atherton

INTRODUCTION

In recent years, there has been considerable interest in classification systems as a means of organizing information (recorded messages) for transfer purposes. Arguments have occurred and positions have been taken with regard to the efficacy of this or that type of system. At the same time, the term "classification" itself has been used with varying degrees of broadness, all the way from a very narrow hierarchical view to a view so broad that it takes in practically everything that can be conceptualized and defined.*

The current concern with classification has had an apparent effect on the various methods of bibliographic control applied to library science literature. Actual analysis of all the methods would make a good topic for a doctoral dissertation and will not be performed here. Only an outline for such a study has been prepared and is presented in brief form as a basis for discussion.

Excerpt from a presentation at 1967 Albany Conference on Bibliographic Access to Library Science Literature.

*The "Elsinore definition" of *classification* will be used by the authors: by "classification" is meant any method creating relations, generic or other, between individual semantic units, regardless of the degree in hierarchy contained in the systems and of whether those systems would be applied in connection with traditional or more or less mechanized methods of document searching. *Classification Research; Proceedings of the Second International Study Conference* held at Hotel Prins Hamlet, Elsinore, Denmark, 14th to 18th, September 1964 (Copenhagen, Munksgaard, 1965), p. 544.

Three major sets of factors are involved in the evaluation of classification systems: evaluation of the system according to *purpose,* according to *design,* and according to *functional operation.* Classification systems are considered in an objective fashion.

Subjective aspects, such as personal factors and individual differences in interpretation and judgment, which would influence application, have not been considered, though conceivably these could affect operation. The objectivity proposed in this outline may be impossible to achieve, but at least an attempt at objectivity should be made so that those factors which are entirely subjective can be recognized separately.

In Part A, we have considered the question, ''Why was this classification made?'' Then in Part B we moved on to ''How is this classification made?'' Finally in Part C we come to ''How well does this classification do what it was made to do?''

PART A. BASIC DETAIL NEEDED FOR EVALUATION OF PURPOSE

Types of classification analyzed for purpose

Type 1) *for books and reports:*
[Dewey Decimal Classification, Universal Decimal Classification, Library of Congress Classification, Bliss Bibliographic Classification, Colon Classification]

Purposes:

To place books, reports in order on a shelf (array in a consistent sequence)

To physically group books on like subjects together (array in a helpful sequence)

To fit into a more general classification

To be used directly (for searching open stacks *by a person* on foot or for browsing)

To be used by student, scholar, practitioner, specialist, general reader

Type 2) *for classified catalogs:*
[Classification Research Group's Faceted Classification, also Dewey, UDC, LC]

Purposes:

To search for all the books in a library on a given subject

To display that subject in its full relationships with generic and specific as well as coordinate subject classes

To avoid the one-book-one-place impasse of physical shelf arrangement *by classification*

To fit into a more general classification

To be used indirectly (as a rule, must use an alphabetical index to learn *notation for area to* be searched, and to request items in closed stacks)

To be used for browsing in one place (in a book or card catalog used as a unit rather than by travelling over floors, levels, buildings)

To be used by student, scholar, practitioner, specialist, general reader

Type 3) *for content of books:*
[Tables of contents]

Purposes:

To display author's or editor's organization and interpretation of his subject

To enable reader to follow author's flow of thought more readily

To enable cataloger, indexer, abstracter to analyze text

To be used by student, scholar, practitioner, specialist

Type 4) *for classified indexes to books:*

Purposes:

To enable author to indicate specific concepts in detail

To be used by reader to pinpoint access by name, subject, etc.; to get at *full* content, regardless of author's organization of his work

To be used by student primarily, but also helpful for scholar, practitioner, specialist

Type 5) *for arrangement of bibliographies:*
a) retrospective
b) current

Purposes:

To order bibliographies in a helpful sequence

To group items in a like subject together, preferably the sequence used by specialists in that subject and not necessarily to fit a more general classification scheme

To permit searching for all the books and articles on a given subject that have been included (though multiple entry is possible, it has rarely been used)

To provide browsing in a list form, often with annotation or critical comment (where used, *selection* is *ipso facto* critical)

To be used by student, scholar, practitioner, specialist

Type 6) *for directories of personnel, research projects, etc:*

Purposes:
To create helpful subsets of classes according to type of specialty
To permit multiple placement where applicable
To be used by all persons needing rather specific information

Type 7) *for classified indexing or abstracting serials covering book, periodical and report literature:*

Note: books are essentially an established literature. Articles and reports are a flexible, mobile, changing literature.

Purposes:
To permit rapid access to totality of references (and possibly abstracts) about CURRENT literature
To achieve speed of access and widest coverage by dividing subjects into manageable portions
To fit a flexible classification needed for current literature on subject material that is not fixed in focus (i.e., frequently changing organization and emphasis)
To be used by scholar, practitioner, specialist, and the advanced student

Type 8) *for thesauri or index term lists:*

Purposes:
To provide a framework for structuring the thesaurus or index term list
To ensure that related terms are grouped so that all (not part) of their significant relationships are caught
To define homographs, uncover synonyms, limit metaphors by indicating class membership
To be used by makers of thesauri or index term lists and as needed by those who consult them

PART B. BASIC DETAIL NEEDED FOR EVALUATION OF DESIGN OF CLASSIFICATION SCHEMES

Note: In all cases, evaluation of design must relate to purpose of the classification dealt with, not to that of some other classification.

1) **Analysis** according to Ranganathan's Canons of Classification: *Prolegomena to Library Classification* 2d ed. (London, Library Assn., 1957).

For Characteristics (Foci)
1. Canon of Differentiation
2. Canon of Concomitance
3. Canon of Relevance
4. Canon of Ascertainability
5. Canon of Permanence
6. Canon of Relevant Sequence
7. Canon of Consistency

For Array
8. Canon of Exhaustiveness
9. Canon of Exclusiveness
10. Canon of Helpful Sequence
11. Canon of Consistent Sequence

For Chain
12. Canon of Decreasing Extension
13. Canon of Modulation

For Filiatory Sequence
14. Canon of Subordinate Classes
15. Canon of Coordinate Classes

For Terminology
16. Canon of Currency
17. Canon of Reticence
18. Canon of Enumeration
19. Canon of Context

For Notation
20. Canon of Relativity
21. Canon of Expressiveness
22. Canon of Mixed Notations

Queries:
a. What parts of Ranganathan's canons are applicable to the eight types of classification mentioned in Part A?
b. Should the characteristics of the different types influence the application of the canons?
c. Are any new canons needed?

2) **Statement of philosophy** governing the classification system.
The introduction to a classification system should include a short explanation of the general philosophy underlying the system. If there is no explanation, one should be derived by a careful inspection of the system itself. This statement should cover the following points enumerated here as queries:

Queries:
a. Is the system hierarchical, faceted, coordinate or other?
b. Is the structure based on logical exposition or on building from words or concepts?
c. Is the system theoretically or empirically derived?

　　d. Are the methods of exposition based on the evolutionary or revolutionary approach to the development of systems?

　　e. What types of concepts are used to express interrelationships among aspects of recorded knowledge being treated in the system? (e.g., scope note, ''prefer'' or ''use'' note, and cross references)

　　f. What are the structural dimensions of the system; what dimensional concept of knowledge underlies the classification? (e.g., philosophical basis used to determine parameters of what constitutes ''knowledge'')

3) **Analysis** to discover helpfulness or hindrance of collateral or sub-parts of a scheme (such as notation, format, dimensions, auxiliary schedules, or similar addenda).

　　Queries:
　　a. Does the notation hinder the display of class relationships?
　　b. Does the format permit representation of a three or four dimensional structure?
　　c. Do the auxiliary schedules provide enough valuable information to counter-balance their awkwardness in usage?
　　d. How many type fonts are necessary for clarity?

PART C. BASIC DETAIL NEEDED FOR EVALUATION OF FUNCTIONAL OPERATION

1) Analysis of each system in terms of how well it does what it was designed to do (from the point of view of its STATED PURPOSE).

2) Analysis of the *adaptability* of a system to different kinds of needs (as given in 1).

3) Analysis of the *adaptability* of a system to mechanization (especially to show how theoretical principles in design will be affected by advantages and limits of computers).

4) User-type of analysis to show what is or will be demanded of a classification by various types of users.* (This should be a user's *use* study, not what the user thinks he wants, which is a matter pertaining to the evaluation of purpose).

　　a. Responsiveness of classification to various types of users according to their backgrounds (e.g., their degree of sophistication will affect their approach to the classification).

　　b. Responsiveness of parts of the classification in use, in terms of class description, structure, index terms, classified index terms, notation,

---

Note: The USER in such studies would be both the user who applies the classification system and the user who makes use of the end-product of such application.

format, ability to accept new data, realignment as conditions change, etc.

CONCLUSION

The mere fact of making an analytic outline has yielded some interesting information. Without analysis as to purpose—even the sketchy one made here—we could not have differentiated eight different kinds of classification systems for the subject, library science. At the same time, we might have considered some of these systems as something other than classification, particularly classification for indexes to books, directories, and thesauri or index term lists. The outline according to *purpose* shows diversity and yet at the same time it indicates the uniformity and perhaps the ubiquity of classification systems. It also indicates the fullness, or lack of it, in almost all schemes.

The *outline for purpose* sets up the basic corpus of material to be studied. The outlines according to *design* and *functional operation* get down to the brass tacks of evaluation. Here the different factors to be considered can be studied for each system, as well as comparatively for all systems—with the provision that the *purpose* be kept in mind in rating design and operation so that a system is not judged in terms of some factor it was never designed to encounter.

The whole outline reveals how much work is still needed in classification research. There are at least four dissertation possibilities here: thorough analysis of the several different classification methods of bibliographic control, evaluation of classification systems according to design, evaluation according to workability and adaptability, and evaluation by thorough user-analysis, considering the interaction of the user-applier and the user-reader.

The literature of library science is a manageable piece with which to work, and at the same time it contains most of the various types of classification systems encountered. This microcosm should be an excellent base for sound studies; the results forthcoming could then be applied to study of classification in other subjects and perhaps eventually even to that of the universe of knowledge itself.

Francis Levy's* study, made for a recent meeting in Marseilles on the "documentation of documentation" is a step in this direction. That meeting and this one in Albany may mark the beginning of much needed study and exploration of our own field's bibliographic control problems and their solutions.

---

*Francis Levy. "Compatibility between Classifications and Thesauri: Evaluation of a First Study in the Field of Information Storage and Retrieval." (Centre National de la Recherche Scientifique, Groupe d'Etude sur l'Information Scientifique, 1967). Report No. COM./30/67/F.L.

Classification as an Online Subject Access Tool: Challenge and Opportunity

Projects as early as 1965–66 demonstrated that searching a classification schedule online could result in a helpful array of related items during the browsing portion of a search and successful results could be obtained from selecting class numbers and using them as search "terms." Projects using the MARC Pilot Project tapes demonstrated that DDC and LCC class numbers, used in conjunction with the *Library of Congress Subject Headings* (*LCSH*) and title keywords, could bring recall up to and over 90%, when no subject access field could do so well alone. Operational online public access catalogs (OPACs) studied by Hildreth in 1981 showed half of them with a "call number" search capability, sometimes truncated. If all this evidence points toward subject access via classification, why are we asking the question? In my opinion it is because the library world does not seem ready for classification to be used as an online subject access tool. To be ready implies more than a mere list of call numbers from MARC records which can be scanned online. To be ready means re-examining the work of classification and the impact of online access on that process; it means viewing the role of classification efforts from the online searcher's point of view and reviewing what can be done to improve his/her satisfactory searching and results. My analysis of this challenge parallels the work Karen Markey and I did for Central ERIC when they asked us to review the impact of online searching (especially free text searching) on the ERIC database (ED 180432). We had to separate suggestions for improvements into three groups, depending on who the initiator for improvements would be. As in that case, I think we must review the role and efforts of:

1. Classification makers and maintainers (DDC and LCC);
2. OPAC designers (at LC, RLG, WLN, CLSI, and a myriad of libraries, including NLM, OSU, Northwestern, etc.); and

Paper presented at a Subject Access meeting sponsored by the Council on Library Resources, Dublin, OH, June 1982.

3. OPAC users as represented by library staff (public and technical), and typical "end" users.

To be ready, as I said earlier, means more than listing LC call numbers and DDC class numbers from the MARC records. It means linking class numbers with subject headings (something promised as early as 1927 in the *LCSH* introduction). Several persons outside LC have tried to do this—to mention only a few: Mannheimer, Williams, and Daily; Nancy Olson; Bowker in their *Subject Authorities*. Because few online searchers will care to check all the LC schedules to learn what their favorite class numbers mean, or the Dewey numbers, either, some attempt will have to be made to "translate" these numbers and develop table look-ups for online display, perhaps similar to the *LC Classification Outline*.

The comparable effort for DDC would be a publication of all DDC summaries. Any effort like this, of course, must be viewed as a publication for the online searcher, or a "table" for the online system to display when needed. If it is not viewed as a user's tool, we will create something only useful for the classifiers and catalogers, the intended audience for all of the above-mentioned attempts to combine subject headings and class numbers.

Issue 1: Shelf arrangement problems have served as a brake on revising classification schedules or on demonstrating their utility as a subject access tool. Can we divorce shelf arrangement as a process from classification as a subject access process so that we can create useful, systematic browsing displays online which would provide a helpful order of items, avoiding the problem of the inherent order of alphabets?

Both Michael Gorman (*American Libraries*, September 1981, p. 498–9) and Nancy J. Williamson (*Library Resources & Technical Services*, April/June 1982, 122+) have addressed this issue briefly.

The preliminary results of the CLR-sponsored OPAC User Evaluation studies have shown that users need assistance when their search results are either too few or too many. They also request viewing "terms related to their search." System designers are perturbed about response time when terms which are "too common" are used. Can class numbers in MARCs record be explained by classification schedules in auxiliary online files? Retrieval system designers will have to be creative in this area, more so than presently evidenced. Perhaps some developmental effort needs to be supported again, as was done in 1965–66 (AIP Project AUDACIOUS, funded by NSF). Beyond using the EXPLODE command via MeSH's tree structures, a quasi-classification, there do not seem to be any ingenious uses of classification to broaden or narrow searches, or to improve response time by translating common terms entered into a system message to prompt the user to narrow their search, etc.

Issue 2: Can a combination of OPAC designers, researchers, and classification owners and maintainers come up with some ingenious uses of class numbers to improve response time online, to guide users to better search strategies, etc.?

Issue 3: What useful links can be forged between *LCSH* and LCC or DDC which will be helpful online in various OPACs?

This is an issue related to both Issue #1 and #2 because most people have missed the value of these links. NLM has not, interestingly enough, in that the schedule they use for CATLINE (Class W) is indexed using MeSH terms as much as possible. Has that day come for LCC? If it did, what would we do with the result online? The data in the Bowker publication could be of some use for such a study, but taken alone, it can not yet show what the potential is online. Even NLM in writing the specifications for Medlars III has not incorporated any use of their Class W Schedule online, even though it is maintained in machine-readable form.

Subject authority control can be viewed as a problem for one system of subject headings or a single classification system, or it can be viewed as a problem of users who search in multiple files, each with their own unique vocabularies or classification systems. If viewed as the latter, something needs to be done to integrate, if not make compatible, the various systems which might be searched. All through the 1960's attempts at compatibility were made, but we have not yet seen any results in this area which have changed the life of online searchers. Retrieval system vendors like SDC, DIALOG, and BRS have attempted multiple-database vocabulary indexes online, but these are the lowest common denominator, simply a merger of lists of terms from database records, with no attempt to show the syndetic structure of each vocabulary or to group these terms into broad related groups. The *Integrated Energy Vocabulary* and the Battelle Switching Vocabulary System are examples of things to come. The application of BSO (Broad System of Ordering; a UNISIST project) is another way to proceed. Which way will lead to the biggest payoff from the least investment?

Issue 4: Are there automatic means for achieving online switching between subject vocabulary and classification systems? Does an effort like BSO have to be imposed before multiple files can be searched adequately online with the least user effort? Is a transparent translation from a user's search terms to the system vocabularies in an OPAC feasible and practicable?

All of the above discussion assumes that we would not get bogged down by the idiosyncracies of our present systems which have tried to accommodate shelf arrangement, format considerations, and interpolation problems. In other words, if we start off assuming classification can serve a useful purpose online, what might these purposes be and how can we get there from existing records, existing schedules, and existing systems?

****

DISCUSSION

One participant mentioned that the authority format allows the use of notes that could help the user know where to look for what he is seeking. Participants in some of the focused interviews conducted as part of the online public access catalog evaluation project have talked about the idea of a ''knowledge tree,'' which could help a user broaden or narrow a search.

Classification as a User's Tool in Online Public Access Catalogs

INTRODUCTION

More and more of the world's library catalogs are in machine-readable form and the older form of card catalogs is being replaced by COM catalogs and online public access catalogs. In the later version the online retrieval system's command language and displays are varied, but tend to resemble the retrieval systems designed in the late 1960's for abstracting and indexing databases. Subject access is usually provided by keyword searching of title words and abstracts and/or descriptors from a controlled vocabulary. Excepting a few databases, this is all the subject-content in the records of these databases. But that is not the case in library catalog records. A rich, untapped source of subject-content is in the call number, or classification number in the record.

As the reports are now coming in from Online Catalog Use studies (1) we are learning that users have difficulties browsing in the online files, reducing or increasing results, and determining alternate search strategies. It is the purpose of this paper to show ways in which the present cataloging records can be scanned, the classification numbers explained and displayed, and the online catalog user aided in their search for just the right amount of information retrieval. The exhibits given here are "idealized" and were not done to fit any one existing system. Instead it is hoped it will focus every system designer's attention on this portion of the bibliographic records and prompt some of them to implement some "table look-ups" similar to the present thesaural displays which come from auxiliary files like a name or subject authority file.

CURRENT WORK

The work upon which this report is based is just now getting underway at Syracuse University, with the assistance of Chen-lin Wu. The project is

Reprinted with permission from *Universal Classification,* Proceedings of the 4th International Study Conference on Classification Research, Indeks-Verlag, 1982.

entitled "Developing a Classification-Based Online Catalog Retrieval System." We will try to add certain features to the experimental version of SULIRS, the online catalog at Syracuse University, Bird Library, and possibly to DIATOM, a simulation of DIALOG at Syracuse University on which we have mounted a file of 12,000 MARC/LC records. We will be exploring the most useful displays of portions of the Library of Congress Classification schedules (edited for naive/inexperienced library searchers), Dewey Decimal Classification schedules, and possibly the National Library of Medicine Classification schedules. In this prototype system we will not be concerned with the needs of classificationists and classifiers for online access to their tool, the classification schedule, but we realize that this is a parallel effort which should be expended if a full search access system from a classification scheme is ever to be developed.

Our research focuses on the need to provide assistance to the user at critical times in the search when he/she may be dissatisfied with the output, the match of search terms, or with the next best step to take in the search. We are assuming that browsing in alphabetically related displays or in a thesaural display (with broader and narrower terms) has not proven to be very satisfactory and that a logical (i.e., classified) display may be helpful.

PREVIOUS WORK

The early work of Freeman and Atherton in 1968 (2), called AU-DACIOUS, was perhaps the first classification-based online retrieval system. The classification system was the Universal Decimal Classification and the database was a file of nuclear science literature. Some of the examples in this paper come from that early work, but the interaction is of a more recent vintage, as the AUDACIOUS software was a precursor of DIALOG and NASA/RECON! This work indicated how far we had to go to provide a fool-proof and effective system for inexperienced users who would not want to be bothered with a full display of a classification schedule, cataloger's notes, and cryptic captions in the outline to explain shelf arrangement problems for different types of materials.

Later work, also at Syracuse, done by Martel and Atherton (3) during the LEEP project, attempted to show how a classification schedule could be coded for machine input so that ranges of class numbers could be displayed or searched, how a KWIC index could be developed from the captions, and how the class numbers could be linked to MARC records. This work, in 1969, preceded the development of MARC II records. We worked with 50,000 MARC Pilot Project records and the Z Schedule from the Library of Congress. Here again we learned how much more effort would have to be expended before these "outlines of knowledge" could be useful to the online searcher.

Since that time there have been a few reports of using Dewey class numbers for SDI; KWIC indexes to LCC were generated by combining the indexes to all parts of the LC Schedules; and several people have made table look-ups between class numbers on MARC records and subject headings assigned or listed in authority files. None of this later work has been done with a focus on its utility for online searching. Subject access problems online seem acute enough already to warrant some careful attention on the utility of information from class numbers. (4) As shown in reference 4, a searcher may enter the term ISLAM and be told it appears in 39 titles and 831 different records (see Figure 3-A in ref. 4). In another online catalog the same searcher might be told that there are 254 subject headings with the word "ISLAM" in it. What does the searcher do next? Will subdivisions of subject headings help? Will a quick scan of the first ten records help? That may be all that can be done at the present time, and that is just not enough.

POSSIBLE COMMANDS AND DISPLAYS ONLINE

Most online catalogs and retrieval systems allow some browsing of an index display before printing bibliographic records. They also allow searching in different fields or data elements of the bibliographic records, combining terms using Boolean operators and displaying records in different orders. These same features can be used on the information about classification numbers and their meaning (or captions). Only a few new data element labels might be needed and some additional flexibility on what systems would allow as an order of search commands. Some systems have already built in too much rigidity and the user has difficulty moving "backwards and forwards." Having observed people at the card catalog and at the shelves, most librarians know that serendipity will only work if the system will allow some free and easy browsing. What the computer-based system can do so well is keep track of that browsing so that valuable information can be collected automatically and used all together after some decisions of relevance have been made.

What follows is not a completely systematic and exhaustive list of illustrations, but it should be indicative of the power we can unleash if we consider the class number in bibliographic records as subject-content and if we develop browsing lists of related concepts in a logical array, following the basic classification schedules such as LCC, DCC, and UDC, to mention only the universal schemes.

Figure 1 could be someone's first display at the online catalog if they chose to scan a summary display from the classification schedule in their area of interest. Some would liken this to a menu-driven system such as that used in videotext systems, but I prefer to think of it as a user-driven command for a logical browse on the most general level. From this screen, the user could go to a "call number" search, a subject term search, or a quick display of a few records with this general class number.

FIGURE 1. Screen Display with Classification Summary

SEARCH: Browse ISLAM/CT Summary

297   ISLAM and religions derived from it

Summary

297.1 Sources, relationship, attitudes of Islam
  .2 Islamic doctrinal theology (Aqaid and Kalam)
  .3 Islamic public worship and other practices
  .4 Islamic religious experience, life, practice
  .5 Islamic moral theology
  .6 Islamic leaders and organization
  .7 Islamic activities
  .8 Islamic sects and other religions derived from Islam

Which line above is closest to your search topic??? _____

Figure 2 could be the display in the classification schedule's index, showing the user the different class numbers but not requiring that they input the numbers of interest. In fact, they could request a further browsing level, deeper into the schedule before they would actually begin to retrieve items. The second display in Figure 2 could give the number of items classified under each number or it could give the number of more specific (narrower) class numbers for each one displayed. For the naive online catalog user this latter information might be confusing. Notice that a (CF.) note appears. If the user were curious and wanted to follow this lead, a simple command would display the related class numbers in context. See Figure 3. At that time the user might be asked to indicate which lines are closest to the search topic. Once named, the system could automatically combine all the "cc7" lines and any other lines specifically requested, giving a retrieval result at this point, with very little keyboarding done by the online searcher.

Moving around in the classification schedule and in the index should be very easy. If found to be confusing, the system could collect all the selections and display them automatically on the top of the screen, as in PaperChase (5), with a set of possible commands available in a line below this.

FIGURE 2. Two Screen Displays—Browsing in Classification

SEARCH: Browse RADIOACTIVITY

c 1 Radioactivity	(539.16)
c 2 Radioactivity in atmosphere	(551.510.7)
c 3 Radioactivity in earth	(550.378)
c 4 Radioactivity in oceans and seas	(551.46:539.16)
c 5 Radioactivity in rivers	(551.48:539.16)
c 6 Radioactivity standards	(539.16.081)

SELECT: C2 Browse

cc 1 Structure, mechanics, and thermodynamics of the atmosphere	(551.51)
cc 2 . . . . Physical properties of the atmosphere	(551.510.3)
cc 3 . . . . Composition of the atmosphere	(551.510.4)
cc 4 . . . . General structure of the atmosphere	(551.510.5)
C 2******Radioactivity in atmosphere	(551.510.7)
cc 5 . . . . . . Natural radioactivity	(551.510.71)
cc 6 . . . . . . Artificial radioactivity	(551.510.72)
cc 7 . . . . Radioactive fall-out (Cf.)	(551.510.721)

FIGURE 3: Screen Display of Related Class Numbers—with Retrieval Result

SEARCH: CF cc7

CF cc7: 614.73,   Caption in Context:

B 1 Public Health and Safety	(614)
N 1 ...Food and Drugs. Sanitary inspection and control	(614.3)
N 2 ...Prevention of infection, epidemics, etc.	(614.4)
N 3 ...Disposal of the dead	(614.6)
N 4 ...Hygiene of air, soil and water. Pollution	(614.7)
cc 7 ******Fall-out in general; For sampling methods, see 614.73:543:053)	(614.73)*****
N 5 ...Accidents. Safety organizations	(614.8)

CF cc7: 628.511, Caption in Context:

B 2 Public Health Engineering	(628)
N 6 ...Water Supply. Drinking Water (General)	(628.1)
N 7 ...Sewage. Disposal of Sewage	(628.3)
cc 7 ******Atmospheric pollution	(628.511)***

FIGURE 3. Screen Display of Related Class Numbers—with Retrieval Result (continued)

CF cc7: 628.511, Caption in Context:

N8 ......Water pollution   (628.515)
N9 ....Industrial waste disposal   (628.543)

???Which line above is closest to your search topic??? cc7 n4

***Your retrieval set includes items classified 551.510.7, 614.73, 628.511 and 614.7. A total of 45 items are retrieved.

FIGURE 4: Example of Search, Display, Caption Scan and Continued Display of Records

---

SEARCH: RAPE/T;TYPE 1/3/1

1 Rape/Title
  -1-
  Call No.:   364.153/Sex Offenses
  Author: Groth, A. Nicholas
  Title: Men who rape.
  PubDate: 1979
  Subjects: 1.   Criminal Psychology   2. Rape

SEARCH: Browse 1/CT

Browse caption 364.153 in context

CT	Caption	Call No.	Items
1	Crime and its alleviation (Criminology)	364	2
2	Offenses	364.1	0
3	Offenses against the person	364.15	6
4	genocide	364.151	12
5	homicide and suicide	364.152	4
6*********	sex offenses	364.153	8
7	abduction	364.154	1
8	other crimes of violence	364.155	3
9	criminal libel, slander, invasion of privacy	364.156	10
10	traffic in drugs	364.157	13

TYPE CT6 NOT S1/3/1

2 364.153/CT
  -1-
  Call No.:   364.153/Sex Offenses

FIGURE 4: Example of Search, Display, Caption Scan and Continued Display of Records (continued)

Author:	Parker, Tony
Title:	The Hidden World of Sex Offenders
PubDate:	1969
Subjects:	1. Sex Crimes—Great Britain

Figure 4 shows how someone could go from a title word search to a record display to a browse display of the class number for that record in the context of the classification schedule, see number of items possible to retrieve, and look at additional records. Of course the system would track any lines selected for a total retrieval score. Figure 5 is a variation on this type of search, the difference being that the system would automatically switch over from a word search to a class caption search if there are no hits. Then the user could browse in that part of the schedule.

FIGURE 5: Search Example with Command for Caption Scan after Record Display

SEARCH: ATOMIC BOMB and WORLD WAR II

1.   0 Atomic Bomb and World War II (Subject Headings)

      Searching further. . . . .
2.   2 Atomic Bomb/SH and World War II/CT

TYPE 2/3/1-2

-1-
Call No.:	940.5442/Campaigns and Battles
Author:	Osada, Arata
Title:	Children of the A-Bomb, the testament of boys and girls of Hiroshima.
Subjects:	1. Atomic Bomb 2. World War, 1939–1945—Personal Narratives, Japanese 3. Hiroshima—Bombardment, 1945

-2-
Call No.:	940.5442/ Campaigns and Battles
Author:	Knebel, Fletcher
Title:	No high ground
Subjects:	1. Atomic Bomb 2. Hiroshima (Japan)

FIGURE 5: Search Example with Command for Caption Scan after Record Display (continued)

EXPAND 2/CT

CT	Caption	Call No.	Items
1	General History of Europe	940	30
2	20th Century, 1918–	940.5	5
3	1918–1930	940.51	2
4	1930–1939	940.52	1
5	World War II, 1939–45	940.53	4
6	Military History of World War II	940.54	0
7	Operations	940.541	0
8	Specific campaigns and battles	940.542	11
9	Aerial operations	940.544	8
10*************** Campaigns and battles		940.5442	3

CONCLUSION

Although the illustrations in this paper come from UDC and DDC, I feel confident that a similar array could be obtained from LCC if the schedules were edited to ready them for the online catalog user. Because classification schedules have been designed to correct for subject scatter, their indexes contain many synonyms pointing to the same class numbers; word forms are not as big a problem; generic relations are handily displayed, and coordination of related topics is accommodated. It would seem a horrible waste not to use all this intellectual effort online. Criticism of subject authority lists like the *Library of Congress List of Subject Headings* may lead to improved online subject searching (6) eventually, but there is indication already that this may be insufficient for the demands of online searchers. The panacea of natural language searching and automatic clustering after relevance feedback is as sought after as the Holy Grail, but may prove to be as illusive. In the meantime, the investment in library classification may have renewed value online if we focus on revising the schedules for online displays during subject searching.

REFERENCES

1. Besant, Larry. "Users of public online catalogs want sophisticated subject access." *American Libraries* 14 (March 1982), 160.

Hildreth, Charles. *The User Interface in Online Public Access Catalogs*. Final Report to Council on Library Resources. Dublin, OH; OCLC, Inc., 1982. (in press as monograph)

"Testing the feasibility of online catalogs" *BRS Bulletin* 3 (June–July 1979), 1.

Cochrane, Pauline A. "Subject Access in the Online Catalog" *Research Libraries in OCLC: A Quarterly*, No. 5 (January 1982), 1–7.

2. Freeman, Robert R. and Pauline Atherton. AUDACIOUS-an Experiment with an On-Line, Interactive Reference Retrieval System Using the Universal Decimal Classification as the Indexing Language in the Field of Nuclear Science. Report AIP/UDC-7 under National Science Foundation Grant GN-433. New York: American Institute of Physics, April 25, 1968.

3. Martel, Frank and Pauline Atherton. The Conversion of the LC Classification Schedules to Machine-Readable Form; An Exploratory Project. LEEP Report. 1969. Syracuse University, School of Library Science.

4. See Cochrane ref. in (1)

5. Horowitz, Gary and Howard L. Bleich. "PaperChase: a Computer Program to Search the Medical Literature" *New England Journal of Medicine* 305 (October 15, 1981), 924–930. See also *American Libraries* (May 1982) p. 303–06.

6. Cochrane, Pauline and Monika Kirtland. Critical Views of LCSH and An Analysis of Vocabulary Control in LCSH. An Information Analysis Product from ERIC Clearinghouse on Information Resources, Syracuse University, 1981.

Part 5

What Can Be Learned from Subject Access Research?

Introduction

The selections in this chapter come from the most popular of all my research projects, the Subject Access Project, which was funded by the Council on Library Resources in 1976–1978. Nothing about our research was novel and innovative; what was new was the idea of augmenting MARC bibliographic records so they would be more useful for subject searching in the online catalogs which were in the planning stage at that time.

What we did was borrow ideas from the information retrieval field—from the online bibliographic services—and apply them to library catalogs. We augmented the MARC records with subject descriptions from the books themselves, in the same way an index editor will add free text from a periodical article or report to augment the indexing record for that item. (The second 1978 selection is a page of conclusions about the use of book indexes for this purpose.)

We used the computer-based system called ORBIT from the System Development Corporation as our "online catalog system" and we asked users to phrase queries much like the ones they are now phrasing as they stand (or sit) at online public access catalogs. The selection from the Final Report of the Subject Access Project, entitled *BOOKS Are for Use*, gives you some idea of how we went about this research, what the augmented records looked like, what types of queries we had from users which were processed on BOOKS/ORBIT, and what we learned from the exercise.

We evaluated the performance of an online library catalog, with and without augmented subject descriptions. The results, published in DATA-BASE in 1982, were impressive, but the library world has not yet embraced the idea we recommend even though there is a great deal of interest in subject augmentation since the results of the Council on Library Resources sponsored research on online catalog users.

BOOKS Are for Use: Final Report of the Subject Access Project

What Was Learned from the Subject Access Project?

In our original proposal for this project we stated that we wanted to find out about the following:

1) Availability of suitable information in books to produce augmented subject descriptions.
2) Cost of inputting these subject descriptions in machine-readable form.
3) Cost of computer storage of a BOOKS data base (MARC-like records augmented with subject descriptions).
4) Costs of online searching of a BOOKS data base.
5) Benefits derived from online searching of BOOKS.

In summary, we found that:

1) Suitable information which met our selection criteria was available in 90% of the books we systematically selected from the University of Toronto Libraries. Two hundred fifty-three books had to be rejected because they contained insufficient information on their contents pages or had no contents page and had no index. A large part of these 253 rejected books came from one part of the collection on post confederation Ontario history.

Suitable information was available to select subject descriptions which averaged about 300 words per title. The subject description we devised was created following selection rules. We had a quota system for each title, roughly 30 *entries* per book (i.e., an entry was a group of terms in a contextual phrase such as a chapter heading or index phrase).

The information (terms and phrases) in the subject descriptions did produce a useful vocabulary for online searching, with

Excerpt from a report to the Council on Library Resources, 1978. ERIC Document 156 131.

half the terms appearing in the subject descriptions for two or more books. Four thousand of the terms appeared in subject descriptions for 6 or more books. About 1,600 of these subject description terms matched with terms found in the Library of Congress subject heading for the books in the file. There were thousands more subject terms from these descriptions than from either the title or subject headings.

2) The cost of selecting and inputting these subject descriptions was about $5.00/title (including overhead) with most of the time and costs being the keyboarding, proofreading, editing and computer processing personnel time. The selection of the subject description took, on the average, 12 minutes per title.

3) At the System Development Corporation the cost of computer storage of our file was about $.30 per record/month. Initial start-up costs were about $1.00 per record. Online use of the file was set at $35/hour with $.08 for each offline print. Updates to the file were not made, but were estimated at approximately $.30 per record. The file was accessible 12 hours per day, 5 days per week via telecommunications ($8/hour).

4) Costs of the average sign-on during the BOOKS demonstration period were $14.00 for twenty minutes. During the controlled test period where actual queries were being searched, the average search required 8 minutes online for a MARC record search and 4 minutes online for a BOOKS record search. The offline prints averaged about six per search. These figures suggest that the average search would cost about $5.00 for MARC searching and $2.50 for BOOKS searching.

5) The benefits derived from online searching of BOOKS included:

   a) Greater access to the books with relevant information.
   b) Greater precision, insuring fewer non-relevant items in the search output.
   c) Less costly online searching than MARC searching.
   d) The ability to answer some queries impossible using today's catalog information.

During controlled tests the present-day catalog record (MARC) and the BOOKS record were searched following a randomized block, repeated measures experimental design. The comparison of the results from 90 searches shows that

   a) MARC retrieved 56 relevant items while BOOKS retrieved 130 relevant items. Only 14 relevant items were retrieved by both MARC and BOOKS searches.

b) The average precision of MARC searches was 35%, BOOKS searches was 46%.

c) The average MARC search took twice as long online.

This comparison did not change when either searches for humanities or social science were studied separately.

REVIEW OF PROJECT PLAN AND OBJECTIVES

"Our general habits of thought can easily blind us to the need for altering our ways of thinking in accordance with the nature of the material under investigation as we penetrate into new domains."
—David Bohm
British Journal Phil. Sci., 12 (August, 1961), pp. 103–116.

To put this final report in a proper setting, we will quote from the original research proposal to the Council on Library Resources, written in the Fall of 1975. The project was funded in late June, 1976 and continued with CLR support until February, 1978. A special grant from the Syracuse University Research Fund will continue the Subject Access Project through June, 1978, while further support is being sought to help answer the question: "Where Do We Go From Here?"

The project plan as written in late 1975 reads as follows:

Specific Aims

This project could result in the redesign of both the data base *and* retrieval systems used in libraries to search by subject and retrieve information about the content of their book collections. It is proposed to sample the holdings of two* large libraries with machine-readable catalogs who are planning to provide online searching of their catalog in 1976, to augment their MARC-like records for this sample with subject descriptions taken from either the table of contents and/or subject indexes in these books, to test the searching of this new data base on a sophisticated retrieval system at Syracuse University,** and to contrast this retrieval method with the more conventional methods employed by these libraries at the present time.

Significance of this Project

The nature of the catalog in libraries is undergoing some significant changes because of the advent of MARC, ISBD, and online retrieval

---

*This was later changed to *one* library.
**This was later changed to the System Development Corporation ORBIT Retrieval Service.

systems for computer-based literature searching. Existing methods and services for subject searching in libraries are rapidly being modified by the potential of these innovations and the availability of data bases representing the machine-readable versions of printed abstracting and indexing services (e.g., Psychological Abstracts, COMPENDEX (Engineering Index), etc.). Reference librarians in academic libraries are now negotiating search requests and developing search strategies which include "free text searching" of the exact words in the formulation of the query and matching these with words found in the abstract, title, and indexing record for journal articles, conference papers, etc. Unfortunately the MARC records, produced by the Library of Congress and elsewhere, do not contain such "free text" as abstracts or annotations for the books they catalog. Also unfortunately, the existing data bases developed by abstracting and indexing services do not cover books to any large extent and very few bibliographic data bases in machine-readable form exist in the humanities or social science fields. In the MARC records covering the book literature of these fields, only the main entry, the book's title, and the few Library of Congress subject added entries are available for searching in the "free text" mode at the present time. These data elements are not too descriptive of the *specific* information in a book on macro-economics, adult education, or World War II, for example.

It is proposed to augment the subject description for books in these and other fields utilizing a set of selection rules for choosing words and phrases found within the books themselves. Free text of this sort could be satisfactory for searching online and might be an economical way to augment the MARC records already in the files of such networks as OCLC, UTLAS, LIBCON, etc. (A field exists in the MARC format at the present time which could be used for this input.)

If various sets of selection rules are tested by this project, perhaps the library world could adopt the most useful set as a standard and plan a cooperative input project similar to the CONSER project which would augment the present files of MARC records in a systematic way.

If the results of this project's demonstration of the new features of our experimental retrieval system are successful, present operational retrieval systems may want to add these features in order to be more responsive to free text searching styles, and book indexers and publishers may wish to take greater care in preparing this "free text."

The data collected will measure the availability of the resources available (does a library collection contain a suitable amount of books with indexes and usable tables of contents); *the cost of inputting, storing and searching these augmented records; and the benefits derived in searching such records.* (Italics added.)

We proceeded to implement this plan when funds were made available by CLR.

In the summer of 1976 we did as planned, quoting again from the original proposal:

PHASE I: SAMPLE DESIGN AND COLLECTION PROCEDURE (5 MONTHS)

1. Develop sampling plan for selecting sample of books from the University of Toronto data base.
   sample size 100 books/category × 24 subject categories* = 2,400
   (1,200 chosen in each library with check for duplicates)
2. Implement computer program to:
   1) draw the sample according to procedure developed
   2) produce tape with a catalog record for each item in the sample from the machine-readable file in each library
   3) print out call number and bibliographic information for each item on a separate form, assign each an identification number (1-2,400)
3. Train and supervise staff for data collection.
   Procedure to be followed for each item:
   1) take the volume from the stacks; Xerox title page, table of contents, and subject index (if the book has one)
   2) staple Xeroxed pages to the computer-printed form for that book
   3) reshelve books
Possible delays due to: books in circulation or books missing.
Any book not available must either be located in a library accessible to the investigators or a Xeroxed copy of title page, table of contents and index can be requested by interlibrary loan.
4. Analysis of data.
   Investigators collect all forms for items and determine:
   1) percent of books by category with subject index
   2) variation in: number of pages/subject index; estimate number of entries/subject index; publisher's practice in indexing books*

PHASE II: DATA BASE AUGMENTATION PROGRAM (8 MONTHS— SOME OVERLAP WITH PHASE I)

1. Select subset of sample collected in Phase I.
   Possibilities:

---

*This was later changed to 10 categories in order to have more books in each category.
*Note: See separate paper by Gratch, Settel and Atherton (in bibliography with this report) as this will not be reported in detail in this report.

    a. select x items from each category,
            or
    b. select categories suggested by reference librarians as being those in which book material is especially valuable.
    (will consider only those items which have indexes)**
2. Consider impact of variations of selection rules.
3. Edit indexes of items to be input according to the ''optimal'' selection rules.
    1) on Xeroxed index pages circle items to be keyed
    2) prepare table of chapter numbers and pages they include
4. Train keypunch or terminal operators to enter data from table of contents and marked index pages according to a specified format with associated chapter numbers.
5. Develop computer programs which can store the three records for each item.
    1) catalog record from Toronto with main entry, title, class number, and LC subject entries as access points
    2) table of contents
    3) subject index entries
6. Development computer programs to build a dictionary for this file.
7. Use computer-based search routines for:
    1) conventional inverted file and Boolean search of MARC-like records. (If OCLC/Basis is available, some searches of that file can be compared with our augmented file searches if records are in OCLC files.)
    2) alternative SMART-like system for searching "free text" augmented records (already available at Syracuse University)
Note: Date from this phase will include:
    1) editing time for each item
    2) keying time for each item
    3) number of characters for table of contents records and subject index records (estimate of number of access points added)
        These permit estimation of entry cost and storage costs if these augmented subject representations were to be used on a continuing basis in operational systems.

PHASE III: TESTING AND RETRIEVAL (5 MONTHS—SOME OVERLAP WITH PHASE II)

1. Solicit queries from reference librarians and library users at University of Toronto, Cornell University and Syracuse University.

**Later changed to indexes and tables of contents.

2. Run searches against:
   1) MARC-like records
   2) table of contents file
   3) subject index file
3. Obtain evaluation of retrieval results by requesters.
   Note: Data analysis from this phase will include:
   Comparison of the number of items retrieved using different subject representations and search methods consider relevance evaluations by requesters, processing time, and results.

AUXILIARY ACTIVITIES (IF TIME AND RESOURCES PERMIT; OTHERWISE, A POSSIBLE FOLLOW-UP PROJECT)

1. Investigate availability of machine-readable subject indexes from publishers who utilize computer composition in book production. We could even experiment with machine selection of subject terms if some indexes could be made available to us in the course of the study.
2. Data base survey—determine available data bases and their current coverage and treatment of book materials (e.g., PRECIS of BNB, Psychological Abstracts, CAIN, etc.).

EXPLORATORY STUDIES IN SUBJECT DESCRIPTION

Introduction

Our efforts to augment the subject description of books were just getting underway in 1975–76 when we learned of related events to improve subject access in library catalogs—PRECIS at the British National Bibliography and an "In-Depth Subject Cataloging Approach" at Brodart, Inc.

We made contact with these activities and have also consulted a few publishers of books and the abstracting and indexing services who cover books in their fields. Time did not permit us to pursue these contacts over an extended period of time, but we thought it best to document our vain attempts to alert interested parties.

In-Depth Subject Cataloging Approach at BRODART, Inc.

At the 1976 ALA meeting we learned that Brodart had undertaken a re-cataloging of all the titles classified by Dewey 300-369 in the *Public Library Catalog*. They hired subject catalogers to add 10 or more subject headings, using Sears *List of Subject Headings* or assigning some "more specific, yet simple heading" and changing to non-Sears subdivisions like "Pro and Con."

They did 810 titles and added 10,780 subject headings, an average of 13.3 subjects per title. They entered these into their COM catalogs.

To our knowledge there has been no expansion of this project.

As we were not covering much of the same titles it was not possible for us to make any comparisons.

PRECIS

There has been a great deal of interest about PRECIS in Canada and the United States in the last few years. Conferences and workshops have been held and some were championing the cause of PRECIS as the next subject indexing scheme for the Library of Congress. Only in January 1978 were these pursuits aborted with the news that L.C. would not adopt PRECIS when it closed its card catalog in 1980.

Even so, we pursued a comparison of our subject descriptions with PRECIS indexing to check out if this preserved-context-indexing system, with its rigorous analytico-synthetic construction, might not be a better means of subject access than our non-intellectually based crude subject descriptions made from what the book contains in its table of contents and/or index.

We examined the differences between BOOKS and PRECIS without performing any careful tests. What follows is our report of these examinations.

BOOKS ON SOCIOLOGY

With the assistance of Mrs. Florence Hayes at Cornell University, we examined the L.C. heading, our subject description and PRECIS string for 10 books in sociology. Figures 5.1a and b illustrate what we found.

BOOKS PUBLISHED IN ENGLAND AFTER 1968

Because we could search the BOOKS data base by date and place of publication, we decided to see how many books in the BOOKS file might be in the BNB and indexed by PRECIS. One hundred twenty-five titles qualified, but time only permitted a check of a few titles in the BNB itself. For 8 books we found the PRECIS string, or at least one manipulation of it. The full BOOKS record is included here with the PRECIS string as we found it in the BNB, along with the BNB number and the Dewey class number. Four different subject areas are represented in the next four figures.

FIGURE 1: MARC, BOOKS and PRECIS Comparison

a)

```
         RSN - 00889901
         SNO - 1767
        ┌CCN - HM131 C7477
        │ME  - Coser, Lewis A., 1913-
        │TI  - Greedy institutions: patterns of undivided commitment
 MARC   │IM  - New York, Free Press, 1974
        │COL - 166p.
        │PY  - 1974
        │LCH - Social institutions: Commitment (Psychology)
        └LCH - Affiliation (Psychology): Power (Social sciences)
         IT  - *ALIENS AS SERVANTS OF POWER (P. 32-46)
         IT  - *BOLSHEVIK PARTY ORGAN IZATION (P. 126-135)
         IT  - *CATHOLIC PRIESTS SACERDOTAL CELIBACY AMONG (P. 150-161)
         IT  - CHRISTIANS AS SERVANTS TO OTTOMAN POWER (P. 40-46)
         IT  - *DOMESTIC SERVANTS OBSOLESCENCE OF (P. 67-88)
         IT  - *EUNUCHS POLITICAL FUNCTION OF (P. 21-31)
         IT  - *FAMILY AS GREEDY INSTITUTION (P. 89-100)
         IT  - GERMANY COURT JEWS IN (P. 34-40)
         IT  - *GREAT BRITAIN DOMESTIC SERVANTS IN (P. 67-77)
         IT  - JESUITS ORGANIZATION OF (P. 118-126)
         IT  - JEWS AS SERVANTS OF GERMAN POWER (P. 33- 40)
         IT  - LOUIS XV MISTRESSES OF (P. 58-63)
         IT  - MAINTENON FRANCOISE DE (P. 56- 60)
         IT  - MARRIAGE : SACERDOTAL CELIBACY AND (P. 150-157) : UTOPIAN
                COMMUNITIES AND (P. 138-142)
         IT  - *MASTER SERVANT RELATIONS (P. 68-88)
         IT  - *MILITANT COLLEC TIVES (P. 117-135)
         IT  - *POLITICAL EUNUCHISM (P. 22-31)
         IT  - *ROYAL MISTRESSES AS INSTRUMENT OF RULE (P. 47-63)
         IT  - *SECTS (P. 103-115)
                *SECTS (P. 103-115)
         IT  - *SEXUALITY : SACERDOTAL CELIBACY AND (P. 150-161) : UTOPIAN
                COMMUNITIES AND (P. 136- 149); *WOMEN FAMILY AND (P. 90-100)
```

PRECIS entry from 1974 BNB:

    Commitment

b)

```
         RSN - 00595160
         SNO - 1790
        ┌CCN - HM133 H4
        │ME  - Herbst, P. G.
        │TI  - Behavioural worlds, the study of single cases
 MARC   │IM  - London, Tavistock Publications, 1970
        │COL - 248p.
        │PY  - 1970
        │LCH - Small groups - Case studies: Social science research
        └LCH - Social sciences - Methodology
         IT  - ANXIETY; BOREDOM; *CONSTRAINTS OF TASK STRUCTURE (P. 74-84)
         IT  - *ENGAGED COUPLE FROM DATING TO MARRIAGE (P. 161-187); HERBST P G
         IT  - LINEAR NETWORKS PROPERTIES OF (P. 41-46)
         IT  - OUTPUT RATE AS FUNCTION OF WORK RATE AND LEVEL OF INTEGRATION (P.
                71-78); STRESS
```

PRECIS entry from 1971 BNB:

    Behavior. Man.

        Research.   (1 entry)

FIGURE 2. MARC, BOOKS and PRECIS—Book in Public Finance

```
            RSN  -  00682872
            SNO  -  1883
           ┌CCN  -  HJ1013 B155
            ME   -  Baker. Norman
            TI   -  Government and contractors: the British Treasury and war
                    supplies. 1775-1783.
            IM   -  London. Athlone Press. 197:
   MARC     COL  -  274p.
            SER  -  University of London. Historical studies. 30
            PY   -  1971
            LCH  -  Gt. Brit. Treasury: Defense contracts - Gt. Brit. - History
           └LCH  -  U.S. - History - Revolution - Supplies
            IT   -  AGENTS PROBLEMS WITH CONTRACTORS' AGENTS (P. 122-126)
            IT   -  AMYAND JOHN M P. APOTHECARY GENERAL (P. 184-188)
            IT   -  *ATKINSON RICHARD CONTROVERSY OVER RUM SUPPLIED BY (P. 165-175)
            IT   -  *BACON ANTHONY AS CONTRACTOR FOR COAL (P. 189-198)
            IT   -  BARING FRANCIS: BARRACK FURNITURE (P. 208-215); BAYNES WILLIAM
            IT   -  BEEF: BLACKBURN JOHN: CAMP EQUIPMENT (P. 208-215); CANADA
            IT   -  CHERRY GEORGE: *COAL (P. 189-199); COMMISSION
            IT   -  CONTRACTORS : ACCOUNTS OF ; FAIL TO OBSERVE FULL TERMS OF
                    CONTRACTS (P. 111-115)
            IT   -  *CONTRACTS ; AS POLITICAL PATRONAGE (P. 216-220) ; PRICING UNDER
                    (P. 35-39 46-55) ; NEGOTIATION OF (P. 43-56) : PROFITS UNDER (P.
                    242-248); *CORK (P. 35-39 64-79 94-101); CORNWALL CHARLES WOLFRAN
            IT   -  COWES I O W; DEVAYNES WILLIAM M P

            IT   -  DRUMMOND HENRY M P (P. 175-183); DURAND JOHN M P
            IT   -  EAST ANGLIA AS A SOURCE OF SUPPLIES (P. 80-86); FLOUR
            IT   -  FRANKS MOSES; FRENCH JAMES BOGLE; GARNIER GEORGE (P. 184-188)
            IT   -  GORDON ROBERT GENERAL ASSESSMENT AS COMMISSARY AT CORK (P. 94-101)
            IT   -  HARLEY RT HON THOMAS M P AS CONTRACTOR FOR SPECIE (P. 175-183)
            IT   -  HENNIKER DEVAYNES AND WOMBWELL; HENNIKER JOHN M P
            IT   -  HOWE GENERAL SIR WILLIAM M P: INDIAN GOODS (P. 199-205)
            IT   -  *IRELAND AS SOURCE OF SUPPLY (P. 66-80); JAMES SIR WILLIAM M P
            IT   -  JENKINSON CHARLES M P
            IT   -  KNOX WILLIAM AS AGENT FOR INDIAN GOODS (P. 201-205)
            IT   -  LONDON CORN EXCHANGE
            IT   -  LOYALISTS CLOTHING AND EQUIPMENT FOR (P. 208-215); MASON KENDER
            IT   -  MAYNE ROBERT M P; MEDICINES (P. 184-188); MILLS WILLIAM
            IT   -  MURE SON AND ATKINSON
            IT   -  NAVY BOARD COMMISSIONERS OF THE NAVY IN CONTROVERSY OVER
                    DELIVERIES IN IRELAND (P. 64-72); NESBITT ARNOLD M P
            IT   -  NESBITT DRUMMOND AND FRANKS
            IT   -  NORTH LORD FREDERICK M P RETAINS CONTRACTING SYSTEM DESPITE
                    DEFICIENCIES (P. 248-253); NOVA SCOTIA; PEAS
            IT   -  POTTER CHRISTOPHER M P
            IT   -  *PROVISIONS ; SHIPMENT OF (P. 91-95) ; DELIVERY OF (P. 66-72) ;
                    LATE DELIVERIES OF (P. 110-114) ; GOVERNMENT RECEPTION AND
                    INSPECTION OF (P. 91-101) ; COMPLAINTS OF QUALITY OF (P. 101-105)
                    : DISPOSAL OF EXCESS OF 1782-3 (P. 147-160); RICHARDSON ANTHONY
            IT   -  ROBINSON JOHN M P
            IT   -  *RUM CONTRACTS FOR (P. 161-175) ; CONTROVERSY OVER (P. 165-175)
            IT   -  SMITH AND FITZHUGH; SPECIE SUPPLY OF (P. 175-183)
            :T   -  STEPHENSON JOHN M P
            IT   -  TREASURY LIASON WITH OTHER GOVERNMEN" DEPARTMENTS (P. 42-48)
            IT   -  VICTUALLING BOARD (P. 42-48); WOMBWELL SIR GEORGE M P
```

```
                            1971
   PRECIS:  B71 - 20336    355.8
              1. Military equipment and supplies
                   War of American Independence
                 - Provision of military supplies to British Army
                   Role of British Treasury
                 Military supplies
              2. Great Britain.  Army.
                   War of American Independence
              3. Great Britain.  Treasury.
                 - Provision.  Role of British Treasury.
                 War of American Independence
                 - Great Britain.  Army.  Military Supplies.
                 Provision.  Role of British Treasury.
```

FIGURE 3. MARC, BOOKS and PRECIS—Book in Urban Planning

```
              RSN - 00745525
              SNO - 0397
             ┌ CCN - HT166 M365
             │ ME  - Massey, Doreen. B.
             │ TI  - The basic: service categorisation in planning
             │ IM  - London, Centre for Environmental Studies, 1971
   MARC      │ COL - 41p.
             │ SER - Centre for Environmental Studies. Working papers, 63
             │ PY  - 1971
             └ LCH - Cities and .owns - Planning - 1945-; Industries. Location of
              CT  - *THEORETICAL DEFINITION OF BASIC AND SERVICE CATEGORIES (P. 9-20)
                    : CATEGORISATION ON FUNCTIONAL CRITERIA (P. 13-20)
              CT  - USE OF BASIC SERVICE CONCEPTS IN LOWRY MODEL (P. 21-29)
              CT  - *USE OF BASIC SERVCIE CONCEPTS IN PLANNING (P. 30-41) ; POLICY
                    TESTING IMPLICATIONS OF THE CONCEPTS (P. 30-41) / ANALYSIS OF
                    LOCATIONAL BASIC SERVICE CONCEPT IN POLICY TESTING CONTEXT (P.
                    36-41)
```

PRECIS: B71 - 22522   338
                            Industries. <u>Basic and Service Categorization</u>

FIGURE 4. MARC, BOOKS and PRECIS—Book in Ethics

```
              RSN - 00617252
              SNO - 1149
             ┌ CCN - BJ1461 M64
             │ ME  - Mortimore, Geoffrey, comp.
             │ TI  - Weakness of will.
             │ IM  - London, Macmillan, 1971
   MARC      │ COL - 255p.
             │ SER - Controversies in philosophy
             │ PY  - 1971
             │ LCH - Will - Addresses, essays, lectures
             └ LCH - Ethics - Addresses, essays, lectures
              CT  - *SOCRATIC PARADOX (P. 29-96) ; EVIL PLATO (P. 29-36) : PLATO'S
                    PROTAGORAS AND EXPLANATIONS OF WEAKNESS SANTAS GERASIMOS (P.
                    37-62) : CONTINENCE AND INCONTINENCE ARISTOTLE (P. 63-68) :
                    ARISTOTLE ON MORAL WEAKNESS HARDIE W F R (P. 69-96)
              CT  - *HARE'S PARADOX (P. 97-176) : ASSENTING TO A MORAL PRINCIPLE
                    GARDINER P L (P. 100-117) ; ASSENT TO MORAL RULE HORSBURGH H J N
                    (P. 118-131) : BACKSLIDING HARE R M (P. 132-146) : MORAL WEAKNESS
                    LUKES STEVEN (P. 147-159) : WEAKNESS OF WILL MATTHEWS GWYNNETH
                    (P. 160-176)
              CT  - *ACTIONS AGAINST BETTER JUDGEMENT (P. 177-246) : ACTING WITH
                    REASON GRIFFITHS A PHILLIPS (P. 177-189) : OUGHTS AND WANTS
                    COOPER NEIL (P. 190-199) : WANTS DESIRES AND DELIBERATION BENSON
                    JOHN (P. 200-215) : OUGHTS AND WANTS COOPER NEIL (P. 216-225) ;
                    OUGHTS AND WANTS BENSON JOHN (P. 226-232) : ACTING AGAINST BETTER
                    JUDGEMENT THALBERG IRVING (P. 233-246)
```

PRECIS: B71 - 04855   123
                            Freedom and Necessity
                            Free Will <u>and</u> Determinism

PRECIS STRINGS AND BOOKS RECORDS—A COMPARISON

Thanks to Dr. Phyllis Richmond who is writing a book on PRECIS, we were able to find the *exact* PRECIS string for some books *identically classified* with books in BOOKS. As the vocabulary is the important aspect to study for retrieval purposes, these records are given here as they appear on the PRECIS indexing record Dr. Richmond photocopied in England. The record in our file and the PRECIS string may not be for the same title, but they are for books classified identically. Four of the ten fields in the BOOKS data base are represented here.

FIGURE 5. MARC, BOOKS, and PRECIS—Book in Drama

```
        RSN -  00632951
        SNO -  2106
       ┌ CCN -  PN1998 A3 R66513
       │ ME  -  Guarner. Jose Luis
       │ TI  -  Roberto Rossellini: Translated by Elisabeth Cameron.
MARC   │ IM  -  London . S tudio Vista. c1970
       │ COL -  144p.
       │ PY  -  1970
       └ LCH -  Rossellini. Roberto. 1906-
         CT  -  THREE FASCIST FILMS (P. 7-11): ROMA CITTA APERTA (P. 13-18)
         CT  -  L'AMORE (P. 25-27): GERMANIA ANNO ZERO (P. 28-32)
         CT  -  LA MACCHINA AMMAZZACATTIVI (P. 33-38)
         CT  -  STROMBOLI TERRA DI DIO (P. 39-43)
         CT  -  FRANCESCO G'ULLARE DI DIO (P. 44-49)
         CT  -  VIAGGIO IN ITALIA (P. 57-63): ERA NOTTE A ROMA (P. 82-86)
         CT  -  VIVA L'ITALIA (P. 87-93): V*NINA VANINI (P. 94-99)
         CT  -  L'ETA DEL FERRO (P. 105-11!)
         CT  -  LA PRISE DE POUVOIR PAR LOUIS XIV (P. 112-117)
         CT  -  *ATTI DEGLI APOSTOLI (P. 121-132) FILMOGRAPHY (P. 137-142)
```

PRECIS: B71 - 06296 791.4302330924
                     Cinema films directed by R.R.

FIGURE 6. BOOKS and PRECIS Records for Book in LC Class HT

```
        RSN -  00703736
        SNO -  0692
       ┌ CCN -  HT169 G7 P5
       │ TI  -  Planning for urban growth: British perspectives on the planning
       │        process. Edited by John L. Taylor.
       │ IM  -  New York. Praeger Publishers. 1972
MARC   │ COL -  194p.
       │ SER -  Praeger special studies in international politics and public
       │        affairs
       │ PY  -  1972
       └ LCH -  Cities and towns - Planning - Great Britain - Congresses
         CT  -  *JAMES JOHN R (P. 3-12): *AREA PERSPECTIVES RAM V. J. (P. 13-26)
         CT  -  *COMMUNICATIONS AND TRANSPORT PLANNING DERBYSHIRE ANDREW (P.
                27-42): *PLANNING LEGISLATION HEAP DESMOND (P. 43-57)
         CT  -  *DEVELOP- MENT AND LAND COMMISSION THOMAS WYNDHAM (P. 57-70)
         CT  -  *PLAN-MAKING PRO- CESS AND STRUCTURE OF URBAN FORM DERBYSHIRE
                ANDREW (P. 71-94)
         CT  -  AGENCIES FOR URBAN DEVELOPMENT THOMAS WYNDHAM (P. 95-100)
         CT  -  LOCATION OF INDUSTRY JAMES JOHN R (P. 101-108)
         CT  -  *TOWN PLANNING PROBLEMS IN BEIRUT SALAAM ASSEM (P. 109-120)
         CT  -  *PLANNING EDUCATION AND TRAINING (P. 121-134)
         CT  -  *EDUCATION FOR PLANNING IN BRITAIN COCKBURN CYNTHIA (P. 155-172)
```

PRECIS

309.2'62'0941   HT169.G7
Great Britain. Urban regions. Social planning$bConference
proceedings
0255629

690000 _Sz11C10SjjGreat Britain$zp1030$aurban regions$z21030$asocial
planning_Sz60010Saconference proceedings
692000 0004219 692000 0007412 043000 e-uk—— 650000 Cities and
towns$xPlanning$zGreat Britain$xCongresses 651000 Great Britain
$xSocial policy$xCongresses 693000 275 28765 '3 DCD: 309.2'62'0942

FIGURE 7.   BOOKS and PRECIS Records for Book in LC Class HJ

```
        RSN - 00069994
       SNO - 1858
     ┌ CCN - HJ135 H5
     │ ME  - Hicks, Ursula Kathleen (Webb) 1896-
MARC │ TI  - Development finance: planning and control
     │ IM  - . Clarendon Press, 1965
     │ PY  - 1965
       CT  - *STRATEGY FOR DEVELOPMENT IMPACT OF FINANCE (P. 1-15)
       CT  - *CHOICE IN PUBLIC EXPENDITURE PROGRAMME PROGRAMMES AGRICULTURE
              EDUCATION PUBLIC HEALTH APPLICATION OF COST BENEFIT ANALYSIS (P.
              16-36)
       CT  - *FINANCE AND FINANCIAL INFRASTRUCTURE FINANCE FROM ABROAD AID AND
              LOAN DIRECT INVESTMENT CENTRAL BANKING IN DEVELOPMENT COUNTRIES
              (P. 37-60)
       CT  - *FISCAL POLICY FOR DEVELOPMENT TAXES ON OUTGOINGS IMPORT DUTIES
              LEVIES SALES AND TURNOVER TAXES TAX RATE ON URBAN LAND AND
              BUILDINGS (P. 61-83)
       CT  - *TAXES ON INCOMINGS MARKET AND EXPORT TAXES PERSONAL INCOME TAX
              GRADUATED PERSONAL TAX TAXATION OF BUSINESS PROFITS TAXES ON
              CAPITAL GAINS AND CAPITAL (P. 84-107)
       CT  - *INTERGOVERNMENTAL FISCAL AND FINANCIAL RELATIONS TAX ALLOCATION
              AMONG FEDERAL STATE AND LOCAL GOVERNMENTS SALES TAX AS A STATE
              LEVY INCOME TAX SHARING (P. 108-130)
       CT  - *ORGANISAT6ION AND EXECUTION OF DEVELOPMENT PLANS (P. 131-156)
       CT  - *BUDGETING AND CONTROL OF EXPENDITURE ESTIMATES CONSOLIDATED FUND
              AND CIVIL CONTINGENCIES FUND FINANCIAL SELECT COMMITTEES OF
              LEGISLATURE (P. 157-182)
```

```
    PRECIS

    336.3                                                        HJ135
    Fiscal policies
    0643696


    690000 $z21030$afiscal policies
    692000 0390984   650000 Fiscal policy   693000 04 330272 6
```

FIGURE 8.   BOOKS and PRECIS Records for Book in LC Class NK

```
        RSN - 00778522
       SNO - 2466
     ┌ CCN - NK5440 B6 W^8
     │ ME  - Wilson, Bill, 1926-
     │ TI  - Nineteenth century medicine in glass, by Bill & Betty Wilson.
MARC │ IM  - Amador City, Calif., Nineteenth Century Hobby & Pub. Co. , 1971
     │ COL - 147.2p.
     │ PY  - 1971
     └ LCH - Medicine bottles - Catalogs
       IT  - BARNES DEMAS: FOUGERA E AND S: MACK JULIUS C
       IT  - NEW YORK PHARMACAL ASSOCIATION: PARK JOHN D: A AND B D SANDS
       IT  - SPIEKER JOHN J: VOGELER CHARLES AND AUGUSTUS: WAKELEE H P
       IT  - WEEKS AND POTTER: WRIGHT INDIAN MEDICINE CO
```

```
    PRECIS

    338.4'3'7488                                              NK5440.B6
    British antique glass bottles. Prices
    0792039


    690000 $z11030$abottles$iglass$iantique$iBritish$zp1030$aprices
    692000 0116149   692000 0149020   692000 0011835   043000 e-ux—
    650000 Bottles, British$xPrices   693000 905447 00 x
```

FIGURE 9. BOOKS and PRECIS Records for Book in LC Class PN

```
        RSN - 00845059
        SNO - 1972
       ┌CCN - PN1998 A2 P48
        ME  - Phillips, Gene D.
        TI  - The movie makers: artists in an industry.
MARC    IM  - Chicago, Nelson-Hall Co., c1973
        COL - 249p.
        PY  - 1973
        LCH - Moving-picture producers and directors - United States
       └LCH - Moving-picture producers and directors - Great Britain
        IT  - *CHAPLIN CHARLIE (P. 25-43); *CUKOR GEORGE (P. 65-79)
        IT  - *FORBES BRYAN (P. 187-97); GIANT (P. 89-94); GREENE GRAHAM
        IT  - *HAWKS HOWARD (P. 45-62); HEPBURN KATHERINE
        IT  - *HOWE JAMES WONG (P. 9-19); *KUBRICK STANLEY (P. 115-29)
        IT  - LEAN DAVID (P. 151-57 159-63); *LOSEY JOSEPH (P. 167-82)
        IT  - PINTER HAROLD (P. 173-77); *REED SIR CAROL (P. 135-48)
        IT  - *RUSSELL KEN (P. 215-31); *SCHLESINGER JOHN (P. 201-13)
        IT  - *STEVENS GEORGE (P. 83-95); *ZINNEMANN FRED (P. 99-112)
```

```
  PRECIS

791.43'0233'C924                                    PN1998.A3C8
American cinema films. Directing. Cukor, George
0774901

690000 $z11030$acinema films$i American$z21030$adirecting$z2C020$a
$z31030$c Cukor, George
692000 000748x  692000 000152x   043C00 n-us——   600010 Cukor$hGeorge
693000 436 09942 x
```

Book Publishers—Improving Subject Access to Books

The *subject descriptions* we added to MARC records depend for their content on what publishers do when they prepare the book for publication. We decided to see how "good" or "bad" the indexes were in the books in our sample. A special study was made of approximately 100 titles in our collection, divided between social science and humanities fields. The full report is to be published in 1978 in *The Indexer*. The paper, written by B. Gratch, B. Settel, and P. Atherton, is entitled "Characteristics of Book Indexes for Subject Retrieval in the Humanities and Social Sciences."

An executive summary of our findings is included here:

The characteristics of indexes in 113 books in nine disciplines of the humanites and social sciences have been measured, analyzed, and compared to the standards and guidelines for indexes established by the American Standards Institute and the British Standards Institution. These books were taken from a representative sample of English Language monographs in these subject fields which had been selected for the Subject Access Project. Categories of analysis include: statistics on the number of index pages, lines per index page, and indexing density; arrangement of index; scope of index; style and format of index headings and subheadings; type and use of locators; type and use of control devices; and the physical appearance of indexes.

The findings reveal some serious inadequacies of book indexes for subject retrieval. Among the most significant findings are: 1) only

55% of the books from which this study's sample was drawn possessed any index at all; 2) 47% of the headings tallied from the second page of these subject indexes were personal names or titles of works of art; 3) 91% of this study's sample lacked an introductory note to explain scope or features of the index; 4) inconsistent policies for indexing front, back and illustrative matter were revealed; 5) 60% of the sample contained index entries having 10 or more undifferentiated locators; 6) 41% of the sample had neither "see" nor "see also" references and 57% had no multiple entries for a multi-term entry.

Recommendations about index improvement in books are given.

Time did not permit a distribution of our findings to publishers, with a follow-up to check on their interest in our project. We did have time to determine that our BOOKS data base was made up of publishers from the following countries: USA 64%, United Kingdom 34%, Canada .5%, other countries 1.5%.

Personal contact was made to two publishers (Bowker and Macmillan). Excerpts of our letter to them follow, with an example of a Collier-Macmillan book in the BOOKS format.

I feel that the key to greater subject access to library book collections rests with publishers. The books you produce provide the *subject descriptions* we can use for our augmented online catalogs of the future. The contents pages and indexes of the book itself can supply the information from which subject descriptions in library catalogs can be made. This is what our project has done—to show librarians, library users, and publishers how an improved library catalog can provide greater access.

The example enclosed with this letter shows what we did with a Macmillan book. Following our rules for selection, we chose entries from the contents and/or index. We have compared these subject descriptions with abstracts in abstracting services like *Psychological Abstracts,* with PRECIS strings from BNB, and with Library of Congress subject headings. We have found through controlled tests that our input is useful for online subject searching. The Library of Congress, National Library of Canada, OCLC, and many research libraries are interested in these developments at this particular time when important decisions are being made about closing card catalogs, changing subject analysis schemes, etc.

It is possible that the library world will buy the idea of *subject descriptions* but not buy that they should come from contents pages and/or back-of-the book indexes. This is a difficult decision and one on which I myself am somewhat ambivalent. As we proceeded on our project, developing subject descriptions for some 2,000 books in ten fields of the humanities and social sciences, we noticed what no one can ignore: contents pages and indexes are of varying quality. Few indexes conform to ANSI, BSI, or University of Chicago standards. The variety of styles and formats caused us to develop a manual of rules for selection which had to be quite detailed because of this variety. Nevertheless, we feel this effort could lead to something fruitful if publishers were willing to give more attention to the by-product use of these two parts of the book. If library users can search and find Etzioni's book because they thought of such words as *democracy, leadership*, or *authoritarian government*, I think we will all be be more satisfied with our information systems. As it is, only headings such as *political sociology* are available for Etzioni's book in our catalogs now and these headings have hundreds of titles listed in alphabetic order by author with no discrimination possible. You could not find "leadership in democracy" or something similar in our library catalog today or tomorrow!

Is there something that we can do cooperatively?

At this writing there has been no response to these letters.

FIGURE 10. Sample Record of BOOKS Entry

Typical Library Catalog entry	RSN - 00331905 SNO - 1743 CCN - HM101 E77 ME - Etzioni, Amital TI - The active society: a theory of societal and political processes. IM - London. Collier-Macmillan, 1968 COL - 698p. PY - 1968 LCH - Social action: Sociology: Political sociology
Subject Access Project (SAP) suggested addition for subject description	IT - ACTION AUTARKY (P. 111-116). ALIENATION (P. 373-381 617-622 FF) IT - ASSETS (P. 323-329 FF); *AUTHORITARIAN GOVERNMENT (P. 507-523) IT - AUTONOMY ; BALANCE OF (P. '16-12C) ; IN RELATION TO CONTROL (P. 111-116); BRITAIN GREAT (P. 374-378) IT - *CHANGE SOCIETAL (P. 387-421); CHINA; COERCIVE POWER (P. 370-375) IT - COLLECTIVITIES (P. 436-443); *COLLECTI VITY (P. 99-103 435-451) IT - *COMMITMENT (P. 555-565FF) IT - *COMMUNICATION RELATION TO POWER (P. 333-342) IT - COMMUNITY OF ASSUMPTIONS (P. 177-182) IT - COMPLIANCE TRENDS OF (P. 375-381) IT - *COMPLIANCE PATTERNS RELATION TO SOC.ETAL GOALS (P. 370-381) IT - CONFLICT (P. 586-592). *CONSCIOUSNESS (P. 223-244) IT - *CONSENSUS (P. 466-494) ; POLITICAL (P. 471-475) IT - CONSENSUS BUILDING (P. 432-436FF); CONSENSUS FORMATION IT - *CONTEXTUATING ORIENTA TIONS (P. 157-168) ; CHANGES IN (P. 157-168) IT - *CONTROL (P. 388-399 422- 446) ; RELATION TO POWER (P. 334-338) IT - *CONTROL CONSENSUS ARTICULATION MECHANISMS FOR (P. 484-494) IT - CONTROLLING OVERLAYER (P. 362-366) IT - CONVERSION PATTERN (P. 323-327) IT - *COST (P. 155-168) ; OF ALTERING KNOWLEDGE CONTEXTS (P. 157-166) IT - *CYBERNETIC FACTORS IN SOCIETAL GUIDANCE (P. 132-273) IT - *DECISION MAKING (P. 249-306); DEMOCRACY (P. 506-511) IT - ELITE COUNTRIES (P. 552-557'); ELITES INTELLECTUAL (P. 182- 189) IT - *EQUALITY (P. 517-535); EXPEPT ELITE (P. 182-189); FRANCE IT - FUNCTIONAL ANALYSIS (P. 79-83 135-143) IT - FUNDAMENTAL CRITICISM (P. '81- 186) IT - *INAUTHENTICITY (P. 633-648FF) ; OF INSTITUTIONS (P. 634-647) IT - INCREMENTALISM (P. 268-273); INNOVATION (P. 239-244); INTEGRATION IT - *KNOWLEDGE (P. 132-151 155-168 172-189) ; IN DECISION MAKING (P. 301- 305); *LEADERSHIP (P. 337-354); *MALLEABILITY (P. 21-30) IT - *MIXED SCAN NING (P. 283-306) IT - *MOBILIZATION (P. 387-422) ; EXTERNAL (P. 412-418) ; INTERNAL (P. 401-411) ; SUPRA UNIT RELATIONS (P. 414-418) IT - *MODERN SOCIETIES (P. 432-455) ; DIFFERENCES FROM POST MODERN SOCIETIES PREFACE (P. 422-446) ; SIMILARITIES WITH POST MODERN SOCIETIES (P. 433-441); PLANNING AGENCIES (P. 487-492) IT - POLITICAL ELITE (P. 182-189) IT - *POST MODERN SOCIETY PREFACE (P. 432-455) IT - *POWER (P. 172-189 350-381) ; AS A SOCIETAL FORCE (P. 313-342) ; IN DECISION MAKING (P. 301-305), ; PER SUASIVE (P. 370-375FF) ; UTILITARIAN (P. 370-377FF); PROJECTS (P. 647- 652) IT - RATIONALITY INSTRUMENTAL (P. 254-262FF) IT - *RESPONSIVENESS (P. 503- 526); *RIGIDITY (P. 506-518) IT - *SOCIETAL ACTION (P. 223-241) ; LANGUAGE OF (P. 70-74) IT - *SOCIETAL CONTEXTS (P. 157-168) IT - SOCIETAL GUIDANCE OF ·NOWLEDGE (P. 207-213)

FIGURE 10. Sample Record of BOOKS Entry (continued)

```
IT  - .'SOCIETAL KNOWLEDGE DISTRIBUTION OF (P. 197-214) : REALLOCATION
       OF (P. 197-214). SOVIET UNION: SUB COLLECTIVITIES (P. 447-455)
IT  - SYNTHESIS (P. 143-148): SYSTEM ANALYSIS (P. 310-314)
IT  - *THEORY OF ACTION (P. 21-36)
IT  - *THEORY OF SOCIETAL GUIDANCE (P. 94-125) : FUNCTIONAL CONCEPTIONS
       IN (P. 79-83) : GENETIC CONCEPTIONS IN (P. 79- 83)
IT  - TOTALITARIAN SOCIETIES: TRANSFORMATION (P. 239-243 327-331)
IT  - TRIBALISM (P. 602-607): UNIFICATION (P. 556-564 596-600)
IT  - *UNITED STATES MOBILIZATION IN (P. 404-540)
IT  - UNITED STATES AS A SUPER POWER
```

Subject Descriptions in Abstracting and Indexing Services

When the Subject Access Project began we made a concerted effort to choose subject fields which were *not* adequately covered by existing online data bases—that is, in all but one case, Psychology. We wanted one field where we could compare book coverage and treatment in an online data base. *Sociological Abstracts* had stopped covering books in 1972 and other online data bases in the social sciences and humanities were just beginning to appear in early 1976 when we began our work.

Time did not permit an exhaustive comparative study, but a quick check showed that BOOKS contained seventeen books published between 1973–1975, which were in an online version of *Psychological Abstracts*. Five of these books were collections of selected readings, the kind of book that gets the standard LCSH subheading: "Addresses, essays, and lectures." One book was a handbook, another an introductory textbook. As chance would have it, seventeen different publishers were represented.

We made no analysis, but merely put the Psychological Abstracts entry next to the BOOKS record (see the following figures). These were sent to the Editor of Psychological Abstracts and to the Executive Secretary of NFAIS. Conversations were cordial when we met in December, 1977, and a tentative agreement was reached to collaborate if the Subject Access Project went into a second phase.

FIGURE 11. Sample Records for Psychology Books in BOOKS and Psychological Abstracts

Psychology Book #1:   <u>Women and Sex</u>

```
BOOKS    RSN - 00784957
         SNO - 1563
Record   CCN - BF692 S24
         ME  - Schaefer, Leah Cahan, 1920-
         TI  - Women and sex: sexual experiences and reactions of a group of
               thirty women as told to a female psychotherapist.
         IM  - New York, Pantheon Books, 1973
         COL - 269p.
         PY  - 1973
         LCH - Sex (Psychology): Woman - Psychology
         CT  - FINDINGS (P. 17-22)
         CT  - *EARLY SEX MEMORIES (P. 23-48) : CHILDHOOD SEX PLAY (P. 39-43)
         CT  - *EARLY SEX EDUCATION (P. 49-66)
         CT  - *ADOLESCENCE MENARCHE AND RELATED EXPERIENCES (P. 67-86)
         CT  - *SELF-STIMULATION MASTURBATION (P. 87-106) : ANXIETY GUILT DENIAL
```

FIGURE 11. Sample Records for Psychology Books in BOOKS and Psychological Abstracts (continued)

```
                    (P. 93-101)
          CT  - *INITIAL INTERCOURSE (P. 107-130) ; INITIAL INTERCOURSE
                PREMARITAL (P. 100-113) ; EXPECTATIONS (P. 116-120)
          CT  - *ORGASM (P. 131-158) ; ORGASM CLITORAL VAGINAL OTHER (P. 137-142)
          CT  - *INTERVIEW JULIA (P. 159-224); FEMALES AND SEXUALITY (P. 232-238)
```

Psychological Abstracts Record

```
                    9
AN   7039 51-4.
AU SCHAEFER. LEAH C.
TI WOMEN AND SEX: SEXUAL EXPERIENCES AND REACTIONS OF A GROUP OF THIRTY
   WOMEN AS TOLD TO A FEMALE PSYCHOTHERAPIST.
SO NEW YORK. N.Y. PANTHEON. 1973. XIV, 269 P. $8.95.
LG EN.
YR 73.
CC 10.
PT 01.
DF BOOK HUMAN-FEMALES PSYCHOSEXUAL-BEHAVIOR.
ID SEXUAL EXPERIENCES & REACTIONS TOLD TO FEMALE PSYCHOTHERAPIST, HUMAN
   FEMALES. BOOK.
```

Psychology Book #2:   Jean Piaget, the Man and his Ideas

```
BOOKS     RSN - 00830161
Record    SNO - 1627
          CCN - BF723 C5 E9
          ME  - Evans. Richard Isadore, 1922-
          TI  - Jean Piaget: the man and his ideas by Richard I. Evans.
                Translated by Eleanor Duckworth.
          IM  - New York, E.P. Dutton, 1973
          COL - 189p.
          SER - Dialogues with notable contributors to personality theory, v. 7
          PY  - 1973
          LCH - Cognition (Child psychology): Psychology; Piaget. Jean, 1896-
          IT  - BEHAVIOR; CONCRETE OPERATIONAL PERIOD IN CHILD: CONSERVATION
          IT  - FORMAL OPERATIONAL PERIOD IN CHILD: FREUD SIGMUND
          IT  - GENEVA SWITZERLAND; *INTELLIGENCE PIAGET'S THEORY OF (P. 78-96)
          IT  - LANGUAGE; LEARNING; LOGIC; MEASURING YOUNG MINDS ELKIND; MOLLUSKS
          IT  - PERCEPTION
          IT  - *PIAGET JEAN : AUTOBIOGRAPHY OF (P. 105-143) : BIBLIOGRAPHY OF
                (P. 143-175) : CHILDHOOD AND ADOLESCENCE OF (P. 105-111) ; EARLY
                THOUGHT OF (P. 112-116) : EARLY WORK OF (P. 117-121) ; ON GENETIC
                EPISTEMOLOGY : INTELLECTUAL DEVELOPMENT OF (P. 105-130) : ON
                KNOWLEDGE : ON PRINCIPLES OF MENTAL GROWTH : RESEARCH OF : ON
                ROOTS OF KNOWLEDGE (P. 78-96) : SCIENTIFIC PUBLICATIONS OF (P.
                143-175)
          IT  - PREOPERATIONAL STAGE IN CHILD TWO SUBSTAGES OF (P. 86-90)
          IT  - REVERSIBILITY: SCHEMES SUBSCHEMES
          IT  - SENSORY MOTOR PERIOD IN CHILD SIX SUBSTAGES OF (P. 80-85) :
                SKINNER B F; STRUCTURES; SYMBOLIC SEMIOTIC REASONING
          IT  - UNITED STATES OF AMERICA
```

Psychological Abstracts Record

```
                    13
AN     11 51-1.
AU EVANS, RICHARD I.
IN U. HOUSTON.
TI JEAN PIAGET: THE MAN AND HIS IDEAS.
SO NEW YORK. N.Y. E. P. DUTTON, 1973. LXI, 189 P. $8.95(CLOTH),
   $2.95(PAPER).
LG EN.
YR 73.
CC 01.
PT 01.
```

FIGURE 11. Sample Records for Psychology Books in BOOKS and Psychological Abstracts (continued)

```
DE BIOGRAPHY PIAGET-JEAN BOOK.
AB PRESENTS PORTIONS OF A CONVERSATION WITH PIAGET WHICH INCLUDE
   DISCUSSIONS OF HIS THEORIES, HOW THEY WERE FORMULATED, AND HIS VIEWS
   ON A VARIETY OF PSYCHOLOGICAL ISSUES (E. G. INTELLIGENCE TESTING,
   PSYCHOANALYSIS, AND R. F. SKINNER). A PORTION OF PIAGET S
   AUTOBIOGRAPHY AND AN ESSAY BY HIM ON GENETIC EPISTEMOLOGY ARE
   INCLUDED ALONG WITH CRITICAL SUMMARIES OF HIS WORK.
ID PIAGET/J. BIOGRAPHY & THEORETICAL DISCUSSION. BOOK.
```

Library Networks—Improving Subject Access to Books

OCLC, BALLOTS, SCORPIO (Library of Congress), and UTLAS had all announced some plans for subject access when our project was getting underway in 1976.

OCLC had awarded a contract to Battelle Memorial Institute to use BASIS (an online retrieval system) with a portion of the OCLC data base (NEMIS records).

BALLOTS had term access to words in the title.

SCORPIO had a subject retrieval component for access to LCSH in the 1ccc, bibl, and other files at the Library of Congress.

UTLAS had an online Call Number Query system, providing subject access via the classification number. . . .

None of these cooperative, shared cataloging systems was augmenting the records in their files or running retrieval tests of the kind we ran. . . .

We kept all groups informed of our progress, gave demonstrations at L.C., University of Toronto, OCLC, and talked to personnel from BAL-LOTS. We were encouraged by their interest. Dr. James Rush at OCLC backed up our letter to publishers with a letter of his own. He also analyzed some 20,000 OCLC records and found that fewer than 5% had any "contents" note (a near equivalent to our subject descriptions). He expressed an interest in getting a copy of the BOOKS data base. Using the OCLC terminal at the School of Information Studies we began a search of OCLC to see how many of the BOOKS records were on OCLC. We estimate over 40%, but our check was aborted because of the press of other projects.

Everyone we contacted agreed that such an augmentation of the MARC record was probably a step in the right direction and that a massive cooperative project via their networks would have to be launched if existing catalog records were to be augmented. No one library could or should make the effort alone, not even the Library of Congress for current publications.

The end of our current funding prevented further exploration of this aspect of the project.

WHERE DO WE GO FROM HERE?

"The effort to maintain one's place on a descending moving staircase is not conducive to innovation."

—*H. C. Brookfield*

What Should Happen Next to Improve Subject Access?

From the experience gained during the Subject Access Project, certain things became clearer:

1) The searcher of an online library catalog record like BOOKS needs vocabulary aids online. To think of all synonyms and all subject heading alternatives is a great burden. If LCSH were online as a searching aid, along with a version of the *Roget's Thesaurus,* the searcher could choose a term and then make selections from the display rather than keying in all the possible synonyms or "index-onyms," which would retrieve relevant items.

2) If subject descriptions like those in BOOKS are developed for the world's library collections, it should be a cooperative effort with further investigation of alternatives to SAP forms of subject descriptions. The length of the description and the rules for selection need to be reviewed critically. The quota system, as we developed it, is probably inadequate and difficult to apply.

   As subject descriptions are merely *extracts* from each book, some effort must be made to improve the contents page and indexes in books so that these extracts will be more content-bearing.

3) The display of subject descriptions online needs to be improved. In searching, we could not locate easily the matched term or phrase in a long subject description. Computer software or reprocessing of the file needs to be done to highlight *where* the match of search terms or phrases occurs in the text of subject description for each item. (The LEXIS system has this feature for their legal files.)

Final Remarks

In Gregory Bateson's *Steps to an Ecology of Mind* (1971) there is an apt quote from Laing, who noted that:

"The obvious can be very difficult for people to see. That is because people are self-correct systems. They are self-corrective against disturbance, and if the obvious is not of a kind they can easily assimilate without internal disturbance, their self-corrective mechanisms work to sidetrack it, to hide it. . . Disturbing information can be framed like a pearl so that it doesn't make a nuisance of itself; and this will be done, according to the understanding of the system itself of what would be a nuisance. This too—the premise regarding what would cause disturbance—is something which is learned and then becomes perpetuated or conserved.

The promising results of our project prompt us to suggest that some effort needs to be launched by a responsible organization if we are ever to get off the dead center of poor subject access to our rich library collections. Either the Library of Congress, the National Library of Canada, the National Federation of Abstracting and Indexing Services or the American Association of Publishers needs to review the present scene and begin to work toward improvements. The published work of Hudson, Lipetz, Bates, McClure and others points to the dire need for greater subject access. Our investment in books is partially wasted and under-used if access is only available to those who come to the library catalog to search for known items.

Interestingly, we in the United States and Canada must look to Europe for avant garde developments in this area, for we have no such national or international developments on our own soil.

a) The Bath University Programme of Catalogue Research has been in existence since 1 September, 1977, funded for three years by a grant from the British Library (Research & Development Department). One of their first projects was an investigation of the provision of subject access to Library Catalogues through Keyword Indexes (SALCKIN).

b) Research at Lund University and Chalmers University in Sweden, funded by the Swedish government, is comparing the indexing of 400 titles in the field of environment and energy. The two systems being compared are PRECIS and our subject descriptions *in Swedish*!

c) European Common Market committees are working on multilingual projects with indexing and abstracting studies *before* the EURONET system gets underway.

The research and development staff at OCLC and BALLOTS, as well as at the Library of Congress and the National Library of Canada, showed great interest in our work, but it isn't clear to anyone who should take the initiative for the next step as network priorities are set by consensus.

The need is great for a redundant but carefully controlled subject access system, according to Marcia Bates in her May, 1977 *J. ASIS* article (p. 161–169).

The present system (LCSH) is controlled but *not redundant,* witness our analysis of L.C. subject headings for the social science and humanities books in our BOOKS data base.

The system we developed of "subject descriptions" is *not controlled*.

It would appear that some combination of the two would be a fruitful way to proceed. Dr. Bates goes on to say:

> With automation . . . we can now use a subject approach . . . that allows the naive user, unconscious of and uninterested in the complexities of synonymy and vocabulary control, to blunder on to desired subjects to be guided, without realizing it, by a redundant but carefully controlled subject access system.

Free text computer searching online is here to stay. Searchers online need assistance. Our next efforts should be to combine the best of the past with the promising features offered by new computer technology. Vocabulary aids for both the controlled portions of catalog records and the uncontrolled portions like the subject descriptions must be an integrated part of the online library catalogs of the future.

Thoreau said, "The book is the most treasured wealth of the world." This statement is part of the mosaic on the inside wall of the entrance to the Library of Congress. Are we the bankers and brokers of that wealth or are we the misers? S. R. Ranganathan, more than 40 years ago, said "Books are for use." We must try to understand all the implications of these phrases as we move into the future of online catalog searching.

THE BOOKS DATA BASE

Examples of Records from Humanities and Social Sciences

These examples are assembled here to exhibit the range of differences in subject description across several fields of knowledge and several "types of *books*."

The treatment of *subject analysis* is seen by looking at the part of each record coded *LCH,* i.e., Library of Congress Subject Heading.

The *subject description*, which comes from the book itself may be in two parts, that selected from the Table of Contents is coded *CT* (i.e., Contents Term) and that selected from the book's index is coded *IT* (i.e., Index Term).

The array of examples shows books published from 1947 to the present, by British, Canadian, and American publishers, commercial and university presses, books by one author or many, festschrift, and histories, translations, theory books and treatises. In all, the collection appears to be very representative of the content of non-serial library book collections.

Arrangement of examples is by call number (CCN). The meaning of the first letters within the L.C. classification number is explained below for ease of browsing through this set of examples.

BC	Logic
BF	Psychology
BH	Aesthetics
BJ	Ethics
DE	Ancient History
DF	Ancient Civilizations
F	Post-Confederation Ontario (Canada) History
GN	Anthropology
HJ	Public Finance
HM	Sociology
HT	Urban and Regional Planning
NB	Sculpture
NE	Print Media
NK	Decorative Arts
PN	Drama, Film, Television

The wealth of additional words for description and access which the CT and IT fields bring to the record is immediately apparent. Oftentimes the CT and IT entries look very much like "subject headings," but more often than not they are only descriptive phrases, names of persons and places, artifacts or concepts. Their value comes in their ability to *describe the book's content* in more detail and *identify for the searcher* if the library has any book which contains some information, no matter how little, on the particular topic, person, or place of interest to him/her.

Perhaps the best example of this is the record for PN1655 (CCN): Tragedy and the theory of drama. If a library user was looking for a book that contained a discussion of Tragedy, contrasting *Agamemnon* and *King Lear,* she/he would be hard put to find this book from scanning the cards in a traditional (*or* online) catalog which contained the existing records for our book collections. He could get as far as "tragedy" by searching under title or subject, but he would never know that this book by Olson is a "hit."

By using the online data base BOOKS on ORBIT, the searcher could do a Boolean search of the words "tragedy" and "Agamemnon" and "Lear." This book would be a "hit." Such a search is shown in the appendix entitled "Samples of Searches." Actually three books were retrieved, all with Tragedy as a subject heading (one with subdivision). If the searcher had gone to the "card catalog" for this book collection she/he would have found eight books to choose from.

An archival tape of the BOOKS data base exists at Syracuse University, in the possession of Professor Atherton. It is in the *print image* format of the SDC/ORBIT program. A copy of a portion of that tape is shown here to show how the "page" is formatted and how the records are "marked off." Inquiries about the use of this tape for study purposes should be made to Professor Atherton.

```
                                            ┌─────────────────┐
                                            │ BOOKS RECORD    │
RSN - 00759652                              │      IN         │
SNO - 1030                                  │ LOGIC (3C71)    │
CCN - BC71 P86                              └─────────────────┘
ME  - Purtill, Richard L., 1931.
TI  - Logic for philosophers
IM  - New York, Harper & Row, 1971
COL - 419p.
SER - Sources in contemporary philosophy
PY  - 1971
LCH - Logic
CT  - *PROPOSITIONAL LOGIC (P. 3-46) ; OPERATORS AND CONNECTIVES (P.
      4-13) ; TAUTOLOGIES CONTRADICTIONS AND CONTINGENTS (P. 14-21) ;
      EQUIVALENCES (P. 22-29) ; IMPLICATION (P. 30-39) ; PHILOSOPHICAL
      DIFFICULTIES (P. 40-44)
CT  - *PROOFS AND DISPROOFS (P. 47-76) ; DIRECT PROOFS (P. 48-54) ;
      DISPROOFS (P. 55-59) ; CONDITIONAL PROOFS (P. 60-64) ; LOGICAL
      SYSTEMS (P. 65-69) ; PHILOSOPHICAL APPLICATIONS (P. 70-75)
CT  - *SYLLOGISTIC LOGIC (P. 77-122) ; STANDARD FORM STATEMENTS (P.
      78-85) ; IMMEDIATE INFERENCE (P. 86-96) ; SYLLOGISMS (P. 97-108)
      ; SORITESES AND ENTHYMEMES (P. 109-116) ; PHILOSOPHICAL
      APPLICATIONS (P. 117-121)
CT  - *CLASS LOGIC (P. 123-154) ; SYLLOGISTIC LOGIC AS CLASS INFERENCE
      (P. 141-147)
CT  - *PREDICATE LOGIC (P. 155-202) ; SUBJECTS PREDICATES AND
      QUANTIFIERS (P. 156-162) ; QUANTIFIER EQUIVALENCES AND
      IMPLICATIONS (P. 163-171) ; PROOFS IN PREDICATE LOGIC (P.
      172-185) ; DISPROOFS IN PREDICATE LOGIC (P. 186-194)
CT  - *EXTENDED PREDICATE LOGIC (P. 203-230) ; PREDICATE VARIABLES AND
      QUANTIFIERS (P. 204-208) ; IDENTIFY (P. 209-213) ; DEFINITE
      DESCRIPTIONS AND THE IOTA OPERATOR (P. 214-218) ; LAMBDA OPERATOR
      (P. 291-225)
CT  - *PROPOSITIONAL MODAL LOGIC (P. 231-260) ; LEWIS SYSTEMS (P.
      243-250) ; PHILOSOPHICAL APPLICATIONS (P. 254-259)
CT  - *EXTENSIONS OF MODAL LOGIC (P. 261-291) ; QUANTIFIERS AND MODAL
      LOGIC (P. 262-268) ; EPISTEMIC LOGIC (P. 269-277) ; DEONTIC LOGIC
      (P. 278-281) ; MIXED MODALITIES (P. 282-286)
CT  - *LOGIC OF ORDINARY LANGUAGE (P. 292-323) ; LOGICAL TRUTH
      LOGICAL FALSEHOOD AND LOGICAL NONSENSE (P. 293-298) ; EQUIVALENCE
      IN ORDINARY LANGUAGE (P. 299-304) ; IMPLICATION IN ORDINARY
      LANGUAGE (P. 305-309) ; VALID APPEALS TO ORDINARY LANGUAGE (P.
      310-316)
CT  - *TOOLS OF ANALYSIS (P. 324-350) ; PROBABILITY THEORY (P. 334-342)
      ; SCIENTIFIC INFERENCE (P. 343-347)
IT  - CARROLL DIAGRAM (P. 138-146)
IT  - CONNECTIVE CLASS PROPOSITIONAL (P. 5-12)
IT  - DOXASTIC LOGIC (P. 273-277) ; ONTOLOGICAL ARGUMENT (P. 256-260)
IT  - *PROOF (P. 47-75 172-182)
```

****

```
                                            ┌─────────────────┐
RSN - 00810250                              │ BOOKS RECORD    │
                                            │      IN         │
SNO - 1330                                  │ PSYCHOLOGY      │
                                            │  (BF38.5)       │
CCN - BF38.5 B44 1973                       └─────────────────┘
ME  - Beloff, John
```

TI - Psychological sciences: a review of modern psychology.
IM - London, Crosby Lockwood Staples, 1973
COL - 361p.
PY - 1973
LCH - Psychology - Methodology
CT - *PSYCHOLOGICAL SCIENCE (P. 1-37) ; OBJECTIVES (P. 1-11) ; REJOINDERS (P. 12-21)
CT - *INTROSPECTIVE PSYCHOLOGY (P. 38-66) ; ANALYTICAL INTROSPECTION (P. 41-48) ;
      PHENOMENOLOGY (P. 49-61)
CT - *COMPARATIVE PSYCHOLOGY (P. 67-91) ; ANIMAL MINDS (P. 69-77) ; INSTINCT IN
      MAN (P. 78-87)
CT - *DIFFERENTIAL PSYCHOLOGY (P. 92-126) ; ABILITIES (P. 95-106) ; TRAITS (P. 107-118)
CT - *BEHAVIOURISTICS (P. 127-161) ; CONDITIONING (P. 128-140) ; BEHAVIOUR THERAPY
      (P. 141-153)
CT - *COGNITIVE PSYCHOLOGY (P. 162-209) ; SKILLS (P. 165-172) ; LANGUAGE (P. 173-185)
      ; CREATIVITY (P. 186-197)
CT - *SOCIAL PSYCHOLOGY (P. 210-240) ; INDIVIDUAL AND GROUP (P. 211-218) ; DISSONANCE
      AND OBEDIENCE (P. 219-231)
CT - *DEPTH PSYCHOLOGY (P. 241-281) ; UNCONSCIOUS (P. 243-251) ; IMPACT OF FREUD
      (P. 252-263) ; *PARAPSYCHOLOGY (P. 282-320)
IT - ABILITIES HUMAN HEREDITY OR ENVIRONMENT AND (P. 96-100)
IT - CONDITIONING RUSSIAN WORK ON (P. 130-134)
IT - *EXTRA SENSORY PERCEPTION (P. 298-307 PASSIM)
IT - EXTRAVERTS (P. 113-117 PASSIM) ; HYPNOTISM HYPNOSIS (P. 267-271)
IT - INTROVERTS (P. 113-117 PASSIM)
IT - MENTAL TESTS (P. 101-107) ; IQ AND (P. 188-192 PASSIM)
IT - PSI FACTOR (P. 299-307 PASSIM)
IT - PSYCHOLINGUISTICS OBJECTIONS TO CHOMSKIAN THEORY (P. 182-186)

****

RSN - 00007244

SNO - 1083

CCN - BH301 S75 F6 1963

ME - Fowlie, Wallace, 1908-

TI - Age of surrealism

IM - Bloomington, Indiana University Press, 1963

COL - 215p.

PY - 1963

LCH - Surealism

CT - *LAUTREMONT TEMPERAMENT (P. 28-44) ; *RIMBAUD DOCTRINE (P. 45-62)

CT - *MALLARME MYTH HERODIADE (P. 63-82)

CT - *APOLLINAIRE POET (P. 83-101) ; *BRETON MANIFESTOES (P. 102-119)

CT - *COCTEAU THEATRE (P. 120-137)

CT - *ELUARD DOCTRINE ON LOVE (P. 138-156) ; *PICASSO ART (P. 157-173)

CT - *SURREALISM IN 1960 (P. 193-204)

> BOOKS RECORD
> IN
> AESTHETICS
> (BH301)

```
IT  - *CHANSON DU MAL AIME (P. 84-98) ; *CHANTS DE MALDOROR (P. 33-44)

IT  - FREUD ; GIDE ; NADJA (P. 115-119) ; ORPHEE (P. 125-130)

IT  - SANGD'UN POETE (P. 129-137)
```

****

```
RSN - 00007309
SNO - 1100                                   BOOKS RECORD
CCN - BJ78 R8 K713 1947                           IN
                                             ETHICS (BJ78)
ME  - Kropotkin, Petr Alekseevich, kniaz', 1842-1921
TI  - Ethics, origin and development, by Prince Kropotkin; authorized
      translation from the Russian, by Louis S. Friedland and Joseph R.
      Piroshnikoff.
IM  - New York, Tudor Pub. Co., 1947
COL - 349p.
PY  - 1947
LCH - Ethics; Ethics - History; Ethics, Evolutionary
CT  - *DETERMINING BASES OF MORALITY (P. 1-18)
CT  - *EVOLVING BASES OF NEW ETHICS (P. 19-31)
CT  - *MORAL PRINCIPLE IN NATURE (P. 32-61)
CT  - *MORAL CONCEPTIONS OF PRIMITIVE PEOPLES (P. 62-83)
CT  - *MORAL TEACHINGS ANCIENT GREECE SOPHISTS SOCRATES ARISTOTLE
      EPICURUS (P. 84-113)
CT  - *CHRISTIANITY MIDDLE AGES RENAISSANCE COPERNICUS GIORDANO BRUNO
      KEPLER GALILEO HUGO GROTIUS (P. 114-146)
CT  - *DEVELOPMENT OF MORAL TEACHINGS IN SEVENTEENTH AND EIGHTEENTH
      CENTURIES CUDWORTH AND CUMBERLAND SPINOZA CLARKE HUTCHESON
      LIEBNITZ MONTAIGNE AND CHARRON GASSENDI BAYLE LA ROCHEFOUCAULD LA
      METTRIE HELVETIUS HOLBACH ENCYCLOPAEDISTS MORELLY AND MABLY
      MONTESQUIEU VOLTAIRE AND ROUSSEAU TURGOT AND CONDORCET (P. 147-212)
CT  - *DEVELOPMENT OF MORAL TEACHINGS IN END OF EIGHTEENTH CENTURY AND
      BEGINNING OF NINETEENTH CENTURY MORAL TEACHINGS IN GERMANY FICHTE
      SCHELLING HEGEL SCHLEIERMACHER (P. 213-230)
CT  - *DEVELOPMENT OF MORAL TEACHINGS NINETEENTH CENTURY MACKINTOSH AND
      STUART JOHN STUART MILL SCHOPENHAUER VICTOR COUSIN AND JOUFFROY
      AND POSITIVISM LITTRE SOCIALISM FOURIER SAINT-SIMON AND ROBERT
      OWEN EVOLUTIONARY ETHICS HUXLEY EGOISM AND ALTRUISM JUSTICE AND
      CHARITY THE STATE (P. 231-332)
IT  - BACON FRANCIS (P. 180-185) ; BENTHAM JEREMY (P. 235-240)
IT  - *CHRISTIANITY (P. 116-133) ; COMTE AUGUSTE (P. 248-256)
IT  - DARWIN CHARLES (P. 32-38N) ; DESCARTES (P. 181-186)
IT  - EPICURUS (P. 103-109) ; FEUERBACH (P. 255-259) ; GUYAU (P. 104-109)
IT  - HOBBES (P. 149-155) ; HUME DAVID (P. 200-205) ; *KANT (P. 213-225)
IT  - LOCKE JOHN (P. 162-168) ; PLATO (P. 90-98) ; PROUDHON (P. 267-279)
IT  - SHAFTESBURY (P. 169-173) ; SMITH ADAM (P. 203-210)
IT  - SPENCER HERBERT (P. 288-322) ; STOICS (P. 109-114)
```

```
                                                          ┌─────────────────┐
                                                          │ BOOKS RECORD    │
                                                          │ IN              │
                                                          │ ANCIENT         │
RSN - 00127257                                            │ CIVILIZATION    │
SNO - 1179                                                │ (DE89)          │
                                                          └─────────────────┘
CCN - DE89 A5
TI  - Ancient society and institutions:  studies presented to Victor
      Ehrenberg on his 75th birthday.
IM  - Oxford, Blackwell, 1966
COL - 312p.
PY  - 1966
LCH - History, Ancient - Addresses, essays, lectures
CT  - BIBLIOGRAPHY OF VICTOR EHRENBERG
CT  - *GOVERNMENT OF CLASSICAN SPARTA ANDREWES A (P. 1-20)
CT  - *THIRD CYRENE EDICT OF AUGUSTUS ATKINSON KATHLEEN M T (P. 21-36)
CT  - *ALEXANDER THE GREAT AND GREEKS OF ASIA BADIAN E (P. 37-70)
CT  - *ATHENIAN SETTLEMENTS ABROAD IN FIFTH CENTURY BC BRUNT P A (P.
      71-92) AESCHYLUS AND ATHENIAN POLITICS 472-456 BC DAVISON J A (P.
      93-108) ; ESTATE OF PHAENIPPUS DE STE CROIX G E M (P. 109-114)
CT  - *ISEGORIA IN ASSEMBLY AT ATHENS GRIFFITH G T (P. 115-138)
CT  - SOLONIAN CRISIS HOPPER R J (P. 139-146)
CT  - *TROY VIII AND LOKRIAN MAIDENS HUXLEY G L (P. 147-164)
CT  - *LYCURGAN RHETRA JONES A H M (P. 165-176)
CT  - *AFTER PROFANATION OF MYSTERIES LEWIS DAVID M (P. 177-192)
CT  - *PERICLEAN IMPERIALISM MATTINGLY H B (P. 193-224)
CT  - TWO HALICARNASSIANS AND A LYDIAN SCULLARD H H (P. 225-232)
CT  - *ORIGIN OF DELIAN LEAGUE SEALEY RAPHAEL (P. 233-256)
CT  - *ANATOMY OF FORCE IN LATE REPUBLICAN POLITICS SMITH R E (P.257-274)
CT  - *VOTING PROCEDURE AT ELECTION OF STRATEGOI STAVELEY E S (P. 275-288)
      ; *RHIANOS HYPOTHESIS WADE GERY H T (P. 289-302)
CT  - *SPARTAN ANCESTRAL CONSTITUTION IN POLYBIUS WALBANK F W (P. 303-312)

    *********************************************************************

                                                          ┌─────────────────┐
RSN - 00479920                                            │ BOOKS RECORD    │
SNO - 1211                                                │ IN              │
CCN - DF220 L76                                           │ ANCIENT HISTORY │
ME  - Luce, John Victor, 1920-                            │ (DF220)         │
                                                          └─────────────────┘
TI  - The end of atlantis:  new light on an old legend
IM  - London, Thames & Hudson, 1969
COL - 224p.
SER - New aspects of antiquity
PY  - 1969
LCH - Civilization, Mycenaean; Thera (Islands); Atlantis
CT  - *PLATO'S ACCOUNT OF ATLANTIS (P. 12-40) ; HISTORICAL ELEMENT IN
      GREEK MYTHS AND LEGENDS (P. 13-32)
CT  - *ATLANTIS AND MINOAN CRETE (P. 41-57) ; ATLANTIC LOCATION OF
      ATLANTIS (P. 41-45) ; MINOAN HYPOTHESIS (P. 46-56)
CT  - *THERA AND ITS VOLCANO (P. 58-95) ; ISLAND OF THERA (P. 58-62)
      ; CHRONOLOGY OF BRONZE AGE ERUPTION (P. 63-73) ; NATURE AND
      INTENSITY OF THERA ERUPTION EVIDENCE OF KRAKATOA (P. 74-83)
```

```
CT  - *EXCAVATIONS ON THERA (P. 96-106)
CT  - *AFTER-EFFECTS AND MEMORIES OF THERA ERUPTION (P. 107-175) ;
      COLLAPSE OF MINOAN SEA POWER (P. 107-113) ; CONVERGENCE OF
      ARCHAEOLOGY AND TRADITION AT KEOS (P. 118-136) ; FLOATING ISLANDS
      (P. 152-170)
IT  - *AKROTIRI (P. 96-105) ; ARGONAUTS (P. 148-152) ; CRETE
IT  - EGYPT ANCIENT RECORDS (P. 52-56)
IT  - EGYPTIANS AND MINOANS (P. 52-56) ; KNOSSOS
IT  - POTTERY MARINE STYLE (PL. 21-26) ; SOLON
IT  - *THERA ; POTTERY (PL. 45-49) ; SETTLEMENTS (P. 96-105)
```

****

```
RSN - 00392141                              ┌─────────────────┐
                                            │  BOOKS RECORD   │
SNO - 0113                                  │       IN        │
                                            │ ONTARIO HISTORY │
CCN - F5545 B69 J65                         │     (F5545)     │
                                            └─────────────────┘
ME  - Johnston, Charles Murray, 1926-

TI  - Brant county; a history 1784-1945.

IM  - Toronto, Oxford University Press, 1967

COL - 181p.

PY  - 1967

LCH - Brant Co., Ontario - History

IT  - AGRICULTURE IMPLEMENTS ; BRANT JOSEPH

IT  - BRANT COUNTY RELIGIOUS ACTIVITIES ; BRANTFORD

IT  - BUFFALO AND BRANTFORD RAILWAY ; BURFORD TOWNSHIP ; CARRON HIRAM

IT  - CHURCH OF ENGLAND ; CONSERVATIVE PARTY

IT  - DEPRESSION OF 1929 (P. 137-142) ; DUNCAN SARA JEANNETTE

IT  - EDUCATION ; FIRST WORLD WAR (P. 120-125)

IT  - GRAND RIVER INDIAN SETTLEMENT ; INDUSTRY TECHNOLOGY

IT  - JOHNSON E PAULINE ; MALCOLM ELIAKIM LIAK ; MOHWAK INDIANS

IT  - NORTON JOHN ; OAKLAND TOWNSHIP ; ONONDAGA TOWNSHIP ; PARIS

IT  - SIX NATIONS' CONFEDERACY OR LEAGUE ; SIX NATIONS' RESERVE

IT  - UPPER CANADA ADMINISTRATION
```

****

```
RSN - 00670542                              ┌─────────────────┐
                                            │  BOOKS RECORD   │
SNO - 0978                                  │       IN        │
                                            │  ANTHROPOLOGY   │
CCN - GN497 T87 1971                        │     (GN497)     │
                                            └─────────────────┘
ME  - Turney-High, Harry Holbert, 1899-
TI  - Primitive war; its practice and concepts.  Foreword by David C.
      Rapoport.  Afterword by Harry Holbert Turney-High.
IM  - Columbia, University of South Carolina Press, 1971
COL - 288p.
PY  - 1971
LCH - War
```

CT - *PRACTICE OF PRIMITIVE WAR (P. 5-140) ; WEAPONS (P. 5-20) ;
THEORY OF WAR (P. 21-38) ; FORMATIONS (P. 39-60) ; DISCIPLINE AND
COMMAND (P. 61-90) ; FUNCTIONAL DESIDERATA (P. 91-106) ;
INTELLIGENCE SURPRISE AND COUNTERSURPRISE (P. 107-122) ; BATTLE
PLANS (P. 123-140)

CT - *CONCEPTS OF PRIMITIVE WAR (P. 141-253) ; SOCIO PSYCHOLOGICAL
MOTIVES (P. 141-168) ; ECONOMIC MOTIVE (P. 169-186) ; MILITARY
VALUES (P. 187-204) ; MILITARY ATTITUDES (P. 205-226) ; WAR AND
ORGANIZATION OF SOCIETY (P. 227-253)

CT - *SURVIVAL AND REVIVAL OF PRIMITIVE WAR (P. 254-265)

IT - AFRICA ; DAHOMEAN ; ENEMY LIFE VALUATION OF (P. 220-226) ; EURASIA

IT - GIBEAH CAMPAIGN AGAINST (P. 32-38) ; GREAT PLAINS AMERICAN

IT - HEAD TAKING (P. 196-200)

IT - HEBREWS EARLY MILITARY OPERATIONS (P. 31-38) ; IROQUOIS ; JIBARO

IT - LAND ECONOMIC (P. 182-186) ; LIFE ATTITUDES REGARDING (P. 210-215)

IT - MELANESIA ; *METHODS TACTICAL (P. 21-38) ; OCEANIA ; OJIBWAY ; OMAHA

IT - *PLANS PRINCIPLE OF SIMPLICITY OF (P. 123-137) ; POLYNESIANS

IT - SAMOAN ; *SEX MOTIVE (P. 151-164) ; SLAVING (P. 178-182)

IT - *SOCIAL ORGANIZATION (P. 227-253) ; *SOCIOLOGY (P. 227-253)

IT - TENSION RELEASE (P. 141-145) ; *WOMEN (P. 151-164) ; ZULU

****

RSN - 00070623
SNO - 1830
CCN - HJ5715 C2 D78

> BOOKS RECORD
> IN
> PUBLIC FINANCE
> (HJ5715)

ME - Due, John Fitzgerald
TI - The general manufacturers sales tax in Canada.
IM - , Canadian Tax Foundation, 1951
PY - 1951
CT - *DEVELOPMENT OF THE TAX (P. 5-22)
CT - *TAX RATES AND TAX YIELD (P. 23-34)
CT - SINGLE STAGE SALES TAXES (P. 35-40)
CT - *STRUCTURE OF TAX AND PROVISIONS TO PREVENT MULTIPLE APPLICATION
(P. 41-58) ; *EXEMPTIONS OF CONSUMPTION PURCHASES (P. 59-72)
CT - *SALE AND SALE PRICE FOR TAX PURPOSES (P. 73-88) ; PRICES ON
DIRECT SALES TO RETAILERS AND CONSUMERS (P. 82-86)
CT - *ADMINISTRATIVE PROVISIONS ORGANIZATION AND PROCEDURES (P. 89-108)
CT - *COMPLIANCE PROBLEMS (P. 109-120) ; SALES TAX CONSIDERATIONS FOR
FIRM AS A SELLER (P. 114-118)
CT - *SHIFTING PYRAMIDING AND INCIDENCE OF SALES TAX (P. 121-140) ;
REACTIONS OF MANUFACTURERS TO TAX (P. 122-126) ; PRICE
ADJUSTMENTS OVER LONGER PERIOD OF TIME (P. 127-131)
CT - *DISTRIBUTION OF SALES TAX BURDEN (P. 141-151)
CT - *ROLE OF SALES TAX IN DOMINION TAX STRUCTURE (P. 152-168) ; SALES
TAX AS PERMANENT ELEMENT IN DOMINION TAX STRUCTURE (P. 152-161) ;
INCREASES IN SALES TAX AS ANTI INFLATIONARY WEAPON (P. 162-168)

CT - *MANUFACTURERS SALES TAXES AND FEDERAL PROVINCIAL SALES TAX
      RELATIONSHIPS (P. 169-188)
IT - DOMINION BUREAU OF STATISTICS
IT - EQUITY OF SALES VS INCOME TAXES (P. 155-159)
IT - *EXEMPTION OF PRODUCERS' GOODS (P. 37-57)
IT - EXEMPTIONS PURCHASERS (P. 110-114)
IT - MANUFACTURERS FORM OF SALES TAX LIMITATIONS OF (P. 170-175)
IT - OLIGOPOLY SIGNIFICANCE FOR SHIFTING (P. 122-127)
IT - RETAIL SALES TAX RELATIVE ADVANTAGES OF (P. 170-176)
IT - VALUATION PROBLEMS (P. 79-87)

****

```
                                              ┌─────────────────┐
                                              │  BOOKS RECORD   │
                                              │       IN        │
                                              │   SOCIOLOGY     │
RSN - 00070919                                │     (HM19)      │
                                              └─────────────────┘
SNO - 1669
```

CCN - HM19 T5 1961
ME - Timasheff, Nicholas Sergeyevitch, 1886-
TI - Sociological theory, its nature and growth.
IM - , Random House, 1961
PY - 1961
CT - *SOCIOLOGICAL THEORIES (P. 3-14)
CT - *COMTE AUGUSTE (P. 15-29) ; STATIC AND DYNAMIC SOCIOLOGY (P.
      22-26) ; SPENCER HERBERT (P. 30-42)
CT - *COMPETING SCHOOLS (P. 59-130) ; SOCIAL DARWINISM (P. 59-71) ;
      PSYCHOLOGICAL EVOLUTIONISM (P. 72-87) ; EVOLUTIONISMS AND
      ORGANICISM (P. 88-96) ; EARLY ANALYTICAL SOCIOLOGY (P. 97-105) ;
      DURKHEIM EMILE (P. 106-118) ; RUSSIAN SUBJECTIVISM (P. 119-130)
CT - *VOGUE OF PSYCHOLOGICAL SOCIOLOGY (P. 131-190) ; DECLINE OF
      EVOLUTIONISM AND RISE OF NEO POSITIVISM (P. 131-140) ; COOLEY
      CHARLES H AND THOMAS W I (P. 141-157) ; PARETO VILFREDO (P.
      158-166) ; WEBER MAX (P. 167-190)
CT - *CONTEMPORY CONVERGENCE IN SOCIOLOGICAL THEORIES (P. 191-302) ;
      NEO POSITIVISM (P. 191-211) / MATHEMATICAL WING OF NEO POSITIVISM
      (P. 199-203) ; HUMAN ECOLOGY AND SOCIOMETRY (P. 212-220) ;
      FUNCTIONAL APPROACH (P. 221-233) ; ANALYTICAL SOCIOLOGY (P.
      234-260) / SOROKIN PITIRIM A (P. 235-241) / PARSONS TALCOTT (P.
      242-249) ; PHILOSOPHICAL SCHOOLS (P. 261-276) / INSTITUTIONAL
      SCHOOL (P. 261-265) / PHENOMENOLOGICAL SCHOOL (P. 266-273) ;
      HISTORICAL SOCIOLOGY (P. 277-288) ; REVIVALS (P. 289-302) / NEO
      EVOLUTIONISM (P. 289-293)
CT - *MID TWENTIETH CENTURY SOCIOLOGY (P. 303-312)
IT - COLLECTIVE CONSCIENCE CONSCIOUSNESS (P. 108-113)
IT - ECONOMIC DETERMINISM EVOLUTIONISM (P. 46-50)
IT - OPERATIONAL DEFINITION (P. 195-199)

```
RSN - 00872975                          ┌─────────────────┐
SNO - 0373                              │  BOOKS RECORD   │
                                        │       IN        │
CCN - HT166 H43                         │ URBAN PLANNING  │
                                        │    (HT166)      │
ME  - Hellman, Harold, 1927-            └─────────────────┘
TI  - The city in the world of the future.
IM  - New York, M. Evans, 1970
COL - 186p.
PY  - 1970
LCH - Cities and towns - Planning
CT  - *NEW BUILDING TECHNIQUES (P. 17-33) ; *HOUSING (P. 34-48)
CT  - *CITY INDOORS (P. 49-60) ; *REBUILDING CITY CENTER (P. 61-78)
CT  - *PLANNING (P. 79-94) ; *NEW TOWNS NEW CITIES (P. 95-108)
CT  - *UNIVERSITY CITIES (P. 109-119)
CT  - *EXPERIMENTAL CITIES (P. 120-135) ; *MEGASTRUCTURES (P. 136-147)
CT  - *CITIES IN SEA (P. 148-165)
IT  - APARTMENTS (P. 38-43) ; CONTINENTAL SHELVES (P. 160-165)
IT  - DISNEY WORLD (P. 120-126) ; DOMES (P. 3-7 52-57)
IT  - *DOWNTOWN AREAS SPECIFIC PLACES GO INDOORS (P. 49-60)
IT  - GAMES COMPUTERS AND (P. 90-94)
IT  - LAND AND REBUILDING CITY CENTERS (P. 67-72)
IT  - *MACHINE STOPS THE (P. 60-70) ; MALL PROJECTS (P. 63-67)
IT  - MODULARIZATION (P. 23-27) ; NEW YORK CITY MANHATTAN
IT  - TRANSPORTATION ; *WEATHER AND INDOOR CITIES (P. 49-60 PASSIM)
*************************************************************
RSN - 00398750                          ┌─────────────────┐
SNO - 2306                              │  BOOKS RECORD   │
                                        │       IN        │
CCN - NB80 F74                          │   SCULPTURE     │
                                        │    (NB80)       │
ME  - Frankfort, Henri, 1897-1954       └─────────────────┘
TI  - Sculpture of the third millenium B.C. from Tell Asmar and
      Khafajah.
IM  - Chicago, University Press, 1939
COL - 87p.
SER - The University of Chicago Oriental Institute Publications, v. 44
PY  - 1939
LCH - Sculpture, Sumerian; Mesopotamia - Antiquities; Tell Asmar, Iraq
LCH - Khafaje, Iraq; Excavations (Archaeology) - Mesopotamia
CT  - WORKS FROM PERIOD OF EARLY DYNASTIC II (P. 19-27)
CT  - LATER REALISTIC STYLE WORKS FROM THE PERIOD OF EARLY DYNASTIC III
      (P. 28-33) ; STONE AND METAL IN MESOPOTAMIAN ART (P. 37-42)
CT  - RELIEFS (P. 43-48) ; DRESS (P. 49-55)
CT  - *CATALOGUE OF SCULPTURES (P. 56-80)
IT  - BITUMEN ON STATUES OR PLAQUES ; CONICAL KILT (P. 20-24)
IT  - COPPER HOARD ; COSTUME (P. 51-55) ; DEITIES (P. 45-49)
IT  - FEMALE FIGURES ; GODDESSES ; HOARDS STATUES
IT  - INSCRIPTIONS (P. 10-15) ; LAGASH TELLOH (P. 9-13)
IT  - PLAQUES (P. 43-48) ; PRIESTS (P. 46-50) ; SHELL INLAYS
IT  - SIN TEMPLE (P. 7-11) ; SINGLE SHRINE TEMPLE (P. 5-9)
IT  - SQUARE TEMPLE (P. 3-11) ; STYLES DEVELOPMENT OF (P. 16-20)
IT  - TEMPLE OVAL AT KHAFAJAH
```

```
RSN - 00607779                                    ┌─────────────┐
                                                  │ BOOKS RECORD │
SNO - 2389                                        │     IN       │
                                                  │ ART (NE1310) │
CCN - NE1310 B5 1960                              └─────────────┘
ME  - Binyon, Laurence, 1869-1943
TI  - Japanese colour prints, by Laurence Binyon and J.J. O'Brien
      Sexton, edited by Basil Gray.
IM  - Boston, Boston Book & Art Shop, 1960
COL - 230p.
PY  - 1960
LCH - Ukiyoe; Color prints, Japanese; Printers' marks - Japan
LCH - Wood-engravers Japan
CT  - 1658 TO 1695 (P. 25-29) ; *1695 TO 1730 (P. 30-41)
CT  - *1730 TO 1764 (P. 42-52) ; *MEIWA PERIOD 1764 TO 1772 (P. 53-71)
CT  - *ANYEI PERIOD 1772-1781 (P. 72-81)
CT  - *TEMMEI PERIOD 1781 TO 1789 (P. 82-97)
CT  - *KWANSEI PERIOD 1789 TO 1801 (P. 98-121)
CT  - *KYOWA AND BUNKWA PERIODS 1801 TO 1818 (P. 122-133)
CT  - *BUNSEI PERIOD 1818 TO 1830 (P. 134-144)
CT  - *TEMPO AND KOKWA PERIODS 1830 TO 1848 (P. 145-154)
CT  - KAYEI PERIOD TO MEIJI 1848 TO 1881 (P. 155-161) ; SECOND KIYONOBU
      PROBLEM (P. 166-170)
CT  - *COLOUR PRINTED BOOKS AND ALBUMS (P. 176-188)
CT  - TABLES TO FACILITATE READING OF DATED BOOKS AND PRINTS (P. 189-197)
      ; CENSORSHIP OF PRINTS (P. 198-204)
CT  - ACTORS' MON (P. 205-210)
CT  - YEDO PUBLISHERS' TRADE MARKS AND SEALS (P. 211-217)
IT  - DAISHO NO TSUKI LONG AND SHORT MONTHS (P. 189-197)
IT  - *HARUNOBU SUZUKI (P. 54-70) ; HIROSHIGE I (P. 156-160)
IT  - *HOKUSAI KATSUSHIKA (P. 134-144)
IT  - KIBYOSHI YELLOW BACK STORY BOOKS (P. 83-87) ; KIYOMASU (P. 48-52)
IT  - KIYONAGA (P. 85-89 105-109) ; *KIYONOBU I (P. 30-41)
IT  - KIYONOBU II (P. 166-170) ; *MASANOBU OKUMURA (P. 44-53)
IT  - MORONOBU (P. 25-29) ; UTAMARO I KITAGAWA (P. 107-111 127-131)

***************************************************************

RSN - 00127871                                    ┌─────────────┐
                                                  │ BOOKS RECORD │
SNO - 2465                                        │     IN       │
                                                  │ ART (NK5344) │
CCN - NK5344 N6 W6                                └─────────────┘
ME  - Woodforde, Christopher
TI  - The Norwich school of glass-painting in the fifteenth century.
IM  - , Oxford University Press, 1950
PY  - 1950
CT  - NORWICH GLASS PAINTERS (P. 9-15)
CT  - *GLASS OF FIVE CHURCHES (P. 16-127) ; ST PETER MANCROFT NORWICH
      (P. 16-41) ; EAST HARLING (P. 42-54) ; NORTH TUDDENHAM (P.
      55-67) ; RINGLAND (P. 68-73) ; LONG MELFORD SUFFOLK (P. 74-127)
CT  - *ANGELS (P. 128-148) ; *LABOURS OF THE MONTHS (P. 149-160)
CT  - *CHARACTERISTICS OF NORWICH FIFTEENTH CENTURY GLASS PAINTING (P.
      161-182) ; *BLASPHEMY WINDOW AT HEYDON (P. 183-192)
```

```
CT  - ENGLISH INSCRIPTIONS (P. 193-201)
CT  - *DESTRUCTION AND LOSS (P. 202-214)
IT  - CLOPTON FAMILY ; COLOUR IN GLASS ; DECORATIVE DESIGN AND PATTERNS
IT  - *EAST HARLING CHURCH MEDIEVAL GLASS (P. 42-55)
IT  - GLASS PAINTING PAINTERS (P. 9-15) ; HERALDIC GLASS ARMS
IT  - *LONG MELFORD SUFFOLK CHURCH (P. 74-127) ; EAST WINDOW (P.
      114-119) ; MEDIEVAL GLASS (P. 114-119)
IT  - *NARRATIVE WINDOWS (P. 183-192)
IT  - *NORFOLK CHURCHES MEDIEVAL ANGELS IN (P. 128-148)
IT  - *NORTH TUDDENHAM MEDIEVAL GLASS (P. 55-68)
IT  - *NORWICH ; ALL SAINTS' CHURCH MEDIEVAL GLASS (P. 179-186) ; ST
      PETER MANCROFT CHURCH (P. 16-42) / EAST WINDOW (P. 20-39) /
      HISTORY OF THE GLASS (P. 16-20) / MEDIEVAL GLASS (P. 20-42)
IT  - SAINTS MARGARET (P. 55-59)
IT  - *SUBJECT MATTER ; ANGELS (P. 128-148) / NINE ORDERS OF (P.
      129-137) / SCROLLS AND (P. 137-143) ; CHRIST INFANCY (P. 23-27)
```

****

```
                                    ┌─────────────────┐
                                    │  BOOKS RECORD   │
                                    │       IN        │
                                    │ DRAMA (PN1655)  │
                                    └─────────────────┘

RSN - 00183277

SNO - 2014

CCN - PN1655 O55

ME  - Olson, Elder, 1909-

TI  - Tragedy and the theory of drama.

IM  - Detroit Wayne State University Press, 1961

COL - 269p.

PY  - 1961

LCH - Drama - History and criticism; Tragedy

CT  - *DRAMA AND DRAMATIC ACTION (P. 3-28) ; *PLOT (P. 29-54)

CT  - *INCIDENT AND CHARACTER (P. 55-86) ; REPRESENTATION AND DIALO

CT  - *EMOTION FICTION AND BELIEF (P. 127-148)

CT  - *DRAMATIC EFFECT AND DRAMATIC FORM (P. 149-170)

CT  - *AGAMEMNON (P. 171-194) ; *KING LEAR (P. 195-216)

CT  - *PHEDRE (P. 217-236) ; MODERN DRAMA AND TRAGEDY (P. 237-260)

IT  - O'NEILL EUGENE MOURNING BECOMES ELECTRA (P. 237-243)

IT  - *PROBABILITY AND REPRESENTATION (P. 90-100)

IT  - *SHAKESPEARE WILLIAM KING LEAR (P. 195-215) ; SHAW GEORGE BERNARD

IT  - WILDER THORNTON
```

```
RSN - 00818902
SNO - 1968                          BOOKS RECORD
CCN - PN1995.9 W4 F4 1973               IN
ME  - Fenin, George N.            FILM (PN1995.9)
TI  - The Western, from silents to the seventies by George N. Fenin and
      William K. Everson.
IM  - New York, Grossman, 1973
COL - 396p.
PY  - 1973
LCH - Western films - History and criticism
CT  - *WESTERN HISTORY AND HOLLYWOOD (P. 3-24)
CT  - *CONTENTS AND MORAL INFLUENCE OF WESTERN (P. 25-46) ; HERO (P. 25-30)
CT  - *PRIMITIVES PORTER EDWIN S AND ANDERSON BRONCHO BILLY (P. 47-60)
      ; GREAT TRAIN ROBBERY (P. 47-51)
CT  - *GRIFFITH DAVID W AND INCE THOMAS H 1909-1913 (P. 61-74)
CT  - *HART WILLIAM SURREY AND REALISM (P. 75-107) ; MY LIFE EAST AND
      WEST (P. 75-81) ; HELL'S HINGES (P. 82-91) ; HART'S PEAK AND
      DECLINE (P. 92-103) ; *MIX TOM AND SHOWMANSHIP (P. 108-121)
CT  - FAIRBANKS DOUGLAS AND FORD JOHN 1913-1920 (P. 122-129)
CT  - *CRUZE JAMES THE COVERED WAGON AND FORD JOHN THE IRON HORSE (P.
      130-145)
CT  - *THE TWENTIES (P. 146-179) ; DIRECTORS WYLER WILLIAM AND HOWARD
      WILLIAM K (P. 161-166) ; SOUND (P. 173-179)
CT  - *WESTERN COSTUME (P. 180-194)
CT  - *THIRTIES (P. 195-225) ; AUTRY GENE AND ROGERS ROY (P. 210-215)
CT  - *WESTERN SERIAL (P. 226-236)
CT  - *FORTIES (P. 237-265) ; HISTORICAL WESTERNS (P. 243-247) ; THE B
      WESTERN (P. 255-265)
CT  - *POSTWAR WESTERN (P. 266-287) ; SEX (P. 266-275) ; NEUROSES (P.
      276-280) ; RACIAL CONSCIENCE (P. 281-287)
CT  - *STUNTMAN AND SECOND UNIT DIRECTOR (P. 288-300) ; STUNT MOVIES
      (P. 295-300) ; *TELEVISION (P. 301-317)
CT  - *WESTERN'S INTERNATIONAL AUDIENCE AND INTERNATIONAL WESTERN (P.
      318-336) ; CONTEMPORARY WESTERN (P. 337-342)
IT  - BILLY THE KID ; BROWN JOHNNY MACK ; CANUTT YAKIMA ; CAREY HARRY
IT  - CLARK DANIEL B (P. 116-120) ; COOPER GARY ; DEMILLE CECIL B
IT  - FAIRBANKS DOUGLAS SR (P. 123-129) ; FOX WILLIAM (P. 113-117)
IT  - GIBSON HOOT ; HAYDEN RUSSELL (P. 255-262) ; HIGH NOON ; JONES BUCK
IT  - MAYNARD KEN ; MCCOY TIM ; SCOTT RANDOLPH ; STAGECOACH
IT  - STARRETT CHARLES ; STEELE BOB ; THOMSON FRED ; TYLER TOM ; VIDOR KING
IT  - WAYNE JOHN
```

BOOKS ARE FOR USE: A USER GUIDE TO THE BOOKS FILE ON SDC/ORBIT

Preface

We have used Ranganathan's First Law of Library Science as a title for this guide. It seems appropriate to recall this law and the other four as we begin to experiment with the new version of library catalogs—*online subject access to library collections.* The laws of library science, promulgated in 1931 by S. R. Ranganathan,[1] the Father of Library Science in India, are as follows:

Books Are for Use
Every Reader His Book
Every Book Its Reader

---

1. S. R. Ranganathan, *Five Laws of Library Science.* Delhi: Asia Publishing House, 1931.

Save the Time of the Reader (and the Staff)
A Library is a Growing Organism

Ranganathan died in 1972 at the age of 81, but the force of his laws can carry a new generation of librarians to seek solutions to the problems associated with the implementation of these laws. On my visit to India in 1970, at his request, I brought news to his students and colleagues about computer-based library services and research. At that time I reported about MARC and LEEP.[2] Now we can go beyond these early beginnings and envision national and international online networks to access the world's library collections from any location where a telephone, electrical outlet and computer terminal can be placed.

This guide is dedicated to Ranganathan's memory and vision which has guided me and my students through our professional careers. Its publication date marks the fifth anniversary of his passing.

Introduction

BOOKS is a new version of an online catalog to a sample library book collection. It is not any one library's collection *per se* (although we chose the titles by means of a random selection of the English language monographs in the classified lists of the holdings of the University of Toronto). It is meant to represent what a library catalog for a single library or a group of libraries could look like *if* we attempted to *describe the subject contents* of our book collections.

Bibliographic records in present-day online catalogs (1ccc on SCORPIO, OCLC, Ballots, UTLAS, etc.) are mainly physical or bibliographical descriptions of library materials, with subject *headings* not subject *descriptions*. What reference librarians can now do to search online for the journal and report literature of several subject fields, they *cannot* do for the book literature in those fields. ERIC, NTIS, MEDLINE, COMPENDEX, INSPEC, PSYCH. ABSTRACTS, INFORM, etc. are online databases which do not primarily abstract and index the book literature of their respective fields.

Our project at Syracuse University, the Subject Access Project, has created a database for the book literature in ten fields of the social sciences and humanities. The Council on Library Resources funded the project for one and a half years in the hope that the library profession could learn something about the cost/effectiveness of augmenting subject descriptions for online subject searching of library catalogs.

---

2. Pauline Atherton, *Putting Knowledge to Work; An American View of Ranganathan's Five Laws of Library Science*. Delhi: Vikas, 1973.

We hope you will try BOOKS on ORBIT, considering it to be a prototype of what your own library or your library network's catalog could be. Once you have searched and found some titles, it will still be necessary for you to check your library catalog for your holdings of the titles in the BOOKS file, but even with this inconvenience and two-step look-up we think you will agree that "BOOKS are for use."

If you are interested in the procedures we followed to produce the records in the BOOKS file, please refer to another Subject Access Project publication by Barbara Settel, "SUBJECT DESCRIPTION OF BOOKS: A Manual of Procedures for Augmenting Subject Descriptions in Library Catalogs."

P.S. We assume that users of BOOKS are Trained SDC/ORBIT searchers. This guide will not explain basic ORBIT commands or features. For aid we recommend ORBIT Training Sessions and Manuals to you.

What is BOOKS in ORBIT???

(a) It's a file of approximately 2,000 books in English taken as a random sample of a large research library's holdings in ten classes of the L.C. Classification:

HUMANITIES

1. Philosophy:
   BC Logic
   BH Aesthetics
   BJ Ethics

2. History:
   DE Graeco-Roman World
   DF Ancient Greece
   DG Ancient Italy
       Rome to 476

3. Arts:
   NB Sculpture
   NE Engraving
   NK Art Applied to Industry
       Decoration & Ornament

4. Literature:
   PN 1560-3300 Drama

5. Post Confederation
   Ontario History:
   F 5520-5547

SOCIAL SCIENCES

6. Psychology:
   BJ 1-990

7. Anthropology:
   GN 1-696

8. Public Finance:
   HJ

9. Sociology:
   HM 1-221

10. Urban Planning
    Urban Redevelopment:
    HT 166-177

(b) The BOOKS database has this profile of its contents:

1) ANTHROPOLOGY (LC Class: GN 1-696), 131 books.
   Ethnology, Man, Kinship, Primitive Societies, Rites and Ceremonies, Human Evolution, various tribes (e.g., Maoris, etc.),
   Race, Anthropometry.
2) ARTS (LC Class: NB, NE, NK), 124 books.
   Sculpture, Art Objects, Pottery, Greek Bronzes, Glassware, En-
   gravings, Batik, Handicraft, Color Prints, Medicine Bottles, Porce-
   lain, Metal Work, etc.
3) DRAMA (LC Class: PN 1560-3300), 256 books.
   Theater, Moving Pictures, Drama, Television Plays, Production
   and Direction, Aesthetics, Stage Setting and Scenery, Acting,
   Actors, Actresses, Western Films, Melodrama, Tragedy, Historical Drama, French Drama, Dancing, etc.
4) GRAECO-ROMAN CIVILIZATION (LC Class: DE, DF, DG),
   130 books.
   Greece, Rome, Civilization, Politics and Government, Social Life
   and Customs, Architecture, Athens, Hellenism, Antiquities, Del-
   phian Oracle, etc.
5) ONTARIO (CANADA) HISTORY, POST CONFEDERATION
   (LC Class: F 5520-5547), 179 books.
   Ontario History, Politics and Government, Canadian Social Life and
   Customs, Indian Trails, Boats and Boating, Land Settlement, etc.
6) PHILOSOPHY (LC Class: BC, BH, BJ), 139 books.
   Logic, Ethics, Conduct of Life, Good and Evil, Free Will and
   Determinism, Aesthetics, Art and Science, Thought and Thinking,
   Reasoning, etc.
7) PSYCHOLOGY (LC Class: BF 1-990), 319 books.
   Emotions, Personality, Child Study, Perception, Consciousness,
   Mental Tests, Motivation (Psychology), Adolescence, Infants,
   Personality Tests, etc.
8) PUBLIC FINANCE (LC Class: HJ), 114 books.
   Taxation, Budget, Fiscal Policy, Income Tax, Value Added Tax,
   Grants-in-Aid, Inheritance and Transfer Tax, Municipal Finance,
   Tariff, Tax Evasion, etc.
9) SOCIOLOGY (LC Class: HM 1-221), 140 books.
   Social Conflict, Social Change, Technology and Civilization,
   Power (Social Science), Social Interaction, etc.
10) URBAN PLANNING (LC Class: HT 166-177), 447 books.
    Planning, Cities and Towns, Urban Renewal, Regional Planning,
    Green Belts, Land, Housing, Zoning, Waterfronts, Urban Trans-
    portations, etc.

FIGURE 12. Explanation of BOOKS Record and its Accessibility on ORBIT

SDC/ORBIT CATEGORY NAME	ABBREVIATION	SEARCHABLE	STANDARD PRINT COMMANDS*		
			PRINT	TRIAL	FULL
Accession Number (Record Serial Number)	RSN	x		x	x
SAP Number	SNO	x		x	x
Call Number (LC or U of T)	CCN	x	x	x	x
Main Entry	ME	x	x	x	x
Title	TI	x	x	x	x
Imprint	IM	-	x		x
Collation	COL	-	x	-	x
Publication Year	PY	x		x	x
Subject Headings (LCSH)	LCH	x (as LCH, LCT)	x	x	x
Contents Terms	CT	x (as CT...)			x
Index Terms	IT	x (as IT...)			x

*Remember you can INCLUDE or EXCLUDE any category in any PRINT command.

FIGURE 13. Sample of BOOKS Record on ORBIT

```
RSN - 00618606
SNO - 1080
CCN - BH221 R93 W47
ME  - West, James D.
TI  - Russian symbolism; a study of Vyacheslav Ivanov and the Russian
      symbolist aesthetic.
IM  - London, Methuen, 1970
COL - 250p.
PY  - 1970
LCH - Ivanov, Viacheslav Ivanovich, 1866-1949; Aesthetics, Russian
LCH - Symbolism in art
CT  - *NINETEENTH CENTURY (P. 5-47) ; VISSARION GRIGOREVICH BELINSKY
      (P. 6-11) ; APOLLON ALEKSANDROVICH GRIGOREV (P. 16-20) ; LEV
      NIKOLAYEVICH TOLSTOY (P. 2:-26) ; ALEKSANDR MIKHAYLOVICH
      SKABICHEVSKY (P. 27-34) ; VLADIMIR SOLOVYOV (P. 35-41)
CT  - *VYACHESLAV IVANOV'S PHILOSOPHY OF ART (P. 48-106) ; ELEMENTS IN
      CONTEMPORAY SYMBOLISM (P. 50-57) ; ART AND THEORY OF KNOWLEDGE
      (P. 58-65) / SELF KNOWLEDGE (P. 61-65) ; ART AND COMMUNICATION
      (P. 66-87) / POET AND CROWD (P. 71-75) / MYTH OF DIONYSUS (P.
      77-81) ; ART AND REALITY (P. 88-92) ; IVANOV AND CASSIRER (P.
      93-106)
CT  - *SYMBOLIST DEBATE (P. 107-:80) ; ART AND LIFE (P. 116-131) /
      LITERATURE AND LIFE (P. 116-120) / INDIVIDUALISM AND TRADITION OF
      SOCIAL COMMITMENT (P. 121-'26) / RETREAT FROM INDIVIDUALISM (P.
      127-131) ; ART AND COMMUNICATION (P. 132-145) ; ART AND REALITY
      (P. 146-180) / INTERPRETATION OF REALISM (P. 153-161) / ART AND
      THEORY OF KNOWLEDGE (P. 162-169) / TRANSFORMATION OF REALITY (P.
      172-180); *POETRY AND THE ABSOLUTE (P. 181-190)
IT  - BELY A BUGAYEV B N; BRYUSOV V YA RUSSIAN SYMBOLIST
IT  - CHULKOV G I SYMBOLIST POET AND CRITIC THEORIST OF MYSTICAL
      ANARCHISM; ELLIS L L KOBYLINSKY SYMBOLIST POET AND CRITIC
IT  - PSYCHOLOGY PSYCHOLOGY OF PERCEPTION
IT  - SOLOGUB F F K TETERNIKOV RUSSIAN SYMBOLIST
```

For ease of searching single and combined categories and for comparison and evaluation studies, several category lists in this database are approachable in different lists, or inverted files.

FIGURE 14. BOOKS Category and List Relationships

List Name

BIW	Basic Index Words	single terms in <u>all</u> searchable fields, e.g., BLINDNESS (BIW)
ST	SAP Terms	all <u>single terms</u> from CT <u>and</u> IT fields, e.g., BLINDNESS (ST)
SP	SAP Phrases	all <u>phrases</u> from CT <u>and</u> IT fields, e.g., PARTIAL BLINDNESS (SP)
SWT	SAP Weighted Terms	all <u>terms</u> in CT <u>and</u> IT fields which meet criteria for weighting (*), e.g., ten or more pages on Psychology (CT) would result in *PSYCHOLOGY (SWT)
SWP	SAP Weighted Phrases	all <u>phrases</u> from CT and IT fields which meet weighting criteria, e.g., Choice theories (p. 258-306) in IT field would result in *CHOICE THEORIES (SWP)
LCT	LC Heading Terms	all terms in LCH field (e.g., PSYCHOLOGY - MATHEMATICAL MODELS) would result in the following terms in LCT field: MATHEMATICAL (LCT), MODELS (LCT), and PSYCHOLOGY (LCT)

Below is a schematic diagram showing the relationship of the <u>word searchable fields</u> (ME, TI, LCH, CT, IT) to the category lists explained above (BIW, ST, SP, SWT, SWP, LCT). All searchable categories are included in the diagram.*

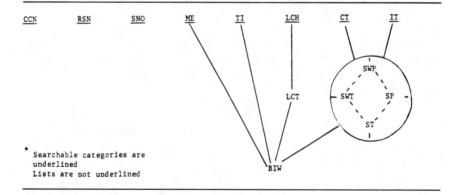

*
Searchable categories are
underlined
Lists are not underlined

BOOKS File: Use of ORBIT Features

ALL

The word ALL should be used before every term or phrase being searched to avoid the Multi Meaning Message, which will always appear because of the multiple listing of terms and phrases (see chart).

The word ALL may be purposely omitted if the searcher desires to know which fields or lists contain the term or phrase being searched, or when checking spelling variations, or a questionable truncation.

NEIGHBOR

The NBR command is useful for obtaining a list of alphabetically adjacent terms in the categories or lists that you want to examine in order to check the number of postings.

```
SS 12 /C?
USER:
"NBR MORAL: (LCH)

PROG:

POSTINGS        TERM
      1         MONETARY POLICY - PAKISTAN
      2         MOORE, HENRY SPENCER, 1898-
      1         MORAL REARMAMENT
      1         MORRIS, DESMOND.  THE NAKED APE
      1         MOSCA, GAETANO, 1858-1941
UP N OR DOWN N?
- - - - - - - - - - - - - - - - - - - - - - - - - - - - - - -
USER:
"NBR MORAL

PROG:

POSTINGS        TERM
      2         MORA (ST)
      1         *MORA (SWT)
     96         MORAL (BIW)
     46         MORAL (CT)
     49         MORAL (IT)
UP N OR DOWN N?
```

Tips on Searching

I. Numeric or Alpha-Numeric Fields
   1. Record Serial Number (RSN) and SAP Number (SNO)
      These fields list the University of Toronto and SAP staff control numbers. They are used to locate and check copies of these records. If the offline print is ordered and sorted by SNO, it will be in L.C. class order because of the way the SAP number was applied.
   2. Classification Call Number (CCN)
      Always truncate the call number you are searching. This will create a subset of the BOOKS file which you can scan as you would a shelf list or book stack.
      The University of Toronto (location of all titles in BOOKS) modified the L.C. numbers to refine the classification of materials (in Class F).

```
SS 12 /C?
USER:
ALL BJ14:   (CCN)

PROG:
SS 12 PSTG (15)
```

3. Publication Year (PY)

To search the records for date of publication, combine a search statement with AND FROM (year) THRU (year).

```
SS 7 /C?
USER:
ALL REGIONAL PLANNING (LCH) AND FROM 1960 THRU 1977

PROG:
SS 7 PSTG (    )
```

II. Word Searchable Fields

4. Main Entry (ME)

The "phrase" in this field is usually a person's or an organization's name, with other information (e.g., birth-death dates). *Search* the person's last name or the organization's name *with truncation*. Without the word ALL a Multi Meaning Message will produce all forms of the name.

Remember that this is *not* the only place in the BOOKS record where "authors" will be found. Only specify (ME) after name if you are looking for an entire book by that author.

```
SS 14 /C?
USER:
SMITH:   (ME)

PROG:
MM (SMITH:)   (13)
              1    SMITH, DAN THROOP (ME)
              :
              :
              9    SMITH, WILLARD MALLALIEU, 1888-  (ME)
             10    SMITH, WILLIAM H., 1917-  (ME)
             11    SMITH, WILLIAM HENRY, OF CNAADA  (ME)
             12    SMITH, WILLIAM LOE, 1855-  (ME)
             13    SMITHELLS, ROGER  (ME)
SPECIFY NUMBERS, ALL, OR NONE
```

5. Title (TI)

The key terms in your search request should be searched in the title field using the ALL and the AND operator. The title field usually contains only one sentence and it is small enough that the words will be in close proximity.

---

i.e., ALL GAY (TI) AND ALL CIVIL (TI) AND ALL RIGHTS (TI)

will retrieve books entitled <u>Gay Civil Rights</u>, <u>Gay People</u>

<u>and Civil Rights</u>, <u>Civil Rights for Gay Men and Women</u>, etc.

---

6. Subject Headings (LCH)

The authority list to check before searching terms and phrases in this field is the *L.C. List of Subject Headings,* 8th ed. (available in print and on microfiche). Remember to truncate to avoid missing relevant items because of subdivision variation. Occasionally key terms may be searched in this field with the AND operator. The OR operator can be used when combining terms if each component term is a relevant subject heading term by itself.

7. Contents Terms (CT) and Index Terms (IT)

Break the phrase expressing your search request into its key component terms and "sentence search" (SENS) the terms combined with a Boolean AND.

```
SS 6 /C?
USER:
ALL GN (CCN)

PROG:
SS 6 PSTG (135)

SS 7 /C?
USER:
SENS 6 (CT) : CULTURE : AND : PERSONALITY

etc.
```

A sentence in the CT and IT categories is defined as the characters, excluding pagination, that exist between semicolons, i.e.,

CT-*Symbolist Debate (p. 107–180); Art and Life (p. 116–131);
            sentence   sentence

By their very nature terms and phrases in these fields are *free* text, as they are chosen by the author or indexer of the book with little regard for controlling the form or expression of concepts. Nevertheless, these fields are rich sources to search for word and phrase matches if the ORBIT features of truncation and word proximity are used.

The *Neighbor* command will be more helpful in the IT field where important words in phrases are often inverted to create the alphabetic index to these important terms in context.

III. Terms and Phrases
1. Term Searching

Using the word MORAL as the key term to be searched, Table 1 lists the various possibilities.

TABLE 1. Word Searching Hints

Form	Description
ALL MORAL	searches all terms in all fields and lists for the key term.
ALL MORAL (LCT)	searches all terms in the field or list specified in parentheses; in this case, the Library of Congress heading terms list. SWT (SAP Weighted Terms) will not be searched, however (see below).
ALL *MORAL	searches the SWT (SAP Weighted Terms) list for the key term.
SENS_ ( ) : MORAL:AND:ACTS ↗ ↖ search field statement (title by default)	searches each sentence in a specific field of a previously designated set for these two key terms.

```
And Don't Forget to use the AND NOT operator
to help exclude false drops.

          SS 2/C?
          USER:
          ALL WALES:
          PROG:
          SS 2 PSTG (16)

          SS 3 /C?
          USER:
          2 AND NOT ALL PRINCE:
          PROG:
          SS 3 PSTG (12)
```

2. Phrase Searching

　　To handle compound or multi-word concepts, consider it as a phrase or as AND-ed terms. Using the phrase MORAL PHILOSOPHY as the phrase to be searched, Table 2 lists the various possibilities for searching specified phrases in BOOKS.

TABLE 2. Phrase Searching Hints

Form	Description
ALL MORAL PHILOSOPHY	searches the CT & IT fields for an <u>exact</u> match. No words or phrases are allowed before or after the key phrase in a sentence to match with this search.
ALL MORAL PHILOSOPHY:	searches the CT & IT fields for a match. Allows letters, words and phrases to be included <u>after</u>, but not before the key phrase in the sentence.
ALL MORAL PHILOSOPHY ( )	searches the list or field specified in parentheses, except SWP (SAP Weighted Phrases),[+] for an exact match. No letters, words or phrases are allowed before or after the key phrase in the sentence.
ALL MORAL PHILOSOPHY: ( )	searches the list or field specified in parentheses, except SWP (SAP Weighted Phrases),[+] for a match. Allows letters, words and phrases to be included <u>after</u>, but not before the key phrase in the sentence.
[+] ALL *MORAL PHILOSOPHY	the asterisk preceding the phrase is used instead of the parentheses after the phrase to designate the SAP Weighted Phrase list. Use with or without truncation.
STRS_ ( ) : MORAL#PHILOSOPHY ⤴ ↖ search　　field statement　(title by default)	searches the specific <u>field</u> of a specific set for a match. No attention is paid to words or phrases preceding or succeeding the phrase.
SENS_ ( ) : MORAL#PHILOSOPHY ⤴ ↖ search　　field statement　(title by default)	searches each <u>sentence</u> of a specific field of a specific set for a match. No attention is paid to words or phrases preceding or succeeding the key phrase. The entire key phrase must occur within a single sentence.

Summary

　　Searching any word searchable field or list for a *specific* term(s) is straightforward and requires little explanation. However, when searching any field or list for a phrase, remember that the search is limited to matching your phrase with a phrase that looks identical to yours at the *beginning*, i.e., the first words in the ''sentence'' in a field must match your first words. The search will not match your phrase if a phrase occurring later in the sentence matches. Consequently, the phrase search may be less than thorough.

> For example: ALL MORAL PHILOSOPHY: (CT) will retrieve a citation containing the (CT sentence, ; Moral Philosophy of the Ancient Greeks (p. 207–243) ;, because of your truncation, but this strategy will *not* retrieve a citation containing the (CT) sentence, ; Development of Moral Philosophy in Ancient Greece (p. 503–521);.

The English language being what it is, it is often possible to phrase a concept in many different ways (oftentimes using the same component terms).

i.e., Culture and Personality, Personality and Culture

Another example can highlight the problem of synonyms. The idea of "urban renewal" might be found under the following entries in the CT and IT fields:

urban renewal	regional planning
urban development	town planning
urban redevelopment	urban housing
urban planning	etc.

Major differences exist for searching controlled vocabulary and free text fields. Few people are accustomed to doing a *combination* of controlled vocabulary and free text searching. This may be the best way for searching BOOKS. Keep in mind that:

1) In a free text search the number of possible terms *you must think of* to express a certain concept will be very large. It is up to you to combine the synonymous terms into phrases to express that concept.

2) Your search strategy can involve combining free-text search terms or phrases in four different subject fields (TI, LCH, CT, IT) and possibly expressing that concept using the Library of Congress Classification Number (CCN).

INTERESTING QUERIES

Social Science #1	Creativity
Social Science #2	Infant Mortality
Social Science #3	Police Personality Characteristics
Social Science #4	Perceived Size & Value of Visual Symbols
Humanities #1	Greek, Roman and Etruscan Imagery on Sarcophagi
Humanities #2	Eliminate the Use of the Deduction Theorem
Humanities #3	Adequate Connectives to Represent all Truth Functions

Note: Seven of the ninety queries used in the controlled experimental searches are analyzed here in depth.

The online strategies used by the MARC searcher and the BOOKS searcher are shown, with the number of items retrieved given after each numbered search statement.

Statistics and measures of precision, estimated recall, and time online are included. . . .

The *analysis* section compared the two methods, diagnosing why the BOOKS or MARC strategy resulted in low recall or low precision, or missed relevant items.

The matched items found by both methods are listed and the relevance assessments, if different, are given.

Sample output is shown for a few queries.

****

Interesting Query Social Sciences #1   Query #SS-1

Creativity, creative ability, or intellectual productivity.

a) MARC SEARCH STRATEGY

```
1 CREATIVE ABILITY: (LCH) OR ORIGINALITY (LCT) OR
  IMAGINATION (LCT)
  NP ORIGINALITY (LCT)
  NP (IMAGINATION (LCT))
  3

2 (LCH) CREATION (LITERARY, ARTISTIC, ETC.): OR CREATIVE THINK-
  ING: OR CREATIVE WRITING: OR CREATIVITY IN LITERATURE:
  NP (CREATION (LITERARY, ARTISTIC, ETC.): (LCH))
  NP (CREATIVE THINKING: (LCH))
  NP (CREATIVE WRITING: (LCH))
  NP (CREATIVITY IN LITERATURE: (LCH))

2 (LCT) INTELLECT OR INSPIRATION
  NP (INSPIRATION (LCT))
  5

3 (TI) ALL CREATIV:
  7

4 3 AND NOT 1
  6

5 ALL CREAT: (TI)
  9

6 5 AND NOT 4
  3

7 ALL IMAGINATION (TI)
  2

8 ALL CREATION (LITERARY, ARTISTIC, ETC.)
  NP (CREATION (LITERARY, ARTISTIC, ETC.)
```

b) BOOKS SEARCH STRATEGY

1 ALL CREATIV:
55

2 ALL PRODUCTIV: OR ALL PROLIFIC: OR ALL FRUITFUL: OR ALL FECUND:
25

3 ALL INVENTIVE: OR ALL INGENIOUS: OR ALL IMAGINATIVE: OR ALL GIFTED: OR ALL TALENTED OR ALL ENDOWED: OR ALL ARTISTIC: OR ALL CLEVER: OR ALL DEMIURGIC:
29

4 ALL INTELLECTUAL:
45

5 ALL CEREBRAL: OR ALL INTELLECT:
17

6 ALL LEARNED: OR ALL SCHOLARLY: OR ALL PENSIVE: OR ALL LIT-ERATE: OR ALL THOUGHTFUL: OR ALL BOOKISH:
11

7 1 OR 2 OR 3 OR 4 OR 5 OR 6
157

8 ALL ABILIT:
57

9 7 AND 8
23

10 1 AND 2
2

11 9 OR 10
23

c) STATISTICS

	MARC	BOOKS	
Total Retrieved	16	23	Estimated No. Relevant Items in
Relevant/Known	0	2	BOOKS = 13 + 2 (2 were suggested
Relevant/Not Known	6	7	by requester and missed by both,
Possibly Relevant	4	6	SNO 1617 & SNO 1571).
Not Relevant	6	8	(2 matches.)

Precision: $\dfrac{10}{16} = 63\%$ $\dfrac{15}{23} = 65\%$

Estimated Recall: $\dfrac{6}{13} = 46\%$ $\dfrac{9}{13} = 69\%$

Time Online: .30 hr.   .17 hr.

d) ANALYSIS

Matches: There were 6 matched items in the MARC and BOOKS searches.

Two (SNO 1479 & SNO 1481) were assessed as Relevant/Not Known both times.
Two (SNO 1491 & SNO 1624) were assessed as Not Relevant both times.
One (SNO 1492) was assessed as Possibly Relevant both times.
One (SNO 1560) was assessed as Possibly Relevant when the MARC record was examined and Not Relevant when the BOOKS record was examined.

MARC: Low recall—six Relevant/Not Known items were found by BOOKS and not by MARC:

a) SNO 1330 LCH: Psychology–Methodology
b) SNO 1490 LCH: Mental tests
c) SNO 1514 LCH: Space–Perception
d) SNO 1568 LCH: Difference (Psychology)
e) SNO 1589 LCH: Personality assessment
f) SNO 1641 LCH: Adolescent psychology

LCSH headings where hits occurred were: Creative ability, Intellect. TITLE words where hits occurred were: creativity, creative, creating, and imagination. The BOOKS search found books using terms: gifted, prolific, literate.

BOOKS: Missed relevant documents—four items (Relevant/Not Known) were found by MARC and not by BOOKS:

a) SNO 1482 LCH: Creation (Literary, Artistic, etc.)
b) SNO 1483 Title: The Crisis of Creativity
c) SNO 1567 LCH: Self-Realization
d) SNO 1781 LCH: Creation (Literary, Artistic, etc.)

The strategy used was a string of synonyms from *Roget's Thesaurus* to describe the terms in the query. *Creation* as a term was not used and the truncated term *Creation:* did not retrieve it.

Note: From a previous search the requester remembered two items (SNO 1617 and 1571) which neither MARC nor BOOKS searches retrieved on this search. This prompts us to think that our estimate of relevant documents is low and benefits searches in both records equally.

****

Interesting Query Social Sciences #2   Query #SS-2

Infant mortality: rates, general causes of.

a) MARC SEARCH STRATEGY

(LCH) CHILDREN—MORTALITY OR INFANTS—MORTALITY OR IN-
FANTS—DISEASES OR INFANTS (NEWBORN)—MORTALITY OR SUDDEN
DEATH INFANTS
NP (CHILDREN—MORTALITY (LCH))
NP (INFANTS—DISEASES (LCH))
NP INFANTS (NEWBORN)—MORTALITY (LCH))
NP (SUDDEN DEATH IN INFANTS (LCH))

1 (LCT) ALL FATAL: OR ALL MORTALIT: OR ALL DEATH: OR ALL
DISEASE#
NP (FATAL: (LCT))
NP (MORTALIT: (LCT))
NP (DISEASE# (LCT))
3

2 (TI) ALL FATAL: OR ALL MORTALIT: OR ALL DISEASE# OR ALL DYING
OR ALL DEATH#
NP (FATAL: (TI))
NP (MORTALIT: (TI))
NP (DISEASE# (TI))
NP (DYING (TI))
8

3 1 OR 2
10

4 (LCT) ALL CHILD OR ALL CHILD'S OR ALL CHILDREN OR ALL BABIES OR
ALL BABY OR ALL INFANT# OR ALL GIRL# OR ALL YOUTH#
NP (CHILD'S (LCT))
NP (BABIES (LCT))
NP (BABY (LCT))
NP (GIRL# (LCT))
NP (YOUTH# (LCT))
38

5 4 OR 3
48

6 4 AND 3
NONE

6 (LCT) ALL CHILDREN OR ALL INFANT# OR ALL CHILD
38

7 (TI) ALL CHILDREN OR ALL CHILD'S OR ALL CHILD OR ALL BABIES OR
ALL BABY OR ALL INFANT: OR ALL GIRL# OR ALL YOUTH
NP (CHILD'S (TI))
NP (BABIES (TI))
NP (BABY (TI))
NP (YOUTH (TI))
21

8 7 OR 4
40

9 8 AND 3
NONE

9 ALL CHILD STUDY (LCH)
25

b) BOOKS SEARCH STRATEGY

1 ALL CHILD: OR ALL INFANT:
230

2 ALL MORTALITY: OR ALL FATALITY: OR ALL DEATH:
80

3 1 AND 2
26

4 ALL CAUSE: AND 3
3

5 ALL FATALIT: AND 3
NONE

5 SENS 3 (IT) : INFANT MORTALITY:
NONE

c) STATISTICS

	MARC	BOOKS	
Total Retrieved	25	3	Estimated No. Relevant Items
Relevant/Known	0	0	in BOOKS = 3
Relevant/Not Known	3	0	(no matches across searches)
Possibly Relevant	3	2	
Not Relevant	19	1	

Precision: $\dfrac{6}{25} = 24\%$ $\dfrac{2}{3} = .66\%$

Recall: $\dfrac{3}{3} = 100\%$ $\dfrac{0}{3} = 0\%$

Time Online: .25 hr. .07 hr.

d) ANALYSIS

MARC: Low precision—searcher settled for all child study (LCH) after mortality synonyms and child terms did not work. (See also attached sample of offline output for MARC search.)

BOOKS: Low recall—missed 3 rated Relevant/Not Known:
(Relevance assessed on basis of subtitle)

   SNO 1621—Child development: the human, cultural, and educational context
   SNO 1611—Human development, from birth thru adolescence
   SNO 1606—Human development in Western culture

Missed 3 Possibly Relevant:
(Relevance assessed on basis of subtitle)

   SNO 1616—The first 2 decades of life
   SNO 1605—Theory & Problems of child development
   SNO 1622—Mental growth & personality development: a longitudinal study

FIGURE 15. Sample of Offline Output for MARC Search

```
CCN  -  BF721 S446
ME   -  Schm: !t. Wilfred H.O.
TI   -  Child development: the human, cultural, and educational context
IM   -  New York, Harper & Row, 1973
COL  -  181p.
LCH  -  Child study
SNO  -  1621
PY   -  1973
RSN  -  00802988



CCN  -  BF698.8 R5 L48
ME   -  Levitt. Eugene E.
TI   -  The Rorschach technique with children and adolescents:
         application and norms by Eugene E.Levitt and Aare Truumaa.
IM   -  New York. Grune & Stratton, 1972
COL  -  146p.
LCH  -  Rorschach test; Child s.udy; Adolescent psychology
SNO  -  1594
PY   -  1972
RSN  -  00747244



CCN  -  BF698 M63
ME   -  Montagu. Ashley. 1905-
TI   -  Touching: the human significance of the significance of the skin.
IM   -  New York. Columbia University Press. 1971
COL  -  338p.
LCH  -  Touch; Skin. Nonverbal communication; Personality; Child study
SNO  -  1582
PY   -  1971
RSN  -  00633101



CCN  -  BF721 G644 1969
ME   -  Gordon. Ira J.
TI   -  Human development. from birth through adolescence by Ira J.
         Gordon.
IM   -  New York, Harper & Row, 1969
COL  -  408p.
LCH  -  Child study; Adolescence; Socialization
SNO  -  1611
PY   -  1969
RSN  -  00556920



CCN  -  BF717 M5 1968
ME   -  Millar. Susanna
TI   -  The psychology of play.
IM   -  Harmondsworth. Penguin, 1968
COL  -  288p.
LCH  -  Play; Child study
SNO  -  1604
PY   -  1968
RSN  -  00413057



CCN  -  BF721 L525
ME   -  Lewis. Morris Michael
TI   -  Language. thought. and personality in infancy and childhood
IM   -  New York. Basic Books. 1964
```

```
COL - 256p.
LCH - Child study; Children - Language
SNO - 1615
PY  - 1964
RSN - 00093690
```

```
CCN - BF721 M86
ME  - Murphy, Lois (Barclay), 1902-
TI  - Personality in young children.
IM  - New York, Basic Books, 1956
LCH - Personality; Child study
SNO - 1617
PY  - 1956
RSN - 00006822
```

```
CCN - BF721 M48 1958A
ME  - Merry, Frieda (Kiefer)
TI  - The first two decades of life.
IM  - New York, Harper & Row, 1958
COL - 642p.
LCH - Child study; Adolescence
SNO - 1616
PY  - 1958
RSN - 00006818
```

```
CCN - BF721 J4 1960
ME  - Jersild, Arthur Thomas, 1902-
TI  - Child psychology.
IM  - Englewood Cliffs, N.J., Prentice-Hall, 1960
COL - 506p.
LCH - Child study; Infants
SNO - 1613
PY  - 1960
RSN - 00006799
```

```
CCN - BF721 E36 1974
ME  - Elkind, David, 1931-
TI  - Children and adolescents: interpretive essays on Jean Piaget.
IM  - New York, Oxford University Press, 1974
COL - 186p.
LCH - Child study; Adolescent psychology; Piaget, Jean, 1896-
SNO - 1609
PY  - 1974
RSN - 00846214
```

```
CCN - BF721 T46
ME  - Thompson, George Greene, 1914-
TI  - Child psychology: growth trends in psychological adjustment.
IM  - Boston, Houghton Mifflin, 1952
COL - 667p.
LCH - Child study
SNO - 1623
PY  - 1952
RSN - 00006856
```

```
CCN - BF721 P533
ME  - Piaget, Jean, 1896-
```

```
TI  - Play. dreams and imitation in childhood.
IM  - New York, Norton, pref. 1951
COL - 296p.
LCH - Child study; Imitation; Play; Symbolism
SNO - 1619
PY  - 1951
RSN - 00006835
```

```
CCN - BF723 I6 J65
ME  - Jorda :. Thomas Edward
TI  - Early developmental adversity and the first two years of life.
IM  - Austin. Tex. . Society of Multivariate Experimental Psychology.
      1971
COL - 80p.
LCH - Infants; Child study; Stress (Physiology)
SNO - 1634
PY  - 1971
RSN - 00818727
```

```
CCN - BF723 D7 C5 1973
TI  - Child art; the beginnings of self-affirmation by Sir Herbert Read
      and others Edited by Hilda Present Lewis.
IM  - Berkeley. Calif. . Diablo Press. 1973
COL - 105p.
LCH - Drawing. Psychology of; Child study
SNO - 1631
PY  - 1973
RSN - 00803992
```

```
CCN - BF721 B38 1970
ME  - Bernrad. Harold Wright. :908-
TI  - Human development in Western culture
IM  - Boston. Allyn and Bacon. 1970
COL - 642p.
LCH - Child study. Adolescence
SNO - 1606
PY  - 1970
RSN - 00639519
```

```
CCN - BF721 A8 1970
ME  - Ausubel. David Paul
TI  - Theory and problems of child development by David P. Ausubel and
      Edmund V. Sullivan.
IM  - New York. Grune & Stratton. 1970
COL - 849p.
LCH - Child study
SNO - 1605
PY  - 1970
RSN - 00610611
```

```
CCN - BF723 D7 B87
ME  - Burns. Robert C.
TI  - Kinetic family drawings (K-F-D); an introduction to understanding
      children through kinetic drawings. by Robert C. Burns and S.
      Harvard Kaufman.
IM  - New York. Brunner/Mazel. 1970
COL - 160p.
LCH - Drawing. Psychology of; Child study; Personality assessment
SNO - 1630
PY  - 1970
RSN - 00590871
```

```
CCN - BF723 M6 P53 1970
ME  - Piaget, Jean. 1896-
TI  - The child's conception of movement and speed; translated from the
      French by G.E.T. Holloway and M.J. Mackenzie.
IM  - London, Routledge & K. Paul, 1970
COL - 306p.
LCH - Motion perception (Vision); Child study
SNO - 1637
PY  - 1970
RSN - 00538591


CCN - BF723 S6 F56
ME  - Flapan, Dorothy
TI  - Children's understanding of social interaction.
IM  - New York, Teachers College Press, 1968
COL - 86p.
LCH - Social perception; Child study
SNO - 1640
PY  - 1968
RSN - 00426142


CCN - BF721 V4
ME  - Vernon, Philip Ewart
TI  - Intelligence and cultural environment
IM  - London, Methuen, 1969
COL - 264p.
LCH - Intellect; Man - Influence of environment; Child study
SNO - 1624
PY  - 1969
RSN - 00413560


CCN - BF723 C65 A7 1968
ME  - Aronfreed, Justin Manuel. 1930-
TI  - Conduct and conscience; the socialization of internalized control
      over behavior
IM  - New York, Academic Press, 1968
COL - 405p.
LCH - Conscience; Socialization; Child study
SNO - 1629
PY  - 1968
RSN - 00346149


CCN - BF723 R3 C5 1963
ME  - Clark, Kenneth Bancroft. 1914-
TI  - Prejudice and your child.
IM  - Boston, Beacon Press, 1963
COL - 247p.
LCH - Race awareness; U.S. - Race question; Prejudices and antipathies
LCH - Child study; Segregation in education
SNO - 1639
PY  - 1963
RSN - 00097544


CCN - BF721 S57
ME  - Sontag, Lester Warren. 1901-
TI  - Mental growth and personality development: a longitudinal study
IM  - Lafayette, Ind. , Child Development Publications, 1958
COL - 143p.
LCH - Child study; Intellect; Personality
SNO - 1622
PY  - 1958
RSN - 00006852


CCN - BF721 C2
ME  - Carmichael, Leonard, 1898-, ed.
TI  - Manual of child psychology.
```

```
IM  - New York, Wiley, 1946
COL - 1068p.
LCH - Child study
SNO - 1607
PY  - 1946
RSN - 00006763


CCN - BF455 L84 1961
ME  - Luri's, Aleksandr Romanovich, 1902-
TI  - The role of speech in the regulation of normal and abnormal
      behavior.
IM  - New York, Liveright Pub. Corp., 1961
COL - 148p.
LCH - Speech (Psychology); Child study
SNO - 1506
PY  - 1961
RSN - 00006442
```

****

Interesting Query Social Sciences #3   Query #SS-3

Police personality characteristics (or other law enforcement personnel).

a) MARC SEARCH STRATEGY

11 ALL POLICE PSYCHOLOGY: (LCH) OR ALL POLICE ETHICS (LCH)
   NP (POLICE PSYCHOLOGY: (LCH)
   NP (POLICE ETHICS: (LCH)

1 ALL POLICE (LCT)
  NP (POLICE (LCT))

1 ALL PERSONALITY A#D OCCUPATION: (LCH) OR ALL PERSONALITY
    ASSESSMENT: (LCH)
  NP (PERSONALITY A#D OCCUPATION: (LCH))
  3

2 (TI) ALL POLICE:
  NP (POLICE: (TI))

2 (TI) ALL LAW AND ALL ENFORCEMENT
  NP (ENFORCEMENT (TI))

2 ALL PERSONALIT### (TI) AND ALL OCCUPATION# (TI)
  NP (OCCUPATION# (TI))
  NONE

2 ALL COP# (TI)
  1

b) BOOKS SEARCH STRATEGY

1 ALL POLICE: OR ALL COPS: OR ALL GUARD: OR ALL PATROL: OR ALL
CONSTABULARY: OR ALL LAW:
243

2 ALL PERSONALITY:
176

3 1 AND 2
31

4 3 AND NOT ALL LAWYER:
31

c) STATISTICS

	MARC	BOOKS	
Total Retrieved	0	31	
Relevant/Known	0	0	
Relevant/Not Known	0	0	Estimated No. Relevant Items
Possibly Relevant	0	2	in BOOKS=0
Not Relevant	0	29	
Precision:	0%	$\frac{2}{31}=6\%$	
Estimated Recall:	---	---	
Time Online:	.08 hr.	.12 hr.	

d) ANALYSIS

MARC: No hits.
The LCH headings "Police psychology" and "Police ethics" had no postings
in the BOOKS file.

The term "Police" did not appear as a term in the LCT list or the Title list.

The two items retrieved by BOOKS which were judged "Possibly Relevant"
had the subject heading, Psychology, applied.

BOOKS: Low precision.

In an attempt to cover all the synonyms for law enforcement personnel, the
terms police, cops, guard, patrol, constabulary and law were entered in
truncated form, e.g., police:, law:. This resulted in many false drops because
of the word "law" which appears in many phrases in subject descriptions for
social science monographs.

The two "Possibly Relevant" items were found because their subject descriptions contained the following:

SNO 1378—Human relations industry and law (p. 318–324)
SNO 1536—Psychology in Law and Criminology; Whitmer (p. 235–256);
Giardini (p. 257–291)

Neither one of these would have been found if "law:" as a search term had not
been used. This type of vocabulary problem poses an insurmountable problem
for the online searcher.

```
************************************************************
```
Interesting Query Social Science #4   Query #SS-4

Accuracy of perceived size and value (brightness) of visual symbols (particularly in regard to cartographic symbols or applications to geography and maps).

a) MARC SEARCH STRATEGY

1   ALL VISUAL: (LCH) OR ALL VISIBILITY (LCT) OR ALL FORM PERCEP-
    TION: (LCH) OR ALL INFORMATION DISPLAY: (LCH)
    NP (VISIBILITY (LCT))
    NP (INFORMATION DISPLAY: (LCH))
    4

2   ALL SIGNS A#D SYMBOLS: (LCH) OR ALL SENSES A#D SENSATION:
    (LCH)
    NP (SIGNS A#D SYMBOLS: (LCH))
    NP (SENSES A#D SENSATION: (LCH))

2   ALL PSYCHOMETRICS (LCT) OR ALL PSYCHOLOGY, PHYSIOLOGICAL:
    (LCH)
    15

3   ALL OPTICS, PHYSIOLOGICAL: (LCH) OR ALL PHOSPHENES (LCT) OR
    ALL OPTICAL ILLUSIONS: (LCH)
    NP (OPTICS, PHYSIOLOGICAL: (LCH))
    NP (PHOSPHENES (LCT))
    NP (OPTICAL ILLUSIONS: (LCH))

3   1 OR 2
    19

4   ALL CARTOGRAPHY (LCT) OR ALL MAP: (LCH) OR ALL TOPOGRAPH:
    (LCH)
    NP (CARTOGRAPHY (LCT))
    NP (MAP: (LCH))
    NP (TOPOGRAPH: (LCH))

4   (TI) ALL MAP# OR ALL CARTOGRAPH: OR ALL TOPOGRAPH:
    6

5   (TI) ALL SYMBOL: OR ALL SIGN:
    11

6   (TI) ALL VISUAL: OR ALL VISION OR ALL OPTIC:
    NP (OPTIC: (TI))
    6

7   4 AND 5
    NONE

7   4 AND 6
    NONE
```
```

7 5 AND 6
  NONE

7 1 AND 4
  NONE
7 1 AND 2
  NONE

7 ALL PSYCHOMETRICS (LCT)
  8

8 ALL PSYCHOLOGY, PHYSIOLOGICAL (LCH)
  8

b) BOOKS SEARCH STRATEGY

1 ALL VISUAL: OR ALL VISION: AND ALL EYE:
  55

2 ALL PERCEPT: OR ALL SIGHT: OR ALL AWARENESS: OR ALL EYESIGHT
  137

3 1 OR 2
  162

4 ALL PHYSIOLOGICAL AND ALL PSYCHOLOG:
  33

5 ALL PSYCHOLOG: AND ALL PHYSICAL:
  42

6 4 OR 5
  68

7 3 AND 6
  32

8 ALL MAP: OR ALL CARTOGRAPH:
  40

9 7 AND 8
  NONE

9 1 AND 8
  2

10 3 AND 8
  3

11 ALL BF: (CCN) AND 6
  56

12 ALL BF: (CCN) AND 7
  30

c) STATISTICS   MARC   BOOKS

	MARC	BOOKS	
Total Retrieved	4	30	
Relevant/Known	0	0	Estimated No. Relevant Items
Relevant/Not Known	0	3	in BOOKS=3(1 match—different
Possibly Relevant	3	4	assessment).
Not Relevant	1	23	

Precision: $\dfrac{3}{4}=75\%$ $\dfrac{7}{30}=23\%$

Estimated Recall: $\dfrac{0}{3}=0\%$ $\dfrac{3}{3}=100\%$

Time Online: .26 hr.   .15 hr.

d) ANALYSIS

Matches: The one match (SNO 1440), classified BF 241, had two subject headings:
Form Perception
Visual Perception
When examined as BOOKS output it was assessed Relevant/Not Known. When examined as MARC output it was assessed Possibly Relevant.

MARC: Low recall. Several subject headings to express visual or optical perception and physiological psychology were used, plus terms in LCT and Title lists for map, cartography, and topography. The eight items retrieved using LCH: Psychology, Physiological, were rejected as a "mixed bag." In this output were some of the relevant items found in the BOOKS search.

The three "Possibly Relevant" items retrieved were matched by the search term "visual:" in the title or subject heading. In two cases the subject heading was "Visual Perception;" in one case "Visualization." In one case "Form Perception" was the subject heading, but the title was "Similarity in Visually Perceived Form."

Two of the Possibly Relevant books were classified: BF 241
One was classified: BF 293

BOOKS: The search was limited to books classified in BF (Psychology). Terms to express vision perception and physiological psychology were used:
a) Visual, vision, eye
b) percept:, sight, awareness, eyesight
c) physical, physiological, psycholog:

When "map" or "cartography" were used, the results were too low.
The resulting output of 30 items was classified as follows.
Not Relevant—B 121, 131, 149, 191, 203, 319.5, 321, 531, 671, 683, 697, 698, 701, 721, 724

Possibly Relevant—BF 121, 131, 295
Relevant—BF 237, 241, 455

According to this scatter of relevant items, someone scanning the book shelves in a library might have some real problems!

A similar problem exists in the subject catalog: The three relevant items had the following subject headings:

a) Form Perception; Visual Perception

b) Psychometrics; Psychology, Physiological

c) Human Information Processing; Pattern Perception

****

Interesting Query Humanities #1 Query #Hum-1

Greek, Roman, and Etruscan imagery (decoration) on sarcophagi (c500 B.C.– 300 A.D.)—no Christian imagery.

a) MARC SEARCH STRATEGY

1 ALL SARCOPHAGI (LCT)
NP (SARCOPHAGI (LCT))

1 ALL GREEK (LCT) OR ALL ROMAN (LCT) OR ALL ETRUSCAN (LCT)
31

2 ALL COFFINS (LCT) OR ALL TOMBS (LCT) OR ALL SEPULCHRAL (LCT) OR
ALL BURIAL (LCT)
NP (BURIAL (LCT))
NP (COFFINS (LCT))
4

3 1 AND 2
NONE

3 ALL GREECE (LCT) OR ALL ROME (LCT)
87

4 1 OR 3
103

5 ALL FUNERAL (LCT)
1

6 5 AND 3
1

7 ALL CHRISTIAN ANTIQUITIES: (LCH) OR ALL CHRISTIAN ART: (LCH)
NP (CHRISTIAN ANTIQUITIES: (LCH)
1

8 (TI) SARCOPHAGI
NP (SARCOPHAGI (TI))

8 (TI) ALL GREECE OR ALL GREEK OR ALL ROME OR ALL ROMAN OR ALL
ETRUSCAN
75

9 (TI) ALL TOMB# OR ALL SEPULCHER# OR ALL SEPULCHRAL OR ALL
    GRAVE# OR ALL FUNERAL
    NP (SEPULCHER# (TI))
    NP (SEPULCHRAL (TI))
    NP (FUNERAL: (TI)
    8

10 8 AND 9
    NONE

10 (TI) ALL STATUE# OR ALL SCULPTURE# OR ALL MONUMENT#
    NP (STATUE# (TI))
    25

11 9 AND 11
    NONE

12 9 AND 10
    1

13 ALL ICONOGRAPHY (LCT, TI)
    NP (ICONOGRAPHY (LCT, TI))

13 ALL ICONOGRAPHY (LCT)
    NP (ICONOGRAPHY (LCT))

13 ALL ICON: (TI)
    1

b) BOOKS SEARCH STRATEGY

1 ALL TOMB: OR ALL SARCOPHAG:
    18

2 ALL GREEC: OR ALL GREEK: OR ALL ROM:
    260

3 1 AND 2
    13

4 3 AND NOT ALL MODERN
    11

c) STATISTICS

	MARC	BOOKS
Total Retrieved	4	10
Relevant/Known	0	0
Relevant/Not Known	2	6
Possibly Relevant	0	2
Not Relevant	2	2

Precision: $\dfrac{2}{4} = 50\%$ $\dfrac{8}{10} = 80\%$

c) STATISTICS   MARC   BOOKS

Estimated Recall: $\dfrac{2}{6} = 33\%$ $\dfrac{6}{6} = 100\%$

Time Online: .23 hr.   .10 hr.

d) ANALYSIS

Matches: Two items were retrieved in both searches and both times the items were assessed Relevant/Not Known.

MARC: Low recall. The four relevant items retrieved by BOOKS but missed by MARC had the following subject headings:

  Civilization, Etruscan
  Etrurians
  Rome—Civilization

  "Tombs—Etruria" and "Funeral Rites and Ceremonies—Rome" were the subject headings for the two items found by searching MARC and BOOKS.

****

Interesting Query Humanities #2   Query #Hum-2

How can I eliminate the use of the deduction theorem?

a) MARC SEARCH STRATEGY

  1 ALL BC: (CCN) AND ALL LOGIC (TI)
    26

  2 ALL BC: (CCN) AND ALL LOGIC (LCH)
    13

  3 1 OR 2
    26

  4 STRS 4 (TI) :DEDUCTI:
    1

  5 STRS 4 (LCH) :DEDUCTI:
    NONE

  5 ALL DEDUCTI: (TI) OR ALL DEDUCTI: (LCT)
    NP (DEDUCTI: (LCT))
    2

  6 5 OR 6
    2

b) BOOKS SEARCH STRATEGY

1 ALL DEDUCTION:
22

2 1 AND ALL THEOREM:
1

c) STATISTICS   MARC   BOOKS

	MARC	BOOKS	
Total Retrieved	2	1	
Relevant/Known	0	0 ⎤	Estimated No. Relevant Items
Relevant/Not Known	0	1 ⎦	in BOOKS = 1 (no matches)
Possibly Relevant	0	0	
Not Relevant	2	0	

Precision: $\dfrac{0}{2} = 0\%$ $\dfrac{1}{1} = 100\%$

Estimated Recall: $\dfrac{0}{1} = 0\%$ $\dfrac{1}{1} = 100\%$

Time Online: .07 hr.   .04 hr.

d) ANALYSIS

MARC: Low precision and recall.
   One book which was retrieved caused the comment "Snicker, Snicker," because a title word search for DEDUCTION turned up the book with the title, "Personal deductions in the federal income tax."
BOOKS: The relevant item was retrieved by a simple search of the two words "deduction" *and* "theorem." The book's title was "Classical Theory of First Order Logic," and its LCH: Logic, Symbolic and Mathematical.
****
Interesting Query Humanities #3   Query #Hum-3

What connectives are adequate to represent all truth-functions?

a) MARC SEARCH STRATEGY

1 (LCH) TRUTH-FUNCTIONS
NP (TRUTH-FUNCTIONS (LCH))

1 ALL BC 171: (CCN)
NP (BC 171: (CCN))

1 ALL BC:
58

2 ALL BC: (CCN)
41

3 STRS 2 (TI) :TRUTH#FUNC:
   NONE

3 STRS 2 (LCH) :TRUTH#FUN:
   NONE

3 STRS 2 (TI) :TRUTH:
   NONE

3 STRS 2 (LCH) :TRUTH:
   NONE

3 STRS 2 (TI) :CONNECTIV:
   NONE

3 STRS 2 (LCT): CONNECTIV:
   NONE

3 ALL CONNECTIV: (TI) OR ALL CONNECTIV: (LCT)
   NP (CONNECTIV: (TI)
   NP (CONNECTIV: (LCT))

b) BOOKS SEARCH STRATEGY

1 ALL CONNECTIVE: AND ALL TRUTH:
   4

c) STATISTICS

	MARC	BOOKS	
Total Retrieved	0	4	
Relevant/known	0	0	Estimated No. Relevant Items
Relevant/Not Known	0	1	in BOOKS = 1
Possibly Relevant	0	3	
Not Relevant	0	0	
Precision	0%	100%	
Estimated Recall:	0%	100%	
Time Online:	.08 hr.	.03 hr.	

d) ANALYSIS

MARC: Attempts to find ''truth'' or ''truth functions'' in the LCH and TI fields proved useless.
BOOKS: A simple search of the terms ''truth'' and ''connective'' retrieved four items.

Characteristics of Book Indexes for Subject Retrieval in the Humanities and Social Sciences

by Bonnie Gratch, Barbara Settel, and
Pauline Atherton

CONCLUSIONS AND RECOMMENDATIONS

Not all significant characteristics of index quality could be studied, but our study and evaluation did use existing guidelines and standards and has revealed some interesting findings about book indexes in the humanities and social sciences. Although our conclusions are not a definitive statement about the quality of indexes in these subject areas, it does represent an expository effort to reveal the status quo and the impact of these conditions on subject retrieval if the book indexes are to serve such a function. Granted, the indexing profile our findings postulate may be related to practices of the past as many of the poorer quality indexes appeared to have earlier publication dates. Remember, however, that the sample was drawn from post-1966 acquisitions, so the likelihood of a majority of cases with pre-1960 publication dates being represented is not that great.

SUMMARY

The following findings reveal the most serious inadequacies of book indexes:

1. Only 55% of the sample drawn by the Subject Access Project possessed an index, suggesting that this leaves almost half a library with no indexes at all—a very discouraging finding, indeed;
2. There is a lack of introductory note to explain the scope of indexes (91% had no introductory note);

Reprinted with permission from *The Indexer*, Vol. 11, No. 1, April 1978. Editor's Note: This is an excerpt.

3. Inconsistent practices result in no indexing for front, back and illustrative matter in books;
4. There is an excess of entries with ten or more undifferentiated locators (60%);
5. Most indexes lack sufficient cross-references (41% have neither 'see' nor 'see also');
6. Multiple access (57% of sample had no multiple entries) is not consistently provided.
7. 35% of the indexes used forms for locators *not* recommended by standards.

The findings for the social sciences generally reveal more desirable index features and less undesirable ones. Nevertheless, the lack of control over scattering of headings and subheadings stands out as a serious inadequacy for the total sample. Certainly, subject access is severely restricted when only 59% of the sample possess cross-references, and 22% of the sample have no control devices whatsoever.

RECOMMENDATION

The most obvious recommendation to remedy these inadequacies is to follow the standards and guidelines that have been created for this purpose. For those features where the standards make no comment or are not in agreement, a further effort should be made to provide direction.

Specific recommendations for improvement of book indexes based on this study:

1. All non-fiction books should have indexes.
2. Illustrative matter should be indexed and the style of index entry should indicate such indexing.
3. If an index entry is followed by ten or more locators, some attempt should be made to subdivide the entry for ease of reference to specific aspects of the subject.
4. 'See' and 'see also' references should be used.
5. Scope notes should be provided.
6. Subheadings and pre-coordination of terms should be used instead of single word index entries.
7. Form of locators should follow existing standards and non-standard forms should not be used.

This study was made to evaluate the effect of the index quality of books on computer-based subject searching using these indexes to form a data base. Clearly, the findings expressed above show that effective on-line subject retrieval is impaired by the existing conditions. Without a syndetic structure on-line data bases such as that recently generated by us (BOOKS on ORBIT, SDC) can be manipulated but existing computer capabilities for free text searching cannot pick up many types of relationships. Variations in word form, spellings, inversions, pre-coordination of words in headings and subheadings will all prove to provide hurdles for the on-line searcher. To some extent spelling variations can be edited at input or corrected for by root searching and variable character searchings; but there is no replacement for greater effort at quality and consistency at the source—in the publisher's office.

Augmenting Subject Descriptions for Books in Online Catalogs

by Barbara Settel and Pauline A. Cochrane

INTRODUCTION

The Subject Access Project, under a grant from the Council on Library Resources in 1976–77, researched and tested a method for improving subject access to the content of books. It did this by augmenting subject descriptions in MARC records with words and phrases from the books' index and/or table of contents. The objective was simple—with many libraries about to convert their catalogs to online systems, this would be an appropriate opportunity to introduce changes in the format and content of book records; that is, we would no longer be bound to the information which could be put on a 3×5 card. We could utilize the capacity of automated systems to manipulate large files of information. We could, in short, enter much more information about a book's subject into a file of online records. Users could then do more meaningful subject searches in book catalogs. Knowing the importance of time and cost constraints, we looked to the subject aids already provided in most books, namely tables of contents and indexes, and we attempted to devise standard rules and guidelines for selection of terms and phrases which could be applied across a divergent group of subjects and a wide range of indexing styles.[1]

The results of our research were reported[2] to the library world and publicized through talks at conferences and workshops and public demonstrations of online searches in the BOOKS database. Interest at the time of the project was keen and many libraries took advantage of our offer to search the BOOKS database on ORBIT. In Sweden at the Lund University Library, Bjorn Tell and his associates translated into Swedish our *Manual of Procedures for Augmenting Subject Descriptions*.[3] They used the

Reprinted with permission from *Database*, December 1982.

method we suggested for the description of Swedish books and government reports.[4] In the latter case they extended our selection rules and added the titles of figures and tables in order to access statistical data in these reports.

Still, to our knowledge, few libraries have actually implemented our selection procedures for input into an online catalog. Some may have considered this, but were reluctant to take on the workload themselves, and had no contact with other libraries who might cooperate. Perhaps others were still not convinced there would be much subject searching in their catalogs or were not yet ready to consider implementing an online catalog, let alone the enhancement of records. Nevertheless the idea is still in the air—witness the editorial in *Database*[5] suggesting the very idea again, and one of the readers writing in to say "It's been done at Syracuse." This renewed interest and the frantic pace at which online public access catalogs are being developed prompted us to believe our work needed to be brought out again to reach a wider, possibly more interested, audience.

As data from the recent online catalog use study indicates,[6] catalog users require improved subject access. We offer our work as one of several possible suggestions for such improvement. Selection of subject descriptions from the books themselves could enhance book records for all if it could be a cooperative venture now. The libraries with online catalogs now may have a more realistic picture of the inadequacies of subject searching those catalogs through existing records. We are reporting our rules and procedures in abbreviated form to solicit comments, suggestions, and trials by others. Only in this way can we expect a concerted effort to begin to improve subject access in online library catalogs.

SELECTION OF SUBJECT DESCRIPTIONS

The flow chart in Table I shows an overview of the steps in the *subject description* selection process. Except for the initial determination to begin with the index or table of contents, the steps (select and underline terms, check quota, format) in the three branches of the selection process are virtually the same. However, the *rules* for selection of entries do vary with table of contents or index and the style of index entries. In this article we will explain the rationale and objectives of each step in the selection process and give summaries of the selection rules for tables of contents and indexes. Examples are included as much as space will allow. Anyone wishing to utilize the selection procedures should refer to the manual for more detailed instructions on the application of individual rules.

TABLE 1. Flow Chart of the Selection Process

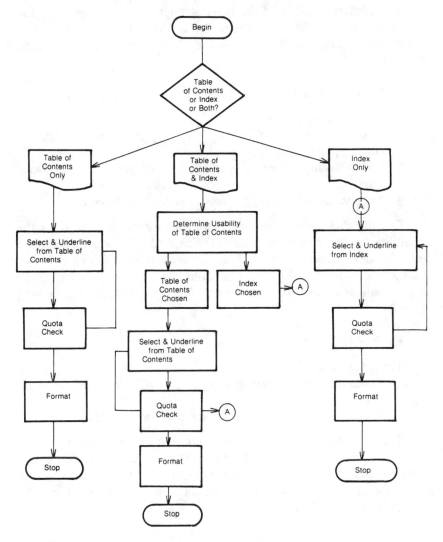

STEPS IN THE SELECTION PROCESS

Step 1: Begin Selection with Table of Contents, Index or Both?

Where a book contains a table of contents alone, or an index alone, selection will be made only from the available section. When both an index and a table of contents are available, a judgment about the "usability" of the table of contents must be made. Tables of contents often contain catchy phrases or headings which are too general to be useful. Selection of entries from these tables is unwarranted when an index is also provided. Therefore, a table of contents must satisfy certain criteria to be usable. These criteria are incorporated into the rules summarized below. A contents table failing to meet any one rule should not be used for selection and the index should be used instead.

RULES FOR CHOICE OF TABLE OF CONTENTS OR INDEX

The table of contents must:
1. *Contain at least one heading for every 25 pages of text, not counting introduction, forward, etc.*
2. *Contain content-bearing headings and not cute phrases or headlines.*
3. *Not contain a significant amount of repetition of terms.*

Because these rules entail subjective judgments, in some cases the "usability" of the contents table cannot be easily decided and a comparison with the index will be necessary. These cases are titled "difficult choices" and include contents, tables with unpaged headings. In these cases, the index should be chosen for selection only if it meets both of the following rules.

RULES FOR DIFFICULT CHOICES

The index must
1. *Contain locators with page ranges, not "ff," "et. seq." or single pages.*
2. *Include ample subject terms, other than names and places.*

The examples below show a table of contents rejected for selection and another deemed "usable." In Example 1, the headings are extremely repetitive, and there are not a sufficient number of headings for the length of text. In this case selection will begin from the index, which will probably be a better indicator of the books' content.

EXAMPLE 1.

EXAMPLE: THE LITTLE WORLD OF MAN BF (PSYCHOLOGY)

CONTENTS

EXAMPLE 2.

EXAMPLE: Zulu Tribe in Transition; GN (Anthropology)
The Makhanya of Southern Natal

No subject headings

Contents

Example 2 illustrates a table of contents which satisfies all the rules above. While selection may extend to the index if a quota allows (quota explained later), the table of contents provides excellent topical headings and it should be used for selection first.

Step 2: Selection of Entries

This step is naturally the most time-consuming and the most important part of the entire process. The selection procedure requires the application of sets of rules to a wide variety of styles of indexes and table of contents. Each set of rules is applied in an order which ensures the selection of the most important entries first.

In general, we use a quantitative measure to determine those important entries. For example, selections from the table of contents are made from entries with page ranges of five or more pages. Selections are made from the index on the same basis, if ranges exist. Where indexes do not contain page ranges, other measures like locators to chapters and entires with many subheadings are used to indicate important entries.

While the basis for selection rules is largely quantitative, we did include a number of devices to inject qualitative measures into the selection process. For example, a heading may be selected from a table of contents because it contains a range of 10 pages, but *only* the content-bearing words are underlined for subsequent input into the book's record. Thus, we apply a stop list of terms to selection of entries from either the index or table of contents. Headings with ranges of five or more pages but with no clear references to a subject would not be selected.

Our selection rules were developed to take advantage of the most common features employed by indexers to point to the subjects most frequently discussed in a book. If our system allows the selection of some irrelevant entries, it is probably because the index misrepresented the coverage of this topic, or we were forced to select entries without page ranges or other features which are better indicators or important topics. Our job was not to test the quality of each index or to try to reindex any book. Rather, working with what the indexer provided, we tried to use the most reliable measures of content (page ranges, chapter locators, etc.) whenever possible.

The section below summarizes the rules for selection and underlining of entries for tables of contents and indexes. Rules for underlining are as important as those for initial selection, because unnecessary terms or terms without clear reference will cost time and money to input, take up storage space, and affect the relevance of retrieval.

RULES FOR SELECTION OF ENTRIES FROM TABLES OF CONTENTS

Select and underline headings and locators with ranges of 5 or more pages according to the following rules:

1. *Do not underline "a," "an," "the" unless essential for meaning.*
2. *Underline headings which are content-bearing and clear indicators of the books' subject. Do not underline headings which resemble headlines or cute phrases. In headings containing a mixture of content and non-content bearing terms, underline only the content-bearing portion.*

EXAMPLE:

Canoes, Sails and Fishing Craft
The First Steamers
The Fleets Come and Go
The Pleasure-Seekers

3. Do not underline headings on the stop list, even if they cover ranges of five or more pages. (Stop list includes terms like forward, introduction, appendix.)
4. Underline terms from chapter and section subheadings only if the concept or term hasn't already been selected from the main heading with inclusive paging.

EXAMPLE:

Values, Rights and Obligations	20-43
The Grounding and Selection of Values	21-27
Values and Rights	28-43
Obligations	36-43

(repetitive of terms in chapter heading with inclusive paging.)

5 . Do not underline headings if you would have to add terms to the headings to supplement or clarify their meaning.

EXAMPLE:

A Lost Consensus	(no reference, vague)
A Comprehensive and Common-Sense Approach	(no reference, vague)
What are the Causes of the Crisis?	(unclear)

RULES FOR SELECTION OF ENTRIES FROM INDEXES

The rules for selection from indexes are grouped by style of index including indexes with page ranges, indexes with "ff," "f," or "et seq," and all other indexes. Because the basic set of selection rules is repeated for each group, indexes which contain a mixture of styles will still be properly selected. For example, an index is predominantly one with "ff" and an occasional page range. The initial rules for indexes with page ranges are repeated in the section for indexes with "ff" so that eligible entries will not be missed.

It is important to apply the rules in the order given, to ensure the selection of the most important entries first. Selection stops when you have a manageable size of selections or all the rules have been exhausted. The subsequent section on the quota explains in more detail how a manageable size can be determined.

EXAMPLE:

Social Characteristics, 206-233, 246-255, 304-306
Social Interaction, 67-70
    and attitude change, 287-288
    and decision process, 62-100, 105
Social perception, 79-100
    accuracy, 82-85
    of leader, 89-96
Sociometry, 8, 23-25, 407-411

4. Where entries have 5 or more subheadings, regardless of page ranges. Do not underline locators.

EXAMPLE:

Behavior, 10
    expressive, 22-24
    instinctive, 106
    learned, 25-27   5 subheadings
    modal, 96
    social, 37-39

5. Where entries have a total of 10 or more page references, not necessarily ranged.

EXAMPLE:

Books, 3, 7, 10, 124, 127, 301, 304, 306, 321, 346   Total pages = 10 Select
Animals, 21-23, 45-47, 58, 104, 107, 201-204
        Total pages = 13 Select
Character analysis, 15-17, 20-23, 28, 30, 32, 50-52   Total pages = 13 Select
Character disorders, 20-23, 26-28
        Total pages = 7 Do not select

In indexes with no page ranges, but with "f", "ff", "et seq", first select and underline all entries and locators which satisfy the rules above, in that order. Then:

1. Select and underline all entries and locators followed by "ff" or "et seq".
2. If necessary, lower the total number of page references from 10 to 5.

In all other indexes (no clear use of page ranges or "ff"), first apply the rules for indexes with ranges. Then:

1. Select and underline all entries with a total of five or more locators.

2. Where five consecutive entries begin with the same word or root and all relate to a common concept, underline this word or root as you would an entry with five subheads.

EXAMPLE:

Suburbs, 13
<u>Suburban</u> industry, 17
Suburban phenomena, 37
Suburban self-government, 123
Suburban shopping, 18
Suburbanization, nature of, 37

3. If necessary, lower the number of subheadings from 5 to 3

Step 3: Applying the Quota—or Knowing When to Stop

As mentioned above, the selection rules are designed to ensure a progressive selection of entries beginning with the most significant entries—those covering a large page range or containing many subheadings—and ending with the less significant entries—those covering fewer pages. The variety of selection rules is necessitated by the varying quality of indexes and tables of contents. Because of this lack of standardization in the arrangement of entries and locators, each index or table of contents will yield a different number of selections. A quota was devised to control the quantity of selection and maintain a database of manageable size which would reflect the major contents of the monograph.

The formula for the quota in the Subject Access Project was based on the average index or table of contents entries in each subject field. Our subject fields were determined by the LC classes of the book sample. As we explain more fully in the manual, even this formula was not totally satisfactory, as it did not take into account the length of the book or the quality of the index or table of contents. Using our formula, some books with short indexes but long in length would receive especially small quotas, restricting the amount of selections possible. At the other extreme were books with lengthy indexes or tables of contents, yet a comparatively short length or text. These cases would have high quotas and yield a disproportionate number of entries for the size of the book.

To compensate for these discrepancies we had to adjust our quotas by using the quota derived from the formula only as a "guideline." We also looked at the average quota for each LC class and the length of the book being selected. Low quotas for lengthy books were increased to be more in line with average quotas for that class. Likewise, high quotas for shorter books were reduced. While it was not always easy to determine the best quota for each book, we did have to have a system for deciding when to stop, and for our purposes, this system did work.

Quotas averaged around forty for each class, as did actual selections for monographs with indexes alone or indexes and tables of contents. The average number of selections for monographs with only tables of contents was about 15. Because you will probably not be working with a small sample like ours, and it will not be feasible to develop a formula by LC class, these figures may serve as a useful gauge in deriving your own formula for a quota.

We should emphasize that whether you select more or fewer entries than the quota depends largely upon the quality of the index or table of contents being selected. It is important to make selections which satisfy the rules and not to make selections merely on the basis of quantity. Never bend the rules or make questionable selections just to get a higher number of selections to meet a quota.

Step 4: Formatting Selections for Computer Input

A system for formatting the entries is necessary to allow for the designation of individual entries and their relation to main headings or subheadings. We used a hierarchy of codes (@;/%) but other methods would work as well. The key is to allow the retrieval system to link terms in each subheading with a main heading, so the searcher can retrieve on terms which occur either in individual entries, or in a cluster of entries representing a unit of main heading and subheadings.

In Example 3, we show a portion of a table of contents. Because of the formatting, *kinship system* will be searchable as an individual entry or in combination with any chapter heading. Each unit representing main headings and subheadings acts like a multiterm descriptor which is searchable as a bound phrase or as separate terms.

EXAMPLE 3. Portion of Contents Table Formatted for Input

@ THE <u>KINSHIP SYSTEM</u> 75-228		
VII.; POPULATION AND FAMILY GROUPS	75	
VIII.; <u>EXTENDED FAMILIES AND DESCENT GROUPS</u>	79- 90	
IX.; <u>DOMINANT DESCENT GROUPS</u>	91-109	
X.; <u>RANK, INHERITANCE AND ARBITRATION</u>	110-122	
XI.; <u>RIGHTS AND OBLIGATIONS: CONSANGUINEAL</u>	123-159	
XII.; <u>RIGHTS AND OBLIGATIONS: AFFINAL</u>	160-173	
XIII.; <u>PAGAN MARRIAGE</u>	174-212	
XIV.; <u>CHRISTIAN MARRIAGE</u>	213-228	
@ <u>THE POLITICO – JUDICIAL SYSTEM</u> 229-318		
XV.; POLITICAL HISTORY	229-241	
XVI.; POLITICAL UNITS	242-252	
XVII.; <u>THE POLITICAL HIERARCHY</u>	253-273	

EXAMPLE 3. Portion of Contents Table Formatted for Input (continued)

There are numerous possibilities for arranging these subject descriptions as part of a book record. The method you choose will depend on the retrieval system employed. If you want to index your records like those on Dialog, SDC or BRS, you might set up two fields, one for contents terms, one for selection from the index. See Example 4. These fields would resemble descriptor fields and each entry would be equivalent to a descriptor. The selections might also be treated together as an abstract, with each complete entry acting like a sentence. If weighting is possible, you could indicate selections with larger page ranges as major entries and search or limit by this feature.

EXAMPLE 4.

```
RSN - 00772823
SNO - 2070
CCN - PN1994  H27
ME  - Harrington, John, 1942-
TI   - The rhetoric of film
IM  - New York, Holt, Rinehart and Winston, 1973
COL - 175p.
PY  - 1973
LCH - Moving-pictures
CT  - *RHETORIC AND.FILM (P. 1-20)
CT  - *RECORDING VISUAL REALITY (P. 21-35), *SOUND
       (P. 36-50)
CT  - *POINT OF VIEW (P. 51-93); -THEME AND UNITY
       (P. 94-111)
CT  - *STRUCTURE AND ORGANIZATION (P. 112-126)
CT  - *RHYTHM AND CONTINUITY (P. 127-143); *RHETORIC
       (P. 144-158)
IT   - COMPOSITION (P. 24-28); DOCUMENTARY (P. 44-50)
IT   - *LENSES (P. 54-67); MONTAGE (P. 137-141); SCRIPTS
       (P. 102-110)
```

Augmentation

SUMMARY OF EVALUATION TESTS

We knew from our time and cost studies that the average number of selections per book was 32.4 and the average time spent on selections was 10 minutes per book. To evaluate and compare the online retrieval results of a BOOKS record (with augmented subject descriptions) compared with a MARC record, we designed the following experiments.

We established a controlled test environment for determining the answers to the following questions:

(1) For subject searching, does the BOOKS-style record aid in the *retrieval of more relevant items* than existing MARC records?

(2) Are the *times and costs* of online subject searching the BOOKS records significantly different from the times and costs associated with online subject searching of MARC records?

(3) Are a significant *number of relevant items missed* when the results of searching BOOKS and MARC records are compared?

(4) Are a significantly higher *number of nonrelevant items retrieved* when BOOKS records are searched? In other words, is the *precision* of BOOKS search lower than MARC?

(5) Are a significant number of items retrieved from a BOOKS search which is matched by a search of MARC records?

(6) Do any of the answers to the questions above change if the subject field of the query changes (i.e., a request for information from a field in the humanities or a field in the social sciences)?

The *unit of analysis* forming the statistical population under investigation was the *searches* performed online using the two subject systems, MARC and BOOKS.

The *criterion variables* used for comparing performance of the two systems on each search were:

(1) the number of relevant books retrieved
(2) the precision ratio of the search
(3) the computer connect time required for each search

As designed we had both *experimental factors* (the two systems MARC and BOOKS) and *classification factors* (searches in two subject areas, social sciences and humanities) which formed a series of related experimental treatments or related classifications.

A split-plot factorial analysis of variance with repeated measures on one factor seemed to be appropriate. With this design the variation among the results of the searches were partitioned into variation due to the indexing systems, the variation due to the subject areas searched, the variation due to the interaction of the indexing system with the subject area, the variation due to differences among the queries and residual experimental error.

To make these tests as "real" as possible we asked for queries from faculty and graduate students at Syracuse University. Eight persons agreed to ask queries on topics of interest to them and they also agreed to assess the results of the search. They rated relevance on a four point scale: Relevant-Known, Relevant-Not Known, Possibly Relevant, and Not Relevant. In all, ninety queries were collected and searched by two different searches, one required to search only the MARC portion of the record and the other searched the BOOKS record en toto.

The results were as follows:

Research Questions 1, 3 and 6—EXPERIMENT ONE:
Criterion = number of relevant documents retrieved.

Searches in *MARC records retrieved 56 relevant* documents in all, while *BOOKS searches retrieved 131*. The results of the analysis, too lengthy to include here, indicate no significant interaction effect, no significant A effect (classification factor) and a significant B effect (indexing system).

Therefore it is concluded that: *searches conducted with BOOKS yield a significantly greater number of relevant documents than do searches conducted with MARC.*
****
Questions 4 and 6—EXPERIMENT TWO:
Criterion= precision ratio per search.

The overall precision of MARC searches was 35% while for BOOKS searches the precision was 45%. The results of the analysis indicate no significant interaction effect, no significant B effect and a significant interaction effect, no significant B effect and a significant A effect.

Therefore it is concluded that: *there is no significant difference between the precision ratios of searches conducted with MARC or BOOKS.*

Based on our analysis of the results by subject field, it is also concluded that: *regardless of subject access system, searches in the humanities have higher precision ratios than do searches in the social sciences.*
****
Questions 2 and 6—EXPERIMENT THREE:
Criterion = computer connect time per search.

MARC searches took twice as long as BOOKS searches (on the average .14 hr. versus .07 hr.). The results of the analysis (not included for lack of space) indicate no interaction effect, a significant A effect and a significant B effect.

It is concluded, therefore that: *regardless of indexing system, searches in the humanities take significantly less time than do searches in the social sciences. Also, searches conducted with the BOOKS subject access system take significantly less time than do searches conducted with the MARC subject access system regardless of whether the searches are in the humanities or the social sciences.*

Comments regarding Question 5: Surprisingly, there were *very few matches.* (5%) in retrieval output. Only *27 of the 90 queries* contained *output* from the MARC and BOOKS online searches *which matched.* Some 1,143 items were "duplicates," or matched output. Only 14 of these 52 items were assessed relevant.

DISCUSSION OF FINDINGS

BOOKS records retrieved at least twice as many of the relevant items for the social science queries (31 versus 61) and three times as many as MARC for the humanities queries (25 versus 70).

The search times online for the 90 searches in the humanities and social sciences had the following overall averages:

	Humanities	**Social Sciences**
MARC	.12 hr.	.15 hr
BOOKS	.06 hr.	.08 hr.

The precision figures for both systems are below 67%! Both MARC and BOOKS retrieved two or three non-relevant items for each relevant item. Both the MARC and BOOKS searches were lower on precision for the social science queries than the humanities.

BOOKS searches failed to retrieve 42 of the known relevant items while MARC searches failed to retrieve 117.

In summary, our results lead us to conclude that we can recommend the BOOKS record as a better record for online subject searching than the MARC record.

REFERENCES

1. Gratch, B., Settel, B. and Atherton, P. "Characteristics of Book Indexes for Subject Retrieval in the Humanities and Social Sciences," *The Indexer,* April 1978, Vol II No. 1: 14–23.

2. Subject Access Project Publications:
Progress Reports to the Council on Library Resources (available through ERIC).
Occasional Newsletter Series, 4 numbers (out of print).
BOOKS Are for Use; A User Guide for the BOOKS File on SDC/ORBIT. Prepared by Jeffrey Simon and Pauline Atherton, September, 1977. 12p. (out of print but included in appendix of final report of project).
Atherton, Pauline, "Improved Subject Access to Books in On-Line Library Catalogs," in First International On-Line Information Meeting, London, 13–15 December 1977. pp. 131–138. (N.Y.: Learned Information).
BOOKS ARE FOR USE. Final Report to the Council on Library Resources. Syracuse University, School of Information Studies, Subject Access Project, Pauline

Atherton, Director. Syracuse, N.Y. 1978. 172 pp. $10.00 when ordered from S.U. Printing Services. Also available as ED 156 131.

3. Subject Description of Books; A Manual of Procedures for Augmenting Subject Descriptions in Library Catalogs. Edited by Barbara Settel. (Syracuse University, School of Information Studies, Research Study #3, 1977. $5.00).

4. Private communication from Bjorn V. Tell, November, 1981.

5. Pemberton, Jeff. "The Linear File," *Database,* March 1980, Vol. 3 No. 1 and June 1980, Vol. 3 No. 2, both pp. 4–5.

6. Markey, Karen. Research Report on Analytical Review of Catalog Use Studies, OCLC. Feb. 1980, 61 pp. Available through ERIC as ED 186041.

Besant, Larry, "Online Catalog Users Want Sophisticated Subject Access, *American Libraries* (March 1982), p. 160.

About the Author
Pauline (Atherton) Cochrane

Since the early 1960s Pauline (Atherton) Cochrane has been working on automated information systems and services. Early in her career her research was funded by the National Science Foundation while she was at the American Institute of Physics. When she left there in 1966 to go to Syracuse University to teach, she continued research but directed it toward improving library education and library service. At Syracuse she served for more than five years as Associate Director of the ERIC Clearinghouse on Information Resources, helping with the Vocabulary Improvement Project and the use of ERIC online. The research and development she did while at Syracuse was supported by the Office of Education, Council on Library Resources, National Library of Medicine and Rome Air Development Center.

Professor Cochrane has been a consultant to the Library of Congress, OCLC, H. W. Wilson Company, System Development Corporation, Unesco, Oak Ridge National Laboratory, Field Enterprises Educational Corporation, and the Minnesota Historical Society. She has been a member of the editorial board of several professional journals and has lectured all over the United States, Canada, Australia, Europe, Scandinavia, and India.

This selection of her writings brings together what has been a central theme throughout her very full career: the improvement of subject access for information seekers.

Index

Compiled by Linda Webster